LIFE-SPAN DEVELOPMENTAL PSYCH

LIFE-SPAN DEVELOPMENTAL PSYCHOLOGY

ANDREAS DEMETRIOU
University of Cyprus

WILLEM DOISE
University of Geneva

CORNELIS F. M. VAN LIESHOUT
University of Nijmegen

JOHN WILEY & SONS
Chichester · New York · Weinheim · Brisbane · Singapore · Toronto

Copyright © 1998 by John Wiley & Sons Ltd,
Baffins Lane, Chichester,
West Sussex PO19 1UD, England

National 01243 779777
International (+44) 1243 779777
e-mail (for orders and customer service enquiries):
cs-books@Wiley.co.uk
Visit our Home Page on http://www.wiley.co.uk
or http://www.wiley.com

Reprinted January 1999

Other Wiley Editorial Offices

John Wiley & Sons, Inc., 605 Third Avenue,
New York, NY 10158–0012, USA

WILEY-VCH Verlag GmbH, Pappelallee 3,
D-69469 Weinheim, Germany

Jacaranda Wiley Ltd, 33 Park Road, Milton,
Queensland 4064, Australia

John Wiley & Sons (Asia) Pte Ltd, 2 Clementi Loop #02–01,
Jin Xing Distripark, Singapore 129809

John Wiley & Sons (Canada) Ltd, 22 Worcester Road,
Rexdale, Ontario M9W 1L1, Canada

Library of Congress Cataloguing-in-Publication Data

Demetriou, Andreas,
    Life-span developmental psychology/Andreas Demetriou, Willem
Doise, Cornelius F.M. van Lieshout.
        p.   cm.
    Includes bibliographical references and index.
    ISBN 0–471–97078–6 (pbk.: alk. paper)
    1. Developmental Psychology.   I. Doise, Willem, 1935–
II. Lieshout, C. F. M. van.   III. Title.
BF713.D446 1997
150–dc21   97–23240
                                                     CIP

British Library Cataloguing in Publication Data

A catalogue record for this book is available from the British Library

ISBN 0–471–97078–6

Typeset in 10/12pt Times by Vision Typesetting, Manchester
Printed and bound by Antony Rowe Ltd, Eastbourne

This book is printed on acid-free paper responsibly manufactured from sustainable forestation,
in which at least two trees are planted for each one used for paper production.

CONTENTS

ABOUT THE AUTHORS

Josie Bernicot is Professor of Developmental Psychology at the University of Poitiers. She is also head of the 'Communication' research team at the Laboratory of the Psychology of Child Development and Education at the University of Paris. Her present research focuses on the field of developmental pragmatics. She has published theoretical and experimental articles on verb acquisition by children, metaphors, production and comprehension of speech acts, metapragmatics, and the transition between the prelinguistic and linguistic periods of development.
Address: University of Paris V, CNRS, Laboratoire PSYDEE, 46 rue Saint-Jacques, 75005, Paris, France.

Caroline Braet is a psychologist and behavioural therapist in the Paediatrics Department of the University Hospital of Ghent. She is a teacher and trainer of the developmental and clinical aspects of childhood therapy, carries out behavioural and family therapy with children and is researching programmes for children.
Address: Department of Paediatrics, University Hospital of Ghent, H. Dunantlaan 2, B-9000 Ghent, Belgium

George Butterworth is Professor of Psychology at the University of Sussex and an Honorary Professor of Psychology at the University of East London. His doctoral research was completed at the Department of Experimental Psychology, Oxford University, and he has carried out many years of research on perception and cognitive development in babies.
Address: Psychology Division, School of Cognitive Science, University of Sussex, Falmer, Brighton, BN1 9QN, UK

Andreas Demetriou was Professor of Developmental Psychology at the Aristotle University of Thessaloniki until September 1996, when he moved to the University of Cyprus as Professor of Psychology. His research interests focus on life-span cognitive development and on the educational applications of cognitive developmental theories. He has proposed one of the so-called neo-Piagetian theories of cognitive development. Currently his research focuses on the relations between cognitive development and personality development.
Address: Department of Educational Sciences, University of Cyprus, P.O. Box 537, 1678 Nicosia, Cyprus

Willem Doise is Professor of Social Psychology at the University of Geneva. His research interests include intergroup relations, social identity, socio-cognitive development, social representations, and explanations in social psychology.
Address: Department of Social Psychology, University of Geneva, CH-1211, Geneva 4, Switzerland

Anne Marie Fontaine has a PhD in Psychology. She is Associate Professor in Differential Psychology and Social Contexts of Differential Development at the Oporto State University, where she is also Head of the Differential Development and Ecological Psychology Research Center. She has conducted and supervised several research projects on the development of motivation and self-concept during adolescence, their relationship with school achievement, and the influence of family and school on their develpment. She is author of the book *Achievement Motivation in the School Context* and has written several chapters and articles for international books and journals.
Address: Faculty of Psychology, University of Oporto, 4000 Oporto, Portugal

Helen Haste has published extensively on moral development, political values and gender. Her most recent book is *The Sexual Metaphor*. Her work in these areas is also reflected in books with D. Locke, J.S. Bruner, and J. Torney-Purta. Her present research is on citizenship, efficacy and social responsibility. Her other research fields include metaphor and culture, with especial reference to the public understanding of science. She holds degrees from the Universities of London, Sussex and Bath. She is Head of the Psychology Department at the University of Bath, and she has held visiting positions at Harvard. She is currently vice-president of the International Society for Political Psychology.
Address: Department of Psychology, University of Bath, Bath, BA2 7AY, UK

Klaus Helkama received his MA and PhD in Social Psychology from the University of Helsinki. He has also studied at the Moscow State University. He spent a year at Harvard with Lawrence Kohlberg, receiving a Certificate of Advanced Study in Human Development in 1980. Since 1986, Klaus Helkama has been Professor of Social Psychology at the University of Helsinki. He has been chairperson of the Finnish Psychological Society, member of the Finnish Research Council for the Social Sciences, and Dean of the Faculty of Social Sciences of the University of Helsinki. During 1996–1997 he was visiting professor at the University of Geneva. He has published seven books and numerous articles on moral development and values, as well as on the history of social psychology.
Address: University of Helsinki, Department of Social Psychology, P.O. Box 4 (Fabian Katu 28), SF-00014 Helsinki, Finland

Dolph Kohnstamm is Professor of Developmental Psychology at Leiden University and a member of the Social Science Research Council of the Royal Dutch Academy of Sciences. His current research is mainly on the changing structure of (perceived) individual differences in temperament and personality in childhood and adolescence; he has worked for many years in programmes for preschool education for socially disadvantaged children and has done several studies to evaluate their effects.

Address: Faculty of Social and Behavioural Sciences, Wassenaarseweg 52, 2300 RB, Leiden, The Netherlands

Diomedes Markoulis is Professor and Head of the Section of Developmental Psychology at the University of Thessaloniki, Greece. He received his doctorate in developmental psychology from the University of Thessaloniki. His major publications focus on cognitive, socio-moral and political reasoning growth throughout the life-span. His recent research concentrates on structural isomorphism in normal and sensory-impaired adolescents and adults.

Address: Department of Psychology, Aristotelian University of Thessaloniki, Thessaloniki 540 06, Greece

Ivan Mervielde is Professor of Personality and Social Psychology at the University of Ghent, President-elect of the European Association of Personality Psychology and a member of the European Association of Social Psychology. His main research interests are in extending the lexical approach to childhood personality measurement and longitudinal behavioural genetic research of childhood personality structure.

Address: Department of Personality and Social Psychology, University of Ghent, H. Dunantlaan 2, B-9000 Ghent, Belgium

K. Richard Ridderinkhof is a Fellow of the Royal Dutch Academy of Sciences and lectures in the Faculty of Psychology, University of Amsterdam. His research interests are in life-span changes in human information processing, selective attention and executive control. He has published articles in *Child Development*, *Journal of Experimental Child Psychology*, *Acta Psychologica*, *Psychophysiology* and *Biological Psychology*.

Address: Department of Psychology, University of Amsterdam, Roetersstraat 15, 1018 WB Amsterdam, The Netherlands

Maurits van der Molen is Professor of Developmental Psychology at the University of Amsterdam. His research interests lie in mental chronometry, cognitive psychophysiology, central and autonomic nervous system approaches to development and childhood psychopathology. He has published articles in *Psychophysiology*, *Biological Psychology*, *Child Development*, and *Journal of Experimental Psychology*.

Address: Department of Psychology, University of Amsterdam, Roetersstraat 15, 1018 WB Amsterdam, The Netherlands

Cornelis F. M. van Lieshout is Professor of Developmental Psychology at the University of Neijmegen. His research interests concern the social and personality development of children and adolescents. He is particularly interested in the development of dyadic relationships and also child and adolescent behaviour in the context of the family and peer groups.

Address: Psychological Laboratory, University of Nijmegen, P.O. Box 9104, HE 6500 Nijmegen, The Netherlands

Leni Verhofstadt-Denève is Professor of Developmental and Personality Psychology at the University of Ghent, where she is also Director of a Guidance Centre for children and adolescents and Director of a day nursery. She was president of the Belgian Psychological Society 1987–1993 and in 1993 was elected a member of the National Committee for the Psychological Sciences, the Belgian Royal Academy of Sciences.

Address: Vakgroep Ontwikkelings- en Persoonlijkheidspsychologie, H. Dunantlaan 2, 9000 Ghent, Belgium

Franz Emanuel Weinert is co-director of the Max Planck Institute for Psychological Research and Research Professor at the Universities of Heidelberg and München. He received his PhD from the University of Erlangen and his habilitation from the University of Bonn. From 1968–1981 he worked as a Professor and Director of the Psychological Institute at the University of Heidelberg. For some years he served as President of the German Psychological Association.

Address: Max-Planck-Institut für Psychologische Forschung, Leopold-strasse 24, D-80802 München, Germany

Sabine Weinert is a teaching and research assistant in the field of of developmental psychology and developmental psychopathology at the University of Bielefeld (Department of Psychology). She received her PhD from the University of Bielefeld in 1990.

Address: Max-Planck-Institut für Psychologische Forschung, Leopold-strasse 24, D-80802 München, Germany

PREFACE

Developmental psychology is a fascinating and a broad science. It includes the whole of psychology under a life-span perspective. This book aspires to present this science as completely and comprehensively as possible to all readers who have an interest in the various facets of human development. The history, the geographical and scientific origin of the authors who contributed to the book, and its organization and contents converge to suggest that we may come close to the fulfilment of this aspiration. Of course, it is up to readers to judge how close we have come.

This book was conceived five years ago, in 1992, at the International Congress of Psychology in Brussels, during a meeting between Michael Coombs and the first two of the Editors. The idea at that time was to produce a textbook in developmental psychology that would be stronger than other textbooks available in at least four respects. The first aim was to provide the students with a holistic picture of development across the life course from the beginning of life to the end. The second aim was to integrate the developmental views of the individual from different angles, such as the biological, the cognitive, the social, the societal, and the historical perspective. The third aim was to bring developmental theorizing and research in Europe and other parts of the world into focus more than is usual in a standard American textbook. The fourth aim was to produce a book that at one and the same time would be both cohesive and representative of the differences in method and theory that characterize the various subfields within developmental psychology. Attention is drawn to the following characteristics of the book.

Topical approach. The book is organized around the main themes or aspects of development rather than chronologically. Thus, after a chapter on the history and theoretical systems in developmental psychology at the beginning, the book includes chapters on the neurological bases of development, perceptual and motor development, the development of communication and language, cognitive development, social development, the development of morality and wisdom, the development of motivation, personality and emotional development, and developmental psychopathology. Each of these chapters deals with the phenomena of interest under a life-span perspective. The main advantages of the topical organization are twofold.

On the one hand it provides an integrated and complete picture of the development of the phenomenon of interest in each chapter. On the other hand it enables one to see clearly the theoretical and methodological differences between the various subfields. From the practical point of view, this approach enables teachers and students to focus on the domains of their interest without unnecessary interference from other domains.

Multiplicity of traditions and orientations. The book represents all theoretical and methodological traditions that have dominated in developmental psychology throughout the century and which mark the field in the present day. This was ensured by a very extensive planning of the general structure and chapters of the book and by a very selective choice of authors from different academic origins. That is, the topical organization of the book enables each chapter author to stress those traditions and methods that dominated the subfield concerned. The preparation of each of the chapters by well-known researchers in each field ensures that all main issues currently under discussion in each subfield will be clearly represented in the book. It needs to be mentioned here that seventeen scholars coming from ten European countries cooperated to produce the ten chapters of the book. At the same time, the editors of the volume took considerable pains to ensure the necessary integration in style structure and cross-references illustrating common concerns and mutual enrichments of different research traditions. Moreover, each chapter is organized along the same dimension: introduction, theoretical paradigms, methods, main findings and ideas about development, explanation of development.

Special Features

The book includes a number of features that will facilitate both the instructor to pass on the message and the student to assimilate it.

1. A number of key concepts are listed at the end of the book. These summarize the gist of each section and they can be used as advanced organizers for studying each chapter and as reminders of the main ideas of the chapter.
2. Each chapter contains a number of boxes which were prepared with the aim to further illustrate or illuminate some of the key ideas elaborated in the chapter.
3. Finally presentation in each chapter is organized at two levels. On the one hand, each chapter is didactically prepared. That is, concepts and ideas are fully explained and exemplified so that they can be grasped by the beginner. On the other hand each of the chapters reviews the research concerned more extensively and in more depth than is usual in psychology textbooks. This makes the book appropriate for both begin-

ners and more advanced readers who need to be informed about the present state of the art in modern developmental psychology.

Overview of the Book

Chapter 1: F. E. Weinert and S. Weinert: History and systems of developmental psychology. This chapter involves five parts. After a short introduction, it outlines the history of developmental psychology and it then specifies the basic premises of the milestones of developmental psychology in the twentieth century (Piaget, Vygotsky, Bowlby and Ainsworth, and the life-span approach). It then moves on to discuss the central issues of modern research and theory and it attempts to anticipate the future. This chapter also presents the reader with the changing views on the developing individual across the history of the discipline.

Chapter 2: M. W. van der Molen and K. R. Ridderinkhof: The growing and aging brain: Life-span changes in brain and cognitive functioning. This chapter focuses on the relationships between brain development and cognitive development. After an introduction to the basic concepts of brain anatomy and functioning, the chapter reviews modern research on the development of various aspects of the brain, such as changes in its structure, in the communication between different parts of the brain, and in the efficiency of its functioning. The chapter explicates how these changes affect cognitive functioning through the life-span. Also, the chapter discusses modern methods for the study of brain functioning, such as the widely celebrated neuro-imaging techniques which enable the researchers to study ongoing brain activity in relation to cognitive activity.

Chapter 3: G. Butterworth: Perceptual and motor development. After a short introduction to Piaget's work about sensorimotor intelligence, this chapter reviews recent evidence on the origins and development of perception and action systems in the life-span. The chapter emphasizes two aspects which seem to dominate in modern thinking. That is, that from early on in life there are complex and well-integrated perception and action systems which have resulted from our evolution as a species and that these systems are involved in the formation of more complex processes, such as attention, drawing and writing.

Chapter 4: J. Bernicot: Communication and Language Development. After introducing the main theoretical and experimental paradigms concerned with the development of language and communication, this chapter focuses on the communicative and representational functions of language, the relationship between language and the communication situation, and the links between language and the non-linguistic facets of communication. The main steps in the development of these processes are outlined. The chapter also summarizes work on second-language learning by children and adults, written language, and communication in the years of maturity.

Chapter 5: A. Demetriou: Cognitive development. This chapter first presents a systematic introduction to Piaget's theory, with an emphasis on those aspects of the theory which have stood up well to the test of time. Then it introduces the so-called neo-Piagetian theories of cognitive development which attempted to integrate the strongest postulates of Piaget's theory with modern information processing and dynamic system theory. Then there is a systematic introduction to research and theory which focused on the development of inductive and deductive reasoning. The section following covers the development of the understanding of different conceptual domains, namely the understanding of the physical and the biological domain and also the so-called theory of mind. Finally, the last section outlines a theory that aims to function as a frame for integrating different models of cognitive development.

Chapter 6: C. F. M. van Lieshout and W. Doise: Social development. This chapter examines development as it occurs in interactions in the contexts of an individual's relationships and groups across the life course. To illustrate these processes the chapter traces the developmental pathways of three central interactive orientations: antisocial behavior, behavioral inhibition and social withdrawal, and social responsibility. Then the chapter elaborates on the role of interactions in the formation and the maintenance of relationships and it discusses the commonalities and differences in the various types of relationships. In the next section, the role of the family group and the school class are described as social contexts for development. The chapter concludes with a discussion of the continuity and discontinuity in social development.

Chapter 7: H. Haste, D. Markoulis and K. Helkama: Morality, Wisdom and the Life-span. In the first part, the main theories in the field of moral development and prosocial behaviour are reviewed. The second part focuses on the various methods which are used to study the development of moral reasoning. The third part presents the main findings on development of moral reasoning and prosocial behaviour. The fourth part discusses research on wisdom and on extraordinary moral responsibility as a contribution to the understanding of moral development in a life-span perspective.

Chapter 8: A. M. Fontaine: Motivation. After a presentation of basic concepts and definitions, eight theoretical paradigms (e.g., classical theories, such as homeostatic theories and expectancy-value theories, and modern theories, such as self-concept and appraisal theories) that have been used over time in the study of motivation are outlined. Thereafter, current methodologies of studying development of motivation are presented and assessed. Then the main results of developmental studies in the realms of achievement motivation, anxiety, self-concept and social comparison are discussed.

Chapter 9: G. A. Kohnstamm and I. Mervielde: Personality Development. This chapter integrates different approaches to the study of temperament and personality across the life-span. Basic issues, such as the dimensional versus holistic character of personality, stability and change of personality across the life-course, and the relation between more transient states and more permanent states, are discussed first. These issues appear to be core features of different theoretical orientations through the history of the study of temperament and personality. Differences and congruences of instruments for the assessment of temperament and personality in different phases across the human life-course are treated next. The chapter concludes with the description of the development of temperament and personality across the life-span and over generations.

Chapter 10: C. Braet and L. Verhofstadt-Denève: Developmental psychopathology. The orientation on psychopathology from a life-course perspective has recently resulted in the outline of a new discipline: developmental psychopathology. The chapter starts with a short history of the discipline and its place amidst other orientations on psychopathology. Procedures for the longitudinal assessment of different developmental pathways of psychopathology are sketched. The chapter concludes with the description of pathways of developmental disorders in different domains, in particular the cognitive, social, emotional and behavioural domains.

Chapter 1

History and Systems of Developmental Psychology

F. E. Weinert

Max Planck Institute for Psychological Research

and

S. Weinert

University of Bielefeld

INTRODUCTION

One of the most basic facts of human existence is that there are typical age differences and age-related changes in most aspects of human functioning: in the physical body, in sensory and motor abilities, in cognitive skills, in behavior, and in subjective experience. These typical changes are part of our common, lay knowledge and provide a good idea of what infants, toddlers, elementary school children, adolescents, adults, and the elderly are like. Thus, chronological age provides a quite general, but universal indicator of a person's physical and psychological state across the life-span.

Although there are important age-related phases and changes that are biologically determined and genetically programmed (i.e. occur similarly in all humans across all cultures), how these phenomena are interpreted and classified has always varied widely across cultural, historical, and societal

Life-Span Developmental Psychology
Edited by A. Demetriou, W. Doise and C. F. M. van Lieshout. © 1998 John Wiley & Sons Ltd.

contexts: 'Although the significance of different ages and the extent and boundaries of the years which form relatively unitary age categories or age grades vary from society to society, we know of no society which does not differentiate between various "ages" and does not define them through the norms and values of its cultural tradition. In every society the basic and common biological facts are marked by a use of cultural definitions which ascribe to each age grouping its basic characteristics' (Eisenstadt, 1956, p. 21ff).

What is interesting and sometimes surprising is that 'facts' that are self-evident and obvious in one culture and time are not necessarily obvious or self-evident in other cultures or at other times. A good example is the length of childhood and adolescence. Although age-spans covered by child-hood and adolescence and the definition of their age-graded tasks may appear natural or necessary to members of industrialized societies, they can be completely different in other cultures. The period of childhood can be shorter or longer, and in some cultures there is hardly a distinction between childhood and adulthood. Adolescence may last many years and (as in our culture) proceed in a relatively unregulated and nonritualized manner, or it may last only a few months and include ritualized preparation for induction into the adult culture (e.g. initiation rituals). Such differences are not just found between more traditional and modern societies—they also occur within single societies as a result of cultural change.

There are also large individual differences in psychological age and aging within any one cultural period. That is, individuals of the same age, from similar backgrounds, vary widely in when specific biological and psychological features of childhood, adolescence, adulthood, and old age appear, how they appear, the form they take, and how they change.

HISTORICAL ROOTS OF DEVELOPMENTAL PSYCHOLOGY

Across history, there have been many varied, intuitive ideas about development, collected as common sense and noted by poets, philosophers, educators, and physicians. People have always made robust generalized statements about human development, provided explanations, and provided us with (sometimes contradictory) advice about the 'best' ways to facilitate development and to avoid developmental problems. Thus, the lay psychology of development offers a rich but very culture-specific set of materials.

A scientifically based developmental psychology has existed for only a little more than 100 years. Although this psychology was built on rich experiential sources of knowledge about development and education, it is nonetheless a typical product of the nineteenth century. Among the many roots of present-day developmental psychology there are two that continue to have an especially important influence: the theory of evolution and the founding of psychology as an empirical science of human behavior.

The Impact of the Theory of Evolution on Developmental Psychology

It is not possible to understand the zeitgeist of the nineteenth century without recognizing the fascination scientists and scholars in almost every discipline had for historical analysis, especially for the concept of development. What was this concept? It was the basic and far-reaching belief that one could only understand biological, psychological, or philosophical phenomena by knowing their place in a historical or developmental sequence. It was also the assumption that every developmental phenomenon followed a regular pattern that proceeded from an indefinite, incoherent homogeneity to a definite, coherent heterogeneity.

This basic idea was more general, pervasive, and far reaching than even the contents of Charles Darwin's epochal work, *On the Origin of Species* (1859). The principles of 'natural selection' as the basis for the evolution of living organisms were laid out in this book long before the discovery of the laws of genetics or the molecular mechanisms of genetic transmission. The basic principles of natural selection are the following: (a) there is a natural genetic variation among individuals; (b) because of limited environmental resources (e.g. food), not all individuals in a population can survive; (c) those who do survive are the fittest, that is, they adapt best to their current environment; (d) there is continuous natural selection that leads to changes in the individuals of the species and (through surviving gene mutations) to the emergence of new forms that in turn contribute to variation. According to Darwin, these fundamental regularities were true not only for the animal world but also for the development 'of each mental power and capacity of man' (1859, p. 488).

Despite the programmatic inclusion of psychology in the theory of evolution, one should not overstate Darwin's (1809–1882) influence on developmental psychology. His contribution was quite varied and was often confused with ideas from many others.

If one were to ask today which consequences of the theory of evolution had the most important effects on developmental psychology when it began in the nineteenth century and when it expanded explosively in the twentieth century, one could receive a variety of different answers. Three are especially noteworthy:

- The 'law of biogenetics' formulated by Haeckel and enthusiastically supported by many of his contemporaries specified 'that ontogenesis is the abbreviated and speedy recapitulation of phylogenesis' (Haeckel, 1866, Vol. I., p. 300). This thesis elicited enormous fascination among developmental psychologists in the United States and in Europe.

  Of course, many developmental psychologists at the time knew that the 'biogenetic law' was not meant to suggest a strict parallelism or a genetically transmitted causal relation between phylogeny and ontogeny. Rather, it specified a vague analogy that is no longer given any scientific credibility.

- Fuelled in part by a search for empirical support for recapitulation theory, comparative studies of all sorts were fostered in developmental psychology—across human and nonhuman species, across cultures, and across age groups.

  This comparative orientation, still important today, considerably enriched the knowledge base available to developmental psychology. Heinz Werner suggested as early as 1926 that general developmental psychology (in addition to specialized theories covering the development of animals, children, the mentally ill) should be established as an integrative science concerned with general laws of mental development in phylogeny, ontogeny, and pathology. This interesting program unfortunately remained caught between single empirical studies and general theoretical speculation.

- The same can be said for a newer research trend that is called sociobiology or human ethology (Wilson, 1975). This field began with the assumption that characteristic, genetically anchored, needs and behaviors universal to all humans arose during phylogeny. This assumption led to comparative animal studies and to comparative cultural studies that attempt to describe the universality, variability, and adaptivity of human behavior.

  There is no question that sociobiological research has produced a good deal of interesting knowledge about 'human nature' and its variability across cultures. However, the scientific contribution of this research paradigm is still quite controversial because of gaps in empirical support and theoretical explanation, which are often filled with 'it could have been' plausibility argumentation and scientifically dangerous 'research story telling.'

Developmental Psychology as a Subdiscipline of Psychology

The fact that psychology became established as an independent science in the last quarter of the nineteenth century plays a less obvious, but no less important role than the theory of evolution in the history of developmental psychology. From the beginning, developmental psychology was a subdiscipline of psychology and was embedded in its scientific as well as its institutional framework.

Most psychologists place the birth of scientific psychology as a discipline independent of physiology and philosophy in 1879, when Wilhelm Wundt established the first experimental laboratory in Leipzig. It was also Wundt who wanted the future scientific psychology to rest on two methodological paradigms: (a) the analysis of the elements, processes, and products of basic human mental functions (e.g. sensory perception, attention, motor actions) as an experimental physiological psychology; and (b) the study of higher mental processes (e.g. thinking, speech) as a comparative-descriptive cultural psychology ('folk psychology'), which Wundt considered to be a comprehensive developmental psychology (including animal psychology and child psychology).

Wilhelm Wundt's (1893) broad conception of developmental psychology as a developmental history of humanity and of individual humans was, as already noted, most notably adopted by Heinz Werner (1926). Wilhelm Wundt doubted that this broad agenda could be accomplished. He cynically predicted that perhaps 90% of all the psychologists of the time would confuse developmental psychology with child psychology. He was probably right: at least in the first half of the twentieth century, child psychology did indeed dominate developmental laboratories and textbooks in all countries. Nonetheless, even with this more limited scope, developmental psychology won and maintained a unique research perspective within the discipline of psychology.

The approach taken by child psychology was quite different from that taken by experimental or differential psychology. The central questions for child psychology were, when specific motor, perceptual, and thinking abilities first appeared in development, and how they changed with age. Because development was primarily conceived as species-general, universal, and similar for all healthy humans, the general belief was that developmental norms could be derived from the observation of single (sometimes more) children. Developmental norms indicated when, on average, children showed a particular behavior and allowed inferences about when basic mental competencies became available. In this approach, age assumed an essential role as a marker variable.

Given that developmental psychology took its own path in its early theories (e.g. the emphasis on maturation models) and methodologies (e.g. systematic observational studies), one might ask what difference it makes that it has always remained a subdiscipline of psychology. From an historical perspective there are two main ways in which general psychology influenced developmental psychology:

- The constant (although often selective) exchange of scientists, theories and themes allowed developmental psychology to import many new ideas and useful variables that were adapted to its descriptive, normative approach.
- The influence of general psychology was especially important in the establishment of required methodological standards. From its beginning, scientific psychology was established as an empirically oriented science of human behavior and had stringent requirements to ensure objective measurement, data reliability, experimental control, and replicability of empirical findings. These standards were also adopted by developmental psychology.

Early Roots of Developmental Research in Psychology

The theory of evolution and the growth of scientific psychology both had important effects on the establishment of developmental psychology at the end of the nineteenth century. Sciences, however, usually have many roots, precursors, and beginnings. This was certainly true of developmental psychology, which experienced a tremendous worldwide growth between 1890 and 1915. In these 25 years no fewer than 21 child psychology journals and 26 university institutes for child research were founded around the world. Despite a general orientation toward a descriptive-normative approach, there were many interesting differences in the research questions and research methods in the early days of developmental psychology. This heterogeneity was probably reinforced by the fact that psychology itself was not a homogeneous entity but rather a concatenation of several, sometimes mutually ignored, sometimes contentiously argued, scientific paradigms (e.g. experimental psychology, psychoanalysis, differential psychology, phenomenological psychology). In the following section we will sketch this heterogeneity by briefly characterizing five particularly important roots of developmental psychology. Each was not only important when the discipline began, but continued to influence the subsequent growth of modern developmental psychology.

Wilhelm Preyer and the systematic observation of child behavior

In contrast to prescientific developmental psychology, which was more often concerned with the problems of handicapped children, educational issues, and fortuitous observation, the orientation in scientific child psychology from the start was toward a more or less systematic observation of child behavior.

In the nineteenth century many parents wrote diaries tracing the development of their children. These diaries provided a first source of empirical data for scientific developmental psychology.

The physiologist Wilhelm Preyer (1841–1897) knew of these documents and criticized them for their imprecise observation and various sorts of confusions. He thoroughly studied the behavior of his own son during his first three years of life and used this and all other data sources available to him to construct an age-graded behavioral inventory for early childhood. This inventory included sensorimotor skills, perception, mental representation, speech acquisition, concept formation, thinking, learning, volition, and the development of consciousness.

Because of this pioneering work, Preyer counts as the originator of developmental psychology's most important empirical research paradigm: the explicit, systematic, methodologically controlled observation of child behavior and age-related changes. Further, he began the tradition of using his findings to give advice to parents and to address child-rearing issues. Of course, Preyer's methods and findings have been subsequently criticized. As we know now, many of his observations were simply false, for example, when he wrote 'the newborn arrives in a bright and noisy world, but it cannot yet see and cannot yet hear.'

Despite the obvious problems with his methods and data, Preyer must be acknowledged as one of the most important developmental psychologists of the nineteenth century. His central contribution was to ensure that behavioral observation became the primary method of the discipline.

Many developmental psychologists followed the path first taken by

Preyer and developed improved strategies, controls, and methods for behavioral observation. One of the most important of these was Arnold Gesell (1880–1961). As director of the well-known Yale Clinic of Child Development he developed improved methods, systematized behavioral observation, introduced technological support (e.g. films), built a huge archive of behavioral data from children of all ages, and outlined regular development sequences for many behavioral domains. This work provided the scientific prerequisites for the construction of developmental assessment tests. These tests allowed the comparison of children's observed developmental states with empirically derived behavioral age norms.

Alfred Binet and the study of development and individual differences

In psychology, the name Alfred Binet (1857–1911) is primarily associated with the construction of the first intelligence test and the concept of 'intellectual age' as a global index of intellectual developmental level. These accomplishments provided the first quantitative measures of intelligence, its developmental level, and its individual differences. Binet's scientific interests were actually much broader than his most famous achievement suggests and included work in experimental, differential, social, developmental, and educational psychology. However, although much of his other work is more important and theoretically relevant to present-day psychology, it has been largely ignored and forgotten. What is remembered is Binet's construction of the first intelligence scales for differentiating normally developing and retarded children (Binet & Simon, 1905), work which made him one of the most cited authors in psychology.

In 1904 the French Ministry of Education asked Binet to find an objective way to distinguish normal and retarded children so that their skills could be appropriately developed in regular or special classes. To accomplish this task, Binet chose to avoid using school achievement tests or teachers' assessments of students and instead concentrated on finding the most objective measure of *intelligence*, which he saw as the central individual factor in school success or failure. His basic idea was the following: those children with more (or higher) intellectual abilities should learn more, faster, and better from everyday experiences than those with less intelligence. Thus, from differences in learning, one could infer differences in underlying intellectual abilities.

Binet's concept of manifest intelligence included different components (sensory and motor skills, general world knowledge, memory, concept formation, and complex problem solving) that were summed up to yield an overall value for general intelligence.

The intelligence test constructed for children by Binet and Simon (1905) became the world-standard model for countless test procedures. A large number of methodological and theoretical contributions on the concept, development, and diagnosis of intelligence have their roots in Binet's scientific and applied research.

Stanley Hall and broad-band studies of children and adolescents

Stanley Hall (1840–1924) was one of the most influential teachers in the early days of psychology. He was the first American student of Wilhelm Wundt, founded the first psychological laboratory and was the first professor of psychology in the United States, and in certain respects turned developmental psychology into a normal science. He was interested in many topics, themes, and developmental phenomena, not only in childhood, but also in adolescence and old age. His basic theoretical perspective on human development was biological-social, and he accepted the validity of the biogenetic law. Within this orientation, Hall was concerned with different aspects of cognitive, social, personal, moral, and religious development. Hall's primary method was to study these areas with extensive questionnaires; in his studies, he addressed a range of topics from simple automatized habits and instincts to complex actions, feelings, volitional impulses, and moral-religious beliefs.

Although his somewhat simplistic questionnaire technique and the resulting data were criticized both by contemporaries and by later psychologists, G. Stanley Hall stands as the originator of the tradition of broad-band, cross-sectional studies in developmental psychology. In this methodology, behavior and attitudes are measured by questionnaires or tests given to relatively large numbers of people of various ages. Age groups are compared and mean differences between them are taken to be valid indicators for individual developmental change. This procedure, however, is only reliable when the variables studied are those that develop similarly in all people, so that individual differences do not play an important role in developmental change. Cross-sectional methodologies, applied within these limits, continue to provide an especially attractive, economical research design in modern-day developmental psychology.

John Watson and experimental child research

John B. Watson (1878–1958), the admired and much criticized founder of radical behaviorism (in which the goal was to limit legitimate psychological research to the measurement of observable behaviors), held the basic laws of learning to be valid independent of age. As a demonstration, he used classical conditioning procedures to show that even infants could acquire a new response to a previously neutral stimulus (e.g fear to an object) when this stimulus (e.g. a piece of fur) was frequently paired with a stimulus that already elicited anxiety (e.g. a very loud noise).

Watson believed that most human behaviors and attitudes were acquired during development by expanding a few inborn reflexes and instincts with such conditioned learning. This belief was expressed in his famous, though controversial, statement: 'Give me a dozen healthy infants, well-formed, and my own specified world to bring them up in and I'll guarantee to take any one at random and train him to become any type of specialist I might select—doctor, lawyer, artist, merchant-chief, and yes, even beggar-man and thief, regardless of his talents, penchants, tendencies, abilities, vocations, and race of his ancestors' (Watson, 1924, p. 104).

Even Watson agreed that this statement went far beyond the results of the infant learning experiments available at the time. His general approach was criticized intensely from the start and, as later research on the heredity–environment issue was conducted, was held to be scientifically untenable.

But it was not primarily his theoretical work that made J. B. Watson important to the history of developmental psychology. Rather, it was his introduction of the experimental method of infant research, still an important research area today, and his empirical demonstrations that learning processes are important not only for cognitive but also for socioemotional development. These ideas were also postulated by some US learning theorists and educational psychologists at the beginning of the century and were later reemphasized and substantiated by B. F. Skinner (1938) and in a more modern way by the social-cognitive learning theorist A. Bandura (1989). In present-day psychological research, the dichotomies of nature and nurture, or maturation and learning no longer express ideological controversy but are seen rather as sets of complementary forces that interact to explain human development and the development of individual differences in behavior.

Sigmund Freud and research on socialization

When the Viennese neurologist Sigmund Freud (1856–1939) developed his psychoanalytical model of personality and personality development as well as his ideas about the origins and treatments of neurotic diseases and symptoms, he was in theoretical and methodological opposition to the 'academic psychology' founded by Wilhelm Wundt. It would be impossible in this chapter to describe or evaluate adequately Freud's monumental contributions or their cultural, scientific, and clinical effects. Thus, only his theory of personality development (Freud, 1917/1963) will be considered as a representative example.

For Freud the motor of psychic development was a set of psychosexual drives. These drives dominate behavior, appear in a regular sequence over childhood and adolescence, and are expressed physically through specifically preferred sources of sexual satisfaction and object attachments. Freud described the sequence of phases as follows: The oral phase (birth to 1 year) is characterized by a dominance of the mouth region and oral activities such as sucking; in the anal phase (1 to 2 years) dominance moves to the anal region and control of excretions; in the phallic-Oedipal phase (2 to 5 years) there is a strong fixation on the opposite sex parent; the latent period (5 to puberty) is a time when early sexual interests no longer play an important role; and the final puberty-genital phase (12–13 through 18–20 years) is a time in which latent infantile sexual impulses give way to adult sexuality.

Freud and many of his followers stated that excessive satisfaction or frustration (or a mixture of excessive satisfaction and frustration) of the latent impulses dominating a particular phase would lead to premature personality fixation at that phase and that especially traumatic experiences in a particular phase could be the basis of later neurotic development. Freud himself believed that personality was often fixed during the fourth or fifth year of life and that later developments only gradually expressed what was already formed.

Freud's psychoanalytical model of development and some important later modifications were combined with psychodynamic learning theories and social-anthropological findings to become the theoretical basis of psychological research on socialization. This work included the study of how children develop within specific societies and the effects of cultural mores, social belief-value systems, and particular parental practices on the developing personality.

Different Models in Early Developmental Psychology

A brief look at the various roots and beginnings of developmental research in psychology shows that there were different ideas about the scope of developmental psychology, how development proceeds, and what the causes of development might be. These different ideas can be captured by briefly summarizing the important early models of development:

1. *Growth model of development.* Development in this model is seen as genetically programmed and directed by processes of maturation. Developmental change is seen as a continuous, quantitative increase in sensory, motor, and cognitive powers, skills, and performances (see Figure 1.1). Empirical examples of this model are Preyer's age-graded behavioral inventory for early childhood and the construction of the first intelligence scales (Binet & Simon, 1905).

2. *Stage model of development.* Development here is also seen as growth in sensorimotor, cognitive, and sociocognitive competencies, but developmental change is characterized as discontinuous, sequential and stage-like, with qualitative differences between successive stages (see Figure 1.2). Noteworthy proponents were Jean Piaget (1970; see section on main perspectives of developmental research, below), Arnold Gesell (1946), and Sigmund Freud (1917/1963).

3. *Differentiation model of development.* In this model, development is neither linear nor stage-like growth, but involves a differentiation of initially more simple, diffuse, holistic patterns of behavior and competencies. These patterns become more differentiated, complicated behavioral systems with higher integration and hierarchical organization (see Figure 1.3). This model has been applied to fields such as language acquisition, motor development, and the development of drawing. Noteworthy proponents of this model were Heinz Werner and Kurt Lewin.

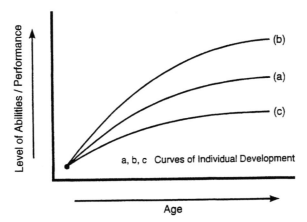

Figure 1.1 Growth model of development

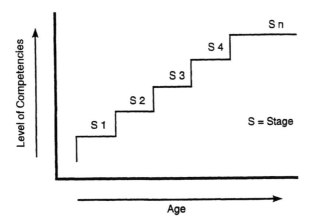

Figure 1.2 Stage model of development

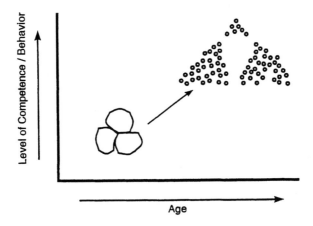

Figure 1.3 Differentiation-hierarchization model of development

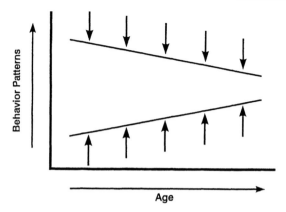

Figure 1.4   Canalization and funnel models of development

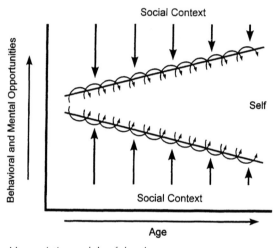

Figure 1.5   Humanistic models of development

4. *Canalization and funnel models of development.* These models assume
    that the range of human behavior or potential behavior is initially very
    broad and plastic at birth and then becomes increasingly reduced in
    scope, fixed in form, and shaped to conform to social norms (see Figure
    1.4). The mechanisms for this include consequences of early childhood
    experiences (e.g. psychosexual impulse fixation/psychoanalysis), and
    early learning (e.g. canalization) that shapes the range of the behavioral
    repertoire.
5. *Humanistic models of development.* Until recently, the concept of the
    individual as an active, increasingly productive constructor of its own
    development, an expression of philosophical ideas from the Enlighten-
    ment, was expressed primarily in psychology by such renegade psycho-
    analysts as Eric Fromm and Abraham Maslow, who were dissatisfied
    with the psychoanalytic emphasis on uncontrollable impulses and
    drives. The concept has become increasingly visible in developmental

psychology in the last few decades. Developmental models from this perspective see the developing individual as more than simply a 'prisoner of age and stage.' They characterize the individual as an organism that is active from birth, increasingly able to direct and control its information-processing activities, to direct and organize its own action possibilities, and to reflect on its own thinking (see Figure 1.5). In some ways, the humanistic model is the opposite of funnel/ canalization models.

Given the variety of developmental models, an obvious question is which is correct, that is, which model best fits the available empirical data about development. The most honest answer is that each of the models is appropriate for describing some aspects of human development. Although this answer does not appear very satisfactory at first, a more fine-grained analysis of human development shows that development is not unitary or homogeneous but rather a collection of very different processes, many with their own local regularities.

FOUR SCIENTIFIC MILESTONES IN THE PROGRESS OF DEVELOPMENTAL PSYCHOLOGY IN THE TWENTIETH CENTURY

Although developmental psychology has its roots in the nineteenth century, the discipline first achieved its present scientific profile and societal importance in the twentieth century. This accomplishment resulted from fundamental theoretical progress and involved contributions from many scientists and many varied research programs. To describe and evaluate the history of these activities comprehensively would require an entire book, and as such is beyond the scope of this chapter.

A flavor of these activities can, however, be conveyed by a description of the most important milestones in the history of developmental psychology in the last 100 years. Four such milestones are especially noteworthy and still strongly influence current empirical and theoretical directions in developmental psychology. These include (1) the monumental scientific contribution of the Genevese scholar Jean Piaget, who postulated and investigated the principle of self-regulation in human development; (2) the contributions of the Russian psychologist L. S. Vygotsky, who emphasized and analyzed the importance of social context for human development; (3) the contributions of John Bowlby and Mary Ainsworth to understanding early personality development, attachment motivation, and the self; and (4) changes in the substance of developmental psychology from a science focused almost exclusively on childhood to a life span psychology. The inclusion of adulthood and old age in developmental psychology demanded a 'new' conceptualization of human development and initiated a revolution in developmental theories. Many developmental psychologists have been involved in this expansion since the middle of the present century.

Jean Piaget and the Principle of Self-Regulation in Human Development

In developmental psychology, as in other disciplines, the productivity of a theory is often measured by the number and range of new and surprising observations it generates. This was certainly the case with Jean Piaget (see Box 1.1). His observations have become an important part of the current store of general knowledge of mental development in children. There is a wide range of nonobvious, even counter-intuitive knowledge that we owe to Piaget. This knowledge resulted in part from his specific methodological procedures and in part from his new theoretical perspectives on development. Piaget's perspective stems from a combination of philosophical ques-

---

Box 1.1 Piaget's work is full of surprising observations. Some examples

At 0;7 (28) [7 months, 28 days] JACQUELINE tries to grasp a celluloid duck on top of her quilt. She almost catches it, shakes herself, and the duck slides down beside her. It falls very close to her hand but behind a fold in the sheet. Jacqueline's eyes have followed the movement; she has even followed it with her outstretched hand. But as soon as the duck has disappeared—nothing more! It does not occur to her to search behind the fold of the sheet, which would be very easy to do (she twists it mechanically without searching at all). But curiously, she again begins to stir about as she did when trying to get the duck and again glances at the top of the quilt.

I then take the duck from its hiding place and place it near her hand three times. All three times she tries to grasp it, but when she is about to touch it I replace it very obviously under the sheet. Jacqueline immediately withdraws her hand and gives up . . . (Piaget, 1937/1968, pp. 36–37).

NAIN (4 years and 6 months): 'Can the moon go wherever it wants, or does something make it move?—*It's me, when I walk.*' And again: '*It comes with me, it follows us.*'

GIAMB (7 years): 'Does the moon move or not?—*It follows us*—Why?—*When we go, it goes.*—What makes it move?—*We do* . . . (Piaget, 1926/1971, pp. 146–147).

KENN (7 years and 6 months): 'If you pricked this stone, would it feel it?—*No.*—Why not?—*Because it is hard.*—If you put it in the fire, would it feel it?—*Yes.*—Why?—*Because it would get burnt.*—Can it feel the cold or not?—*Yes* . . . (Piaget 1926/1971, p. 176).

VEL (8 years and 6 months): 'Is the sun alive?—*Yes.*—Why?—*It gives light.*—Is a candle alive?—*No.*—Why not?—*(Yes) because it gives light. It is alive when it is giving light, but it isn't alive when it is not giving light* . . . (Piaget, 1926/1971, p. 196).

tions of epistemology (how is knowledge possible) and a biological-natural science orientation (e.g. the adaptation of behavior types to environmental constraints). Piaget's goal was to construct a biology of knowledge by empirically investigating knowledge structures and their development (see Box 1.2).

Piaget's experiences with the Binet–Simon intelligence test procedures convinced him that a true picture of children's thinking and cognitive development could be found more in an analysis of children's typical errors than in their correct answers. Both errors and types of problem solving characteristics of different ages suggested to Piaget that cognitive development consisted of qualitative changes in thinking that could not be reduced

---

Box 1.2   Jean Piaget's (1896–1980): Biological sketch

Piaget's interests in the natural sciences, especially biology, and his interest in philosophical questions were evident early in his career. He was just 11 years old when his first publication—a one-page description of an albino sparrow that he had observed in the park— appeared in a journal of natural history. Over the next few years his scientific activities included the investigation of mollusks, and he published more than 20 articles relevant to this topic. Piaget's godfather, concerned that Piaget not specialize too early, awakened the young scientist's interest in philosophical issues. These two themes, a basic biological orientation and an interest in philosophical questions of epistemology, remained important in Piaget's work for the rest of his life.

In 1918 Piaget finished his studies in the natural sciences at the University of Neuchâtel, receiving his doctorial degree at the Faculty of Science. His intensive involvement in the development of children's thinking began when he was working in Paris on the development of Binet and Simon's intelligence tests. In the following years Piaget worked at the Jean-Jacques Rousseau Institute in Geneva and at the University of Neuchâtel. During this time, he completed five widely read books on children's early speech, the development of rules of games and moral judgments, children's perceptions of dreams, and their concepts of causality. Later Piaget taught and conducted research at the University of Geneva and Lausanne, and also at the Sorbonne in Paris. After 1955 he was the director of the Center for Genetic Epistemology in Geneva.

His first published books were followed by more than 50 books and hundreds of articles about cognitive development and what cognitive development tells us about human ways of knowing.

Initially, Piaget's work received only little attention in the scientific community. However, since the 1960s, developmental psychologists all over the world have considered Piaget the most important developmental theorist of this century.

to a simple increase in the number of correctly solved tasks. Piaget believed that the types of knowledge a child had constructed at a particular point in time determined how that child would perceive a new problem, what sorts of problem-solving activities were possible, and which errors were most likely to occur. In other words, the child's thought structures (which developed in a regular sequence) determined what and how he/she could think about the world.

To measure such qualitative developmental differences, Piaget used the 'clinical interview' in which children were asked somewhat standardized questions embedded in carefully constructed problem contexts.

He interpreted the results of his empirical observations and interviews as support for the idea that knowledge states and such basic and (to adults) obvious concepts as space, time, speed, and causality developed slowly over the course of cognitive development. For example, infants do not know what is obvious to older children and adults: that an object (e.g. a toy) continues to exist and occupy space when it is no longer perceptible because it is covered by a cloth (object permanence); similarly, young children do not know that the amount, number, and volume of objects do not change when they are simply rearranged in space (conservation).

According to Piaget's perspective, these concepts and their stages of development (types of knowing) were neither genetically preformed nor acquired from external conditions. Rather, development was seen as an active construction of reality, during which the child's cognitive structures changed to better adapt to the environment. Mental development was thus described as 'the establishment of cognitive or, more generally, episte-mological relations, which consist neither of a simple copy of external objects nor of a mere unfolding of structures preformed inside the subject, but rather involve a set of structures progressively constructed by continu-ous interaction between the subject and the external world' (Piaget, 1970, p. 703).

In this active-constructivist perspective, the developmental processes of knowledge construction were continuous, but the knowledge structures and the ways in which the child could know the world were discontinuous, and changed in a regular sequence of stages. The single developmental stages were seen to develop in an invariant, unidirectional, irreversible, and univer-sal (e.g. the same for all humans) way.

In the course of these qualitative developmental changes the available mental structures become increasingly flexible and allow the child to process increasingly nonobservable, complex information, that is, to represent in-formation symbolically and to manipulate it mentally.

According to Piaget, the development of cognitive structures is driven by an innate tendency to adapt to new experiences on the basis of available knowledge structures. The infant is active from birth on and strives to use its knowledge structures to understand the world (assimilation). As avail-able knowledge structures confront the constraints and demands of the external world, they, in turn, slowly adapt (accommodation). The innate tendency to search constantly for a better balance between the two processes of assimilation and accommodation is the foundation of the fundamental mechanism of self-regulation, which directs and maintains cognitive development.

To conclude: Piaget's theory of cognitive development differs from the mainstream perspective dominant at the beginning of the twentieth century in several ways:

- In contrast to maturation theory and radical learning theory, Piaget stressed the importance of childhood *activity* and *self-regulation* in development. According to Piaget, development should be seen neither as passive, genetically controlled processes of unfolding nor as passive, environmentally controlled processes of learning, but rather as active processes of construction.
- Because Piaget stressed the *interaction* between child and environment in explaining developmental change, he avoided characterizing development as controlled unilaterally by either internal or external factors.
- A change away from monocausal developmental models allowed new ways of thinking about developmental processes and mechanisms that included an innate tendency for self-regulated adaptation (assimilation and accommodation) and the gradual construction of cognitive structures of increasing complexity, flexibility, abstraction, and operational efficiency.
- These processes do not only change observable behavior and problem solving. Basic knowledge and the possible modes of action are determined by the quality of the available overall cognitive system, and this system is slowly and systematically constructed, independent of any particular content domains.

It is hard to portray how important Piaget's theoretical perspective and his empirical evidence were for the history of developmental psychology in the twentieth century. His work caused a revolution in developmental theory (with the system of such concepts as activity, adaptation, self regulation, construction, and cognitive structures occurring in a universal sequence of qualitatively different developmental stages). Since the time Piaget introduced his concepts, they have become an integral part of the background shared by the international developmental community.

L. S. Vygotsky and the Concept of Social Learning in Human Development

Most developmental approaches, especially Piaget's universalistic theory, portray child development as an individual, intra-psychic process that is largely independent of social interaction and sociocultural contexts. This is not true for Vygotsky. His analyses of the *social origin* of higher mental functions such as conscious attention, consciously controlled memory, and

Box 1.3   L. S. Vygotsky (1896–1934): Biographical sketch

Lev Semyonovich Vygotsky was born northeast of Minsk in Belarussia in 1896, the same year as Jean Piaget's was born. After completing his studies, he first taught literature and psychology for six years in a school in Gomel in the vicinity of Chernobyl. In 1924 he received an offer to be a research assistant for experimental psychology at the University of Moscow, largely on the basis of his presentation to the second Neuropsychology Congress. This was the beginning of a short but brilliant scientific career during which Vygotsky served as professor in several institutions and wrote more than 180 articles and books.

During his career, Vygotsky addressed issues in such different domains as perceptual development, memory, thinking, emotion and volition in childhood, concept acquisition, the relation between thought and speech, the problem of consciousness, the relation between development and learning, the acquisition of writing, developmental diagnostics, the importance of play in development, and instructional principles. He also studied different developmental disorders ('defectology') including the development of blind, deaf/dumb, mentally retarded, and 'difficult' children. Vygotsky died of tuberculosis on June 11 1934, when he was 38 years old.

Although some of his work was translated into English as early as the 1930s, it was not until the beginning of the 1960s and the translation of a greatly abbreviated version of 'Language and Thought' that Vygotsky's perspective attracted wide attention. Since then, especially since the 1980s, interest in Vygotsky's work has increased immensely around the world, and it has had a large impact on many newer developmental theories.

volition have received increased attention in the last few years, so that his work is of importance not only historically but also as a part of the current developmental perspective (see Box 1.3).

Vygotsky stressed the importance of the social dimensions for defining such constructs as mind, cognition, memory, and consciousness, constructs that are typically attributed to the individual in most psychological theories as well as in everyday lay terms. According to Vygotsky, the higher mental functions do not develop in the individual but in the social interaction: 'Any function in the child's cultural development appears twice, or on two planes. . . . First it appears between people as an interpsychological category, and then within the child as an intrapsychological category. This is equally true with regard to voluntary attention, logical memory, the formation of concepts, and the development of volition . . . Social relations or relations among people genetically underlie all higher functions and their relationships' (Vygotsky, 1981, p. 163).

Thus, higher cognitive functions are manifested first in the social plane, between people, and only then slowly get internalized by the child (interiorization). An especially good example of this process is the acquisition of conscious action plans and selective attention in complex problem-solving situations. The development of these higher mental functions is closely related to the interiorization of outer, external speech to internal speech or the transition from social to self control.

How can this process be portrayed? First, speech provides an especially important social-cultural means for controlling social exchange. It is used to negotiate different social purposes, for example to influence others, to draw their attention to events or memories, to draw attention to a particular part of a task, or to hold a discussion with others in a problem-solving situation. According to Vygotsky, the most important qualitative change in ontogeny that leads to higher, consciously controlled mental functions is the interiorization of such social control by cultural means.

This perspective on mental development differed equally from radical biological and from extreme environmentally oriented developmental theories that dominated the first half of the twentieth century. Social exchange and the resulting learning processes were given little importance in biologically oriented theories because either the whole developmental process or the developmental mechanisms were considered to be biologically determined. They were also given little importance by extremely environmentally oriented theorists who considered learning and development to be synonymous.

The either-or contrast between inner and outer control of development was resolved in Vygotsky's considerations. For him developmental processes underlying thinking, memory, or attention are neither internally controlled maturational processes or self-regulation processes nor the result of social interaction and learning. Rather, social interaction provides sociocultural means that are actively taken up by the child, slowly interiorized, and thus transformed into new available means for problem solving.

The implication of this view is that the analysis of developmental changes in cognitive functions requires more than isolated studies of single children. The child must be studied more in its social interactions with experienced members of its society. This consideration has had both important theoretical as well as practical and diagnostic consequences that are especially evident in the now well-known concept of the 'zone of proximal development.'

The zone of proximal development marks the difference between the levels of shared and interiorized functions: it is defined as the distance between the 'actual developmental level as determined by independent problem solving' and the higher level of 'potential development as determined through problem solving under adult guidance or in collaboration with more capable peers' (Vygotsky, 1978, p. 86).

The (individually different) zone of proximal development has acquired importance as a developmental diagnostic tool as well as a useful concept in instruction.

A comparison of Vygotsky's and Piaget's theoretical positions shows some important similarities and differences:

- Both theorists stressed the importance of activity and action for cognitive development. These are neither the result of preformed maturational processes nor are they acquired by elementary learning experiences.
- For both, the goal was to better understand higher cognitive processes by looking at their sources and developmental changes. The study of developmental changes was thus given a central role in psychological theories.
- Development means more than change in external forms of behavior. It is characterized by qualitative changes in basic cognitive structures (Piaget) or in mental functions (Vygotsky).
- For Piaget, developmental changes were universal, directed by the child's confrontation with the specific (physical) environment and by an innate drive for adaptation, organization, and self-regulation. For Vygotsky, the sociocultural world was more important. Contrary to Piaget's perspective, Vygotsky believed that the actual course of the process of development of the child's thinking does not take place in the direction going from the individual to the socialized state but rather, starts from the social and proceeds to the individual.
- The differences between the two developmental positions are shown especially clearly in their treatment of the role of instruction in development. Both agree that the effectiveness of teaching and learning depends on the developmental level of the child. For Piaget, instructional processes cannot modulate any essential developmental changes but are dependent on developmental changes. In contrast, for Vygotsky, instructional processes play a major role in the development of higher mental processes.

John Bowlby, Mary Ainsworth, and their Contributions to the Study of Socioemotional Development

What are the social and psychological conditions that are most important for the future mental health of a child? What are the causes of mental illness? Such questions about the variables affecting personality development occupy a central position in the theoretical and applied deliberations of both developmental and clinical psychologists. The importance of early experience to later personality development was emphasized especially strongly in a report written by John Bowlby for the World Health Organization (WHO) in 1951 (see also Box 1.4).

Bowlby summarized his conclusions at the beginning of the WHO report as follows: ' . . . what is believed to be essential for mental health is that the infant and young child should experience a warm, intimate, and continuous relationship with his mother (or a permanent mother-substitute) in which

---

Box 1.4 John Bowlby (1907–1990) and Mary Ainsworth (born in 1913): Biographical sketch

---

John Bowlby was born in 1907. After completing his undergraduate studies in medicine at Cambridge University, he did volunteer work at a school for maladjusted children and decided to begin training as a child psychiatrist and in psychoanalysis. After the Second World War, Bowlby was invited to become head of the children's department of the Tavistock Clinic in London, which, to highlight his beliefs in the importance of the parent–child relationship, he promptly renamed the 'Department for Children and Parents.'

Commissioned by the World Health Organization, Bowlby produced an influential report in 1951 on mental health in postwar Europe that documented the significance of the quality of parental care and the disastrous effects of early childhood separation on the future mental health of a child. The search for a satisfactory theoretical explanation of the significance of early relationships and deprivation experiences on young children remained Bowlby's primary scientific interest for the rest of his career.

Mary Ainsworth, born in 1913, took a position in London at the Tavistock Clinic with John Bowlby. She worked on a project investigating the effect of early childhood separation on personality development.

Attachment theory is the joint work of John Bowlby and Mary Ainsworth: 'John Bowlby, using concepts from ethology, cybernetics and psychoanalysis, formulated the basic outlines of the theory. We owe to him a new way of thinking about the infant's tie to the mother, and its disruption through separation and deprivation. Mary Ainsworth not only translated the basic tenets of attachment theory into empirical findings, but also helped us to expand the theory itself. Her two major theoretical contributions were the explanation of individual differences in attachment relations and the concept of the caregiver as secure base' (Bretherton, 1991, p. 9).

---

both find satisfaction and enjoyment. . . . It is this complex, rich, and rewarding relationship . . . that child psychiatrists and many others now believe to underlie the development of character and of mental health' (Bowlby, 1951, p. 13).

An obvious question was how to explain the significance of early relationships to later development. Why can an early childhood separation from the caretaker (who need not be the biological mother) have such dramatic consequences for a child's subsequent development? In Bowlby's opinion, neither the psychoanalytic perspective prevailing at the time nor the social learning theories that dominated developmental psychology could adequately explain the empirical facts. Both perspectives emphasized the satisfaction of primary needs (hunger, thirst, sexuality), and early social relationships were regarded as derived from primary need satisfaction, feeding in particular. Bowlby took a very different stance: ' . . . he conceived attachment behavior as a major component of human behavioral equipment, on a par with eating and sexual behavior, and as having protection as its biological function, not only in childhood but throughout life' (Ainsworth & Bowlby, 1991, p. 336).

From a psychological point of view, attachment describes the emotional bond that develops between a child and his or her caretaker. From a functional point of view, this emotional bond serves as a key element in balancing the infant's needs for safety and the need for exploration and varied learning experiences. Many things are novel and exciting to 1- to 2-year-old children, but those things that attract babies may also cause them harm. Attachment was seen as the mechanism that keeps interest and fear in balance and that protects children. Bowlby hypothesized that attachment is a control system, somewhat analogous to a thermostat: If a situation is strange or frightening or if the distance between the attachment figure and the child threatens to become too large, attachment behaviors will be initiated by the mother or the child to keep the system within bounds. According to Bowlby, the basis for this regulatory activity is an evaluation of the situation, which is based on prior experience, and inner working models of the self and the attachment figure.

Attachment does not only depend on the proximity-seeking behavior of the child, it also depends on the responses of the attachment figure. If the attachment figure satisfies the child's needs for protection and exploration, the child will develop a working model of its caretaker as reliable and a working model of the self as valued and competent. Conversely, frequent rejection, neglect, or caretaker unavailability will lead to an uncertain model about the caretaker's behavior and to a working model of the self as unworthy and incompetent. These working models are the basis for expectations as well as action plans and thus have a strong influence on behavior and socioemotional development.

John Bowlby's and Mary Ainsworth's ethologically oriented attachment theory has stimulated a large amount of subsequent research, ranging from the examination of the stability of early attachment patterns, to their predictive power for later socioemotional and cognitive development, to the investigation of cultural similarities and differences in attachment patterns, and to the analysis of attachment patterns in adolescence and adulthood. Many researchers have investigated the role of attachment in special populations, for example among neglected and abused children, or children whose parents exhibit socioemotional disorders.

The works of Bowlby and Ainsworth represent classics in the strict sense of the word, both within the attachment research tradition and in the wider field of socioemotional development more generally. Their contribution is a milestone in the history of developmental psychology.

From Child Research to Life-span Developmental Psychology

Another milestone in the history of developmental psychology in this century cannot be attributed to the work of individual scientists but is the result of a collective effort by many scientists to redefine developmental psychology so that it includes the entire life-span, from birth to death (see Baltes, 1987).

Of course there were earlier attempts to include at least old age in developmental research, because it was believed that development during the latter part of the life-span may mirror development during childhood. There were also a few individual scientists who were interested in psychological development across the entire life-span. An explicit attempt to conceptualize developmental psychology as life-span psychology, however, first began in the 1960s and 1970s.

The focus of this new conceptualization was not just to expand the range of developmental research to include adulthood and old age; rather, it presented a fundamentally new theoretical orientation. Although theoretical models of childhood development differed in many respects, an implicit and dominant assumption was that development was directed by processes of biological maturation. For example, according to Flavell (1972, p. 247) the fundamental developmental changes during childhood were species-specific and uniform, unavoidable, significant, directed toward achieving the mature adult state, and irreversible.

Life-span psychology (exemplified by Baltes, 1987, and many others) attempted to replace or at least expand this strongly biological orientation with a more open, liberal, and pluralistic concept of psychological development. If one considers psychological changes across the life-span as a whole, the following characterization emerges:

- Development is a life-long process. No age period, not even in early childhood, totally determines subsequent development.
- Development is multidirectional: there are increases and decreases in behavior at all age levels (even when growth processes dominate in childhood and processes of decline dominate in old age). In other words: there are gains and losses in behavioral possibilities at every age and at every developmental level (typical losses in early childhood include the reduction of conditioning readiness and a narrowing of the phonological repertoire as a consequence of exposure to particular languages; typical examples of gains in old age are increases in expert knowledge in different domains and greater wisdom).
- In contrast to canalization models, the life-span approach assumes life-long individual plasticity for 'new' developments. Although genetic factors, learning processes in early childhood, and a variety of life experiences, as well as the effects of critical life events, can strongly and permanently influence the behavior of an individual, it is nonetheless a tenet that there are always developmental opportunities as well as developmental constraints across the entire life-span.

- Most proponents of life-span developmental psychology also espouse a contextualized concept of development. They assume that human development is a complex, dynamic phenomenon in which biological and intrapsychological factors, mechanisms, and tendencies interact dialectically with social-interactive, societal, cultural, historical, and idiosyncratic events and experiences. A three-factor model has been proposed to represent these developmental influences systematically (see Baltes, 1987). These are:

1. Age-graded influences: Biological (e.g. maturation) and age-dependent social effects (e.g. normatively determined school entry) lead to interindividual similarities in development.
2. Historically graded influences: Historical-cultural events or changes (wars, economic crises, industrialization, etc.) affect the development of certain age cohorts in similar ways, and lead to larger similarities among the members of a cohort (similar year of birth and similar secular developmental conditions) and larger differences between adjacent cohorts.
3. Non-normative influences: These events (e.g. illnesses, loss of close relationships, large change in economic status) do not follow any general or predictable patterns; thus, they tend to increase individual differences between persons of the same cohort or the same sociocultural contexts.

The life-span approach has generated many empirical studies focused on specific questions, usually across longer age-spans. It is notable that these studies frequently involve a multidisciplinary focus and collaboration which include such disciplines as biology, medicine, demography, psychology, sociology, and education.

A look at the current international literature shows that developmental psychology has assumed a life-span orientation. A more liberal concept of development becomes more frequent, and psychological development is increasingly understood to include all longer-term changes in behavior, cognition, and personality. It is important to note, however, that within this broad conceptual framework there are still classes of behavioral changes, mostly in early childhood and in old age, that suggest a more narrow, biologically oriented developmental concept.

MAJOR CHANGES AND CENTRAL ISSUES IN MODERN DEVELOPMENTAL PSYCHOLOGY

Looking at just the last 30 years of developmental psychology, there are different trends that help to characterize the field in its current form. Three are especially important:

1. The significance and influence of developmental psychology has in-

creased within the field of scientific psychology. Research findings are used to prevent and solve serious problems involving children, adolescents, and older adults. This has led to a large international expansion in developmental research.

2. The time of the 'large theories' and broad theoretical controversies is past. Micromodels and microtheories covering limited ranges of application have dominated the field for some time. This trend has its advantages and disadvantages. Advantages include the fact that present theoretical models acknowledge the variability of observed phenomena and empirical data. Disadvantages are that such models are less likely to provide a scientifically solid, comprehensive picture of a specific age group or of the life-span development of particular psychological functions such as memory, thinking, or the self concept.

3. The empirical findings, theories, and applications in developmental psychology have become more complex and less transparent. It is often difficult to process the mosaic research findings to answer general theoretical or practical questions. This is not only because many developmental psychologists prefer micromodels. It also occurs because human development is in fact a complex and complicated phenomenon that can be seen from many different perspectives (Bruner, 1990).

Main Perspectives of Developmental Research

It has already been noted that developmental phenomena can be approached from different perspectives, and that the perspective one takes leads to different research questions.

1. The general goal from the *universal perspective* is to describe the laws of human ontogeny, that is, to analyze those aspects that characterize the development of all humans at all times (maturation, universal sequences of adaptation, degeneration).

    If empirical results suggest that individual variability in the development of a certain feature is small, one can make generally valid theoretical claims on the basis of data from fewer individuals (in the extreme case, from one person). This was a strategy followed, for example, by Jean Piaget.

2. The explicit goal of the *differential perspective* is to describe and explain individual differences in cognitive and personality development. To illustrate the scientific potential of this area (which is somewhat ignored by mainstream developmental psychology), one only needs to think of the obvious and often large differences among adults in many aspects of psychological functioning and abilities. How do these differences develop? What are their causes? Is it possible to influence differential developmental pathways intentionally by altering the environment, instruction, or caregiving style? These questions can be asked and answered on different levels:

- Some interindividual differences appear in similar ways in all cultures. Good examples are psychological differences between males and females. Such sex differences have been the subject of intense debate for years. We still lack a sufficiently solid empirical base to provide scientifically, and not ideologically, based answers to these very difficult questions.

- There are large, culturally mediated interindividual differences. The range of variation in human behavior and experience across cultures is impressive, and includes massive, culture-specific sex role differences, differences in belief and value systems, and differences in many cognitive skills and personality styles. Despite acknowledging unexplained genetic differences between members of different ethnic groups, the results from cross-cultural research always demonstrate strong effects of culturally transmitted habits, norms, skills, and child-rearing practices.

- There are large interindividual differences within each culture and society. For example, despite the many cultural, historical, and social similarities among the developed, highly industrialized countries of Europe and North America, there are still enormous interindividual differences in intellectual skills, cognitive abilities, personal characteristics, and social patterns. To explain such interindividual differences, it is necessary to analyze the life-span development of many different individuals. This is necessary to bring a scientific approach to the old nature–nurture problem, rather than simply continuing the controversial discussions. In such a life-span analysis the relative importance of genetic factors and environmental conditions in the genesis and development of interindividual differences can be assessed. Because contributions from molecular biology are presently not able to explain psychological phenomena, two classic methods are still used to assess genetic and environmental effects: twin and adoption studies. These methods allow a rough estimation of heritability, that is, the relative influence (in a particular population and in a particular historical period) of genetic factors and environmental conditions on variation in the development of psychological characteristics. However, it is not possible to make general statements about the impact of genetic and environmental influences for single individuals or for the human species in general. This restriction is often ignored or misunderstood.

3. The focus of the *individual perspective* is on lawful characterizations of the development of single individuals. It is difficult for psychology to take the single individual as the object of research, because psychology is a nomothetic science that searches for general laws of behavior. What contribution can the development of the single individual make to such a science? There are two ways in which the relation between general developmental laws and individual development has been approached:

- The individual is taken as the intersection point of a large number of psychological variables and developmental changes. For example, one can construct a psychological profile from an individual's scores on intelligence tests, standardized cognitive tasks, personality questionnaires, and behavioral rating scales. Such a profile allows the characterization of that person's developmental status and shows graphically how that individual differs from the mean values for its particular age group.

- Beginning in the nineteenth century proponents of a phenomenological-hermeneutic perspective have argued that it is impossible to use quantitative measures to describe individual uniqueness, consciousness, or intentionality, and that it is impossible to explain development by nomothetic laws. They propose adopting a more phenomenological orientation to be able to characterize and understand the individual personality and its development in more qualitative ways. This argument is based on a fundamental misunderstanding of what the science of psychology is. As a science, psychology must study universal, differential, and individual regularities in development. This means that scientific psychological studies can only address parts of the developing person, not the whole and not the unique.

From General Models to Specific Information-Processing Approaches

The *fact* that a person's behavior, experience, and performance changes with age over the course of development from infancy to old age seems self-evident. The answer to the question of *what* it is that actually changes during the course of development is not at all self-evident. Should the changes be described only on the level of isolated behaviors or patterns of behavior, as radical behavior theories would assume? Or should they be characterized as changes in general competencies and cognitive abilities? Are there empirically testable patterns and relations among single aspects of development in behavior, experience, and performance, so that it is justified to speak of changes in psychological structures, systems, and functions? Piaget's answer to this question was clear: important developmental changes during childhood do not occur at the level of observable behavior, but at the level of the domain-general cognitive structures that underlie action and thought. Piaget's theory thus constituted an integrative, general competence theory: regardless of the contents or the specific psychological function (e.g. speech, perception, thought), how a child understands or can understand is determined by that child's current cognitive developmental state.

There were some empirical results that led theorists to question seriously whether such a general structural perspective could fully account for developmental changes:

- The development of concepts that were formally and logically similar seemed more heterogeneous and domain-specific than a general developmental model would predict.
- Children's thinking and problem-solving skills were more task-specific than a structuralist theory would predict.

An example will illustrate these points: According to Piaget's theory, children of about 4 years have an 'egocentric' representation of the world and do not consider the prior knowledge, wishes, or perspectives of adult communication partners (more exactly, they *cannot* take this information into account). However, children of this age do adapt to special situations, for example, they simplify their speech when communicating with younger children. Generally, what the empirical findings show is that preschool children's thinking is not always centered on their own perspective in every situation and every task, nor is their thinking always static and irreversible. Thus, under some conditions the general features that Piaget described as developmentally prototypical do not characterize young children's thought in general. This suggests that it is too simplistic to say that some cognitive abilities are either present or not present at a particular age; rather, whether cognitive skills are available or not depends on specific situational conditions.

Why a child can solve a problem under some conditions but not under others, or in some domains but not in others, cannot be adequately explained by a developmental theory that posits only general abilities, independent of task and content.

This of course raises the question of whether theoretical advances are more likely to come from studies of the development of general, overarching cognitive structures, or from studies of those different situational demands and cognitive prerequisites that make a task difficult or easy for a child. This would shift the focus from a search for general, age-typical competencies and deficits, to the study of those components and processes important for the encoding, processing, and use of information in the context of concrete tasks. In such an undertaking, task analysis, that is, a fine-grained analysis of the processes involved in the solution of specific tasks, would be especially important.

The research carried out from this information-processing perspective has produced a variety of models for specific developmental changes and has led to a considerably more complex picture of what it is that develops, namely a diverse set of competencies, rather than only a single entity.

From a Focus on Competence Deficits in Childhood and Old Age to the Search for the Competent Young Child and the Competent Old Adult

Regardless of any particular underlying theoretical orientation, the focus of developmental research has often been on the deficits of particular age groups, not their competencies. This research specified what younger children cannot yet do and what older adults can no longer do. The list of appropriate examples is long. To begin with infancy, Preyer characterized newborns as blind and deaf; Piaget emphasized the poor coordination between sensory and motor abilities in early infancy; William James described early infancy as a 'blooming, buzzing confusion'; radical learning theorists characterized the cognitive state of the newborn as a 'tabula rasa.' These deficit characterizations do not stop with infancy but apply at later developmental stages as well: In comparison to an older child, the 5-year-old solves fewer tasks in an intelligence test, does not take another person's perspective, does not possess appropriate memory strategies, and so on.

This deficit perspective also dominated the description of developmental changes in old age. For example, an early hypothesis (called the 'degeneration hypothesis') was that older adults and children have similar 'deficits' and process information more slowly, less efficiently, and less flexibly than young adults.

As general overarching models were differentiated into more domain-specific developmental models, such deficit-oriented perspectives were increasingly replaced by research that focused on competencies. A variety of studies on developmental changes in old age showed that there was not a uniform, general degeneration across all functions and content domains, at least in healthy adults. Further, training studies showed astounding learning and performance reserves in old age in addition to declines. And last, naturalistic studies of changes in areas where individuals had extensive expertise showed improvement in performance well into old age.

The perspective also changed in child-oriented research. More and more researchers focused on the competencies of infants and young children. In their introduction to the book *The Competent Infant*, Stone, Smith, and Murphy wrote in 1973: 'We have ample reason now to think that it [the nature of neonatal experience] is neither a buzzing nor a confusion, though certainly blooming. So much does the evidence of recent research belie the earlier contentions, so much does it underscore the competence of the young infant, that we have chosen the title of this book to crystallize the single overriding trend of these findings' (1973, p. 4).

A LOOK FROM THE PAST TO THE FUTURE OF DEVELOPMENTAL PSYCHOLOGY

Developmental psychology has always been both a basic and an applied science. It emerged both from nineteenth-century ideas of the theory of evolution, and from a need to address a variety of disorders and educational problems in children and adolescents. Thus developmental research has always been both theory driven (basic research) and problem driven (applied research). This dual orientation will, and must, continue into the future.

Can We Expect Theoretical Progress in Describing, Explaining, and Predicting Developmental Phenomena?

The saying, 'Past behavior is the best predictor of future behavior' applies not only to individual development, but also to developmental psychology itself. Therefore, we may expect an expansion of developmental research in the future, with more scientists conducting more research projects and reporting their results in increasingly more publications. It is also certain that the present range of content areas studied, questions asked, and developmental research results published will increase. The remark that developmental psychology can be defined in terms of what developmental psychologists do will be even more apt than before.

The expansion of developmental research will not only increase our knowledge of the details of development but should lead to general theoretical progress as well. An important indicator for this positive expectation is the increasing attention to the problems of taking chronological age as a developmental variable.

Over the more than 100-year-old history of developmental psychology, chronological age has been the dominant independent variable in empirical research. In other words, the mean age at which some psychological change occurs has been studied again and again, with a focus on when infants, children, and adolescents first show particular cognitive or social competencies, how long these abilities and skills take until they have reached their maximum level (asymptote), and when (in adulthood) they eventually decline. Chronological age has served not only as a temporal ordering variable to describe developmental changes but also as a (pseudo) explanation for those changes.

Age got its status as an indicator variable simply because the timing and length of many maturational processes (and degenerative processes in old age), many learning processes, and many processes of knowledge acquisition, as well as culturally normed educational opportunities are highly correlated with chronological age. It was a long time before chronological age was recognized to be an empty variable (Wohlwill, 1973) that has no explanatory value. Recognizing this, more and more researchers are presently attempting to delineate the psychological prerequisites, relevant environmental conditions, dynamic processes, and moderating variables of developmental changes, rather than simply using age as an illusory explanation for those changes. It is only in this way that both descriptive and explanatory models of human development will be significantly improved.

Do such improvements in descriptive and explanatory models also automatically improve developmental predictive accuracy? Unfortunately, this is not always the case, because most developmental changes are too complex and multicausally determined. This is especially true for the acquisition and modification of more advanced abilities, knowledge, motivations, aspirations, and attitudes.

Developmental Psychology as a Source of Scientific Knowledge for Solving Practical Problems

In the course of a critical analysis of traditional theoretical approaches, Kaplan defined developmental psychology as 'a practico-theoretical discipline, a policy discipline, concerned with the perfection (including liberation or freedom) of the individual' (Kaplan, 1983, p. 188). Two things are especially noteworthy and unusual in this definition: first, that developmental psychology is seen not just as an empirical-theoretical discipline but also as a pragmatic-political one; and second, that both scientific and pragmatic activities within the discipline must be oriented toward current social values. There is little doubt that most developmental psychologists doing applied work follow both of these perspectives in their work. However, research scientists best address their theoretical and pragmatic goals when they are as unbiased as possible in their search for reliable and valid insights. They do this by studying the values, convictions, attitudes, and political orientations of the developing individual as empirical facts. This allows the acquisition of the most 'objective' knowledge, which can then be applied to achieve practical goals, even goals within a sociopolitical context.

The sorts of questions asked by developmental psychologists cover a broad range, from issues of early detection and prevention of developmental problems, to treatment, child rearing, child competence in courts of law, and cognitive or personal problems in old age. Responsible and scientifically well-founded answers to such questions can, of course, only be as good as our knowledge base. All reliable, valid empirical findings and all empirically supported theoretical models help to increase our understanding of practical problems (here we pay homage to Kurt Lewin, who said that there is nothing more practical than a good theory!). However, this is not sufficient. In addition, we need a specialized applied knowledge, acquired from practical experience and systematic research. We have made much progress in this direction in the last decades, but we must continue to expand this practice-oriented knowledge, especially in the following areas:

- *Developmental psychopathologies.* Psychopathological development (e.g. disorders or impairments in cognitive, motor, sensory, linguistic, emotional, personal, or social development) frequently cannot be fully understood from the context of normal development. Rather, the particular phenomena, symptoms, possibilities for change, spontaneous remissions, and interventions must be explicitly studied.
- *Diagnosis.* Before one can provide advice and help for developmental problems, it is necessary to be able to diagnose the problem. A child's developmental level must be determined for different psychological functions, the particular dysfunctions must be localized, and remedial possibilities must be identified. There are many tests available (developmental scales, developmental tests, tests for estimating the zone of proximal development, microgenetic methods to analyze simulations of

change, standardized behavioral observation scales, and methods for obtaining medical histories).

- *Predictions and prognoses.* There are some developmental problems that spontaneously occur and then spontaneously disappear. There are also long-term problems and problems that progressively increase in severity. It is important to know which kind of problems require intervention. One may forgo intervention for the first type of problem, because it is not required or might even cause problems. However, in the second case, intervention is usually most effective when it is begun as early as possible.

- *Interventions.* The professional techniques used in counseling, remedial instruction, training programs, and different forms of therapy must be evaluated for whether they are indicated or contraindicated in specific types of situations.

- *Evaluation.* What effects do specific interventions have on different developmental problems in different individuals in different social contexts? Are undesired side-effects likely to accompany desired main effects? There are no general recipes for answering these questions. Each intervention is an experiment, guided by hypotheses, that requires monitoring of possible effects and side-effects and continuous diagnosis of the initial problem. The results from such work will provide information for optimizing treatments under specific concrete conditions.

Because it is both a basic and an applied science, developmental psychology is well equipped to improve its practical competencies. Indeed, it has made great progress in the last 100 years in doing just this. However, it is necessary to increase theoretical and empirical efforts to come even closer to the goal put into the mouth of the renaissance scientist Galileo Galilei by the German poet Bertold Brecht: 'To my mind, the only purpose of science is to lighten the toil of human existence.'

REFERENCES

Ainsworth, M. D. & Bowlby, J. (1991). An ethological approach to personality development. *American Psychologist*, **46**, 333–341.

Baltes, P. B. (1987). Theoretical propositions of life-span developmental psychology: On the dynamics between growth and decline. *Developmental Psychology*, **23**, 611–626.

Bandura, A. (1989). Social cognitive theory. *Annals of Child Development*, **6**, 1–60.

Binet, A. & Simon, T. (1905). Application des méthodes nouvelles au diagnostic du niveau intellectuelle chez des enfants normaux et anormaux d'hospice et d'école primaire. *L'année Psychologique*, **11**, 245–336.

Bowlby, J. (1951). *Maternal Care and Mental Health*. Geneva, Switzerland: World Health Organization.

Bretherton, J. (1991). The origins of attachment theory. John Bowlby and Mary Ainsworth. *Developmental Psychology*, **28**, 759–775.

Bruner, J. T. (1990). *Acts of Meaning*. Cambridge, MA: Harvard University Press.

Darwin, C. (1859). *On the Origin of Species by Means of Natural Selection.* London: John Murray.

Eisenstadt, S. N. (1956). *From Generation to Generation.* New York: Free Press.

Flavell, J. H. (1972). An analysis of cognitive developmental sequences. *Genetic Psychology Monographs*, **86**, 279–350.

Freud, S. (1963). *Introductory Lectures on Psycho-analysis. Part III: General Theory of the Neuroses* [English translation of Vorlesungen zur Einführung in die Psychoanalyse, 3. Teil, Neurosenlehre. Leipzig und Wien, Heller Verlag, 1917]. London: Hogarth Press.

Gesell, A. (1946). The ontogenesis of infant behavior. In L. Carmichael (Ed.), *Manual of Child Psychology* (pp. 295–331) New York: Wiley.

Haeckel, E. (1866). *Generelle Morphologie der Organismen.* [General morphology of organisms]. Berlin: Reimer.

Kaplan, B. (1983). A trio of trials. In R. M. Lerner (Ed.), *Developmental Psychology: Historical and Philosophical Perspectives* (pp. 185–228). Hillsdale, NJ: Erlbaum.

Piaget, J. (1926/1971). *The Child's Conception of the World.* London: Routledge & Kegan Paul.

Piaget, J. (1937/1968). *The Construction of Reality in the Child.* London: Routledge & Kegan Paul.

Piaget. J. (1970). Piaget's theory. In P. H. Mussen (Ed.), *Carmichael's Manual of Child Psychology* (Vol. 1, pp. 703–732). New York: Wiley.

Preyer, W. (1895). *Die Seele des Kindes.* [The mind of the child] (4th edn). Leipzig: Grieben.

Skinner, B. F. (1938). *The Behavior of Organisms.* Engelwood Cliffs, NJ: Prentice-Hall.

Stone, L. J., Smith, H. T. & Murphy, L. B. (1973). *The Competent Infant—Research and Commentary.* New York: Basic Books.

Vygotsky, L. S. (1978). *Mind in Society: The Development of Higher Psychological Processes.* Cambridge, MA: Harvard University Press.

Vygotsky, L. S. (1981). The genesis of higher mental functions. In J. V. Wertsch (Ed.), *The Concept of Activity in Soviet Psychology* (pp. 144–188). Armonk, NY: Sharp.

Watson, J. B. (1924). *Behaviorism.* New York: People's Institute Publishing.

Werner, H. (1926). *Einführung in die Entwicklungspsychologie* [Introduction to developmental psychology]. Leipzig: J. A. Barth.

Wilson, E. O. (1975). *Sociobiology: The New Synthesis.* Cambridge, MA: Belknap Press of Harvard University Press.

Wohlwill, J. F. (1973). *The Study of Behavioral Development.* New York: Academic Press.

Wundt, W. (1893). *Grundzüge der physciologischen psychologie* [Fundamental of physiological psychology], Vol. 1. Leipzig: Englemann.

Chapter 2

The Growing and Aging Brain: Life-span Changes in Brain and Cognitive Functioning

Maurits W. van der Molen and K. Richard Ridderinkhof

University of Amsterdam

INTRODUCTION

For a long time, developmental psychology has been relatively 'brainless'. Until recently, developmental psychologists have generally failed to consider the behavioral implications of the growing brain. They assumed either that the *in vivo* brain cannot be accessed in the developing child, or that the neural hardware is irrelevant for theories of the developing software, or even that the dependence of the developing mind on the maturing brain is inexplicable in principle. This seems ironic, since the founding father of developmental psychology as an academic discipline, Wilhelm Preyer, was concerned specifically with brain–behavior relations (see van der Molen, 1990). Unfortunately, the study of developmental psychology and the experimental analysis of brain–behavior relations have grown apart rapidly during the turn of this century. Even to date, many developmental psychologists seem willing only to pay lip service to the importance of biologically plausible theories (for a critical assessment see Segalowitz, 1994, p. 67). However, recent years have shown an increasing appreciation of the relevance of the neural underpinnings of developmental processes, as witnessed by the recent publications of special issues, journals, and volumes that try to bridge the gap between developmental psychology and the neurosciences (e.g. Crnic & Pennington, 1987; Dawson & Fischer, 1994; A. Diamond, 1990a; K. Gibson & Peterson, 1991; Johnson, 1993; Schore, 1994; Segalowitz & Rose-Krasnor, 1992). These reports have stimulated a growing awareness among developmental psychologists that the progress in the neurosciences and the availability of innovative, non-invasive methods for studying brain–behavior relations are creating new and interesting possibilities to incorporate brain maturation in developmental theorizing.

A deeper understanding of the growing and aging brain should provide a challenge for theories that aim to integrate nervous system function and performance across the life-span. Obviously, an exhaustive treatment of developmental changes in brain–behavior relations cannot be given within the limited scope of this chapter. Our main thrust will be to identify major trends in brain growing and aging, with some emphasis on brain plasticity. These trends will be highlighted with illustrative studies that used non-invasive methods to assess brain–behavior relations across the life-span. The illustrations were selected to emphasize the connection between the developmental and aging ends of the life-span continuum. In this regard, the current discussion is kaleidoscopic rather than exhaustive. The chapter will be concluded by a discussion of the life-span perspective relating the speed of performance to the inhibitory control supposedly exercised by the frontal cortex. We hope that this chapter will contribute to a further appreciation of interdisciplinary research on age changes in brain–behavior relations, and promote the formulation of life-span theories that incorporate our current understanding of the growing and aging brain.

THE WORKING BRAIN

In order to appreciate the implications of the findings emerging from the neurosciences for developmental theorizing, the reader should have a basic understanding of brain structure and function. In his monograph *The Working Brain*, Luria (1973) provided a concise integrative account of brain structure and function, which will be reviewed briefly below. Luria's views are still accepted widely, and his notions of the special functions of the frontal cortex are now being incorporated in developmental theories (e.g. Dempster, 1992). According to Luria (1973), mental functions are not strictly localized but are supported by many brain regions that act in concert. This view led him to propose three major functional systems of the brain that are involved in many types of mental activity. Box 2.1 provides an example of how nineteenth-century localizationists made an attempt to chart the unknown brain territory.

Nervous System Anatomy

Before considering Luria's (1973) scheme of cerebral organization, it is necessary to provide a brief sketch of the functional anatomy of the central

Box 2. 1   Brain mapping of complex mental functions

Psychology has a long history relating brain to behavior. In the late eighteenth century, the Viennese neuroanatomist Gall wished to establish a new science which would be an anatomy and physiology of the brain and at the same time a psychology (e.g. Gall & Spürzheim, 1810). Gall was convinced that specific areas of the brain subserve specific psychological functions and that it was possible to obtain objective measurements of the development of these functions by charting the surface of the head. Gall postulated that the brain is not a unitary organ but a collection of at least 35 specific brain centers, each corresponding to a specific mental function. He believed that even complex mental functions such as 'spirituality' and 'self-esteem' were mediated by distinct brain organs. In the left panel of Figure B2.1:1 it can be seen that the phrenologists used ingenious tools to surface the human skull and in the right panel a detailed brain map is shown depicting a wide array of psychological functions resulting from the analysis of the bumps on the scalp.

3 The organ of Inhabitiveness
4 The organ of Adhesiveness
5 The organ of Combativeness
6 The organ of Destructiveness
7 The organ of Constructiveness
8 The organ of Covetiveness or Acquisitiveness
9 The organ of Secretiveness
10 Self-Love or Self-Esteem
11 Love of Approbation
12 Organ of Cautiousness
13 Organ of Benevolence
14 The organ of Veneration, or of Theosophy
15 The organ of Hope
16 Ideality, or the Poetical Disposition

1 The organ of Amativeness
2 The organ of Philopogenativeness

Figure B2.1:1   Phrenological machine (left panel). Phrenological map of the psychological make-up of the brain (right panel).

Obviously, the extreme localizationist view of the phrenologists lacked a factual basis and the brain charts resulting from their fanciful enterprise were soon forgotten. The first empirical attempt to localize brain function originated from the work of the French neurologist Broca (1865) who described the case of a patient who was able to understand but not to produce language. Postmortem examination revealed that this patient had a lesion in the posterior portion of the left frontal brain. This site was included in lesions observed in similar cases, which led Broca to conclude that this part of the brain comprises the center for speech production, and that a lesion of this site results in the loss of expressive speech. Several years later, Wernicke (1874) described cases where lesions including another part of the brain were associated with the loss of ability to understand speech while production was still intact. Thus, this region was identified as the center for speech perception. The discovery that complex mental functions, like speech perception and production, were localized in circumscribed areas of the brain aroused a renewed interest in the functional structure of the brain.

Sources: Broca, P. (1865). Sur le siége de la faculté du language articulé. *Bulletin of the Society of Anthropology*, **6**, 377–296. Gall, F. J. & Spürzheim, G. (1810). *Anatomie et physiologie du système nerveux en général, et du cerveau en particulier, avec des observations sur la possibilité de reconnaître plusiers dispositions intellectuelles et morales de l'homme et des animaux, par la configuration de leurs têtes*. Paris: Schoell. Wernicke, C. (1874). *Der Aphasische Symptomenkomplex*. Breslau, Poland: Cohn & Weigert.

nervous system. The central nervous system consists of four major parts, the *spinal cord, brain stem, diencephalon*, and *cerebral hemispheres* (see Figure 2.1). During the course of embryonal development, nerve cells are organized into a tubular structure which persists in the adult. The portion that ends up in the head develops into the brain and the remainder forms the spinal cord.

The spinal cord contains afferent pathways for sensory information to the brain and efferent pathways descending from the brain to the motor system. The spinal cord also receives information from internal organs, and is involved in many autonomic functions. It continues upwards into the brain stem which consists of three parts, the *medulla, pons*, and *midbrain* (from bottom to top). The medulla includes several control centers for vital autonomic functions, such as breathing and heart rate. The pons contains an important relay center for information from the cerebral hemispheres to the *cerebellum*, a system which is important for the parametrization and fine-tuning of movement. The midbrain controls many sensory and motor functions, including eye movement. Above the brain stem lies the diencephalon that comprises two major structures, the *thalamus* and *hypothalamus*. The thalamus is a major relay system for information coming

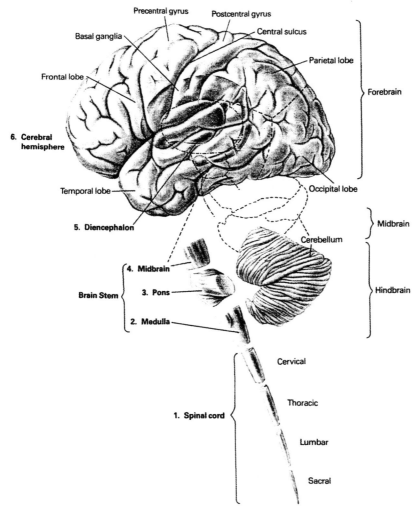

Figure 2.1   The six main anatomical regions of the central nervous system. From Kandel, E. R., Schwartz, J. H. & Jessell, T. M. (Eds) (1991). *Principles of Neural Science* (third edition). New York: Elsevier. Reproduced by permission of Elsevier Science.

from lower regions of the brain to the cerebral cortex. The hypothalamus, lying just below the thalamus, is important for the regulation and integration of autonomic, endocrine, and visceral functions. Overlying and surrounding the diencephalon are the cerebral hemispheres. They consist of the *cortex* (whose function is described in more detail below) and deeper lying structures, including the *basal ganglia*, participating in the control of motor behavior, the *hippocampus*, involved in memory storage, and the *amygdala*, which is a coordination center for autonomic and endocrine responses associated with emotional states. The central nervous system surrounds an interconnected system of four cavities, the *ventricles*, that contain cerebrospinal fluid.

Box 2.2   Brain images of complex functional systems

Luria (1973) emphasized that mental functions are not confined to a single brain region but are mediated by a widely distributed network of brain mechanisms. This view is illustrated nicely by recent brain images of human subjects performing a series of hierarchically organized language tasks (Posner & Raichle, 1994). At the lowest task level, subjects were asked to fix their gaze on a small crosshair in the middle of a monitor while an image of their brain activity was obtained using positron emission tomography (PET). At the second level, subjects continued to look at the crosshair but now common English nouns were presented just below the crosshair or spoken over headphones. At the third level, subjects were asked to pronounce the words they viewed or heard. Finally, the fourth level required subjects to generate a use for the word they either viewed or heard.

The basic idea is that subtracting the first level from the second would isolate brain areas concerned with visual or auditory perception. Subtraction of the second level from the third level would iden-tify the regions involved in speech production, and, finally, subtraction of the third level from the fourth level would index the areas concerned with the access of the meaning of a word. The PET scans revealed that blood flow is concentrated in different brain regions depending on the language process isolated using the subtraction technique. The occipital lobe brightened up when subjects were passively viewing words whereas the temporal lobe was lightened when they listened to the nouns. When the task required speech production, blood flow was shifted to the motor cortex. Finally, when subjects were generating verbs, brain areas in the temporal and frontal lobes were activated. These findings demonstrate that the posterior parts of the brain are primarily devoted to the reception and initial analysis of sensory information whereas the anterior brain regions are involved in production, control, and memory.

These findings provide strong support for Luria's (1973) contention that complex functions cannot be strictly localized in particular areas of the brain. Moreover, the functional systems of the brain are also highly flexible with regard to their componential organization. Analogous to an orchestra which may play the same tune by using different instruments, complex functional systems perform invariant tasks by using variable mechanisms. Finally, Luria pointed to the dynamics of the functional systems of the brain. This aspect has important implications for developmental psychology. Obviously, the change of higher mental functions due to training or in ontogeny has important implications for their cerebral organization. In the early stages of training or development of a complex mental function it will rely on rather primitive brain mechanisms, but in subsequent stages the mental functions will acquire a more complex structure and, evidently, will invoke very different brain structures. Basically, Luria's argument is

that a decomposition of the mental function is needed prior to analyzing which brain mechanisms act in concert to produce the complex
mental activity.

Sources: Luria, A. R. (1973). *The Working Brain: An Introduction to
Neuropsychology*. London: Penguin. Posner, M. I. & Raichle, M. E.
(1994). *Images of Mind*. New York: Scientific American Library.

The wrinkled surface of the cortex consists of clefts and ridges that
separate the major cortical regions: the frontal, parietal, and occipital lobes
(from anterior to posterior) and the temporal lobe (lateral to the other
lobes). The major division lines are formed by the *sagittal fissure*, a cleft that
separates the brain along the midline into the two hemispheres, connected
by the *corpus callosum*; the *central sulcus* that separates the frontal lobe from
the more posterior regions; the *parietal-occipital sulcus* that separates the
parietal and occipital lobes; and the *Sylvian fissure* that demarcates the
temporal lobe. Most of the cerebral cortex is involved in sensation and
action. Broadly speaking, the anterior parts of the brain are involved in
production whereas the posterior regions are committed to perception (for a
systematic treatment of these issues, the reader is referred to Kandel,
Schwartz & Jessell, 1991).

Functional Brain Systems

Luria (1973) distinguished three principle functional systems of the brain
that are involved in any type of mental activity. The first functional system is
concerned with the regulation of activation; the second is concerned with
information processing; and the third is concerned with the programming,
regulation, and verification of action. Box 2.2 provides an example of how
functional systems may act in concert to perform complex operations.

The reticular activation system

Luria's first functional brain system is concerned with the regulation of
cortical tone or activation. This system is located in the subcortex and brain
stem, and consists of a neural net (called the *reticular formation*) over which
excitation can spread in order to gradually modulate the state of the nervous
system. Some of the fibers of this formation comprise the *ascending reticular
activation system*, and run upwards to terminate in higher nervous structures including the cortex. The ascending part of the reticular formation is
committed to the regulation of cortical activation. Other fibers comprise the
descending reticular activation system; they arise from the cortex and run
down to terminate in the brain stem. Via the descending part of the reticular
formation, the cortex exert control over the tonus of the nervous system.

The information processing system

The basic function of Luria's second functional system is information processing: it is involved in the reception, analysis and storage of information. This system occupies the lateral regions of the posterior cortical surface, including the occipital, temporal, and parietal areas. The information processing system is formed by projection and association zones of the cortex. The projection (or primary) areas consist of neurons with high specificity, responding only to particular stimulus features. The primary regions are surrounded by secondary areas that subserve a synthetic function. These areas include many associative neurons enabling specific information to be combined in functional patterns. Finally, the tertiary zones lie on the boundaries between occipital, temporal, and parietal cortex. Luria (1973) ascribed the tertiary zones the principal function of the spatial organization of information coming from different regions and the transformation of successive information into simultaneously organized patterns.

The hierarchical organization of the information processing system has important ontogenic implications. Early during childhood, the proficiency of higher zones depends on the integrity of the lower zones. Thus, an early deficit in the primary zones will lead inevitably to the incomplete maturation of the tertiary zones later in development. During the course of development, however, the higher zones come to assume control over the lower cortical zones. In the adult person, the sensory information derived from the lower zones is fitted into the schemes produced by the tertiary zones. In this vein, the tertiary zones may compensate for damage at lower cortical levels.

The action system

The third functional system of the brain is responsible for the programming, regulation, and verification of action. This action system is also organized hierarchically, with the lowest level formed by the spinal cord. It is responsible for organizing automatic and stereotyped responses to stimuli. The second level consists of the brain stem which operates as an important relay center that integrates motor commands descending from higher levels and information ascending from the spinal cord. The third level in the hierarchy is the *motor cortex*, located anterior to the cental gyrus. The motor cortex receives information from other cortical areas and issues motor commands to the lower levels and to the muscular system. The fourth and highest hierarchical level of the action system consists of the *premotor cortex* and *supplementary motor area*, which are responsible for motor programming and preparation, and the *prefrontal cortex*, an executive control center.

The most important part of the third functional system is the frontal lobe, which contains almost one quarter of the total mass of the brain. As indicated above, the frontal cortex has two-way connections to the brain stem. This rich system of activating and inhibitory connections allows the frontal cortex to finely tune the state of the cerebrum and to adjust the energy level of the organism in response to changing needs of the internal milieu and the demands of the environment. The frontal lobe is also connected to the thalamus, hypothalamus, amygdala and other subcortical structures. Most of these connections are reciprocal: the frontal cortex receives and integrates impulses arriving from virtually all subcortical areas, allowing it to organize efferent impulses so that it can regulate all the structures. Finally, the frontal cortex is connected intimately and reciprocally to a wide array of other cortical areas, including the motor cortex and the association areas, making it a 'superstructure' above all other parts of the cortex. This applies foremost to the prefrontal cortex which, in Luria's (1973) scheme, is considered the tertiary association zone of the frontal lobe.

In reviewing the complex mental functions mediated by the frontal cortex, Luria (1973) noted that this structure does not mature completely until very late during ontogeny. He reported data from the Moscow Brain Institute showing that the surface area of the frontal lobe increases rapidly around the age of 3 with a second jump towards the age of 7 or 8. The long maturational period of the frontal cortex has important implications for cognitive development. Young children may show behaviors comparable to the inadequate performance of frontal-lobe lesioned patients. For example, both young children and frontal patients experience considerable difficulty in suppressing prepotent responses. The next sections will discuss age-related changes in the brain across the life-span, in order to facilitate an appreciation of the significance of age changes in brain–behavior relations.

THE GROWING BRAIN

Brain maturation is an epigenetic process. The total genetic information available to the developing organism—perhaps 10^5 genes in mammals—is not sufficient to specify the total number of neuronal connections—perhaps 10^{15}. Epigenetic influences arise both from within the embryo and from the external environment. Internal influences include factors such as surface interactions between cells and hormonal changes into the blood flow. External influences include factors such as nutrition and sensory experience. The interplay of these factors controls the proper differentiation of individual neural cells and the patterning of neural connections. This process occurs in a series of ordered steps that are precisely timed with a temporal sequence that is relatively fixed and characteristic of a particular neural structure.

Prenatal Development

Prenatal development can be divided in several periods: the *germinal, embryonic,* and *fetal* stages. The first phase, the germinal stage, lasts from conception until implantation, when the developing organism is firmly attached to the wall of the uterus. After implantation, the organism enters the embryonic stage, when the embryo begins to differentiate into three distinct layers: the *ectoderm* or outer layer, that will later develop into the nervous system, but also sensory cells, skin glands, hair, nails, and parts of the teeth; the *mesoderm* or middle layer, from which will develop the muscles, skeleton, and the circulatory and excretory systems; and the *endoderm* or inner layer, which will develop into gastrointestinal tract, bronchi, lungs, and other vital organs such as the liver and pancreas. Development during the period of the embryo takes place at an extremely rapid rate. Although the embryo is only a quarter of an inch long at one month after conception, it is 10 000 times the size of the zygote from which it developed. The last seven months of pregnancy, the fetal stage, involve primarily a process of refining all the primitive systems that are already in place. Brain growth does not stop at birth. Indeed, between the seventh prenatal month and a child's first birthday, the brain increases in weight by more than a milligram per minute. At birth, the newborn's brain is about 25% of its adult weight, but by the second birthday it is about 75%. It is not surprising, then, that the last prenatal months and the first two years have been termed the period of *brain growth spurt*. The amazing growth of the human brain is illustrated in Box 2.3.

Neural development

The human brain and nervous system consists of more than one trillion highly specialized cells that are involved in the transmission of electrical and chemical signals across trillions of connective spaces between the cells. There are two distinct classes of cells in the nervous system: *nerve cells* (or *neurons*) and *glial cells*. Neurons are the basic information processing units of the brain and nervous system, and are all formed by the end of the second trimester of pregnancy. Neurons consist of a cell body and two types of outgrowths: *dendrites* and the *axon*. Dendrites, branching out in a treelike fashion, serve as the main apparatus for receiving signals from other nerve cells. In contrast, there is typically one axon that is the main conducting unit of the nerve cell for transporting signals. Near its end, the axon branches out to make contact with other neurons at contact points called *synapses*. Interneuronal communication at the synapse is accomplished with the help of chemical *neurotransmitters*.

Box 2.3 The amazing growth of the human brain

For the human organism, the time frame of gestation is 40 weeks following the last menstrual period. During gestation, the brain develops at a spectacular rate. Assuming that the fully developed human brain contains approximately one hundred billion neurons and that virtually no new neurons are added after birth, the developing brain must generate neurons at a rate of approximately 250 000/min. The rapid growth of the brain during the embryonic and fetal stages of development is depicted in Figure B2.3:1. During intra-uterine development, the brain grows from virtually nothing to approximately 350 grams at birth. At this point, it is important to note that brain maturation is not limited to the gestation period. Most of the postnatal growth occurs within the first few years after birth but some measures of brain maturation continue to reveal development change even after the seventh or eighth decade of life. Brain growth can be subdivided into many sequential processes. The precise timing of these processes may provide potentially important information on the factors controlling the development of the nervous system, as a later occurring process cannot possibly influence an earlier process whereas a preceding process may have an effect on a subsequent process.

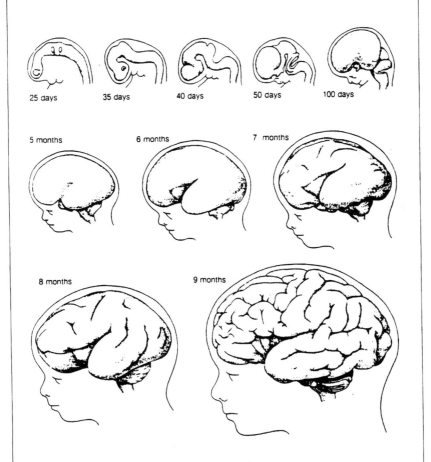

25 days   35 days   40 days   50 days   100 days

5 months   6 months   7 months

8 months   9 months

Figure B2.3:1 Prenatal development of the human brain
From Cowan, W. M. (1979). The development of the brain. *Scientific American*, **214**, 112–133. Reproduced by permission.

Glial cells are far more numerous than neurons, and they continue to form throughout the life of the organism. Glial cells are probably not essential for neural transmission. They are thought to serve several other roles. Glial cells nourish neurons and provide firmness to the brain as supporting elements. Some types of glial cells produce a waxy substance called *myelin*, forming a sheath that covers most large axons. Myelination acts like an insulator to speed up neural impulse transmission. Other types of glial cells have nutritive functions, remove debris after cell death and injury, or may be implicated in the creation of the blood–brain barrier, in the migration of neurons, or in the outgrowth of axons.

The initial formation of neurons and their migration to the appropriate regions of the brain are events that occur almost entirely during the prenatal period. In broad outline, there are two classes of postnatal neural changes: *formative* and *regressive* changes. Formative changes include the proliferation, migration, and differentiation of the nerve cells, the myelination of neural pathways, and the increase in the number of connections among neurons. The regressive changes include the elimination of neurons and the decline in synaptic connections. Interestingly, the child has many more neurons and connections just after birth than is typical when (s)he is an adult. The marked changes in the nervous system during development may well comprise one of the important constraints on the development of motor skills, language and cognitive abilities.

Nerve Cell Proliferation and Migration

The proliferation of nerve cells begins at the inner surface of the neural tube. The cavity of the neural tube gives rise to the ventricular system of the central nervous system. The inner wall of the neural tube will generate all the neurons and glial cells of the nervous system. However, cell proliferation is not uniform along the length of the neural tube. Individual regions expand differentially to develop the various specialized structures of the mature nervous system.

A characteristic feature of nerve cells is that they migrate from the sites of their proliferation in the ventricular zones to their ultimate positions. In broad outline, there are two different ways in which neurons migrate to their final destination. In some parts of the developing nervous system, migration takes the form of passive displacement. That is, after leaving the proliferation zone, cells travel initially over a short distance, but are then displaced farther away from their original position by the migration of newly produced cells. Thus, cells that are generated earlier are positioned farther away from the proliferative zone. Regions of the nervous system showing this *inside-to-outside* spatiotemporal gradient include the thalamic areas and many parts of the brain stem and spinal cord. In many cases, however, the migrating neuron contributes actively to its displacement away from the proliferative zone. When this happens, more recent neurons may bypass neurons generated previously, thereby creating an *outside-to-inside* pattern which is found in most parts of the cerebral cortex (Nowakowski, 1987).

An essential question in the study of brain growth is how migrating neurons travel to their final destination. Soon after the formation of the neural tube, many cells begin to proliferate but a distinct group of cells, radial glial cells, retain contact with both surfaces of the neural tube. In the primate cortex, many neurons use radial glial cells for navigating from the proliferative zone to reach their target destination. This observation led Rakic (1988) to propose the radial glial hypothesis, suggesting that the proliferative zone is already segmented in distinct units. Each unit is assumed to give rise to generations of neurons that use the same radial glial pathway to reach their proper destination. In this vein, the array of discrete proliferative units constitutes a *proto-map* of specialized regions of the mature cortex. The radial scaffolding is assumed to provide the basis for the cortical columnar parcellation. This compartmentalization of the mature cortex has important implications for its functional organization. For example, studies of the visual cortex have shown that when a microelectrode penetrates along a perpendicular track, all cells tend to respond in the same manner to the visual orientation of the stimulus (Hubel & Wiesel, 1962, 1963). When the electrode moves to a neighboring site, all cells respond again in the same manner, but this time to a different orientation of the stimulus. Similar modular circuits have been reported for other brain areas (for a review see Purves, 1994). At this point, however, it should be noted that radial glial cells cannot provide the whole story, since many neurons migrate in regions of the nervous system in which radial glial cells have not been found. Furthermore, the preformationist view adopted by Rakic (1988) has been challenged, as illustrated in Box 2.4.

Synapse Formation

Once a cell reaches its final destination, and sometimes even before, it enters the differentiation phase. During differentiation, it begins to grow an axon which terminates in a swelling called the *growth cone* that navigates itself to a precise target. Although the mechanisms of this path-finding are not yet fully understood, chemoaffinity has been established to be one important factor. It has been demonstrated, for example, that growth cones orient themselves toward a target that releases a protein labelled *nerve growth factor*, suggesting that growth cones can sense and follow chemical tracks over considerable distances.

Within a few hours after reaching its destination, the growth cone is transformed into a nerve terminal that gradually takes on the form of a mature synapse. Synapse formation is an intricate and complicated process. Formation of the synapse begins with the immobilization of the growth cone to its target. Then the receptor molecules accumulate beneath the terminal while the density of receptors beyond the synaptic site is reduced considerably. When receptor molecules stabilize under the growth terminal, other axons arrive and may attach themselves to the same target. The one

---

Box 2.4   Preformation versus epigenesis

The preformation hypothesis defended by Rakic (1988) can be contrasted by the epigenetic view. The latter position is consistent with the
observation that neurons remain uncommitted for some time when
they aggregate in the cortex, which may suggest that the cortical plate
forms a 'tabula rasa' inscribed by circumstantial situations (Creutzfeldt, 1977). The epigenetic hypothesis assumes that the heterogeneity
of cortical areas is due to influences impinging on the plastic cortical
plate from other brain structures. Some evidence supporting the epigenetic view comes from the study of the somatotopic representation
of whiskers in the rodent brain which suggests that brain maps can be
altered by peripheral manipulations. These and similar observations
have been interpreted as support for the hypothesis that the heterogeneity of the cortical plate is induced by the periphery rather than
originating from an intrinsic source. Along similar lines, it has been
suggested by Bayer and Altman (1991) that the proliferating ventricular zone is neither a genetically determined mosaic nor a strict tabula
rasa but rather a rough-grained structure which underlies the epi-
genetically determined fine-grained columnar organization of the mature cortex. The prefatory patterning of the ventricular zone provides
only the background for the cytoarchitectonic diversity and functional
specialization of the mature cortex. The conclusion that seems to
emerge from these observations is that the parcellation of the cortex is
induced by powerful epigenetic influences exerted by afferent inputs
from thalamic relay nuclei.

Sources: Bayer, S. A. & Altman, J. (1991). *Neocortical Development.*
New York: Raven Press. Creutzfeldt, O. D. (1977). Generality of the
functional structure of the neocortex. *Naturwissenschaften*, **64**, 507–
517. Rakic, P. (1988). Intrinsic and extrinsic determinants of neocortical parcellation: a radial unit model. In P. Rakic and W. Singer (Eds),
Neurobiology of the Neocortex (pp. 5–27). New York: John Wiley.

---

that arrived first is not necessarily the one that will persist, however. Indeed,
some synapses will be eliminated even though the overall number of contacts continues to grow. An important function of the selective elimination
of synapses is not only to fine-tune synaptic connections but also to modify
or even eliminate components of neural pathways. Some important implications of synapse eliminations are detailed in Box 2.5

Neuronal Interaction

Interneuronal communication is regulated by chemical substances, the
neurotransmitters, that operate in the synaptic cleft. Electrical signals travel

Box 2.5 Selective stabilization of synaptic contacts

There is an interesting phylogenetic trend in the synaptogenesis in the cerebral cortex. In rodents there is little evidence for overproduction of synapses. In the rat brain, synaptic density reaches a maximum which is only 10% greater than the adult value. In the kitten, the maximum value is 50% above the adult value and for the monkey and human the maximum is about 75–95% above the adult value. In the human visual cortex (area 17), only 10% of the maximum value is found around birth. The maximum is reached around eight months followed by a decrease to 50–60% of the maximum at age 11. Synaptogenesis is different for the frontal cortex (middle frontal gyrus). Maximum synaptic density is reached only at around the first birthday and the subsequent decrease does not become evident until age 7, not reaching adult levels before age 16 (Huttenlocher, 1990, 1994).

The observation that human brains comprise a large initial excess of synaptic connections which is then pruned to sustain only some connections whereas others are removed, resulted in epigenetic theories of brain development which rely heavily on notions of selective stabilization (e.g. Changeux, 1985; Edelman, 1987). The theory that epigenesis contributes to the specification of neuronal networks seems to offer a plausible explanation for the apparent discrepancy between the complexity of the brain and the simplicity of the genome. There is, for example, no simple relation between the quantity of DNA, the material of heredity, and the complexity of the brain. From mice to man, the level of organization and performance of the brain increases spectacularly while the total quantity of DNA in the nucleus of the fertilized ovum does not change significantly. In the same vein, the epigenetic theory may offer an explanation for the immense connectivity of the brain coded by only a limited number of genes. The theory of epigenesis by selective stabilization may also provide an account of critical periods or sensitive phases in the development of the organism that correspond to stages of maximal connectivity in which synaptic contacts are still in a labile state (Changeux & Dehaene, 1989). The presence of large numbers of labile contacts may provide the anatomical substrate for neural plasticity during development. Finally, the prolonged period of synaptogenesis may have implications for psychopathology. For example, a disturbance of synapse elimination has been suggested to be involved in the etiology of diseases such as schizophrenia (e.g. Feinberg, 1982).

Sources: Changeux, J.-P. (1985). *Neuronal Man: The Biology of Mind.* New York: Pantheon. Changeux, J.-P. & Dehaene, S. (1989). Neuronal models of cognitive functions. *Cognition*, **33**, 63–109. Edelman, G. M. (1987). *Neural Darwinism: The Theory of Neuronal Group Selection.* New York: Basic Books. Feinberg, I. (1982). Schizophrenia: Caused by a fault in synaptic elimination during adolescence. *Journal* *of Psychiatric Research*, **17**, 319–334. Huttenlocher, P. R. (1990). Morphometric study of human cerebral cortex development. *Neuropsychologia*, **28**, 517–527. Huttenlocher, P. R. (1994). Synaptogenesis in human cerebral cortex. In G. Dawson & K. W. Fischer (Eds), *Human Behavior and the Developing Brain* (pp. 137–152). New York: Guilford Press.

along the axon into the nerve terminal. At the synapse, these signals are then carried by neurotransmitters across the synaptic cleft. A variety of small molecules can serve as transmitters, and their effect is determined by the properties of the receptors rather than the chemical nature of the transmitter. Thus, a particular neurotransmitter may serve to excite some postsynaptic cells while inhibiting others. The classical transmitter substances include *acetylcholine, dopamine, noradrenaline* (or *norepinephrine*), *serotonin,* and *GABA*.

The cholinergic transmitter system is critically involved in attentional functioning, perhaps by increasing the signal-to-noise ratio of salient information. Animal studies have shown that the cell bodies of neurons that make use of acetylcholine are generated early during gestation but adult levels are attained only after the first decade of life.

Dopaminergic neurons can be found in the midbrain and have widespread projections to the limbic system and the cerebral cortex, most densely to the prefrontal cortex. This transmitter system is engaged in the activation of behavior and, more specifically, in the planning of and switching between response sets. Although dopamine fibers penetrate the rat cortex early after birth, dopamine concentrations in neonatal brains are considerably lower than in adult brains.

Noradrenergic neurons are also found in the midbrain and project to the hippocampal formation, the cerebellum, and the neocortex. This transmitter system is involved in the orienting reaction resulting in the inhibition of ongoing behavior, an increase in arousal, and heightened attention to salient features of novel stimuli. The noradrenergic system appears to be more extensive at birth than when the brain has matured; it has therefore been suggested that this transmitter system may promote cortical plasticity.

The serotonergic transmitter system originates in the brain stem and projects most strongly to the hippocampal formation, the basal ganglia, and the frontal cortex. Manipulations of this transmitter system have been observed to result primarily in behavioral inhibition. Serotonin levels increase rapidly after birth but are shown to decline throughout adulthood.

Finally, GABA is a major transmitter of inhibitory neurons in the brain and spinal cord. GABA-ergic neurons are widely distributed throughout the brain and are implicated in movement control. In the rat brain, the amount of GABA around birth is only half of the adult amounts.

The rapidly growing literature on developmental changes in neurotransmitter systems makes at least three important points. First, it should be noted that these systems are concurrently active so as to optimize human information processing. Second, the developmental status of the neuro-transmitter systems may impose considerable constraints on information processing during the life-span. And third, these combined neurobiological findings indicate that brain growth is not limited to early development but seems to persist into adult life. (The interested reader is referred to Fillenz (1990) and Stellar and Stellar (1985) for an introduction to, respectively, the noradrenergic and dopaminergic neurotransmitter systems and their implications for psychological functioning.)

Axonal Transmission

Information processing in the brain is facilitated by myelination. In parallel with the dendritic changes, many axons acquire a myelin sheath. Myelinated fibers fire more rapidly and with greater functional specificity than non-myelinated ones. They have shorter refractory periods and lower thresholds to stimulation. Thus, they can fire more frequently and with less presynaptic stimulation. As axons can propagate impulses prior to myelination, the presence of a myelin sheath is an indicator of functional efficiency and specificity rather than of functional onset.

The myelination of the human brain has been reviewed aptly by K. Gibson (1991). The human brain is myelinated only moderately at birth. At that point in time, no myelin exists in any cortical layer. Neocortical layers begin to myelinate during the first month after birth. Cortical myelination begins first and proceeds most rapidly in areas directly interconnected with the brain stem and in primary sensory and motor areas. Myelination begins last in and proceeds most slowly in tracts and layers concerned with intracortical connections and in association areas. Sensory and motor areas generally complete their myelination before the second year of life, but integrative systems may continue to myelinate much longer. Fibers in the reticular formation continue to myelinate into the second decade of life as do interhemispheric association fibers. Finally, cortical intrahemispheric association fibers may continue myelination even into the third decade of life (Yakovlev & Lecours, 1967).

Myelination sequences have been taken to provide a crude index of regional brain development, and several attempts have been made to correlate myelination to behavioral development (e.g. Konner, 1991). Box 2.6 provides an illustration of the relation between myelination and cognitive development as conceived within neo-Piagetian theory. It should be noted, however, that neurological function begins before myelin appears and that demyelination does not always result in loss of function. Moreover, myelination is only one indicator of brain maturation, and other neural indices may provide different information.

Box 2.6   Myelination and cognitive development

Developmental psychologists have been speculating about the relationship between myelination and cognitive development. Case (1985), for example, suggested, as a working hypothesis, that successively higher levels of cognitive operation are controlled by successively higher levels in the brain, and he assumed that each of these systems has its own characteristic period of myelination. More specifically, he assumed that the brain systems that myelinate between 1 to 4 months are those for controlling isolated sensory and motor functions whereas the systems that myelinate from 4 months to 1.5 years are those for coordinating such sensory and motor functions. Thus he suggested a close correspondence between the myelination of different brain systems and the developmental timing of cognitive operations subserved by those systems.

How does myelination facilitate cognitive operations? Case (1985) pointed to two primary functions of myelin. One is the speeding of neural transmission and the other is to act as an insulator preventing leakage across neural pathways. Thus, before myelination, linear transmission from one neural assembly to a target assembly would be slow due to the absence of a myelin sheath, and lateral transmission to competing assemblies would be high due to a lack of myelin insulation. In contrast, after myelination, linear transmission speed would be high and lateral transmission negligible. As a consequence, the efficiency of neural transmission is greatly improved which will increase the subject's processing space, allowing the performance of cognitively more demanding tasks (see also Bjorklund & Harnishfeger, 1990).

Sources: Bjorklund, D. J. & Harnishfeger, K. K. (1990). The resources construct in cognitive development: Diverse sources of evidence and a theory of inefficient inhibition. *Developmental Review*, **10**, 48–71. Case, R. (1985). *Intellectual Development: Birth to Adulthood*. New York: Academic Press.

THE AGING BRAIN

Specifying the time of entering old age is not always straightforward. For some species, there is a rapid onset of deterioration at some time after maturation, such as the Pacific salmon which dies after the first period of reproduction. For other species, such as mammals, maturation is followed by a slow and progressive phase of senescence (cf. Masoro, 1995). Moreover, the rate of deterioration varies considerably among individuals so that chronological age provides only a rough marker of senescence. In fact, many studies of aging report larger variances for older adults than for younger groups, suggesting that the uniqueness of the individual increases with the passage of time. It has been pointed out, however, that the increased variance in the aged is inflated because of the association between senescence and diseases. This observation led to the introduction of the concept of 'primary aging' as distinct from 'secondary aging' (e.g. Busse, 1969). Primary aging refers, then, to fundamental processes which are universal within a species, intrinsic to the organism, deleterious to its functioning, and increasing the probability of dying. Much of senescence, however, is thought to be secondary to these processes and may consist of compensatory or non-deteriorative responses that are then comprised under the concept of secondary aging.

Models of Primary Aging

Over the years, a great deal of effort has been invested to identify the nature of the basic aging processes, and many models of primary aging have been proposed. These models can be classified into two broadly defined categories: *genetic* and *homeostatic failure* theories. Theories assuming that genetic factors play a central role in primary biological aging are based on observations that the maximum life-span differs reliably across species and that differences in life-span tend to cluster within families. Unfortunately, the mechanisms by which genes promote longevity are not known. Homeostatic failure theories of primary aging emphasize the progressive inability of the organism to prevent deterioration. For instance, early 'wear and tear' theories of senescence suggest that the organism is similar to a machine and that over time the parts wear out. This view has been modified because in some systems, continued or chronic use can actually improve its functioning. It has been argued that this 'use it or lose it' principle might apply to the brain, given that activation of nerve cells has been shown to lead to maintenance of neurons during aging (Swaab, 1991). For most systems, however, repair processes fail to keep pace with deterioration, resulting in a failure to maintain the structural and functional properties of the organism.

Homeostatic failure has been identified both at local cellular levels and at the level of cells in homeostatic control systems. Local age-related cell death may stem from the damaging effects of free radicals, chemical compounds that arise largely during the course of normal metabolism and that may alter the structure of cellular proteins. The formation of free radicals increases with age.

If aging affects specific cells functioning in homeostatic control systems, inadequate control may then result in damage elsewhere in the organism that is secondary to dysfunction of homeostatic control. Thus, age-related changes in immune and neuroendocrine systems may contribute to a wide range of degenerative processes. It should be noted, however, that in spite of the great variety of homeostatic failure theories and other perspectives on primary aging, the causal role of the alleged basic aging process is yet to be established (see Masoro, 1995, for a review and discussion).

Aging in the Central Nervous System

Although primary aging processes are difficult to identify and disentangle from secondary aging processes, it is beyond doubt that chronological age is associated with widespread changes in the central nervous system. These changes vary from gross neuroanatomical changes to microscopic changes in dendritic arboring and neuronal loss, and appear to be region-specific.

Gross changes

One of the best documented findings refers to the age-related decrease in overall brain weight and volume. Brain weight has been reported to vary from 930 to 1350 grams in normal 70–89 year olds (Katzman & Terry, 1983). These authors reported a study in which shrinkage of the brain is expressed in terms of the ratio of cerebral volume to cranial volume. They observed a reduction of 10% between the ages of 20–49 and 80–89. Some researchers have pointed to a cohort effect due to lower brain weights of those born around World War II. In studies that corrected for cohort effects, virtually no change was observed between the ages of 20 and 50 years, followed by a decrease of 2% per decade through age 90 (see La Rue, 1992).

Another gross change in brain morphology, *gyral atrophy*, refers to shrinking of the cortical ribbon in particular regions of the brain. Atrophic changes may occur in widely separated areas of the brain while intermediate brain tissue appears normal. The convexities of the frontal pole of the cortex are affected most by gyral atrophy. The ratio of gray to white matter also increases in old age from 1.13 in the sixth decade to 1.55 by the tenth decade (cf. Katzman & Terry, 1983), indicating a reduction in the number of myelinated axons relative to nerve cell bodies and dendrites. These findings suggest an age-related loss of myelin which has been observed to be more pronounced in regions where myelination is completed relatively late during development; that is, in the anterior regions of the brain rather than the posterior areas. Animal studies of demyelination show a wide array of functional alterations, including decreased conduction velocity, more frequent conduction failure, increased refractory period, temporal dispersion of impulses, cross-talk between neighboring axons, and increased susceptibility to temperature and mechanical influences. On the other hand, anatomically specific demyelination does not always result in the expected function loss (Konner, 1991).

Regional specificity

Age-related changes in brain morphology appear to be highly selective (Scheibel, 1996). There are virtually no studies available examining the effects of aging on the brain stem. The limbic system shows varying degrees of age-related change depending on the specific areas that have been studied and on the methods of analysis. Several systems have been studied in the hypothalamic region. Again, the pattern of age-related changes reveals a high degree of specificity. Brain-imaging techniques have been used to identify hippocampal atrophy. Subjects with marked atrophy were found to have verbal-memory deficits. This bird's eye view indicates that brain aging is a highly specific process rather than being a global deterioration affecting the various brain structures and functions equally.

Microscopic changes

Deterioration is most obvious at the microscopic level. Neuronal loss is well documented and shows wide variations by cortical regions. Frontal and temporal areas lose approximately 20–30% with age, while primary sensory areas seem to lose only 12–15%. The hippocampus and parts of the amygdala lose 25% of their cells. The cell loss in some parts of the brain stem (e.g. locus coeruleus) is considerable but other parts of the motor brain stem areas seem to have a stable population. In contrast, midbrain nuclei (e.g. substantia nigra) show a significant cell loss of almost 50% by the ninth decade (Horvath & Davis, 1990). Note that both the locus coeruleus and substantia nigra are implicated in Parkinson's disease.

Some nuances are noteworthy, however. Studies using new techniques for examining neurodegeneration seem to indicate the absence of neuron loss in the hippocampus across a variety of species (see Gallagher & Rapp, 1997). In addition, neuronal loss of large cell bodies has been found to concur with a simultaneous neuronal increase in small cells (Terry, DeTeresa & Hansen, 1987). This finding may suggest that large neurons shrink into smaller ones rather than being eliminated during aging. Thus, it would be important to consider neuron size in cell counting studies (La Rue, 1992). Finally, the gradual cell loss during normal aging is very modest compared to the loss of neurons early in development.

Even when neurons themselves survive, their cell bodies, axons, and dendrites may reveal atrophy. A characteristic pattern of degenerative changes consists of an initial swelling of the cell body followed by a loss of dendritic branches. Obviously, the loss of dendritic branches reduces the number of interconnections between cells. Indeed, a 13% decrease of synapses has been found in 74–90 year olds compared to 16–72 year olds (cf. Katzman & Terry, 1983). Interestingly, an increase in dendritic growth has been found in the hippocampus and cortical areas around 50 years of age followed by a regression around the eighth and ninth decades. It has been suggested that the initial dendritic branching may reflect a compensatory response of viable neurons to cope with decremental dendritic changes of their neighbors. It seems that this compensatory ability fails in very old neurons (Coleman & Flood, 1987).

Changes in neurotransmitter systems

Detailed information concerning the age-related decline in neurotransmission is still limited. A concise review of the normal aging of neurotransmitter systems is provided by DeKosky and Palmer (1994). Age-related declines in the cholinergic system have been reported in the hippocampus, and to a lesser extent in the cerebral cortex. Cholinergic deficiencies have been suggested to provide the neurochemical substrate for some of the symptoms seen in patients with Alzheimer's disease. Unfortunately, attempts to improve the mental status of patients with Alzheimer's disease by administering precursors of acetylcholine have not been successful.

The cerebral cortex and the hippocampus have not been observed to show age-related changes in the dopaminergic system; reduction of dopamine seems to be restricted largely to the striatum (DeKosky & Palmer, 1994). The striatum is part of the brain stem and plays an important role in voluntary movement. Striatal dopamine depletion has been observed to result in a difficulty of initiating and maintaining motor actions (Robbins, 1986). These difficulties are clearly observed in Parkinson's disease in the form of bradykinesia and rigidity. In some respects, the performance of normal old people is similar to patients with Parkinson's disease (e.g. a decline in response speed). These similarities suggest that dopamine depletion may underlie some of the behavioral deficits seen during senescence.

The noradrenergic system appears to be stable with age. The largest group of noradrenergic neurons is found in the locus coeruleus. Reductions in noradrenaline content have been found in the locus coeruleus and hypothalamus, but there is little change in the cerebral cortex. Similar observations have been reported for the serotonergic system (Morgan & May, 1990). Some changes in serotonin receptors have been observed for the cerebral cortex and have been suggested to underlie the increased incidence of sleep disturbance and mood disturbances that occur in older adults (DeKosky & Palmer, 1994). Finally, most studies examining GABA have reported age-related declines in the hippocampus and cerebral cortex.

In sum, aging of the central nervous system does not appear to involve single large deficits in neurotransmission. Several lines of evidence suggest that normal aging occurs as the result of a complex series of small changes which may induce imbalance between neurotransmitter systems. Obviously, conglomerate changes in neurotransmission may have a widespread impact on the functional output of the brain (Cotman, Kahle & Korotzer, 1995).

Similarities between normal and neuropathological aging

At this point, it should be noted that 'normal' aging is difficult to disentangle from brain deterioration associated with dementia and other diseases of old age. Some age-related changes, including decreased brain weight, loss of neurons or myelin, and gyral atrophy, show a considerable overlap in distribution for normal aging and dementia. Other changes have a limited distribution in normal brains but are more numerous and widespread in Alzheimer's disease (La Rue, 1992). These changes include increases in the formation of free radicals and *amyloid*. Free radicals arise largely during the course of normal metabolism. As described above, the formation of free radicals is known to increase with age, and some investigators hold this increase responsible for neuronal loss in the aging brain (e.g. Harman, 1984). Amyloid is associated with *neuritique plaque*, a complex material that binds elements of degenerating neurons and synapses. In Alzheimer's disease, these plaques are more dense and more frequent than in normal aging. Although the formation of free radicals and amyloid is accentuated in typical aging diseases, they do occur in significant proportions of seemingly healthy old people. It might be possible, of course, that a considerable subset of healthy older adults are actually in preclinical stage. However, Dickson, Crystal, Mattiace et al. (1991) failed to find a relation between performance on neuropsychological tests and cortical plaque counts in a carefully controlled prospective study. This negative finding suggests that behavioral deficits in older subjects may require quite different explanations in spite of the similarities between normal and neuropathological aging (cf. Katzman, 1995, p. 338).

THE MALLEABLE BRAIN

Until the early 1960s it was not generally accepted that brains can change structurally with experience. Most scientists believed that after a rapid development *ex utero* the brain becomes structurally stable. With age the brain may increase and decrease in size, but it was not widely recognized that its morphology can change in response to alterations in the environment. The plasticity of the brain has now been established beyond doubt, not only for the immature brain, but for the aging brain as well. This radical change in view will be illustrated by reviewing some of the major findings concerning plasticity in the maturing and the aging brain. The illustrations have been selected from four paradigms adopted in brain-plasticity studies. The *enrichment* paradigm has been employed to examine the impact of a variety of environmental influences on the structure of animal brains. By contrast, the *deprivation* paradigm has been used to study the detrimental effects of environments that lack the stimulation assumed to promote brain growth. The *grafting* paradigm is an invasive procedure in which neurons are transplanted from one brain region to another. A somewhat similar procedure is the *rerouting* paradigm in which input from one sensory modality is directed artificially to another modality. Although the studies that employed these paradigms reveal a seemingly unlimited plasticity, it must be noted that there are also important constraints. Within the context of this chapter, it should be asked whether the factor aging is among those constraints.

Box 2. 7   Brain training for language-impaired children

The observation that the structure of adult brains is modulated by experience led to a wide array of studies which examined the effects of training and exercise on the structure of specific brain areas. Some studies, reviewed in Kaas (1991), examined how somatosensory brain maps in monkeys may change as the result of experience. In one experiment, when monkeys were trained to use their middle finger performing a particular task, their brain map representing the middle finger became larger. In another experiment, one finger of the monkey's hand was amputated. It was expected that the corresponding brain area would deteriorate due to loss of stimulation. Instead, the brain area representing the amputated finger responded almost immediately to stimulation of the other fingers. Similarly, training was found to improve the temporal 'sharpening' in monkeys by remodelling their brains (Merzenich, Allard & Jenkins, 1990). These combined findings suggest not only that adult brain structure can be influenced by exercise but also that neural brain circuitry may change dynamically in response to experience.

Tallal found in a series of studies that language-impaired children have trouble distinguishing syllables such as 'ba' and 'da' that begin with consonant sounds that last only tens of milliseconds (e.g. Tallal, 1980). This finding led Tallal and her co-workers to hypothesize that the brains of language-impaired children are unable to process information on time scales of tens of milliseconds. In a recent *Science* article, Merzenich, Jenkins, Johnston et al. (1996) demonstrated that the temporal processing deficits of language-impaired children can be ameliorated by training. The investigators reasoned that if training could improve the temporal sharpening in monkeys by re-shaping their brains, similar exercises might improve the temporal discrimination in language- and reading-impaired children. They devised a series of adaptive computer games requiring children to follow spoken commands, but speech was stretched by 50%, and rapidly changing speech components were emphasized by making them louder. During a 4-week period, the children played the games repeatedly, and while their performance improved the sounds were shortened and less emphasized. After training, the children's performance on a battery of language tests was considerably improved; a gain of 1 to 2 years of language ability. This gain was maintained when the children were tested again after 6 weeks, suggesting that the children actually improved their language ability.

Sources: Kaas, J. H. (1991). Plasticity of sensory and motor maps in adult mammals. *Annual Review of Neuroscience*, **14**, 137–167. Merzenich, M. M., Allard, T. & Jenkins, W. M. (1990). Neural ontogeny of higher brain function: Implications of some neurophysiological findings. In O. Franzén & P. Westman (Eds), *Information Processing* *in the Somatosensory System* (pp. 239–311). London: Macmillan. Merzenich, M. M., Jenkins, W. M., Johnston, P., Schreiner, C., Miller, S. L. & Tallal, P. (1996). Temporal processing deficits of language-learning-impaired children ameliorated by training. *Science*, **271**, 77–81. Tallal, P. (1980). Auditory temporal perception, phonics, and reading abilities in children. *Brain and Language*, **9**, 182–198.

Enrichment

The effects of the environment on postnatal maturation in the rat brain have been examined extensively by Diamond (for a review see M. Diamond, 1991). She showed that cortical thickness grows rapidly for the first 10 days and then continues to grow more slowly until between 26 and 41 days of age. Beyond this age, a gradual decrease in cortical thickness begins that continues until death. Cortical areas change in a similar fashion, with only small regional differences. In addition, the increase of cortical thickness reveals gradual change rather than growth in spurts.

Diamond used these data as background for the evaluation of environmental influences. In one study, rats were placed in a non-enriched cage whereas others lived in cages containing objects to explore, climb, and sniff. The results of this experiment indicated that the maturation of the rat's cortex can be accelerated by a stimulating environment. As early as eight days after being placed in the enriched condition, the somatosensory cortex showed increases in thickness of 7–11% and some occipital areas increased as much as 16%.

After demonstrating that brain maturation can be accelerated by placing the rat in a stimulating environment, Diamond examined whether the detrimental effects associated with aging can be counteracted by the positive effects of enrichment. She addressed this interesting issue by forming three groups. Twelve rats were placed in a large enriched cage with stimulus objects that were changed frequently. Other rats aged in a standard colony with three rats in a small cage and no toys. The third group consisted of rats who were exposed to impoverished conditions; one rat per cage and no toys. The results from this experiment demonstrated significant morphological changes. The enriched environment induced an increase in cortical thickness at any age throughout the life-span, suggesting that brain plasticity is preserved in the elderly rat. By contrast, impoverished conditions reduced cortical thickness. Both beneficial and detrimental effects were most pronounced when the rats were first placed in the standard colony and then transferred to the enriched or impoverished condition. Interestingly, impoverished conditions were less detrimental when the reduction in number of animals per cage took place gradually and the beneficial effects of enriched environments were maintained only with frequent replacement of toys. The latter effect is suggestive of the adverse influence of boredom (cf. M. Diamond, 1991, p. 115).

Further studies, summarized in M. Diamond (1991) and Rosenzweig

(1996), revealed enrichment effects on a variety of other brain parameters in addition to cortical thickness. Thus, enrichment increases the sizes of neuronal cell bodies and nuclei, increases the numbers of glial cells, enhances dendritic branching patterns, alters the number and size of dendritic spines, and alters the number of synapses per neuron. These studies encouraged an increasing number of investigators to examine the effects of training and exercise on brain structure. In Box 2.7, an example is given of how experience may alter primate brain structure and ameliorate the performance of language-impaired children on speech discrimination tests.

Deprivation

Greenough (1986) argued that brain plasticity involving events unique to the experience of the individual can be distinguished from brain plasticity involving environmental information shared by all members of a species. An important aspect of the latter type of brain plasticity appears to be that the nervous system is sensitive to external influences only during certain portions of its development. These *critical periods* in brain ontogeny have been investigated most thoroughly in the developing visual system with regard to the effects of monocular deprivation. Visually deprived animals show deficits in visual acuity, pattern recognition, form perception, and possibly orienting (Tees, 1986). When one eye is occluded, neurons respond exclusively to the normal eye and stop to respond to the deprived eye. Monocular deprivation results in a decrease in the number of dendritic spines in the hemisphere contralateral to the deprived eye in rats. The period during which cortical spine density in the monkey cortex can be altered by monocular deprivation spans the first 10 weeks after birth (see review in Boothe, Vassdal & Schnek, 1986).

It should be noted, however, that the duration of critical periods has been observed to depend on the experiential history of the animal. In cats, for example, the critical period for the adverse effects of monocular deprivation can be prolonged almost infinitely by rearing the animal in the dark from birth (see review in Tees, 1986). Observations that experience may alter temporal aspects of critical periods raise the question of whether critical periods are really critical. Moreover, true critical periods require the irreversibility of effects but, as indicated by Tees (1986), many adverse effects have been shown to change for the better when the animal is exposed to more favourable conditions. On a more fundamental level, Greenough and co-workers asked why evolution would design organisms that will be forever damaged if they are not exposed to species-appropriate information at the right time (Greenough, Black & Wallace, 1987). Their answer was that throughout the evolutionary history of the species, the animal has come to expect 'normal' experience. If a deviant experience occurs, such as monocular occlusion, the fine-tuning on interneuronal contacts during development may go astray and result in a (sometimes irreversible) aberrant neuronal organization.

Grafting and Misrouting

The enrichment and deprivation studies of cortical development reveal an impressive plasticity of the brain. The notion of cortical plasticity is reinforced further by grafting studies. O'Leary (1989) reviewed studies demonstrating that when visual cortical neurons are transplanted to the sensorimotor region of a newborn rat, they extend and retain permanent axons to the spinal cord, a subcortical target of the sensorimotor cortex. Conversely, sensorimotor cortical neurons transplanted to the visual cortex extend and retain a projection to the superior colliculus, a subcortical target of the visual cortex. These findings suggest that many of the area-specific features of the adult cortex are not predetermined but emerge from epigenetic influences that operate during cortical development areas that are initially pluripotential.

Similar conclusions can be drawn from misrouting studies showing that when visual input is directed artificially to the somatosensory cortex of newborn hamsters cells in this area can respond both to visual and somatosensory stimuli in modality-appropriate ways (e.g. Frost & Metin, 1985). In a similar vein, the auditory cortex of ferrets can be made to respond to visual input (Sur, Pallas & Roe, 1990). These findings provide strong support for the conclusion that the areas in the primary sensory cortex process information in a fundamentally similar way, suggesting that the basic organization of cells that underlies the functional specificity of these areas is also similar (O'Leary, 1989).

Constraints on Plasticity

The extensive cortical plasticity may create the impression that functional specificity is simply imposed by environmental input on the 'tabula rasa' of cortical equipotentiality. It should be emphasized, however, that experience is only one factor shaping cortical circuitry, albeit an important one. For instance, retinal signals never induce cortical changes when the animal is paralyzed or anaesthetized while being exposed to visual patterns. In a similar vein, retinal stimulation may induce changes in the visual cortex of one hemisphere but not in the other when the attentional state of the latter is compromised by subcortical damage. These findings led Singer (1986) to conclude that, according to its central state, the developing brain must be able to select the instances at which experience can assume the role of a shaping factor (p. 288).

Johnson (1993) categorized limitations in brain plasticity into two broad categories: *extrinsic* and *intrinsic* constraints. Extrinsic factors include aspects of the environment which are invariant for most members of a given species such as the exposure to patterned light or gravity. For humans, the exposure to language sounds would be part of the species-specific environment whereas exposure to a specific language (e.g. Dutch) would belong to an individual-specific environment. Indeed, Werker and Tees (1984) observed that infants are initially able to discriminate speech sounds taken from a wide range of disparate languages but lose this ability during the first year of life. Most likely, only those neurons in the auditory system that continue to be stimulated are selected while the others will die. These findings provide an illustration of how environmental stimulation may contribute to the species- and individual-specific cortical organization (see Butterworth, ch. 3 this volume, and Bernicot, ch. 4 this volume).

Extrinsic constraints may refer to limitations imposed by the sequential development of different sensory systems, which may provide structure to the emerging perceptual organization (Turkewitz & Kenny, 1982). A corollary of this notion is that premature reduction of sensory limitations would be detrimental rather than beneficial to perceptual development. A further extrinsic factor that constrains cortical plasticity refers to specific orienting predispositions that serve to select and organize experience. An example of human predispositions comes from the domain of language learning. Greenough et al. (1987) have suggested that an innate predisposition of the infant to smile and make noises could serve the infant by shaping the caretaker's speech toward a form of linguistic input that is optimal for organization and maturation of the infant's perceptual system.

Intrinsic constraints on cortical plasticity seem to be twofold (e.g. Johnson, 1993). The first type of constraints relate to the layered structure of the cortex and its inside-out pattern of growth. The fact that maturation proceeds from deeper layer to more superficial ones may have important implications for the connectivity of a cortical region. As development proceeds upwards through the layers, progressively more afferent and efferent pathways will become functional. The second type of constraints refer to the uneven rate of maturation in different cortical regions. Primary sensory and motor cortices mature earlier than the rest of the cortex. Thus information reaching the early maturing regions may be trapped there until other regions have matured to a level capable of transmitting information. The differential rates of development between cortical layers and in different cortical regions may impose considerable constraints on the functions a cortical mechanism can subserve at a given point in development (see Johnson, 1993, for a detailed discussion of the issue). Such constraints may in fact have a beneficial effect on development, as can be seen in Box 2.8.

Age as a constraint

It seems reasonable to ask whether age might operate as a constraint on brain plasticity. Most of the deprivation and enrichment studies have examined brain plasticity in the immature brain rather than in the mature brain of young animals (but see M. Diamond, 1991). Synapse remodelling occurs to the greatest extent in fetal and neonatal development, suggesting that with advancing age the brain becomes less malleable. Brain plasticity is apparent in the aged brain as well. One of the most important implications of the

---

Box 2.8 The earlier the better?

Turkewitz and Kenny (1982) pointed to the uneven rate of development and sequential onset of sensory systems and suggested that reduced intersensory competition and limited intrasensory competition at early stages during development may facilitate perceptual development in the absence of interference from competing input. Once a system is organized, the introduction of competing input may result in a disruption of the current system followed by a more advanced reorganization. In this fashion, the patterning of sensory limitations during ontogeny promotes current adaptive functioning and provides the basis for subsequent perceptual organization and a highly functional organization of neural space (see also Turkewitz & Mellon, 1989). A corollary of this view is that premature reduction of sensory limitations would be detrimental rather than beneficial to perceptual development. There is some evidence indicating disruption of function when input is made available earlier than normal. Turkewitz and Kenny (1982) described experiments focusing on homing behavior in kittens which are born with their eyes sealed but with a neurophysiologically functioning system. It has been demonstrated that the homing behavior of kittens is initially under the control of thermal or olfactory cues. The eyes of kittens begin to open approximately six or seven days after birth. During this time visual information is gradually incorporated into the perceptual system resulting eventually in visual dominance and the modification of homing behavior. If the eyes of the kitten are opened artificially, the visual stimulation will interfere with the organization of tactile, thermal, and olfactory inputs, and thus, homing behavior will be disturbed. These and similar findings led Turkewitz and Kenny (1982) to conclude that child rearing based on the view that 'earlier is better' may impede rather than accelerate development.

Sources: Turkewitz, G. & Kenny, P. A. (1982). Limitations on input as a basis for neural organization and perceptual development: A preliminary theoretical statement. *Developmental Psychobiology*, **15**, 357–368. Turkewitz, G. & Mellon, R. C. (1989). Dynamic organization of intersensory function. Special Issue: Infant perceptual development. *Canadian Journal of Psychology*, **43**, 286–301.

enrichment studies reviewed by M. Diamond (1991) is that environmental stimulation can have beneficial effects on the brain at any age. Research examining plasticity in the aging brain has been reviewed by Woodruff-Pak (1993). Her conclusion is that the neural substrate for plasticity is maintained in the brain from fetal development throughout adulthood and old age. This conclusion is almost opposite to the long-held belief that there is little or no recovery of function in older brains. Until recently, most investigators did not even include older animals in plasticity studies because they thought it would be pointless to examine this phenomenon in the aging brain.

The plasticity of the older brain can be examined from different perspectives. One is the loss and renewal of synapses. Cotman and Nietro-Sampredo (1982) amassed evidence to suggest that synaptic growth and remodelling is a continuous process involved in the development and maintenance of brain circuitry. Synapse renewal in the adult brain can be readily demonstrated by partial denervation of brain structures. Lesion-induced synaptogenesis has been identified in peripheral structures, such as the spinal cord, but also in central structures, such as the hippocampal formation. Partial denervation of peripheral or central structures causes intact fibers to sprout new nerve endings and to form new synapses that replace those lost as a consequence of the lesion. Interestingly, synapse remodelling has also been observed in areas located outside the denervated zone. Finally, Cotman and Nietro-Sampredo (1982) indicated that synaptic renewal may occur in the absence of tissue damage. Demonstrations of environmental influences on several cortical features in adult animals provide impressive evidence for spontaneous synaptic renewal. These findings suggest that 'use it or lose it' provides a better description of the aging brain than 'wear and tear'.

A word of caution is in order here. Greenough and his colleagues (reviewed in Greenough, 1993) showed that while motor learning was associated with synaptic increase in the cerebellum, motor exercise increased the number of capillaries, the blood vessels that mediate transfer of nutrients from blood to brain. This pattern of findings was interpreted to suggest that learning involved a remodelling of brain circuitry to incorporate the ability to perform novel skills, whereas exercise involved an increase in capillaries to support cerebellar involvement in mediating routine but taxing motor output. Importantly, these authors demonstrated also that the capacity to increase capillary numbers is greatly reduced in the old rats, suggesting that although the brain might retain the ability to form new synapses it loses the ability to support them metabolically with advancing age (Black, Isaacs, Anderson, Alcantara & Greenough, 1990). Thus, the beneficial effects of experience may be constrained by the age-related breakdown of support systems (Black, Isaacs & Greenough, 1991).

THE TRANSPARENT BRAIN

Relating maturation and aging of the brain to age-related changes in behavior requires the availability of designated tools. For a long time, brain methods consisted primarily of the detailed investigation of postmortem brains, or the careful analysis of deviant behaviors in patients with well described lesions. Standardized tests have been devised to elicit behavior characteristics that reliably discriminate lesioned patients from healthy controls. The usual procedure is to construct tasks that yield performance deficits in patients with lesions in one brain region (e.g. the frontal lobe) while showing normal performance for patients with lesions in other regions (e.g. the parietal or temporal lobes). These neuropsychological tests are then used to examine performance deficits in subjects suspected of brain dysfunction. The nature of the performance deficits revealed by neuropsychological testing is thought to provide a behavioral window on the alleged dysfunction of the brain.

Along similar lines, it has been proposed that neuropsychological procedures can be used to examine brain maturation (e.g. A. Diamond, 1990b). Under the hypothesis that the frontal lobes are the last to mature fully, children should reach asymptote performance on frontal tasks later than on non-frontal tasks (Welsh & Pennington, 1988). Unfortunately, the brain remains invisible in neuropsychological evaluations. Brain functions must be inferred from test scores using a complex analogy reasoning based on brain–behavior relations observed in clinical samples.

More recently, imaging techniques have been developed to provide images of the intact human brain. Magnetic resonance imaging allows the evaluation of brain structure (MRI) and brain function (fMRI). Positron emission tomography (PET) can be used to examine activation patterns of the brain during task performance. These neuroimaging techniques have greater spatial resolution but lower temporal resolution than electrophysiological techniques based on non-invasive measurements of brain electrical activity. The latter techniques, including the magnetoencephalogram (MEG), electroencephalogram (EEG), and event-related potential (ERP) procedures, allow the assessment of brain activation with a temporal resolution of less than 1 ms. The brain electrical and neuroimaging techniques provide a window to the intact brain, thereby opening exciting research possibilities for exploring changes in brain structure and brain function during development and senescence. A rapidly growing literature describes attempts to examine brain function in children and older adults. The interested reader is referred to Lyon and Rumsey (1996) for a review of neuroimaging techniques and their use on the diagnosis of developmental disorders. The following sections provide illustrations of how the various brain methods have been used to make brain structures and states transparent during normal development and successful aging. Studies were selected to highlight the connection between maturation and senescence; unfortunately, relatively few studies have made an attempt to cover the complete life-span.

Brain Size

From an ontogenetic perspective, the relation between brain size and cognition is not clear. In a series of studies, Epstein (1974a,b) derived his *phrenoblysis* hypothesis (the Greek word 'phreno' stands for skull or mind while 'blysis' refers to welling-up of matter), suggesting that the brain grows in spurts with peaks in growth rate occurring between 6–8, 10–12, 14–17, and

Box 2.9   Heritability of human brain electrical activity

Development can be described as the process by which the genotype comes to be expressed as the phenotype. The genotype is the material inherited from the ancestors making the individual genetically unique, and the individual's phenotype is the collection of measurable or observable characteristics. Genetic influences have been documented for a wide range of human behavior (Plomin & Rende, 1991). For example, a large body of research on genetics and intelligence indicates that about 50% of the difference in the way individuals score on IQ tests is due to the genetic make-up of the test-takers (Plomin, 1990). The genetic influences in individual differences in human behavior are most likely expressed via the brain, but surprisingly little is known about the heritability of human brain functioning.

In a recent study, van Beijsterveldt (1996) used the electroencephalogram (EEG) to provide a window on human brain functioning, and the twin method to partition phenotypic variance into genetic and environmental contributions. The EEG was recorded during rest from electrodes placed on frontal, central, parietal, occipital, and temporal scalp locations over both hemispheres. The EEG was then submitted to spectral analysis to obtain the power values for the delta (1.5–3.5 Hz), theta (4–7.5 Hz), alpha (8–12.5 Hz), and beta (13–25 Hz) bands. The EEG was obtained from 91 monozygotic and 74 dizygotic adolescent twins. Monozygotic or identical twins are genetically identical to each other while dizygotic or fraternal twins share, on average, 50% of their genetic potential. If hereditary affects a trait, the phenotypical resemblance should be approximately two times larger for identical twins. If the trait is determined by the environment, the phenotypical resemblance should be similar in identical and fraternal twins. Van Beijsterveldt (1996) found striking similarities in the EEG for monozygotic twins as compared to dizygotic twins. More specifically, the variance explained by genetic factors as 76%, 89%, 89%, and 86% for, respectively, the delta, theta, alpha, and beta band. These values indicated that there is only little differentiation between frequency bands. Heritability was also similar for anterior compared to posterior brain regions, left compared to right hemisphere, and male compared to female subjects. These findings are intriguing on at least two counts. First, with values of over 80%, EEG power belongs to the most heritable human traits. Second, the lack of differences in heritability between brain regions and sex seems to suggest that morphological and functional variability are manifested in the behavioral genetics of brain electrical activity.

Sources: Van Beijsterveldt, T. (1996). *The genetics of electrophysiological indices of brain activity: An EEG study in adolescent twins.* Doctoral dissertation. University of Amsterdam. Plomin, R. (1990). *Nature and Nurture: An Introduction to Human Behavioral Genetics.* Pacific

Grove, CA.: Brooks/Cole. Plomin, R. &. Rende, R. (1991). Human behavioral genetics. *Annual Review of Psychology*, **42**, 161–190.

possibly also between 2–4 years of age. Most interestingly, these periods of increased brain growth seem to coincide with jumps in mental growth as indexed by intelligence tests. The correlated patterns of peaks and troughs in brain growth and mental development suggested to Epstein (1978) a link with Piagetian theory. The spurts in brain growth would precede and prepare stage transitions in cognitive development. Since Piaget did not specify a stage transition after age 16, Epstein (1978) predicted a post-formal-operations stage to occur after that age. He suggested also that discontinuities in brain growth may have important implications for educational policy: children should learn new material and concepts during periods of rapid, not slow, brain growth. He speculated, for example, that at age 15, during a growth spurt, children could acquire the same input in about one fourth of the time it would take them during the slow growth period around age 13 (cf. Epstein, 1974b, p. 223). Accordingly, the phreno-blysis hypothesis may have important implications for educational practitioners and curriculum reform. The phrenoblysis hypothesis has attracted severe criticism, however. Several authors indicated that re-analyses of the data that form the basis for Epstein's ideas fail to support the hypothesized pattern of two-years-low growth and two-years-high growth (e.g. Harmon, 1984; Marsh, 1985; McCall, 1990). Others obtained data that are only partly consistent with Epstein's results (e.g. McCall, Meyers, Hartman & Roche, 1983). Indeed, interindividual variability in developmental growth renders it unlikely that spurts will be evenly spaced (cf. Marsh, 1985, p. 1060).

There are only a few studies examining the relation between brain size and cognitive aging. Although it is generally held that the brain decreases in size with age, investigators obtained little evidence for shrinking. Eslinger and co-workers examined the relation between brain size, as indexed by the ventricle-to-brain ratio, and performance, as indexed by neuropsychological evaluation (Eslinger, Damasio, Graff-Radford & Damasio, 1984). The results provided some support for a relation between brain morphology and cognitive performance during senescence. Although these findings are consistent with the hypotheses of parallel change in brain size and performance, it should be noted that most of the current evidence is coming from clinical studies. Attempts to establish relations between brain-size measures and performance during normal aging have proven even more difficult (Scheibel, 1996).

Spectral Analysis of Brain Electrical Activity

The non-invasive measurement of central nervous system function began with Berger's discovery of the human electroencephalogram in 1931. The EEG is a record of the oscillatory electrical activity measured from electrodes placed at different positions on the scalp. Segments of EEG can be submitted to spectral analysis for a decomposition of the oscillating signal into four major frequency bands: the alpha (8–12 Hz and 5–100 μV), beta (18–30 Hz and 2–20μV), delta (0.5–4 Hz and 20–200 μV) and theta (5–7 Hz and 5–100 μV) bands (e.g. Lindsley & Wicke, 1974). The amount of energy (the power) in a particular frequency band can then be used as an estimate of the excitability of neuronal ensembles (Nunez, 1981). The findings summarized in Box 2.9 indicated that there is a surprisingly strong genetic factor influencing EEG power.

A now classic study by Matousek and Petersén (1973) reported developmental changes in EEG amplitudes for the four standard frequency bands. These data have been transformed to EEG power by John (1977), who showed that the power in the alpha frequency band recorded over occipital-parietal regions revealed periods of rapid growth that alternate with periods of slow growth. Several authors cited those data to support stage theories of brain maturation. Epstein (1986), for example, noted the strong resemblance between the apparent periodicity in the Matousek and Petersén (1973) data and his own peak and trough periods derived from head-size and mental-performance data. The peaks in EEG alpha power occurred at approximately the same ages as the spurts in head size and mental performance detected by Epstein—4, 8, 12, and 15 years. Hudspeth and Pribram (1992), who conducted a thorough re-analysis of the Matousek and Petersén (1973) data, also pointed to the close correspondence between the stage demarcations of EEG power and the Piagetian timetable of cognitive growth, which may suggest that brain maturation is a critical factor in determining the time course of cognitive development; a conclusion echoing Epstein's hypothesis formulated almost 20 years earlier.

A more elaborate analysis of growth spurts in human EEG has been performed by Thatcher (1994, for a review) in a series of studies. This investigator collected 19 channels of EEG from 557 subjects between the ages of 2 months to 26.4 years. The focus was on EEG coherence, a spectral measure that provides an index of the functional coupling of neural generators. Thus Thatcher was primarily concerned with the organization of intracortical connections during postnatal development. He observed a marked difference between hemispheres. Developmental changes in the left hemisphere involved a progressive lengthening of intracortical connections between sensory areas and frontal regions. In contrast, developmental change in the right hemisphere consisted primarily of a contraction of long-distance frontal connections to shorter distance sensory connections. These findings led Thatcher to assume that the left-hemisphere expansion reflects a process of functional integration of cortical subsystems whereas the right-hemisphere contraction would be a manifestation of functional differentiation of previously integrated subsystems. Thatcher observed further that these changes in cortical organization are repeated during three major developmental cycles with transitions at approximately 6 and 10 years. These findings were interpreted to provide support for neo-Piagetian views of cognitive development. More specifically, the analysis of EEG

Box 2.10   Uneven EEG changes with advancing age

The age-related trends in EEG activity during senescence have been examined in great detail by Duffy, McAnulty and Albert (1993). They recorded the EEG from 202 subjects spanning a 30–80-years-old age range. Their findings show that age-related change in the EEG is not a simple linear process. Although these investigators observed a broad trend for decreased slow and increased fast activity consistent with previous reports on EEG aging, the specific changes varied between EEG frequencies and age decades. Only a few measures of slow EEG activity showed a linear decrease with age. In contrast, the majority of fast EEG activity changed in a nonlinear fashion. For example, measures of beta activity revealed cubic trends with an increase in activity from approximately 30 to 45 years of age, followed by stability, and a second increase at about 65 to 79 years of age. Finally, Duffy et al.'s data did not reveal an increased prevalence of slow activity with age, which suggested to them that the aging of brain electrical activity does not fall on the same continuum with changes observed in Alzheimer's disease.

Sources: Duffy, F. H., McAnulty, G. B. & Albert, M. S. (1993). The pattern of age-related differences in electrophysiological activity of healthy males and females. *Neurobiology of Aging*, **14**, 73–84.

---

coherence was assumed to indicate some of the physiological processes that may be associated with the emergence of cognitive stages (Thatcher, 1994, p. 250). It should be noted, however, that the hypothesis of cognitive development driven by iterative and sequential brain-growth cycle remains to be demonstrated by studies showing consistent relations between individual differences in brain growth and cognitive development. Such evidence should be derived preferably from longitudinal studies.

The literature on EEG changes during senescence has been reviewed by Dustman, Shearer and Emmerson (1993). Four distinct types of change have been observed consistently; (a) slowing of the alpha rhythm; (b) shifts in the amounts of beta activity; (c) diffuse slowing (increased delta and theta); and (d) focal slowing and sharp waves recorded over temporal areas, usually the left hemisphere. The adult alpha rhythm of 10.2–10.5 Hz is attained by early adolescence and remains at that level until the age of 60. Beyond this age the alpha rhythm slows by 1 Hz until age 80 and an additional 1 Hz decrease is reached in the very old (100–105 year olds). It should be noted that alpha rhythms lower than 8.0 Hz are generally considered to be pathological. The occurrence of low-voltage, fast beta activity increases with age until about 60 and then decreases somewhat during senescence. Dustman et al. (1993) indicated that fast EEG activity in old age may be a favourable sign for preserved intellect, while EEG slowing is usually associated with cognitive loss. The findings reviewed in Box 2.10

indicate, however, that EEG aging is much more complex than just a progressive slowing of rhythms.

In addition to examining age-related trends in EEG activity, Dustman and colleagues used the EEG to investigate the functional communication among cortical areas (see review in Dustman et al., 1993). They reasoned that when two cortical areas are communicating, the EEG waves recorded over these areas would be more similar (coherent) than when the areas are not functionally related. Dustman and co-workers found that EEG activity was more coherent between frontal and central recordings than between frontal and occipital recordings. Most important, they observed a greater EEG coherence in older subjects compared to young adults. Similar comparisons were made for spectral power within each of the four standard EEG frequency bands. It appeared that for each EEG frequency, EEG power was more homogeneous across scalp sites for older compared to younger subjects. These findings suggested to Dustman et al. (1993) a functional breakdown of the autonomy of specific cortical areas in older adults; that is, the aging brain seems to respond in a more homogeneous or global fashion (p. 379). They proposed that the decreasing heterogeneity in brain electrical activity is due to an age-related loss in inhibitory functioning.

Event-related brain potentials

In addition to spectral analysis, the EEG can be analyzed to obtain event-related brain potentials. ERPs represent changes in the electrophysiological activity in the brain in response to a physical or mental event or in association with a movement. ERPs consist of a series of time-dependent voltage changes that are most apparent in averages of EEG activity associated with repeated occurrences of the critical event. The voltage–time fluctuations exhibit a typical series of peaks and troughs that are labelled according to their polarity (positive or negative) and latency. Thus, the P3 refers to the third positive component of the brain potential. The composite of peaks and troughs has been categorized in early, exogenous components that reflect the obligatory activation of neuroanatomical structures in the stimulated primary pathways, and later, endogenous components, such as P3, which are sensitive to the information processing demands of a task and relatively insensitive to the physical characteristics of the eliciting event (for a concise introduction see Ridderinkhof and Bashore, 1995). A review of studies focusing on developmental changes in endogenous ERP components can be found in Friedman (1991).

A speculative account of how developmental changes in ERP components may be related to brain maturation has been submitted by Courchesne (1990), who distinguished between quantitative and qualitative changes in ERPs when children grow older. The quantitative changes refer to age-related reductions in the latency and amplitude of ERP components and are assumed to be manifestations of increased processing efficiency, whereas

---

Box 2.11   Brain-potential analysis of cognitive stage transition

---

A relatively direct test of Courchesne's (1978) hypothesis that relates ERP morphology to developmental changes in processing mode has been undertaken by Stauder and colleagues (Stauder, Molenaar & van der Molen, 1993). They selected children on the basis of their conservation ability and required them to perform two tasks, a standard ERP oddball task and an experimental analogue of the Piagetian conservation-of-liquid-quantity task. In Piagetian conservation tasks, children are first shown pairs of stimuli that are known to be equal in some particular aspect (e.g. liquid quantity). The experimenter then proceeds to deform the particular aspect of one of the stimuli. Following the deformation, children are questioned as to whether the stimuli are equal, and they are asked to justify their response by argument. Responses and arguments are then used to categorize the children as conservers and non-conservers. In the Piagetian literature, the ability to conserve is one of the hallmarks of the transition from the pre-operational stage to the concrete-operational stage.

Stauder et al. (1993) reasoned that task demands on the child's conservation ability should elicit different ERP morphologies in conservers and non-conservers. Thus, they constructed an experimental conservation analogue having the format of a signalled choice reaction time task. On each trial, a warning display was presented depicting a partly colored vertical rectangle ('A glass of lemonade'). After a few seconds, the warning display was replaced by a respond display depicting the same, but now uncolored rectangle, flanked by two partly colored rectangles that differed in the size and height of the colored area ('The lemonade of the first glass is now poured into one of the other glasses'). The child was asked to indicate, by a right-hand or left-hand button press, the rectangle containing the colored area of rectangle depicted in the warning display ('The glass that now contains the lemonade of the first glass').

The performance results reported by Stauder et al. (1993) yielded the expected increase in response speed with age. The error data were more interesting in showing that conservation ability, but not age, affected response accuracy. The performance of concrete-operational children was considerably more accurate than that of pre-operational children. Moreover, a detailed analysis of the error patterns suggested that, at least for some items, pre-operational children did not simply guess but used alternative, pre-operational problem-solving strategies such as a 'height-only' rule for guiding response selection. This finding is important in suggesting that pre-operational and concrete-operational children used qualitatively different modes for processing the stimuli presented in the experimental conservation-of-liquid-quantity task. Most important, brain potentials elicited by the respond stimuli presented in the experimental analogue elicited a broad positive component with a centroparietal scalp distribution that discriminated

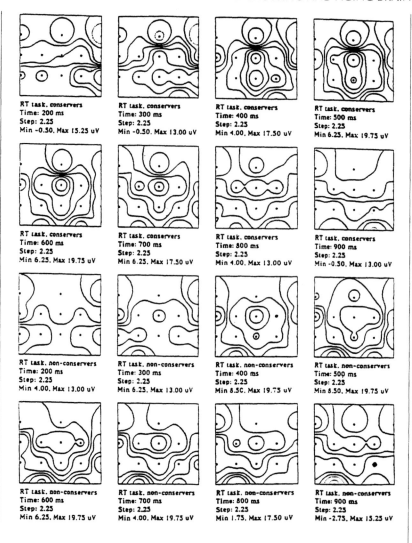

Figure B2.11:1 Equipotential maps of the scalp potential fields to the re-spond displays of the experimental analogue of the conservation of liquid quantity task

The equipotential lines are drawn in steps of 2.3μV. The amplitude range of the equipotential lines and the time of the scalp potential fields are given beyond each map. Solid lines refer to positive potentials and dotted lines refer to negative potentials. The dots in the maps refer to the electrode positions on the scalp. The top of the maps refers to anterior electrode placements and the bottom of the maps refers to posterior locations. The bottom rows present the equipotential maps of the non-conservers and the maps of the conservers are presented in the top rows

From Stauder, J. E. A., Molenaar, P. C. & van der Molen, M. W. (1993). Scalp topography of event-related brain potentials and cognitive transition during childhood. *Child Development*, **64**, 769–788. Reprinted with permission.

between pre-operational and concrete-operational children but not between young and old children. Figure B2.11:1 presents equipotential maps of the brain potential at four different time points (see figure caption for explanation). The maps show a distinct centroparietal distributed positivity (solid equipotential lines) for the conservers at 500 and 700 ms post-stimulus that is preceded by an anterior negativity and followed by a posterior positivity. Little change can be observed for the non-conserving children. The difference in scalp distribution was taken to reflect a developmental change in processing mode when children proceed from a pre-operational to a concrete-operational cognitive stage. In this regard, the findings reported by Stauder et al. (1993) contribute to the rapidly emerging evidence in support of the biological underpinnings of the Piagetian concept of stage transitions in cognitive development (see also Thatcher, 1994).

Sources: Stauder, J. E. A., Molenaar, P. C. M. & van der Molen, M. W. (1993). Scalp topography of event-related brain potentials and cognitive transition during childhood. *Child Development*, **64**, 769–788. Thatcher, R. W. (1994). Cyclic cortical reorganization: Origins of cognitive development. In G. Dawson & K. W. Fischer (Eds), *Human Behavior and the Developing Brain* (pp. 232–266). New York: Guilford.

qualitative changes refer to differences in ERP topography or morphology and are assumed to reflect developmental changes in the mode of information processing. Both types of developmental change have been observed in a now classic study reported by Courchesne (1978), who presented different age groups, between 6 and 36 years, with trains of stimuli. The trains consisted of standard stimuli, interspersed infrequently with target stimuli and with novel stimuli; participants were asked to respond only to targets and ignore all other stimuli. Target stimuli elicited a P3 that peaked over parietal areas. This scalp distribution did not differentiate between age groups, but the latency of the P3 decreased with age (along with reaction time), suggesting to Courchesne that with age children were able to detect and process target stimuli with increasing efficiency. Novel stimuli elicited in adults a P3 that was maximal over frontal regions, and in children a P3-like wave with a peak amplitude over parietal regions. Novels elicited also a negative wave, termed Nc, in the ERP of children but not adults. These combined findings suggested to Courchesne that adults may use different modes in processing novel, not pre-categorized, stimuli than children, and he related this developmental change in processing mode to stage-wise cognitive development of the kind hypothesized in the Piagetian literature (see also Wijker, 1991; Demetriou, ch. 5 this volume). A study specifically designed to examine this hypothesis is reviewed in Box 2.11.

Oken and Kaye (1992) examined P3 changes in healthy volunteers ranging in age from 20 to 99 years of age. The latency of P3 elicited by rare auditory stimuli increased with age from 304 ms in the 20 year olds to 364 ms in the 90 year olds with an average rate of 0.84 ms per year. These findings provide a useful baseline against which to interpret aging of the P3.

Friedman and Simpson (1994) used P3 to examine the hypothesis that aging is associated with a change in frontal-lobe function. Clinical research using frontal-lobe lesioned patients has validated that the P3 elicited by novel stimuli requires intact frontal lobes (e.g. Knight, 1984). Thus, Friedman and Simpson presented a target/novelty task similar to the one employed by Courchesne (1978) to young adults (24 year olds), middle-aged persons (49 year olds) and healthy older subjects (70 year olds). The P3 findings replicated the results reported previously in the literature for young adults but not for the elderly. For young adults, target stimuli elicited a P3 with a parietal maximum whereas novel stimuli elicited a more frontally distributed P3. For the elderly, however, both P3s were frontally distributed. Interestingly, it was observed that during the initial stages of task performance young adult subjects also showed frontally oriented P3s. But this pattern changed rapidly during the course of performance. In the elderly, the frontally oriented pattern continued to exist as if they continued to produce 'novelty' responses. These findings were replicated and extended in a follow-up study in which subjects also performed the Wisconsin Card Sorting Task (WCST) to explore the relation between age-related changes in frontal-lobe functioning and P3 topography (Fabiani & Friedman, 1995). The new findings indicated a marked difference in P3 topography elicited by novel and target stimuli for young adults but not for the elderly as in the previous study. Interestingly, it was observed that a failure to maintain set on the WCST was associated with more frontally oriented P3s. These findings were taken as support for the hypothesis that decreased frontal functioning in the elderly is associated with increased frontal electrical activity, perhaps through disinhibition or compensation by other subregions.

There are relatively few studies in the developmental literature that chart age-related changes from early childhood into senescence. One such study has been published recently by Dustman and co-workers who examined life-span changes in electrophysiological measures (Dustman, Emmerson & Shearer, 1996). These authors pointed to a series of observations that led them to assume that with advancing age the brain responds in a more homogeneous or global manner. They examined this hypothesis using two different paradigms. The first paradigm is based on the observation that brain potentials evoked exogenously by patterned and unpatterned flashes are markedly different. Dustman et al. suggested that this difference reflects inhibitory processes elicited by patterned flashes, serving to enhance contrast in the visual system. ERPs were recorded using this paradigm in 220 subjects aged 4 to 90 years. The results were consistent with the predictions. The dissimilarity in the ERPs elicited by patterned and unpatterned flashes increased progressively during childhood, remained fairly constant during adulthood, and decreased again throughout senescence. These findings were taken to support the hypothesis that inhibition within the visual system is less effective during childhood and old age than during young adulthood.

In the second paradigm, exogenous ERPs were recorded to light flashes of different intensities. The amplitude of the evoked potentials increases as a function of flash intensity. Dustman et al. (1996) found that the slope of this function was flatter for young adults compared to children and older subjects. This finding was interpreted to suggest that young adults were better able than children and older adults to inhibit the impact of intense flashes. In other words, these findings provide support for the hypothesis that inhibitory control waxes and wanes during the life-span. In this respect, the findings reported by Dustman and colleagues are consistent with the results reported by Friedman and co-workers (e.g. Fabiani & Friedman, 1995) by converging on the notion of a frontally-based inhibition deficit in the elderly. The notion of inhibitory control as an important developmental dimension will be discussed further *vis-à-vis* life-span changes in speeded responses in a later section. Interestingly, Dustman et al. observed also that slopes were flatter for old adults who engaged frequently in strenuous exercise than for those who seldom exercised. This finding was interpreted to suggest that exercise may counteract the age-related decrease in inhibitory functioning during senescence. These findings are consistent with the results reported by Spirduso & MacRae (1990) and others that suggest that aerobic fitness and training may reduce detrimental changes in nervous-system functioning in aging subjects (see also Bashore & Goddard, 1993).

Neuroimaging: PET Studies

Positron emission tomography became available in the early 1980s. PET uses radioactive isotopes to provide quantitative measures of regional cerebral blood flow or glucose metabolism as indices of neuronal activity. This technique allows the construction of brain images with a spatial resolution in the order of several millimeters and a temporal resolution of about 15s to one minute. PET is a relatively expensive technique and its use is limited by the fact that children are more sensitive to radiation effects than adults (for more details, see Krasuski, Horwitz & Rumsey, 1996).

Chugani and co-workers used PET to examine the distribution of glucose-metabolic activity during the first year of life in clinically referred children who, in retrospect, did not suffer from neurological events affecting development (for a review see Chugani, 1994). The ontogeny of glucose-metabolic patterns seemed to proceed in phylogenetic order. The second and third months of life showed a progressive increase in the cortical mediation of behavior. Glucose-metabolic activity increased rapidly in large areas of the parietal, occipital, and temporal cortex, but remained low in most of the frontal lobe. The frontal cortex is the last region to undergo a maturational rise in glucose-metabolic activity, where functional maturation of the lateral portion (6 to 8 months) precedes the phylogenetically more recent dorsal regions (8 to 12 months). This development is suggested to coincide with the emergence of higher cognitive abilities (cf. Chugani, 1994, p. 159).

Neonatal glucose-metabolic rates, that are about 30% lower than in the young adult, increase rapidly to reach adult values by about the second year. The rise does not stop, however, and glucose-metabolic rates begin to exceed adult levels during the third year until a plateau is reached during the fourth year that extends until about 9 years. A gradual decline is then observed until adult rates of glucose-metabolic activity are reached by the end of the second decade. Chugani (1994) suggested that the rapid increase in glucose-metabolic activity corresponds to the period of rapid over-production of synaptic connections.

PET studies failed initially to reveal dramatic changes in brain metabolism during senescence. More recent studies, however, using PET cameras with improved resolution, show an inverse relation between brain metabolism and age; moreover, some brain areas are more vulnerable than others. De Santi, de Leon, Convit et al. (1995) examined brain metabolism in various areas in the frontal lobe, temporal lobe, hippocampus, and cerebellum. Metabolic reductions in older adults relative to young adults were observed in all frontal regions and the temporal lobe but not for the cerebellum. More specific analysis indicated that age-related decline in frontal-lobe metabolism was larger than the decline in temporal-lobe metabolism which, in turn, was larger than the decline in the metabolism of the hippocampus. Similar findings have been reported by Loessner, Alavi, Lewandrowski et al. (1995) using a larger sample. These authors reported a considerable reduction in metabolic activity on the frontal lobes with only a small trend during the third and fourth decades and a more dramatic decline after the sixth decade. These findings are consistent with many reports suggesting that the frontal lobes are most sensitive to the effects of aging (e.g. Terry et al., 1987). At this point, studies are needed relating age-related changes in brain metabolism to cognitive performance.

Neuroimaging: MRI Studies

Magnetic resonance technology was used initially to examine the atomic constituents of chemical samples. Later it was developed into an imaging technique that can be used to distinguish different body tissues based on their chemical compositions. MRI techniques are based on the principle that the frequency of a radiowave emitted by an atomic nucleus depends directly upon the strength of a surrounding magnetic field. When the head is placed into a homogeneous magnetic field, the signals coming from the brain can be translated into images by adding a small gradient onto the static magnetic field. fMRI, or dynamic MRI, uses conventional MRI scanners with fast imaging techniques to detect changes in blood flow and blood volume in tissue activated during task performance. Major advances over PET include higher temporal and spatial resolution and the lack of radiation and invasiveness, allowing its use in normal children. One of the major limitations is the greater sensitivity to movement artifacts. Consider-able subject cooperation is needed during task performance (cf. Krasuski et al., 1996).

MRI has been used to assess gray-matter volumes in the brains of normal subjects ranging in age from 8 to 35 years (Jernigan, Trauner, Hesselink &

Tallal, 1991). These results suggested regional variation in cortical maturation. Significant change was observed for superior cortical regions, comprising mostly the frontal and parietal areas, but not for the inferior cortical
regions. The age-related decrease in frontal gray matter seems to coincide
with the reduction in synaptic density in the frontal cortex observed by
Huttenlocher (1994). Jernigan et al. suggested the possibility that the observed structural changes in specific cortical regions may relate to the
decrease in cortical plasticity thought to occur during childhood and adolescence (see also Chugani, 1994).

A study that examined normal brain growth in children and adolescents
ranging in age from 5 to 17 years failed to find evidence of brain growth as
indexed by total cerebral volume (Reiss, Abrams, Singer et al., 1997).
However, the data revealed considerable age-related declines in cortical gray
volume and complementary gains in white matter volume. The former result
was interpreted in terms of regressive events aimed at the refinement of
neuronal connections, whereas the latter finding was taken to indicate
increased myelination, in particular of the prefrontal brain areas implicated
in executive functioning. Finally, Reiss et al. obtained a significant correlation of intelligence with brain volume, in particular with the volume of gray
matter in the prefrontal area of the brain. Interestingly, their results seem to
indicate that increases in cerebral volumes are associated initially with
increases in intelligence, but later on the increase in intelligence levels off, and
still later gives way to a decrease when cerebral volume continues to increase.
These findings suggest the possibility that increases in brain size beyond an
optimal range may have detrimental effects on intellectual functioning.

MRI studies have also contributed to the picture of highly specific brain
changes during the later stages of life. In a study that examined healthy
subjects ranging in age from 21 to 70 years, MRI measurements indicated
that hippocampal volumes and temporal-lobe white matter did not change
with age, temporal-lobe gray-matter volumes decreased with age, and ventricular volumes increased with age (Sullivan, Marsh, Mathalon et al.,
1995). Interestingly, memory performance was not related to hippocampal
volumes, but mild declines in some memory measures were related to
ventricular enlargement. These findings suggested that age-related atrophy
of the cortex adjacent to hippocampal structures plays a role in the memory
declines observed in old age. A substantial decrease in hippocampal gray
volume in older adults was revealed in an MRI study that examined participants in their ninth decade (Coffey, Wilkinson, Parashos et al., 1992).

Changes in brain morphology across the life-span (from 3 months to 70
years) have been charted by Pfefferbaum et al. (1994). MRI was reported to
demonstrate differential developmental trajectories in head size, gray and
white matter, and cerebrospinal fluid. Head size showed a significant linear
increase until age 10 years followed by a cessation in growth. Cerebrospinal
fluid, by contrast, remained fairly constant from birth to the age of 20–30
and was then seen to increase into old age. Cortical gray matter was found
to increase rapidly until the age of 4 years, followed by a gradual decline.
Cortical white matter increased steadily from birth to about 20 years and

then levelled off. The latter finding is consistent with previous reports suggesting that myelination continues well into adolescence, as myelination and axonal growth are likely to contribute to the increase in white-matter volume. The rise and decline of gray matter is consistent with the trajectories of cell growth, arborization, synaptogenesis, and cell proliferation, which are likely to contribute to the increase in cortical gray-matter volume during the first years of life. The initial reduction in gray-matter volume which then follows was assumed by Pfefferbaum et al. to be due to synaptic and axonal pruning. The later reduction in gray-matter volume together with the increase in cerebrospinal volume may signal cortical atrophy. More specifically, Pfefferbaum et al. suggested that the onset of ventricular enlargement between age 20 and 30 years may provide a demarcation point between the maturational process of neuronal pruning and the atrophic processes of normal aging.

In this respect, Pfefferbaum and co-workers seem to have adopted the 'hill metaphor' of life-span development which assumes that developmental progression will stop at a certain age beyond which the deterioration associated with aging will begin. The following section will examine whether the 'hill' suggested by electrophysiological and brain imaging studies is manifested also at behavioral levels.

THE PROCESSING BRAIN

One of the most robust findings in the developmental literature is that children respond faster in speeded-up performance tasks as they grow older. At the other end of the life-span, the recurrent observation is that older subjects respond more slowly with advancing age (see Demetriou, ch. 5 this volume). The age-related changes in the speed of responding have been interpreted by some authors to suggest a *global* change in the information processing system. That is, it is assumed that all elements of the information processing system mature and decline at the same rate. Others have interpreted age changes in response speed to be process-specific. Unfortunately, the neural mechanism underlying the trends in the efficiency of performance, be they global or process-specific, have not been elaborated extensively. Some explanations point to the frontal lobes and can be couched into a 'last-in-first-out' scenario of brain–behavior relations during the life-span.

The Global-Difference Hypothesis

Age-related changes in processing speed have been documented extensively in the human performance literature (for a review see Cerella & Hale, 1994). The amounts by which the speed of responding in simple tasks changes with age are relatively small compared to the changes in more complex tasks (see e.g. Birren, 1964, 1965; Goldfarb, 1941, cited in Welford, 1959). Considerable changes in processing speed during childhood have been observed in

tasks involving visual search (e.g. E. Gibson & Yonas, 1966), letter discrimi-
nation (e.g. Lane & Pearson, 1983), letter matching (e.g. Hale, 1990),
memory search (e.g. Kail, 1988), name retrieval (e.g. Bisanz, Danner &
Resnick, 1979), mental addition (Kail, 1991), mental rotation (Kail, 1988;
Hale, 1990), and response selection (e.g. Ridderinkhof, van der Molen,
Band & Bashore, 1997). Similarly, significant differences in processing speed
during senescence have been observed in tasks involving visual search (e.g.
Rabbitt, 1965), letter discrimination (e.g. Simon & Pouraghabagher, 1978),
letter matching (e.g. Cerella, DiCarra, Williams & Bowles, 1986), memory
search (e.g. Anders & Fozard, 1973; Bashore, 1990), mental addition (e.g.
Allen, Ashcraft & Weber, 1992; Birren, 1964), mental rotation (e.g. Cerella,
Poon & Fozard, 1981), and response selection (e.g. Kay, 1954; Ruch, 1934;
Salthouse & Somberg, 1982).

The diversity of this assortment of tasks suggests that age-related changes
in response speed may refer to a global rather than a specific information
processing mechanism. In order to assess the hypothesis that advancing age
has a generalized slowing effect, Cerella and co-workers regressed the RTs
of older subjects, taken from a large number of studies in which age-related
changes in response speed were assessed on a wide range of tasks varying in
complexity, against those of young adults (Cerella, Poon & Williams, 1980).
They obtained a linear regression function with a slope of about 1.4 that
accounted for over 90% of the variance. This pattern led Cerella et al. to
conclude that a single parameter, represented by the slope of the regression
function, characterizes the age effect across tasks of increasing complexity.
The assumptions underlying the notion of generalized change in response
speed and a hypothetical data-pattern consistent with this notion are given
in Box 2.12.

A very similar pattern has been obtained by Kail (1991) who adopted
Cerella's procedures for analyzing developmental changes in processing
speed. This author performed an exhaustive search of the developmental
literature from 1964 to 1989 and identified 72 studies reporting latencies for
groups of children and young adults. A meta-analysis showed that the
spread of points could be fitted to linear functions with slopes greater than
1.0. The slopes ranged from approximately 3 in 4 year olds to 1.25 in 14 year
olds. These findings were taken to suggest that developmental changes in
processing speed involve a global mechanism underlying performance in a
wide variety of speeded tasks.

A variety of mechanisms have been invoked to explain global changes in
processing speed. Kail and Salthouse (1994), for example, likened the speed
of information processing to the clock speed of a microcomputer. For an
individual with a higher clock speed, all processing takes place at a faster
rate than for individuals with a lower clock speed. As young children's clock
speed increases, the speed of processing in all cognitive processes increases
until the adult level is reached, beyond which clock speed may decrease
again, resulting in slower responses across information processing tasks.
A more elaborate hypothesis has been proposed by Myerson and colleagues who assumed that differences in response speed between age

Box 2.12   Global or process-specific age changes?

The analytical procedure entertained by Cerella and others is based on the assumption that (a) reaction time (RT) consists of the sum of durations of several component processes, and (b) advancing age affects all component processes indiscriminately both within and between tasks. Support for these assumptions is derived from analyses in which the RT data of children or older adults are regressed on those of young adults either across levels of a task or across tasks differing in complexity. The slope of the regression function is then assumed to reflect the age-related change in the speed of information processing. This is illustrated by the following hypothetical example presented in Figure B2.12:1. In the left panel of the figure, mean RTs are depicted for four different age groups (5, 8, 11, and 21 year olds) in three experimental conditions (A, B and C). The RTs of each group of children can be regressed against those of the adults and the resulting linear regression lines are depicted in the right panel of the figure. Multiplying adults' RTs from each condition by the slope of the corresponding regression function yields accurate estimates of each group of children's RTs. For example, adults' RT in the slowest condition is 500 ms. When this value is multiplied by $b=2.0$ the youngest children's RT of 1000 ms is obtained.

The studies reviewed by Cerella and Hale (1994) reported regression results relating groups of children or older adults to young adults' RTs and observed that simple regression analyses were quite accurate in describing the relations between the RTs of different age groups. Almost without exception, the fit of the regression equation has been

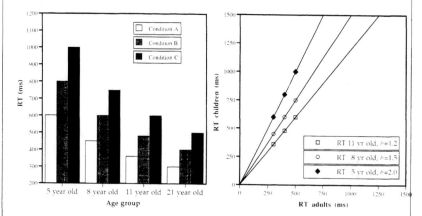

Figure B2.12:1   Hypothetical reaction time data from 5-, 8-, 11-, and 21-year-old subjects in conditions A, B, and C (left panel). Regression functions drawn on the basis of the hypothetical data shown in the left panel (right panel)

From Ridderinkhof, K. R. & Van der Molen, M. W. (1997). Mental resources, processing speed, and inhibitory control: A developmental perspective. *Biological Psychology*, **45**, 241–261. Reprinted by permission.

found to account for almost all of the variance in the group means, with r^2 typically higher than 0.90. A recent anomaly, however, has been published by Ridderinkhof and van der Molen (1997). They re-analyzed data from a previous study in which children of different ages and young adults performed on a selective attention task. During task performance, the EEG was recorded to obtain brain potentials that signal the completion of stimulus analysis and the onset of selective response preparation. Task-relevant stimuli elicit a brain potential comprising a positive component reaching peak amplitudes over the parietal regions. This component has been coined P3 in the psychophysiological literature and is assumed to be a manifestation of stimulus evaluation. Voluntary responses elicit negative-going changes in brain electrical activity that are larger over motor cortex sites contralateral to the limb involved in the motor response. The onset of the lateralized readiness potential (LRP) has been used to index preferential response activation (for more details see van der Molen, Bashore, Halliday & Callaway, 1991).

Ridderinkhof and van der Molen (1997) reasoned that if P3 latency, LRP onset, and RT reflect the durations of, respectively, stimulus evaluation, stimulus evaluation plus response selection, and all component processes, and if age would affect all processing components indiscriminately, then the same regression parameters should accurately describe not only the relation between young adults' and children's RTs, but also between their P3 latencies and between their LRP onset latencies. Their results are plotted in Figure B2.12:2. Ridderinkhof and van der Molen fitted growth functions to each of these measures for the three age groups of children and the young adults. The growth functions provided adequate descriptions of the relations between children's and young adults' speed measures but, importantly, the rate parameter was not equivalent across speed measures. It was substantially larger for P3 latency than for LRP onset

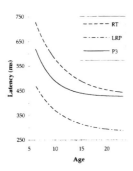

Figure B2.12:2 Growth functions of LRPs, P3s, and RTs calculated on data from Ridderinkhof and van der Molen (1995)
From Ridderinkhof, K. R. & van der Molen, M. W. (1997). Mental resources, processing speed, and inhibitory control: A developmental perspective. *Biological Psychology*, **45**, 241–261. Reprinted by permission.

and RT. As can be seen in the figure, asymptote latencies are reached at a more rapid rate and earlier in development for P3 than for LRP and RT. This pattern indicates that perceptual component processes, indexed by the P3, develop at a faster rate than response-related processes associated with the LRP. These findings are clearly inconsistent with the global-difference hypothesis predicting that age-related changes in the speed of responding pertain to all components of the reaction process to the same degree. In this vein, the results reported by Ridderinkhof and van der Molen (1997) contribute to the growing evidence that age-related changes in response speed may be process-specific and not always generalized.

Sources: Ridderinkhof, K. R. & van der Molen, M. W. (1997). Mental resources, processing speed, and inhibitory control: A developmental perspective. *Biological Psychology*, **45**, 241–261. Van der Molen, M. W., Bashore, T. R., Halliday, R. & Callaway, E. (1991). Chrono-psychophysiology: Mental chronometry augmented with psycho-physiological time markers. In J. R. Jennings and M. G. H. Coles (Eds), *Handbook of Cognitive Psychophysiology: Central and Autonomic Nervous System Approaches* (pp. 9–178). Chichester, UK: John Wiley.

groups are largely determined by the communication efficiency of processing elements activated during task performance (e.g. Myerson, Hale, Wagstaff et al., 1990). More information is lost between processing steps in older adults, resulting in slower processing compared to young adults.

Alternatively, it has been proposed that the observed age-related changes in processing speed may be mediated to a significant extent by changes in the ability to inhibit. According to this view, young adults are better able to screen out irrelevant information from working memory compared to other age groups; thus, more functional capacity will remain available for the processing of relevant information and the selection of the appropriate response (e.g. Bjorklund & Harnishfeger, 1990; Hasher & Zacks, 1988). It is further proposed that age-related changes in inhibitory control are mediated by the frontal lobes (e.g. Dempster, 1992). The relatively late functional maturation and relatively early deterioration of the frontal lobes suggested the possibility that age-related changes in frontal-lobe functioning are closely related to cognitive development and aging (e.g. Dempster, 1993; Segalowitz & Rose-Krasnor, 1992; see also Clark, 1996, for a detailed discussion of the relation between frontal lobes and inhibitory control).

Critical Notes

The global-difference hypothesis invoked to provide a unified account of life-span changes in the speed of information processing has been challenged on various counts. The criticisms focused on (a) the generality of the findings, (b) the methods used for analyzing age-group differences, (c) the models developed to account for the alleged global change, and (d) the brain mechanism(s) assumed to participate in the waxing and waning of response speed.

Generality of findings

One problem facing the hypothesis of generalized change is domain-specificity. It has been observed that age-related changes in response speed are different between lexical and nonlexical processing. The relation between the latencies of older and younger adults performing various lexical tasks can be well described by a linear function with a slope of approximately 1.5 (e.g. Lima, Hale & Myerson, 1991). By contrast, the relation between the latencies of older and younger adults performing nonlexical tasks is non-linear and can be well described by a positively accelerating power function (e.g. Hale, Myerson & Wagstaff, 1987). Lima et al. (1991) observed that the rate of change is smaller in the lexical compared to the nonlexical domain. The finding that the lexical and nonlexical domains are associated with different mathematical functions predicting the latencies of older adults from those of young adults, indicates that age-related changes in response speed are not as general as suggested by the global-difference hypothesis. Lima et al. interpreted this domain specificity in terms of crystallized and fluid abilities, in that lexical tasks may depend primarily on crystallized intelligence and nonlexical tasks on fluid intelligence. In this vein, their findings would be consistent with the psychometric literature indicating that crystallized and fluid intelligence tests are differently susceptible to age-related effects (e.g. Horn, 1985).

A psychophysiological critique of the global-difference hypothesis has been presented by Bashore, Osman and Heffley (1989). These authors increased analytical precision by augmenting the analysis of response latencies with P3 as a psychophysiological time marker of stimulus analysis (see, e.g. Van der Molen et al., 1991). Thus, Bashore and co-workers performed a search of the psychophysiological literature and identified a large number of studies in which age-related changes were examined using both overt performance measures, including RT, and brain-potential measures, including P3 latency. These data were then subjected to regression analysis. Both RTs and P3 latencies data yielded linear functions that explained more than 90% of the variance, suggesting that information processing speed in older adults could be predicted accurately and globally from speed in young adults. The slope of the regression function for RT was significantly larger than 1.0. However, the slope of the regression on P3 data approximated 1.0. Under the hypothesis that P3 latency provides an index of the completion of the evaluation of the stimulus, it must be concluded that the speed of stimulus-related processing is less sensitive to the effects of advancing age compared to response-related processes, a conclusion that contradicts the global-difference hypothesis. A developmental study showing similar results is summarized in Box 2.12.

Methods of analysis

An even more damaging criticism of the global-difference hypothesis focused on the use of regression analysis to evaluate age-related changes in processing speed. It has been demonstrated that the outcomes of the regression analysis are very sensitive to the results included in the meta-analysis. Moreover, it has been shown that the regression analysis may conceal task-specific changes that can be identified by subjecting latency data to ANOVA (for a review of this debate see Bashore, 1994). The latter criticism led some investigators to augment regression analysis with ANOVA (Madden, Pierce & Allen, 1992). In this procedure, reaction times from different age groups are first subjected to regression analysis and the parameters of the best-fitting regression function are then used to transform the latency data. The rationale of the transformation is as follows: if children's or older adults' RTs can be predicted accurately from young adults' RTs through a global regression function, the transformation based on the parameters of this regression function will align the response times such that age group by task interactions in the ANOVA should be absent. The occurrence of any such interaction after transformation would indicate the presence of task-specific age effects that cannot be attributed to generalized change in processing speed. Madden et al. (1992) applied this procedure on data from a visual search task and found that an age group by task interaction remained after transformation, indicating local differences between age groups beyond the effects predicted by the global-difference model (see also Ridderinkhof & van der Molen, 1997).

Models of global change

The models invoked to explain generalized change also elicited considerable debate. Molenaar and van der Molen (1994), for example, presented a series of simulations demonstrating that the information-loss proposed by Myerson et al. (1990) failed to identify specific effects of aging on the information processing flow even when the model that was used to simulate response latencies was constructed to embody localized effects on the communication efficiency between successive elements of the information processing system. This result led Molenaar and van der Molen to conclude that the information-loss model cannot be used to decide between generalized versus process-specific effects of advancing age on the speed of information processing.

Capacity models of generalized age-related changes in processing speed have been criticized for various reasons. Some investigators, while accepting the capacity view of information processing, proposed a view that is almost diametrically opposed to the inefficient-inhibition hypothesis (e.g. Bjorklund & Harnishfeger, 1990; Hasher & Zacks, 1988). Rather than making working-memory capacity available for speeded information processing, inhibitory control itself *requires* working-memory capacity, as demonstrated by the finding that the ability to inhibit a prepotent response depends on the amount of capacity allotted to a secondary task (e.g. Roberts, Hager & Heron, 1994). Other theorists rejected the notion of a single-capacity reservoir and amassed evidence to suggest multiple domain-specific capacity pools (e.g. Wickens, 1984). As indicated by Kail (1993), explaining generalized change in terms of multiple resources would require either that speeded information processing tasks all draw from one and the same capacity pool, or that multiple resources develop at a similar rate.

Further, it has been argued that information processing bottlenecks do not arise because of capacity limitations but rather are due to structural interference between incompatible actions (e.g. Allport, 1993; Neumann, 1987). This line of reasoning has been adopted by Brainerd and Reyna (1989) and provides an alternative to the inefficient-inhibition view. More specifically, Brainerd and Reyna assumed that the response selection mechanism becomes more articulated during childhood, resulting in a richer assortment of responses and thus less structural interference. Within this context, age-related changes in response speed are interpreted in terms of the efficiency of action selection. This view is compatible with findings suggesting that response-related processing is more susceptible to age effects than stimulus-related processing (for a review see Bashore, 1994). Finally, it should be noted that the concept of inhibitory control may not be a unitary phenomenon or a unidimensional construct. The term 'inhibition' has been used for a wide range of phenomena (e.g. Dagenbach & Carr, 1994). The application of this concept to explain generalized change in processing speed would therefore seem to imply that all inhibitory behaviors change in concert. This possibility has been suggested but rejected by Dempster (1992) who pointed to different developmental trends for perceptual, linguistic, and motor inhibition.

Brain mechanisms of global change

How successful is the frontal-lobe hypothesis in providing a unified account of life-span changes in the speed of responding, as suggested by Dempster (1992) and others? Obviously, the frontal-lobe hypothesis is consistent with a great variety of findings emerging from the neurosciences, suggesting that the frontal lobes are late to mature and early to decline. Furthermore, the frontal-lobe hypothesis is compatible with numerous observations that these structures are implicated in inhibitory control and working memory (for reviews see Pennington, 1994; West, 1996). More specifically, the frontal-lobe hypothesis is in accordance with the neuropsychological view that the prefrontal cortex controls information processing by way of a dynamic filtering or gating mechanism that inhibits extraneous activity (e.g. Shimamura, 1995). Effective gating increases the availability of relevant sensory and cognitive signals by filtering out signals from irrelevant noise (cf. Shimamura, 1995, p. 810).

It should be noted, however, that frontal-lobe damage may result in a wide array of cognitive and behavioral deficits, suggesting that the frontal lobes are not associated with just one specific function. The complexities of frontal-lobe functioning are well illustrated by the frontally damaged patients described in Box 2.13. Functional specialization within the frontal cortex has been well established (for a review see e.g. Fuster, 1989). The modular function of the frontal cortex is revealed for instance by findings showing that dorsal lesions result predominantly in deficits in spatial processing, whereas ventral lesions are specifically associated with recognition-memory impairments, and medial lesions with motor (planning) dysfunction (e.g. Gazzaniga, 1995). It has been argued, however, that a multitude of behavioral and cognitive impairments do not arise because different regions of the frontal lobes are serving different functions, but because different areas of the frontal lobes are inhibiting different posterior brain areas which themselves serve different behavioral and cognitive functions (Shimamura, 1995). More research is clearly needed to decide whether the concept of inhibitory control mediated by the frontal lobes as a general development factor is ultimately tenable. At this point, however, the application of the frontal-lobe hypothesis may be productive in generating data that are highly relevant to the intriguing issue of life-span changes in processing speed, whether global or local in nature.

CONCLUSION

This chapter has been inspired by the belief that knowledge gained by integrating psychological and neurobiological perspectives will lead to a more complete understanding of human development and aging. Obviously, the research reviewed in this chapter represents only the tip of an ever growing iceberg. The psychological and neurobiological literatures cover vast domains and both are extremely diverse with regard to the topics under examination and the methods used to examine age-related change in behavior, brain structure, and brain function. Nonetheless, interesting attempts have been made to bridge the apparent gap between disciplines. Brain–behavior relations have sometimes been suggested by theoretical speculation associating spurts in cognitive development to brain growth (e.g. Fischer & Rose, 1994) or by linking widespread behavioral change to biochemical alterations in the aging brain (e.g. DeKosky & Palmer, 1994). But brain–behavior relations are based increasingly on fastidious task analyses to illuminate the psychological meaning of behavioral indices of developmental changes, on non-invasive analyses of human brain activity during task performance (e.g. Friedman, 1991), and on the construction of animal models, in an attempt to understand how the abilities required by the task are implemented in the brain (e.g. Diamond, 1990b; see also Gallagher & Rapp, 1997).

Box 2.13   The mystery of the prefrontal brain

For a long time, it was assumed that the frontal lobes did not participate in essential mental capacities. Ladd (1890), for example, argued
that experimental and pathological evidence does not warrant an
interpretation of the frontal lobes as the seat of intelligence. Massive
lesions were seen to occur in the frontal lobes without notable changes
in intellectual function whereas small lesions in the posterior parts of
the brain are most frequently associated with a profound loss of
mental capacity. The view that the frontal lobes do nothing much and
are basically expandable is expressed most clearly by the neurologist in
the recent movie *Regarding Henry* (1991). Henry, a young and energetic lawyer, played by Harrison Ford, has been shot in the head
during a hold-up. When he has recovered from his injuries and is
visiting the neurologist, the doctor informs him that he has been very
lucky: 'The bullet passed only through the frontal lobes which have
expendable systems and fortunately, did not hit other parts of the
brain supporting vital mental functions.'

Recently, Damasio (1994) offered a penetrating description of a
frontal-lobe-damaged patient showing vital changes. This patient,
referred to as Elliot, was a businessman in his thirties and happily
married. Unfortunately he developed severe headaches which were
diagnosed to result from a rapidly growing tumor compressing both
frontal lobes upward, from below. The tumor and frontal-lobe tissue
damaged by the tumor were removed successfully, but Elliot was no
longer Elliot.

He needed prompting to get started in the morning and prepare to go to work.
Once at work he was unable to manage his time properly; he could not be
trusted with a schedule. When the job called for interrupting an activity and
turning to another, he might persist nonetheless, seemingly losing sight of his
main goal. Or he might interrupt the activity he had engaged, to turn to
something he found more captivating at that particular moment. Imagine a
task involving reading and classifying documents of a given client. Elliot
would read and fully understand the significance of the material, and he
certainly knew how to sort out the documents according to the similarity or
disparity of their content. The problem was that he was likely, all of a sudden,
to turn from the sorting task he had initiated to reading one of those papers,
carefully and intelligently, and to spend an entire day doing so. Or he might
spend the whole afternoon deliberating on which principle of categorization
should be applied: Should it be date, size of the document, pertinence to the
case, or another? The flow of work was stopped. One might say that the
particular step of the task at which Elliot balked was actually carried out *too*
well, and at the expense of the overall purpose. (Damasio, 1994, p. 36).

The behavioral changes in Elliot described by Damasio (1994) are
consistent with the observations which have been reported by Luria
(1973) who described the behavioral changes of frontal-lobe-damaged
patients in terms of his organizational framework. Frontal damage
may lead to the disintegration of complex action programs and to
their replacement by simpler and stereotyped forms of behavior.

Speech no longer regulates action, resulting in the loss of behavioral control. Frontal-lobe-lesioned patients do not display primary memory deficits but rather an inability to maintain cognitive schemes active in working memory and to switch from one scheme to another. Obviously, such a deficit is very disruptive to intellectual functioning. Simple cognitive tasks do not present a problem for frontal-lobe-damaged patients; they fail when tasks demand the formation and execution of complex schemes involving priority setting and switching between alternative actions along the way.

Sources: Damasio, A. R. (1994). *Descartes' Error: Emotion, Reason, and the Human Brain*. New York: Putnam. Ladd, G. T. (1890). *Elements of Physiological Psychology*. London: Longmans, Green & Co. Luria, A. R. (1973). *The Working Brain. An Introduction to Neuropsychology*. Harmondsworth: Penguin.

The rapid progress in electrophysiology and brain-imaging techniques is likely to alter dramatically our current understanding of brain–behavior development and aging. The imaging of the brain has only just begun. Most of the research is concerned with clinical populations and only a limited amount of studies examined brain structure and function during normal development or senescence. The picture painted by studies examining brain growth in healthy children strongly suggests that the frontal lobes are the last to mature. This picture emerged from EEG studies (e.g. Thatcher, 1994), ERP studies (e.g. Courchesne, 1978, 1990), MRI studies, (e.g. Jernigan et al., 1991), and PET studies (e.g. Chugani, 1994). Conversely, the data reported by imaging studies of the aging brain in healthy older subjects seem to converge on the conclusion that the frontal lobes are the first to deteriorate. The greater vulnerability of the frontal lobes compared to other brain regions was demonstrated in ERP studies (e.g. Friedman & Simpson, 1994; Fabiani & Friedman, 1995), MRI studies (e.g. Coffey et al., 1992) and PET studies (e.g. Loessner et al., 1995).

A rapidly growing literature documents the growing and aging brain in relation to age-related changes in behavior. Contributions to this literature include studies that are inspired by a well-defined theoretical framework and have examined brain–behavior relations during task performance (e.g. Stauder et al., 1993; Friedman & Simpson, 1994) as well as studies inspired by more speculative frameworks of brain–behavior relations (e.g. Epstein, 1974a, b; Thatcher, 1994). In between are studies employing correlational analyses of the relation between brain structure or function parameters and psychometric indices of intellectual functioning (e.g. Ylikowski, Ylikowski, Erkinjuntti, et al., 1993). More studies are needed using brain imaging during task performance. This approach has already been adopted in the electrophysiological literature (e.g. Friedman, 1991). In the brain-imaging literature, PET has been used to delineate the brain systems activated when subjects perform attention-demanding tasks (e.g. Posner & Raichle, 1994).

This work provides exciting illustrations of how brain-imaging techniques may help to identify brain areas associated with specific mental operations. In addition, it is likely that techniques of molecular biology will be applied increasingly to study the growing and aging brain. Future investigations of membrane functions, cellular metabolism, and trophic factors are likely to extend the current understanding of the nervous system beyond that given by the measurements of neurotransmitters, and will give a higher-resolution look at the brain metabolism (DeKosky & Palmer, 1994).

The findings emerging from plasticity studies will have important implications for theorizing. These findings are anticipated to shed new light on the developmental psychology evergreens 'nature–nurture' and 'critical periods' but may also challenge the traditional 'hill metaphor' of life-span change. One of the challenges for the life-span analysis of brain–behavior relations will be answering the fundamental question of where development stops and aging begins (e.g. Pfefferbaum et al., 1994) or whether progressive developmental and regressive aging phenomena may coincide (for a more detailed discussion of these questions the interested reader is referred to Birren & Schroots, 1996). Plasticity studies seem to provide one answer by suggesting that progressive and regressive phenomena may both occur during development and aging. Another answer can be derived from studies examining age-related changes in neurotransmitter systems and myelination which seem to suggest that growth may be a characteristic of the brain throughout life (cf. Benes, 1994).

Attempts to integrate findings from developmental psychology and neurobiology within a life-span framework provide a perspective highlighting research areas in which new insights can be gained using electrophysiological or brain-imaging techniques. Only a handful of studies made an attempt to examine brain structure or function across the life-span. Pfefferbaum et al. (1994) reported life-span changes in different brain-structure indices which may have important implications for cognitive functioning. From the perspective of brain–behavior relations, the electrophysiological work done by Dustman and colleagues (e.g. Dustman et al., 1996) is perhaps most significant. These authors advanced the hypothesis that inhibitory control is compromised in children and older adults, and they were able to amass empirical support for this hypothesis by using different experimental paradigms and electrophysiological indices. Their life-span approach has extended knowledge about the relation between brain electrical activity and attention and provided a more detailed picture of changes in the ability to inhibit with advancing age.

The usefulness of a life-span orientation is also demonstrated by studies of age-related changes in the speed of information processing. The life-span perspective revealed that the methods used to examine performance changes are similar at both ends of the life-span, and that the models invoked to account for the increase in response speed during development and its decrease with advancing age are almost identical (e.g, Bashore & van der Molen, 1994). It can be expected that a brain–behavior analysis of these life-span changes in information processing speed will soon follow to test and refine the model of inhibitory control mediated by the frontal lobe that has been invoked to provide an account of the life-span changes in information processing speed.

ACKNOWLEDGEMENTS

The preparation of this chapter has been supported in part by grants to the first author from the Netherlands Organization for Scientific Research (NWO #575–63–092C and #575–63–093). The research of the second author has been made possible by a Fellowship of the Royal Netherlands Academy of Arts and Sciences. Most of the chapter was written while Maurits van der Molen stayed at the Laboratoire de Psychophysiology Cognitive et de Neuropsychiatrie (director Dr P. Robaey) at the Hôpital Sainte-Justine, Montreal, Canada, supported by the Fonds de la Recherche en Santé du Québec (#941754–104). The comments of Dr Sonia Robaey are highly appreciated.

REFERENCES

Allen, P. A., Ashcraft, M. H. & Weber, T. A. (1992). On mental multiplication and age. *Psychology and Aging*, **4**, 536–545.

Allport, A. (1993). Attention and control: Have we been asking the wrong questions? A critical review of twenty-five years. In D. E. Meyer & S. Kornblum (Eds), *Attention and Performance*, Vol. XIV (pp. 183–218). Cambridge, MA: MIT Press.

Anders, T. R. & Fozard, J. L. (1973). Effects of age upon retrieval from primary and secondary memory. *Developmental Psychology*, **9**, 214–217.

Bashore, T. R. (1990). Age-related changes in mental processing revealed by analyses of event-related brain potentials. In J. Rohrbaugh, R. Parasuraman & R. Johnson (Eds), *Event-related Brain Potentials: Basic Issues and Applications* (pp. 242–275). New York: Oxford University Press.

Bashore, T. R. (1994). Some thoughts on neurocognitive slowing. *Acta Psychologica*, **86**, 295–325.

Bashore, T. R. & Goddard, P. H. (1993). Preservation and restoration effects of aerobic fitness on the age-related slowing of mental processing speed. In J. Cerella, J. Rybash, W. Hoyer & M. L. Commons (Eds), *Adult Information Processing: Limits on Loss* (pp. 205–228). New York: Academic Press.

Bashore, T. R., Osman, A. & Heffley, E. F. (1989). Mental slowing in elderly persons: A cognitive psychophysiological analysis. *Psychology and Aging*, **4**, 235–244.

Bashore, T. R. & van der Molen, M. W. (Eds) (1994). Life-span changes in human performance [Special Issue]. *Acta Psychologica*, **86**, 106–325.

Benes, F. M. (1994). Development of the corticolimbic system. In G. Dawson & K. W. Fischer (Eds), *Human behavior and the developing brain* (pp. 176–206). New York: Guilford.

Birren, J. E. (1964). *The Psychology of Aging*. Englewood Cliffs, NJ: Prentice-Hall.

Birren, J. E. (1965). Age changes in speed of behavior: Its central nature and physiological correlates. In A. T. Welford & J. E. Birren (Eds), *Behavior, Aging and the Nervous System* (pp. 191–216). Springfield, IL: Charles C. Thomas.

Birren, J. E. & Schroots, J. J. F. (1996). Concepts, theory, and methods in the psychology of aging. In J. E. Birren and K. W. Schaie (Eds), *Handbook of the Psychology of Aging*, Fourth Edition (pp. 3–24). New York: Academic Press.

Bisanz, J., Danner, F. & Resnick, L. B. (1979). Changes with age in measures of processing efficiency. *Child Development*, **50**, 132–141.

Bjorklund, D. J. & Harnishfeger, K. K. (1990). The resources construct in cognitive development: Diverse sources of evidence and a theory of inefficient inhibition. *Developmental Review*, **10**, 48–71.

Black, J. E., Isaacs, K. R., Anderson, B. J., Alcantara, A. A. & Greenough, W. T. (1990). Learning causes synaptogenesis, whereas motor activity causes angiogenesis, in cerebellar cortex of adult rats. *Proceedings of the National Academy of Sciences*, **87**, 5568–5572.

Black, J. E., Isaacs, K. R. & Greenough, W. T. (1991). Usual vs successful aging: Some notes on experiential factors. *Neurobiology of Aging*, **12**, 325–328.

Boothe, R. G., Vassdal, E. & Schneck, M. (1986). Experience and development in the visual system: Anatomical studies. In W. T. Greenough & J. M. Juraska (Eds), *Developmental Neuropsychobiology* (pp. 295–315). New York: Academic Press.

Brainerd, C. J. & Reyna, V. F. (1989). Output-interference theory of dual-task deficits in memory development. *Journal of Experimental Child Psychology*, **47**, 1–18.

Busse, E. W. (1969). Theories of aging. In E. W. Busse & E. Pfeiffer (Eds), *Behavior and Adaption in Late Life* (pp. 11–32). Boston: Little, Brown.

Cerella, J., DiCarra, D., Williams, D. & Bowles, N. (1986). Relations between information processing and intelligence in elderly adults. *Intelligence*, **10**, 75–91.

Cerella, J. & Hale, S. (1994). The rise and fall in information-processing rates over the life span. *Acta Psychologica*, **86**, 109–197.

Cerella, J., Poon, L. W. & Fozard. J. L. (1981). Mental rotation and age reconsidered. *Journal of Gerontology*, **36**, 620–624.

Cerella, J., Poon, L. W. & Williams, D. M. (1980). Age and the complexity hypothesis. In L. Poon (Ed.), *Aging in the 1980s: Psychological Issues* (pp. 332–340). Washington, DC: American Psychological Association.

Chugani, H. T. (1994). Development of regional brain glucose metabolism in relation to behavior and plasticity. In G. Dawson & K. W. Fischer (Eds), *Human Behavior and the Developing Brain* (pp. 153–175). New York: Guilford.

Clark, J. M. (1996). Contributions of inhibitory mechanisms to unified theory in neuroscience and psychology. *Brain and Cognition*, **30**, 127–152.

Coffey, C. E., Wilkinson, W. E., Parashos, I. A, Soady, S. A. R., Sullivan, R. J., Patterson, L. J., Figiel, G. S., Webb, M. C., Spritzer, C. E. & Djang, W. T. (1992). Qualitative cerebral anatomy of the aging human brain: A cross-sectional study using magnetic resonance imaging. *Neurology*, **42**, 527–536.

Coleman, P. D. & Flood, D. G. (1987). Neuron numbers and dendritic extent in normal aging and Alzheimer's disease. *Neurobiology of Aging*, **8**, 521–545.

Cotman, C. W., Kahle, J. S. & Korotzer, A. R. (1995). Maintenance and regulation in brain of neurotransmission, trophic factors, and immune response. In E. J. Masoro (Ed.), *Handbook of Physiology*, Section 11, *Aging* (pp. 345–362). New York: Oxford University Press.

Cotman, C. W. & Nieto-Sampredo, M. (1982). Brain function, synapse renewal, and plasticity. *Annual Review of Psychology*, **33**, 371–395.

Courchesne, E. (1978). Neurophysiological correlates of cognitive development: Changes in long-latency event-related potentials from childhood to adulthood. *Electroencephalography and Clinical Neurophysiology*, **45**, 468–482.

Courchesne, E. (1990). Chronology of postnatal human brain development: Event-related potential, positron emission tomography, myelinogenesis, and synaptogenesis studies. In J. W. Rohrbaugh, R. Parasuraman & R. Johnson, Jr (Eds), *Event-related Brain Potentials: Basic Issues and Applications* (pp. 210–241). New York: Oxford University Press.

Crnic, L. S. & Pennington, B. F. (1987). Developmental psychology and the neurosciences: An introduction. *Child Development*, **58**, 533–538.

Dagenbach, D. & Carr, T. H. (Eds) (1994). *Inhibitory Processes in Attention, Memory, and Language*. New York: Academic Press.

Dawson, G. & Fischer, K. W. (Eds) (1994). *Human Behavior and the Developing Brain*. New York: Guilford Press.

De Santi, S., de Leon, M. J., Convit, A., Tarshish, Ch., Rusinek, H., Tsui, W. H., Sinaiko, W., Wang, G.-J., Bartlet, E. & Volkow, N. (1995). Age-related changes in brain: II. Positron emission tomography of frontal and temporal lobe glucose metabolism in normal subjects. *Psychiatric Quarterly*, **66**, 357–370.

DeKosky, S. T. & Palmer, A. M. (1994). Neurochemistry of Aging. In M. L. Albert & J. E. Knoefel (Eds), *Clinical Neurology of Aging*. Second edition (pp. 79–101). New York: Oxford University Press.

Dempster, F. N. (1992). The rise and fall of the inhibitory mechanism: Toward a unified theory of cognitive development and aging. *Developmental Review*, **12**, 45–74.

Dempster, F. N. (1993). Resistance to interference: Developmental changes in a basic processing mechanism. In M. L. Howe & R. Pasnak (Eds), *Emerging Themes in Cognitive Development*, Vol. I (pp. 3–27). New York: Springer Verlag.

Diamond, A. (Ed.), (1990a). The development and neural basis of higher cognitive functions. *Annals of the New York Academy of Sciences*, **608**, 267–317.

Diamond, A. (1990b). Developmental time course in human infants and infant monkeys, and the neural bases of inhibitory control in reaching. In A. Diamond (Ed.), The development and neural bases of higher cognitive functions. *Annals of the New York Academy of Sciences*, **608**.

Diamond, M. C. (1991). Environmental influences on the young brain. In K. R. Gibson & A. C. Peterson (Eds), *Brain Maturation and Cognitive Development* (pp. 107–124). New York: Aldine De Gruyter.

Dickson, D. W., Crystal, H. A., Mattiace, L. A., Masur, D. M., Blau, A. D., Davis, P., Yen, S.-H. & Aronson, M. K. (1991). Identification of normal and pathological aging in prospectively studied nondemented elderly humans. *Neurobiology of Aging*, **13**, 179–189.

Dustman, R. E., Emmerson, R. Y. & Shearer, D. E. (1996). Life-span changes in electrophysiological measures of inhibition. *Brain and Cognition*, **30**, 109–126.

Dustman, R. E., Shearer, D. E. & Emmerson, R. Y. (1993). EEG and event-related brain potentials in normal aging. *Progress in Neurobiology*, **41**, 369–401.

Epstein, H. T. (1974a). Phrenoblysis: Special brain and mind growth periods I. Human brain and skull development. *Developmental Psychobiology*, 7, 207–216.

Epstein, H. T. (1974b). Phrenoblysis: Special brain and mind growth periods II. Human brain and skull development. *Developmental Psychobiology*, 7, 217–224.

Epstein, H. T. (1978). Growth spurts during brain development: Implications for educational policy and practice. In J. S. Chall & A. F. Mikky (Eds), *Education and the Brain: The Seventy-seventh Yearbook of the National Society for the Study of Education*. Part II (pp. 343–370). Chicago: Chicago University Press.

Epstein, H. T. (1986). Stages in human brain development. *Developmental Brain Research*, **30**, 114–119.

Eslinger, P. J., Damasio, H., Graff-Radford, N. & Damasio, A. R. (1984). Examining the relation between computed tomography and neuropsychological measures in normal and demented elderly. *Journal of Neurology, Neurosurgery, and Psychiatry*, **47**, 1319–1325.

Fabiani, M. & Friedman, D. (1995). Changes in brain activity patterns in aging: The novelty oddball. *Psychophysiology*, **32**, 579–594.

Fillenz, M. (1990). *Noradrenergic Neurons*. New York: Cambridge University Press.

Fischer, K. W. & Rose, S. P. (1994). Dynamic development of coordination of components in brain and behavior: A framework for theory and research. In G. Dawson & K. W. Fischer (Eds), *Human Behavior and the Developing Brain* (pp. 3–66). New York: Guilford Press.

Friedman, D. (1991). The endogenous scalp-recorded brain potentials and their relation to cognitive development. In J. R. Jennings & M. G. H. Coles (Eds), *Handbook of Cognitive Psychophysiology: Cental and Autonomic Nervous System Approaches* (pp. 621–656). New York: Wiley.

Friedman, D. & Simpson, G. V. (1994). ERP amplitude and scalp distribution to target and novel events: effects of temporal order in young, middle-aged and older adults. *Cognitive Brain Research*, **2**, 49–63.

Frost, D. O. & Metin, C. (1985). Induction of functional retinal projections to the somatosensory system. *Nature,* **317,** 162–164.

Fuster, J. M. (1989). *The Prefrontal Cortex, Anatomy, Physiology, and Neuropsychology of the Frontal Lobe* (2nd ed.). New York: Raven Press.

Gallagher, M. & Rapp, P. R. (1997). The use of animal models to study the effects of aging on cognition. *Annual Review of Psychology,* **48,** 339–370.

Gazzaniga, M. S. (Ed.) (1995). *The Cognitive Neurosciences.* Cambridge, MA: MIT Press.

Gibson, E. J. & Yonas, A. A. (1966). A developmental study of visual search behavior. *Perception and Psychophysics,* **1,** 169–171.

Gibson, K. R. (1991). Myelination and behavioral development: A comparative perspective on questions of neoteny, altriciality, and intelligence. In K. R. Gibson & A. C. Peterson, (Eds). *Brain Maturation and Cognitive Development* (pp. 29–63). New York: Aldine De Gruyter.

Gibson, K. R. & Peterson, A. C. (Eds) (1991). *Brain Maturation and Cognitive Development: Comparative and Cross-Cultural Perspectives. Foundations of Human Behavior.* New York: Aldine de Gruyter.

Greenough, W. T. (1986). What's special about Development? Thoughts on the bases of experience-sensitive synaptic plasticity. In W. T. Greenough & J. M. Juraska (Eds), *Developmental Neuropsychobiology* (pp. 387–407). New York: Academic Press.

Greenough, W. T., Black, J. E. & Wallace, C. S. (1987). Experience and brain development. *Child Development,* **58,** 539–559.

Hale, S. (1990). A global developmental trend in cognitive processing speed. *Child Development,* **61,** 653–663.

Hale, S., Myerson, J., & Wagstaff, D. (1987). General slowing of nonverbal information processing: Evidence for a power law. *Journal of Gerontology,* **42,** 131–136.

Harman, D. (1984). Free radical theory of aging: the 'free radical' diseases. *Age,* **7,** 111–131.

Harmon, D. S. (1984). Brain growth theory and educational psychology. *Psychological Reports,* **55,** 59–66.

Hasher, L. & Zacks, R. T. (1988). Working memory, comprehension, and aging: A review and a new view. In G. K. Bower (Ed.), *The Psychology of Learning and Motivation,* Vol. 22 (pp. 193–225). San Diego, CA: Academic Press.

Horn, J. (1985). *Handbook of Intelligence, Theories, Measurements, and Applications.* New York: Wiley.

Horvath, T. B. & Davis, K. L. (1990). Central nervous system disorders in aging. In E. L. Schneider & J. W. Rowe (Eds), *Handbook of the Biology of Aging,* Third edition (pp. 306–329). New York: Academic Press.

Hubel, D. H. & Wiesel, T. N. (1962). Receptive fields, binocular interaction and functional architecture in the cat's visual cortex. *Journal of Physiology,* **160,** 106–154.

Hubel, D. H. & Wiesel, T. N. (1963). Receptive fields of cells in striate cortex of very young, visually inexperienced kittens. *Journal of Neurophysiology,* **26,** 994–1002.

Hubel, D. H. & Wiesel, T. N. (1970). The period of susceptibility to the physiological effects of unilateral eye closure in kittens. *Journal of Physiology*, **206**, 419–436.

Hudspeth, W. J. & Pribram, K. H. (1992). Psychophysiological indices of cognitive functioning. *International Journal of Psychophysiology*, **12**, 19–29.

Huttenlocher, P. R. (1994). Synaptogenesis in human cerebral cortex. In G. Dawson & K. W. Fischer (Eds), *Human Behavior and the Developing Brain* (pp. 137–152). New York: Guilford Press.

Jernigan, T. L., Trauner, D. A, Hesselink, J. R. & Tallal, P. A. (1991). Maturation of human cerebrum, observed *in vivo* during adolescence. *Brain*, **114**, 2037–2049.

John, E. R. (1977). *Functional Neuroscience*: Vol 2. *Neurometrics*. Hillsdale, NJ: Erlbaum.

Johnson, M. H. (Ed.) (1993). *Brain Development and Cognition*. Cambridge, MA: Blackwell.

Johnson, M. H. (1993). Constraints of cortical plasticity. In M. H. Johnson (Ed.), *Brain Development and Cognition*. (pp. 703–721). Cambridge, MA: Blackwell.

Kail, R. (1988). Developmental functions for speeds of different processes. *Journal of Experimental Child Psychology*, **45**, 339–364.

Kail, R. (1991). Developmental change in speed of responding during childhood and adolescence. *Psychological Bulletin*, **109**, 490–501.

Kail, R. (1993). The role of a global mechanism in developmental change in speed of processing. In M. L. Howe & R. Pasnak (Eds), *Emerging Themes in Cognitive Development*, Vol. I (pp. 97–119). New York: Springer Verlag.

Kail, R. & Salthouse, T. A. (1994). Processing speed as a mental capacity. *Acta Psychologica*, **86**, 199–225.

Kandel, E. R., Schwartz, J. H. & Jessell, T. M. (Eds) (1991). *Principles of Neural Science*. Third edition. New York: Elsevier.

Katzman, R. (1995). Human nervous system. In E. J. Masoro (Ed.), *Handbook of Physiology*, Section II, *Aging* (pp. 325–344). New York: Oxford University Press.

Katzman, R. & Terry, R. (1983). Normal aging of the nervous system. In R. Katzman & R. Terry (Eds), *The Neurology of Aging* (pp. 15–85). Philadelphia, PA: Davis.

Kay, H. (1954). The effects of position in a display upon problem solving. *Quarterly Journal of Experimental Psychology*, **6**, 155–169.

Knight, R. T. (1984). Decreased response to novel stimuli after prefrontal lesions in man. *Electroencephalography and Clinical Neurophysiology*, **59**, 9–20.

Konner, M. (1991). Universals of behavioral development in relation to brain maturation. In K. R. Gibson & A. C. Peterson (Eds), *Brain Maturation and Cognitive Development* (pp. 181–223). New York: Aldine de Gruyter.

Krasuski, J., Horwitz, B. & Rumsey, J. M. (1996). A survey of functional and anatomical neuroimaging techniques. In G. R. Lyon & J. M. Rumsey (Eds), *Neuroimaging: A Window to the Neurological Foundations of*

Learning and Behavior in Children (pp. 25–55). London: Brookes.

La Rue, A. (1992). *Aging and Neuropsychological Assessment*. New York: Plenum.

Lane, D. M. & Pearson, D. A. (1983). Attending to spatial locations: A developmental study. *Child Development*, **54**, 98–104.

Lima, S. D., Hale, S. & Myerson, J. (1991). How general is general slowing? Evidence from the lexical domain. *Psychology and Aging*, **6**, 416–425.

Lindsley, D. B. & Wicke, J. D. (1974). The electroencephalogram: Autonomous electrical activity in man and animals. In R. F. Thompson & M. Patterson (Eds), *Bioelectric Recording Techniques* (pp. 3–83). New York: Academic Press.

Loessner, A., Alavi, A., Lewandrowski, K-U, Mozley, D., Souder, E. & Gur, R. E. (1995). Regional cerebral function determined by FDG-PET in healthy volunteers: Normal patterns and changes with age. *Journal of Nuclear Medicine*, **36**, 1141–1149.

Luria, A. R. (1973). *The Working Brain. An Introduction to Neuropsychology*. Harmondsworth: Penguin.

Lyon, G. R. & Rumsey, J. M. (Eds) (1996). *Neuroimaging: A Window to the Neurological Foundations of Learning and Behavior in Children*. London: Brookes.

Madden, D. J., Pierce, T. W. & Allen, P. A. (1992). Adult age differences in attentional allocation during memory search. *Psychology and Aging*, **7**, 594–601.

Marsh, R. W. (1985). Phrenoblysis: Real or chimera? *Child Development*, **56**, 1059–1061.

Masoro, E. J. (1995). *Handbook of Physiology*, Section 11, *Aging*. New York: Oxford University Press.

Matousek, M. & Petersén, I. (1973). Frequency analysis of the EEG in normal children and adolescents. In P. Kellaway & I. Petersén (Eds), *Automation of Clinical Electroencephalography* (pp. 75–102). New York: Raven Press.

McCall, R. B. (1990). The neuroscience of education: More research is needed before application. *Journal of Educational Psychology*, **82**, 885–888.

McCall, R. B., Meyers, E. D., Hartman, J. & Roche, A. F. (1983). Developmental changes in head-circumference and mental performance growth rates: A test of Epstein's phrenoblysis hypothesis. *Developmental Psychology*, **16**, 457–468.

Molenaar, P. C. M. & van der Molen, M. W. (1994). On the discrimination between global and local trend hypotheses of life-span changes in processing speed. *Acta Psychologica*, **86**, 273–293.

Morgan, D. G. & May, P. C. (1990). Age-related changes in synaptic neurochemistry. In E. L. Schneider & J. W. Rowe (Eds), *Handbook of the Biology of Aging* (3rd edition, pp. 219–254). New York: Academic Press.

Myerson, J., Hale, S., Wagstaff, D., Poon, L. W. & Smith, G. A. (1990). The information-loss model: A mathematical theory of age-related cognitive slowing. *Psychological Review*, **97**, 475–487.

Neumann, O. (1987). Beyond capacity: A functional view of attention. In H.

Heuer & A. F. Sanders (Eds), *Perspectives on Perception and Action* (pp. 361–394). Hillsdale, NJ: Erlbaum.

Nowakowski, R. S. (1987). Basic concepts of CNS development. *Child Development*, **58**, 568–595.

Nunez, P. L. (1981). *Electrical Fields of the Brain*. New York: Oxford University Press.

Oken, B. S. & Kaye, J. A. (1992). Electrophysiological function in the healthy, extremely old. *Neurology*, **42**, 519–526.

O'Leary, D. D. M. (1989). Do cortical areas emerge from a protocortex? *Trends in the Neurosciences*, **12**, 400–406.

Pennington, B. F. (1994). The working memory function of the prefrontal cortices: Implications for developmental and individual differences in cognition. In M. M. Haith, J. B. Benson, R. J. Roberts, Jr & B. Pennington (Eds), *The Development of Future-oriented Processes* (pp. 243–289). Chicago: University of Chicago Press.

Pfefferbaum, A., Mathalon, D. H., Sullivan, E. V, Rawles, J. M., Zipursky, R. B. & Lim, K. O. (1994). A quantitative magnetic resonance imaging study of changes in brain morphology from infancy to late adulthood. *Archives of Neurology*, **51**, 874–887.

Posner, M. I. & Raichle, M. E. (1994). *Images of Mind*. New York: Scientific American Library.

Purves, D. (1994). *Neural Activity and the Growth of the Brain*. Cambridge: Cambridge University Press.

Rabbitt, P. (1965). Age and discrimination between complex stimuli. In A. T. Welford & J. E. Birren (Eds), *Behavior, Aging and the Nervous System* (pp. 35–53). Springfield, IL: Charles C. Thomas.

Rakic, P. (1988). Intrinsic and extrinsic determinants of neocortical parcellation: A radical unit model. In P. Rakic & W. Singer (Eds), *Neurobiology of the Neocortex* (pp. 5–27). New York: Wiley.

Reiss, A. L., Abrams, M. T., Singer, H. S., Ross, J. L. & Denckla, M. B. (1997). Brain development, gender and IQ in children: A volumetric imaging study. In press.

Ridderinkhof, K. R. & Bashore, T. R. (1995). Using event-related brain potentials to draw inferences about human information processing. In P. A. Allen & T. R. Bashore (Eds), *Age Differences in Word and Language Processing* (pp. 294–313). Amsterdam: Elsevier Science Publishers.

Ridderinkhof, K. R. & van der Molen, M. W. (1995). A psychophysiological analysis of developmental differences in the ability to resist interference. *Child Development*, **66**, 1040–1056.

Ridderinkhof, K. R. & van der Molen, M. W. (1997). Mental resources, processing speed, and inhibitory control: A developmental perspective. *Biological Psychology*, **45**, 241–261.

Ridderinkhof, K. R., van der Molen, M. W., Band, G. P. H. & Bashore, T. R. (1997). Sources of interference from irrelevant information: A developmental study. *Journal of Experimental Child Psychology*, **65**, 315–341.

Robbins, T. W. (1986). Psychopharmacological and neurobiological aspects of the energetics of information processing. In G. R. Hockey, A. W. K. Gaillard, & M. G. H. Coles (Eds), *Energetics and Human Information*

Processing (pp. 71–90). Dordecht: Martinus Nijhoff.

Roberts, R. J., Hager, L. D., & Heron, C. (1994). Prefrontal cognitive processes: Working memory and inhibition in the antisaccade task. *Journal of Experimental Psychology: General*, **123**, 374–393.

Rosenzweig, M. R. (1996). Aspects of the search for neural mechanisms of memory. *Annual Review of Psychology*, **47**, 1–32.

Ruch, F. L. (1934). The differentiative effects of age upon human learning. *Journal of General Psychology*, **11**, 261–286.

Salthouse, T. A. & Somberg, B. L. (1982). Isolating the age difference in speeded performance. *Journal of Gerontology*, **37**, 59–63.

Scheibel, A. B. (1996). Structural and functional changes in the aging brain. In J. E. Birren & K. W. Schaie (Eds), *Handbook of the Psychology of Aging*, Fourth edition (pp. 105–128). New York: Academic Press.

Schore, A. N. (1994). *Affect Regulation and the Origin of Self: The Neurobiology of Emotional Development*. New York: Erlbaum.

Segalowitz, S. J. (1994). Developmental psychology and brain development. In G. Dawson & K. W. Fischer (Eds), *Human Behavior and the Developing Brain* (pp. 67–92). New York: Guilford Press.

Segalowitz, S. & Rose-Krasnor, L. (Eds) (1992). The role of frontal lobe maturation in cognitive and social development [Special Issue]. *Brain and Cognition*, **20**, 1–213.

Shimamura, A. P. (1995). Memory and frontal lobe function. In M. S. Gazzaniga (Ed.), *The Cognitive Neurosciences* (pp. 803–813). Cambridge, MA: MIT Press.

Simon, J. R. & Pouraghabagher, A. R. (1978). The effect of aging on the stages of information processing in a choice reaction time task. *Journal of Gerontology*, **33**, 553–561.

Singer, W. (1986). Neuronal activity as a shaping factor in postnatal development of visual cortex. In W. T. Greenough & J. M. Juraska (Eds), *Developmental Neuropsychobiology* (pp. 271–293). New York: Academic Press.

Spirduso, W. W. & MacRae, P. G. (1990). Motor performance and aging. In J. E. Birren & K. W. Schie (Eds), *Handbook of the Psychology of Aging*. Third edition (pp. 183–200). New York: Academic Press.

Stauder, J. E. A., Molenaar, P. C. M. & van der Molen, M. W. (1993). Scalp topography of event-related brain potentials and cognitive transition during childhood. *Child Development*, **64**, 769–788.

Stellar, J. R. & Stellar, E. (1985). *The Neurobiology of Motivation and Reward*. New York: Springer Verlag.

Sullivan, E. V., Marsh, L., Mathalon, D. H., Lim, K. O. & Pfefferbaum, A. (1995). Age-related decline in MRI volumes of temporal lobe gray matter but not hippocampus. *Neurobiology of Aging*, **16**, 591–606.

Sur, M., Pallas, S. L. & Roe, A. W. (1990). Cross-modal plasticity in cortical development: Differentiation and specification of the sensory neocortex. *Trends in Neurosciences*, **13**, 227–233.

Swaab, D. (1991). Brain aging and Alzheimer's disease: 'Wear and tear' versus 'use it or lose it'. *Neurobiology of Aging*, **12**, 317–324.

Tees, R. C. (1986). Experience and visual development: behavioral evidence. In W. T. Greenough & J. M. Juraska (Eds), *Developmental Neuropsychobiology* (pp. 317–361). New York: Academic Press.

Terry, R., DeTeresa, R. & Hansen, L. (1987). Neocortical cell counts in normal human adult aging. *Annals of Neurology*, **21**, 530–539.

Thatcher, R. W. (1994). Cyclic cortical reorganization: origins of cognitive development. In G. Dawson & K. W. Fischer (Eds), *Human Behavior and the Developing Brain* (pp. 232–266). New York: Guilford Press.

Turkewitz, G. & Kenny, P. A. (1982). Limitations on input as a basis for neural organization and perceptual development: A preliminary theoretical statement. *Developmental Psychobiology*, **15**, 357–368.

Van der Molen, M. W. (1990). Energetics of cognitive development. In W. Koops, H. J. G. Soppe, J. L. van der Linden, P. C. M. Molenaar & J. J. F. Schroots (Eds), *Developmental Psychology behind the Dikes* (pp. 123–139). Delft: Centuron.

Van der Molen, M. W., Bashore, T. R., Halliday, R. & Callaway, E. (1991). Chronopsychophysiology: Mental chronometry augmented with psychophysiological time markers. In J. R. Jennings & M. G. H. Coles (Eds), *Handbook of Cognitive Psychophysiology: Central and Autonomic Nervous System Approaches* (pp. 9–178). Chichester, UK: Wiley.

Welford, A. T. (1959). Psychomotor performance. In J. E. Birren (Ed.), *Handbook of Aging and the Individual* (pp. 562–613). Chicago: University of Chicago Press.

Welsh, M. C. & Pennington, B. F. (1988). Assessing frontal lobe dysfunction in children: Views from developmental psychology. *Developmental Neuropsychology*, **4**, 199–230.

Werker, J. F. & Tees, R. C. (1984). Cross language speech perception: Evidence for perceptual reorganization during the first year of life. *Infant Behavior & Development*, **7**, 49–63.

West, R. L. (1996). An application of the prefrontal cortex function theory to cognitive aging. *Psychological Bulletin*, **120**, 272–292.

Wickens, C. D. (1984). Processing resources in attention. In R. Parasuraman & D. R. Davis (Eds), *Varieties of Attention* (pp. 63–102). New York: Academic Press.

Wijker, W. (1991). *ERP Ontogenesis in Childhood*. Doctoral dissertation, University of Amsterdam.

Woodruff-Pak, D. S. (1993). Neural plasticity as a substrate for cognitive adaptation in adulthood and aging. In J. Cerella, J. Rybash, W. Hoyer & M. L. Commons (Eds), *Adult Information Processing: Limits on Loss* (pp. 13–35). New York: Academic Press.

Yakovlev, P. I. & Lecours, A. R. (1967). The myelinogenetic cycles of regional maturation of the brain. In A. Minkowski (Ed.), *Regional Development of the Brain in Early Life* (pp. 3–70). Oxford: Blackwell.

Ylikovski, R., Ylikovski, A., Erkinjuntti, E., Sulkava, R., Raininko, R. & Tilvis, R. (1993). White matter changes in healthy elderly persons correlate with attention and speed of mental processes. *Archives of Neurology*, **50**, 818–824.

Chapter 3

Perceptual and Motor Development

George Butterworth

University of Sussex

INTRODUCTION

This chapter will provide an overview of the development of perception and motor skills in humans. Most attention will be devoted to the origins of these abilities in infancy where much recent research has clarified the foundations of the developmental process but perception and action in early childhood and through the life-span will also be considered. The chapter presents some difficulty in organisation, not only because it covers such a vast field of enquiry but also because perception and action systems are so intimately related. It is not really feasible to separate fully the acquisition of knowledge through perception from the influence of skilled action in learning and we do not mean to give the impression that these are truly separate domains. The chapter begins with an initial discussion of perceptual development, followed by a section on the early acquisition of motor skills, and it concludes with some examples of the interaction of perception, cognition and action in the development of selective attention and in children's drawing. The divisions are made merely for ease of exposition with no implication that cycles of perceiving, acting and knowing can be readily compartmentalised at any time in development.

Life-Span Developmental Psychology
Edited by A. Demetriou, W. Doise and C. F. M. van Lieshout. © 1998 John Wiley & Sons Ltd.

PERCEPTION IN INFANCY

The nineteenth-century philosopher and psychologist William James famously described the world of the newborn baby as a 'buzzing, blooming confusion, where the infant is seized by eyes, ears, nose and entrails all once'. This vivid phrase conveys an image of a passive infant, inundated by meaningless sensations, with little coherent awareness of self or of the outside world. The newborn was thought to have little more than reflex control of action and to be capable of seeing or hearing very little. The nature of early visual perception has been a particularly contentious question. The paradox to be resolved by any theory of perceptual development is that the two-dimensional surface of the eye, the retina, on which visual images of the world are projected lacks the third dimension and yet we perceive the world as three dimensional and extended in space. Philosophers have suggested that our experience of visual space must be derived from the sense of touch and from motor activities.

Many theorists assumed that babies have to learn to see by correlating touch with vision during the early months of life. The assumption has been that, even though the visual system is functional at birth, the visual sensations received by the baby are initially meaningless. The baby's experience would not be of reality as adults know it; it could only be a world of meaningless sensations. This is why James argued that early experience would be a buzzing, blooming confusion. The effect of importing these assumptions into developmental psychology is that it is necessary to explain how the infant can organise experience in order to progress in understanding the visual world beyond such chaotic beginnings. This perspective implies that the very process of visual perception is learned by correlating different experiences early in life.

One of the major scientific achievements of the last 25 years has been radically to revise this nineteenth-century preconception in favour of an image of the infant as 'competent' and well adapted to the demands of the physical and social environment. This change in the preconceptions governing studies of babies has had an impact on how perceptual development has come to be understood. Rather than following the traditional assumption that babies must learn to perceive, the contemporary view tends to be that the founding perceptual abilities are themselves very important in allowing babies to learn. The results of contemporary investigations raise questions about the role of perception in intellectual development, since perceptual systems are functional from the beginning. Before considering the evidence in more detail we will explore some historical and methodological issues which have proved important in guiding modern ideas about perceptual development.

Piaget's Theory of Infant Perception

Jean Piaget (1896–1980) was among the most influential theorists of percep-

Table 3.1 Piaget's hierarchical theory of intellectual development in infancy

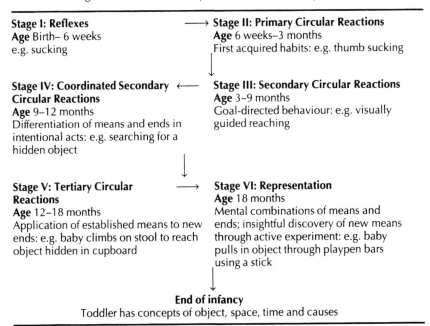

Stage I: Reflexes **Age** Birth– 6 weeks e.g. sucking	⟶ **Stage II: Primary Circular Reactions** **Age** 6 weeks–3 months First acquired habits: e.g. thumb sucking
Stage IV: Coordinated Secondary ⟵ **Circular Reactions** **Age** 9–12 months Differentiation of means and ends in intentional acts: e.g. searching for a hidden object	**Stage III: Secondary Circular Reactions** **Age** 3–9 months Goal-directed behaviour: e.g. visually guided reaching
Stage V: Tertiary Circular ⟶ **Reactions** **Age** 12–18 months Application of established means to new ends: e.g. baby climbs on stool to reach object hidden in cupboard	**Stage VI: Representation** **Age** 18 months Mental combinations of means and ends; insightful discovery of new means through active experiment: e.g. baby pulls in object through playpen bars using a stick

End of infancy
Toddler has concepts of object, space, time and causes

tual development. He took the traditional view that perception itself develops from more primitive beginnings. He postulated that development begins with a limited number of innate reflex actions which are triggered by specific sensory experiences. For example, babies are born with the sucking reflex which serves their nutritional needs. Soon however, the baby applies the reflex to other objects, in repetitive exploration (circular reaction) and thus learns something of the variety of shape, texture and consistency of objects.

Other biologically based reflexes, such as looking, or listening or grasping, are also applied to a variety of objects in exploration of the world; the senses become inter-coordinated and actions are hierarchically organised (Table 3.1). Through acting on the world the baby acquires basic knowledge of cause and effect and of the properties of physical and social objects.

Piaget shared the starting assumption that 'touch tutors vision' in early development. He suggested that the visual world of the newborn is two-dimensional and lacking in depth. Perception of shape and size develop only slowly, during the first 6 months of life. Piaget assumed that the senses are initially separate and become coordinated through the child's own activities. In the first 3 months seeing and hearing become coordinated but remain separate from touching and looking. Then, between 3 and 6 months, these two coordinations form a new, multisensory coordination which incorporates touch, vision and hearing. Only when this has happened does the infant become capable of knowing that the same physical object can simultaneously give rise to tactile, visual and auditory sensations.

Piaget (1954) argued that the baby gradually comes to know about the properties of objects through her own activities. A very important aspect of his theory concerns the acquisition of the 'object concept'. The object concept is defined by Piaget as a belief that physical objects are:

> Permanent, substantial, external to the self and firm in existence even though they do not directly affect perception and to conceive of them as retaining their identity whatever the changes in position (Piaget, 1954, pp. 5, 7)

Piaget described a series of six stages in the development of the object concept whereby this knowledge slowly gives structure to the baby's early perception. An example of one of these stages is given in Weinert and Weinert (ch. 1, this volume). Piaget's theory of early perception assumes very limited perceptual abilities indeed in the first 6 months of life. Piaget recognises both the intrinsic biological processes of growth and the role of the infant's actions in the construction of knowledge. However, recent research has shown that Piaget may have underestimated the abilities of infants and this work needs to be taken into account to give a contemporary overview of perception and its contribution to the early development of the child.

Gibson's Alternative

A radical alternative to the traditional view of visual perception was developed by James Gibson (1966). He argued that perception should be considered as an active process of seeking after information, with no one sense being more important than any other. According to Gibson, the different senses are 'tuned' to different ranges of the available energy impinging upon them but they are able to yield equivalent information about the real world. Hearing depends on mechanical transmission of patterned sound, touch depends on mechanical transmission of object properties through the skin, seeing depends on radiant transmission of the patterned light reflected from complex, structured surfaces, while taste and smell depend on patterned chemical transmission.

Gibson stressed that space is not empty, but full of textured objects and surfaces. He argued that perception of visual space occurs because terrestrial space is filled with structures that are perceived in relation to the surfaces of the earth. These textured surfaces reflect light to the eye and the pattern of texture is preserved in the image which falls on the retina, the light-sensitive surface of the eye. The relative distance of objects from the observer is preserved in the retinal image because the pattern or texture of the retinal image becomes more fine grained as the distance from the observer increases. These texture gradients vary systematically with distance from the observer. The pebbles on a beach receding into the distance appear more densely packed the further away they are. Since the beach is formed of pebbles packed at nearly identical density, the gradient of change in texture provides the eye with direct information about the structure and distance of visual space.

Gibson emphasises that while each of the senses has specialised functions, such as the visual perception of colour or cutaneous perception of temperature, there is also information common to different senses, such as rhythmic patterns that can be perceived either by eye or by ear. The implication of Gibson's theory is that perceptual systems have evolved to put the infant in direct contact with the real world from the outset; babies may be able visually to perceive the world before they can act upon it.

Methods of Studying Perception in Babies

Even young babies show spontaneous visual preference, preferring to look at one thing rather than another. This means that it is possible to study what the infant chooses to look at. The pioneer of the visual preference method was Robert Fantz (1965). The infant, who may be lying down, or who can be specially supported, is presented with a pair of visual targets, one to the left and the other to the right of the midline. The investigator notes the direction of the baby's first eye movement and the total amount of time that the infant fixates the target. On succeeding trials, the targets are alternated from left to right, so that any bias a baby may have for looking to one side or the other cancels out. The fact that babies show spontaneous perceptual preferences means that it is possible to study what the infant chooses to look at. In the early studies, it was established that babies prefer to look at patterns over plain surfaces, and in one variation, it was found that newborns showed a preference for a face-like stimulus.

An extension of the visual preference technique involves presenting babies with the same stimuli repeatedly. This is called the habituation method, since it involves accustoming the baby to the visual object, so that it becomes progressively less interesting. Then, once the infant's attention has declined a new object will be presented and any recovery of visual interest by the baby is measured. Where there is no initial preference between stimuli, this method creates the potential for discriminating between familiar stimulus and a new one, once again revealing what the baby perceives. Furthermore, the method also implies that the baby remembers something of the stimulus, since the procedure relies on the test material becoming increasingly familiar.

Many contemporary studies of infant perception use variations of the visual preference and habituation methods, to study not only vision but also aspects of auditory perception, such as perception of phonemes, to be discussed later.

The Perceptual World of the Newborn

Contrary to William James's assumption that the world of the newborn is a buzzing, blooming confusion, even very young infants will actively seek out what stimuli they will attend to. Modern evidence suggests that all the basic sensory systems are functional from birth or before; even the newborn will show preference in vision, in hearing, in taste and smell. This implies that babies are not passive recipients of stimulation nor are they simply captured by sensory stimulation. We will briefly review the sensory capacities of the newborn before turning to research on the information which the senses make accessible to the baby.

Vision

Relative to adult standards, the acuity of vision in the newborn is poor. They cannot pick out such fine detail as will become possible later. The eyes have a fixed focal length of 21 cm, which arises because the lens does not accommodate properly until about three months. This means that objects are seen clearly at the distance of 21 cm but will become out of focus at greater distances. However, the fixed focal length of 21 cm coincides with the average distance of the mother's face from the baby, when the infant is held at the breast. So, even though distant objects will be blurred, important social objects can be seen from birth. There are various ways of measuring visual acuity in newborns. With static cards on which stripes of various width have been drawn, newborns can discriminate between stationary black and white stripes 1/8th of an inch wide and a uniform grey surface. This is shown by their preference to look at the patterned rather than the plain card. Moving the stripes to attract visual following movements actually yields much finer measures of visual discrimination. Measuring the electrical activity of the visual areas of the brain with special electroencephalographic methods yields evidence for even finer discrimination, which is comparable to adults by 8 months (Shea, 1995). It is also known that newborns see in colour, probably trichomatically, as in normal (non-colour blind) adults. Van der Molen and Ridderinkhof (ch. 2, this volume) provide extensive information both about the methods used to investigate the neurological bases of perception and also about the condition of sensorimotor areas of the brain early in life.

Stereoscopic binocular vision, which is particularly useful for depth perception, does not begin to develop until about 13 weeks. This seems partly to be a function of poor control over the convergence of the eyes (when we focus both eyes on the same object the eyes converge differentially according to the object's distance), partly a function of changes in the axes of alignment of the eyes in the early weeks of life, and partly a function of 'tuning' the visual cortex of the brain so that the neural cells responsible for binocular vision receive the same information from both eyes. Extensive research indicates that binocular aspects of visual functioning depend on early visual experience during a 'sensitive' period when the binocularly activated cells in the visual nervous system undergo fine tuning as a result of visual experience. There are important implications for the treatment of squints (strabismus). The effect of a squint is that binocular cells do not receive the same input from equivalent regions of the two eyes, so it is important surgically to realign the squinting eye if stereoscopic vision is not to be adversely affected.

Newborn infant eye movements are very similar to those of adults. Successive shifts of visual fixation from object to object are known as saccades. Newborn infants follow moving objects by making a series of saccadic jumps; whereas smooth tracking movements of the eyes develop at about two months. The scanning pattern is internally generated and not simply a reaction to incident visual stimulation. This is important because it again suggests that the newborn is well prepared to explore the visual environment. Newborns are particularly prone to picking out the external edges of visual objects, although they will shift their gaze to the interior of the object if it has internal movement. They do not simply search at random, newborn infants are scanning for salient features of objects (Atkinson & Braddick, 1989).

Hearing

The auditory system is functional from before birth. The inner ear has reached its adult size by the 20th week of gestation. The middle ear, with its complex structure of bones and membranes which mediate hearing, is well formed by the 37th week of pregnancy, although it continues to change shape and size into adulthood. The external ear acquires its adult shape at the 20th gestational week but it continues to grow in size until the child is about 9 years of age.

It is becoming increasingly clear that infants are attentive to sounds from before birth. Since the middle ear of the fetus is filled with amniotic fluid, the conduction of sound will be quite different in utero than postnatally. The most likely source of sound to be internally transmitted is the mothers speech, especially the patterning of sound onset and offset, at frequencies that are not masked by the internal noise of the mother's heart beat and blood circulation.

Recent studies have shown that newborns can distinguish their mother's voice from the voice of another female, which suggests that aspects of the mother's voice may have become familiar to the fetus in utero (DeCasper & Fifer, 1980). Newborn babies generally prefer voices in the female range (average frequency 260 cycles per second) to the male range (on average one octave lower at 130 cycles per second). Adults and even children will adopt a higher pitched tone of voice when addressing babies, as if this is a particularly effective way of speech 'getting through'. Eimas, Siqueland, Jusczyk and Vigorito (1971) invented an ingenious technique for studying babies' auditory perception of speech sounds. In this procedure babies are first trained to suck on a nipple attached to a pressure transducer at a consistent rate. They soon learn to suck consistently in return for the reward of hearing a particular phoneme over earphones. For example, the baby may be trained to respond to the sound 'b'. After several repetitions of the same sound the infant becomes familiar with it and the sucking response drops in frequency as the baby habituates. Once this decline in sucking occurs, the experimenter introduces a new sound 'p', and if the baby can perceive the difference, a recovery in the amplitude of sucking takes place. The phoneme 'p' differs from 'b' not simply in acoustic properties but also in the effect the change of sound has on the meaning of words, as in /p/in and /b/in. The research of Eimas et al. (1971) suggested that babies may perceive sound in a manner appropriate to the perception of speech. This important study set in train many further investigations of the extent to which human auditory perception specifically prepares the infant to be receptive of speech sounds and we will return to this question later.

Smell and Taste

Newborns show a similar aversion to a sour taste as do adults. They can also discriminate sweetness and show contented emotional expressions to sweet liquids. Newborn babies show a similar range of expressions when presented with smells that are unpleasant (rotten eggs), or pleasant (a milky smell, honey, chocolate). Neonates also recognise the smell of their own mother's breast milk within the first six days of life (MacFarlane, 1975).

Perception in Adulthood and Old Age

The review so far has simply shown that very young babies can perceive the world as they encounter it. This does not mean that visual and auditory acuity are fully formed at birth. In fact, visual and auditory acuity are usually at their peak in young adults (20 years for vision and 13 years for hearing). The progressive honing of specialised skills, as in musicians and artists, allows finer and finer perceptual discrimination to continue to develop well into adulthood.

Changes in vision and hearing are well documented from 25 to 70 years consequent upon the physical changes which occur with ageing. Changes in visual acuity are noticeable at about 40 years of age and by 70 years, less than 30% of individuals still have perfect vision. Hardening and discolouration of the lens may eventually lead to cataract and blindness, which occurs in 20 to 25% of 75-year-old people. The older eye needs more light to see clearly. As much as 100 times more illumination is required for a 70 year old than for a 20 year old, to see an object in conditions of low light. Colour vision is also impaired, especially in the blue region of the spectrum. The iris and the lens take longer to adjust as the elasticity of the muscles decreases. The cells of the retina may show damage due to decreased blood circulation in people above the age of 55 years.

There are also changes in the auditory system. There is a general loss of auditory acuity with ageing as the hair cells transmitting sound from the inner ear to the brain deteriorate. High frequency consonant sounds are particularly affected whereas hearing for low frequency vowels remains relatively intact. The effect is to interfere with clear reception of speech.

About 15% of adults over 75 years are deaf and some hearing loss can be measured in most adults from 50 years onwards.

Of course, changes in auditory and visual acuity can be compensated to some extent with spectacles and hearing aids. However, there are also changes in perception with ageing which are caused by changes in the processing capacity of the regions of the brain responsible. As individuals age there is cell death in the brain and the connections become less numerous. It has been estimated that 16% of the retinal ganglion cells in the visual system, responsible for detecting fine detail in focal vision, are lost between the ages of 50 and 70 years. This may be sufficient to result in a significant change in the processing capacity of the brain for visual detail (Lehmkuhle, 1995). Measures of the overall electrical activity of the brain suggest that there is increasing sluggishness in the electroencephalogram (EEG), with a decrease from 10 cycles per second of alpha waves at 20 years, to 9 cycles per second at 60 and 8 cycles per second at 80 years (Schroeder, 1992).

It is well established therefore that the physical basis of ageing contributes to difficulties in sensory processing. However, just as spectacles may compensate for loss of visual acuity, people also find strategies of behaviour to compensate for the effects of ageing in their everyday lives. A well established distinction between crystallised and fluid intelligence, first proposed by Cattel (1963), illustrates how old people may rely on accumulated wisdom (crystallised intelligence) to compensate for changes in speed of reaction, memory and sensory perception (fluid intelligence).

Perception of Complex Object Properties in Early Infancy

Two very important features of visual perception are size and shape constancy. Changes in distance or orientation of an object from the observer result in differences in the projection of the retinal image. Size constancy refers to perceiving the real size of an object, despite the fact that the size of the retinal image varies greatly with the distance of the object. Shape constancy is the ability to perceive an object's real shape, despite any changes in orientation with respect to the observer which will result in changes in the projected shape of the retinal image.

Piaget believed that babies have to learn to coordinate touch with vision to perceive size and shape constancy. He suggested that having learned to grasp the object, the baby could twist and turn it, bring it further and nearer in the field of view and gradually make the discovery of size constancy. The assumption is that 'touch tutors vision' in early development. Piaget suggested that the visual world of the newborn is two dimensional and lacking in depth and that perception of shape and size constancy develops only slowly, during the first 6 months of life.

Gibson (1966) argued that perception should be considered an active process of seeking after information, with no privileged relation of any one sense over any other. While each of the senses has specialised functions, such as visual perception of colour or cutaneous perception of temperature, there is also information common to different senses. The implication of Gibson's theory is that perceptual systems have evolved to put the infant in direct contact with the real world from the outset. The evidence from infancy therefore enables a choice between these two theories of perceptual development.

In fact, there have been several demonstrations that babies show shape and size constancy before they could have learned to perceive these complex properties of objects by coordinating vision with touch. The first demonstration of size and shape constancy in 3-month-old babies was made by Bower (1966). His finding has since been replicated in newborns by Slater (see Slater, 1989). In recent years, many new findings about the complex relations in early perception have come to light. These studies present a novel picture of the 'competent' infant, well able to gain information about the world through perception.

Auditory-visual Coordination

Wertheimer (1961) first showed in a test of his newborn baby daughter that there is an innate coordination between seeing and hearing, such that when the newborn baby hears a sound, the eyes will be oriented toward the sound. These results have subsequently been confirmed by several investigators. Castillo and Butterworth (1981) showed that newborns would look to a distinctive visual feature of the environment for the source of a sound. Vision and audition interact in sound localisation from birth. This is not to say that these coordinations are fixed and unchanging. In fact, there is a rather complex development; the innate coordination lasts for the first two months and then eye movements to sound become increasingly difficult to elicit until 5 months, when the coordination re-emerges. Such U-shaped functions are rather common in early development and imply developmental reorganisation of subsystems to give rise to new abilities.

Perception of Physical Objects

Piaget considered that extensive touching, grasping and looking at objects was necessary for gradually piecing together knowledge about object properties.

Evidence against the theory that 'touch tutors vision' came from ingenious experiments which demonstrated that infants are capable of picking up visual information that an object is about to collide with them. Bower, Broughton and Moore (1970) made objects move rapidly towards the faces of young infants. The infants, aged 6 to 21 days, rotated their heads upward and pulled away from the 'looming' object. Looming is characterised by rapid expansion of the retinal image, as the object approaches, and this specifies an imminent collision. In another study Bower (1971) also suggested that babies perceived a 'virtual object' as solid. The virtual object was produced by projecting a polarised light shadow of a stationary cube which infants viewed using polarising goggles. They were surprised when their hand passed through the object as they swiped at it.

These early studies were the first to suggest that very young babies may perceive that objects are solid before they have had extensive experience of touching things. Other studies have demonstrated that very young babies may also extract basic visual information about objects that they have touched but not seen. Meltzoff and Borton (1979) tested babies aged 29 days in a task where the baby was given a pacifier of a particular shape to suck. Some babies received a smooth dummy, others received a knobbly dummy but, in both cases, the dummy was placed in the baby's mouth without being seen by the baby. The baby actively explored the dummy with lips and tongue. Then large-scale models of both dummies were placed to left and right in the baby's visual field. Babies preferred to fixate the shape which they had explored orally. The experiment shows that active oral exploration conveys something to the baby, through touch, of what the object looks like.

As adults we know that when one object is occluded by another, the hidden object continues to exist and retains its physical and spatial properties. Furthermore, the movements of the object and its transformations are subject to regular physical laws and are therefore predictable. This is known as the 'object concept', a shorthand way of expressing the fact that objects are permanent, substantial and possessed of constant shape, size and identity.

According to Piaget the object concept stands at the foundations of thought. He was of the opinion that until the child is about 18 months old, appearances and disappearances are not understood as the movements of single objects in space. His evidence came from infants' failure to search manually for hidden objects before 9 months. Indeed, he argued that for the young baby the object is a 'mere image', lacking permanence, substantiality and identity (Piaget, 1954). Piaget's theory rests heavily on the assumption that perception is insufficient to inform the developing child about the physical world (we should remember that he was writing in 1935). According to Piaget infants fail to search for a hidden object because they do not perceive that it continues to exist once it disappears. If Piaget's interpretation of search failures is correct, then the physical universe of the infant must be very different to that of the adult.

Another source of evidence came from infants born without arms or legs, following the thalidomide tragedy. These babies often showed normal intellectual development, despite the fact that they lacked the opportunity for extensive physical interaction with objects. In particular, they often lacked experience of simultaneously holding and looking at objects, a condition Piaget considered essential for learning that objects are solid (DeCarie, 1969). Other evidence came from ingenious experiments based on the possibility that the infant may be capable of picking up information through the distal senses, especially through vision. Baillargeon (1991) has systematically measured infants' perception of physical objects. Her studies involve repeated presentation of a visual display so that the infant loses interest in it (i.e. the baby becomes habituated to the display). Then, a variant on the display is presented and if the infant notices the change, she will recover interest and start to look again (i.e. the baby becomes dishabituated). Changes in looking patterns reveal which combinations of physical events babies perceive as possible or impossible.

Baillargeon's experiments on perception of substantiality test the babies' reaction when the principle that a solid object cannot move through the space occupied by another is violated (Baillargeon, 1991). Babies of 3.5 months observed a screen, in the form of a drawbridge, seen end on by the infant, which was rotated repeatedly in a 180 degree arc. Once the infant was habituated to this display, a large box was placed behind the screen and the infant was shown one of two test events. In one event, the physically possible case, the screen stopped rotating when it was obstructed by the box. In a second, impossible event, the screen continued to rotate through a full 180 degrees, as if the box were no longer behind it. Babies looked longer at the impossible event than at the possible event. This suggests that infants did perceive the continued existence of the hidden box and that they also perceived that the screen could not rotate through it. In subsequent experiments, Baillargeon (1991) went on to demonstrate that by 6.5 months babies not only understand that the screen should stop when there is a box behind it, but also that the screen will stop at different positions depending on the height of the box, or depending on whether the object behind the screen can be compressed or not. That is, the baby appropriately perceives occlusion and the possible physical interactions between rigid and elastic objects, and finds it unusual when the experimenter presents the baby with visual events which violate basic physical laws. This evidence suggests that infants do perceive that solid objects cannot travel through the space occupied by other solids.

There is evidence that perceptual systems provide information for other aspects of basic physical knowledge. For example, Antell and Keating (1983), using the habituation method, showed that newborn babies discriminate sets of two objects from sets of three objects. The baby was repeatedly presented with a picture containing two (or three) objects and, once familiar with the display, the number of objects was changed, to three (or two) objects. Babies looked longer at the new picture which suggests that they notice the change in number.

Starkey, Spelke and Gelman (1983) showed that the ability to perceive small numbers is not restricted to visual perception. Babies can detect the correspondence between the number of sounds they hear and the number of objects they see. Infants from 6 to 9 months of age were played a soundtrack of a drum beating in a regular rhythm, either of two or three beats. They preferred to look at whichever of two pictures contained the same number of objects as corresponded with the number of drum beats. Thus, babies perceive that the number of objects in a small set changes if one is added or taken away and they perceive the correspondence between small sets of objects perceived in auditory and visual modalities. This is not achieved by counting the number of objects, rather it seems that number in small sets of up to four objects can be apprehended directly. It is possible that perceptual abilities such as these lie at the very foundation of mathematics learning (Nunes & Bryant, 1996).

Spelke (1991) has discussed the implications of infant's perception of the physical world for the acquisition of knowledge. She suggests that perception operates around a set of core principles which are progressively enriched through experience. These include the perception of physical causality, as in billiard ball collisions, and basic aspects of space and time perception, all of which lay the foundations for acquiring knowledge of the world. On this view, basic constraints which govern physical reality, such as the principle that solid objects cannot pass through each other, operate in perception from the outset to form a core constraint to guide subsequent cognitive development. However, other physical phenomena, such as perceiving that objects falling under gravity must continue on their path of motion until they reach a solid surface, appear not to constrain perception, at least in the first 6 months. This suggests that perceptual development through repeated experience may be responsible for the infant anticipating the trajectory of falling objects. It is not clear why some physical principles act as core constraints on perception and other physical principles do not.

In summary, contemporary research suggests that vision and touch function as correlated modalities; the infant does not require extensive tactile experience to perceive basic properties of substance. In general, these findings lend support to the views of Gibson, rather than Piaget, and they suggest that perceptual systems contribute to the development of knowledge, as well as being influenced by foreknowledge once it is acquired.

Social Perception

As was mentioned earlier, infants recognise their mother's voice soon after birth and there is also evidence for an early olfactory preference for the mother. Could there also be an early visual preference for the mother? Bushnell, Sai and Mullin (1989) tested this hypothesis in a very carefully controlled study of 5-day-old babies. The baby was seated facing a large white screen into which had been cut, at head height, two apertures on either side of the infant's midline. The mother and a female stranger, of similar hair length and hair colour, were seated, silently, behind the screen so that their heads were visible through the apertures. The screen itself was liberally sprayed with an air freshener to eliminate any olfactory clues. It was found that the neonates preferred to look at their own mother approximately 61% of the time. This preference was eliminated when mother and stranger wore identical wigs, which suggests that something about the mother's hairline may be distinctive for visually recognising the mother in the very early days. Prenatal familiarity with the mother's voice, coupled with an innate tendency to look where a sound is heard, may be sufficient for the baby to learn rapidly the distinctive aspects of the mother's appearance. Within a few months there is definite evidence that babies remember the sound of the mother's and the father's voice. In one study by Spelke and Owsley (1979) the baby heard a tape recording of the mother's voice played over a loudspeaker placed exactly between the mother and father. The parents sat without talking or moving the mouth, so there was no information in visual synchrony with the sound. Babies from 3 months looked toward the mother when they heard the mother's voice and toward the father when the father's voice was played. This suggests that correlated aspects of auditory and visual information, characteristic of each parent, must be remembered by 3 months. Even though there need not be a very precise auditory-visual memory the infant is nevertheless acquiring some familiarity with the sound and sight of the caregiver.

Kuhl and Meltzoff (1982) examined another aspect of auditory-visual coordination in 4-month-old babies who were presented with two video-recorded faces of strangers to left and right of the midline. One face was shown repeating the vowel 'i' while the other repeated the vowel 'a'. However, the baby heard only one sound track, to correspond with one of the visually presented sounds. Babies preferred to look at the face which corresponded with the sound track. This suggests that the babies must detect a correspondence between the auditory and visual information for the vowel sound. This ability might be very useful in acquiring language since it means that visual and auditory information for speech are to some extent overlapping (or redundant). An elementary level of lip reading may also help the young infant in producing appropriate speech sounds, as well as to perceive them. Further evidence in support of this hypothesis comes from difficulties that blind children have in learning to produce certain sounds (Mills, 1987).

That perception of movements may facilitate their production has been demonstrated by Meltzoff and Moore (1977). These investigators showed that newborns can imitate tongue protrusion, mouth opening and lip pursing movements. It is worth noting that imitation of tongue protrusion has now been observed in newborn infants in cultures as diverse as North America, Switzerland, Sweden and a nomadic tribe in Nepal (Reissland, 1988).

Vinter (1986) replicated and extended these results. She showed that newborns can also imitate sequences of finger movements. The ability to imitate was demonstrated only when babies actually saw the action being carried out by the adult; they did not imitate if only a stationary model was observed. For example, tongue protrusion occurred on seeing the tongue actually in motion, not if the baby only saw the protruded tongue in its final stationary position. The implication is that newborns depend on the dynamics of the perceived event in order to imitate it.

As in many other newborn behaviours, a U-shaped developmental function was found with imitation of hand movements dropping out at about 7 weeks and tongue and mouth imitation dropping out at about 3 months. The abilities reappeared at 7 months and 12 months respectively. It is worth noting that Piaget observed symbolic imitation at 14 months, when his daughter used tongue protrusion movements in an attempt to understand how the sliding drawer of a matchbox might work. This observation reinforces the argument that founding abilities observed in the neonate should not be confused with their more developed forms.

A final observation concerns the significance of infant perceptual competence for acquiring speech and language. Obviously, auditory-visual perception is particularly useful for perceiving the communicative actions of another person. Babies learn to communicate through speech in a very few months, and one important problem for developmental psychology is to explain how this achievement is possible. Spelke and Cortelyou (1981) suggest that there are three aspects of auditory-visual coordination that may contribute:

1. Young infants are able to locate a person when they hear a voice. There is a basic, innate spatial coordination between vision and hearing such that the auditory system will seek out a visual object to help locate the sound.
2. By 4 months, perhaps earlier, babies are able to determine whether a person they can see speaking is the source of the voice by perception of the synchrony between the face and the voice.
3. Also by 4 months there is evidence that infants begin to have specific expectations about which face goes with which voice, at least in the case of the highly familiar mother and father.

Thus, this aspect of social development depends upon preadapted perceptual systems providing information that is specific to the individuals with whom the baby interacts.

Speech Perception

Babies are well equipped to recognise speech in the sense that they have an innate or very early learned ability to recognise speech sounds (or phonemes). Different languages have different phonemes and a phonemic distinction in one language may not occur in another language, even one that is closely related. There appears to be a critical period for setting the boundaries of phonemes and once they have been set in one way as a child it is very difficult as an adult to master a different set of phonemes that draws distinctions in a way that is incompatible with the first language. For example, /r/ and /l/ are different phonemes in English, but not in Japanese, which is why the Japanese people who learn English as adults have great difficulty in hearing the difference between the two.

Babies very rapidly learn the phonemes of the language that they hear. Indeed, they have no difficulty in learning the phonemes for two or more different languages if they are being reared in a multilingual family. The ability to hear the difference between phonemes is not restricted at birth to the language that the child hears at home. Japanese babies can hear the difference between /l/ and /r/ even though monolingual Japanese adults find this difference very difficult to detect. But the language that the baby hears soon starts to have an influence because, by about 8 months, babies begin to show a marked decrease in their ability to distinguish between phonemes that are not present in the language that they hear around them.

The ability to make phoneme distinctions is not uniquely human as chinchillas can also discriminate between synthetic phonemes (Kuhl & Miller, 1978). This suggests that this ability has developed from some more basic auditory perceptual ability. However, there is no evidence that animals show the selective learning that is demonstrated by infants for whom phonemic contrasts take on communicative significance.

Other aspects of intersensory perception in young babies have important implications for the acquisition of speech and language. Kuhl and Meltzoff (1982) showed that babies detect a correspondence between the auditory and visual information for vowel sounds. This ability to 'lip read' might be very useful in acquiring language since it means that visual and auditory information for speech are to some extent overlapping (or redundant). As mentioned earlier, Meltzoff and Moore (1977) showed that newborns can imitate tongue protrusion, mouth opening and lip pursing movements and it is possible that this capacity for imitation may be fundamental to the development of communication. Thus, there may be a developmental link between early perception and subsequent acquisition of symbolic capacities and the development of speech.

One way to understand this complex developmental issue is to consider language acquisition to build upon the ways in which the auditory system naturally categorises sounds. To comprehend the symbolic meaning of words requires the infant to attend not only to the sounds she hears but also to the adult's behaviours and contextual factors which will provide important information about the meaning which language is intended to convey.

Early pre-speech abilities include the sound perception system which may involve a universal perceptual capacity for the sounds from which individual languages have been built. The counterpart to the sound perception system is found in the baby's production of babbling. There is now good evidence that auditory experience plays an important role in the development of speech by selectively tuning the auditory system to the sounds typical of the infant's linguistic community. For example, newborns are able to discriminate the sounds /l/ and /r/ whether they are Japanese or English babies. The capacity to make this discrimination is retained in English speakers but Japanese adults are unable to perceive the difference between these phonetic contrasts. There is now a great deal of evidence that language-specific phonetic contrasts are lost by the end of the first year of life, if they do not occur in the particular speech community in which the infant is immersed (Burnham, Earnshaw & Quinn, 1987).

Other perceptual-motor processes enter into language acquisition too. Social interaction skills, such as 'turn taking' between infant and mother, the emotional attunement of the infant to the mother, attending jointly to objects and events with the mother, all lay the ground work for communication. Motor development enables the infant to gain control over the articulatory and gestural systems while cognitive development enables their use in intentional communication, both in gestures such as pointing and in speech. Babies comprehend single words at about 9 months, for example by responding to their name, and babies will produce single words at about the same age. Subsequent development, which is described by Bernicot (ch. 4, this volume) proceeds rapidly as babies enter the 'one-word stage' and discover the names of objects. The first sentences, two-word combinations, begin at around 18 months and thereafter the child acquires the rudiments of grammar.

Summary

This part of the chapter has reviewed the contemporary literature on perception in young babies based on the philosophical and historical preconceptions which have informed theories of cognitive development in infancy. We examined Piaget's theory, that action gives structure to perception and an alternative account, based on Gibson, which stresses the informative value of perception. Simple methods of studying infant perception, based on the spontaneous and learned preferences of babies, reveal that they do indeed perceive complex object properties, such as size and shape constancy, solidity, and permanence early in development before they have had the opportunity to construct these properties through their own activities. Babies also show important abilities to imitate, which may be implicated in the acquisition of speech and which also imply that they may recognise other people as importantly similar to themselves. The implication is that complex perceptual systems are part of our evolutionary heritage.

THE DEVELOPMENT OF SKILLED ACTION

Traditional accounts of early motor development begin at birth and present the infant as very limited indeed in motor abilities. In recent years a great deal of evidence has accumulated for aspects of motor development in the prenatal period and this has revealed important new information, relevant to the perceptual and motor repertoire of the newborn, which needs to be taken into account. Until recently little was known about foetal behaviour. Pregnant women often note feeling foetal movements at about 16 weeks gestation but they are only aware of the most gross movements. In fact, up to 20 000 movements per day can be recorded. The advent of real time ultrasonic scanning in the 1970s has offered a safe means of imaging foetal movements in utero. Ultra high frequency sound (outside the audible range), is transmitted into the pregnant woman's abdomen. The echoes of the sound are picked up electronically and converted to a visual image which provides a view of the foetus as it moves.

De Vries, Visser and Prechtl (1984) have described 15 distinctively different movement patterns in the 15-week fetus, these include foetal breathing movements, where the amniotic fluid is regularly inhaled and exhaled, stretching movements, turning movements, and slightly later, thumb suck-

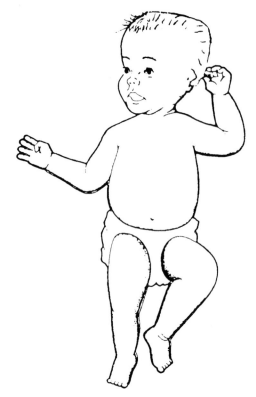

Figure 3.1 The asymmetric tonic neck reflex or 'fencer' posture as in the newborn baby.

ing. These well-coordinated movement patterns occur under the relatively weightless conditions of the foetal environment. Some, like the foetal breathing movements, seem related to similar action patterns in postnatal life.

After the 24th week, finer degrees of movement control are observed, including expressive facial movements. Foetal activity resumes, in the increasingly cramped living quarters, and is now subject to sleep–wake cycles.

The first postural reflex, to be observed at 28 weeks, is the tonic neck reflect (TNR). This pattern of coordinated muscular activity extends the arm and leg on the side to which the head is turned, while the opposite arm and leg are flexed, as shown in Figure 3.1. This so called 'fencer posture' continues to the 8th postnatal month. The typical orientation of the majority of infants is with head and arm to the right, whereas a small minority typically face the extended left arm. This spontaneous, asymmetric posture of head and arm is thought to predict whether the baby will eventually be right- or left-handed.

The general explanation of many of the fetus's spontaneous movement patterns is that they serve to exercise the developing system and to aid the growing joints take their correct shape. Another possible function of prenatal activity is that it provides a high level of input to the developing ears, eyes and other sensory receptors. The cutaneous (skin), taste and olfactory (smell) receptors and the vestibular and auditory systems are functional by the 24th gestational week. The visual system is functional by the 26th week. Finally, the continuous rotation and 'crawling' movements of the young fetus may prevent adhesion to the uterine wall. Spontaneous movement, graceful and patterned, is generated by the fetus of 15 weeks.

It is very likely that there is a continuous relationship between some foetal movement patterns and postnatal forms of behaviour. De Vries, Visser and Prechtl (1984) describe a stretch and yawn pattern at 10 weeks foetal age which suggests continuity in the organisation of yawning and stretching movements throughout life. Less obviously, there may also be continuity across locomotor patterns. The crawling movements of the 6-month-old baby and the typical alternating walking movements of upright locomotion maybe related to the so-called 'stepping reflex', a cyclic stepping movement made by newborns when supported in an upright posture. The stepping movements may in turn be related to foetal crawling movements which prevent adhesion to the uterine wall (Thelen, 1989). Thus, in seeking evidence for the founding abilities underlying the acquisition of motor skills, we find that the developing fetus is already equipped with a repertoire of motor movements which may be incorporated in developmental processes following birth.

Motor Development in Infancy

Such observations on foetal behaviour have therefore led to a re-evaluation of the status of the newborn both in terms of the origins of motor abilities and in terms of the functioning of perceptual systems. The normal Western baby at birth, around 40 weeks, weighs about 7 pounds and is about 21 inches long. The head, which has grown fastest in utero, is disproportionately larger than the body. Head and neck take up about 30% of the total body volume by comparison to 15% at 6 years and only 10% in adults. It is worth remembering that the changing proportions of the body pose particular problems in gaining motor control, not only in infancy but also in later periods of the life-span where rapid changes in body proportions, as in adolescence, create new biomechanical constraints to be overcome.

The radical shift in environmental from pre- to postnatal life, the extra weight of the body, especially the head, rapid growth and new possibilities for the control of action through vision may all contribute to the apparent 'helplessness' of the newborn. However, the period of intra-uterine life may have been rather effective in preparing the baby for independent existence, particularly in the basic repertoire of motor movements which were laid down under relatively weightless conditions. The developmental problem for the infant may lie not in acquiring basic movement synergies but in bringing the action system under voluntary control.

Perception has a particularly important part to play in the acquisition of skills in infancy. A motor skill is an organised sequence of goal-directed activity which is guided or corrected by feedback. Among the most important developmental precursors of skills are gaining control over the posture of the head, by about 3 months, over sitting by about 6 months, and standing toward the end of the first year. Each of these skills has a mechanical aspect in that the infant must acquire the necessary strength to support the heavy weight of the head and the body. In addition, vision serves an important role in stabilising posture since visual feedback from the stationary environment can be used to monitor involuntary swaying movements when learning to sit or stand (Butterworth & Cichetti, 1978). The onset of independent locomotion by crawling and walking also depends on good prior control of static postures in sitting and standing. Visual perception serves an intrinsic role in the acquisition of such gross motor skills and it is not surprising that babies born blind are severely impaired in learning to sit, crawl and walk (Fraiberg, 1974).

Acquiring control over head and trunk enables further, fine motor skills to be acquired, such as reaching and grasping, which depend on gross postural stability for their effective deployment. Fine motor activities such as acquiring delicate finger grips have a prolonged period of development and it is not surprising that infants with visual impairments are also delayed in the development of prehension (Fraiberg, 1974).

The basic developmental process once again builds upon an innate repertoire of elementary perceptual-motor coordination. In some motor domains such as sucking, the baby soon acquires very skilled control over the pressure and vacuum produced by the mouth in obtaining milk. In other domains, such as reaching to grasp something or in acquiring independent locomotion, only the most basic elements of the visual-motor coordinations can be observed and skilled control takes many months to be acquired.

A clear example concerns the development of reaching to grasp an object. There is now quite extensive evidence for an innate basis to eye–hand coordination. Bower (1982) demonstrated that newborns will attempt to make gross swiping movements of the hand and arm in the vicinity of an attractive object suspended within reach in the field of view. As the baby's aim gets better, contacts become more frequent and by about 4 months, the baby succeeds in grasping the object after contacting it. The actions of visually elicited reaching and tactually elicited grasping have become increasingly 'anticipatory' and the hand begins to open before contact with the object so that by 5 months both reaching and grasping are coming under visual control. In fact, developments in the grips of babies can be observed well into the second year of life, as the infant becomes able to grasp objects and then gains finer and finer control over the fingers. Babies first grasp predominantly by pressing all the fingers against the object in the palm of the hand with little by way of precise finger control. The so-called palm grips progressively give way to more precise finger grips, so that by the end of the first year, the baby is able to pick up rather small objects in a 'pincer grip' between the end of the index finger and the tip of the thumb. The fully opposed pincer grip, with finger tip to thumb tip contact, is species-specific

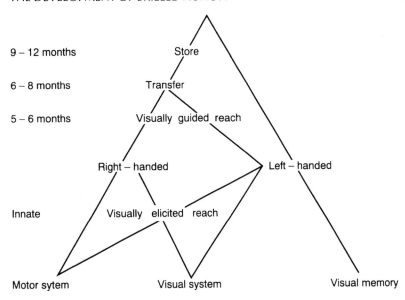

9 – 12 months   Store

6 – 8 months   Transfer

5 – 6 months   Visually guided reach

                          Right – handed   Left – handed

Innate   Visually elicited reach

Motor sytem   Visual system   Visual memory

Figure 3.2   Hierarchical integration of vision, action and memory in development of reaching and grasping.

to humans and may be essential for very skilled tool use, as for example in sewing or drawing.

Figure 3.2 illustrates the hierarchy of processes involved in acquiring reaching and grasping skills in infancy.

These observations once again show that the amount of pre-adaptive structure available in early development is greater than traditional theories would suppose but development is still a complex process. The baby only slowly gains the skills required to put the innate eye–hand coordination to use. Contemporary theorists of motor development emphasise the extent to which such processes are self-organising. Development begins from pre-adapted systems which become inter-coordinated into more complex systems, themselves stable within certain dynamic limits. Reaching behaviour, as one example of this general process, becomes more stable and less likely to be perturbed by unexpected events as it becomes more skilled. Ineffective behaviours drop out of the repertoire, as the effective ones are selected and integrated to form a new level of self-organisation (Thelen, 1989).

Many other motor skills also come under visual control during infancy. Table 3.2 shows month by month the progress in motor development to be expected in the average child (Griffiths, 1954). It should be noted however, that the sequence of 'motor milestones' is not inevitable, as was once thought. Babies need not acquire all the skills, nor is their order of acquisition always the same. Some babies never learn to crawl before they walk, some crawl after they walk and some never crawl at all! Neither is progress in motor development the simple consequence of maturation, as was once assumed, since as we have seen, acquisition of motor skills depends upon progressive coordination of action systems with perception and memory.

Table 3.2   Motor development in the first two years

Months	Behaviour
1.	Lifts chin when prone; holds head erect for a few seconds
2.	Lifts head up when prone
3.	Rolls from side to back
4.	Lifts head and chest when prone; holds head erect
5.	Rolls from side to side
6.	Sits with slight support
7.	Can roll from back to stomach, stepping reactions
8.	Tries vigorously to crawl, sits alone for short time
9.	Can turn around when left on floor, makes some progress crawling
10.	Stands when held up
11.	Pulls self up by holding on to furniture
12.	Crawls on hands and knees; side steps around furniture
13.	Stands alone
14.	Walks alone
15.	Climbs stairs
16.	Trots about well
17.	Climbs on a low chair, stoops
18.	Can walk backwards
19.	Climbs stairs up and down
20.	Jumps, runs

Source: Adapted from Griffiths (1954).

Motor Development in the Life-span

The account so far has concentrated on motor development in infancy because that is where the most obvious and rapid changes occur. However, motor development continues through the pre-school years into adulthood and is much influenced by the changing proportions of the body which arise through physical growth. Overall physical growth slows down markedly by comparison with the rate of growth in infancy but it continues, with bursts and pauses, until adult stature is attained. Between the ages of 2 and 6 years children gain on average three inches in height per year and about four and a half pounds in weight (Johnston, 1986).

There are also marked changes in body proportions, with the relative growth rate of the head and trunk slowing down while the growth rate of the arms and legs speeds up. At 2 years, the head is about 25% of the total height of the child, whereas by 5 years, the proportion falls to about 16%. The top-heavy infant starts to acquire proportions that are more adult-like. Motor development proceeds apace and the child becomes much more skilled in movement as baby fat is lost. The changes in body proportions have the effect of moving the centre of gravity downwards and this enables the toddler to perform feats that require strong muscles and good balance, such as running, throwing and catching. Fine motor skills also improve rapidly so that between 3 and 5 the child becomes capable of building with bricks, and she acquires the fine coordination needed to hold a pencil, to use scissors, to button her own clothes and lace her shoes.

The rapid changes in physical development which comprise the 'growth spurt' typically correlated with puberty mark the onset of adolescence. There is a wide variation, both between and within the sexes, in the onset and rate of change during the transition to adolescence. In boys, the growth spurt may begin as early as 10 years, or as late as 16 years. In girls, the same process may begin as early as 8 years or not until 12 or 13 years. Other physical changes include increases in strength, a doubling in the size of the heart, greatly increased lung capacity and changes in the balance of sex hormones released by the pituitary gland of the brain, including an increase in testosterone in males and in oestrogen in females. On average, sexual maturity is reached 18 to 24 months earlier in girls than in boys. In girls, rapid change in height usually precedes the development of secondary sexual characteristics, whereas in boys, the height spurt generally occurs after the genitals have begun to grow (Coleman, 1980).

Biological growth continues into young adulthood. For example, between 17 and 30 years the long bones of the skeleton and the vertebral column continue to grow and this may add up to 1/4 inch to men's height (less for women). Some bones of the skull continue to grow throughout life (Tanner, 1978). Physical strength increases to peak efficiency at between 25 and 30 years. Rutter and Rutter (1992) give two examples from athletics: the 10 000 metre runner Paavo Nurmi ran his fastest race at the age of 27 and the hammer thrower Karl Hein reached his peak at 30. However, both athletes showed less than a 5% decline in performance over the next 20 years, possibly because they continued to take vigorous physical exercise. Examples such as these illustrate a number of points: that the peak of physical prowess occurs in early adulthood; that a significant physical decline need not occur and that protective factors, such as physical exercise, may be important in successful ageing. Finally, sex differences in life expectancy and during the life course may have important consequences for motor development into adulthood.

Summary

Contemporary researchers on motor development would not view the loco-motor milestones as the inevitable consequence of maturation. There is now rather strong evidence that some of the repetitive, rhythmic motor pattern observed in crawling and walking may be continued from foetal movements and provide the basic patterning observed in the walking movements of the toddler. Crawling is not an inevitable substage before walking. Some babies never crawl before they walk, others get about by shuffling along on their bottom, there are alternative pathways to the final upright posture which means that motor development is flexible, rather than rigidly pre-programmed.

Gaining control in many motor skills requires not only physical strength but also sensitivity to various kinds of feedback. Gaining control of head, trunk and legs is assisted by the visual flow pattern (visual proprioception) contingent on body movement. Good control over static balance is a prerequisite for control of dynamic balance, as in walking or running.

Static balance is also a prerequisite for the emergence of visually guided reaching. Here again, an innate coordination becomes modified by feedback, so that by the fifth month, the visually elicited reach of the newborn has become the visually guided reach. Further development enables the infant to gain control over the wide variety of grips of which the human hand is capable. Hierarchical integration of reaching with memory enables reaching to be used in later skills, such as searching for hidden objects, and thus motor skills become a constituent process in cognitive development.

Motor development is closely correlated with the changes in body proportions which occur with growth. As the child grows, so the coordination between different parts of the body must be recalibrated to allow for the different bio-mechanical consequences of changing body form. Such changes continue into adulthood. Decline in physical proficiency is not inevitable since practised athletes can maintain proficiency over many years.

DEVELOPMENT OF SYSTEMS OF PERCEPTION AND ACTION

We have considered the foundations of perception and action in infancy and have traced the general course of their development in the life-span. Perception and action are interrelated aspects of adaption to the world. Perception is a system of exploration by which information is obtained about the world and it is through action that the world may be transformed. Perceptual systems are deployed in increasingly skilled ways as the child actively explores the environment. Action systems may themselves give rise to perceptual effects, as in learning to draw, which further illustrates that it is impossible to make dichotomous categories between perceptual and action systems. Perception and action are inextricably entwined in the child's acquisition of knowledge.

Selective Attention

We have argued that the Gibsonian theory of perception, as a process specifically adapted to the pick-up of environmental information, most closely agrees with the evidence from infancy. From birth babies selectively attend to the environment, exploring some aspects in preference to others. They reveal that they actively seek information in their encounters with reality. However, there is so much information available that may be differentially relevant depending on the particular needs of the child, that the scope for the development of selective attention is truly enormous. A classical study by Gibson and Gibson (1955) illustrates the general principle of 'perceptual differentiation' which occurs as people learn to attend selectively to those aspects of the environment which allow successful discrimination between objects. In this task, children aged 6 to 11 years and adults were asked to identify patterns made in the shape of a spiral whorl. A target spiral figure was shown for 5 seconds and the 34 cards were presented successively in which the spiral whorl differed in the number of loops, the degree of compression of the loops and their orientation in 30 cases (4 cards in the set of 34 were identical to the target card). Younger children confused more of the non-identical spirals with the standard than did adults. However, as the experiment progressed, even the youngest children improved and the adults who were already performing nearly correctly, became faster in making correct identifications. The more dimensions along which the comparison stimuli differed from the standard, the better the learning in both children and adults.

Gibson and Gibson (1955) argued that repeated perception of the figures enabled the subjects progressively to isolate the relevant dimensions along which the stimuli varied from the standard. They call this process 'perceptual differentiation' and argue that it is the basic mechanism of perceptual development both in children and in adults. Perceptual differentiation is defined as isolating the richly informative aspects of the world. The information that is relevant will vary, depending on the nature of the task and on how effective it is in allowing discrimination between otherwise similar objects. Thus, in difficult tasks such as determining the sex of chicks, where very little perceptual information exists to differentiate the males and the females, it takes time to acquire the appropriate skills and even adults may not perform this type of problem well without training.

On simpler tasks, children may differentiate between objects less well than adults not because they cannot perceive the information available but because they are less systematic in the deployment of their attention among available alternatives. Vurpillot (1976) reviews some classic studies in this field carried out in Russian and French laboratories in the 1960s. For example, Zaporoshets and Zinchenko (1966) filmed the eye movements of children aged from 3 to 6 years. Patterns of eye movement were compared when they were first scanning an unfamiliar picture and after the children had been given the opportunity to familiarise themselves with the visual display. At 3 years children made relatively few exploratory eye movements and they tended to explore around only one part of the display during the familiarisation phase of the experiment. When presented with the same targets again, in a recognition task, they tended to scan other, different parts of the display with the result that identification of the target was somewhat haphazard. By 6 years however, the scanning strategy was much more systematic. Children showed extensive scanning during familiarisation which was sufficient for accurate recognition after brief scanning. Systematic search of the figures by an exhaustive scanning strategy was not fully developed until 6 years of age.

In a more complex variation of the task Vurpillot (1968) compared

Figure 3.3 Apparatus used by Vurpillot (1976) to investigate selective attention in young children
Reproduced from E. Vurpillot, *The Visual World of the Child*, London: George Allen & Unwin, 1976, by permission of HarperCollins Publishers

scanning strategies of children aged from 3.5 to 9.5 years in a task in which the child had to scan between two pictures of houses to say whether they were exactly the same or not. The houses were each of identical outline with six windows. Three of the pairs of houses were identical in all respects but the three remaining pairs differed in one, three or five ways in the contents of the windows (e.g. shutters, plant pots, light bulb present or absent in corresponding windows; Figure 3.3).

Children in the youngest age groups (3.5 to 5 years) would prematurely terminate search before giving their judgement. From 6 years scanning became more exhaustive and more pairs of windows were fixated when the pairs were actually identical, then when there were a large number of differences (hence allowing early termination of search). Children became faster as the experiment progressed, but the youngest group were always slower to complete the tasks than the older children. The decrease in attention time among the younger children was attributed to their shorter attention span and loss of interest in the task. This has the paradoxical effect that the amount of useful information they extract actually decreases as the task goes on. The older children extract the same amount of information but they do so in progressively less time as they become more familiar with the problem. The pattern of eye movements also varied with age, with children from 6 years making more systematic horizontal eye movements between corresponding windows than the younger children. This strategy ensures that homologous parts of the houses are being compared. Vurpillot suggests that for the younger children part of the difficulty in the systematic deployment of visual attention may actually arise because the task does not permit the child to direct her own eye movements by pointing manually to the target. Thus, if this suggestion is correct, voluntary attention in young children may be assisted by visual-manual coordination. The use of pointing may help ensure that the child's focus of vision is directed to the most informative part of the display. Among older children, attention may be deployed increasingly on the basis of a cognitive model of the task to be achieved. Such representational solutions require not only systematic strategies of logically exhaustive search but also considerable memory for the combinations of relevant information that will allow an accurate decision.

These examples of selective attention therefore illustrate the extent to which development, even in the presence of complex perceptual abilities, nevertheless depends upon differentiation of relevant information. For specialised tasks, such as determining the identity or difference of objects experienced successively, it is not sufficient to deploy attention at random, or merely to attend to the most interesting part of a display. In this case, it is necessary to perform logically exhaustive search with systematic deployment of attention. Performance on tasks of this kind continues to develop well into the tenth year and indeed, there are large differences between individuals even as adults, in tasks requiring sustained visual attention (Mackworth & Bruner, 1970). Finally, some loss of systematicity in attention deployment may be found in extreme old age, or in the cases of adults with damage to the frontal lobes of the brain, where the capacity for sustained attention is affected in ways reminiscent of the inconsistencies in the performance of young children.

From Scribbles to Graphic Symbols

In the final section of this chapter we will consider an example of the interaction of perception, action and cognitive processes in development. The earliest drawings of the child, aged from 18 to 30 months, are often scribbles, which may reflect little more than that energetic movements of the child making visible marks on a surface. It has proved possible to classify early drawings into 20 basic types which are very similar worldwide (Kellogg, 1969). These simple forms include geometric shapes such as circles, squares, triangles, crosses and simple combinations such as the mandala (a cross enclosed by a circle) and sun drawings (a circle with straight lines radiating in all directions). The basic elements combine to form the first graphic symbols as the child begins to perceive meaning in the visual patterns produced.

A drawing of a person by a 3 year old may consist of a 'tadpole figure' comprising a circle for the head, with two vertical lines for legs, some dots for facial features and the arms extending horizontally from the head, as in Figure 3.4. A similar tadpole schema, drawn horizontally, may be used to represent animals, such as a cat or dog. This propensity for the combination

Figure 3.4 A child's drawing of a tadpole figure

of geometric forms serves a general symbolic function in representing visual objects. It is remarkable that congenitally blind children, when asked to draw the human figure, also do so using combinations of circles and straight lines, just like the sighted child (Millar, 1975).

Luquet (1927), one of the early students of child art, argued that children's drawing passes through several stages. Following the '*fortuitous realism*' of the scribbling stage, the early symbolic period in drawing was described as the stage of '*intellectual realism*'. Although the drawing of pre-school children bears some resemblance to what is being depicted, its primary purpose is to represent an object by symbolic means. The drawing is not an attempt at a photographic type of depiction, rather, it is an iconic symbol that incidentally resembles what it represents. Luquet argued that young children, by combining simple geometric elements, are drawing 'what they know' rather than what they see. On this account, knowledge acts in a 'top-down' way to give meaning to the child's visual depiction. Intellectual realism gradually gives way to *visual realism* as the child attempts to master the intricacies of representing life-like three-dimensional objects, so that the drawing actually resembles physically the object depicted.

Piaget and Inhelder (1967) followed Luquet's classification of stages, especially in Piaget's theory of the child's conception of space, where he argued that it is not until age 7 or 8 years that the child would adequately be able conceptually to coordinate different points of view and understand proportionality to make use of such devices in visually realistic spatial depictions.

Freeman and Janikoun (1972) provided some evidence for a transition from intellectual to visual realism. They asked children to draw a cup which was presented in such a way that the handle could not be seen but a prominent feature, a flower decoration on the cup, was in full view. Children below 8 years included the non-visible handle and omitted the visible flower decoration from their drawings. They know that a cup has a handle and their drawing symbolically depicts what they know about cups. Children aged over 8 years omitted the handle and included the flower, since, it is argued, they draw realistically what they can see from a particular viewpoint. Note however, that another interpretation of this study is that the younger child simply prefers to draw the symbol for a cup rather than the cup as seen from a particular viewpoint.

Ingram and Butterworth (1989) showed that children as young as 3 years would attempt to draw a pair of plain wooden blocks of different size from a particular viewpoint. The blocks were presented in different positions (either vertically one on top of the other, horizontally one next to the other or in-depth, one behind the other). The finished drawings of the vertical pile and of the in-depth file were both drawn in the vertical plane and the final products were virtually indistinguishable. However, the process of drawing revealed that the children had different pictorial strategies for depicting height and depth. Piles were drawn with the bottom block first, then the second block drawn above and touching the first block. Files were also drawn vertically but the near block was always drawn first and the far one second and not touching the first. Thus even the 3-year-old children were preserving something of the specific spatial viewpoint in their drawings. Furthermore, the different temporal order of production of the blocks shows that different spatio-temporal 3D processes may still result in very similar 2D products. Not until about 5 years of age did the children begin to represent depth by perspective interposition of the cubes. These data show that even young children are attempting a visually realistic depiction which includes the point of view of the observer.

Ingram and Butterworth (1989) showed that this early visual realism can easily be suppressed in favour of intellectual realism. Facial features were added to the blocks so that the pair of blocks resembled a doll. In whatever orientation the blocks with doll features were presented, children between 3 and 7 years always drew the doll vertically. In fact, some of the youngest children drew the featured blocks as a vertical tadpole figure, just a head and legs, even though the model had a body and lacked arms and legs! Such tadpole drawings never occurred to the blocks without features. Figure 3.5 summarises the developmental sequences in the transition from tadpole drawings to perspective representations of the human figure in children.

It seems that the blocks alone lack any symbolic significance and hence even young children can depict them realistically in a drawing. However, as soon as human features are added, the child invariably draws the person schema, in the typical frontal vertical orientation. These data suggest that drawing some types of objects does involve conceptual knowledge, consistent with Luquet's theory of intellectual realism. However, even very young

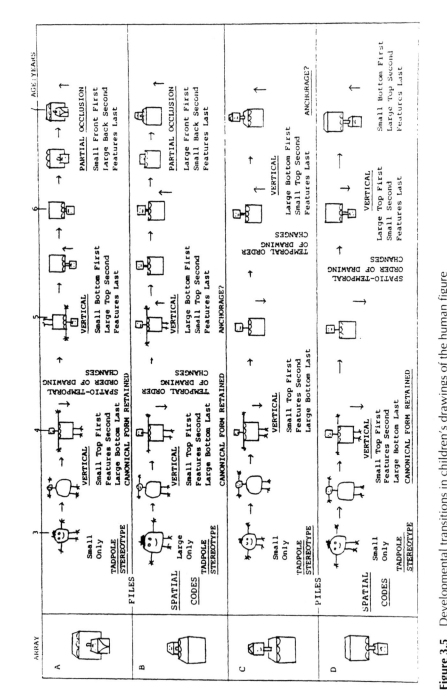

Figure 3.5 Developmental transitions in children's drawings of the human figure

children, at Luquet's stage of fortuitous realism, will draw what they see from a particular viewpoint if the overwhelming effects of the symbolic representation can be circumvented. Thus, the motor activity of drawing in young children taps both visuo-spatial processes and symbolic cognitive processes in the act of depiction. Individual development in artistic skills can continue into adulthood, according to talent, practice, and the culturally transmitted norms of pictorial representation which vary from one society to another.

CONCLUSION

This chapter has reviewed perceptual and motor development through the life-span. Contemporary evidence suggests that infants are much better able to perceive reality than had been traditionally assumed. The infant is equipped with perceptual systems whose function is to make contact with reality. From the outset, infants selectively explore the perceptual world and their very early development consists largely in selectively tuning perceptual systems to the particular characteristics of the environment encountered. This principle is especially evident in the development of auditory perception of phonemes but it applies to other perceptual systems also.

Motor development is similarly richly endowed from the outset. Development consists in selective retention of some aspects of an innate repertoire of motor abilities, the coordination and hierarchical integration of actions with perception, so that actions become progressively more skilled and accurately anticipate their outcome. Action patterns eventually come under the control of memory and cognitive processes so that activity may apply not only to objects that are directly present but action also applies to imagined objects. Thus perception changes from providing an 'engine' in early development which supplies information from the 'bottom up' to become partially driven by stored information or expectations that drive perceptual exploration from the 'top down'.

Once perception and selective attention are driven by representational processes the child begins systematically to seek after information in a logically consistent fashion. Development is not so much a question of changes in the mechanisms of perception but one of how perceptual systems are deployed, in the economical search for information. Much development in the pre-school and early school period occurs as perception interacts with logic, as in the classification of objects in typical sorting tasks.

The development of children's drawing also shows how the child's cognitive and motor activities may actually create objects for visual perception. The interaction of motor skills with symbolic and visuo-spatial processes is particularly apparent in the early development of human figure drawing. The symbolic component of drawing can be dissociated from its visuo-spatial aspect, with both types of representation being simultaneously available. In pre-school children, the symbolic representation tends to suppress the visual-spatial form. This suggests that symbolic processes must be separate, and at least to some extent, independent of other forms of visuo-spatial representation.

The examples in this chapter serve only to define the most basic phenomena in perceptual and motor development. Perception is not a process we outgrow as we get older. It is always at the core of the acquisition of knowledge. The chapter has outlined some of the ways in which perception and action provide the foundation for development from infancy to adulthood and how the child's developing knowledge may itself come to influence attention, perception and action.

ACKNOWLEDGEMENTS

Some sections of this chapter were previously published as Butterworth, G. E. (1994). 'Infancy' in A. M. Coleman (Ed.), *Encyclopedia of Psychology*, London: Routledge. Figure 3.1 is after Capute, A. J., Accardo, P. J., Vining, E. P. G., Rubinstein, J. E. and Harryman, S. (1978). Primitive reflex profile. *Monographs in Developmental Pediatrics*, 1, 40. Figure 3.3 is courtesy of HarperCollins Ltd, Glasgow. Thanks to Nigel Ingram for permission to reproduce Figures 3.4 and 3.5 which appeared in his doctoral dissertation 'Representation of three-dimensional spatial relationships on a two-dimensional picture surface', University of Southampton, UK, 1983.

REFERENCES

Antell, S. E. & Keating, D. P. (1983). Perception of numerical invariance in neonates. *Child Development*, **54**, 695–701.

Aslin, R. (1985). Effects of experience on sensory and perceptual development. In J. Mehler and R. Fox, *Neonatal Cognition: Beyond the Buzzing, Blooming Confusion* (pp. 157–184). Hillsdale, NJ: Erlbaum.

Atkinson, J. & Braddick, O. L. (1989). Development of basic visual functions. In A. Slater and G. Bremner (Eds), *Infant Development* (pp. 3–36). Hillsdale, NJ: Erlbaum.

Baillargeon, R. (1991). The object concept revisited: New directions in the investigation of the infant's physical knowledge. In C. E. Granrud (Ed.), *Visual Perception and Cognition in Infancy. Carnegie-Mellon Symposia on Cognition*, Vol. 23. Hillsdale, NJ: Erlbaum.

Bower, T. G. R. (1996). The visual world of infants. *Scientific American*, **213**, 80–92.

Bower, T. G. R. (1982). *Development in Infancy*, 2nd edn. San Francisco: Freeman.

Bower, T. G. R. (1971). The object in the world of the infant. *Scientific American*, **225**, 31–38.

Bower, T. G. R., Broughton, J. M. & Moore, M. K. (1970). The coordination of visual and tactual input in infants. *Perception and Psychophysics*, **8**, 51–3.

Bremner, J. G. (1994). *Infancy*, 2nd edn. Oxford: Blackwell.

Burnham, D. K., Earnshaw, L. J. & Quinn, M. C. (1987). The development of categorical identification of speech. In B. M. McKenzie and R. H. Day, *Perceptual Development in Early Infancy*. Problems and Issues (pp. 237–272). Hillsdale, NJ: Erlbaum.

Bushnell, I. W. R., Sai, F. & Mullin, J. T. (1989). Neonatal recognition of the mother's face. *British Journal of Developmental Psychology*, 7, 3–15.

Butterworth, G. E. & Cicchetti, D. (1978). Visual calibration of posture in normal and motor retarded Down's syndrome infants. *Perception*, 7, 513–525.

Campos, J. J., Barrett, K. C., Lamb, M. E., Goldsmith, H. H. & Stenberg, C. (1983). Socioemotional development. In Haith, M. M. and Campos, J. J., *Handbook of Child Psychology*, Vol. 2 (pp. 783–916). New York: Wiley.

Castillo, M. & Butterworth, G. E. (1981). Neonatal localisation of a sound in visual space. *Perception*, 10, 331–338.

Cattel, R. B. (1963). Theory of fluid and crystallised intelligence: A critical experiment. *Journal of Educational Psychology*, 57, 253–270.

Chomsky, N. (1980). *Rules and Representation*. New York: Columbia University Press.

Coleman, J. (1980). *The Nature of Adolescence*. London: Methuen.

De Vries, J. I. P., Visser, G. H. A. & Prechtl, H. F. R. (1984). Fetal motility in the first half of pregnancy. In H. F. R. Prechtl (Ed.), *Continuity of Neural Function from Prenatal to Postnatal Life* (pp. 46–64). London: Spastics International Medical Publications.

DeCarie, T. G. (1969). A study of the mental and emotional development of the thalidomide child. In B. M. Foss (Ed.), *Determinants of Infant Behaviour*, Vol. IV. London: Methuen.

DeCasper, A. J. & Fifer, W. (1980). Of human bonding: Newborns prefer their mother's voices. *Science*, 208, 1174–1176.

Eibel-Eibesfeldt, I. (1989). *Human Ethology*. New York: De Gruyter.

Eimas, P., Siqueland, E. R., Juscyk, P. & Vigorito, J. (1971). Speech perception in infants. *Science*, 171, 303–306.

Fantz, R. L. (1965). Visual perception from birth as shown by pattern selectivity. *Annals of the New York Academy of Sciences*, 118, 793–814.

Fraiberg, S. (1974). *Insights from the Blind*. New York: Basic Books.

Freeman, N. F. & Janikoun, R. (1972). Intellectual realism in children's drawings of a familiar object with distinctive features. *Child Development*, 43, 1116–1121.

Gibson, J. J. (1966). *The Senses Considered as Perceptual Systems*. London: Allen & Unwin.

Gibson, J. J. & Gibson, E. J. (1955). Perceptual learning. Differentiation or enrichment? *Psychological Review*, 62, 32–41.

Griffiths, R. (1954). *The Abilities of Babies*. London: University of London Press.

Hofer, M. (1981). *The Roots of Human Behaviour*. San Francisco: Freeman.

Ingram, N. & Butterworth, G. E. (1989). The young child's representation of depth in drawing. Process and product. *Journal of Experimental Child Psychology*, **47**, 356–379.

Inhelder, B. & Piaget, J. (1958). *The Growth of Logical Thinking from Childhood to Adolescence*. New York: Basic Books.

Johnston, F. E. (1986). Somatic growth in the pre-school years. In F. Falkner and J. M. Tanner (Eds), *Human Growth: A Comprehensive Treatise*, Vol. 2. New York: Plenum Press.

Kellogg, R. (1969). *Analyzing Children's Art*. Palo Alto, CA: National Press Books.

Kuhl, P. & Meltzoff, A. N. (1982). The bimodal perception of speech in infancy. *Science*, **218**, 1138–1141.

Kuhl, P. K. & Miller, J. D. (1979). Speech perception by the chinchilla: Identification functions for synthetic VOT stimuli. *Journal of the Acoustical Society of America*, **63**, 905–917.

Lehmkuhle, S. (1995). Deficits in parallel visual processing in children with reading disability and in the elderly. In L. F. DiLalla and S. M. Clancy Dollinger (Eds), *Assessment of Biological Mechanisms across the Lifespan* (pp. 29–52). Hillsdale, NJ: Erlbaum.

Luquet, G. H. (1927). *Le dessin enfantin*. Paris: Delachaux et Niestle.

MacFarlane, A. (1975). Olfaction in the development of social preferences in the human neonate. In *Parent Infant Interaction* (CIBA Foundation Symposium 33). Amsterdam: Elsevier.

Mackworth, N. S. & Bruner, J. S. (1970). How adults and children search and recognize pictures. *Human Development*, **13**, 149–177.

Meltzoff, A. N. & Borton, R. W. (1979). Intermodal matching by human neonates. *Nature*, **282**, 403–404.

Meltzoff, A. N. & Moore, M. K. (1977). Imitation of facial and manual gestures by human neonates. *Science*, **198**, 75–78.

Millar, S. (1975). Visual experience or translation rules? Drawing the human figure by blind and sighted children. *Perception*, **43**, 63–371.

Mills, A. E. (1987). The development of phonology in the blind child. In B. Dodd and C. Campbell (Eds), *Hearing by Eye: The Psychology of Lip Reading*. Hillsdale, NJ: Erlbaum.

Nunes, T. & Bryant, P. E. (1996). *Children doing Mathematics*, Oxford: Blackwell.

Piaget, J. (1954). *The Construction of Reality in the Child*. New York: Basic Books. (First published in French 1937.)

Piaget, J. & Inhelder, B. (1967). *The Child's Conception of Space*. London: Routledge & Kegan Paul.

Reissland, N. (1988). Neonatal imitation the first hour of life—observations in rural Nepal. *Developmental Psychology*, **24**, 464–469.

Rubel, E. W. (1985). Auditory system development. In G. Gottlieb and N. A. Krasnegor (Eds), *Measurement of Audition and Vision in the First Year of Postnatal Life* (pp. 53–90). New Jersey: Ablex.

Rutter, M. & Rutter, M. (1992). *Developing Minds: Challenge and Continuity across the Lifespan*. Harmondsworth: Penguin Books.

Schroeder, B. A. (1992). *Human Growth and Development*. New York: West Publishing.

Shea, S. L. (1995). From the lab to the clinic: Recent progress in the assessment of developing vision. In L. F. DiLalla and S. M. Clancy Dollinger (Eds), *Assessment of Biological Mechanisms across the Lifespan*. Hillsdale, NJ: Erlbaum.

Sinclair, D. (1978). *Human Growth after Birth*, 3rd edn. Oxford: Oxford University Press.

Slater, A. (1989). Visual memory and perception in early infancy. In A. Slater and G. Bremner (Eds), *Infant Development* (pp. 43–71). Hove: Erlbaum.

Spelke, E. & Cortelyou, A. (1981). Perceptual aspects of social knowing, looking and listening in infancy. In M. E. Lamb and L. R. Sherrod (Eds), *Infant Social Cognition*. Hillsdale, NJ: Erlbaum.

Spelke, E. & Owsley, C. J. (1979). Intermodal exploration and knowledge in infancy. *Infant Behaviour and Development*, **2**, 13–24.

Spelke, E. (1991). Physical knowledge in infancy. Reflections on Piaget's theory. In S. Carey and R. Gelman, *The Epigenesis of Mind. Essays on Biology and Cognition* (pp. 133–170). Hillsdale, NJ: Erlbaum.

Spelke, E., Breinlinger, K., Macomber, J. & Jacobson, K. (1992). Origins of knowledge. *Psychological Review*, **99**, 4, 605–632.

Starkey, P., Spelke, E. & Gelman, R. (1983). Detection of intermodal numerical correspondences by human infants. *Science*, **222**, 179–181.

Steiner, J. (1979). Human facial expression in response to taste and smell stimulation. In H. Reese and L. P. Lipsitt, *Advances in Child Development and Behaviour*, **13**, 257–295.

Tanner, J. M. (1978). *Foetus into Man*. London: Open Books.

Thelen, E. (1989). Self organization in developmental processes. In M. Gunnar and E. Thelen, *Systems and Development. The Minnesota Symposium in Child Psychology* (pp. 77–117). Hillsdale, NJ: Erlbaum.

Vintner, A. (1986). The role of movement in eliciting early imitation. *Child Development*, **57**, 66–71.

Vurpillot, E. (1968). The development of scanning strategies and their relationship to visual differentiation. *Journal of Experimental Child Psychology*, **6**, 632–660.

Vurpillot, E. (1976). *The Visual World of the Child*. London: Allen & Unwin.

Wertheimer, M. (1961). Psychomotor coordination of auditory and visual space at birth. *Science*, **134**, 1692.

Zaporoshets, A. V. & Zinchenko, V. P. (1966). Development of perceptual activity and the formation of a sensory image in the child. In *Psychological Research in the USSR* (pp. 393–421). Moscow: Progress Publishers.

Chapter 4

Communication and Language Development

Josie Bernicot

University of Paris and University of Poitiers

For thirty or so years, the study of the development of communication and language has followed the general trends of psycholinguistics, i.e. the areas of interest have become increasingly specialized, and the studies more and more specific. The researcher no longer talks about communication or language in general, but looks instead at the more local, well-defined characteristics of one or the other. With respect to general cognitive psychology, certain features of life-span developmental psychology in the area of child communication and language have led developmental psychology along a path of its own. In particular, some of the aspects examined here more than elsewhere are the communicative and representational functions of language, the relationship between language and the communication situation, and the link between language and the nonlinguistic facet of communication. In the area of communication and language, as in all other domains of psychology, European research is in step with the major international trends.

The purpose of this chapter is to define the concepts which will allow us to situate the current research, not only with respect to the various ways in which communication and language are analyzed and to the history of research in this field, but also in regards to the experimental paradigms used, from both the procedural and data processing standpoints. This chapter will then describe the stages in the development of communication and lan-

Life-Span Developmental Psychology
Edited by A. Demetriou, W. Doise and C. F. M. van Lieshout. © 1998 John Wiley & Sons Ltd.

guage. The steps involved in the child's acquisition of the mother tongue are presented, along with a brief description of second language learning by both adults and children, written language acquisition, and the development of communication and language in the elderly. The chapter ends with a discussion of the developmental and psycholinguistic theories which attempt to account for how communication and language progress with age.

BASIC CONCEPTS AND DEFINITIONS

To understand the development of communication and language, we need some precise definitions of the basic concepts used in the field. These basic concepts concern language functions, language activities, linguistic forms, nonverbal communication, and the communication situation itself.

Language Functions

Language has two major and essential functions: representation and communication. The main theories of development give precedence to one or the other. Piaget (1964), for example, considered the representation function to be fundamental, whereas for Vygotsky (1985), communication prevailed.

The representation function. The representational function of an utterance is to describe reality. Language is thus considered as a means of depicting reality, an instrument for breaking down the world. As such, it plays a major role in the construction of knowledge and in the processing and storage of information. The function of an utterance such as 'An apple is a kind of fruit' or 'Stick A is longer than stick B' is clearly representational.

The communication function. The communication function of an utterance is to transmit information to an uninformed addressee, or to persuade or act upon others. As such, language participates in social relations, becoming an instrument of action in relations among individuals. Language in this case is a system, defined by a set of rules, conventions, and shared knowledge, all of which not only underlie verbal communication but also every other social activity. The function of utterances such as 'Please tell me a story' or 'I'm going to play basketball with Nicholas' is clearly communicative.

Language Activities

A child can carry out three main activities with language: comprehension, production, and metalinguistic activity.

Comprehension. The child is the listener—the addressee in current terminology—and as such, must interpret messages addressed to him or her.

Production. The child is the speaker, and as such, must produce messages and address them to a listener.

Metalinguistic activity. The child is the 'observer', and as such, must talk about language and reflect upon certain properties of language. If, outside a communication situation, a child is asked to state the definition of a word or judge the grammatical correctness of an utterance and explain why, then he or she is engaging in metalinguistic activity.

In our review of the research, we must determine which type of activity is under study in each case. This is all the more important since the results obtained vary substantially across activities. As a general rule, children perform better in comprehension than in production (a point which could be debated and developed at length), arriving finally at successful metalinguistic activity.

Linguistic Forms

Double articulation

Language differs from other modes of communication in its double articulation (Saussure, 1960, 1916) along two axes: the syntagmatic axis and the paradigmatic axis (see Figure 4.1).

The syntagmatic axis, where linguistic units are lined up, is the axis of the necessarily linear chain of speech: only one word can be pronounced at a time.

The paradigmatic axis, where units can be substituted for each other, is the axis of the relationships between the actual units of the utterance, and other units which can be mentally associated with them. For example, 'Barbara speaks [French, Russian, Chinese, German, etc.].'

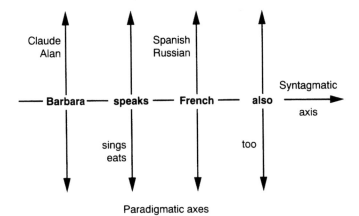

Paradigmatic axes

Figure 4.1   Representation of the syntagmatic and paradigmatic axes
Reproduced with permission from Bernicot, J. (1994a). Les méthodes d'étude de l'acquisition du langage. L'acquisition du langage: étapes et théories. In J. Crépault (Ed.), *Développement et intégration des fonctions cognitives. Cours de Psychologie*, Vol. 3 (pp. 292–306, 408–426). Paris: Dunod.

SIGNIFICATUM	CONCEPT	
SIGNIFICANS	ACOUSTIC SIGNAL	AIRCRAFT

Figure 4.2   Saussure's two-part representation of the sign

Linguistic signs

Another crucial concept in the definition of language is that of linguistic sign. Saussure (1960, 1916) proposed a two-part definition of the linguistic sign, whereas Pierce's (1867–1908) definition was three-part. Saussure's is the one most frequently used, while Pierce's definition has been found to be particularly applicable in recent work on pragmatics (cf. Bernicot, 1992).

Two-part definition of the linguistic sign. The linguistic sign has two faces, the significans (also called the signifier) and the significatum (also called the concept signified). The significans is the acoustic signal corresponding to the word produced, 'dinosaur' for instance. The significatum is the concept associated with the word (see Figure 4.2). The link between the significans and the significatum is arbitrary, that is, the acoustic signal does not depend in any way on the concept. Take the case of CAT: the link between the word and the concept is arbitrary; it is not arbitrary with the word MEOW. When a child produces MEOW to refer to a cat, he or she is in fact using the animal's cry, in which case there is a dependency relationship between the word and the corresponding concept.

Three-part definition of the linguistic sign. In this definition, the linguistic sign has three faces, the 'representamen', the 'object', and the 'interpretant'. The representamen is the sound signal or graphic transcription of the sign: for example, the French word *grenade* (this has three distinct meanings: hand grenade, pomegranate, and Granada, the city in Spain). The interpretant is the equivalent or more detailed sign created in the mind of the person to whom the representation is addressed (in the case of *grenade*, the interpretant is either a weapon, a kind of fruit, or a city). The object is the thing that corresponds to the sign (for example, the city of Granada, see Figure 4.3). When the word *grenade* is used in front of a number of persons, the interpretant will vary, depending on the addressee's profession or preoccupations: a soldier will think of a weapon, a grocer will consider a piece of fruit, and a traveller will imagine a city. This three-part definition of the linguistic sign is better able to account for polysemous words, so frequent even in everyday vocabulary.

Levels of analysis

Four levels of language analysis are defined: phonological, syntactic, semantic, and pragmatic.

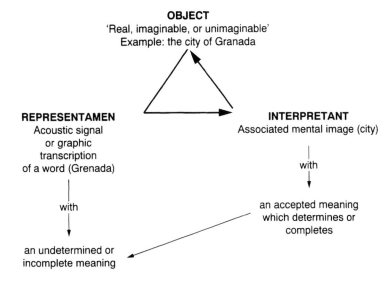

Figure 4.3   Peirce's three-part representation of the sign

The phonological level is the sound level. One question that might be asked at this level is: At what age do children acquire the phonological system of their mother tongue, and is there an order in which sounds or combinations of sounds are acquired? We are also interested at this level in the important question of intonation.

The syntactic level is the grammatical level, that is the order of words and the location of words in sentences relative to their function. For example, in sentences expressed in the active voice, the agent of the action is at the beginning of the utterance, whereas in the passive voice it is at the end. These two word orders are acquired independently, both in comprehension and in production. The syntactic level also includes the morphological aspects of language, that is variations in the form of words according to their function, as in 'woman / women' (singular vs plural) or 'he is / they are' (third persons singular vs plural of the verb 'to be').

The semantic level refers to the meaning off words and utterances. Words change meaning with age. For example, the verb 'to buy' is thought initially to have the same meaning as the verb 'to take'. It is not until a later stage that the child's meaning of 'to buy' incudes an exchange of money.

The pragmatic level relates the form of the utterance to the communication situation. At this level, the meaning of a word or utterance is considered to be determined not only by its form, but also by the inferences authorized by the context, whether linguistic or situational. The necessity of a context-based interpretation is clearly evidenced by linguistic phenomena such as hinting, insinuation, irony, and metaphor. Context is also needed to account for everyday utterances like 'Can you pass me the salt?' used as an illustration by Searle (1979). From a linguistic point of view, this utterance is a question about whether or not the listener is able to carry out a certain action; it therefore calls for a yes or no answer. From a social standpoint, this utterance produced in the context of a meal cannot be understood as a question but as a request to pass the salt.

Language and Nonverbal Communication

Researchers interested in language acquisition have shown that the nonverbal aspects of communication occupy an important position, both in language acquisition and language use (Bruner, 1983; Lock, 1978). A number of studies have been conducted on behaviors such as the direction of gaze, pointing, facial expressions, and forward or backward body movements (Van Der Straten, 1991).

Cosnier's (1982) classification of communicative gestures—some parts of which are presented below—distinguishes quasi-linguistic gestures from syllinguistic ones.

Quasi-linguistic gestures are capable of ensuring communication without the use of speech. Some examples are 'Stop', expressed by raising one arm, with the palm of the hand facing upwards and outwards, or 'Shh' expressed by placing the first finger vertically across closed lips.

Speech-accompanying gestures are produced in conjunction with speech to provide further specification or reinforcement of the linguistic message. They may be coverbal, in which case they illustrate discourse, as in pointing with the finger to the object being discussed. Or they may serve to synchronize the interaction by maintaining and monitoring the contact between the speaker and the listener, as in eye contact, head shaking, and so on.

The Communication Situation

Figure 4.4 indicates the main parameters of the communication situation currently being considered in research on language acquisition. They are related to the place and time of the communication, as well as to the characteristics of the participants and the different types of rapports between them.

METHODS FOR STUDYING COMMUNICATION AND LANGUAGE DEVELOPMENT

The specific methods used to study the development of communication and language can be illustrated by looking at the history of the related research, the characteristics of the subjects who have participated in the experiments, and the materials and experimental designs used.

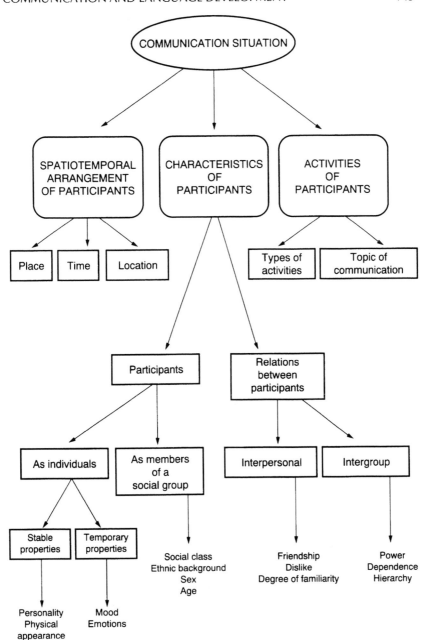

Figure 4.4 Characteristics of the communication system
From Bernicot (1992; 1994a)

History

Although child language is an age-old interest, and although the awareness of the importance of language for humans is marked by the etymology of the word 'infant' (he who does not speak), formal studies on this subject date

---

Box 4.1   Text by Herodotus (circa 500 BC)

SECOND BOOK—EUTERPE

II. Before the reign of Psammetichus, the Egyptians believed they were the most ancient people on earth. This prince having wanted to find out, at the advent of his crowning, which nation had the greatest right to this title, the Egyptians assumed from that time on that the Phrygians had come before them, but that they themselves had come before all other nations. The attempts of this prince having long remained fruitless, he thought up the following scheme: he took two newborn children of low lineage and gave them to a shepherd to be raised among the herds, ordered him to prevent whosoever from pronouncing a single word in their presence, keep them closed up in a cabin which no one could enter, bring them at certain times to the goats to be fed, and when they were satisfied, go about his other occupations. In giving these orders, the prince wanted to find out what would be the first word these children would pronounce when they had stopped returning inarticulate sounds. This plan worked well. Two years after the shepherd had begun taking care of the children, as he was opening the door and entering the cabin, the two children, crawling towards him, began to cry 'Bekos', stretching out their hands. The first time the shepherd heard them pronounce this word, he said nothing; but having noticed that, when he entered to take care of them, they frequently repeated the same word, he informed the king, who ordered him to bring them to him.

Psammetichus, having heard them speak himself, and having found out which people used the word *bekos* and what it meant, learned that the Phrygians called bread as such. The Egyptians concluded from this experiment and came to the agreement that the Phrygians were older than they.

---

back only to the beginning of the twentieth century. Moreover, since classical times, and especially since the turn of the twentieth century, the research themes and objectives have evolved tremendously.

Classical times. The oldest study appears to be the one conducted by Herodotus, the Greek historian (circa 500 BC.). The text of his study is given in Box 4.1. Apparently, the Pharoah's goal was both philosophical and political: to determine, by means of the language, the age of a culture and hence the status of dominance of that culture and that language. His story is also a testimony to the belief in the totally innate nature of the most ancient language. Despite a great concern for accuracy, note in particular the lack of respect for the basic principles of ethics (isolation of the children for several months), the use of a small number of subjects, and as far as the interpretation is concerned, failure to relate the words /bekos/ to the common cry of the goat.

Scientific observations proper were not truly undertaken until the nineteenth century. Before that, the reflections were exclusively philosophical and/or oriented towards child-raising, as in Rousseau's (1762) eighteenth-century writings.

The nineteenth century. The first nineteenth-century studies consisted of regular if not daily note-taking by one of the parents during his or her child's initial years of language acquisition. The observer wrote down the words and expressions produced and understood by the child, in their order of appearance, along with the child's pronunciation and the corresponding meanings. Initiated in the nineteenth century, these studies continued on into the early 1900s. The work done by Grégoire (1937, 1947) for French, Pavlovitch (1920) for French and Serbo-Croatian, Gvozdev (1949) for Russian, and Léopold (1939, 1947, 1949) for English and German are among the most well known. Note also the work by G. Stanley Hall (1883) in the Untied States, later to become the source of a large body of work.

These initial studies, produced in the most cultivated and educated of milieus, were centered on what the child says and understands. They were not concerned with the structural components of the language (vocabulary, syntax, etc.) and their acquisition.

As in antiquity, this period also exhibited a philosophical preoccupation with the origin of language. Darwin's (1877) observation of one of his sons is a good illustration of this interest. Another example of this tendency is the enthusiasm spurred by Itard's (1807) book about Victor, the wild child of Aveyron who was brought up with very little human contact until a relatively late age.

First half of the twentieth century. During this period, data were gathered from all social milieus, in a child-raising and relatively normative perspective. The studies looked at the differences between the sexes and the social classes, and the causes of learning difficulties. Samples of children were tested for questions related to sentence length and various types of grammatical or pronunciation errors (Carmichael, 1946).

The sixties. Chomsky's model of language (1965), which followed the main principles of the School of Port Royal (cf. Arnauld & Lancelot, 1660) triggered an abundance of research on the acquisition of grammar by the child. The idea was to follow a small number of children as they began to learn to speak. Roger Brown (1973), for example, studied the development of language in three children (Adam, Eve, and Sarah). Researchers visited the children in their home once a month, and recorded their verbal productions. The recordings were transcribed and analyzed in the laboratory, and the first syntactic acquisitions of the children were thus discovered.

The seventies. This decade was characterized by the study of the semantic aspects of language, and in particular, of the semantic relations expressed in children's initial utterances. The beginning of an awareness of context was noted. This is also the period during which the speech adults use to address children was examined. The purpose of a large part of the research was to contribute to the discussion on the innate versus acquired nature of language. Another area of interest was the link between linguistic and cognitive development, especially in the framework of Piaget's theory (1964). One question raised was whether the words used to express spatial relations (e.g. in

---

Box 4.2   Summary of a study by Bernicot and Legros (1987)

UNDERSTANDING OF DIRECTIVES BY 3- TO 8-YEAR-OLD
CHILDREN

The comprehension of direct requests (e.g. 'Shut the window') and
unconventional indirect requests (e.g. 'It's cold in here') was examined
using 3- to 8-year-old children. From a theoretical standpoint, this
study relies on both the psychological perspective, which emphasized
the social and cognitive factors of language acquisition, and the philosophy of language. Three groups of 24 children (ages 3–4, 5–6, and
7–8) completed comic strip stories. In addition to examining the usual
variables, the children's age and the type of utterance (direct request or
unconventional indirect request), the study was concerned with the
role of the production context (strong or weak). The following results
were obtained. (1) In contrast to other studies, direct requests were
better understood than unconventional indirect requests (hints). (2)
The context strength played an important role: direct and indirect
request comprehension was found to depend on the utterance production context. (3) As expected, for both types of requests, performance
increased with age. The results are discussed in terms of levels of
comprehension, i.e. comprehension of the to-be-performed action,
and comprehension of the speaker's intention. From a developmental
point of view, it seems that children understand the action before they
understand the speaker's intention.

---

front of, behind, on, next to, in the middle) are necessary to the acquisition of
the corresponding concepts, or whether, on the contrary, the concepts are
acquired before the words. The debates between Piaget and Chomsky during
a colloquium at Royaumont Abbey in 1975 (cf. Piatelleli-Palmarini, 1979) are
a good illustration of some of the major issues raised at the time.

The eighties and nineties. The characteristic feature of these years is their
emphasis on the pragmatic aspects of language, that is, on variations in the
form and meaning of utterances as a function of the communication situation (cf. Bernicot, 1992). This framework is the basis for studies on developmental changes in speech acts, particularly requests, excuses, and
metaphors, and so on. Phenomena such as stylistic variations and humor
are also studied. This period has witnessed the birth of a new interest in the
connection between linguistic and social development, relying not only on
theories of pragmatics like Searle's (1979) but also on theories of development like Vygotsky's (1985) and Bruner's (1983). Today, research dealing
simultaneously with all four essential aspects of language (phonology, syntax, semantics, and pragmatics) is being conducted in various laboratories.
The summary of a recent study presented in Box 4.2 points out the obvious
change in the research goals and methods since classical times or even the
nineteenth century. The once very broad and philosophical objectives have
become very 'local' and centered on the operation of a single linguistic

subsystem. The methods have also evolved, both as to the number of subjects and the types of procedural controls.

Subjects

Research on language acquisition is generally conducted with subjects between the ages of 3 and 12 years. Note however, that there has been a recent increase in the number of studies dealing with children in the 18 month to 3 year range.

The number of children used as subjects varies considerably from one study to the next. Some of the research consists of case studies, where the author is only interested in a small number of subjects, usually between one and five. In the larger studies, the current tendency is to include between ten and sixty subjects in each group, defined by the conditions of the experiment.

The socio-cultural origin of the children, a factor which must be carefully controlled by researchers, also varies across studies. Contrary to the situation in the nineteenth century where only the most cultivated social classes participated, today's research pertains to all children. Most studies look at group averages (means, medians, and variance) rather than individual child data, which can be analyzed and perhaps later summarized.

Equipment and Materials

Since 1950, the gradual appearance of new technological devices such as tape recorders, video cameras, and computers has considerably enhanced and facilitated data collection and analysis. In the past, researchers used techniques called 'eye–pencil–paper', which severely limited the quantity, objectivity, and even the level of accuracy and hence the reliability of the data collected.

Apart from studies on phonology, which necessitate complicated and costly equipment such as a voice frequency analyzer, almost any study can be conducted with commonplace, readily available materials and equipment. In many cases a good tape recorder is sufficient, with the occasional addition of a cordless microphone, for example, to record children in a school courtyard during recess. In other cases, a video camera is needed to study variables such as direction of gaze and gestures during speech, or to get a better feeling for the comprehension or production context. Moreover, this type of standard, lightweight equipment (tape recorders and/or video cameras) makes it possible to record in the home without upsetting family routines. Another way of decreasing the disturbing effects of the presence of equipment and experimenters is to have the subjects do the recording themselves.

The next step after recording is transcribing. This is a difficult step, due both to the amount of work involved and to the decisions that must be made concerning *what* should be transcribed and *how*. Strict rules must be followed, and they must be suited to the research objectives. Some of the things that need to be decided are what notation to use for intonation, whether gestures accompanying speech should be noted, and how particular pronunciations and contractions should be transmitted (e.g. 'gotta' for 'have got to').

Once the recordings have been transcribed, the data must be coded and processed. In recent years, a number of computer programs have been developed for assisting researchers with these two operations. Among these are text analysis programs and data management systems such as FX by Pierre Plante (1993a,b) in Canada. Another important research asset today is the availability of databases containing corpora of children's productions. The ChiLDES system (Child Language Data System), implemented in 1984 in the United States by Brian MacWhinney and Catherine Snow, is a good example of such a system. This database was designed to contain corpora from all languages, and to be supplemented and used by researchers throughout the world (cf. Flecher & MacWhinney, 1995). Some more recent projects take into account a broader range of language constituents (cf. Edward & Lampert, 1993), or focus on a particular language, as in the PERGAME database of corpora from French-speaking children (developed under the initiative of Josie Bernicot). These software packages and databases help to standardize and automate coding, and facilitate access to information via a large variety and number of criteria.

Research Designs

As in all other branches of psychology, research in the field of language acquisition relies both on the experimental method in the traditional sense of the term (cf. Claude Bernard, 1815), and on observation. Note, however, that for obvious ethical and deontological reasons, phenomena like the effect of surrounding individuals' attitudes can only be captured by observation. Conventionally, either the cross-sectional method (comparison of different subjects of different ages) or the longitudinal method (comparison of the same subjects at different ages) is employed.

Experimental method: causal links

The overall goal of the experimental method is to establish a cause–effect link between two parameters.

CAUSES. As far as language acquisition is concerned, the causes or independent variables essentially correspond to the characteristics of the subjects, their speech, and the communication situation.

Characteristics of the subjects. The subjects are described by their age, sex, socio-economic or cultural background, native language, school grade, intelligence quotient, position in the family, and so on.

Characteristics of the subjects' speech. A subject's speech is described by variables such as the types of words used, types of syntactic marks, verb or article categories, sentence forms (e.g. negative or interrogative), and so on.

Characteristics of the communication situation. The communication situation is described by the topic of conversation, the content of the productions, the context, the characteristics of the addressees, the types of psychological or social relationships between the conversing partners, and so on.

TASKS. A link between two parameters is detected by using a task in which all subjects are asked to perform the same activity. In a large number of experiments, the task is accomplished individually by each subject. Researchers have displayed a great deal of imagination in this area; the current tendency consists of proposing tasks which are similar to the children's daily activities, or tasks in which role-playing puts them in situations where they really have something to say or understand. It is not possible here to draw up a complete list of the tasks used. Here are a few examples among the many others; repeat an utterance, follow instructions, produce certain utterances to make people carry out certain actions while playing 'house' with dolls and miniature equipment, understand stories by answering questions, retell stories, fill in comic strips by pretending to be one of the characters, describe a picture or other type of object to either the experimenter or another child who has to identify the described object.

EFFECTS. The effects or dependent variables are defined in each experiment by measuring the subjects' performance on the task. A few examples of dependent variables commonly used in production are mean utterance length, number of verbs, articles, or spatial or causal terms; number of sentences with a given linguistic form; and number of requests, assertions, or speaking turns. In comprehension, some of the frequently studied dependent variables are the number of correctly understood, recalled, or completed stories; the number of properly followed instructions; the number of correctly identified objects or characters. For the assessment of metalinguistic knowledge, the main tasks are utterance judgment tasks, with subsequent explanation of one's response.

Observation: coexistence and covariation

Observation is defined as the investigation of a natural or cultural phenomenon without the intervention of reaction of the researcher as the phenomenon is taking place. Of course, one cannot 'observe everything'. The researcher must therefore decide what to observe, one consequence being that the decision made is always subject to debate.

When the observation method is used, the researcher has much less control over the conditions of study than in the experimental method. In many cases, causal links cannot be detected by means of observation. This limits the potential explanations that might be given for a phenomenon. However, observation can be highly effective in detecting covariation and coexistence. In the study of language learning, observation is particularly suitable for examining the role played by the surrounding individuals.

A good illustration of the problem of covariation is how mothers adapt their speech to fit their child (cf. Moreau & Richelle, 1981). For language acquisition, it has been shown that maternal speech is adjusted to the level just above the child's. To establish a causal link in this case, one would have to 'find' or 'create' mothers who do not do this type of adaptation. Otherwise, the only thing that one can claim is that the mother's speech level covaries with that of her child.

To illustrate coexistence, let us consider Suzuki's study (1992), whose purpose was to define the circumstances under which Japanese 2 year olds learn requests. To teach direct and indirect requests to their children, Japanese mothers systematically use scripts (structured, routine contexts based on knowledge shared by mother and child). Suzuki's (1992) study is very interesting, but it does not get around the classical criticism: nothing proves that the child's acquisition of requests depends on the mother's use of scripts, since the experiment does not show that when scripts are lacking, requests are not learned or are learned in some other way. No causality is shown: scripts and requests simply coexist.

Research on language acquisition calls upon concepts from various domains (linguistics, psychology, sociology), all necessary not only for analyzing language, but also for understanding the communication situation. The research methods and designs are the same as in general psychology or developmental psychology, that is the experimental method and observation. However, the complex and highly situation-dependent nature of child language has often led researchers either to design specific paradigms for experimentation or, perhaps more often than in other areas, to use controlled observation, the only appropriate way to grasp certain phenomena.

COMMUNICATION CAPABILITIES AND CHARACTERISTICS THROUGHOUT THE LIFE-SPAN

It is not possible here to present a comprehensive picture of all the diverse aspects of the development of communication and language. Priority is given to the child's acquisition of the mother tongue. However, other topics including second language learning by children and adults, written language acquisition, and aging-related issues are also discussed.

Native Language Acquisition

There are four main periods in the development of communication and language: the prelinguistic period, the one-word utterance period, the two-word utterance period, and finally, the sentence period, with its long and complex evolution which continues until adulthood and sometimes even beyond. Added to these main periods are important steps such as the acquisition of different types of sentences and the use of strategies. The emphasis is usually placed on production, although the problem of comprehension is sometimes brought up at certain crucial points. The results reported here generally concern the syntactic and semantic analysis levels, and to a lesser extent, the pragmatic level. The ages indicated for each stage are of course only rough indicators, not absolute norms.

Prelinguistic period (before age 1)

Over the past few years, a great deal of research has focused on the prelinguistic period, both in production and reception. The findings have radically changed our picture of infants. At the production level, the vocal and gestural communication behavior of infants in some respects obeys the same rules as their later linguistic communication behavior. At the reception level, infants at birth already possess the perceptual mechanisms needed to distinguish the speech sounds produced by individuals in their surroundings. Specialized language learning capabilities exist, and certain behaviors appear at an extremely early age.

Production. Vocal activity evolves rapidly in the course of the first year, going from the newborn's cries to the beginnings of articulatory control (5 or 6 months), observed in the babbling and vocalizations of the child getting ready to pronounce his or her first words.

Somewhere around the age of 6 or 7 months, iterated sequences of two-sound 'syllables' emerge in the production repertoire (ta ta . . ., pa pa . . .). At approximately 9 or 10 months, children can produce nonrepetitive syllable chains (apabuyi . . ., tadi . . ., etc.). Shortly after that, children produce a variety of fluent, well-articulated vocal sequences, giving the impression that they are using a jargon which is an expressive imitation of adult speech. One is always surprised by the speed at which vocal productions evolve between birth and the first spoken words. Note that it is very difficult to explain this rapid progress from a theoretical point of view. In particular, when does child babbling become similar to the speech of the surrounding individuals? In an attempt to answer this question, a French specialist (Boysson-Bardies, 1984) compared the babbling of French children living in Paris, Arab children living in Tunis, and Cantonese children living in Hong Kong at 6, 8, and 10 months. Until the age of 6 months, infants produce a very wide range of phonemes (sound units), far more than those occurring in their native language. After 8 months, these vocal productions begin to sound like the phonemes of the mother tongue.

During the prelinguistic period, the child gradually shifts from a global form of communication, involving the entire body, to a more differentiated form which requires vocal activity and the beginnings of verbal comprehension. In addition, as this is the stage where the sounds of the native language are learned, it is marked by the child's entry into the basic mechanisms of communication (Bruner, 1983; Deleau, 1990). For example, certain rules for referencing in dialogue or joint action (cooperation) are acquired between 9 and 18 months. At the end of this period, children begin to adapt their nonverbal messages to the addressee and to the communication situation, according to rules analogous to those used during the linguistic period (Marcos & Bernicot, 1994).

Reception. Children exhibit striking capabilities when it comes to language reception. Already by the age of one month, infants can distinguish the human voice from other sounds, and before they are two months old, they respond to the voice of their mother and to that of a stranger (Mehler, Bertoncini, Barrière & Gerschenfeld, 1978). Another even more surprising finding is that babies only a few days old can be trained to produce different responses to the presentation of two artificial stimuli such as 'ba' and 'ga' (Bertoncini & Mehler, 1978). In studies of this type, the so-called nonnutritive sucking response is used. For a more detailed description, see Butterworth's chapter (ch. 3, this volume). Other indexes are also used to establish a habituation curve, including heartbeat, blood flow, and visual target fixation time. It can be shown that infants even distinguish sounds that adults in their surroundings are incapable of differentiating. For example, Japanese babies can distinguish an 'r' from an 'l', even though this distinction does not exist in Japanese, and Japanese adults have trouble producing it. From a theoretical point of view, this means that children's inborn perception system allows them to discriminate speech sounds on the basis of almost any phonetic feature.

One-word utterances (1 year olds)

The production of the first word is considered to be an important step since it marks the point at which the child has truly gained access to the linguistic system. However, determining this exact moment for a given child is very difficult because it involves defining the boundary between the vocal and the linguistic. A sound must be recognized as a word by an adult. A wide range of interpretations exist, because children do not always articulate correctly and their words do not always have the same meaning as those of adults. Also, the recognition of a sound as a word by an adult varies with the adult's degree of familiarity with the child. As a general, rule, the first words begin to appear about 1 year (varying between 9 and 18 months). The characteristic feature of this phase is the production of isolated words, that is utterances containing only one word. Some examples of one-word French utterances interpreted by the surrounding individuals as sentences are *papa*, *mama*, *a'voir* (for *au revoir*, meaning goodbye), *pati* (for *parti*, meaning gone).

Since the turn of the century, numerous authors have concentrated on the one-word utterances of very young children. For some, the child starts by naming concrete objects, both animate and inanimate. According to Bloom (1973) however, concrete names play a relatively minor role during this first phase. At 16 months, it is mostly prepositions, negations, adverbs, and verbs that appear to be employed (relational words).

If we go along with Nelson (1973), not all children talk about the same things. Some children's utterances are more reverential, that is object-oriented. For other children the initial utterances are expressive, that is communication-oriented (requests, refusals, calls, etc.). Bloom (1973), who studied the use of person names, showed that at first children use names to greet, call, or simply name someone who enters into the scene. Then names serve to refer to objects that belong to the named person, and finally, they are used to designate the agent of a predicted or upcoming action.

As a general rule, these isolated words (holophrases) are interpreted by the individuals in the home as meaning something as complex as that usually expressed by a sentence. In theory, the words produced by children have an undetermined or ambiguous meaning. When saying 'Daddy', the child may mean 'Here's Daddy', 'Daddy come help me', or 'Daddy has a new sweater', and so on. In practice, these utterances are easily interpreted in the light of the communication situation, and in fact allow children to interact satisfactorily with surrounding individuals. A child's words only take on meaning—sometimes even a complex meaning—through the interpretation adults make of them. The very existence of words as sentences is a testimony to the importance of the adult's interpretation of a child's words, not only as the language is being used, but also and above all, as it is being learned.

The growth of a young child's vocabulary is spectacular. The comprehension curve increases in a nearly linear fashion from 50 words at the age of 18 months to 2500 words at the age of 6. There is also qualitative progress, which sometimes continues until quite a late age (9 or 10 years for certain complicated French verbs). In many cases, children start with their own private meanings for words. Adult meanings are gradually acquired, following the rules described by Clark (1973) in the framework of semantic feature theory.

Two-word utterances (2 year olds)

As soon as several words are combined in the same utterance, the problem of how to arrange them according to their function arises, that is the problem of syntax. In French, English, and numerous other languages, it is important to order words correctly in an utterance so that successful communication can be achieved.

From the age of 2 on, a child produces two-word utterances which are organized according to a grammar called a pivot grammar, proposed by Braine (1963) from a corpus of English-speaking children. This grammar distinguishes two classes of words: the pivot class (P) and the open class (O). The possible two-word utterances are O+P and P+O. There are only a few pivot words, and for a given child, each pivot word has a fixed position in the utterance (first or second position). Open words are more numerous. For a given child, the position of open words varies across utterances. Table 4.1 gives some examples of two-word utterances taken from Oléron (1976) and Hurtig and Rondal (1981).

The pivot grammar is an original solution to the problem of word order, in so far as it is based on rules which do not exist in the adult grammar. For

Table 4.1   Examples of two-word utterances

Pivot word		Open word	
aussi	(too)	*bonbon*	(candy)
aussi	(too)	*du pain*	(Bread)
encore	(more)	*banane*	(banana)
encore	(more)	*du pain*	(bread)
encore	(more)	*manger*	(eat)
encore	(more)	fromage	(cheese)
encore	(more)	*le bonbon*	(candy)
Open word		**Pivot word**	
auto	(car)	*ama (à moi)*	(t'me)*[a]
ballon	(ball)	*ama (à moi)*	(t'me)
clè	(key)	*ama (à moi)*	(t'me)
bonbon	(candy)	*ama (à moi)*	(t'me)
camion	(truck)	*broum-broum*	(vroom-vroom)
auto	(car)	*broum-broum*	(vroom-vroom)
moto	(motorcycle)	*broum-broum*	(vroom-vroom)
grue	(crane)	*broum-broum*	(vroom-vroom)

Notes: French words in italics; translations in parentheses.
[a]In French *à moi* (literally 'to me') is a form of possession and simply means 'mine' as in *Ce livre est à moi* (This book is mine).
Source: Reproduced (translated into English), with permission, from R. Ghiglione & J. F. Richard (Eds), Développement et intégration des fonctions cognitives. *Cours de Psychologie:* Vol. 3. Paris: Dunod.

this reason, although functional until the age of 2, this grammar is a sort of linguistic dead-end which is quickly abandoned by the child. The means by which children move from two-word utterances to sentences are still not totally clear, and the theories proposed so far have been systematically verified. One idea is that a more complex grammar is built by dividing classes P and O into subclasses.

In children's two-word utterances, the are various types of semantic relationships between the pivot word and the open word: existence, disappearance, iteration, attribution, localization, possession, benefit, instrumentation, agent–action, and action–patient. By the age of 2, then, children's use of speech already demonstrates some degree of specialization and complexity.

Sentences (3 year olds and older)

The sentence is defined as an utterance of more than two words containing a noun phrase (NP) and a verb phrase (VP), for example, 'the terrible dinosaur (NP) ran through the forest at top speed (VP).'

Noun phrases.   The acquisition of the noun phrase is dependent upon the acquisition of the following units: noun, pronoun, article, adjective, preposi-

Table 4.2a Order of appearance of the main non-nominal constituents of the noun phrase in French children's speech

---

24 MONTHS
Personal pronouns
moi (me as object of a preposition)
Prepositions and adverbs
Prepositions of possession and benefit :*à* (to), *de* (of), *pour* (for)

---

30 MONTHS
Articles
Indefinite
Personal pronouns
je (I), *tu* (you as familiar singular subject), *toi* (you as familiar singular object of a preposition)

---

36 MONTHS
Articles
Indefinite, Gender agreement with modified noun
Personal pronouns
il/elle (he/she/it as subject), *le/la* (him/her/it as direct object)
Possessive pronouns
mon mien (literally 'my mine', incorrect infantile form of mine)
Prepositions and adverbs
Adverbs of place: *dedans* (inside), *dessus* (on top), *devant* (in front), *derrière* (underneath)

---

42 MONTHS
Articles
Definite, Number agreement with modified noun
Personal pronouns
vous (you as polite singular or plural subject or object), *me* (me as direct object), *te* (you as familiar singular direct object), *nous* (we, us), *on* (one as subject)
Possessive pronouns
ton tien (literally 'your yours', incorrect infantile form of familiar singular yours)
son sien (literally 'her hers' etc., incorrect infantile form of hers/his/its)
Preposition and adverbs
Prepositions of place: *à* (at), *dans* (in), *sur* (on), *sous* (under), *près de* (near), *en* (in) and accompaniment: *avec* (with)

Note: French words in italics; English translations in parentheses.
Source: Reproduced with permission from Hurtig, M. & Rondal, J. A. (1981). *Introduction à la psychologie de l'enfant*. Bruxelles: Mardaga.

tion, and adverb. A complete overview of the studies dealing with this question would be too lengthy to present here, so a table (see Table 4.2) is given in illustration. This table shows the steps in French children's acquisition of the main units of the noun phrase between the ages of 2 and 6.

Verb phrases.   Verb phrase acquisition requires learning the verb tenses and moods (past, present, future, indicative, conditional, etc.). The entire set of forms is produced by French children between the ages of 4 and 6. Although substantial interindividual differences exist, some general tenden-

Table 4.2b Order of appearance of the main non-nominal constituents of the noun phrase in French children's speech

---

48 MONTHS
Articles
Tendency to use indefinite articles instead of definite ones
Personal pronouns
Other personal pronouns
Prepositions and adverbs
Avec (with) expressing instrumentation

---

60 MONTHS
Prepositions and adverbs
Adverbs of time: *aujourd'hui* (today), *hier* (yesterday), *demain* (tomorrow), *maintenant* (now), *tout de suite* (right away), *d'abord* (first), *tout à l'heure* (in a while), etc.

---

66 MONTHS
Possessive pronouns
le mien (correct for of mine)
le tien (correct form of familiar singular yours)
Prepositions and adverbs
Prepositions of time: *avant* (before), *après* (after), *pendant* (during)

---

72 MONTHS
Articles
Correct article usage
Possessive pronouns
le sien (correct form of hers/his/its)
le nôtre (correct form of ours)
le vôtre (correct form of polite singular or plural yours)
le leur (correct form of theirs)

Note: French words in italics; English translations in parentheses.
Source: Reproduced with permission from Hurtig, M. & Rondal, J.A. (1981). *Introduction à la psychologie de l'enfant*. Bruxelles: Mardaga.

cies can nevertheless be noted.

The earliest form is the third person singular of the verb 'to be' as in 'the cake is good'. This form is usually acquired before the age of 30 months. The verbs 'to be' and 'to have', the infinitive forms, and the present indicative are acquired between ages of 30 months and 4 years. The future in its immediate form appears at approximately age 4, as in 'He is going to come' and 'It's going to be my birthday'. The simple future appears later. The imperfect and conditional forms also come later, between the ages of 5 and 6. A 5-year-old child employs nearly all possible verb forms. It is important to note, however, that children do not generally use verb forms to situate an action in time (past, present, future). In this respect, the linguistic behavior of children clearly differs from that of adults. In child productions up to the age of 6, verb forms serve above all to mark the aspect of an action, that is its time-independent properties (Bronckart, 1976). Four examples of verb aspect are given below.
1.　The distinction between an action currently taking place and an

atemporal action: 'She is taking her piano lesson' vs 'She takes piano lessons.'
2. The distinction between the unfolding of an action and a completed action: 'He was eating caviar' vs 'He ate caviar.'
3. Agreements about an imaginary situation: 'I was the policeman and you were the thief.'
4. The expression of a wish: 'It's going to be my birthday soon.'

Sentence types

This section will be illustrated by Halliday's work (1985). Halliday studied the verbal and nonverbal productions of a single child, his son Nigel, between the ages of 9 months and $22\frac{1}{2}$ months. His data analysis pointed out two phases in the child's progress in production.

During phase 1, between 9 and $16\frac{1}{2}$ months, the child did not combine words, or words and gestures. Six functions (usages) were sufficient to describe the child's productions.

1. The instrumental function, used to obtain something from the addressee.
2. The regulatory function, used to control another person's behavior.
3. The interactional function, for greetings, marks of politeness, and making contact with others.
4. The personal function, for self-expression and the expression of one's interests, satisfaction, dissatisfaction, etc.
5. The heuristic function, aimed at increasing one's knowledge.
6. The imaginative function, used to express one's own conception of the environment and the world.

These functions appeared in the order listed above. Each utterance was characterized by a single function and concerned the speaker.

During phase 2, between $16\frac{1}{2}$ and $22\frac{1}{2}$ months, combinations of words and gestures, and then of several words appeared, along with a seventh function, the informative function, used to exchange information between interlocutors. An utterance could fulfil a combination of functions, and the meaning of a given utterance was dialogue-dependent. Two types of combinations appeared, giving rise to two new functions: the pragmatic function, where language serves as a means of acting upon the outside world (combination of the instrumental, regulatory, and interactional functions), and the mathetic function, where language serves as a means of learning (combination of the personal, heuristic, and imaginative functions).

According to Halliday, there is also a third phase, not observed in Nigel. This phase corresponds to the child's entry into the adult system, where the number of functions is unlimited.

The idea of a universal acquisition order for the functions of language has been questioned and contested. Dale (1980), who analyzed the productions of 20 one year olds, showed that the number of functions does increase with

Table 4.3   Examples of relative clauses beginning with *qui* and *que* in French.[a]

Examples of *qui* clauses
Le président qui salue la foule (reversible)
The president that greets the crowd
La foule qui salue le président (reversible)
The crowd that greets the president
Le chat qui mange la souris (irreversible)
The cat that eats the mouse
Examples of *que* clauses
Le président que salue la foule (reversible)
The president that the crowd greets
La foule que salue le président (reversible)
The crowd that the president greets
La souris que mange le chat (irreversible)
The mouse that the cat eats

[a] In French, the *qui/que* opposition in relative clauses has nothing to do with the 'who/that' distinction in English. It is used to mark the grammatical function of the noun being replaced. Accordingly, *qui* at the beginning of a relative clause replaces the subject, while *que* replaces the direct object. Direct object replacement is achieved in English by changing the word order ('The president that the crowd greets') rather than by changing the relative pronoun.

age, but a given age cannot be said to correspond to a particular function. While Halliday's work has not always been confirmed, its heuristic value is nevertheless great in so far as it triggered a very fruitful research trend.

Strategies

A child learning to speak adopts a different attitude towards the verbal messages of the surrounding individuals than the one adopted by an adult who speaks the language perfectly. These attitudes in the child, which rely on certain regularities, are called strategies. Such strategies are defined by Oléron (1979) as devices employed by children to interpret (often complex) utterances on the basis of syntactic cues. It should be noted that these strategies are not used deliberately or consciously by children, but are in effect regularities in the way they approach speech.

This perspective has been used to study the comprehension of passive sentences, pronouns and relative clauses beginning with *que* and *qui* (that, which, who, whom) by French children (e.g. Ségui & Léveillé, 1977). Relative clause acquisition will be developed here. Table 4.3 gives some examples.

In relative clauses beginning with *qui* in French, the standard agent–action–patient order is not altered: the person doing the action is stated first, followed by the action performed, and finally, the recipient of the action. In relative clauses beginning with *que*, that order is modified: the recipient of the action comes first, followed by the action, and finally, the person performing the action. Relative clauses are said to be reversible when interchanging the agent and patient makes a semantically acceptable sentence. They are said to be irreversible when this swapping is semantically impossible.

The comprehension of *qui* clauses (whether or not they are reversible) does not cause any more of a problem than standard sentences in the active voice: a comprehension score of 100% is obtained between the ages of 3 years 7 months and 4 years 8 months.

In contrast, irreversible and reversible *que* clauses are not understood at the same age (3 years 7 months and 10 years 6 months, respectively). It looks as though, for irreversible *que* clauses, children use a strategy based on semantic information. For reversible ones, this same strategy leads to two different meanings, so children use a strategy based on the standard word order. This unfortunately leads them to an erroneous interpretation until a relatively late age (10 or 11).

Second Language Learning by Children and Adults

There are more people in the world who use two or more languages than there are who use only one. A second language can be learned under a wide variety of conditions, whether in the home or school, or early or late in life (cf. Perdue, 1995). Different learning conditions generate different kinds of 'bilinguality', a term used by Hamer and Blanc (1989) to refer to the psychological state of an individual who has access to at least two linguistic codes. The accessibility of the two codes varies along a number of psychological, cognitive, linguistic, sociological, and cultural dimensions, as summarized in Table 4.4.

This chapter will deal specifically with the role of age in the acquisition of bilinguality. The traditional question raised is what is the optimal age for learning a language. No single or straightforward answer can be given to this question, since second language acquisition depends on the sociocultural context in which the language is learned. The relative ease with which young children manage to master more than one language, compared to the substantial amount of effort required of adults learning a foreign language, has long been a puzzling question for researchers.

The hypothesized existence of an optimal language-acquisition period somewhere between infancy and puberty (cf. Lenneberg, 1967) has been examined extensively. This hypothesis seems to have been validated for a language's phonological features, which are more accurately and easily acquired by young children. The findings for the other aspects of language (syntax, semantics, and pragmatics) have not been conclusive as to the existence of any one, biologically determined age for second language learning. However, introducing a second language at an early age is advantageous because it makes for a longer learning period. In addition, the level of linguistic competence a young child must achieve in order to rank alongside same-age native speakers is not as great, making acquisition take less time. Accordingly, the cognitive benefits drawn from childhood bilin-

Table 4.4 Table summarizing the dimensions of bilinguality according to Hamer and Blanc (1989). L1 and L2 denote two languages spoken by a given individual

Analysis dimensions		Explanations
A. According to relationship between language and thought	1. Composite bilinguality	Unit in L1 ⎫ Equivalent ⎬ conceptual unit unit in L2 ⎭
	2. Coordinated bilinguality	Unit in L1=conceptual unit I Equivalent unit in L2=conceptual unit II
B. According to level of competency in the two languages	1. Balanced bilinguality 2. Dominant bilinguality	L1 competence=L2 competence L1 competence > L2 competence (with variations in degree of dominance)
C. According to age at which the two languages were acquired	1. Early simultaneous bilinguality 2. Early consecutive bilinguality 3. Adolescent bilinguality 4. Adult bilinguality	L1 and L2=native languages L2 acquired by age 10 or 11 L1=native language L2 acquired between ages 4 or 5 and 10 or 11 L2 acquired between ages 10 or 11 and 16 or 17 L2 acquired after age 16 or 17
D. According to relationship between the socio-cultural status of the two languages	1. Additive bilinguality 2. Subtractive bilinguality	L1 and L2 both high status, complementary role: bilinguality develops harmoniously L2 high status is detrimental to L1, competitive role: L2 acquired at the expense of L1
E. According to cultural identity and membership	1. Bicultural bilinguality 2. Monocultural bilinguality 3. L2–acquired bilinguality 4. Acculturated bilinguality	Dual cultural identity and membership Cultural allegiance and identity in L1 only Cultural allegiance to L2, cultural identity in L2 Hesitation about cultural allegiance Ill-defined cultural identity

Source: Reproduced with permission from Hamer, J. F. & Blanc, M. (1989). *Bilingualité et Bilinguisme*. Bruxelles: Mardaga.

guality suggest that, as far as second language learning is concerned, the earlier the better. This conclusion is reinforced by the fact that under certain circumstances, an additive type of bilinguality, which Lambert (1974) opposes to a subtractive type, can develop.

Additive bilinguality occurs when the home or community environment attributes a positive value to both languages. By learning the second language, the child adds a tool for communicating and thinking to his or her cultural equipment. In subtractive bilinguality, the two linguistic-cultural entities are competing. This type of bilinguality occurs whenever the community regards one of the languages as culturally and socio-economically superior to the other. In this case, the contribution of the second, more prestigious language is detrimental to the acquisition of the mother tongue. This situation exists for children of ethnolinguistic minority groups, whose schooling takes place in the national language. The effects of subtractive bilinguality are found at both the linguistic and cognitive levels, as well as in personality development.

Clearly, then, bilinguality can be beneficial for the overall development of the child. However, it is always dependent upon the sociocultural context. The psychosocial dimension, that is social values, attitudes, and linguistic and cultural prejudices, is a determining factor.

Acquisition of Reading and Writing

Acquisition of the written language is a major step in the life of a child: it determines proper adjustment and success in school. In line with speaking competence, writing competence is defined as an individual's ability to describe the world and communicate using the written code (Garton & Pratt, 1989). Like the spoken language, the written language has two facets: comprehension (reading) and production (writing), although the oral and written languages differ in a number of ways. The written language emerged late in the history of humanity (circa 3500 or 3000 BC) and is a relatively rare cultural creation (only a minority of the spoken communication and languages possess a written form). The native spoken language is acquired starting very early in life, during daily activities in the home. Moreover, it is not explicitly taught by adults and does not require any conscious learning efforts on the part of the child. The conditions under which the written language is acquired are quite different: the process begins later on (age 3 at the earliest), usually occurs in the schools, and is explicitly taught by adults with conscious learning efforts on the child's part.

This chapter will illustrate written language acquisition by looking essentially at the process of learning to read, and in particular with reading stages, learning difficulties, and teaching methods.

Learning to read can be considered to occur in four stages (cf. Frith, 1985; Goswami, 1993). The first step is logographic. The child guesses a word using cues within or around it. For example, the child guesses that the word is 'Coca Cola' when seeing the picture of the trademark, or the child recognizes his or her name by simply identifying the first letter. The second step is analogical. The child uses spelling knowledge of words he or she can already read, to produce the oral form of new words. For example, what is already known about the word 'good' is used to correctly oralize the word 'wood'. The third step is alphabetic. The child intentionally relies on the written code, while using phonology as the primary mediator (word recognition is based on sound recognition). During the fourth, orthographic step, the visual analysis of the word leads to its recognition without mandatory phonological mediation.

Certain children exhibit a learning disorder called dyslexia. Dyslexia refers to a difficulty or set of difficulties strictly limited to reading and encountered in intelligent children who do not have any apparent social or emotional problems and are not from an underprivileged social class. Dyslexia seems to be primarily due to a specific difficulty in breaking down the spoken language into its phonological constituents and mapping with letters. The hypothesis that certain information processing mechanisms (especially phonological ones) are dysfunctional, probably due to a hereditary disorder, has gained substantial support (cf. Rack, Hulme & Snowling, 1993). However, because no virus, specific brain lesion, or biochemical perturbation has been discovered to explain the origin of dyslexia, it is not a disease in the medical sense of the term (Siegel, 1993). The estimated rate of dyslexia in the literate population as a whole ranges from 3% to 6%.

Comprehension problems can also exist in reading even after several years of learning. This illiteracy problem is currently very widespread, particularly in adolescents and young adults. In many cases, reading comprehension deficits are not caused by a loss of reading skills, but by their inadequate and insufficient acquisition and a lack of automation of what has been learned.

Numerous debates have been launched about the various possible methods for teaching children how to read (ranging from the more analytical ones to the more global ones) and about how to determine which is the best. Still no scientific answer has been found to resolve this issue. Most authors acknowledge that the reading activity involves decoding, comprehension, and goal-oriented management of the reading process. All of these dimensions and their interactions must be studied and considered when choosing a method for teaching reading.

Communication and Language in the Elderly

Communication and language during adulthood and old age have not yet been studied in a systematic manner (cf. Bideaud, Houdé & Pédinielli, 1993). One can predict—and of course hope—that this type of research will undergo an upsurge in the years to come. However, research conducted in other areas such as memory, has provided some interesting information on this subject. For example, the short- and long-term memory capacity for storing information is know to have an impact on the individuals ability to enter into and pursue communication with another person. The decline in memory functions is generally considered as a critical factor in age-related effects.

The effects of aging have generally been studied by comparing the performance of young adults (age 25 to 35 or 40), or middle-aged adults (age 40 to 65 or 70), and elderly adults (70 or older) on immediate recall tasks where items from a read text must be retrieved (words and/or concepts). The effects of aging found in these studies appear to be quite complex.

A study by Simon et al. (1982) clearly showed that short-term recall of an intentionally memorized story does not decline with age. On the other hand, story recall under other conditions (making a value judgment about a text or stating one's opinion about a text) is better for young adults than for the elderly.

Dixon et al.'s (1984) experiment illustrates the effect of the structure of the task and of the subject's personal characteristics on memory performance in the elderly. In this text-recall experiment, elderly adults had trouble remembering the main ideas as well as the details of a text, regardless of whether the concepts were simple or complex. However, the differences between the young and elderly adults varied with their vocabulary level. Elderly subjects with a poor vocabulary had more trouble recalling the main ideas than younger subjects did, but no difference was noted for details. Elderly subjects with a good vocabulary did just as well as young adults on the main ideas but had greater difficulty with the details.

The role of prior knowledge in memorization was investigated by Hultsch and Dixon (1983). These authors asked young and elderly adults to read and recall biographies of movie stars (actors from different generations). The results showed that for the biographies of 'young' actors, the young adults recalled more information than did the elderly, while for the biographies of 'old' actors, the elderly adults recalled more information than did the younger ones.

With a few exceptions, the performance of young adults is superior to that of the older subjects on tasks involving the recall of memorized lists of numbers or words. However, when the recall no longer involves words but the concepts in a meaningful text, the differences are not so clear-cut. Factors other than recall capacity, such as the type of task and the characteristics of the subjects, play an important role.

Now that the stages of communication and language acquisition have been presented, we need to call upon some theories to help account for the patterns. The theories are illustrated with examples pertaining essentially to native language acquisition by the child. Their scope obviously extends beyond that of spoken language and adolescence, and their explicative power also applies to the other aspects of communication and language addressed in this chapter.

CAUSATION AND MECHANISMS OF COMMUNICATION AND LANGUAGE CHANGE

As for all other major kinds of learning, four main theoretical bases can be proposed to account for language acquisition: empiricism, innatism, constructivism, and functionalism. Empiricism emphasizes the subject's experience, innatism (the Chomskian and neo-Chomskian perspectives), the subject's genetic potential, constructivism (Piaget's perspective), the interaction between the subject's experience and genetic potential, and functionalism (Vygotsky's and Bruner's perspectives and pragmatic theories of language), the social meaning of learning for the subject. For each major theoretical trend, the place granted to the situation in the acquisition of communication and language will be indicated here.

Empiricism

In empiricism, the communication situation is a necessary object (it is the meeting place of the stimulus and the response), but its particular characteristics are irrelevant. In the field of language acquisition, empiricism was used as the prevailing perspective from Saint Augustin's time (AD 354–430) until the 1950s. Saint Augustin described the language acquisition process in a very simple way. No doubt referring to his own childhood, he wrote, 'When persons named something, and in doing so turned towards that thing, I saw—and remembered that they were referring to—that which could be designated by the name being pronounced . . . And so, by constantly hearing words as they occurred in various sentences, I was able little by little to understand what they meant; and once my mouth was used to these signs, I became able to say what I wanted to say' (our translation).

A modern version of Saint Augustin's ideas can be found in Watson's behaviorism of the early 1900s (1924). According to this point of view, nothing can be considered as specific to language. Language, like all other behaviors, can be explained in exactly the same manner as any set of responses to stimuli. Behaviorism relies on the postulate that all behavior corresponds to the establishment of a link between a stimulus and a response (S–R). This link is subject to the laws of classical Pavlovian conditioning: contiguity, repetition, habituation, extinction, and so on. A stimulus is any event which is external or internal to an organism and is likely to be captured by its receptors and trigger a reaction. A response is a unit of behavior, placed under the control of one or more stimuli. Figure 4.5 shows how a more complex analysis of the S–R system can account for the acquisition of certain verbal behaviors.

Language learning is thought to be very much like the learning of meaningless syllables, except that it is backed by imitation: the child mimics a model and is encouraged when performing correctly. Words rather than grammar are emphasized (cf. Osgood, 1953). Hence, this approach almost

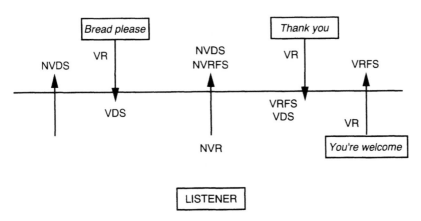

Figure 4.5 Illustration of the applications of the S–R system to the analysis of verbal response chains
Reproduced with permission from Hurtig, M. & Rondal, J. A. (1981). *Introduction à la psychologie de l'enfant.* Bruxelles: Mardaga
Note: The presence of a listener provides an occasion for the speaker to formulate a request in view of obtaining a piece of bread (the setting is at least two people having dinner). The presence of a listener is coded as a nonverbal discriminatory stimulus (NVDS). Next comes the verbal response (VR) 'Bread please', which serves as a verbal discriminatory stimulus (VDS) for the nonverbal response (NVR) of passing the bread to the speaker. Obtaining the bread is the nonverbal stimulus that reinforces (NVRFS) the speaker's request and serves at the same time as the discriminatory stimulus (NVDS) for the production of the response 'Thank you'. In other words, the likelihood that the speaker will behave in exactly the same way in future identical circumstances is increased by the fact that the request was successful. At the same time, the occasion arises for thanking the listener for his gesture. This is what the speaker does with the verbal response 'Thank you' (VR). This response serves as a verbal reinforcement stimulus (VRFS) for the listener. The reinforcement of the listener's behavior increases the likelihood that he will behave in the same way in future identical circumstances. The listener in turn reinforces the speaker's thanking response by means of the verbal response (VR) 'You're welcome'.

totally ignores the combinatory and generative possibilities, inherent to syntax, which enable children to continuously construct sentences they have never heard before and cannot be imitating, because they do not exist in the adult language (e.g. the pivot grammar, or erroneous creations such as 'drinked' for 'drank' in English, or *rier* for *rire* and *combatter* for *combattre* in French, which have the infinitive ending of another verb class).

Original Generative Grammar

The innatist perspective, the communication situation is a nonexistent object. It was the American linguist Noam Chomsky (1965) who proposed

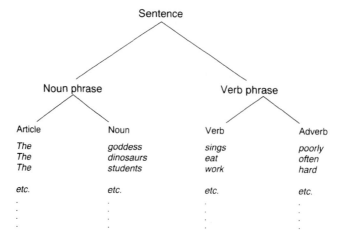

Figure 4.6   Some rules for generating utterances

this alternative to behaviorism: nativism. According to Chomksy, the acquisition of the language structure depends on a language acquisition device (LAD) whose basis is the universal grammar, innately possessed by all humans without learning.

In Chomsky's view, language is a grammar for which theory can provide a formal model. Language acquisition by the child amounts to learning that grammar. The structure of the language is thought to be derived in some sense from the general principles of cognition. For example, the subject–verb–object order of sentences corresponds to the order of daily experience: the one who carries out the action, the action, and the object to which it is applied. The analogy between known cognitive principles and grammatical structures is what is assumed to permit rapid language learning. The child is sensitive to linguistic marks because they reflect the cognitive categories he or she already possesses. To learn language, one must have already grasped what language describes.

According to McNeill (1970), who further developed Chomsky's theory in a language acquisition perspective, the child, like a linguist facing a foreign language, makes several assumptions about the grammar of the language. These assumptions are generated by an innate language acquisition device (LAD) and then tested against the linguistic productions of surrounding individuals. From a structural standpoint, the LAD contains the rules shared by all languages, concerning, for instance, word order, or the place (pre-posed or post-posed) of grammatical marks indicating a semantic relationship (cf. Slobin, 1982). The child's first assumption consists of hypothesizing that a sentence is a word, so the child expresses him/herself in one-word utterances. The pivot grammar constitutes the second assumption, which will be abandoned in turn for a more complex grammar. One specific characteristic of Chomsky's grammar is that it allows for the creation of an infinite number of utterances based on these rules (see Figure 4.6); hence the name generative grammar.

Table 4.5   Example of surface and deep structures

Take the following two utterances:
(1) The cat ate the mouse
(2) The mouse was eaten by the cat

(1) and (2) have different surfaces structures: the sounds
produced and the order of the words are different. They
have the same deep structure: the event described in (1)
and (2) is the same.

Chomksy's theory is a theory of competence, defined as the theoretical set of all utterances that can be generated by the grammar. Competence is opposed to performance, defined as the set of all utterances actually produced by the speakers of a given language.

The set of rules constituting the grammar is divided into three components: the syntactic component, the phonological component, and the semantic component. For each sentence, the phonological component produces a system of sounds which is related to the system of meanings produced by the semantic component. The phonological interpretation is applied to the surface structure, obtained by transformation of the deep structure to which the semantic component is applied. The syntactic component is divided into two sets of rules. The basic component contains the rules which produce the deep structure. The transformational component contains the rules enabling the transition from the deep structure to the surface structure. The notions of surface structure and deep structure can be better grasped by considering the example presented in Table 4.5

The LAD is programmed to take the surface structure of any natural language and recognize its deep structure or universal grammar. It is used to extract the grammatical rules specific to a given language, and thereby allows the speaker to correctly produce all possible utterances in that language (see the notion of competence). No preliminary nonlinguistic knowledge is required; no communication with some privileged addressee is necessary. The only thing the child needs is to be in contact with the language, and fragmented samples without much context are sufficient. The sole constraints for linguistic development are related to mental limitations in performance such as the childs limited attention span and memory capacity.

Slobin (1982) attempted to validate this position by means of cross-cultural studies, that is by comparing the linguistic development of children from very different cultures such as western cultures, Samoan, Kaluli, and Maya. Parental behavior regarding child language differs considerably in these diverse societies. Some consider the child to be initially endowed with verbal communication, while others do not even raise the question. Apparently, no matter what the parent's attitude is towards child language, whether it be teaching-oriented or totally indifferent, the language is learned anyway. For Chomsky's followers, this type of finding is interpreted as an argument in favor of the existence of an innate language acquisition device.

We now have two theories about language acquisition. One, behaviorism, is impossible; the other, nativism, is miraculous. The theories we are now going to analyze represent attempts to bridge the gap between the impossible and the miraculous.

Neo-Chomskian Theories and Constructivism

For these two perspectives, the communication situation is an embarrassing object. Indeed, although the results obtained have either suggested or proven that the communication situation plays a definite role in the acquisition of language and communication, the theoretical constructs do not really include it as a fundamental element.

Neo-Chomskian theories

It was while studying the meaning of words that researchers were confronted with the potential role of the communication situation (cf. Bramaud du Boucheron, 1982). The following example of a neo-Chomskian theory points out some of the contradictory aspects of the issues examined in this type of research.

Starting in 1973, a large number of studies were conducted in the framework of Clark's (1973) theory of semantic features. The basic postulate of this theory is that the definition of a word is composed of minimal units of meaning (corresponding to the inherent features in the original theory). This very rich theory is highly effective for operationalizing concepts and making various predictions about the order of acquisition of words in the same semantic field, or about the meaning children attribute to words. From this theory, one can deduce five hypotheses, all of which have been tested experimentally.

1. Overextension hypothesis. Children incorrectly attribute meanings to words by overextension. The basis of these overextensions is perceptual (for example, 'tutu' is first used to refer to a train and then to all vehicles with an engine; 'wa-wa' is first used to refer to a dog and then to all animals).
2. Feature composition hypothesis. The semantic features defining the meaning of a word are acquired by successive additions and combinations.
3. General and specific features hypothesis. Within a given semantic field, say for example verbs of possession or movement, the features comprising the meaning of a word are acquired in the general-to-specific order. A large number of studies have dealt with the acquisition of verbs. The verb 'take', for instance (whose meaning is composed of the Exchange-of-Object feature) is acquired before 'buy' (Exchange-of-Object + Exchange-of-Money), in such a way that the child first attributes the meaning of 'take' to 'buy'.

4. Perceptual features hypothesis. The initial features composing the meaning of a word are perceptual in origin (e.g. the meaning of 'ball' would consist of the features 'round' and 'red').
5. Transparency hypothesis. The way a child uses a word is tightly linked to the meaning he or she attributes to it: the referent of a word always has all of the properties of the meaning it has for the child. This excludes the use of a word in a situation which only partially corresponds to the attributed meaning.

The above hypotheses have been both partially validated and partially invalidated. The semantic feature theory in fact has many counter-examples. Several different factors have been used in an attempt to explain them, including the characteristics of the communication situation and the notion of features which are important for the child, and features which are part of the child's experience. However, while each new experiment has pointed out some of the limitations of the theory, no one has yet proposed a new theoretical framework which effectively integrates the role of the communication situation. Note that the same problems have been encountered in the study of the production and comprehension of metaphors (see Gombert, 1990). For certain authors, metaphors are understood very early (at approximately the age of 4), whereas for others, their comprehension comes much later (age 9 or 10). It is indeed very difficult to account for metaphors if word meanings are considered to be composed of inherent features. The characteristic property of metaphors is precisely that the meaning changes with the situation (e.g. 'This man is a lion' and 'The ship plows the seas').

Constructivism

The author most often associated with constructivism is of course Jean Piaget. For constructivists, language, like all other major functions (such as perception and memory), is acquired through the subject's activity and exchanges with the environment. Language acquisition is thus achieved via the interaction between the subject's genetic potentials (of which his or her activity is a testimony) and his or her experiences (i.e. exchanges with the surroundings).

For Piagetian pyscholinguists such as Hermine Sinclair de Zwart the primary components of language are structural and representative; they act as the motor of a machine. The minor aspects are contextual and communicative; they act as the operating instructions of the machine. Concepts borrowed from formal linguistic theories become indispensable, providing a sort of algebra of language. Here, language acquisition is subordinate to the exercise of the symbolic (or semiotic) function. The symbolic function serves to represent currently nonperceivable objects or events, by evoking them via differentiated symbols or signs. The symbolic function allows the child to execute five main types of behavior, which appear in the order listed below.

Box 4.3   An example from one of Sinclair de Zwart's studies

Two groups of children are selected, one obviously preoperational, i.e. with no notion of conversation, and one which understands this notion and can explain it using reversibility and compensation arguments. The two groups are shown pairs of objects (e.g. one big and one small; a set of 4 or 5 marbles and a set of 2 marbles; an object which is both shorter and wider than another, etc.) and simply asked to describe each pair, one of which is given to one character, and the other, to another character, without any mention of conservation. The two groups consistently express themselves in totally different ways: in the same cases where the first group uses nothing but 'scalars' (in the linguistic sense of the term), 'He has a big one, and he has a small one' or 'She has a lot and she has a little,' the second group uses 'vectors,' 'That one has a bigger one than the other' or 'One has more,' etc. In cases where the first group only considers one dimension at a time, the second group says, 'This pencil is longer and narrower,' etc. In short, there is a striking correlation between the way children express themselves and the reasoning mode they use. A second study demonstrated the same close tie between the stages of development of seriation and the structure of the terms used.

---

1. Deferred imitation of a previously attended scene (e.g. imitating the cries of a child who has just left).
2. Pretending (e.g. pretending to sleep).
3. Drawing: graphic representations, a midpoint between play and mental imagery (e.g. drawing a man).
4. Mental images: reproductive and then anticipatory internal imitation (e.g. evoking or imagining a scene).
5. Language: verbal representation (e.g. saying 'meow' for a cat). This stage precedes the use of language as an arbitrary sign system where the child refers to a cat by saying 'cat', a conventional sign which holds no analogy with the designated object.

It is Sinclair de Zwart's (1967) work that best represents the Piagetian perspective in the area of language acquisition. This research focuses on the relationship between language and intelligence or cognition. Numerous studies have been conducted on the period around the age of 6. In Piaget's theory, this period marks the beginning of the concrete operations stage and the appearance of the first conversations. The concept of conversation is used from a cognitive point of view to distinguish 'conserving' children from 'non-conserving' ones. For physical matter, for example, a child is said to be conserving if he or she understands that when the shape of a ball of modelling clay is modified (by flattening it out or breaking it up) it contains the same amount of matter as before the transformation. The child must also be able to correctly explain this constancy. The concept of conservation can be applied to many domains like length, number, area, liquid, volume, and so on. The question raised by Piagetians deals with the relationship between cognitive development and language development. Box 4.3 briefly presents an example from one of Sinclair de Zwart's studies. The Piagetians conclude from this type of experiment that language is not the source of intelligence, but on the contrary, is structured by it.

The Chomskian, neo-Chomskian, and Piagetian perspectives reduce language to grammar and do not take the communication situation into account. The advocates of this view have a certain number of arguments in their support. It is a safe view, void of ambiguity: words are labels attributed to facts or preexisting images; words have one and only one meaning that anyone can recognize. These limitations have always been presented as necessary from a methodological standpoint. The limits of the 'studiable' were defined by Saussure (1960, 1916) in his statement that the science of language as the study of grammar can do without the other elements of language, but only if those other elements are not brought into the picture.

Other authors claiming to be functionalists defend the idea that the limits of the 'studiable' can be placed beyond language, in speech. They consider that the explanation of the use and acquisition of language as a communication system does not reside solely in its structure, but must also be sought in the communication context, and in the relationship between that structure and that context.

Functional Theories

In the functional perspective, the communication situation becomes an interesting object. It is one of the fundamental parts of the explanation of the development of communication and language. The main idea (cf. Ervin-Tripp & Mitchell-Kernan, 1977) is that by focusing on the communication situation, it is possible to define a set of prerequisites likely to contribute to progress in language-acquisition research: study natural conversation, analyze larger units than the sentence, consider the extralinguistic context, take variability across individuals or social groups into account, and finally, consider the diverse functions of language. Indeed, language is not just a grammar; it is also a set of strategies used by children to structure their social actions and to control and carry out communicative activities.

Studies which take the communication situation into account are conducted in the framework of an interactionist development theory (like Vygotsky's or Bruner's) or in the framework of pragmatic psycholinguistics, that is a psycholinguistics which is more interested in the utilization, usages, and functions of language than in its structure. This perspective approaches the problem of acquisition by asking the question, 'What does language do and what do children use it for?'

Vygotsky's and Bruner's perspectives

For Vygotsky (1985) a linguistic sign begins as, and always remains, a means of attaining a social end, a means of influencing others. It is not until later that it becomes a means of influencing oneself. Moreover, for Vygotsky, the essential function of language in adults and children alike is communication, and a child's initial speech is purely social. The concept of interaction format developed by Bruner is also of particular interest here. For Bruner (1983) the adult is constantly interpreting the child's behaviors and tends to standardize certain forms of joint action. It is this standard form of a joint action that Bruner calls a 'format'. A format is a typical exemplar of a social relation, like the peek-a-boo game played with young children.

In this perspective, language is the tool, the instrument of cognition. Language thus precedes cognition (this viewpoint is the opposite of an innatist or constructivist one). To speak is to be engaged in a behavior governed by rules. From a developmental viewpoint, this means studying how the child produces and interprets language through a set of rules, conventions, and shared knowledge which subtend, not only verbal communication, but also all social activities. Language acquisition thus implies that the child be aware of these rules, conventions, and shared knowledge, and that he or she manifest linguistic behavior in accordance with them. Language acquisition requires the establishment of relationships between the social rules and the language structures.

The Oxford School and Speech Act Theory

Current pragmatic theories converge in many points with theories of development like Vygotsky's and Bruner's (cf. Bronckart, 1985; Deleau, 1990; Bernicot, 1994b). Following Austin's work (1962), Searle (1979) defined five functions or possible uses of language, called 'speech acts.'

1. Assertives, such as stating or assuming: the speaker commits to the existence of a state of affairs or the truth of an expressed position.
2. Directives, such as ordering or suggesting: the speaker attempts to make the listener do something.
3. Commissives, such as promising or threatening: the speaker is forced to adopt a given behavior in the future.
4. Expressives: the speaker expresses a psychological state (e.g. satisfaction or fear) about the state of the world.
5. Declarations: once accomplished, declarations establish a correspondence between their content and reality (e.g. for an employer, saying to someone that he is employed, or for a teacher, telling a student that she has passed).

From a language-learning standpoint, the speech act most frequently studied is the directive, commonly called a request. Direct requests are distinguished from indirect requests. A request is direct when the formal characteristics of the utterance correspond exactly to the social act accomplished. In this case, the speaker 'says' what he or she 'means' (e.g. 'Give me the pen'). A request is indirect when the formal characteristics of the

Table 4.6 Examples of productions of 6 and 7 year olds

Categories	Action request	Information requests
Direct order	Give me Minnie back	Tell me where the flowers are or Where are the flowers?
Embedded imperative	Can you give me Minnie back?	Can you tell me where the flowers are?
Expression of a need or a wish	I want you to give me Minnie back	I'd like you to tell me where the flowers are
Permission	Could I have Minnie back?	Could I know where the flowers are?
Directive question	Where did you hide Minnie? Did you kidnap Minnie?	What happened to the flowers? Have you seen Minnie?
Hint	I've to take Minnie back	We can't find the flowers
Negotiation	If you give me Minnie back I won't tell the police	Be a good kid, tell me where the flowers are
Justification	Give me Minnie back, she's not your friend	Where are the flowers? They're for Minnie

Source: Reproduced with permission from Bernicot, J. & Mahrokhian, A. (1988). La production des demandes par les enfants: le rôle de la nature de la demande et du statut de l'interlocuteur. *Revue Internationale de Psychologie Sociale*, 1, 391–407. [Reproduit avec l'autorisaton des Editions Privat, Toulouse—extrait de la Revue Internationale de Psychologie Sociale, No. 1/1988.]

utterance do not totally correspond to the social act accomplished. In this case, the speaker 'means' something other than what he or she 'says' (e.g. 'Can you give me that pen?', 'Does your pen still work?', or 'I can't find anything to write with.'). Table 4.6 gives some examples of the productions of 6- and 7-year-old children.

Request production has given rise to a coherent body of research on children between the ages of 2 and 10 (cf. Bernicot, 1992). The production of requests, and in particular their directness or indirectness, also depends on certain characteristics of the communication situation, including the content of the request (action, information, right, favor) and the type of listener (friend, enemy, social role). Moreover, in a given situation, producing an effective request involves making a subtle trade-off between two paradoxical rules: the more direct an utterance, the more understandable it is for the addressee, and the more indirect an utterance the more acceptable it is. In learning to make this subtle adjustment, children go back and forth between the two rules. Effective request production thus involves becoming skilful at applying these rules and understanding the effects of their combinations. For example, if a speaker anticipates the addressee's cooperativeness, then the form of the request will be more or less direct; if the speaker is addressing someone of a higher status, then the form of the request will be more indirect. Children seem to acquire a certain number of rules of this type between the ages of 4 and 6.

These rules should not be confused with the precursors of good manners. Clearly, the learning how to request is not learning how to be polite. It is not a question of knowing how to say 'Hello', 'Please' and 'May I . . .', but rather of learning, in order to realize one's intention in an appropriate situation, to address an appropriate linguistic form, to an appropriate listener. Research on requests has shown once again that language acquisition must be studied within a communicative situation framework, for the communication situation is not a mere medium but an integral part of language production, defined by both the situation and the utterance.

CONCLUSION

In conclusion, remember that this brief chapter is but an initial approach to the problem of the development of communication and language. It began with definitions of the basic concepts employed in this field: language functions, language activities, linguistic forms, nonverbal communication, and the communication situation itself. Then, the major steps which, since ancient times, have led us to our current state of knowledge were described. After an analysis of the research methods and their merits and shortcomings, the principal stages in the development of language and communication in the child, the adult, and the elderly were presented. Emphasis was placed on the acquisition of the mother tongue. Other topics addressed were second language learning by children and adults, now crucial due to the increasing mobility of the worlds' populations; written language acquisition, so essential to success in school and in society in general; and issues related specifically to the elderly.

With respect to theoretical considerations, the field of communication and language has followed the same patterns as psychology as a whole. The conditions of language acquisition and use include neurological maturation, socio-cultural milieu, and differences among individuals and how they are raised and educated. The impact of these conditions has been assessed in many studies. It is generally agreed that all of these factors indeed play a role, but the respective weight of each differs according to the theoretical viewpoint of the author. In the empiricist view, language is acquired through a general associative learning capacity (Richelle, 1976); in the innatist view, it is acquired via the action of a specialized structure specific to humans (McNeill, 1970). In the constructivist view, communication and language is acquired like all other cognitive functions, through the subject's activity and exchanges with the environment (Sinclair de Zwart, 1967). Finally, a more recent view stresses the link between the child's socialization and the development of language and communication (Oléron, 1979; Beaudichon, 1982; Bernicot, 1992).

The scientific study of the acquisition of communication and language by the child is less than 30 years old. It has undergone rapid theoretical growth and given rise to an impressive number of studies. It is currently a very exciting line of research, where so much remains to be discovered.

ACKNOWLEDGMENTS

Special thanks are extended to Vivian Waltz for translating this chapter.

REFERENCES

Arnauld, A. & Lancelot, C. (1969). *Grammaire générale et raisonnée*. With remarks by Duclos, preface by Michel Foucault. Paris: Republications Paulet (first edition: 1660).

Austin, J. L. (1962). *How To Do Things with Words*. Cambridge, MA: Harvard University Press.

Beaudichon, J. (1982). *La communication sociale chez l'enfant*. Paris: Presses Universitaires de France.

Bernard, C. (1815). *Introduction à l'étude de la médecine expérimentale*. Paris: J. B. Baillère et Fils. New edition in 1965, Paris: Hammarion.

Bernicot, J. (1992). *Les actes de langage chez l'enfant*. Paris: Presses Universitaires de France.

Bernicot, J. (1994a). Les méthodes d'étude de l'acquisition du langage. L'acquisition du langage: étapes et théories. In J. Crépault (Ed.), *Développement et intégration des fonctions cognitives. Cours de Pyschologie*, Vol. 3 (pp. 292–206, 408–426). Paris: Dunod.

Bernicot, J. (1994b). Speech acts in young children: Vygotsky's contribution. *European Journal of Psychology of Education*, **9**, 311–320.

Bernicot, J. & Legros, S. (1987). Direct and indirect directives: What do young children understand? *Journal of Experimental Child Psychology*, **7**, 267–293.

Bernicot, J. & Mahrokhian, A. (1989). To ask and to insist after a refusal: How do 6–7-year-old children proceed? *International Journal of Psychology*, **24**, 409–428.

Bertoncini, J. & Mehler, J. (1978). Syllables as units in infant speech perception. *Infant Behavior and Development*, **4**, 247–260.

Bideaud, J. , Houdé, O. & Pédinielli, J. L. (1993). *L'homme en développement*. Paris: Presses Universitaires de France.

Bloom, L. (1973). *One Word at a Time*. La Haye: Mouton.

Boysson-Bardies, B. (1984). Discernable differences in the babbling of infants according to target language. *Journal of Child Language*, **11**, 1–15.

Braine, M. (1963). The ontogeny of English phrase structure: the first phase. *Language*, **39**, 1–14.

Bramaud du Boucheron, G. (1982). *Le développement de la mémoire sémantique*. Paris: Presses Universitaires de France.

Bronckart, J. P. (1976). *Genèse et organisation des formes verbales chez l'enfant*. Bruxelles: Dessart et Mardaga.

Bronckart, J. P. (1985). Vygotsky une oeuvre en devenir. In B. Schneuwly & J. P. Bronckart (Eds), *Vygotsky aujourd'hui*. Neuchâtel: Delachaux et Niestlé.

Brown, R. (1973). *A First Language*. Cambridge, MA: Harvard University

Press.

Bruner, J. S. (1983). The acquisition of pragmatic commitments. In R. M. Golinkoff (Ed.), *The Transition from Prelinguistic to Linguistic Communication*. Hillsdale, NJ: Erlbaum.

Carmichael, L. (1946). *Manual of Child Psychology*. New York: Wiley.

Chomsky, N. (1965). *Aspects of the Theory of Syntax*. Cambridge: MIT Press.

Clark, E. V. (1973). What's in the word? On the child's acquisition of semantics in his first language. In T. E. More (Ed.), *Cognitive Development and the Acquisition of Language*. New York: Academic Press.

Cosnier, J. (1982). Communications et langages gestuels. In J. Cosnier, J. Couon, A. Berrendonner & C. Orecchioni (Eds), *Les voies du langage*. Paris: Dunod.

Dale, Ph. (1980). Is early pragmatic development measurable? *Journal of Child Language*, **7**, 1–12.

Darwin, C. (1877). Biographical sketch of an infant. *Mind*, **2**, 285–294.

Deleau, M. (1990). *Les origines sociales du développement mental*. Paris: Armand Colin.

Dixon, R. A. et al. (1984). Verbal ability and text structure effects on adults' age difference in text recall. *Journal of Verbal Learning and Verbal Behavior*, **23**, 569–578.

Edward, J. A. & Lampert, M. D. (Eds) (1993). *Talking Data. Transcription and Coding in Discourse Research*. Hillsdale, NJ: Erlbaum Associates.

Ervin-Tripp, S. & Mitchell-Kernan, C. (1977). *Child Discourse*. New York: Academic Press.

Frith, U. (1985). Beneath surface of developmental dyslexia. In K. E. Patterson, J. Marshall & M. Coltheart (Eds), *Surface Dyslexia. Cognitive and Neuropsychological Studies of Phonological Reading*. Hillsdale, NJ: Erlbaum.

Flecher, P. & MacWhinney, B. (1995). *The Handbook of Child Language*. Oxford: Blackwell.

Garton, A. F. & Pratt, C. (1989). Learning to be literate. *The Development of Spoken and Written Language*. Oxford: Blackwell.

Gombert, J. E. (1990). *Le développement métalinguistique*. Paris: Presses Universitaires de France.

Goswami, U. C. (1993). Towards an interactive analogy model of reading development: Decoding vowel graphemes in beginning reading. *Journal of Experimental Child Psychology*, **56**, 443–475.

Grégoire, A. (1937, 1947). *L'apprentissage du langage. Vol. 1: Les deux premières années. Vol. 2: La troiséme et les suivantes*. Bibliothèque Philosophie et Lettres, Université de Liège.

Gvozdev, A. (1949). *Formation chez l'enfant de la structure grammaticale de la langue russe*. Akademica Pedagogika Nauka, Moscow.

Hall, G. S. (1883). Contents of children's minds. *Princeton Review*, **11**, 249–272.

Halliday, M. A. K. (1985). *An Introduction to Functional Grammar*. London: Arnold.

Hamer, J. F. & Blanc, M. (1989). *Billingualitè et Bilinguisme*. Bruxelles: Mardaga.

Hérodote (1980). *Histoires* (p. 59) Paris: François Maspéro.

Hultsch, D. F. & Dixon, R. A. (1983). The role of pre-experimental knowledge in text processing in adulthood. *Experimental Aging Research*, **9**, 17–22.

Hurtig, M. & Rondal, J. A. (1981). *Introduction á la psychologie de l'enfant*. Bruxelles: Mardaga.

Itard, J. (1964). Mémoire et rapport sur Victor de l'Aveyron. In L. Malson, *Les enfants sauvages*. Paris: Union Générale d'Editions (first edition: 1807).

Lambert, W. E. (1974). Culture and language as factors in learning and education. In F. Aboud and R. D. Meade (Eds), *Cultural Factors in Learning*. Bellingham: Western Washington State College.

Lenneberg, E. (1967). *Biological Foundations of Language*. New York: Wiley.

Léopold, W. (1939). *Speech Development of a Bilingual Child: Vocabulary Development in the First Two Years*, Vol. 1. Evanston, Ill: Northwestern University Press.

Léopold, W. (1947). *Speech Development of a Bilingual Child: Sound Learning in the First Two Years*, Vol. 2. Evanston, Ill: Northwestern University Press.

Léopold, W. (1949). *Speech Development of a Bilingual Child: Grammar and General Problems in the First Two Years*, Vol. 3. Evanston, Ill: Northwestern University Press.

Lock, A. (1978). *Action, Gesture and Symbol: the Emergence of Language*. New York: Academic Press.

Marcos, H. & Bernicot, J. (1994). Addressee co-operation and request reformulation in young children. *Journal of Child Language*, **21**, 677–692.

McNeill, D. (1970). *The Acquisition of Language*. New York: Harper.

Mehler, J. , Bertoncini, J., Barriére, M. & Gerschenfeld, D. (1978). Infant recognition of mother's voice. *Perception*, **7**, 491–497.

Moreau, M. L. & Richelle, M. (1981). *L'acquisition du langage*. Bruxelles: Mardaga.

Nelson, K. (1973). Structure and strategies in learning to talk. *Monographs of the Society for Research in Child Development*, **38**, (no. 149).

Oléron, P. (1976). L'acquisition du langage. In H. Gratiot-Alphandéry and R. Zazzo (Eds), *Traité de psychologie de l'enfant, tome 6: les modes d'expression*. Paris: Presses Universitaires de France.

Oléron, P. (1976). *L'acquisition du langage*. Paris: Presses Universitaires de France.

Osgood, C. E. (1953). *Method and Theory in Experimental Psychology*. New York: Oxford University Press.

Pavlovitch, M. (1920). *Le langage enfantin: acquisition du serbe et du français par un enfant serbe*. Paris: Champion.

Peirce, C. S. *Ecrits sur le signe*. Translated and commented by G. Deledalle (1978). Paris: Editions du Seuil.

Perdue, C. (1995). *L'acquisition du français et de l'anglais par des adultes.* Paris: CNRS Editions.

Piaget, J. (1964). *La formation du symbole chez l'enfant.* Neuchâtel: Delachaux et Niestlé. (first edition, 1945).

Piatelleli-Palmarini, M. (Ed.) (1979). 'Théories du langage et théories de l'apprentissage. Le débat entre Jean Piaget et Noam Chomsky (pp. 255–257). Paris: Editions de Seuil.

Plante, P. (1993a). FX—*La programmation en faisceaux.* Centre ATO.CI, Université du Québec à Montréal.

Plante, P. (1993b). FXS—*Les faisceaux de saillance.* Centre ATO.CI, Université du Québec à Montréal.

Rack, J. P., Hulme, C. & Snowling, H. J. (1993). Learning to read: A theoretical synthesis. In H. W. Reese (Ed.), *Advances in Child Development and Behavior,* Vol. 24. New York: Academic Press.

Richelle, M. (1976). *L'acquisition du langage.* Bruxelles and Liège: Dessart et Mardaga.

Rousseau, J. J. (1964). *Emile ou l'éducation.* Paris: Garnier (first edition: 1762).

Saussure, F. (1960). *Cours de linguistique générale.* Paris: Payot (first edition: 1916).

Searle, J. R. (1979). *Expression and Meaning.* Cambridge: Cambridge University Press.

Ségui, J. & Léveillé, M. (1977). Une étude sur la compréhension des phrases par l'enfant. *Enfance,* **1**, 105–115.

Siegel, L. S. (1993). The development of reading. In H. W. Reese (Ed.), *Advances in Child Development and Behavior,* Vol. 24. New York: Academic Press.

Simon, E. W. et al. (1982). Orienting task effects on text recall in adulthood. *Journal of Gerontology,* **31**, 575–580.

Sinclair de Zwart, H. (1967). *Acquisition du langage et développement de la pensée: sous-système linguistiques et opérations concrètes.* Paris: Dunod.

Slobin, D. I. (1982). Universal and particular in the acquisition of language. In E. Wanner & L. Gleitman, (Eds), *Language Acquisition: the State of the Art.* Cambridge: Cambridge University Press.

Suzuki, R. (1992). Rôle des scripts et acquisition de la demande en japonais. In J. Beaudichon, J. Bernicot, & H. Marcos (Eds), La communication prélinguistique et linguistique. *Bulletin de Psychologie,* **409**, 42–50.

Van Der Straten, A. (1991). *Premiers gestes, premiers mots.* Paris: Editions du Centurion.

Vygotsky, L. S. (1985). *Pensée et langage.* Paris: Editions Sociales de France.

Watson, J. (1924). *Behaviorism.* Chicago: University of Chicago Press.

Chapter 5

Cognitive Development

Andreas Demetriou

University of Cyprus

INTRODUCTION

Basic Concepts and Definitions

The psychology of cognitive development studies the development of cognitive functions, processes, and abilities. That is, it examines the acquisition and transformation of those processes that enable humans to (i) understand the world in which they live, (ii) cope with the problems that the world presents to them and (iii) store and organize their knowledge and experience about the world.

In simple terms, *understanding* may be defined as the process of making sense of something. But what is making sense? First of all, to make sense of an object, situation, or event one needs to build a representation, a mental model that somehow involves the characteristics of the entity represented. For example, a mental image of an animal will represent the animal *cat* if it involves all those characteristics which make one person think of a real cat. The same is true for many other representations we use to refer to world entities, such as the words of our language, mathematical symbols, and so on. Second, to generate understanding, a representation must not stand alone, it must be connected to other representations. Thus, understanding may be better defined as the process of interconnecting representations rather than simply activating isolated representations, and is therefore by

Life-Span Developmental Psychology
Edited by A. Demetriou, W. Doise and C. F. M. van Lieshout. © 1998 John Wiley & Sons Ltd.

definition associated with the processes that enable the thinker to specify how representations are interrelated. These processes are denoted by the terms *reasoning* or *inference*.

What is *problem-solving?* We first define *a problem* as a situation in which a kind of imbalance, disturbance, or gap exists, and which calls for a response that will reinstate the balance, remove the disturbance, or fill in the gap. So defined, a problem may come from any sector of the world. For instance, it may be related to a change in the behavior of another person which, once understood, allows us to adjust our behavior accordingly. Or it may be related to a change in the behavior or appearance of an object or complex of objects, such as, for example, when a driver drives at a constant speed on a free road and suddenly sees at a close distance a child jumping into the road. Or it may be any of the problems teachers give to students at school, such as arithmetic, science, or language problems. Thus, problem-solving refers to all those processes humans employ to generate answers or assemble and deploy responses with the aim, in general, to transform a situation such that a goal or satisfactory condition can be more easily achieved.

Acquisition of knowledge and expertise refers to two things. With regard to knowledge, it refers to increases in the information one has about the world. For instance, we get to know more about the weather, other countries, machines, other people or ourselves as we grow older. Expertise refers to an increase in the number of skills one has in relation to a given realm of the world or a given category of problems, and an improvement in the facility and the flexibility with which these skills can be used. For instance, with time and practice a doctor becomes more proficient in the diagnosis and treatment of illness and a chess player becomes more skillful and flexible at his game.

Understanding, problem-solving, and the acquisition of knowledge and expertise are closely interrelated. Understanding involves the construction, activation, and interconnection of representations which stand as models or tokens of our knowledge about the world. At the same time, representations acquire their meaning as a result of the processes through which they are interconnected, such that the acquisition of knowledge and expertise cannot be wholly separated from the development of understanding. Finally, both the development of understanding and the acquisition of knowledge and expertise can be seen as a kind of problem-solving. Thus, to understand means to use your skills in manipulating mental representations and then to apply these skills to representations which are already available in order to generate answers or assemble solutions to problems, whether physical, social, or personal.

Understanding, problem-solving, and the acquisition of knowledge and expertise are the focus of a number of fields in psychology. Cognitive psychology and cognitive science attempt to highlight these processes in their mature, adult state. Developmental psychology, by definition, adopts a developmental perspective: it focuses on the evolution of these processes with the aim to answer three types of questions: (i) what changes with development, (ii) how changes occur, (iii) why changes occur. Developmental researchers try, first, to map the conditions of understanding, problem-solving, knowledge acquisition and expertise at the successive phases of life. That is, they examine how various aspects or states of the world, such as the very existence and nature of things, their number, their movement in space and causal interactions, or social interactions between persons and ensuing inner experiences are understood from infancy through adulthood and they try to specify the underlying processes of thought and reasoning. Next, they attempt to ascertain those factors responsible for any changes in these processes from one age phase to the next. For instance, how are maturation and the environment related to the changes in a certain aspect of understanding, problem-solving, or knowledge acquisition? Finally, they look at the mechanisms that bring the changes about, that is, what processes mediate the possible effects of maturation and the environment so that a change in understanding, problem-solving, and knowledge acquisition begins, evolves, and arrives at a conclusion? A concept that dominated the field in this regard is the concept of *stage*. Technically speaking, stage refers to a phase of life which bears a particular set of characteristics and abilities which distinguish this phase from the preceding and the following phases. Thus, stage theorists attempted to specify what stages exist in cognitive development, how they are organized, and why and how transition occurs from the one stage to the next. In the section below we will outline the basic characteristics of the methods researchers use to study cognitive development.

Methods for Studying Cognitive Development

The study of cognitive development is a relatively old field in developmental psychology (see Weinert & Weinert, ch. 1 this volume) and it is very wide in the phenomena that it covers. As a result, it is very difficult to describe the methods used in this field in general terms because they vary both as a function of the historical period or the phenomena of interest. Thus, in this section we will only describe the general rationale that guides the design of cognitive developmental studies and present more details about particular methods in each of the various sections to follow. The presentation will be organized around the three types of questions that developmental psychologists attempt to answer.

   1. *What kinds of concepts can thinkers understand and what kinds of problems can they solve as they develop?* To answer this question, two research strategies are generally used. The first is the *same problem–different answers strategy*. That is, the same problem or task is presented to persons at different ages and the answer or solution given by the subjects at each age is taken as a basis for charting the pattern of development of the concept or skill of interest. For instance, persons are given objects similar to each other in some respects and different in others and they are asked to classify them. Or they are asked to draw a house or a man or the earth itself. Their

performance is allocated to different categories or levels according to the qualities and the complexity and the methods of their productions. Then the developmental pattern of these productions is established by specifying what productions can be constructed at the successive years of age. For instance, what types of classification or drawings can be constructed at the age of 3, 7, 10, and 13 years? The second is the *different problem–different answer strategy*. That is, a set of problems is constructed which differs systematically in one or more dimensions. For example, persons of different ages are given arithmetic problems to solve which require them to operate on single, two, and three digit numbers. Or they are given problems which involve no, one or two unknowns. In this kind of problem, the developmental pattern is established by specifying which type of problems can be solved at each age.

   2. *How does change occur?* In the mind of many developmentalists (see Fischer & Bidell, 1998; van Geert, 1994) this question is equivalent to asking: Is cognitive development stage-like? That is, does it occur in spurts or in a smooth and continuous fashion? The methods summarized above can be used to answer these questions. That is, if children of different ages provide radically different answers or productions to the problems given to them this would indicate that the mind is organized or structured differently at different ages. To specify how organizational or structural changes occur, cognitive developmentalists try to specify the rate or speed of change throughout the age period of interest. For example, is there any acceleration of development at a given age such that a given process or ability is quickly transformed from a given level L to the next more advanced level L+1 and it then stays at the new level for the period of time which presumably corresponds to this level? To answer this question researchers study the age period of interest by gathering data at the appropriate intervals by any of the methods described above. Then they chart productions as a function of age in order to specify the nature of change. For example, changes of the type shown in graph a of Figure 5.1 would suggest that development is continuous; changes of the type shown in graph b of this figure would suggest that development is stagelike. There are many variations of this general method. For instance, instead of researchers simply charting answers and productions as they are provided spontaneously by persons at different ages, persons may receive practice and specify their sensitivity to it at different periods. It is assumed that at phases of stage reorganization persons would be more sensitive to practice and thus more prone to change quickly as a result of it as contrasted to phases at which a stage is rather well established (Fischer & Bidell, 1998).

   3. *Why does change occur?* This question is equivalent to asking 'does a factor A or B cause development?' For example, does the education of the parents affect the rate of cognitive development? Or does a particular type of practice affect the development of a given concept or skill? The methods used to obtain answers to these types of questions obey the general rules of semi-experimental or experimental methods used in other areas of psychology. For example, problems designed to uncover abilities at different ages

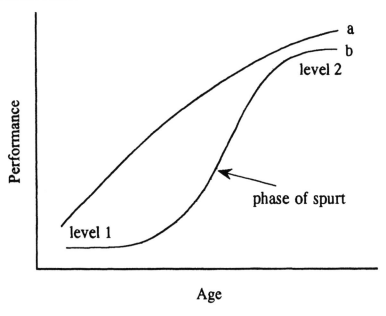

Figure 5.1   Alternative models of cognitive development: (a) continuous development; (b) stage-like development
Note: One may note that in continuous development the improvement of performance is smooth and uniform throughout the age phase concerned. In discontinuous
development successive levels are separated by a period of rapid change which
transforms the system from the one level to the other.

are given to children of educated and uneducated parents and their performance is charted as a function of age and parents' education in order to
specify if their development is similar or different. Or different groups of
subjects are formed so that each can be subjected to a particular form of
practice related to a given concept or ability and their development is
charted to see if they differ in their facility to use this concept or ability.
Obviously, depending upon the particular needs of the researcher, any
combination of the methods summarized above can be used.

Outline of the Chapter

This chapter will discuss the various theories and research which have
addressed these issues over the last 70 years or so. Piaget's theory of
cognitive development will be presented first, since it is the bedrock upon
which subsequent theorizing and research on cognitive development have
been built. Piaget's theory is a gigantic opus which totals of over 40 000
pages. We will focus here on those concepts and phenomena which constitute Piaget's permanent contribution to our knowledge of the human mind
and which still attract the interest of researchers in various fields. Despite its
immense contribution, Piaget's theory, like any theory in science, has been
plagued with a number of problems. These problems will be addressed

through discussion of contemporary theories and research which have attempted to resolve them, namely, the so-called neo-Piagetian theories, which have built on the strong points of Piagetian theory and current research in modern cognitive psychology. This discussion will show how the study of cognitive development gradually shifted emphasis from the theory of Piaget to other traditions in psychology. Then presentation will focus on current research on the development of reasoning and logical thought. The aim will be to show how reasoning as such develops. Next we will consider recent research on the development of the child's understanding and knowledge of the physical, biological, and psychological world. To conclude, we will examine a theory on the organization and development of the human mind, which aimed to integrate theories from different traditions into a comprehensive system. We will also summarize research and theorizing about development in the years of maturity.

PIAGET'S THEORY

As Weinert (this volume) stated in his introduction, Piaget was a biologist with epistemological interests who set himself the task to advance a theory about the origin, nature, and adaptive functions of knowledge and intelligence. That is, his life goal was to uncover and describe the underlying mechanisms that enable humans to understand the basic categories of reason, such as quality, quantity, causality, space, and time. Below we will first outline Piaget's model of the nature of intelligence. Then we will describe the sequence of stages that he proposed as descriptions of the forms that intelligence takes from birth to maturity. Finally, his model of cognitive change and an evaluation of the theory will be offered (Piaget, 1950, 1977).

The Nature and the Adaptive Functions of Intelligence

Piaget believed that reality is a dynamic system of continuous change, and as such could be defined in reference to the two conditions that define dynamic systems that change. Specifically, he argued that reality involves *transformations* and *states*. Transformations refer to all manners of changes that a thing or person can undergo. States refer to the conditions or the appearances in which things or persons can be found between transformations. For example there might be changes in shape or form (for instance, liquids are reshaped as they are transferred from one vessel to another, humans change in their characteristics as they grow older), in size or distance (e.g. a series of coins on a table might be placed close to each other or far apart), in placement or location in space and time (e. g. various objects or persons might be found at one place at one time and at a different place at another time). Thus, Piaget argued, if human intelligence is to be adaptive, it must have functions to represent both the transformational and the static aspects of reality. He proposed that *operative intelligence* is responsible for the representation and manipulation of the dynamic or transformational aspects of reality and that *figurative intelligence* is responsible for the representation of the static aspects of reality (Piaget & Inhelder, 1973).

Operative intelligence is the active aspect of intelligence. It involves all actions, overt or covert, undertaken in order to follow, recover, or anticipate the transformations of the objects or persons of interest. Figurative intelligence is the more or less static aspect of intelligence, involving all means of representation used to retain in mind the states (i.e. successive forms, shapes, or locations) that intervene between transformations. That is, it involves perception, imitation, mental imagery, drawing, and language. Therefore, the figurative aspects of intelligence derive their meaning from the operative aspects of intelligence, because states cannot exist independently of the transformations that interconnect them. Piaget believed that the figurative or the representational aspects of intelligence are subservient to its operative and dynamic aspects, and therefore, that understanding essentially derives from the operative aspect of intelligence.

At any time, operative intelligence frames how the world is understood and it changes if understanding is not successful. Piaget believed that this process of understanding and change involves two basic functions: *Assimilation* and *accommodation*. Assimilation refers to the active transformation of information so as to be integrated into the mental schemes already available. Its analog at the biological level might be the transformation of food by chewing and digestion to fit in with the structural and biochemical characteristics of the human body. Accommodation refers to the active transformation of these schemes so as to take into account the particularities of the objects, persons, or events the thinker is interacting with. Its analog at the biological level might be the adaptation of eating and digestion to the particulars of the different kinds of food we eat. For Piaget, none of these functions can exist without the other. To assimilate an object into an existing mental scheme, one first needs to take into account or accommodate to the particularities of this object to a certain extent; for instance, to recognize (assimilate) an apple as an apple one needs first to focus (accommodate) on the contour of this object. To do this one needs to roughly recognize the size of the object. We will see below that development increases the balance or equilibration between these two functions. When in balance with each other, they generate mental schemes of the operative intelligence. When the one dominates over the other, they generate representations which belong to figurative intelligence. The relations between the different functions and aspects of intelligence are shown in Table 5. 1.

From this conception Piaget theorized that intelligence is active and constructive. In fact, it is active even in the literary sense of the term as it depends on the actions (overt or covert, assimilatory or accommodatory), which the thinker executes in order to build and rebuild his models of the world. And it is constructive because actions, particularly mental actions, are coordinated into more inclusive and cohesive systems and thus they are raised to ever more stable and effective levels of functioning. Piaget believed that this process of construction leads to systems of mental operations better

Table 5.1 The stages and general characteristics of cognitive development according to Piaget

PERIODS OF DEVELOPMENT	FUNCTIONAL INVARIANTS OF THE MIND		
	ASSIMILATION transformations	+ ACCOMMODATION states	→ ADAPTATION schemes and structures
	FIGURATIVE INTELLIGENCE		OPERATIVE INTELLIGENCE
SENSORIMOTOR PERIOD 0–2 years	SYMBOLIC SCHEMES	IMITATION Imitation of movements with the model present	SENSORIMOTOR SCHEMES Exercise of reflexes Circular reactions Object permanence
REPRESENTATIONAL INTELLIGENCE PREOPERATIONAL PERIOD 2–5 years	SYMBOLIC PLAY	STATIC REPRESENTATIONS Deferred imitation Static mental images Global verbal descriptions	PRELOGICAL THOUGHT Interiorized but uncoordinated mental actions
5–7 years			INTUITIVE THOUGHT Intuitions about the identity of object, functional logic, intuitive grasp of logical relations
OPERATIONAL PERIOD 7–11 years	CONSTRUCTIVE PLAY	CONSTRUCTIVE REPRESENTATION Transformational and anticipatory mental images, differentiated verbal descriptions, etc.	CONCRETE THOUGHT Mental actions coordinated into reversible first-order logical structures which are applied on the concrete aspects of reality
11–16 years			FORMAL THOUGHT Second-order mental structures able to conceive of the possible, test hypotheses, and construct models about the world

Note: Vertical arrows show the direction of development. Horizontal arrows show interactions between different functions. Solid arrows indicate that, according to Piaget, operative intelligence shapes figurative intelligence, although it is affected by it to a certain extent (dotted arrows).

able to resist the illusions of perceptual appearances and thus less prone to error. In other words, the gradual construction of the system of mental operations involved in the operative aspect of intelligence enables the developing person to grasp ever more hidden and complex aspects of the world. Below we will summarize the development of operative intelligence.

The Stages of Operative Development

Table 5.1 presents an outline of the stages of cognitive development as conceived by Piaget. Development is divided into two major periods on the basis of the kind of representation that dominates at each. Specifically, there is the period of sensorimotor intelligence, which lasts from birth to the end of the second year and the period of representational or symbolic intelligence, which appears thereafter and continues throughout life. Representational intelligence is divided into two major periods. The first, which begins at age 2 and continues to about age 7, is preoperational, that is, it is representational but mental actions on representations are not yet coordinated into operative structures. For Piaget (1950), the foremost criterion of operational coordination is reversibility, which involves understanding that a given action (actual or mental) can be canceled or undone by another action. We will see below that the kind of reversibility associated with the successive stages of development defines what aspects of the world can be understood at each of these stages. At the age of 7 mental operations are integrated into reversible structures, thus preoperational intelligence is transformed into operational intelligence. Operational intelligence is concrete until approximately age 11–12 years when it becomes formal. Formal intelligence continues to develop until about the end of adolescence.

Sensorimotor intelligence

Piaget's (1954) views on sensorimotor intelligence are discussed by Butterworth (ch. 3 this volume) in his chapter on perceptual and motor development. Thus, the presentation here will focus on Piaget's views concerning the development of object permanence. Object permanence refers to the belief that objects exist on their own and are not dependent on the infant's perceptions or the actions in relation to them. Grasping object permanence is important for two reasons. First, specifying infants' beliefs in regard to the permanence of objects can help us to clarify how the world appears to humans at the outset of life. Second, the construction of the mental structure which is associated with each of the major stages of cognitive development culminates in a particular kind of ontological understanding. Ontological understanding refers to what one believes about the existence and nature of things. Object permanence is the ontological understanding which comes from the construction of the structure of sensorimotor intelligence.

According to Piaget, at the beginning of the sensorimotor period, when the senses are still not interconnected or coordinated with the actions that can be effected on objects, infants believe that objects cease to exist when they are not seen, heard, or touched. Until the age of about 8–10 months, objects are nothing more than simple projections of the infant's actions in relation to them. For instance, when the infant's mother walks out of the room, he fixates his gaze on the door where the mother's figure was last seen. At best, by the end of this period, the infant may move his head along the mother's imaginary track as though the mother were a projection of his gaze. By integrating perceptions and actions on objects and persons, the infant accredits more stability to the existence of objects at the end of the first year.

Still, however, objects do not exist independently of the infant's actions, as she commits the so-called A-not-B error. This phenomenon is highly interesting. Imagine a baby playing with her ball, and that the ball rolls under sofa A. At this age the infant has no difficulty in recovering the ball from under the sofa as she believes that there is a ball under there. If a little later, however, the ball leaves her hands and rolls under sofa *B in front of her eyes* the baby will again look for the ball under sofa A, where she successfully recovered it earlier. Thus, the present behavior indicates that although the infant's notion of object permanence has advanced beyond the eye fixation and tracking of the previous stage it is limited in that it is not completely independent of her actions.

This independence is achieved by the end of the next phase, at about 15–16 months, when objects can be recovered from where they were last seen to disappear. In fact, in the period of transition from sensorimotor to representational intelligence (18–24 months) infants can recover objects which have been hidden at a succession of places imperceptibly. For instance, Piaget first concealed his watch in his hands and then he concealed his hands under a pillow, where he left the watch and withdrew his hands empty. His daughter was able to look directly under the pillow, indicating that she was able to reconstruct the sequence of movements mentally and execute a corresponding plan of movements. This indicates clearly that actions have been interiorized and integrated into plans of mentally executable actions. In fact, the representation of objects as recoverable and therefore permanently existent, springs out of these integrated mental actions. Thus, a new and long journey begins, the journey towards the development of representational intelligence (Piaget, 1954).

The construction of representational intelligence I: from preoperational to concrete thought

The interiorization of sensorimotor schemes generates mental schemes (i. e. patterns of actions that can be executed mentally). Although at the early stages of representational intelligence mental schemes are present, they are not coordinated into reversible structures. Thus, while children at this phase have ideas and concepts about the world, themselves and other persons, their concepts represent isolated states—usually the dominant and most impressive ones—of the world or privileged personal experiences rather than a cohesive and balanced interpretation in which a concept is judged in relation to other concepts. As a result, children's reasoning at this stage is prone to errors since things are judged superficially, primarily by appearances. The weaknesses of this stage will be illustrated below with the examples of some of Piaget's most well-known tasks, which have become his trademark and which are also considered among the most classic tasks of developmental psychology.

Piaget (1950) believed that the foundations of operative intelligence are associated with the ability to grasp the logic of classes and relations since this ability involves all the operations needed to understand all other categories of reason such as—in Kantian terms—quantity, causality, space, time, and even social rules and moral reasoning. In a sense, Piaget believed that the mental operations underlying the logic of classes and relations constituted reason itself.

Piaget defined the membership of different elements in a class (for instance, the membership of various kinds of flowers, such as roses and daisies, in the class 'flowers') in reference to two complementary types of mental action: on the one hand, by the recognition of a common property that is shared by all members of the class (for instance, they are all colorful and they smell nice) and, on the other, by mentally ignoring their differences (e.g. differences in shape, size, smell). However, the logic of relationships requires focusing on the differences between elements and ignoring their similarities. For instance, when ordering a number of pencils of varying lengths according to their size, properties like color and shape are irrelevant to seriation. Below we will describe two tasks, one addressed to the logic of classes and the other to the logic of relations, to illustrate Piaget's belief that reasoning processes which outwardly appear different actually emanate from the same underlying structure of mental operations.

The class inclusion problem is one of the most well-known problems used by Piaget (Inhelder & Piaget, 1964) to study the development of categorical reasoning. In this problem (see Box 5.1) children are shown objects belonging to two complementary classes, such as four roses (class A) and two daisies (class A'), which also belong to a higher-order class that includes them both, such as the class of flowers in the example given here (class B). The child is first asked to describe the objects to ensure that she knows all of the classes and the corresponding names. Then she is asked the classic class inclusion question: 'Are there more flowers (i.e. Bs) or more roses (i.e. As) on the table?' That is, she is invited to compare the superordinate class B with one of the subordinate complementary classes, which in the standard task is always the most numerous class.

Children in the preoperational stage respond with 'there are more roses because the daises are only 2 and the roses are 4'. According to Piaget's analysis, this answer indicates that the superordinate class 'flowers' does not exist in the mind of the children at this stage and so their only alternative is to compare the two groups of visible objects. Piaget ascribed this weakness to a lack of reversibility in their mental operations. Further, he held that the child can only construct the superordinate class if she can first focus on the properties common to the A and the A' objects and then reduce or compose them into a higher-order class identified in reference to this common property. However, if she is able to compare this class with any of the subordinate classes, the child must be able to invert in her mind the operation of composition in order to recover the particular classes involved in the superordinate class. It is only when composition and inversion can be applied simultaneously that the child will be able to move between the subordinate and the superordinate classes and specify their quantitative relationships of inclusion.

Children at the intuitive stage generally make one of two mistakes: they either give the right answer (that is, that flowers are more than roses) but cannot explain it; or they say that 'they are the same'. Both responses indicated to Piaget that the child has an intuitive grasp of the superordinate class but because his mental actions have not yet been integrated into a fully reversible structure of mental operations, he is unable to move up and down the class hierarchy with a clear understanding of both the general and the particular classes. Those difficulties are removed when children enter the stage of concrete operations. At this stage they can give both the right answer and explanations indicating that the structure of concrete operations has been established. Using the same example, they now say that 'flowers are more than roses because daisies are flowers too; (i.e. flowers=roses+daisies) or that 'flowers are more because roses are not the only flowers on the table' (i.e. flowers−roses=daisies).

Piaget (Inhelder & Piaget, 1964) maintained that the understanding of the transitivity of relationships is equivalent to understanding the inclusion of classes. In the simpler version of the transitivity task, three sticks are involved such that, for instance, $A < B < C$. The children are first shown the rods A and B together and then the rods B and C together; rods A and C are never shown together. They are then asked to infer their relationship. As in the case of the class inclusion problem, preoperational children cannot solve the problem, intuitive children can find the right answer but they cannot explain, and finally, concrete-stage children answer correctly and provide an explanation, indicating that they can integrate the two premises by means of reversible mental operations. (That is, that once B is longer than A and C is longer than B, C has to be longer than A.) According to Piaget, this understanding indicates a reversibility different from that required by classificatory reasoning. Specifically, in the logic of relationships the inverse of an operation does not cancel out the effects of the previous operation, but only functions as its reciprocal, that is, it compensates for the results of its application without annihilating or undoing them. Being both bigger than one thing and simultaneously smaller than another does not affect the identity of an object, but only the perspective from which it is seen.

We have gone to some lengths in presenting these two tasks and the answers they evoke at different stages because they are very crucial in understanding Piaget's position on the structure and development of thought. Specifically, attention is drawn to the fact that the task addressed to the logic of classes is, on the surface, different from the task addressed to the logic of relationships. Even the child's answers to these tasks appear, at first, to be different. Remember that in the first case the children evaluate classes of flowers, and in the second they compare size relationships between sticks. Despite these differences, however, Piaget maintained that solutions to these tasks required similar mental operations. In the case of the class inclusion (and other classification) tasks, children have to focus on a given attribute (the 'flowerness' of different kinds of flowers) and compose a general class by mentally reducing all different kinds to this class. At the same time, they have to be able to 'decompose' this class or, more technically, to reverse the mental act of composition so as not to lose sight of the different kinds involved. It is only under this condition that they can move horizontally and vertically in classification hierarchies and understand their inclusion relationships. In the case of transitivity and other seriation tasks, children have to focus primarily on the differences rather than the similarities (i.e. between the rods), and compose them such that a smoothly ascending structure can be mentally constructed. In a sense, this structure corresponds to the superordinate class in the case of the logic of classes of relationships. It is only under this condition that movement along this structure can become bidirectional, enabling children to proceed productively to construct a mental picture and grasp the transitivity of relationships.

Piaget believed that the understanding of all other domains of reality results from a kind of synthesis of the logic of classes and relationships described above. In fact, he was very ingenious in devising tasks representing many different domains prone to show that their understanding evolves through the same stages and is governed by the same structure. Reference here will be made to only two of the conservations, namely those of number and of quantity (Piaget, 1952; Piaget & Inhelder, 1974). In the classic conservation of number task, the experimenter sets before the child a series comprised of a certain number of things, for instance a series of five coins, and arranges them about 2 cm apart. He then invites the child to take coins out of a box and make another series which will comprise the same number. Children in the preoperational stage do not really focus on number as such. They focus on the most dominant dimension of the series—which here is length—and then make a series whose ends coincide with the model series, with little attention to the number of coins. Children in the intuitive stage are able to replicate the model series, which indicates that they have a global grasp of numerosity. This understanding is still dependent on perceptually dominant but number-irrelevant appearances, however, proven by their judgments on the quality of the two rows when one is extended so that it appears longer. In this case they think that 'this row has more coins because it is longer'. Children in the concrete stage are not deceived by transformations which affect the perceptual but not the numerical aspects of the rows, because they have the operational structure necessary to compensate for these transformations or place them in perspective. Thus, when the one of the two rows is elongated, concrete-stage children say 'the number is still the same, because nothing has been added or taken away.' When it is suggested that 'this row seems to have more because it is longer,' they resist by saying that 'it may be longer but there is also more empty space between the coins' (which is an argument which stands for reciprocity), and 'you can see that they are still the same if you bring them back to their original position' (which is an argument which stands for inversion or negation).

Testing the conservation of quantities proceeds in a similar fashion (see Box 5.1). For example, two similar glasses are presented to a child, who is asked to use the liquid (e.g. orange) of an adjacent jar and 'make these two glasses have the same amount of orange.' After this is done, the contents of one glass are transferred to another, usually, longer and thinner glass. Then the standard question is asked: 'Do they still have the same amount?' Preoperational children give a nonconservation answer and a nonconservation explanation: 'No, this one has more because it is longer.' Intuitive children may give a conservation answer which they cannot explain—and which they can abandon faced with counter suggestion—or they may fluctuate between a nonconservation and a conservation answer. Moreover, intuitive children conserve the identity of the material involved, that is, they understand that it is still the same water over the different transformations. Finally, concrete-stage operational children conserve and explain their answer operationally: 'It still is the same because nothing has been added or taken away and it may be longer but it is also thinner and if you pour it back it will again appear the same'.

In conclusion the organization of concrete operations into a cohesive ensemble of mental operations enables schoolchildren, according to Piaget, to acquire a stability in their conception of the fundamental dimensions and properties of reality in the same way that the organization of the sensorimotor actions into cohesive schemes of perception and behavior enables infants at the end of the second year to acquire ontological stability. Likewise, the construction of the structure of concrete operations provides children with the framework within which they can build concepts about every aspect of the physical and the social world since it provides a cohesive reasoning mechanism that can interconnect various seemingly unrelated appearances. Concrete thought, however, causes two important limitations. First, being dependent on the observable properties of reality, it needs to structure each fresh concept anew; that is, it is incapable of constructing a general frame into which, ideally, everything can fit. An example of this limitation is the so-called horizontal decalage phenomenon. That is, the conservation of different aspects of reality is acquired at different stages although it is based on the same underlying structure of mental operations. A classic example in this regard is the conservation of identity, quantity, weight, and volume which is acquired at the age of 5, 7, 9, and 11 years, respectively. The second limitation is probably more serious: there are many aspects of reality which cannot be understood by concrete thought. In this category are phenomena that involve multiple factors which interact in complex and concealed ways, and which need to be reconstructed mentally

Box 5.1   Tasks that can be solved at different Piagetian stages

Class inclusion

Are there more flowers or more roses?
Preoperational answer: More roses because the daisies are only two.
Intuitive answer: More flowers. Why? I don't know.
Concrete answer: More flowers because all of them are flowers.

Conservation of quantity

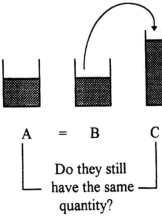

A   =   B   C

Do they still
have the same
quantity?

Preoperational answer: No, it has more (C) because it's taller.
Intuitive answer: Yes. Why? I don't know.
Concrete answer: Yes, it looks to have more because it is taller but it is also thinner and you can pour it back to see that they are the same as before.

The bending rods task

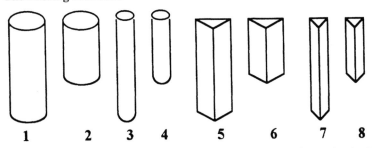

1   2   3   4   5   6   7   8

Choose a pair of rods that would be a fair test of the hypothesis that long rods bend more than short rods.
Concrete solution: Rods 2 and 3 because this would make their difference clearer.
Formal solution: Rods 3 and 4 because they have to be the same in all respects but length.

to be understood. For this to occur, however, a new structure of thought is required which will make concrete operations melt into a new and higher order synthesis. This structure is constructed at the next stage of formal operations (Inhelder & Piaget, 1958).

The construction of representational intelligence II: from concrete to formal thought

Piaget argued that the foremost structural attainment at the stage of formal thought is the integration into a single system of the two forms of reversibility. He considered this as the basis for the transition from the stage of concrete to the stage of formal thought. Therefore, the structure and the workings of this system will be described first, followed by discussion of the more common characteristics of this structure.

While the attainment of the structure of concrete operations was sufficient to ensure the actual or mental manipulation of observable properties of reality, separation of the two forms of reversibility at this stage does not permit manipulations that go beyond or contra reality. An example is the well-known problem of the bending rods, which addresses the ability to understand the isolation of variables in order to uncover causal relationships between possible causes and effects that require explanation. This ability is obviously very important, as it is the basis of empirical science.

An example of this problem is shown in Box 5.1, which illustrates several rods defined by three dimensions, length (long and short rods), width (thin and thick rods), and shape (round and triangular rods). The children were asked to propose a pair of rods that would constitute a fair test of the hypothesis: 'long rods bend more than short rods.' Obviously, any pair that would involve two rods similar in every respect but length is a fair test of this hypothesis, because their possible difference in flexibility can only be ascribed to their length. Piaget believed that this type of reasoning can only be achieved if inversion and reciprocity are integrated such that the thinker can understand their equivalence. Specifically, in the hypothesis above, the ideally fair test would be one which would involve rods composed of *nothing but length*. Imagining such a rod is tantamount to negating or nullifying, in thought, all those properties of the rods that need to be controlled in the experiment. In reality, of course, there are no such rods and so negation in this case is not possible. However, any effects of the factors that need to be controlled can be canceled out if they are made the same, and thus they will affect flexibility to the same degree. Thus any difference between the rods in flexibility can be ascribed to their differences in length. The reader is reminded that canceling out or compensation is the basis of reciprocity. According to Piaget, the understanding that the one form of reversibility can be used in place of another signifies the construction of a structure which integrates both of them into a single ensemble.

All of the characteristics of formal thought derive from the attainment of this structure d'ensemble. The first and more general of these characteristics is the ability to conceive of the possible. It was explained earlier that the integration of the two forms of reversibility leads to the mental construction of states that mimic 'reality that does not exist'; that is, rods which have no other property but length. A more straightforward example of the ability to conceive of the possible is the conservation of reality properties that transcend empirical verification, such as the principle of inertia. Imagine, for instance, that the adolescent is experimenting with a series of balls systematically differing in various dimensions, such as size (which affects air resistance to their movement), weight (which affects friction) and so on. If he has attained the structure of formal operations he can design experiments, such as the one described above, in order to specify the effect exerted on the movement of balls by each of these factors. He can formalize the results of his experimentations, via models that express the relationships discovered, and can also operate on the positions themselves and thus conceive of possibilities that can never be observed. For instance, once he can conclude that 'the balls stop moving because of air resistance, friction, etc.' he can also infer, by negating these factors in thought, that 'the ball would continue moving forever if there was no air resistance, no friction, etc.' He has understood the principle of inertia of movement, a principle which took humanity a few thousand years to grasp.

A number of more specific abilities are derived from the ability to conceive of the possible. Foremost is combinatorial thought which uses a systematic method to generate all possible combinations and even to combine the combinations themselves. In the examples given above the adolescent can first make use of the possibilities afforded by concrete operations and produce classes of rods or balls defined by various combinations of properties (e. g. long–thin, long–thick, short–thin, short–thick). He can then take these products as inputs to further activity, that is, he can combine these combinations to test specific hypotheses (e.g. the combination of long–thin and short–thin rods to test the role of length, or the combination of a long–thin and a long–thick rod to test the role of width). A more conventional test of combinatorial thought is to set out a box full of different coloured balls and ask the child to specify all possible orders in which the balls can be retrieved from the box.

A second ability is propositional thinking, wherein the mind casts the possibilities or combinations it conceives into verbal propositions and then combines these propositions into propositional arguments, that is, arguments where emphasis is placed on the logical relationships between the propositions rather than on their content. This makes formal thought a kind of second-order thought which takes concrete thought as its input in the same way that concrete thought takes real actions or isolated representations as its input.

Being propositional and second-order, formal thought is also hypothetico-deductive, that is, it conceives all possibilities at the beginning and then specifies their implications by logically manipulating the propositions in which the possibilities are cast. It also understands both that reality is a part of the possible, and that specification of this part requires testing by using the method of experimental control described above.

Finally, formal thought has the ability to understand complex dynamic systems whose functioning is governed by multiple interactive forces. Systems of mechanical equilibrium, such as communicating vessels or balances, are examples of these systems. Formal thought can also conceive of complex mathematical relationships, such as proportional relationships. These are second-order relationships because they involve at least two different ratios, which, in turn, indicate a relationship between two numbers. For example, to understand that 2/3 is the same as 4/6 presupposes an understanding that a relationship exists within each of the two ratios.

To conclude, then, Piaget believed formal thought to be the perfectly equilibrated system of thought toward which all development moved, and that once attained, it provided stability in the relationships between the thinking person and the environment, because is could assimilate potentially anything and it could compensate any disturbance. The organization of sensorimotor actions into a coherent structure and the subsequent internalization of this structure enable the infant to attain ontological stability; that is, the understanding that things exist beyond perception. The structure d'ensemble of concrete operations enables the schoolchild to attain conceptual stability; that is, the understanding that a thing's basic properties, such as identity, size and so on, remain invariant despite misleading perceptual cues. Finally, the structure d'ensemble of formal operations enables the adolescent to attain ideational stability, that is, the realization that assumptions are necessary once they ensue from a logical argument even if they can never be verified empirically.

The development of the other aspects of intelligence

Based on his conviction that the mind develops across a sequence of general structures, Piaget maintained that understanding in many other domains, such as those of space, time, and even social understanding, develops in accordance to the development of operative intelligence. For example, Piaget showed that preoperational children are perceptually and socially egocentric. That is, children under 5 find it difficult to understand that the same mountain can appear differently depending on the angle from which it is viewed. Likewise, it is not easy for them to take the other's stance and understand their differences of opinion, since they can only use information available to themselves. Also, the various aspects of figurative intelligence bear the limitations of the structures of operative intelligence. For instance, preoperational children cannot form mental images of transformations, such as the gradual transformation of a plastic arc into a straight line, and keep them in memory as transformations; moreover, they tend to use static verbal descriptions to describe reality structures which call for more dynamic representations (see Bernicot, ch. 4 this volume). These weaknesses are removed when children enter the stage of concrete operations which enables them to take multiple views into account and to follow and represent the dynamic aspects of reality transformations. Finally, their understanding of moral principles is supposed to evolve along a sequence of stages which are structurally isomorphic to the stages of operative intelligence (see Haste, Markoulis & Helkama, ch. 7 this volume)

The Mechanisms of Change in Piaget's Theory

Piaget's theory is often taken as a theory of a simple succession of stages. However, it is more a theory of cognitive change than a stage theory. To Piaget, the stages above were nothing more than transient states of the upward movement of an ever-changing system which tended toward a condition which would make the person able to mentally cope with any form of change in the environment. Thus, he believed that even the final stage of formal operations was, by its very nature, a system of incessant change and expansion of thought. This conception of development is most clearly evident in his last books, which aimed to explain equilibration, Piaget's mechanisms of cognitive development (e.g. Piaget, 1977).

Why does cognitive development occur? Piaget argued that change is necessary when the present cognitive structure yields an incomplete or faulty understanding which generates inconsistencies and conflicts between what the individual understands or does and the present situation. For example, a classification system which ascribes the quality of life to objects in reference to the properties of self-propelled movement will eventually generate conflicts between what is considered to be alive and what is really alive. (Obviously, some objects, such as cars, move on their own but are not alive; some objects, such as plants, do not move but are alive.) Number conservation is a less apparent example. Remember that children believed that the physical length of a series of coins determined the number of coins it held. At some time, this belief will be falsified, either because of the child's actions (as when she counts the coins), or because of another's correction. Piaget believed that noting these divergences between expectations and reality generated cognitive conflicts which had to be removed. He termed the mechanism that removes conflicts 'reflective abstraction'.

In his later work, Piaget identified reflective abstraction as a two-phase process. At the beginning of a developmental cycle it functions as *reflecting abstraction*, that is, it takes successive actions and their results and amalgamates them into a new system which is free of the conflicts and inconsistencies that tantalized the previous system. Let's take the example of a child who believes that longer implies more but she realizes that the actual counting of different arrangements of the same set results in the same number name, which contradicts her belief. Reflecting abstraction is the process which compares successive counting actions, notices their common element (for instance, that all three rounds of counting yielded five), takes it out of context (for instance, in the first round the coins were arranged in along row, next in a circle, and finally in a pile, and no coins were added or taken away), and reduces it (Piaget would say projects or reflects it) to a new concept or scheme: *Aha! it is always five, it is always the same!* In conclusion, reflective abstraction is the mental mechanism that amalgamates a series of actions and their results into a new structure that removes conflicts and inconsistencies generated earlier. Once constructed or discovered, the new concept can itself become the object of reflection. For example, the concept of number can be related to the concept of length to structure one's representation of space in a more accurate way. This is reflected abstraction. In this sense, reflective abstraction is equivalent to reflection: thinking about thinking itself.

The Current Status of Piaget's Theory

Piaget's theory attracted massive interest in the 1960s and 70s. He was among the few psychologists lucky enough to see their theory recognized, discussed, and evaluated not only by psychology but also by other sciences such as education and philosophy. As a result, there is a solid body of empirical evidence on most aspects of Piaget's theory. This evidence enables us to draw certain conclusions regarding the validity of his theory, the permanent contributions that it has made to our understanding of the organization and development of human thought, and even about its potential further contributions.

The studies that evaluated Piaget's theory can be classified into two broad categories. One group of studies were conducted to test the validity of the phenomena Piaget maintained he had discovered; for instance, is it true that children cannot solve the various conservation tasks before the age of 7? The second group of studies, which chronologically followed later, asked a deeper question: Is the theory itself right? This question is an important one because it reflects the difference between evidence and theory. Theories go beyond the evidence on which they were developed. Thus, while it might be true that the phenomena that led to the formation of a theory are valid, the theory itself could be wrong because there are other relevant phenomena which were not accounted for.

Researchers have replicated Piaget's tasks in thousands of studies, covering the whole spectrum of ages, processes, and domains represented in Piaget's studies. They have tested the development of object constancy in infancy, the development of all kinds of concrete and formal operations, and also development of various other processes such as egocentrism and memory. This research can be summarized quite easily in a single statement: Whenever a replication study remained close to the original Piagetian conditions, the same phenomena were observed in more or less the same way at more or less the same age. In the sensorimotor stage, children at about the age of 8 months commit the A-not-B error; in the next phase children fail the class inclusion, transitivity, and conservation tasks until about the age of 7; children become able to grasp these concepts during their primary school years; however they do not take an 'if-then' stance to problems and they cannot reason propositionally, design experiments by systematically controlling variables, or understand proportionality before adolescence even when they are highly intelligent (according to intelligence test scores). Thus, it is safe to conclude that Piaget was right both in the phenomena he discovered and in their approximate age of occurrence (see the studies summarized in Brainerd, 1978; Dasen, 1977).

But is the theory right? The answer to this question is neither simple nor straightforward. In fact, the question itself must be formulated more specifically for a fair and accurate evaluation of the theory to be made. Here only two issues will be raised: one concerns the processes presumably reflected by responses to Piaget's tasks; the other refers to the organization of these processes into the structures he proposed.

The question on processes asks if performance in Piaget's tasks really reflects the processes Piaget thought that they reflect. For instance, does a child's failure to solve the transitivity task really indicate that this child cannot reason logically? One of the first and most influential studies that undermined Piaget's position that his tasks tap logical reasoning processes was Bryant and Trabasso's (1971) study on transitivity. Remember that in this task children are shown the A and B and the B and C terms together and are then asked to infer the relationship between A and C terms. Piaget asserted that failure to make the correct inference implied a lack of the logical structure to produce the inference. There was an important question, however, that Piaget failed to consider. What would happen if children did not remember the A and B and B and C comparisons—or if they did not represent them correctly? Obviously, they would fail the task. In this case, however, their failure would not indicate a lack of logical reasoning, because it could result from a memory lapse or representational inefficiency. This is precisely what Bryant and Trabasso found; that is, that preschool children either forgot the comparisons or they misremember them. For example, instead of representing the premises in their mind in comparative terms (e.g. 'the red stick is longer than the green stick') they represent it in absolute terms (e.g. 'the red stick is long'). Moreover, Bryant and Trabasso have shown that preschool children can infer transitive relations if they are systematically trained to correctly represent and remember the premises.

Hundreds of such studies proved the early presence of practically every concept and ability associated with Piaget's concrete thought, and pinpointed the factors responsible for failure in Piaget's tasks. In short, it was clearly demonstrated that when extra-logical factors such as memory, language and communication, familiarity with tasks and testing procedures, and interest are controlled, supposedly preoperational children can (or can be trained to) classify and grasp class inclusion, seriate and grasp transitivity, conserve number and quantity, understand another's perspective and decipher causal relationships (see Donaldson, 1978; Gelman & Gallistel, 1978). Similarly, studies focusing on formal thought attempted to show that conception of the possible, combinatorial reasoning, the scientific method of controlling variables, and proportional reasoning are present or can be trained before adolescence. These studies have shown that some components of these abilities may indeed be discernible or trainable during the primary school years (Goossens, 1992; Adey & Shayer, 1994). It is equally correct, however, to conclude that overall these studies suggest that the results of training do not generalize to situations and contexts remote from those used in the training experiments. Thus, children continue to fail the Piagetian tasks, despite the training.

Other studies focused on the organization of the processes involved in the understanding of different domains rather than on their age of first attainment. These studies aimed to test whether Piaget was right to assume that each developmental stage had an overarching structure that governed understanding over different domains. Thus, in these studies, children were tested by large numbers of tasks designed to represent different domains, such as space, number, causality, and so on. The notion of the structure of the whole suggests a synchronous development in different domains and therefore that tasks would be performed at equivalent developmental levels, regardless of domain. This expectation was not confirmed. On the contrary, these studies showed systematically that individuals usually operate on different levels in different domains. These findings suggested that there may be factors governing the organization of cognitive processes that go beyond Piaget's notion of the structure of the whole (Demetriou & Efklides, 1985; Fischer & Bidell, in press; Shayer, Demetriou & Pervez, 1988).

Obviously, we need a theory that can accommodate these apparent inconsistencies. Evidence suggests that, although in some sense the types of thought described by Piaget are real and present, these types do not seem to be organized or to change exactly as he maintained. Moreover, they seem to coexist with certain phenomena unnoticed or disregarded by Piaget. In the following sections we will represent several alternative theories that attempted to clarify these issues.

THE NEO-PIAGETIANS: INTEGRATING PIAGET WITH INFORMATION PROCESSING THEORY

The first theories that grew out of Piaget's work took as their basis the so-called 'standard theory' of Piaget, primarily identified with his model for the development of operative intelligence. The reader is reminded that this model involves a descriptive part which specifies the successive stages of cognitive development and an explanatory part which specifies the mechanisms which cause the transition from the one stage to the next. The reader is also reminded that empirical scrutiny of this theory revealed that both its descriptive and its explanatory postulates require revision. Thus, theorists following the present line of research attempted to redefine the successive stages of development with structures better able to accommodate the organization of mental operations, and they sought more basic mechanisms of cognitive change. This line of work on cognitive development began in the late 1960s and early 70s, when the dominant paradigm in mainstream cognitive psychology was the information-processing paradigm, which emphasized the informational and procedural aspects of the mind rather than its logical aspects. Thus, researchers at this time imported concepts and methods from information-processing theory in their attempt to explain cognitive development more satisfactorily than Piaget. Therefore, a short introduction to information-processing concepts will first be given, followed by the basic assumptions of some of the most representative theories which evolved in this tradition. The theories, which have come to be known as the neo-Piagetian theories of cognitive development, have been presented and evaluated in two volumes edited by Demetriou (1988) and Demetriou, Shayer & Efklides (1992).

The model of the human mind proposed by scholars who took the computer as an analog assumes that information deriving from the environment is registered first by the senses. It is then sent to a temporary memory store where it can be transformed, processed, and understood in relation both to the goals of the moment and to the available relevant knowledge and experience which is located in the permanent memory store and is directly connected to the short-term store.

What kinds of change can such a system undergo? In general, two kinds of change may be observed. The first type of change refers to the quality and the amount of information that can be registered and processed by any of the three main systems involved. For example, improved sensory registers will provide the organism with more information on a given domain of the environment. Such improvements would naturally lead to more accurate and complete representation of those aspects of the environment which are of interest to the person. Improved capabilities of the short-term memory store would allow more elaborate or more complex relationships among the reality elements sent from sensory registers to be constructed. This would result in more complex representations about the environment. Second, an improvement in the long-term store would result in a larger knowledge base and greater efficiency in using it, bringing more flexibility and expertise in dealing with current problems.

Juan Pascual-Leone (1970) was the first to propose a model of cognitive development that systematically attempted to integrate the fundamental assumptions of information-processing theory with Piagetian theory. Specifically, he proposed that human thought is organized as a two-level system. The first and more basic level involves a number of constructs and functions which define the volume of information an individual can represent and process at a given time, and also the style and preferred method of processing. As such, the constructs involved at this level define an individual's potential or capacity with regard to what, how much, and in what ways information can be processed. The second level involves the mental operations a thinker can execute and his world knowledge. Actually, Pascual-Leone accepted that this level involves the structures of thought as described by Piaget. Therefore, in Pascual-Leone's theory, the first level of mental architecture originates in information-processing theory and the second originates in Piaget's theory. Pascual-Leone invoked the first level to explain the functioning and the development of the second.

Mental power or *Mp* is the most well known and most studied construct that Pascual-Leone proposed, and it closely resembles the construct of working memory discussed earlier. *Mp* refers to the maximum number of independent information units or mental schemes that can be held simultaneously in the mind at a given moment in order to envisage relationships or to solve a problem. However, Pascual-Leone's *Mp* is broader and more active than the construct of working memory. That is, it is coupled with attention which is purposefully directed by the individual at some schemes or stimuli at the expense of not attending to others. Further, he believed that the mental power available for the representation of mental schemes relevant to the goal which directs understanding or problem-solving at a given moment increases systematically with age. Specifically, *Mp* can boost one scheme or unit of information at the age of 3, increasing by one unit every second year until the age of 15, when it reaches its maximum capacity of 7 units of information.

Pascual-Leone also attempted to show that the increase in *Mp actually causes* the transition from one Piagetian stage (or substage) to the next, and he presented analyses suggesting that the classic Piagetian stages are dependent on *Mp* levels. Specifically, he posited that tasks solved at the preoperational stage require an *Mp* of 1 mental scheme, intuitive 2, early concrete 3, late concrete 4, transitional from concrete to formal 5, early formal 6, and late formal thought 7. Thus, as *Mp* capacity increases, likewise the capacity for understanding increases (Pascual-Leone & Goodman, 1979).

In conclusion, Pascual-Leone's research was highly important because it demonstrated that human cognition may be organized on different levels and that a more basic process-free, context-free, and nonlogical level may determine what and how many processes can be executed at a given moment, what reality structures can be understood and, ultimately, what kinds of logical structures can be constructed. Thus, Pascual-Leone opened the way for the development of more process-oriented theories of cognitive development. One of these theories has been advanced by Robbie Case and his colleagues (Case, 1985, 1992; Case, Okamoto, Griffin, McKeough, Bleiker, Henderson & Stephenson, 1996). This theory will be summarized below.

The Theory of Robbie Case

Robbie Case integrated into his theory some of the most fundamental assumptions of Pascual-Leone's theory. That is, Case believes, in agreement with Pascual-Leone, that the mind is organized in two levels, one defined by processing capacity and one by mental structures. He also believes that the direction of causality runs primarily from processing capacity to mental structures. However, Case introduced several innovations into his analysis of the constructs involved in the two levels, which considerably enhanced the theory. Specifically, he examined the effects of certain important factors that had been underestimated by Pascual-Leone. Next we will detail Case's theory, with emphasis on those aspects that go beyond Piaget and Pascual-Leone.

Structures and stages in Case's theory

Case's analysis of cognitive structures is much closer to mainstream cognitive psychology than to Piaget's or Pascual-Leone's analysis. Specifically, Case analyzed mental structures as systems of goal-directed representations and strategies assembled in a particular sequence until a desired solution is attained. In his own words, understanding and problem-solving are organized as *executive control structures*.

> By definition, an executive control structure is an internal mental blueprint, which represents a subject's habitual way of construing a particular problem situation, together with his or her habitual procedure for dealing with it. All executive control structures will be presumed to contain at least three components: (1) a representation of the *problem situation*, that is, a representation of the conditions for which the plan is appropriate, and in which children sometimes find themselves; (2) a representation of their most common *objectives* in such a situation, that is, the conditions which they desire, and toward whose achievement their plan is directed; and (3) a representation of the *strategy* they employ, that is, the set of mental steps that they develop for going from the problem situation to the desired situation, in as efficient manner as possible. (Case, 1985, pp. 68–69)

These ideas derive directly from the classic work of Newell and Simon (1972) on problem-solving.

Case's definition of cognitive structures allows both the structural or componential composition of what children can represent or do and the processes enabling them to attain a goal to be specified simultaneously. To exemplify the interdependency between the structural and the procedural aspects of mental structures, Case introduced a specific notation, an example of which is given here in reference to a rather simple situation.

Imagine, for instance, a young infant who wants to grasp an interesting object but in order to satisfy this desire she must first remove another object which stands in the way. This structure can be viewed either as a description of the processes that the child must go through to solve the problem, or as a description of the components involved at the various phases of this process. As a process description, the child's engagement with the problem begins by noting the object in her visual field and by activation of the desire to play with it. The attempt to grasp the object makes the child realize that another object stands in the way. This realization generates a second subgoal, which is to remove this object in order to attain her primary goal. Once this is understood, the problem is psychologically solved because the child knows what steps are required to reach the desired final state. Thus, the deployment of strategies evolves in the reverse order from that of the goals and the relevant representations, that is, the problem arises because the strategies deployed to achieve a goal must first be those required to remove the barriers and, subsequently, those needed to realize the ultimate goal. Case analyzes two aspects of mental structures: first, he describes the different types of representations, conditions, and processes involved; second, he describes the complexity of a mental structure, in so far as it specifies the number of representations, goals, and strategies that the child must be able to keep in mind and then coordinate in order to solve a problem. An example of the conventions Case (1985, p. 69) uses to represent executive control structures is given below.

PROBLEM SITUATION   OBJECTIVES
*Interesting object (toy) at X   *Play with object at X
*Second object on path to X   *Move second object out of path
*Second object within reach at Y   *Move hand from Z to Y

STRATEGY
1. Move arm in direction Y.
2. Push object at Y with hand,
    until it moves.
3a. Check availability of object at
    X. If available, go to 3b;
    otherwise, return to Step 2.
3b. Move hand toward object at X.
4. When object touches at X, pick
    it up and begin to play with it.

Stages in Case's theory

Case maintained that executive control structures are the building blocks of developmental stages, which undergo two types of change with the progression of age. Specifically, structures change in the *type* of mental units they involve and in the *number* of units that can be assembled or integrated into a plan of action.

Case posited four types of executive control structures: sensorimotor, interrelational, dimensional, and vectorial. Sensorimotor structures evolve in the age phase from 1 to 18 months and the units involved here are perceptions and actions that can be performed on the objects. For instance, the perception of an object may cause a desire (e.g. I want to hold this object in my hand) which in turn activates the actions that can satisfy the desire (e.g. extend hand towards the object and grasp when hand touches on the object). Interrelational structures evolve between ages from 1 and a half to 5 and then basic units are simple relationships between actions or representations. For instance, children at this phase have a basic understanding of relational systems such as balance beams in which case they can understand that the arm of the beam will tip to the side bearing the most weight. Dimensional structures evolve from age 5 to 11, and involve relationships between the relationships of the preceding stage. They constitute dimensions in the sense that representations or concepts about the same reality are placed along a continuum which provides information about their variations, such as increases or decreases. As a result, at this phase intradimensional relationships can be grasped easily as can global relationships between dimensions, such as the relationships between weights and their distances from the fulcrum in the balance. Vectorial structures evolve between age 11 and 19, when the relationships between dimensions are fully elaborated so that complex relationships of covariation, such as those found in proportional relationships, can be grasped. Note that the four types of structures correspond to Piaget's sensorimotor, preoperational, concrete operational, and formal operational stages.

Development within each of these four main stages evolves along a sequence of four levels or substages: operational consolidation, unifocal coordination, bifocal coordination, and elaborated coordination. As implied by their names, increasingly complex structures can be understood or assembled at each of the four levels. Successive stages are not unrelated, however, for Case posited that the final level of a given stage is also the first level of the next stage. Thus, development is recycling; that is, when the structures of a given stage reach a given level of complexity (which corresponds to the level of elaborated coordination) a new mental unit is created and the cycle begins anew. It must be noted here, however, that the concept of recursion or recycling in development was first introduced by Piaget. The reader is reminded that each of the three major stages of development was expected to result in a specific kind of conservation, namely object permanence at the sensorimotor stage, conservation of physical properties at the concrete stage, and conservation of logically conceived possibilities at the formal stage.

At the level of operational consolidation the basic unit of a given stage gets formulated and established. In one of the tasks used by Case to study development during the sensorimotor stage, a simple balance beam was devised that could be operated by young infants. This beam involved a flat arm which went up and down if pushed. At either end a bell could be fixed which produced a sound when hit by the arm. Infants at the first level can look at the arm producing the sound and refixate their eyes correctly on the correct arm when it is moved by the experimenter, but they cannot strike the arm themselves to produce the sound. This coordination is effected at the second level of unifocal coordination. At this level, the infant can strike the arm at one end in order to make the bell which is under this end ring. This is so because, according to Case, at this level the child can represent situations involving two integral components, such as the sound and the movement of an adult which caused the sound. At the next level (bifocal coordination) the bell is fixed above the end opposite to the one that must be pushed down. Thus, although the movement to be produced is the same, the infant must be able to monitor what is going on at the other end, in addition to the movements of the preceding stage. Finally, at the level of elaborated coordination infants can build complex sensorimotor structures which have the characteristics of reversibility in action. Thus, at this level the bell is placed beneath the end, opposite to that which will make the bell ring, and the infant must understand that the downward movement of the end that hits the ring is caused by pulling the other end up.

This structure is already interrelational because it involves relationships between different and opposing actions which are integrated to produce a desired result. When attained, they are equivalent to the level of operational consolidation of the interrelational stage, and when consolidated, they can be coordinated in pairs. Thus, at the stage of unifocal coordination the child can understand how the movement of the beam is stopped by a block placed under it so that he first removes the block and then pulls the beam up to make the bell ring at the other end. At the subsequent level of bifocal coordination the child understands all of the aforementioned relationships and in addition understands how to use a peg to move the arm. Finally, at the level of elaborated coordination, children understand how the upward-downward movement of the two sides of the arm can be produced by using a light weight on the one side and a heavy weight on the other side.

The attainment of this structure implies that weight is already represented as a dimension, and therefore the interrelational elaborated coordination corresponds to the first level of the dimensional stage. At this level, children examining a normal balance beam (which can balance with various combinations of weights hung at various distances from the center), can approximately specify the weights on each of the two sides and accordingly predict which side will go down. At the next level (unifocal coordination), children count the weights on each side of the balance and determine that the side with more weights will go down. At the level of bifocal coordination, children take distances into account as well, such that if the number of weights on the two sides are (about) equal, they understand that the side with weights further from the center will go down. Finally, at the level of the elaborated coordination, children predict the side to go down based on consideration both of the weights and the distances on each side are counted and of their multiplicative effect.

Obviously, this structure is already vectorial as the forces on each side are conceived as products of two interrelated factors (i.e. weights and distances) and it is indicative of the first level of the vectorial stage. At the vectorial unifocal , bifocal and elaborated coordination stages, adolescents become able to apply increasingly complex mathematical procedures to determine the relative torque exerted on each side of the beam.

Vertical and horizontal structure

Remember that one criticism of Piaget's theory was that it failed to satisfactorily explain variations in task performance, when the solution was supposedly dependent on the same underlying structure. Case and Pascual-Leone believed that Piaget confounded the operations necessary to solve the tasks and the task content itself, making it difficult to determine which caused the variations in performance. Thus, to accurately test if development at successive levels of representation evolves through the same sequence of levels, as supposed by Case's model of recycling development, three requirements need to be met. First, the content of the tasks must be the same across all stages. This is the reason that the same balance beam task was adjusted to be appropriate for testing sensorimotor, preschool, school age children, and adolescents. Second, it must be possible to structure the tasks so as to tap the representational characteristics of each developmental phase. Third, within each level, it should be possible to systematically vary task complexity in terms of the goals and strategies required for their solution, since this is the only way to verify formal equivalence between the sequence of substages involved in each of the main levels.

To test that the level sequence holds over different contents one needs to proceed the other way, that is, tasks must be constructed both to represent different domains and to scale along the same sequence of levels. For example, if the level sequence is (as assumed by the theory), a staircase whose levels are defined and constrained by the constructional characteristics of the human mind, then all tasks representing a given level would have to be solved or failed across the board and independently of their content. Case presented evidence in favor of this interpretation, when he showed that the sequence of levels described above holds for the development of mathematical thought, spatial thought, social thought, and drawing (Case, 1992).

Nature, functions and development of processing capacity in Case's theory

Case used the term *executive processing space* to refer to processing capacity, which he posited to involve two integral components, namely operating pace and short-term storage space (STSS). Operating space refers primarily to the operations that must be performed to attain the problem goal. STSS refers to the maximum number of mental schemes that the thinker can focus on at a single centration of attention. More specifically, STSS involves pointers or cues that help one to remember the products of operations already executed or of operations to be executed at the next processing step. An example is when one has to count the number of elements involved in several groups of objects and then recall all values. In this example the operation of counting occupies the operating space component and the values resulting from counting occupy the STSS.

Case believes that the contents of the operating space change with development, so that at each of his four stages, the operating space is occupied by sensorimotor, relational, dimensional, and vectorial operations. He posits that the development of processing capacity recycles through the same stages in relation to the structure of problem-solving skills and processes.

It is also notable that Case believes that total processing space does not change with development, although he does not deny that both the operating space and the STSS change with development. In fact, he proposed that the execution of the operations occupying the operating space becomes more efficient and thus less demanding of processing resources with age. This results in more available processing space for remembering mental schemes representing either the results of the application of operations or of more objectives in regard to a situation. In fact, Case argues that this inverse trade-off between operating space and STSS results in three changes in each main stage which corresponds to the three substages or levels already described. Thus, the total processing space available at the substages of operational consolidation, unifocal coordination, bifocal coordination, and elaborated coordination is 1, 2, 3, and 4 schemes, respectively.

Case (1985) offered extensive evidence to support his position. To show that the development of STSS recycles through the same levels across the four main developmental stages, he and his colleagues devised STSS tasks appropriate to each of the four stages, which required the child to keep in mind sensorimotor actions (such as seeing or grasping), relational representations (such as words or mental images), dimensional representations (such as numbers), and vectorial representations (such as ratios of numbers). In the test addressed to dimensional STSS children are shown sets of cards marked with several dots. They are instructed to count the dots on each card as soon as it appears, retain the number in memory, and recall all numbers when the last card of a set is presented. Sets usually involve 2 to 7 cards, which require children to store and recall 2 to 7 digits representing the number of dots on each card of the successive sets. The test addressed to the vectorial STSS is similar in all respects but one: dots are of two different colors on each card and the child is asked to find out how many green dots there are on the card for each red one and store in memory the result of this operation. The operation of counting in the first test is dimensional because it involves only one kind of element, which can be placed along a single dimension; it is vectorial in the second test because it has to integrate two different dimensions into one.

In a second series of experiments Case tried to show that increases in STSS are related to increases in processing efficiency. In these experiments, children's operational efficiency was assessed by recording the speed with which they were able to execute the required operation, which was appropriate for each stage. In the task addressed to operational efficiency in the dimensional stage children were asked to count the elements of successive sets as quickly as possible. Also their STSS of the same sets was measured. Thus, the relationship between the two could be specified. This experiment was also directed to adults, who were asked to count and remember the number values in artificial words specifically invented for the experiment. The results of this experiment are summarized in Figure 5. 2 where we can see that the relationship between these two dimensions of processing capacity is almost perfectly linear; that is, the faster children were able to execute the counting operation, the more items they were able to store in STSS. Interestingly, the adults working in an artificial language recorded both a

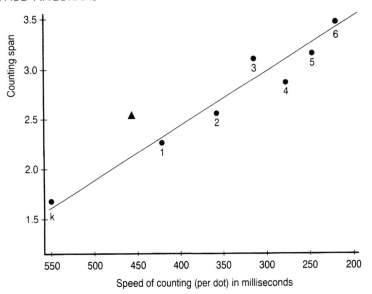

Figure 5.2   Relationships between speed of counting and counting span. Triangles indicate the performance of untrained adults tested in an artificial language
Note: One may note that the faster the subjects were able to count, the more digits they were able to hold in working memory
Reproduced with permission from Case, R. (1985). *Intellectual Development: Birth to Adulthood.* New York: Academic Press.

counting speed and an STSS of a 6–7-year-old child. Given massive practice in counting in this artificial language, however, the adults attained a counting speed and an STSS normal for their age. According to Case, these findings come in support of his position that variations in operational efficiency cause variations in STSS.

How is processing capacity involved in the development of the executive control structures associated with the course of cognitive growth? Both Case and Pascual-Leone asserted that processing capacity sets the limits for the structures a person can learn, because regardless of age, the structures that can be assembled cannot involve more schemes than those that can be simultaneously held in working memory. Case attempted to empirically substantiate this position through a series of learning experiments, in which he trained children to assemble new structures in various domains that either met their diagnosed STSS or were higher. Case found that these studies suggest that potentially everything up to a child's STSS limit is learnable; whatever is above the limit cannot be learned unless it can be reorganized by some kind of strategy which will bring its maximum requirements within the processing limits of the subject's substage (Case et al., 1996).

What causes the actual changes in processing capacity itself? Case posits two main factors. The first is related to maturationally determined changes in the underlying brain structures responsible for the representation and processing of information (see van der Molen & Ridderinkhoff, ch. 2 this volume). The second is practice of a given operation. Practice establishes stable connections between the neural assemblies, allowing the operation to be subsequently executed more efficiently. This explains why the adults' counting performance returned to normal after practice. We must note, however, that the developmental level of the brain sets limits on the degree to which performance can improve as a result of learning. Case (1985) has shown that even after massive practice in counting, first-grade children were no more efficient in counting than second-grade children who had received no practice. In conclusion, Case theorized that maturationally based changes make it possible for practice and learning to improve efficiency; which in turn creates more space for storing information, resulting in increased available STSS. At this point more complex executive control structures can be assembled, which, once they have become operational, lead to the next substage of development.

Executive control structures and central conceptual structures

Case's view of development resembles that of Piaget's in an important respect, that is, it suggests that understanding and problem-solving in different domains, such as the social, mathematical, and spatial domains, involve equivalently complex structures at each level of development, and that they progress from one level to the next at the same pace. Of course, Case related these constraints to processing capacity rather than to the underlying logical structure of mental operations. Case has recently modified his view of development, recognizing now that variations may occur in both the organization and development of different domains, due to differences in how meaning is organized in each of the domains. Specifically, Case recognized that there are *central conceptual structures*.

He defined these as 'networks of semantic notes and relations that have an extremely broad (but not system-wide) domain of application and that are central to children's functioning in that domain' (Case et al., 1996, p. 5). In their studies, Case and his colleagues (Case, 1992; Case et al., 1996), in line with the findings of other researchers to be presented later (e.g. Demetriou & Efklides, 1985; Demetriou, Efklides & Platsidou, 1993a), identified central conceptual structures for quantities, space, social behavior, narrative, music, and motor behavior. Each of these structures is supposed to involve a set of core processes and principles which serve to organize a broad array of situations; for example, the concept of more and less for quantities, adjacency and inclusion relationships for space, and actions and intentions for social behavior. Thus, these are very broad structures in which many executive control structures may be constructed, relative to an individual's experience and needs. For example, in the central conceptual structure that organizes quantities, executive control structures to solve arithmetic problems, to operate balance beams, to represent home locations according to their street address, and so on, may be constructed. In short, central conceptual structures function as frames and they provide the basic guiding principles and raw conceptual material for the construction of more locally focused concepts and action plans, when the need for them arises.

Figure 5.3 shows how Case represents the semantic organization and development of two conceptual structures, namely space and quantity. It can be seen that from the semantic point of view these two structures are considerably different as they involve different notions and defining charac-

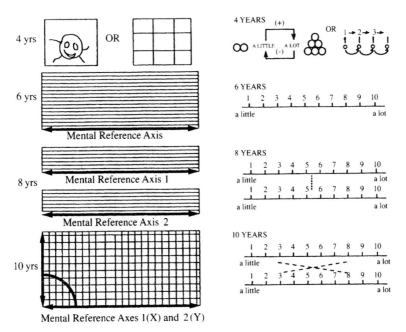

Figure 5.3   The general organization of the spatial and the quantitative central conceptual structure from 4 to 10, according to Case's theory. The similarities and differences between the two structures can easily be inspected.

Note: (a) The spatial central conceptual structure: At 4, children possess preaxial schemas enabling them to represent the component shapes of an object and an object's location in a rectangular field. At 6, a uniaxial schema is established that enables children to conjointly specify an object's internal shape and spatial relation and its location relative to the edge of a field. At 8, a biaxial schema is established enabling children to set up two discrete representations in different locations each referenced to a different axis. At 10, children integrate the two axes so that they can conjointly reference a whole field of objects in relation to both of them at once.

(b) The quantitative central conceptual structure: At 4, children represent quantity globally and also numbers are a sequence of tags associated with objects numbered consecutively. At 6, the two are integrated into a unidimensional schema (the mental counting line) which conjointly represents number and quantity. At 8, a bidimensional schema is established which enables children to represent two quantitative dimensions or scales and their relations. At 10, the integrated bidimensional schema enables children to represent the reversible relations between two scales and generalize this to an entire system.

Reproduced with permission from Case, R., Okamoto, Y., Griffiths, S. et al. (1996). The role of central conceptual structures, in the development of children's thought. *Monographs of the Society for Research in Child Development,* **61**, (1–2, Serial No. 246).

teristics. However, from the developmental point of view, the two structures involve organizations of equivalent complexity at corresponding developmental levels. Therefore, Case still believes in the presence of powerful system-wide constraints in cognitive development despite his recent recognition of variations due to semantic and content differences between cognitive structures. These constraints reflect the capacity of the STSS (Case et al., 1996).

Thus, learning the core elements of a central conceptual structure opens the way for fast acquisition of a wide array of executive control structures, although this does not generalize to other conceptual structures. It remains limited within the one affected, indicating that there may be variations both within and across individuals in the executive control structures that can be constructed within each central conceptual structure. These variations depend on the environmental support provided to each structure and on the individual's particular preferences and involvement. The mechanisms that regulate environmental support and personal involvement are summarized below.

Regulatory mechanisms leading to hierarchical integration and stage transitions

Changes in the underlying hardware of cognition (i.e. the brain) and in its functional manifestations (i.e. the processing capacity), open the way for new structural constructions. However, these changes are not sufficient in and of themselves to produce new executive control structures. These must somehow be worked out of the present structures. Case proposed four mechanisms relevant to the construction of new structures: *schematic search, schematic evaluation, schematic retagging, and schematic consolidation*. Schematic search refers to the need to simultaneously activate the requisite schemes so that they can be interrelated and combined into something new. Schematic evaluation refers to a process which compares alternative groupings or sequences of schemes and then evaluates their relevance to the present goal. Schematic retagging refers to the process which gives an 'identity' to the new structure so that it can be recovered independently of the schemes involved in its construction. Schematic consolidation involves reworking and rehearsing the new structure until it is mastered.

These mechanisms of change are activated in the context of three distinct but rather common general processes which regulate and direct cognitive functioning, namely, *problem-solving, exploration, and mutual regulation*. Problem-solving involves the search for new relationships among existing mental schemes, evaluating the solution's relevance to the goal, somehow symbolizing the finally acceptable solution, and practice and consolidation. The same processes apply in explorations, although explorations may be initiated simply out of curiosity, whereas problem-solving is directed by a goal. Finally, mutual regulation refers to the process involved in situations implicating goal-directed interaction between two or more human beings. In these situations, both parties search for schemes allowing them to follow or copy the other's actions (schematic search), to evaluate their success in regard to the goal (schematic evaluation), to somehow represent the new construction (schematic retagging), and to practice it until it reaches an acceptable functional level (schematic consolidation).

Other Neo-Piagetian Theories

Pascual-Leone and Case were not alone in advancing theories alternative to Piaget's theory. Two equally well known theories were proposed by Graeme Halford, (1988, 1993) and Kurt Fischer (Fischer, 1980; Fischer & Bidell, in press; Fischer and Pipp, 1984).

Halford focused on processing capacity complementing Case's research. He emphasized the aspect of capacity which is necessary for the initial problem representation as opposed to the subsequent representation of objectives and strategies. In other words, Halford accounts for changes in the *kind* of representations that can be constructed rather than for changes in how the given representations can be interrelated. As such, he explains capacity's role in the transition from one major stage to the next, rather than the transition between substages. Halford determined that the stages of element, relational, system, and multiple-system mappings involve representations that require simultaneous consideration of 1, 2, 3, and 4 dimensions, respectively. These stages correspond to Case's sensorimotor, relational, dimensional, and vectorial stage, respectively.

Fischer's conception of the stages of cognitive development is very similar to that of Case. That is, he describes four major stages which coincide by and large with Case's major stages. Moreover, like Case, he believes that development within each major stage recycles over the same sequence of four structurally identical levels. However, Fischer's theory differs from the other neo-Piagetian theories in a number of respects. One of them is in the way it explains cognitive change. Specifically, although Fischer does not deny the operation of information-processing constraints on development, he emphasizes environmental and social rather than individual factors as causes of development. To explain developmental change he borrowed two classic notions from Lev Vygotsky (1962; see Weinert & Weinert, ch. 1 this volume), that is, *internalization* and the *zone of proximal development*. Internalization refers to the processes that enable children to reconstruct and absorb the products of their observations and interactions in a way that makes them their own. That is, it is a process which transforms external, alien skills and concepts into internal, integral ones. The zone of proximal development expresses Vygotsky's idea that at any age the child's *potential* for understanding and problem-solving is not identical to his *actual* understanding and problem-solving ability. Potential ability is always greater than actual ability: the zone of proximal development refers to the range of possibilities that exist between the actual and the potential. Structured social interaction, or scaffolding, and internalization are the processes that gradually allow potential (for understanding and problem-solving) to become actual abilities (concepts and skills).

Fischer used these concepts to explain many of the phenomena that plagued Piaget's theory. He argued that variations in the development and functioning of different mental skills and functions from the one domain to the other may be the rule rather than the exception. In his opinion these variations are to be attributed to differences in the experience that individuals have with different domains and also to differences in the support that they receive when interacting with the various domains. In addition, he posited that an individual's true level, which functions as a kind of ceiling for all domains, is the level of his potential, which can only be determined under conditions of maximum familiarity and scaffolding. Under these conditions, development appears to occur in spurts which affect a wide array of particular skills. Thus, development shows its real stage-like character. Under conditions of low familiarity and support the development of different processes appears less intercoordinated and continuous. Thus, under these conditions there is noise which masks the actual nature of development.

From Piaget to Dynamic Systems Theory: Models for Formalizing Cognitive Development

The neo-Piagetian theories of cognitive development represent the developing mind as a universe of dynamically interacting and constantly changing processes and functions. Moreover, in agreement with Piaget's theory, the theories represent development as a process with a strong stage-like component. In recent years there has been an increasing interest in theories and methods that show promise for capturing and modeling the regularities underlying multiply interacting and changing process. Dynamic systems theory is one of them. When multiple processes interact in complex ways they very often appear to behave unsystematically and unpredictably. In fact, however, they are interconnected in systematic ways, such that the condition of one process at a given point of time t is responsible for the condition of another process, at a next point of time $t+1$, and together they determine the condition of a third process, at a time $t+2$, which then influences the conditions of the other two processes at a time $t+3$ and so on. Dynamic systems theory can reveal and model the dynamic relationships among different processes and specify the forms of development that result from different types of interaction among processes. The aim is to explain the order and systematicity that exist beneath a surface of apparent disorder or 'chaos'. It needs to be noted that there is no limitation as to what processes may be involved in this kind of modeling. That is, the processes may belong to any of the levels of mind, such as the level of the processing capacity and the level of problem-solving skills.

Paul van Geert (1994) was the first to show the promise that dynamic systems theory holds for the understanding of cognitive development. Van Geert assumed the basic growth model to be the so-called 'logistic growth model', wherein (in its simplest form) a given ability follows an S-like pattern of change (see graph b in Figure 5.1). That is, change is very slow and hardly noticeable initially; after a given point in time, however, it occurs very rapidly so that the process of ability spurts to a much higher level in a relatively short period of time; finally, as this process approaches its end state, change decelerates until it stabilizes.

According to van Geert, logistic growth is a function of three parameters: the present level, the rate of change, and a limit on the level that can be reached, called the carrying capacity of the system. The first parameter, that is, the present level, indicates the potential that a process has for further development. Obviously, the more a process departs from its end state the more its potential of change would be. The second (the rate of change), is an augmenting or multiplying factor applied to the present level, in a way similar to the interest rate applied to a no-withdrawal savings account. That is, this is a factor that indicates the rate at which an ability changes in order to approach its end state. The third parameter (carrying capacity) refers to the resources available for development. For example, in a theory such as Case's the short-term storage available may function as the carrying capacity of the development of cognitive processes which may belong to any domain. In fact, the rate of change is directly connected to the carrying capacity so that changes in one of them affect the conditions of the other and both of them together define the form of development that a process will take in the long run.

Investigations in this context have a strong theoretical component. That is, the researcher systematically varies the value of each of the parameters mentioned above in order to see the form that the whole curve will take along the age period of interest. Thus, the developmental functions may take a variety of forms relative to the value given to each parameter involved. The graphs shown in Figure 5.1 show two very simple examples of growth, one for exponential growth (graph a) and one for logistic (graph b). If the researcher wants to model the reciprocal exchange of influences, he or she may involve several processes and specify that each contributes to the development of the others in a certain way, as implicated in the discussion above. In this way, one can develop models of connected growth. This kind of modeling was called 'experimental theoretical developmental psychology', because the form and the implications of various models are explored and specified mathematically before actual experimentation is undertaken. Then the researcher can go out in the field and carry out real experiments. The pattern of growth suggested by empirical findings is then specified and compared to the theoretical curves, and the theoretical model closest to the empirical model is taken as the best representation of the actual course of cognitive development.

Van Geert (1994) himself, Fischer (Fischer & Bidell, in press) and Case (Case et al., 1996) presented a series of studies exploring the implications of these methods for the understanding of cognitive development. The models shown in Figure 5.4 represent Case's explorations. In the first model, Case explored the development of five specific processes within the same central

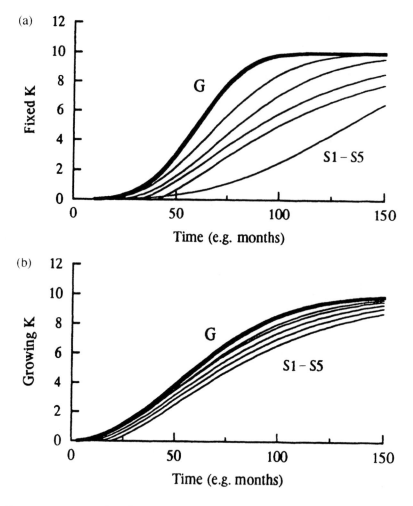

Figure 5.4 Hierarchically linked growth curves: *(a) One-way connection.* This figure depicts five specific cognitive processes (S1–S5) which feed a more general process (G) as they develop. It can be seen that the general process changes faster than the specific processes and that the changes of the specific processes are not very tight. *(b) Two-way connection.* This figure depicts reciprocal connection. The specific processes feed the general process and the general process feeds the specific ones. It can be seen that all processes develop faster and that they change in a more concerted way.
Reproduced with permission from Case, R., Okamoto, Y., Griffiths, S. et al. (1996). The role of central conceptual structures in the development of children's thought. *Monographs of the Society for Research in Child Development,* **61**, (1–2, Serial No. 246).

conceptual structure, and a general process representing the general pro-cessing mechanisms of this structure. It is assumed that each of the specific processes changes as its own rate of change and that it contributes to the development of the general process proportionate to its own rate of change. Under this condition, the general process attains its final level more quickly than the specific processes; moreover, the specific processes appear to follow widely diverging developmental trajectories. In the second model, the assumption that the general process contributes to the development of each of the five specific processes is also posited. Two consequences follow from the addition of this assumption; first, all functions grow more rapidly than before; and second, the growth rate of each specific function becomes more similar and the functions exhibit a tighter pattern of change. These methods have caused a revival of interest in the grand picture of development and the nature of developmental stages, which appeared to diminish after the disenchantment with Piaget's classical theory. Overall, these methods suggest that under some conditions cognitive development does occur in spurts which lead to catalytic, broad, and qualitative transformations of cognitive processes. This picture lends support to Piaget and the neo-Piagetians.

THE DEVELOPMENT OF REASONING

Piaget aspired to describe the development of reasoning and he invoked logic as a model of the stages of cognitive development. However, he has only indirectly focused on reasoning per se. The reader is reminded that his primary aim was to specify what aspects of the world can be understood at different stages and what methods are at the disposal of the individual in exploring the world. Thus, Piaget's theory is not an account of the development of reasoning because it only vaguely specifies the kinds of reasoning that can be mastered at the successive stages of cognitive development. This is true for the neo-Piagetian theories as well which, although they may have elaborated extensively on the processes of problem representation and strategy development, do not address logical reasoning as such. In other words, they did not study the types of inference used to construct a representation of the problem space or how the various types of inference are employed to choose problem-solving strategies and formulate an action plan. Thus, in this section we will summarize the research relevant to the nature and development of logical reasoning.

Reasoning is thinking that involves inference. Generally speaking, inference refers to processes that enable thinkers to transfer meaning from one representation to another. This transfer normally occurs on the basis of properties, observed or conceived, which are present in both the initial (or base) representation and the target representation. In inference, these common properties are used as an intermediary between two representations such that properties characterizing the base representation (apart from common properties) are also ascribed to the target representation. For instance, a 4-year-old child thoughtfully concludes: 'If it doesn't break when I drop it, it's a rock . . . It didn't break. It must be a rock' (reported by DeLoache, Miller & Pierroutsakos, 1998). The two things to be connected here are the notion of the rock and the present object, their common property being that they don't break when dropped. By virtue of this common property, the property of 'rockiness' and other derivative properties (such as rocks are heavy, hard, etc.) may also be transferred to the present object.

There are several types of reasoning, the two most inclusive types being *inductive* and *deductive*. Inductive reasoning is a freer kind of reasoning which can involve any kind of representation, such as perceptions, mental images, and propositions of one's language. Moreover, in inductive reasoning, inference goes from the particular to the general or from the particular to the particular and the conclusion is not necessary but only probable. An example follows:

> All developmental psychologists I met were bright.
> Therefore, all developmental psychologists are bright.

Obviously this conclusion is only probable because in the future we may meet development psychologists who are not bright.

Deductive reasoning is a more constrained kind of reasoning. First, it only involves verbal statements or propositions, or other symbols which stand for propositions. Thus, inference in deductive reasoning is the process which transfers meaning from one set of propositions (the premises) to other propositions (the conclusion). Second, in deductive reasoning the inferential process always proceeds from the general (the premises) to the specific (the conclusion), and the conclusion follows necessarily from the premises. This occurs because in deductive reasoning the premises must be accepted as given, thus the conclusion is mandatory. An example is given below:

> All developmental psychologists are bright.
> Dr X is a developmental psychologist
> Therefore, Dr X is bright.

Obviously, once both premises of this argument are accepted as true, the conclusion is necessarily true—no matter who this Dr X is or what we know about her.

Both inductive and deductive reasoning implicate a number of different varieties, each of which comprises several inferential processes. For example, inductive reasoning involves analogical reasoning, which focuses on relational similarity, and statistical reasoning, which focuses on probabilities. Deductive reasoning involves categorical reasoning, which is concerned with class relations and conditional reasoning, which is examining the relationships between 'if . . . then' type propositions. The study of the development of reasoning aims to highlight the types of inferences that can be made at different ages and how reasoning develops with age. Next we will summarize the research and theory relevant to the development of inductive and deductive reasoning from infancy to adulthood.

The Development of Inductive Reasoning

Reasoning based on perceptual and conceptual similarity

Perceptual similarity is the most readily apparent form of similarity and so it is the basis for the earliest forms of inductive reasoning. Research with young infants has shown that they can make judgments based on perceptual similarity very early in life, if not at birth. In fact, the very methods used to study infants' cognitive abilities, such as the habituation method of the visual preference method (see Butterworth, ch. 3 this volume), assume that they are able to recognize and register similarities and differences among various stimuli.

From as early as 2 and a half years of age children use perceptual similarity as a basis for drawing inductive inferences. For instance, Gelman and Coley (1990) showed their subjects a particular bird and told them that 'it lives in a nest'. Children at this age readily inferred that another bird which was virtually identical to the target would also live in a nest; they were unsure about other birds which differed from the target bird in some respects; and they concluded that other creatures, like a stegosaurus which differed markedly from the target, would not live in a nest. Moreover, other experiments showed that associating an object with a novel name (for example 'this is a dax' or 'this is a diffle') leads children as young as 3 and a half to expect that other objects of the same shape would also be 'dax' or 'diffle' (Becker & Ward, 1991; Landau, Smith & Jones, 1988).

Conceptual similarity was also found to function as a basis of inductive inferences in infancy. Kotovsky and Baillargeon (1995) showed that 10-and-a-half-month-old infants may choose to make inferences on the basis of functional rather than perceptual similarity. They showed the infants a cylindrical container into which they first poured salt, and from which they then poured it out. Subsequently they poured salt either into a container identical to the first in all respects except that it had no bottom and thus could not function as a container, or into another object which was perceptually different from the original container but which could function as a container because it had a bottom. The infants showed surprise when the perceptually similar but functionally inappropriate object appeared to hold the salt, indicating that they were able to formulate a category based on functional rather than perceptual properties and generate inductive inferences accordingly. The work of S. Gelman (see Gelman & Markham, 1987) and Keil (1989) has shown convincingly that by the age of 3–4 children organize their knowledge of the world into elaborate categories which they use as a basis for very powerful inferences. This work will be examined in the next section; here it suffices to say that empirical evidence suggests that with increasing knowledge and experience inductive inference tends to rely increasingly on conceptual rather than perceptual similarity, although perceptual similarity is never abandoned as a basis of inference. Thus, with increasing expertise, inference tends to rely more on attributes indicating category membership than on simple perceptual similarity.

Analogical reasoning

Analogical reasoning involves similarity between relationships rather than similarity between the objects themselves. The classic structure of problems which require analogical reasoning is represented by the following formula: a : b : : c : d. A verbal analogy of this type might be as follows: Nicosia is to Cyprus as Paris is to France. A numerical analogy might be as follows: 2 : 4 : : 3 : 6. In the classic set up for the study of analogical reasoning, one of the terms in the second pair, usually the second one, is missing and the subject is asked to specify this term. A correct response is taken as an indication that the subject can abstract the relationships between the terms in the first pair ('it is the capital of' in the verbal analogy above or 'it is the double of' in the numerical analogy above), assume that the same relationship connects the terms in the second pair and finally apply this relationship to the term given to generate the missing term. Halford (1993) defined the process that enables the thinker to transfer the relationship between the terms of the first pair to the terms of the second pair as structure mapping: 'Structure mapping is a rule for assigning elements of one structure to elements of another, in such a way that any functions or relations between elements of the first structure will also be assigned to corresponding functions or relations in the second structure' (Halford, 1988, p. 105). That is, the c : d pair is mapped onto the a : : b pair so that the terms c and d in the second pair are taken to correspond to the terms a and b in the first pair, respectively, and thus to be related by the same kind of relationship.

It must be noted that structure mapping does not require any perceptual similarity among the terms of the analogy. For example, all of the analogies following are acceptable: [Marantona : football : : Senna : car racing]; [Beethoven : music : : Einstein : science]; [Alexander the Great : Greece : : Napoleon : France]. We can even imagine a relationship running through all three analogies (for example, excellence, distinction, and dominance) although we can hardly see any perceptual similarity between any of the terms. Thus, analogical reasoning operates on the principles organizing perceptual evidence of knowledge about the world, rather than on perceptual evidence itself, and therefore it is a second-order inferential process. For this reason Piaget believed analogical reasoning to be a product of formal operations. Theories of intelligence also ascribe an important role to analogical reasoning. In both classic (Spearman, 1927) and modern theories of intelligence (Gustafsson, 1994) analogical reasoning is considered one of the most central mechanisms of general intelligence.

Contrary to the popular belief that analogical reasoning is a late attainment, recent research suggests that very young infants are sensitive to analogical relationships. For example, Wagner, Winner, Cicchetti & Gardner (1981) showed that 9-month-old infants preferred to look at an arrow pointing up when hearing an ascending tone and at an arrow pointing down when hearing a descending tone. That is, they appeared to be able to decode the analogy 'ascending tone : ↑ : : descending tone : ↓'. Based on this and similar evidence Goswami's (1992) argued 'that the ability to recognize relational similarity may not develop at all' (p. 13) because it 'could be an inherent quality of human reasoning' (p. 15). Moreover, Goswami and Brown (1989) showed that children can solve classic analogies of the a : b : : c : d type once they involve familiar objects and transformations. For example, children were presented with pictures organized in an analogy as follows: chocolate : melted chocolate : : snowman : ? Their task was to choose the missing term d from among five pictures. Many 3 and almost all 4 and 5 year olds were able to solve this kind of task.

This precocious presence of analogical reasoning, however, is largely dependent on the surface or perceptual similarity of the terms. Even school-aged children are prone to fail on analogies which involve very common objects and functional relationships, if there is no obvious perceptual similarity. For example, Case (1985) found that the analogy ink : pen : : paint : brush is understood at about the age of 10 years. Second-order relations which involve abstract relationships, such as food : body : : water : ground are not understood until well into adolescence. Finally, according to Sternberg and Downing (1982), third-order analogies such as sand : beach : : star : galaxy : : : water : ocean : : air : sky are understood only at college age.

In conclusion, analogical reasoning seems to be present at a very early age. Initially it involves relationships between sensorimotor experiences or actions. During the preschool years it can structure many different types of relationships once the objects and the transformations are familiar and there is some kind of surface similarity to direct the inferential process. During the primary school years there is a shift that enables the child to reason on the basis of underlying functional relationships. This kind of reasoning is actually the beginning of abstract reasoning, which fully manifests in adolescence. Finally, at college age, analogical reasoning can structure third- or higher-order relationships of various types.

The Development of Deductive Reasoning

According to Braine (1990), the development of deductive reasoning is a process that leads from *primary reasoning* to *formal* or *secondary reasoning*. Primary reasoning 'provides some elementary information integration processes serving primarily two purposes. The first purpose is to facilitate verbal interaction by providing a set of inferences that are made automatically in processing discourse. The second purpose is to integrate information received from different sources or at different times' (Braine, 1990, p. 134). For example, primary reasoning underlies the ability to follow everyday conversations like the following:

> *Child*: Where is my pencil?
> *Mother*: I am not sure, I think I saw it on the kitchen table or on your father's desk, oh no, it wasn't in the kitchen.
> *Child*: Ah, okay, I am going to my father's study.

In this kind of conversation, 'the comprehension process uses all the information available—what the comprehender knows about the speaker and the speaker's motives, specific knowledge of the world, general conventions about speaking, as well as the words used and their grammatical organization within the sentence being decoded. This kind of comprehension is typical of conversation and reasoning for pleasure. It is ordinarily a fast process since it takes place at conversation and reading speeds. We can take it for granted that all normal human beings have a lot of practice at ordinary comprehension and develop to a fair degree at it' (Braine & Rumain, 1983, p. 267).

However, there are problems which call for formal or secondary reasoning. An example of these problems is given below:

> Birds fly.
> Elephants are birds.
> Elephants fly.

Obviously, the conclusion that *Elephants fly*, is logically valid, although factually false. That is, although we know that elephants are not birds and they do not fly, we have to accept that it necessarily follows from the premises. In other words, we assume that 'if it were true that elephants are birds' then, 'given that we accept that birds fly', we would also have to accept that 'elephants fly'.

Note two differences in the approach required to solve this kind of problem in contrast to problems that can be solved by primary reasoning. First, analytic rather than ordinary comprehension is required; that is, one must focus on the meaning of each sentence as given in the argument and ignore any other previous knowledge or information related to the words in the sentences. Second, it must be understood that an argument involves a network of relationships systematically arranged which can be used as a basis for decoding the relationships. Thus, in order to grasp the logical relationships implied by a logical argument, one must be able to break down or analyze the argument into the premises involved and focus on their logical or formal relationships independent of content. The formal relationships implied by the argument's premises are normally hinted at or suggested by particular words of natural language, such as the conditionals, 'if . . . then', the disjunctives 'either . . . or', and so on. When this approach is taken, one is, in principle, ready for formal or secondary reasoning.

Moshman (1990, 1994) proposed that the development of deductive reasoning evolves through four stages. These stages appear as steps which lead from primary to formal reasoning. The crucial factor in this course of development is an increasing awareness about the inferential processes themselves, their underlying logical properties, and their relationships. Additionally, increased awareness is usually accompanied by an increasing will to control and improve inferential processes. Moshman described the development of reasoning as more a matter of 'metareasoning' than simple inference and logic:

> Metareasoning strategies are strategies of reasoning that go beyond simply assimilating premises to unconscious inference schemata. They involve an explicit distinction between premises and conclusions and a purposeful use of inference to deduce the latter from the former. Such strategies are typically

conscious or at least accessible to consciousness. They include, for example, strategies for systematically generating multiple possibilities consistent with premises, actively seeking counterexamples to potential conclusions, or coordinating several inference schemata to construct a line of argument. (Moshman, '1990, p. 208).

Thus, Moshman's stages (to be summarized below) describe the course from the automatic use of inference schemata to explicit, self-guided logical reasoning. The general characteristics of these stages are summarized in Table 5. 2.

Stage 1: explicit content–implicit inference. This stage appears during the preschool years, when children reason logically *using inferences but do not think about inference.* This is evident in both the children's, ordinary comprehension and in their everyday speech production. That is, when they speak, they correctly use most of the connectives and conditionals involved in inference schemes; specifically, by age 2–3 children correctly use *and, but, or, because* and *if.* Moreover, at this stage or a little later they are able to respond to commands which require the correct decoding of the relationship expressed by the conditional. For example, at approximately age 2, children perform both actions in response to the command *Do A and do B*; at age 4 they perform one of the two actions in response to the command *Do A or do B* (Beilin & Lust, 1975; Johansson & Sjolin, 1975). At this age children also understand the meaning of the conditional *if* when it is embedded in permission schemes; that is, in stories in which an action is permitted to occur if a given condition is met (e.g. 'if you want to play outside you must put your coat on'). Harris and Nunez have recently shown that 3 and 4 year olds can recognize breaches of permission rules by specifying when the child 'is being naughty and not doing what her mum told her' (1996, p. 1574). Of course, understanding of the subtle and more strictly logical meaning of at least some of the conditionals follows a little later. One such example is the directionality *if*; that is, understanding that events paired by *if* are necessarily ordered in a particular time sequence. According to Emerson (1980), it is not until age 5 that children can recognize which of the four following sentences is 'silly': *If it starts to rain I put up my umbrella; I put up my umbrella if it starts to rain; If I put up my umbrella it starts to rain; It starts to rain if I put up my umbrella.* At age 6 children could also correct the silly sentences to make them sensible.

At this stage children do not think about premises and conclusions, but about the actual elements mentioned in the premises. Thus, they run into trouble when faced with a problem which in some way deviates from the standard form of inference schemas. For instance, they cannot solve the problem below, given as an example of problems that can be solved at the next stage. Stage 1 children do not recognize a problem in this argument and they derive a conclusion by choosing one of the two alternatives (plants or machines). This answer indicated that children at this stage have no understanding of the inference processes, that is, they are not aware that the premises constrain the conclusion.

Stage 2: explicit inference–implicit logic. This awareness appears for the first time by about age 5 or 6, marking the transition to the second stage. With this type of awareness, stage 2 children realize that no conclusion can be drawn from the argument below:

Sprognoids are animals or plants or machines.
Sprognoids are not animals.
Therefore, sprognoids are plants.

They realize that because the first premises involves three alternatives and the second premise cancels only one of them, it is uncertain which of the two remaining alternatives is valid. This understanding indicates, according to Moshman, that children at this stage are able to view the premises and conclusions as different parts of an argument. It also indicates that they recognize the fact that the different parts of the argument are connected by inference. In other words, children at this stage are explicitly aware of the inferential process that connects premises and conclusions into coherent arguments, and are sensitive to logical necessity. This stage is consolidated between age 6 and 10, although logic as such is still implicit in their reasoning and does not function as a frame to explicitly guide reasoning. Thus, they fail on problems in which the logical form of the argument must be explicitly differentiated from its content. The previous argument on elephants that can fly is an example of the problems which cannot be solved by children at this stage, because they focus on the content of the argument (which they find to be consistent with what they know about elephants) and do not recognize that this argument is formally identical to many of the arguments and inferences they spontaneously use or understand in their everyday interactions.

Stage 3: explicit logic–implicit metalogic. Preadolescents, aged 11–12, are able to solve the above problem, indicating an understanding of the distinction between logical form and empirical truth. In other words, they understand that 'an argument is valid if, regardless of the empirical truth of its premises and conclusions, it has a logical form such that, *if* the premises were true, the conclusion would have to be true as well' (Moshman, 1990, p. 212). Therefore, at this stage children are explicitly aware of logic as a system of rule-bound relationships between arguments and conclusions, which implies differentiation between formal logical relationships and the language in which they can be expressed.

This differentiation was clearly demonstrated by Osherson and Markman's (1975) study, in which children and adults were asked to evaluate the truth of statements such as 'The chip in my hand is white and it is not white,' or 'The chip in my hand is not red or it is red.' These statements are *nonempirical*, that is, their truth does not depend upon the external world but on the consistency between the assertions involved in the statements. Thus, to determine the truth of these statements, one must both understand that empirical information about the color of the chips is irrelevant and have an 'objective attitude toward language' (Osherson & Markman, 1975, p. 225). In turn, this understanding indicates that children represent logical relationships as something different from empirical reality. Children

Table 5.2 The general characteristics of deductive reasoning at different phases

Age	Stage	Explicit object of understanding	Knowledge implicit in reasoning (subject)	Inference schemas	Comprehension	Reasoning
2–5	Explicit content Implicit inference	*Content*	*Inference:* Conclusions deduced and thus distinct from premises	There is a cat: There is an apple/∴ There is a cat and an apple. There is a grape, and there is a lemon or an egg/∴ There is a grape and a lemon, or there is a grape and an egg.	Automatic; metalinguistic awareness is implicit	Primary
6–10	Explicit inference Implicit logic	*Inference:* Conclusions deduced from and, thus, related to premises	*Logic:* Form of argument distinct from empirical truth of premises and conclusions (necessity)	There is a dog and a tiger; There is not a dog and there is not a tiger/INCOMPATIBLE If there is either a cow or goat, then there is a pear; There is a cow/∴ There is a pear. There is a strawberry or a blackberry; There is not a strawberry/∴ There is a blackberry.	Ordinary; basic metalinguistic awareness	Primary
11–18	Explicit logic Implicit metalogic	*Logic:* Relation of argument form and empirical truth of premises and conclusions (validity)	*Metalogic:* Formal logical system distinct from natural language	Schemes of suppositional reasoning: given a chain of reasoning of the form 'suppose p & and q' one can conclude that if p is present q will also be present. Subjects also start to understand that when q is present, however, it does not follow that p would have to be present	Analytic; complex metalinguistic awareness	Secondary
19–24	Explicit metalogic	*METALOGIC:* Interrelations of logical systems and natural languages	*Metametalogic:* Differentiation and reconstruction of metalogic	All of the above as means for the creation and formation of logical systems that formalize inferential processes or systems about the mind	Reflective; metametalinguistic awareness	Meta-systematic

Note: Based on Moshman (1990), Table 10.1 and Braine (1990), Table 7.1. The symbol /∴ stands for 'Therefore'.

younger than 10 stated that they could not decide on the truth of these statements, indicating that they are not aware of this differentiation. Full development of this stage does not appear before approximately age 16–18.

Even at this stage, adolescents still lack an explicit metalogic, that is, a system enabling them to analyze logical systems, explicitly specify their formal relationships, and possibly build a logical system incorporating relationships and differences among logical systems. As a result, they fail on tasks which require this metalogic. One example of a task that cannot be solved at this stage is the classic version of Wason's (Wason & Johnson-Laird, 1972) 'selection task', which is described below.

Stage 4: explicit metalogic. At this stage an individual can function as a theorist of reasoning, that is, he can consider the characteristics of different types of inference or even those characteristics of different logical systems and specify their similarities and differences. Subjects at this level can therefore solve Wason's task. This task involves four cards marked with a letter on one side and a number on the other. In the experiment, the cards presented to the subject were as follows: A, D, 3, and 7. The subject was told that the 'following rule applies to the four cards and may be true or false: *If there is an A on the one side of the card, then there is a 3 on the other side of the card.*' The subject was then asked to indicate which cards would need to be turned over to decide whether the rule is true or false. The correct answer is A and 7. A is relevant because it is stated in the rule. If there is anything but 3 on its other side the rule would be proved false. D is irrelevant because the rule does not refer to cards with letters other than A. The card with the 3 appears relevant but it is not because the rule specifies what must follow if A occurs and does not state what must follow if 3 occurs. Thus, even if an A does not appear on the other side of the 3 card the rule is not contradicted because the rule does not state what should be marked on the back side of 3. Finally, the card with the 7 is relevant because it might have an A on the other side. This is not permitted by the rule because if there is an A there should be a 3. Thus, turning the 7 card is relevant because it can falsify the rule. Most adult subjects involved in the original experiment selected the A and 3 cards, indicating that they operated as though the 'If A then 3' rule were equivalent to the 'If 3 then A' rule, which of course is not the case for the reasons already explained.

Logicians or psychologists studying reasoning, by definition, function at this stage. Some adults can also function at this stage without formal instruction in logic or cognitive psychology. Work on metasystematic reasoning is relevant here. According to Commons, Richards and Kuhn (1990), metasystematic reasoning enables thinkers to specify the formal characteristics of each of a number of different systems and then specify the higher-order similarities and differences between these systems. Our studies showed that only a small minority of college students, a meager 10%, who were advanced formal thinkers according to their performance on Piagetian formal tasks, demonstrated metasystematic reasoning. Moreover, these subjects exhibited a high level of awareness of their own mental processes (Demetriou, 1990). Being able to function at this stage provides a clear advantage; specifically, it enables the individual to adopt the particular approach required by different types of logical problems and apply the most appropriate inferential process.

Explaining the Development of Reasoning

Where does reasoning come from and how is it elevated from the state of implicit inference about the actual world to the state of explicit inference, logical necessity, and explicit reflection on inference and even on the rules underlying inference?

We have seen that the investigators of inductive reasoning believe that this fundamental form of inference may be part of the human makeup (Goswami, 1992). Macnamara (1986) and Fodor (1975) believe the same about the logical notions of truth and falsity, which constitute the foundations of deductive reasoning. In their opinion, the notion of truth is implicit in the assertions that children make very early on, because making assertions about something implies ascribing a truth value to it. Thus, these authors posit a language of thought which involves the basic logical relations underlying reasoning and which is available before children learn their mother language. Braine (1990), in an attempt to elaborate on this position, argued for ready-made inference schemas corresponding to particular patterns of events and occurrences in the environment. The most common of these patterns are *joint iteration*, which refers to repetitions of actions, events, or objects; *iteration of alternatives*, which applies to a situation wherein one event or object is present and another event or object may or may not be present; and *contingencies*, which refer to time-dependent sequences, which may or may not be causal (examples of these schemes are given in Table 5.2). Learning spoken language, according to these theorists, is equivalent to learning a translation into the language of thought. In other words, learning the connectives *and, or*, and *if*, which correspond to the three patterns mentioned above, is equivalent to mapping them onto the corresponding connectives of the language of thought. The power of the implicit inferences that can be drawn at the first stage of reasoning development (outlined above) lends strong support to this position.

Modern evolutionary psychology suggests a rationale for the assumption that the basic mechanisms of inference are innate. Specifically, Cosmides and Tooby (1994) proposed that reasoning appeared at the point in human evolution when humans began to have organized social life. Social life makes mutual controls necessary because the various goals, interests, promises, and actions of social beings may not coincide. Therefore, members of a social group need to be able to check each other's assertions for consistency—either with other assertions or with the realities referred to—in order to avoid possible cheating and deception. Therefore Cosmides and Tooby proposed that the adaptive function of reasoning was to enable humans to avoid cheating and deception.

While primary reasoning may be present very early, formal or secondary reasoning is acquired gradually over a very long period of time. This transformation of primary into secondary reasoning seems to be related to three interdependent factors: language learning, education, and self-directed reflection.

Language and associated conversational interactions are important because they provide ready-made and clearly coded inference patterns that can structure and direct the inferential process. Falmagne (1990) quite succinctly described the role that native language acquisition plays in the development of reasoning: 'I will argue that logical knowledge is derived both from an apprehension of the structure of the language itself, and from the correspondence between linguistically expressed propositions and empirical states of affairs' (Falmagne, 1990, p. 113). One may imagine many examples of conversations in which the linguistic and the actual structure of events are in direct correspondence: 'If you drop it, it will break into pieces, you see'. 'I told you, I would buy a present for you only if you were the first or the second in your class, so you have to wait until the next time.' The assumption is that noting the correspondence between the linguistic schemas and the actual patterns of events may be the starting point for elaborations that will lead from primary or automated reasoning to more self-directed or formal reasoning. In line with this assumption, permission schema theory (Cheng & Hollyoak, 1985) posits that these inductions occur in the context of permission rules which specify the conditions under which a given action can or must occur (Harris & Nunez, 1996).

Acquisition of analytic comprehension has been considered one of the conditions responsible for the transformation of primary reasoning into secondary reasoning. The reader is reminded that analytic comprehension enables the reasoner to differentiate between the various kinds of meaning implicated in verbal statements, that is, literal, implied, and factual meanings, and to operate on the type of meaning most relevant to the reasoning requirements of the moment. It is generally accepted that one of the main functions of education is to develop analytic comprehension, because education trains students to focus on meaning as such and on the alterative ways one may use to represent it (Bruner, 1968). Thus education shapes the strategies that make the acquisition of formal or secondary reasoning possible.

None of the factors above—that is, nature, language learning, social exchanges, or education—would suffice to explain the very existence and development of reasoning without the reasoner's own awareness of and about reasoning. According to Brown and Kane (1988) and DeLoache et al. (1998) the progression from analogies dependent on surface similarity to abstract and higher-order analogies requires an awareness of analogies per se. That is, given that the terms of many analogies may be interrelated by several alternative relationships, grasping the right relationship requires the thinker's knowledge of this fact, so that he will withhold judgment until he has sought alternative relationships, tried them as possible interpretations, and finally chosen the most appropriate one. Moreover, it is this awareness that enables the reasoner to differentiate between premises and conclusions in deductive reasoning, such that he can decide whether a conclusion can be derived from the premises. And it is this awareness that enables the thinker to subsequently differentiate between inference schemata, which allows him to formulate a framework that can suggest what is and what is not valid. Thus, the capacity of humans to be aware of and reflect on their own mental activity is necessary if all of the factors, such as language, learning and education, can exert an influence (Moshman, 1990, 1995). In the section following we will present research that highlights the development of self-awareness and reflection.

THE DEVELOPMENT OF CHILDREN'S THEORIES ABOUT CORE DOMAINS: THE PHYSICAL, THE BIOLOGICAL, AND THE PSYCHOLOGICAL WORLD

In science, the term theory is used to refer to an organized body of knowledge and ideas about a particular aspect of the world, which aims to coherently describe and explain the phenomena of interest. For example, in psychology we speak of learning theory or Piaget's theory of cognitive development. Once in place, theories function as frames which allow the theory holder to represent and understand the world in theory-specific ways. For instance, a psychologist who espouses Piaget's theory would tend to view children's mental actions as organized into Piagetian structures. At the same time, however, scientific theories are modified if evidence contradicts their postulates and assumptions. Sometimes a new piece of evidence or a new concept may be incorporated into the theory, with no abandonment or alterations to the existing concepts. Other times, however, there may be catalytic or massive reorganizations causing the old theory to be dismissed and a new one adopted. Obviously, changes of this kind result in a transformation of how one sees and understands the world thereafter.

In recent years, many researchers in the field of cognitive development took the theory model as a prototype of how children's representation of the world may be organized, functioning, and changing. These researchers attempted to provide answers to questions like those following: Do children have a single overarching and coherent theory about the world which governs their understanding of the physical, the biological, and the social world or, alternatively, do they have a separate theory about each of these three aspects of the world? Where do these theories come from? That is, do they have a kind of innate origin or kernel which recognizes, so to speak, itself in the world whenever it meets relevant information, thereby framing how the world is to be understood and represented from the beginning? Or, alternatively, do these theories reflect conventional ways of organizing information about and actions on the world?

Ontological Distinctions

An important issue to be addressed first regards the ontological status of the physical, biological, and psychological worlds in the mind of children. Are these three aspects of the world distinct initially, so that characteristics, functions, and processes are correctly ascribed? For instance, do young children realize that a chair (a physical thing) is not the same as thinking about this chair (a psychological thing); or do they realize that 'eating food' (a biological function) and 'wanting not to get fat' (a desire which is a psychological function) are not the same? Do they understand that the stature of a person or animal (a physical object) is not the same as the person herself or the animal itself (a living being)?

There has been a proliferation of studies in recent years investigating these and similar questions. The evidence generated by these studies indicates that by the age of 3 (if not earlier) children can discriminate between the physical and the psychological worlds. Harris, Brown, Marriot, Whithall & Harmer (1991) conducted a study wherein children were told of a boy who has a dog and another boy who is thinking about a dog, and then were asked to judge which dog could be seen, touched, and petted. The 3 year olds realized that only the first boy's dog could be available for these activities.

Gelman's (1987) study examined the *animate–inanimate distinction.* Specifically, she asked children to report the contents of the insides of various animate creatures and inanimate things. She found that even 3-year-old children report that living beings have blood, bones, and muscles inside them whereas inanimate things have materials such as cotton, paper, hair, or 'hard stuff' inside. Likewise, Massey and Gelman (1988) showed that from the age of 3 years children discriminate between animates and inanimates on the basis of life-specific characteristics, such as self-initiated movement and the capacity to grow. They showed, for instance, that children classify very realistic statues of animals with inanimate objects (for instance, they were judged unable to move up a hill) and they group highly atypical animals (e.g. porcupines) with other animals. It must be noted, however, that not every aspect of the animate–inanimate distinction is understood at this early age. Carey's (1985) work shows that children younger than about 10 do not consider plants to be 'alive', which indicates that despite the early distinction between these two aspects, they are not fully understood until quite late in development.

A similar conclusion can be drawn from research addressed to the distinction between the psychological and the biological world. The evidence shows that from an early age, children can make judgments about the outcome of biological and psychological processes which are in conflict. Inagaki and Hatano's study (1988) asked children to predict who would become fatter, a girl who wants to get fat but eats less, or a girl who wants to get slim but eats more. It was found that as of age 4 children predict correctly, indicating that they understand that a bodily process is affected by biologically relevant behavior rather than by will, which is a psychological function. The same study showed, however, that, although able to make the distinction, children do not understand in detail many biological processes which go on inside the body, such as perspiration and digestion.

Causal Distinctions

The three aspects of the world under discussion are distinguished by certain characteristics mutually exclusive. Once these particular characteristics are identified, certain relational judgments can be made. Each of these three aspects is governed by dynamic relationships between the elements, components, dimensions, functions, and processes which are also particular to their domain. In short, within each aspect there are causal relationships, which are specific to that aspect alone, and it is of interest to researchers to see if and when there is a grasp of the causal relationships in each of these domains.

Physical causality. The studies reviewed by Butterworth (ch. 3 this volume) suggest that very young infants are sensitive to patterns of interaction or contact between physical bodies, which implies that they grasp specific types of causal relationships such as transmission of movement, the nature or the direction of movement itself, physical support or occlusion relations, and so on. This body of evidence is highly important because it suggests that our perceptual systems, vision in particular, are able to abstract, more or less automatically, certain types of causal relationships.

Research with young toddlers suggests that the ability to represent causal relationships appears at about age 3. According to Shultz (1982) the first representation of causality is dynamic or generative. That is, children think that there is a causal relation if there is transmission of energy or power from one physical body to another. Interestingly, this understanding of causality as a generative relationship overrides its understanding as a covariation relationship, a similarity relationship, or a relationship defined by temporal and spatial contiguity. In one of his experiments Shultz (1982) used a candle, two air blowers, and a shield located between the candle and the blowers. The experimenter lit the candle in front of the child, turned on one of the blowers, and then removed the shield so that the candle went out. Children as young as 2 were able to identify which blower made the candle go out and in their explanations they invoked generative transmission: 'the white one because it blew it. The green one didn't because it didn't go.'

Despite this precocious sensitivity to causal relations, understanding the causal structure of the world is a slow and cumbersome process. Research on the understanding of common aspects of the world such as force and motion and the day/night cycle, indicates that misconceptions may persist for a long time in development. For example, even adults have difficulty in integrating into their model of motion the Newtonian principle that we can have motion without any cause (Bliss & Ogborn, 1994). Likewise, they believe that the sun and the moon move up and down at the opposite sides of the earth. Frequently, misconceptions coexist side by side with the scientific models of the world. For instance, to reconcile their intuition that the earth is flat with the scientific model that the earth is round, many adults believe that earth is a hollow sphere with people living on a flat surface in the middle of it (Vosniadou, 1994).

Biological causality. Biological causality refers to the transfer of effects which are limited to animates as such and they are related to their living identity as distinct from other characteristics which they may have as physical bodies. For example, living beings inherit structural or functional characteristics; this is not true of inanimate objects. Springer and Keil (1989) conducted a study to test understanding of this concept. Their experiment showed that toddlers believed that a baby animal whose parents had a peculiarly colored pink head was more likely to have a pink head compared to a baby animal whose parents had a normally colored head. However, genetic mechanisms are not fully understood even by educated adults (Caravita & Hallden, 1994).

In conclusion, the evidence summarized above suggests that children's representation of the world is organized in a way that honors the three broad domains it involves. That is, children seem able to abstract the specific ontological and dynamic characteristics of the physical, biological, and psychological aspects of the world and organize their knowledge and behavior accordingly. This evidence implies that human thought is somehow sensitive to the particular ontological and dynamic characteristics of each domain, which thus can explain why from this early age children are able to discriminate between the three domains and why their knowledge of them is both quite advanced and coherent. At the same time, however, we need not overestimate these early achievements because they coexist with misconceptions which persist for a long time.

The Child's Theory of Mind

The mind is the force underlying practically every aspect of human behavior and experience. That is, our actions and feelings depend on how we register and represent the world, and on our thoughts and ideas based on these representations. In short, our personal experience, behavior, and interpersonal relationships depend on the mental states we create as persons. In fact, we might even say that our everyday life is basically a dialogue of minds: the mind is in dialogue with itself or with another's mind.

Due to the importance of the mind's role, the study of the child's theory of mind has probably been the most active field of research in developmental psychology in the last ten years. Research in this line asks three interrelated questions:

1. Do children understand the mind as something different from reality? That is, do they understand that the thoughts or ideas that they may

have about an object or person cannot be identified with this object or person?

2. Do they understand the causal role of mental activity and of its products? That is, do they realize that what people do and how they do it depends on their thoughts, ideas, guesses, fantasies, beliefs, desires, wishes, and the like?

3. Do they understand how mental activity is organized and functioning? That is, do they have any understanding of the mind as a very complex and diversified system which involves many different functions, such as attention, memory, and reasoning, which are responsible for different mental jobs and which may function differently?

In short, the three sets of questions refer to the understanding of the ontological status, the causal role or agency, and the nature and functioning of the mind, respectively. We will summarize the findings about the three aspects of mind below.

Understanding the ontological status of the mind. In the previous section we presented evidence to show that children as young as 3 understand that thinking about an object is not the same as the object itself, although this understanding is not very stable until many years later. For example, in the Harris et al. (1991) study about rabbits and monsters, 4-year-old children had no difficulty in understanding that a rabbit and a monster they were asked to imagine were not real. However, when told that the experimenter would leave the room, many of the children were frightened (to imagine a monster). Even many 6 year olds told the experimenter they were afraid that there might be a monster in the box. These findings confirm our experience that many children continue to be frightened by their thoughts well into the school years. It is well known that some mentally ill patients, such as schizophrenics, cannot clearly distinguish the boundaries between the real and imaginal. This evidence suggests that the imaginary may be distinguished from the real at quite an early age. However, this distinction continues to develop for many years and under certain conditions it may break down quite easily at any age.

Understanding of the mind as a causal agent. The experimental paradigm used to study children's understanding of this aspect of the mind is rather simple. In general, the experimental set-up is organized so that the child has access to two representations of a given arrangement such that the second representation follows the first as a result of some kind of transformation; however, another person who participates in the experiment has access only to the first representation. For instance, the experimenter places a candy in box A in front of both the child and an assistant. The assistant leaves the room and the experimenter moves the candy from box A to box B. The assistant returns and the child is asked to indicate in which box the assistant will look for the candy. Box A corresponds to the assistant's representation of the candy's location; box B corresponds to the child's representation of the present place of the candy. Tasks designed according to this paradigm have come to be known as the *false belief tasks.* Children who indicate location A are obviously able to understand that the representation of a given situation depends on available information and that a person's behavior stems from his representation. Children who indicate position B are obviously unwilling to recognize that others may represent a situation differently than they themselves will represent it. Many studies have shown that 3-year-old children cannot solve this kind of task, whereas four-year-old children can, leading to the conclusion that 3 year olds do not have a theory of mind whereas 4 year olds have. These studies suggest that 3 year olds may have a representational deficit which does not allow them to differentiate their own mind from another's or to recognize that different persons may have different beliefs which can lead to different behavior. We will come to the issue of representation in the next section.

Interestingly, however, 2 and 3 year olds who fail the false belief tasks are quite capable of deception. From a cognitive point of view, deception implies that the deceiver recognizes that there may be alternative representations of the same reality and that it is possible to create in the other's mind a representation which is different from the representation that she herself holds. In their experiments, Chalder, Fritz and Hala (1989) showed that by the age of 2 children understand that withholding or destroying evidence can deceive someone and by the age of 3 they understand the role of lying. In fact, there is evidence indicating that 3 year olds can pass false beliefs tasks if they are embedded in a context of deception.

Deception is not the only context in which children demonstrate an understanding of the other's mind. Wellman (1990) carried out extensive research to show that children younger than 4 are much more sensitive to desires than beliefs as mental states which can produce a response. In his experiments he showed that 3 year olds can solve problems like the following: 'Sam wants to find his puppy. It might be hiding in the garage or under the porch. Where will Sam look for his puppy (garage or porch)?' The 3 year olds were able to correctly predict Sam's behavior even when the representations seemingly changed, as indicated in the following story: 'Before Sam can look for his puppy, Sam's mother comes out of the house. Sam's mom says she saw his puppy in the garage. Where will Sam look for the puppy?' According to Wellman, these findings indicate that 3 year olds have a theory of mind, and he argued further, that as the child's theory of mind develops, importance of desires as causal agents of behavior lessens in favor of beliefs. This seems to imply that the theory of mind is originally geared to mental states associated with the dynamic aspects of people's behavior (i.e. states which are related to emotion and motivation) and it then extends to include those states relevant to the cognitive aspects of behavior. However, recognizing cognitions as causes of behavior is very global at this age. For instance, Carpendale and Chandler (1996) have shown that understanding the interpretative nature of mind (e.g. that different characters may interpret the phrase 'wait for a ring'—a phone call or a diamond ring—differently depending upon the information they have) is attained at the age of 7–8, that is about 2–3 years after understanding false beliefs. Obviously, understanding of interpretation requires a more complex understanding of the nature of the mind. Next we will summarize research related to the child's under-standing of the nature of functioning of different cognitive functions and processes.

Understanding the organization and functioning of the mind. The mind is a very complex system, involving many different functions, processes, and abilities which interact in multiple ways. Therefore research on the develop-ment of the child's understanding of the organization and functioning of the mind should highlight how, if at all, different cognitive functions and processes are understood at different ages. Flavell and his colleagues pres-ented a series of highly ingenious studies about the development of children's knowledge about thinking, which they 'broadly and minimally defined as mentally attending to something' (Flavell, Green & Flavell, 1995, p.v). According to these studies, the development of even this simple under-standing is a process that evolves over many years. Specifically, pre-schoolers seem to 'have at least a minimal grasp of the bare-bones essentials of thinking: namely that it is some sort of internal, mental activity that people engage in that refers to real or imaginary objects or events' (p. 78). They also realize that thinking is different from perceiving and that it is different from other cognitive processes such as knowing. One of their experiments showed that 3 year olds understand that a person who is blindfolded and has her ears closed cannot see or hear an object but she can think about this object. Another experiment showed that 3 and 4 year olds equally understand that a person is thinking when she is in the process of choosing one out of a number of available objects or when she tries to understand how a curious thing happened such as how a large pear fitted into a bottle with a narrow neck. And another study showed that young preschoolers understand that a person can have knowledge of things she is not currently thinking about.

However, there are important aspects of thinking that preschoolers do not understand. Specifically, there is compelling evidence that they do not understand what William James called the 'stream of consciousness', that is, they do not realize that thinking is a process which goes on continuously in people's minds even when they sit quietly and do nothing. In one of Flavell et al.'s studies, preschoolers ignored very clear cues about the continual presence of thought activity. For instance, the large majority of preschoolers refused to agree with the statement 'something is always going on in people's minds, so there must be something going on'.

Neither did preschoolers seem to realize that cognitive activities such as looking, listening, reading, and talking necessarily entail thinking. Even when they attribute mental activity to a person, preschoolers seem unable to specify the content of the person's thinking despite very clear and indicative signs. Flavell et al. conducted an experiment confirming this: with a pre-school child as the subject, one experimenter (A) asked another (B) a thought-provoking question about an object in the room. B said to A, 'That's a hard question. Give me a minute', and she turned to one side giving nonverbal cues that she was trying to find an answer to the question. Preschoolers were not able to indicate that experimenter B was thinking about the object named in the question and many continued to have difficulty with this seemingly simple problem even when experimenter B stared at and touched the object while she was thinking about it. In fact, preschoolers seem to have difficulty in specifying the content of their own thoughts. For example, when asked to name the room in their house where they keep their toothbrush they did not mention either a toothbrush or a bathroom when asked what they had been thinking about.

Because they cannot identify the content of their thought, they are unaware of the associative nature of the mind, which Flavell et al. called *cognitive cueing*. That is, they do not realize that one idea or thought triggers another, which triggers another, and so on. For example, when told a story about a child who thinks of beautiful flowers while on the beach, they cannot explain why that child thinks of the beach when he later sees some beautiful flowers. Finally, preschoolers do not seem to understand that thought is partly controllable and partly uncontrollable, that is, that you can start thinking about something if you decide to but you cannot always stop thinking about something just because you want to. All of these difficulties diminish considerably or are removed by the age of 7–8.

The studies reviewed above suggest that preschoolers differentiate thinking from other cognitive (i.e. perception) and noncognitive activities (e.g. movement) but that they do not yet understand how thinking is activated or how it works. Fabricius and his colleague (Fabricius & Schwanenflugel, 1994) reported a series of studies concerned with a complementary question in which they examined whether children understood the similarities and differences between different cognitive functions such as memory, reasoning, and comprehension. Their studies involved 8- and 10-year-old children and adults. These subjects were given simple descriptions of list memory (e.g. getting all the things at the store that your mother asked you), perspective memory (e.g. saying happy birthday on the right day to your friend who told you her birthday a long time ago), comprehension (e.g. learning a new board game from the instructions on the box), attention (e.g. listening to what your friend is saying to you in a noisy classroom), and inference (e.g. figuring out what your friend wants when he says, 'boy, that cookie looks good'). The subjects were asked to contrast each sentence with all of the sentences and indicate the degree of similarity among the processes referred to in each pair of sentences. It was found that from the age of 8 children can distinguish between memory and inference. For both 10 year olds and adults, but not 8 year olds, the involvement of memory in tasks is taken as an indication of similarity between the processes supposedly involved. Unlike adults, however, neither 8 nor 10 year olds could distinguish between comprehension and attention or between different kinds of memory. Thus, it seems that by late childhood children begin to distinguish between different cognitive processes. This differentiation is very global however, and limited to processes which have clear experiential differences.

Research undertaken in our laboratory focused on understanding of the similarities and differences between the processes involved in solving different types of problems, such as mathematical and spatial problems, and problems requiring designing an experiment to test a hypothesis. In other words, our studies focused on various inferential processes rather than on the differences between different cognitive functions. The method was similar to that used by Fabricius and colleagues, and we examined 10- to 17-year-old subjects. Our studies showed clearly that no differentiation between different problem-solving or reasoning strategies like the above is possible before the age of about 13 years. At the age of 14 adolescents start to notice the differences between spatial thought and experimental and mathematical thought, although they do not differentiate between these two types of thought. Some differentiation appears at about the age of 16 and it culminates in the college years (Demetriou et al., 1993a).

Representational Stability and Complexity

Despite their precocious sensitivity to quite complex aspects of the world and their own mind, children's representations lack adult-like stability and they are quite simplistic and rigid. Evidence indicates that a child's ability to differentiate among the physical, biological, and psychological entities does not itself guarantee that they think of objects and persons as having an identity which is largely independent of superficial changes in appearance. That is, research on what is known as the *appearance/reality distinction* strongly indicates that changes in the appearance of objects or living beings lead young children to believe that they also change their very identity. Moreover, other evidence indicates that children have difficulty in understanding the role of symbols as entities which convey information about other entities.

Flavell and his colleagues (Flavell, Flavell & Green, 1983; Flavell, Green & Flavell, 1986; Taylor & Flavell, 1984) in a series of very carefully designed studies provided convincing evidence that children younger than 4 years do not understand the appearance/reality distinction. Flavell and colleagues presented children with very familiar things, which were made to appear different in a clearly identifiable way. For example, in front of their subjects, these researchers transferred milk from a regular into a red glass, and the children were asked two questions: 'How does it look to your eyes right now?' and 'How is it really and truly?' Children younger than 4 persisted that the milk transferred to the red glass 'really and truly' was red. In fact, children continued to commit this *phenomenism error* even after they were trained to make the appearance/reality distinction (Flavell, Green, Wahl & Flavell, 1987).

Children are also prone to another type of error which is complementary to the phenomenism error, the so-called, *intellectual realism error*. Children will mistakenly believe that the object they see (sponge) looks like the object they know it to be (sponge), although the object has been made to look like something else (rock). That is, they impose what they know on what they see. Flavell and his colleagues (1986) attribute both errors to the inability of children younger than 3–4 to keep in mind *dual encodings* for the same object (i.e. to simultaneously represent an object in two different ways). Their judgment is based on the only representation available to them, which is generally the most salient feature of the object or situation.

DeLoache (DeLoache et al., 1998) advanced a similar interpretation for the difficulties children have in understanding the role of symbols and in using them as sources of information about the objects they refer to. Specifically, DeLoache and her colleagues showed that by 2 and a half years of age, children can use a picture to find where a toy was hidden. This indicates that they understand the relation between the picture and its referent. However, at this age, children have difficulty in using a scale model of a room to retrieve an object from the room. That is, although they are asked to examine the scale model in order to see where to look for the object in the room represented by the model, children younger than 3 fail to use this seemingly realistic information and retrieve the object. According to DeLoache, this difficulty stems from the fact that scale models require *dual representation*. That is, they require to understand that scale models have a concrete aspect which makes them what they are, that is, objects which have an identity of their own, and an abstract function, which makes them symbols of something else. To be able to look for the correspondence between the scale model and the room, children must be able to differentiate between the concrete aspect and the abstract function and focus on the second. Children younger than 3 do not represent the abstract function of the model. Thus, they deal with it as though it is an object to be used on its own. DeLoache has conducted an ingenious experiment to show that when the need for dual representation is eliminated 2 and a half year olds can use scale models as a source of information for the room. Specifically, she led children to believe that the real room was put into a 'shrinking machine' that shrunk the room into the scale model. Under this condition, the model is not a symbol of the room any more; it is the room itself. Thus, no assumptions about the representational nature of the models are required to retrieve the information about the room. The ability for dual representation is established by the age of 4. As a result children become able to use various types of symbol systems, such as maps, to guide their actions in actual environments.

Explaining the Development of Core Theories

Three conditions must be met if a theory is to change. First, increasing experience with the aspect of the world concerned that generates information that shows the theory to be inadequate to describe or explain phenomena that fall into the field of its application. Second, the thinker's mind should possess the minimum representational capabilities that are required for an adequate representation of these phenomena. For instance, a theory of mind, by definition, requires at least dual encodings or representations because to be a theory of mind it should recognize that the same reality can be represented in at least two different representations either by the same person or by two different persons. Third, metaconceptual awareness. That is, understanding that theories are just complex representations about the world and not the world itself and thus are amenable to falsification and improvement.

Explaining the development of the theory of mind needs special attention because of its peculiar status as a theory about the creator of theories, that is, the mind. Two hypotheses have been advanced to explain why children's theory of mind changes as they grow older and these are complementary rather than incompatible.

The first ascribes the development to the increased activation and functioning of one's own mind. That is, as they grow older, children engage in activities and problem-solving which require them to activate different mental functions and which are frequently initially unsuccessful. For example, when an unpleasant thought pops into their mind which they want to stop they may realize that this is not always possible as the thought comes over and over again. Or, when asked to explain something to somebody, they may realize that they do not have all the information and skill necessary to do so (Flavell et al., 1995). Later, in school, as they begin to engage in problem-solving activities in different domains, children start to realize that each domain requires mental operations. On these occasions, children gradually come to 'see', so to speak, their actual mental processes as processes rather than just as products of the functioning of these processes, such that they become sensitive to the presence of different functions and purposefully act to make them work efficiently. This implies that the development of theories and problem-solving about other domains of the world is conducive to the development of the theory of mind itself.

The second hypothesis stresses the social dimension of the discovery of the mind. According to this hypothesis, problem-solving in humans frequently occurs in groups. Thus, people have the opportunity to observe others trying to solve the same problem. Of course, what is going on in another person's mind is completely private. However, people, especially in environments targeted to problem-solving, such as school, exchange experiences and the one may project onto the other her own mental experiences and check directly or indirectly if they are right. These experiences generate information, concepts, hypotheses, and models which gradually become more refined, focused, differentiated and accurate (Demetriou & Efklides, 1984; Demetriou et al., 1997b). Thus, the theory of mind is gradually geared in three assumptions. Specifically, that the mind is (i) private (thus disclosable at will but also capable of or subject to deception); (ii) complex (thus involving many different functions); and (iii) constructive (thus frequently imposing its own organization on reality which may contradict it to some degree). It seems plausible that the development of the theory of mind provides mental and representational flexibility that facilitates the development of reasoning itself and the theories about other aspects of the world. The theory to be presented below deals directly with the dynamic relations between the various levels and structures of the mind.

TOWARD A COMPREHENSIVE THEORY: A THREE-LEVEL THEORY OF THE DEVELOPING MIND

Piaget's theory provided a fairly accurate description of the general characteristics and orientations of thought at different phases of life. However, this theory underestimated the processing aspects of cognitive functioning, the role of self-understanding as a means of self-regulation, and the possible differences between different domains of thought. The various neo-Piagetian models developed concepts able to account for the processing aspects of cognitive functioning and they generated a rich database on the development of processing capacity throughout childhood and adolescence. However, they also underestimated the problem of possible domains of thought and they ignored almost completely the problems of self-understanding and self-regulation. The research on the development of reasoning has been able to reveal the reasoning capabilities of different ages, although it has not investigated how the development of reasoning is related to the development of processing capabilities, or the fact that the various domains may require different inferential processes. Research on the development of foundational theories pointed to the early appearance and development of understanding in regard to important domains. Studies on the theory of mind, in particular, provided fascinating evidence on how the child's understanding of the mind develops. However, this line of research did not investigate the relationship between the development of these foundational theories and that of the various types of understanding studied by Piaget himself, the neo-Piagetians, or the reasoning-oriented researchers. This state of affairs suggests that the field is in need of a theory that would be able to integrate the achievements of the different lines of research into a comprehensive framework. This has been the explicit aim of the theory that I proposed with my colleagues. In its present form, this theory is summarized in Demetriou (1993, 1996; see also Demetriou & Efklides, 1994) and it is empirically substantiated in a number of more technical publications (e.g. Demetriou et al., 1993a; Demetriou, Kazi, Platsidou, Sirmali & Kiosseoglou, 1997a; Demetriou, Pachaury, Metallidou & Kazi. 1996; Demetriou, Platsidou, Sirmali, Zhang & Spanoudis, 1997b).

The Architecture of Mind

According to this theory, the mind is an open system whose organization and functioning is governed by the following principles:

1. *The principle of domain specificity.* According to this principle, the mind and the environment are functionally and structurally attuned to each other. Thus, the mind involves domain-specific systems to represent and

process different domains in the environment. These systems are called *Specialized Capacity Spheres* (SCSs).

2. *The principle of procedural specificity.* The principle above suggests that the various SCSs will differ in the kind of information units or representations they involve. For example, in some problems the information units are words of one's native language; in other problems these units must be defined in relation to the coordinates of three-dimensional space. As a result, each of the domain-specific systems must comprise those operations and processes required by its particular information units and relations. For example, some problems require operations that can ensure the conjunction and disjunction of propositions in inference patterns (e.g. 'if p then q', or 'either p or q'); other problems require the mental rotation of a given image or object.

3. *The principle of symbolic bias.* According to this principle, each domain-specific system is biased toward those symbolic systems (or subsystems) most conducive to the representation of its own properties and relationships and most efficient in its operations. For instance, the system specializing in representation of the quantitative domain is most efficient if it applies mathematical symbol systems. The system specific to the representation of spatial relationships operates more efficiently if it uses mental images rather than words or numbers.

4. *The principle of self-mapping.* Many other cognitive systems involve domain-specific, procedurally specific, and symbolically biased cognitive functions—such as other animals and computers—but do not have minds. To have a mind, a cognitive system must satisfy the principle of self-mapping. This principle states that mind is possible only if cognitive experiences, which differ in regard to domain specificity, procedural specificity, and symbolic bias, are felt or cognized by the problem-solver as distinct. Otherwise, they have to be felt or cognized as functionally similar or equivalent. Positing this principle implies that humans generate and update maps and models of their own mental functions. These models can be retrieved so that the individual can determine the most appropriate course of mental action whenever problem-solving efforts are frustrated, or suggest various alternative plans, strategies, or skills that may be used.

The four principles above suggest that the mind comprises two levels of knowing. The first level involves the SCSs, which are environment-oriented. Thus, the input to the SCSs is information coming from the environment and their output is mental acts of understanding or actions which are directed to the environment. The second level stands over and above the SCSs, and the input to this system is actually information coming from the functioning of the SCSs and its output is (self) instructions purporting to direct their functioning. We call this second-order level of knowing the *hypercognitive system* (the adverb 'hyper' in Greek means 'higher than' or 'on top of', or 'going beyond'). Finally, in line with other neo-Piagetian theories, the theory recognizes a third level in the organization of the mind.

This level involves structures and functions which are more or less content-free but which constrain the complexity of the knowledge structures or problems (either environment-oriented or self-oriented) that the individual can deal with at a given age. The systems involved in the three levels of the mental architecture are described below and shown graphically in Figure 5.5.

Specialized capacity spheres

Empirical research in our laboratory led to identification of five environment-oriented SCSs: the qualitative-analytic, the quantitative-relational, the casual-experimental, the spatial-imaginal, and the verbal-propositional (Demetriou & Efklides, 1985, 1989; Demetriou, Efklides, Papdaki, Papantoniou & Economou, 1993b; Demetriou et al., 1996; Demetriou et al., 1997a; Shayer et al., 1988). Each SCS is itself a complex system which involves various rules, processes, and skills that enable the individuals to represent and process the various elements and relations involved in the reality domain concerned.

The qualitative-analytic SCS. This SCS refers to qualitative reality, and specifically, is the basic production mechanism underlying the construction, representation, and processing of categorical structures. Therefore, this SCS is oriented to the processing of similarity–difference relations, and so involves processes such as browsing, scanning, and selection that enable one to note or locate object properties that are of relevance to the task at hand. It also involves inductive reasoning and classification strategies that enable one to construct classes and categories. Thus, the functioning of this SCS underlies the construction of the various concepts involved in the foundational theories about the world which were discussed in the previous section.

The quantitative-relational SCS. This SCS is concerned with the representations and processing of the quantitative aspects of reality, such as aggregation or separation, increase or decrease, splitting or concentration of objects in space or time. Thus, it involves skills of quantitative specification, such as counting acts (e.g. pointing, bringing in, removing, and sharing) and the four basic arithmetic operations. It also comprises the rules and operations that enable one to specify various overtly observable quantitative dimensions, such as distance or speed, and elaborate their relationships to build more complex dimensions, such as acceleration and velocity. Piaget's tasks addressed to the understanding of numbers and quantities are dependent on the functioning of this SCS.

The causal-experimental SCS. All varieties of interactive reality structures in which some elements function as causes and others as products or effects constitute the domain of the causal-experimental SCS. The functioning of

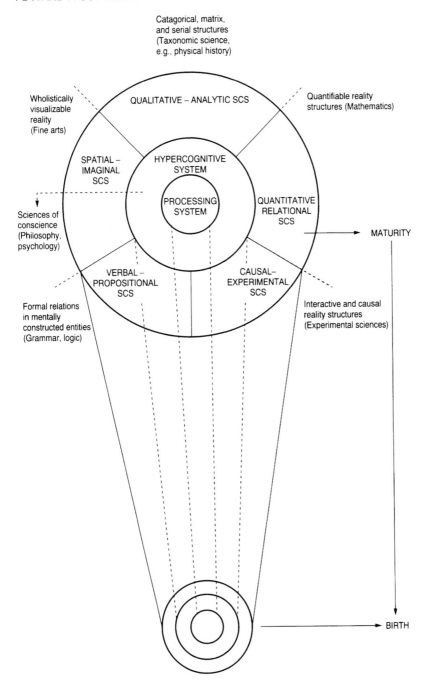

Catagorical, matrix,
and serial structures
(Taxonomic science,
e.g., physical history)

Wholistically
visualizable
reality
(Fine arts)

QUALITATIVE – ANALYTIC SCS

Quantifiable reality
structures (Mathematics)

SPATIAL –
IMAGINAL
SCS

HYPERCOGNITIVE
SYSTEM

PROCESSING
SYSTEM

QUANTITATIVE
RELATIONAL
SCS

Sciences of
conscience
(Philosophy,
psychology)

MATURITY

VERBAL –
PROPOSITIONAL
SCS

CAUSAL–
EXPERIMENTAL
SCS

Formal relations
in mentally
constructed entities
(Grammar, logic)

Interactive and causal
reality structures
(Experimental sciences)

BIRTH

Figure 5.5   The general model of the developing mind, according to Demetriou's
theory.
Reproduced with permission from Demetriou, A., Efklides, A. & Platsidou, M.
(1993a). The architecture and dynamics of developing mind: Experiential structuralism as a frame for unifying cognitive developmental theories. *Monographs of the
Society for Research in Child Development*, **58**, (5–6, Serial No. 234).

this SCS is directed at dissociating cause–effect relationships and thus involves various processes, such as processes that enable one to formulate hypotheses, design experiments, and construct models about the phenomena of interest. This SCS underlies some aspects of Piagetian formal thought, such as combinatorial thought and the isolation of variables ability. It is also related to the differentiation among the physical, biological, and psychological worlds as it enables one to understand that causality may function differently in each.

The spatial-imaginal SCS. This SCS is directed to the representation and processing of those aspects of reality which can be visualized and processed mentally as integral wholes. It is also implicated in orientation and movement in space. This system therefore comprises the skills and processes needed to formulate, activate, and visualize mental images and to plan movement in space.

The verbal-propositional SCS. This SCS involves processes and functions which correspond roughly to Braine's (1990) primary and secondary reasoning. These processes were considered above as the basic components of deductive reasoning.

The hypercognitive system

The hypercognitive system involves *on-line* or *working hypercognition* and *long-term hypercognition*. *Working hypercognition* involves self-directed processes and processes directed to other minds. The self-directed processes enable thinkers to monitor their own cognitive functioning, regulate functioning according to the present goals and evaluate the results of functioning *vis-à-vis* those goals. The processes directed externally enable thinkers to decode the mental states and intentions of others. *Long-term hypercognition* codifies the products of the functioning of working hypercognition, and as such it involves knowledge and rules related to the mind's nature and organization, its functions, and operations in order to be of use to the person.

According to our theory, long-term hypercognition involves three distinct but interrelated kinds of knowledge and processes. Specifically, it involves *a theory of mind, a theory of intelligence*, and *the cognitive self-image*. The theory of mind involves one's representations about the mind. The research reviewed in the section above about children's theory of mind belongs to this part of the hypercognitive system. The theory of intelligence involves one's knowledge and beliefs about what is and is not intelligent in a given environment and time, such as, for example, that people must learn quickly, speak fluently and accurately, be socially flexible and considerate or must control their behavior, and so on. In other words, this model specifies how individuals must use their mind to achieve personal goals without conflicting with their social or cultural group (Sternberg, Conway, Ketron &

Bernstein, 1981). The cognitive self-image resides at the intersection of one's theory of mind and theory of intelligence, that is, it involves the representations individuals have about themselves as intelligent cognitive systems. Thus, this model involves questions such as: How flexible or intelligent or wise am I? Which kinds of problems am I good at solving and which ones am I not so good at solving? How efficient am I in using different cognitive functions, such as memory, imagery, problem-solving and so on? (Demetriou et al., 1993a, 1997a)

The processing system

The processing system is viewed as dynamic field continually occupied in varying proportion by elements of the other two hierarchical levels. Specifically, the input to this system is environment-relevant information, skills, and processes, which pertain to an SCS, and management and evaluation processes, which pertain to the hypercognitive system. We have proposed that working hypercognition is the system responsible for the management of the processing system (Demetriou et al., 1993a, Platsidou & Demetriou, 1995). According to our theory, the functioning of this system may be analyzed in terms of three dimensions: *speed of processing, control of processing*, and *storage*.

Speed of processing basically refers to the minimum speed at which a given mental act may be efficiently executed. Speed of processing is a basic parameter of cognitive functioning because of the very nature of our cognitive system. That is, given that memory traces tend to decay due either to the simple passage of time or to the interference of other stimuli (Baddeley, 1991), it follows that the mental processing related to the current goal must be completed before the activation of any of the units involved falls below a certain threshold. Control of processing refers to a mechanism which functions under the guidance of the task-goal like a filter permitting only goal-relevant schemes to enter the processing space. Control is important as a parameter of processing because it regulates the information to be attended, inhibited, rejected, or postponed within the time and activation limitations of our cognitive system (noted above). That is, the more efficient this mechanism is, the more probable it is that the mind will grasp or effect the interconnections needed at the appropriate time. Storage refers to the maximum number of schemes the individual can keep active above a minimum level of trace strength for the time required in order to grasp their meaning and/or relations as suggested by the moment's current goal. Thus, this part of the theory builds on other neo-Piagetian theories, most notably those of Pascual-Leone and Case, to specify in detail the organization and development of the basic processes related to processing capacity.

It must be noted that the architecture of mind sketched above was not shaped as a synthesis of the research and theorizing undertaken by other researchers. It is derived from the empirical research conducted in our laboratory at the Aristotle University of Thessaloniki. In fact, our research program, for the most part, was concurrent with the other post-Piagetian research programs described in this chapter. Thus, it is encouraging that the picture of mind suggested by this integrative program of research is harmonious with other, more locally focused research programs. This convergence suggests that we may be on the right track in our search for the nature of the human mind.

This convergence is all the more interesting because our methodology was very different from that traditionally used in the field of cognitive development. Specifically, a large part of our research was based on a psychometric-like approach, that is, in our various studies we examined relatively large numbers of subjects with many tasks selected so as to represent many different functions. For example, in one of our recent studies, each subject was examined by three sets of tasks addressed to: all three dimensions of the processing system; different aspects of the various SCSs; and various aspects of the hypercognitive system, such as theory of mind and self-image. The subjects represented many different age groups and performance was analyzed with modern modeling methods, developed specifically to test hypotheses related to the organization of various processes or characteristics into different hierarchical levels and their structures. This methodology is termed 'structural equations modeling' (Bentler, 1989), and is directly relevant to the question of the architecture of mind. These methods allow researchers to test alternative models about the organization of cognitive processes into broader structures and hierarchical levels. Figure 5.6 provides a basis for deriving structural models that would have to be found consistent with the subject's performance in studies like the one described above (Demetriou, Platsidou, Efklides, Metallidou & Shayer, 1991; Demetriou et al., 1993a, 1993b, 1997a,b).

Development Along the Three Levels of Mind

This theory posits the mind to be a hierarchical and multidimensional universe, and therefore requires constructs to encompass the development of all the mind's systems and functions, at all the various levels, and including all their interactions. Below we will summarize the propositions of this theory in regard to what develops, how it develops, and why.

The development of the processing system

Figure 5.7 summarizes our research on the development of the three functions involved in the processing system. We can see from this figure that all three functions improve systematically from middle childhood to adolescence, peaking between ages 20 and 30. Likewise, all three functions deteriorate systematically from middle to old age, such that by age 60 or 70, they return to the level of an 11-year-old preadolescent.

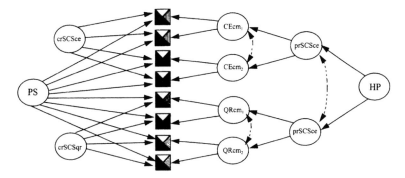

Figure 5.6   The structure of mind as represented in Demetriou's theory in terms of the conventions of structural modeling
Note: According to the conventions of structural modeling, squares symbolize individual tasks or observed variables and circles symbolize more general underlying processes or latent variables. The present representation involves the minimum number of components possible. That is, in pairs, it involves two tasks addressed to each of two components (i.e. cm_1 and cm_2) in each of two different SCSs. At a full scale, the figure would have to involve all five SCSs and all component processes involved in each of them. The reader is invited to note that performance on each task is considered to be associated with all levels of the mental architecture. It can be seen that performance on every task is associated with the processing system (PS), the underlying specific process that stems from a given component (cm), and from the more general or core (cr) processes that characterize each SCS such as (crSCS). Also each of the two components of an SCS is integrated into the SCS through the operation of the organizational principles (prSCS) and the hypercognitive system (HP)
From Demetriou, A., Efklides, A., Papadaki, M. et al. (1993b). The structure and development of causal-experimental thought. *Developmental Psychology*, **29**, 480–497. Copyright © 1993 by the American Psychological Association. Reprinted with ermission.

The development of the SCSs

Space limitations do not allow presentation of the development of all five SCSs, even in rough outline (see Demetriou, 1993; Demetriou et al., 1993a). Therefore, only two SCSs will be examined, the quantitative-relational (Demetriou et al., 1991) and the causal-experimental SCS (Demetriou et al., 1993b). The aim of this presentation is to provide the basis for the causal model of development which will be discussed in the next section.

Between the ages of 3 and 5, *quantitative* thought functions on the basis of what Resnick has called proto-quantitative schemas (Resnick, Bill & Legold, 1992). For instance, a broad concept of numerosity can be used by the child to solve simplified one-to-one correspondence tasks (see Gelman and Gallistel, 1978). Overt quantifying acts, such as pointing or finger counting, are very powerful means of quantifying the world, until as late as age 7.

The ability to mentally execute the basic arithmetic operations is established during the primary school years. Initially, this ability is limited to only one operation on two numbers, and it expands gradually to comprise all

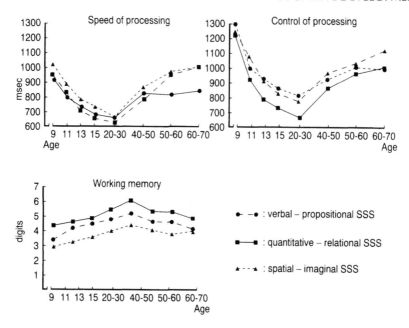

Figure 5.7 Changes in speed of processing, control of processing and working memory as a function of age and SCS
Note: It can be seen that response times in speed and control of processing tasks decrease systematically until the age of 20–30 and they then increase so that by the age of 60–70 years they are very close to those attained at the age of 9 years across all three SCSs. Memory span increases until 20–30 years of age and it then decreases across all three SCSs. This pattern of change suggests that the processing system operates as an integrated whole.
Reprinted from Demetriou, A. & Efklides, A. (Eds), *Mind, Intelligence and Reasoning: Structure and Development,* Copyright 1994 (pp. 75–109), with kind permission from Elsevier Science—NL, Sara Bingerhartstraat 25, 1055 KV Amsterdam, The Netherlands.

four operations and many numbers. If defined on the basis of the number of operations to be executed, this ability develops in four levels. Theses are acquired, one almost every second year, beginning at about age 7 until age 12. Proportional reasoning first appears as an ability to grasp intuitively supported proportional relations at age 11–12 (e.g. problems involving numbers which are multiples of one another, such as 2/4 to 4/8). It gradually increases through a sequence of four levels until at age 14–15 it is able to grasp complex and counter-intuitive relationships (e.g. 4/5 to 7/8). Interestingly enough, however, the development of algebraic reasoning spans the entire period from about age 8 to 15. At the beginning it allows specification of quantitative relations on the basis of well-defined elements (for example, 8-year-old children can solve the problem: $8-x=5$) and it culminates, at about age 15 in the ability to specify relationships by coordinating symbolic structures on the basis of their logical relationships (for example, specify x if $x+y+z=39$ and $x=y+z$). Thus, the ability to execute the four arithmetic operations appears initially to alternate with the acquisition of the lower levels of algebraic reasoning. The development of proportional reasoning appears to alternate with the highest levels of algebraic reasoning (Demetriou et al., 1991, 1996).

The development of the *causal-experimental* proceeds in a similar fashion. That is, up to the age of 5–6 causal understanding can only provide descriptions of observable reality. That is, it creates representations which for the most part preserve the order of events in time. Trial-and-error predominates as a means for studying cause–effect relationships. From age 7 to about 10 causal-experimental thought begins to change from descriptive to theory guided. However, theories at this period are nothing more than implicit theories in action (Karmiloff-Smith & Inhelder, 1974).

It is not until about age 11 that thought acquires a proper experimental orientation to questions regarding causal relationships. According to our studies (Demetriou et al., 1993b), combinatorial abilities begin to appear at about age 11 and are consolidated at about age 15. Simple experimentation and hypothesis formation abilities appear simultaneously at approximately 12–13 years of age, and continue to grow until college years. Model construction abilities, that is, the ability to integrate hypotheses with experimental data into a unified theory, appears at around the age of 15 and may not be very solid even at the graduate level. Signs of a 'personal epistemology' regarding the causal structure of the world were not observed before late adolescence. These involved a grasp of the limits both of the mechanisms an experimenter uses to produce empirical evidence and of the models to which experimentation may eventuate; that is, understanding that experimentation is prone to error due to the presence of confounding variables and that the models are, to a large extent, heuristic tools which, in principle, are always refutable.

The development of the hypercognitive system

The hypercognitive system also changes extensively in all of its components. We described earlier many of the developmental changes in the theory individuals hold about cognition (see section on the theory of mind). Thus, presentation here will focus on the development of one's understanding of intellectual competence and related aspects of self-image (see also Fontaine, ch. 8 this volume).

Three tendencies are well established in the development of the understanding of intellectual competence and the related changes in one's self-image. First, they become differentiated and better articulated with increasing age. For example, Harter (1990) found that in early childhood, middle/late childhood, adolescence, college, and the adult years individuals describe themselves in reference to 4, 5, 8, 12, and 13 domains, respectively. These evolve from a global self-concept which involves gross representations of the physical, social, and intellectual self to a differentiated one, in which each domain is analyzed into many dimensions. Second, understanding of the dimensions that define intellectual competence becomes more objective and more norm-referenced with age. Specifically, preschool children do not differentiate intellectual ability per se (which is associated with the possession of certain qualities that enable one to learn fast and apply learning to efficient problem-solving), from other peripheral characteristics, such as work habits and conduct. Thus, young children think that intellectual ability may be increased with practice and hard work. These differentiations appear gradually during the elementary school years. However, it is only in adolescence that a distinction between effort and ability is made and its relationships to intelligence understood. Thus, self-evaluations of intellectual competence and academic achievement become more accurate and more modest with increasing age. A standard finding in this regard is a clear decline in self-evaluation scores and academic self-esteem from late childhood to early adolescence (Demetriou et al., 1997a; Nicholls, 1990; Phillips & Zimmerman, 1990; Stipek & McIver, 1989).

In conclusion, all systems and subsystems of mind appear to change systematically from birth to maturity in various ways across the SCSs. At some phases in development, such as around 2 or 11 years, there are representational changes across all SCSs. However, there are important differences among the SCSs even at corresponding levels of complexity, because the structures that can be handled by each SCS cannot be reduced either to the same number of units or to the same relationships between units. The implication is that one should be careful to differentiate between descriptions of the general orientations of thought at a particular age and descriptions of how thought works in particular domains. Although descriptions of general orientations offer a useful picture of the general characteristics of the mind, one needs a domain-specific analysis if one is to understand what operations are involved in the mind's functioning when focusing on this domain or how these operations are used. Case's semantic analysis of different domains (see Figure 5.3 above) may be a good starting point in the direction of devising a language appropriate for the analysis of different domains that would at the same time be able to capture their common characteristics.

Explaining Cognitive Development

How the architecture of mind explains the development of mind

The present theory seeks to explain development in reference to the very nature of the mind itself, the nature of the environment, and the nature of the mind–environment relationships. Specifically, the theory assumes that if any cognitive system is to change and develop, it must satisfy three requirements. First, there must be a mechanism which causes misapplications, errors, inefficient or insufficient operation of the available processes, such that the individual's understanding or problem-solving skills are unable to meet the current requirements and are thus in need of change. Second, there should also be some kind of representations of the true state of affairs which suggests which of the variations is closer to the goal. These representations can function as criteria which can guide the selection process. Third, there must be a recording device to register both the criterion representations and any variations that can be tried as possible solutions. Finally, there must also be a right-and-wrong marking device which can determine the correct alternative.

The architecture proposed by the present theory seems able to satisfy these requirements. Specifically, the mechanism which generates variations between the system's representations or attempted solutions and the immediate goal resides partially in the environment and partially in the mind itself. The environment is rarely, if ever, constant, so that these variations may be explained by the slight variations in the information that the environment will provide at any two points in time. Most important, however, this mechanism may be a property of the very nature of the mind itself. For instance, memory failures or varying motivation may result in differing representations or attempted solutions. Moreover, from about age 4, children understand that individuals often represent the same state differently, which may be another cause for variations within minds when they interact on a given state (see section on the theory of mind). It seems, therefore, that it is the very nature of the environment and the mind that ensures the instability necessary for change to occur in the mind's representations and coping operations for the environment.

The second mechanism responsible for furnishing examples of the correct is related to the SCSs involved in the environment-oriented level of knowing. Very early in an individual's life, each SCS possesses mechanisms that abstract SCS-specific meaning from corresponding patterns of information. Our theory assumes that these patterns serve as criterion representations to evaluate the more complex and/or less accurate representations generated at different points in time. Take as an example the infant who has some understanding that numerosity remains constant, such as when she has sets with fewer than three or four elements. When presented with situations wherein numerosity does not appear to be constant, as when the elements are arranged such that they seem to involve more or less, she will try to understand why. Thus, the system is self-corrective because construction always involves a grasp of some aspects of the true state of affairs.

We have stated that selection among variations requires a register-and-compare function, and we assume that the processing system is responsible for this function. Comparisons, error-making activities, and decision-making are the responsibilities of the hypercognitive system. Because of its monitoring, regulation, and selection processes, the hypercognitive system contributes to all three major aspects of development noted above. That is, gradually, it establishes increasingly powerful interpretation, processing, and action networks that can be called upon in the future, thereby expanding the field of application of the environment-oriented SCSs.

We emphasize in this section that the three-level mental architecture proposed by this theory, together with the very nature of the world, make cognitive development possible. However, this alone cannot explain how change, once activated, evolves and spreads over other systems in the mind, as we have attempted to explain. In the following two sections an attempt will be made to highlight the dynamics and the mechanisms of change.

The dynamics of development

Our theory assumes that the levels and systems of the mental architecture are simultaneously distinct and functionally attuned to each other. Thus, a change initiating in one system in the mind may cause changes to other systems, which may then loop back and cause further changes to the first system, and so on. However, depending upon the system in which they originate, changes will exhibit different characteristics. Three general types of changes can be described: bottom-up, top-down, and horizontal.

Bottom-up changes originate in the more basic levels of the mental architecture and spread to the more advanced levels. The most typical characteristic change of this type is that which initiates in the most basic function in the processing system, namely speed of processing, and then spreads upward until it affects structures within the hypercognitive system, such as cognitive self-image. Our theory posits that the lower level changes alter the conditions under which the higher level systems function, such that the changes in the higher level become necessary to cope with the consequences of the lower level change. Specifically, increased speed of processing necessitates improved control of incoming information, because the faster processing increases the likelihood that irrelevant information may pass into the system, requiring the mind to improve processing control. In turn, improved control of information enables the system to better exploit its available storage space or capabilities, since it minimizes the risk of interference due to irrelevant information entering the storage space. All these changes then enhance the possibility that new SCS-specific skill can be constructed, since all these changes eventually affect the functioning of the hypercognitive system. Our studies have shown that these changes contribute to the refinement and differentiation of the individual's hypercognitive maps, and moreover they affect her cognitive self-image. Thus, faster processing leads to acquisition of more powerful reasoning strategies, enabling the individual to learn more and think more logically (Demetriou et al., 1997b).

Top-down changes refer to changes which initiate in the hypercognitive system and spread downward to effect concomitant change in the lower levels. Changes in the hypercognitive system first affect the knowledge individuals have about their own mind or their skills in regulating its functioning. The recent proliferation of research examining the effects of metacognitive training on various conceptual domains highlights this type of change transfer across the levels of mental architecture. In these studies children are trained to observe their own cognitive functioning, try alternative processes to ascertain their varying effectiveness, and code them so as to make them easily retrievable. This research, which purports to help students 'learn how to learn', showed that acquiring awareness of one's own strategies and skills for monitoring and regulating beneficially affects the functioning of the processing system per se, domain-specific skills or processes, and even of deductive and analogical reasoning. That is, learning of this kind generalizes across the levels of the architecture of mind and across different domains within a level, such as the SCSs (Adey & Shayer, 1994; Boekaerts, 1997; Brown & Kane, 1988; Brown & Campione, 1990).

Horizontal changes affect systems at the same hierarchical level. These are essentially changes which affect the relationships between component processes either within the same or across different SCSs. Due to space considerations, discussion here will focus on changes within the same SCS. The development of the causal-experimental SCS is taken as an example. The reader is reminded that in this SCS combinatorial skills first appear at about age 11 and continue to develop until approximately age 14 or 15. Model construction skills appear at about age 14–15 and are neither fully nor well developed until after college age. Skills in experimentation and hypothesis formation develop concurrently with these two sequence levels. According to our theory, this alternation of developmental levels from the one sequence is itself a cause of change, because each improvement in one sequence lays the ground for the other sequences to move further along their own trajectory of levels. This model of developmental synergy within SCSs is explained in the passage below in reference to the causal-experimental SCS.

> Combinatorial abilities of the lower levels serve to set up the mental space in which the first hypotheses can be formulated. At a subsequent phase, hypothesis formation abilities enable the young adolescent to fix the combinations he or she conceives in structures that can function as frames that can direct his or her manipulations of reality. Thus, systematic experimentation begins to be possible. Once it is acquired, experimentation acts in two directions. On the one hand, it provides strategies that can be put into the service of the combinatorial ability itself. As a result, the construction of the higher level combinatorial abilities is facilitated. On the other hand, it generates a data space that has to be understood. Evidently, a good way to gain an understanding is to map this data space onto the space of the hypotheses that served as the starting point of experimentation. This is the beginning of model construction. In turn, when model construction advances to a certain level, it functions as a frame for the conception of more complex hypotheses and consequently for the design of more sophisticated experiments. These then may loop back by providing the material, external or mental, for the construction of more complex model, and so on and so forth. (Demetriou et al., 1993b, p. 495).

Two points need to be noted here. First, changes within an SCS do not automatically generalize to other SCSs, although they may be effected by the same mechanisms. This is due to the fact that SCS-specific changes produce mental units which are of direct use only to the SCS concerned. This has been corroborated by learning experiments which showed that transfer across SCSs is very limited, if present at all (Case et al., 1996; Demetriou et al. 1993a). The second point is concerned with the nature of development itself. That is, the alternation of developmental changes from the one sequence to the other suggests that transformation and reorganization is a more or less permanent condition of the mind. Thus, from this point of view, development is continuous rather than discontinuous.

Mechanisms of change

The previous discussion on developmental causality has explained how each system can function as a cause of change in another system, although the kinds and the degrees of change will vary. According to this theory, different types of change are effected via different mechanisms, that is, there are mechanisms which transfer changes (a) across the hierarchical levels of the mental architecture, (b) within hierarchical levels, that is, from one SCS to the other, and (c) from one component to the other within a given SCS.

Specifically, bottom-up changes affect the flow of information in the mind. For example, an increase in speed of processing lets more information enter into the mind. Therefore, it necessitates better information management than before so that, for example, redundant information is not taken into account. Thus, these changes require mechanisms related to information handling and management, such as *orienting, information search*, and *selective attention*. These mechanisms enable the person to direct processing onto information relevant to the present goal and ignore irrelevant information.

Top-down changes affect the individual's approach to her own cognitive functioning. Greater awareness of cognitive processes leads to better perception of their similarities and differences and thus to the construction of better focused or more generally applicable processes. *Metarepresentation* is the primary top-down mechanism of cognitive change. Simply defined, metarepresentation is a process which looks for, codifies, and typifies similarities between mental experiences (past or present) to enhance understanding and problem-solving efficiency. So defined, metarepresentation is the functional aspect of working hypercognition. In logical terms, metarepresentation is analogical reasoning applied to mental experiences or operations, rather than to representations of environmental stimuli. For example, when a child realizes that the sequencing of the *if . . . then* connectives in language is associated with situations in which the event or thing preceded by *if* always comes first and that it produces the event or thing introduced by *then*, this child is actually formulating an inference schema that leads to predictions and interpretations specific to this schema. When abstracted over many different occasions, and somehow tagged (or symbolized) in the mind it becomes the frame which guides reasoning by implication. Thus, according to this theory, metarepresentation, which is inductive reasoning applied to cognitive experiences, is the mechanism that drives the development of deductive reasoning from primary to secondary reasoning, that is from automated inference to explicit logic and metalogic. Obviously, this conception concurs with Moshman's theory on the development of deductive reasoning.

Horizontal changes involve the SCS. The theory postulates that the mechanisms for transferring change across different SCSs are not the same as those for transferring change within the same SCS. *Bridging* refers to the construction of a new mental unit by establishing relationships between skills and processes which belong to different SCSs. These relationships are necessary for the solution of complex problems that require the activation of more than one SCS. An example of bridging would be the use of graphical representations (spatial SCS), to express covariation relations (quantitative SCS). Another example would be the use of algebraic functions (quantitative-relational SCS), to express causal relations. *Interweaving* is a mechanism that builds new mental units within the same SCS. However, integrating units within SCSs through this mechanism engenders a preference for the use of the new unit and an ensuing reduction in the isolated use of the units involved in the integration, although these units may still be available. For example, interweaving hypothesis formation capability with the isolation of variables ability within the causal-experimental SCS results in model construction skills. Although both specialized skills may always be present, the model construction skills, once established, will dominate (see Demetriou et al., 1993b). The theory describes several other mechanisms to explain how mental units are differentiated and refined with development, or how they are eliminated when are no longer useful. However, space limitations do not allow the explication of these mechanisms.

In conclusion, this theory assumes that development affects architecture as much as architecture affects development. That is, the new units created as a result of development may not dramatically alter the architecture of mind as there will always be an environment-oriented and a self-oriented level of functioning. However, the construction of new units considerably alters the communication between the levels and structures of mind. That is, the new units induce the person to see the objects or relations which are characteristic of one domain of the environment or the self from the perspective of the objects or the relations which reside in other domains. Thus, the conception of mind advanced by this theory is consistent with the basic assumptions of dynamic systems theory which were summarized above.

It also needs to be noted that the present theory was advanced with the aim of accounting for individual differences in cognitive development. Thus, it is assumed that there may be intra-individual and inter-individual differences in the organization and development of any of the SCSs or the domain-general levels described by the theory. Moreover, there may be differences in how the mechanisms of change described above are activated and used by different individuals. Differences of this kind underlie individual differences in learning styles. Our theory specifies a number of mechanisms which are responsible for these individual differences (Demetriou & Efklides, 1987; Demetriou et al., 1996). However, the issue of individual differences is beyond the concerns of the present chapter.

THE LIFE-SPAN APPROACH TO COGNITIVE DEVELOPMENT

The general assumption underlying the theory and research summarized above is that of continuous growth, that is, that development always results in improvement and augmentation or, in other words, in more and better cognitive skills and knowledge across all dimensions. Although this growth model of development may not be entirely accurate across all ages, it seems to have some justification for the early years of life. However, it is overly apparent that after a certain point, changes associated with age result in both gains and losses in various systems, functions, and/or dimensions of the mind. Thus, the dominant model in the study of cognitive development in adulthood is based on a 'gain–loss dynamic'. According to this model, losses in the strength or flexibility of cognitive functions at one level of the mind may be associated with adaptations and reorganizations at another. These changes may increase the 'adaptive fitness' of the person in those contexts and functions which are of importance to the current phase of life (Baltes, 1991).

Recent research and theorizing on cognitive development is fully consistent with the hierarchical and dynamic conception of mind previously outlined. Research in our own (Demetriou et al., 1997b) and other laboratories (Schaie, Willis, Jay & Chipuer, 1989) suggests that the levels and systems of mind are always in place. In the words of Schaie et al. (1989) the mind is structurally invariant across the life-span. Baltes, a leading authority in the study of cognitive aging, suggests that we will have to differentiate between changes in the *mechanics* of mind and changes in the *pragmatics* of mind. In relation to the previous theories, Baltes' mechanics correspond to the processing system; pragmatics correspond to the environment-oriented and the self-oriented levels of the architecture of mind. The gain–loss dynamic conception of life-span cognitive development postulates that negative changes or losses in the mechanics of the mind may be associated with positive changes or gains in its pragmatics.

The empirical evidence seems to support this general model (see Salthouse, 1991). Specifically, it is clear that the various functions of the processing system, such as speed of processing, inhibition and control of processing, and short-term storage, level off at the end of the second decade of life or the beginning of the third and they stabilize at this level until about the middle of the fourth decade, when they start to deteriorate. That is, processing slows down, indicated by higher response times in speed of processing tasks; inhibition and control effected with more difficulty and less efficiency, indicated by lapses and higher response times for tasks which require control; and reduced short-term memory span, indicated by the fact that fewer units of information can be retained in short-term memory tasks. These changes are clearly shown in Figure 5.7, where we can see that all three functions enter a period of negative change around age 35 and they continue to decline systematically, so that by the seventh decade of life they return to the values they had in the first decade.

The environment-oriented systems, such as categorical, analogical, verbal, mathematical, and spatial thought seem to follow more or less the same course, although they begin to decline a few years later (i.e. in the fifth decade) than information processing. Two points need to be noted here. First, it seems that not all domains of thought exhibit negative changes at the same time; for instance, spatial reasoning appears to decline earlier than verbal reasoning. Second, there is no conclusive evidence to prove whether these changes are centered on the processes involved in these domains themselves, or whether they are caused by the changes in the various parameters of processing system (Salthouse, 1991).

The processes and functions involved in the self-oriented system and the ensuing management skills seem to undergo a more positive change. In fact, the evidence suggests that the losses in the functions at the more fundamental levels of the architecture of mind are compensated by gains in many of the functions and skills associated with self-understanding, self-management, and management of complex social and interpersonal issues.

Research focusing on these processes originally attempted to examine whether there were stages following Piaget's stage of formal operations or if, as Piaget claimed, this was the final stage of cognitive development. Patricia Arlin (1975) was the first to propose a fifth stage of cognitive development, a stage which followed formal thought and which she termed a *problem-finding stage*. This stage is characterized by an ability to identify inconsistencies or gaps in the solutions to problems or in the existing knowledge, evaluate the importance of problems, and plan appropriate actions. This problem-finding approach is conducive to the production of new knowledge and skills because it makes individuals dissatisfied with their current knowledge and skills. Just as formal operations build on concrete operations to construct a system of second-order thought, so the problem-finding stage builds on the robust problem-solving skills of the formal stage to motivate individuals to advance their own cognitive functioning. The problem-finding stage is posited to appear in the third decade of life.

Several other authors have argued that postformal thought becomes *dialectical* after a certain phase (Labouvie-Vief, 1990; Pascual-Leone, 1983; Riegel, 1973). Dialectical thought enables the individual to envisage and accept alternative conceptions of the same aspect of reality and achieve a higher-order synthesis. In this synthesis each of the alternative conceptions is recognized for whatever unique or valuable contribution they make in the process of understanding. Obviously, problem-finding is implicated in dialectical thought, because dialectical synthesis would not occur had not lags and inconsistencies been noted first. All of these theorists believe that dialectical thought requires explicit reflection. According to Moshman, dialectical thought presupposes explicit metalogic as a means for first noting and then integrating alternative views of a given reality (Moshman, 1998).

Dialectical thought is highly useful to adults due to a life-style which involves multiple roles, that is, parent, spouse, and professional, which are frequently in conflict. For instance, family demands frequently conflict with professional pressures and dialectical thought can aid in reconciling opposing needs and inconsistencies. Many authors believe that dialectical thought appears in the middle 30s, culminating during middle age.

Dialectical thought is also implicated in the acquisition of wisdom, which is supposed to come with age. According to Baltes and Smith (1990), wisdom is 'exceptional insight into human development and life matters, exceptionally good judgment, advice, and commentary about difficult life problems' (p. 95). Wise judgment integrates factual knowledge of the events and pragmatics of life, strategies for dealing with them, knowledge which considers uncertainties, and a relativist attitude towards life values and goals. The attainment of wisdom is highly useful for both the individual and the social group, since it can integrate the best interests both of the individuals and of their social group into balanced decisions and policies. Moreover, wisdom enables the individual to accept the negative changes that aging brings, such as the cognitive changes noted above and the decline in general physical fitness and health.

In relation to the gain–loss dynamic, Pascual-Leone (1983) posited that the negative changes in the processing system are partially responsible for the acquisition of dialectical thought and wisdom. He argued that the slowing of cognitive processing and the relaxation of control processes enable the middle-aged person to envisage alternatives that would not be possible under conditions of strict logical validity and consistency. This more holistic approach provides, in turn, a basis for the relativism necessary for dialectical thought and wise judgment.

It must also be noted that negative changes are more prominent under conditions of low familiarity and practice. That is, the negative effects of aging first appear under conditions where new skills and knowledge are required, rather than in the context of normal functioning. This is easily explainable. The processing system (or the mechanics of the mind) is demanded more at the phase of the acquisition of new skills, rather than later when they are in place and need only to be activated. Thus, negative changes in this system will affect any other processes in which it is involved. Finally, it must be noted that 'with aging the balance between gains and losses becomes less positive or even negative' (Baltes, 1991, p. 847). That is, after a certain age, deterioration may start to accelerate rapidly and generalize over all functions and levels of the mind. This usually occurs in association with deteriorating health, especially related to the condition of the brain (see van der Molen & Ridderinkhoff, ch. 2 this volume). At this final phase, the deterioration may lead to more or less complete cognitive disengagement.

CONCLUSIONS

The theory and research discussed in this chapter converge on a number of points. These are summarized below:

1. *The mind evolves from being perceptually driven and action-bound to*

being self-guided, reflective and self-aware; from holding few and reality-referenced representations to holding many and reciprocally referenced representations; and from global and less integrated to differentiated but better integrated mental operations.

Specifically, it is indeed true that pre-language infants are able to recognize and abstract meaning from complex patterns of configurations and relationships in the environment. However, no one would disagree that pre-language infants are highly attracted by the variation in their perceptual environment and that they are primarily action-oriented rather than thinking-oriented. Moreover, they seem aware neither of themselves nor of their representational nature.

Preschoolers represent the world and the mind and they operate on representations. However, they are frequently clumsy in their attempts and they are easily deceived by appearances. They are much more efficient when they work with single as opposed to dual or multiple encodings. Moreover, they are more adept under conditions in which both the meaning and the solutions are overtly suggested, rather than under conditions which require analysis and reorganization.

During primary school, children become increasingly able to manipulate multiple encodings; they become increasingly resistant to deception from appearances, thereby acquiring considerable conceptual stability; their knowledge of the world and the mind becomes fairly differentiated and accurate; and they begin to reason on the basis of logical relationships rather than on automatic application of inference schemata. However, their general attitude to problem-solving is descriptive rather than inquisitive, and they think with rather than about representations.

From adolescence onward, the individual begins to view representations from the perspective of other representations, which enables concepts that can represent the most complex and dynamic aspects of reality to be constructed. Thus, the entire approach of the adolescent to the world is gradually differentiated from that of the child, that is, the balance shifts gradually from the description of reality to suppositions about it, and to inquiry about those suppositions. In other words, there is a shift in the focus of understanding from reality itself to its representations so that knowledge of the mind and the self becomes increasingly differentiated, accurate, and codified. Codes of mind raise inferential processes to the level of metareasoning, which enables the individual to think in reference to criteria of logical validity and adequacy. The end-product of the shift is a model-construction, model-testing, and even a model-modeling strategic approach. This gradually generates models of the world which are recognized as such, skills for their testing, either empirical or conceptual, and even skills for formalizing and communicating the models.

Later, in the years of maturity, alternative models of reality and action may be envisaged and simultaneously accepted. As a result, relativism prevails and wisdom starts to guide action. The positive sides of advancing age coexist, from a certain phase onwards, with a slowing in mental efficiency, which is made evident under conditions of low familiarity. Late in life limited efficiency, flawed reasoning, and even cognitive disengagement may prevail.

2. *The mind is a hierarchical, multisystemic, and multidimensional universe.* How is it possible that each of the successive phases of life is marked with characteristic strategies and orientations to the understanding and yet there is so much variation in performance and development? The explanation is found in the architecture of mind, which the research reviewed here strongly suggests involves both domain-specific and do-main-general systems organized on a number of different levels. A similar picture of the mind's architecture is suggested by research in other fields, such as the psychology of individual differences (Gustaff-son, 1994), evolutionary psychology (Cosmides & Tooby 1994) and neurosceince (Diamond & Taylor, 1996; Thatcher, 1994).

    The domain-general systems involve encoding, storing, and control processes. At a basic level of organization, these processes define how much information the mind can hold and how efficiently it can be operated on. At a higher or a hypercognitive level, these processes direct self-mapping and the mapping of other minds and are used to steer cognitive functioning according to immediate demands and goals. The domain-specific systems involve processes specializing on the represen-tation and processing of different types of relationships or structures in the environment. In Gelman and William's words (1998), 'environ-ments and minds share universal structures, not universal surface char-acteristics' (p. 16). Thus, there are systems of mind which evolved to cope with corresponding systems of the environment. Interestingly enough, developmental neurosciences advance models about the learn-ing processes underlying the engrafting of different environmental structures onto the cortex so that environmental specificity is reflected in the specificity of cortical areas and neural networks and this is reflected in the specificity of representational structures (Quartz & Sejnowski, in press).

    Overall then, the domain-general processes constrain, boost, and direct the functioning and development of domain-specific systems and the functioning and development of the domain-specific systems feed, inform, and expand the functioning and development of the domain-general systems. Thus, according to this conception, the architecture and functioning of mind merge to co-define each other into *dynamic systems.* In these systems structure cannot easily be dissociated from function because it refers to the 'dynamic patterning and relating of components that sustain the organized activities that define life and living things' (Fischer & Bidell, 1998, p. 9) in their interpenetration and internetworking with their environments.

3. *Learning can take place at any hierarchical level or in any system of mind.* The assumptions that a hierarchical and multisystemic mind comprises structures that participate both with each other and with the structures of the environment bear some important implications for learning and

development. Specifically, these assumptions suggest that the various hierarchical levels and systems of mind evolved to learn different aspects or organizational levels of the world. Thus, we have to assume both domain-specific and domain-general learning. Domain-specific learning refers to changes in the knowledge, processes, and skills which are activated by particular domains of the environment and which are required to cope with the particular demands posed by these environments. Thus, domain-specific learning springs from, and affects the functioning of, the domain-specific modules; domain-general learning always involves, somehow, the hypercognitive system, and therefore it affects the functioning of the other systems. Domain-specific learning involves mechanisms which ensure that the newly generated skills and concepts will honor the particular domains. Domain-general learning refers to changes in the knowledge, processes, and skills which are concerned with knowing and handling the functioning of the mind itself. Domain-general learning involves mechanisms, such as reflective abstraction and metarepresentation, that generate and refine general patterns of mental action. Logical reasoning is the most important product of these mechanisms. This picture of the nature of mind and learning carries significant implications about the nature of development and individual differences in development.

4. *Intra- and inter-individual variability is the rule in development.* Assuming a hierarchical and multisystemic mind provides an excellent frame for understanding intra- and inter-individual differences in cognitive development and functioning, because there is no reason to assume that all levels or functions are identical either within or across individuals. In fact, to assume variability becomes almost mandatory if we assume (as we have in this chapter) that neither the same individual nor the environment are entirely identical across occasions even in respect to the same module or function. Remember that we have also assumed that the relationships between systems within minds and between the mind and the environment are dynamic and interparticipatory. This implies that a particular difference between any two systems within an individual or any difference between any two individuals in regard to any system at a particular time t_1 may cause more variations at a later time t_2, which will further multiply at time t_3, and so on. In short, the very architecture and dynamics of mind provide for differentiation and variability rather than for similarity and uniformity. However, the very same reasons that generate variability in learning and development also constrain its range. The operation of the domain-general systems and the dynamic relationships between different modules suggest that the rate of change between different processes cannot vary beyond a certain limit at a given phase (Case et al., 1996; Demetriou et al., 1993a; Fischer & Bidell, 1998).

5. *Development occurs at multiple levels and it has many faces.* Our conception of development and learning suggests different kinds of developmental change, whose nature and form will depend on the system and

the level of analysis selected for their examination. Viewed at a refined level of analysis, that is, intervals of hours, days or even weeks, the mind appears constantly changing as a result of variations in the world, or simply due to its own functioning—which is directed either to the understanding of the world or of itself because environmental variations or the changing condition of one system will require micro-adaptations in many other systems. Thus, at this refined level, development appears to be a permanent state of the system. Working on this assumption, Kuhn, Garcia-Mila, Zohar and Andersen (1995) and Siegler (1995) were able to show, via a microgenetic method which records development at this refined level of days or weeks, that at any given time period there is always a kind of cognitive fermentation. Specifically, at any time, some ways of thinking are initially prevalent and then decrease in frequency; others are very weak and infrequent initially but gradually increase in frequency until they dominate; others remain weak and infrequent although they are always present, and still others fluctuate in their level of frequency throughout the given period of time. At this level of analysis it is difficult to specify when there is a change in developmental cycles or stages. We may not even be able to speak of stages, because the concept of stage presupposes, by definition, a certain degree of stability, consistency, and duration. Thus, at this level development appears to be continuous rather than discontinuous.

However, on a broader level of analysis development appears to occur in spurts and to result in the acquisition of new forms of understanding rather than in the addition of more of the same skills. One example is the changes associated with representational shifts, such as the move from sensorimotor to representational intelligence or from desire to belief psychology, and so on. Frequently, these shifts are seen as cutting points which demarcate the end of one developmental cycle and the beginning of another. The age phases which coincide with these shifts are usually regarded as phases during which there is an acceleration of development, which indicates a qualitative transformation of the cognitive system (i.e. a substantial reorganization of functions and processes which generates new possibilities for the thinker). Acquisition of these new possibilities enables the individual to quickly construct new abilities in various domains. In conclusion, at one level of analysis development seems discontinuous for certain processes, whereas at another level it appears to be continuous for other processes.

6. *Being hierarchical and multisystemic, the mind can be modeled in multiple ways.* We have seen that different scholars have used different ways to model the mind. Piaget used logic to model the organization of mental operations. Case used charts of processing steps to represent executive control structures and semantic networks to represent central conceptual structures. Researchers of reasoning provide general patterns of inference and arguments to model reasoning. In my work, the conventions of structural modeling are used to model the levels and systems of mind. Dynamic systems theorists use *n*-dimensional figures to model the

rate and form of development along time. None of these ways of representing the mind is necessarily wrong or better than any other. Any of them can be acceptable and useful in so far as it serves its purpose; that is, to convey how a scholar concurs with the structural, functional, and developmental characteristics in relation to the aspects of developing mind he is researching. At the same time, however, it is to be hoped that, with development, we the researchers of the developing mind, will become tolerant and knowledgable of each others' language.

ACKNOWLEDGEMENTS

Special thanks are due to Robbie Case and Wolfgang Schneider for their comments on an earlier version of this chapter. Thanks are also due to Smaragda Kazi for compiling the reference list and taking care of the art work and to Kathleen Stephanides for copy-editing the chapter.

REFERENCES

Adey, P. & Shayer, M. (1994). *Really Raising Standards: Cognitive Intervention and Academic Achievement*. London: Routledge.

Arlin, P. K. (1975). Cognitive development in adulthood: A fifth stage? *Developmental Psychology*, 11, 602–606.

Baddeley, A. (1991). *Working Memory*. Oxford: Oxford University Press.

Baltes, P. B. (1991). The many faces of human aging: Toward a psychological culture of old age. *Psychological Medicine*, 21, 837–854.

Baltes, P. B. & Smith, J. (1990). Toward a psychology of wisdom and its ontogenesis. In R. J. Sternberg (Ed.), *Wisdom: Its Nature, Origins, and Development* (pp. 87–120). New York: Cambridge University Press.

Becker, A. H. & Ward, T. B. (1991). Children's use of shape in extending novel labels to animate objects: Identity versus postural change. *Cognitive Development*, 6, 3–16.

Beilin, H. & Lust, B. (1975). A study of the development of logical and linguistic connectives. In H. Beilin (Ed.), *Studies in the Cognitive Basis of Language Development*. New York: Academic Press.

Bentler, P. M. (1989). *EQS: Structural Equations Program Manual*. Los Angeles, CA: BMDP Statistical Software.

Bliss, J. & Ogborn, J. (1994). Force and motion from the beginning. *Learning and Instruction: The Journal of the European Association for Research on Learning and Instruction*, 4, 7–25.

Boekarts, M. (1997). Self-regulated learning: A new concept embraced by researchers, policy makers, educators, teachers, and students. *Learning and Instruction: The Journal of the European Association for Research on Learning and Instruction*.

Braine, M. D. S. (1990). The 'natural logic' approach to reasoning. In W. F. Overton (Ed.), *Reasoning, Necessity, and Logic: Developmental Perspec-

tives (pp. 133–157). Hillsdale, NJ: Erlbaum.

Braine, M. D. S. & Rumain, B. (1983). Logical reasoning. In J. H. Flavell & E. M. Markman (Eds), *Handbook of Child Psychology: Cognitive Development*. Vol. III (pp. 263–340). New York: Wiley.

Brainerd, C. J. (1978). *Piaget's Theory of Intelligence*. Englewood Cliffs, NJ: Prentice-Hall.

Brown, A. L. & Campione, J. C. (1990). Communities of learning and thinking, or a context by any other name. In D. Kuhn (Ed.), *Developmental Perspectives on Teaching and Learning Thinking Skills*. Basel: Karger.

Brown, A. L. & Kane, M. J. (1988). Preschool children can learn to transfer: Learning to learn and learning from example. *Cognitive Psychology*, **20**, 493–523.

Bruner, J. (1968). *Towards a Theory of Instruction*, New York: W. W. Norton.

Bryant, P. E. & Trabasso, T. (1971). Transitive inference and memory in young children. *Nature*, **232**, 456–458.

Caravita, S. & Hallden, O. (1994). Re-framing the problem of conceptual change. *Learning and Instruction: The Journal of the European Association for Research on Learning and Instruction*, **4**, 89–111.

Carey, S. (1985). Are children fundamentally different kinds of thinkers and learners than adults? In S. F. Chapman, J. W. Segal & R. Glaser (Eds), *Thinking and Learning Skills*, Vol. 2. Hillsdale, NJ: Erlbaum.

Carpendale, J. I. & Chandler, M. J. (1996). On the distinction between false belief understanding and subscribing to an interpretive theory of mind. *Child Development*, **67**, 1686–1706.

Case, R. (1985). *Intellectual Development: Birth to Adulthood*. New York: Academic Press.

Case, R. (1992). *The Mind's Staircase: Exploring the Conceptual Underpinnings of Children's Thought and Knowledge*. Hillsdale, NJ: Erlbaum.

Case, R., Okamoto, Y., Griffin, S., McKeough, A., Bleiker, C., Henderson, B. & Stephenson, K. M. (1996). The role of central conceptual structures in the development of children's thought. *Monographs of the Society for Research on Child Development*, **61** (1–2, Serial No. 246),

Chandler, M., Fritz, A. S. & Hala, S. M. (1989). Small scale deceit: Deception as a marker of two-, three-, and four-year-olds' early theories of mind. *Child Development*, **60**, 1263–1277.

Cheng, P. W. & Hollyoak, K. J. (1985). Pragmatic reasoning schemas. *Cognition*, **17**, 285–313.

Commons, M., Richards, F. A. & Kuhn, D. (1982). Systematic and meta-systematic reasoning: A case for levels of reasoning beyond Piaget's stage of formal operations. *Child Development*, **53**, 1058–1069.

Cosmides, L. & Tooby, J. (1994). Beyond intuition and instinct blindness: Toward an evolutionary rigorous cognitive science. *Cognition*, **50**, 41–77.

Dasen, P. R. (1977). *Piagetian Psychology: Cross-cultural Contributions*, New York. Gardner Press.

DeLoache, J. S., Miller, K. F. & Pierroutsakos, S. L. (1998). Reasoning and problem solving. In D. Kuhn and R. Siegler (Eds), W. Damon (Series

Ed.), *Handbook of Child Psychology (5th edn): Vol. 2: Cognition, Perception and Language*. New York: Wiley.

Demetriou, A. (Ed.) (1988). *The Neo-Piagetian Theories of Cognitive Development: Toward an Integration*. Amsterdam: North-Holland.

Demetriou, A. (1990). Structural and developmental relations between formal and postformal capacities: Towards a comprehensive theory of adolescent and adult cognitive development. In Commons, M., Armon, C., Kohlberg, L., Richards, F. A., Grotzer, T. A. & Sinnott, J. D. (Eds), *Adult Development, Vol. 2: Models and Methods in the Study of Adolescent and Adult Thought* (pp. 147–173). New York: Praeger.

Demetriou, A. (1993). On the quest of the functional architecture of developing mind. *Educational Psychological Review*, **5**, 1–18.

Demetriou, A. (1996). Outline for a developmental theory of cognitive change: General principles and educational implications. *The School Field*, **7**, 7–41.

Demetriou, A. & Efklides, A. (1985). Structure and sequence of formal and postformal thought: General patterns and individual differences. *Child Development*, **56**, 1062–1091.

Demetriou, A. & Efklides, A. (1987). Towards a determination of the dimensions and domains of individual differences in cognitive development. In E. De Corte, H. Lodewijks, R. Parmentier & P. Span (Eds), *Learning and Instruction: European Research in an International Context, Vol. 1* (pp. 41–52). Oxford: Leuven University Press and Pergamon Press.

Demetriou, A. & Efklides, A. (1989). The person's conception of the structures of developing intellect: Early adolescence to middle age. *Genetic, Social, and General Psychology Monographs*, **115**, 371–423.

Demetriou, A. & Efklides, A. (1994). Structure, development, and dynamics of mind. In A. Demetriou, & A. Efklides, (Eds), *Mind, Intelligence, and Reasoning: Structure and Development* (pp. 75–109). Amsterdam: Elsevier.

Demetriou, A,. Efklides, A. & Platsidou, M. (1993a). The architecture and dynamics of developing mind: Experimental structuralism as a frame for unifying cognitive development theories. *Monographs of the Society for Research in Child Development*, **58**, (5–6, Serial No. 234).

Demetriou, A,. Efklides, A., Papadaki, M., Papantoniou, G. & Economou, A. (1993b). The structure and development of causal-experimental thought. *Developmental Psychology*, **29**, 480–497.

Demetriou, A,. Kazi, S., Platsidou, M., Sirmali, K. & Kiosseoglou, G. (1997a). Self-image, thought styles and cognitive development: Modularity and transmodularity in the development of mind. Unpublished monograph.

Demetriou, A,. Platsidou, M., Efklides, A., Metallidou, Y. & Shayer, M. (1991). The development of quantitative-relational abilities from childhood to adolescence: Structure, scaling and individual differences. *Learning and Instruction: The Journal of the European Association for Research on Learning and Instruction*, **1**, 19–44.

Demetriou, A,. Platsidou, M., Sirmali, K., Zhang, X. & Spanoudis, G

(1997b). The structure and development of the processing system across the life-span. Unpublished Monograph.

Demetriou, A., Pachuary, A., Metallidou, Y. & Kazi, S. (1996). Universal and specificities in the structure and development of quantitative-relational thought: A cross-cultural study in Greece and India. *International Journal of Behavioral Development*, **19**, 255–290.

Demetriou, A,. Shayer, M. & Efklides, A. (Eds) (1992). *The Neo-Piagetian Theories of Cognitive Development: Implications and Applications for Education*. London: Routledge.

Diamond, A. & Taylor, C. (1996). Development of an aspect of executive control: Development of the abilities to remember what I said and to 'Do as I say, not as I do'. *Developmental Psychobiology*, **29**, 315–334.

Donaldson, M. (1978). *Children's Minds*. Glasgow: Fontana/Collins.

Emerson, H. F. (1980). Children's judgments of correct and reversed sentences with 'if'. *Journal of Child Language*, **7**, 137–155.

Fabricius, W. V. & Schwanenflugel, P. J. (1994). The older child's theory of mind. In A. Demetriou & A. Efklides (Eds), *Intelligence, Mind, and Reasoning: Structure and Development* (pp. 111–132). Amsterdam: North-Holland.

Falmagne, R. J. (1990). Language and the acquisition of logical knowledge. In W. F. Overton (Ed.), *Reasoning, Necessity, and Logic: Developmental Perspectives* (pp. 111–131). Hillsdale, NJ: Erlbaum.

Fischer, K. W. (1980). A theory of cognitive development: The control and construction of hierarchies of skills. *Psychological Review*, **87**, 477–531.

Fischer, K. & Bidell, T. R. (1998). Dynamic development of psychological structures in action and thought. In R. Lerner (Ed.), W. Damon (Series Ed.), *Handbook of Child Psychology (5th edn): Vol. 1: Theoretical Models of Human Development*. New York: Wiley.

Fischer, K. W. & Pipp, S. L. (1984). Development of the structures of unconscious thought. In K. Bowers & D. Meichenbaum (Eds), *The Unconscious Reconsidered* (pp. 88–148). New York. Wiley.

Flavell, J. H., Flavell, E. R. & Green, F. L. (1983). Development of the appearance–reality distinction. *Cognitive Psychology*, **15**, 95–170.

Flavell, J. H., Green, F. L. & Flavell, E. R. (1986). Development of knowledge about the appearance–reality distinction. *Monographs of the Society for Research in Child Development*, **51** (1, Serial No. 212).

Flavell, J. H., Green, F. L. & Flavell, E. R. (1995). Young children's knowledge about thinking. *Monographs of the Society for Research in Child Development*, **60** (1, Serial No. 243).

Flavell, J. H., Green, F. L., Wahl, K. E. & Flavell, E. R. (1987). The effects of question classification and memory aids on young children's performance on appearance–reality tasks. *Cognitive Development*, **2**, 127–144.

Fodor, J. A. (1975). *The Language of Thought*. Cambridge, MA: Harvard University Press.

Gelman, R. (1987). 'Cognitive development: Principles guide to learning and contribute to conceptual coherence.' Invited address to American Psychological Association Meeting, New York.

Gelman, R. & Gallistel, R. (1978). *The Child's Understanding of Number.* Cambridge, MA: Harvard University Press.

Gelman, R. & Williams, E. M. (1998). Enabling constraints for cognitive development and learning: Domain-specificity and epigenesis. In D. Kuhn & R. Seigler (Eds), W. Damon (Series Ed.), *Handbook of Child Psychology (5th edn): Vol. 2: Cognition, Perception and Language.* New York: Wiley.

Gelman, S. A. & Coley, J. D. (1990). The importance of knowing a dodo is a bird: Categories and inferences in 2-year-old children. *Developmental Psychology*, **6**, 796–804.

Gelman, S. A. & Markman, E. M. (1987). Young children's inductions from natural kinds: The role of categories and appearances. *Child Development*, **58**, 1532–1541.

Goossens, L. (1992). Training scientific thinking in children and adolescents: A critical commentary and quantitative integration. In A. Demetriou, M. Shayer & A. Efklides (Eds), *Neo-Piagetian Theories of Cognitive Development: Implications and Applications for Education* (pp. 160–179). London: Routledge.

Goswami, U. (1992). *Analogical Reasoning in Children.* Hillsdale, NJ: Erlbaum.

Goswami, U. & Brown, A. (1989). Melting chocolate and melting snowmen: Analogical reasoning and causal relations. *Cognition*, **35**, 69–95.

Gustafsson, J.-E. (1994). Hierarchical models of intelligence and educational achievement. In A. Demetriou & A. Efklides (Eds), *Intelligence, Mind, and Reasoning: Structure and Development* (pp. 75–110). Amsterdam: North-Holland.

Halford, G. S. (1988). A structure-mapping approach to cognitive development. In A. Demetriou (Ed.), *The Neo-Piagetian Theories of Cognitive Development: Toward an Integration* (pp. 103–136). Amsterdam: North-Holland.

Halford, G. S. (1993). *Children's Understanding: The Development of Mental Models.* New York: Erlbaum.

Harris, P. L., Brown, E., Marriot, C., Whithall, S. & Harmer, S. (1991). Monsters, ghosts and witches: Testing the limits of the fantasy–reality distinction in young children. *British Journal of Developmental Psychology*, **9**, 105–123.

Harris, P. L. & Nunez, M. (1996). Understanding permission rules by preschool children. *Child Development*, **67**, 1572–1591.

Harter, S. (1990). Causes, correlates, and the functional role of global self-worth: A life-span perspective. In R. J. Sternberg and J. Kolligian, Jr (Eds), *Competence Considered* (pp. 67–97). New Haven, CT: Yale University Press.

Inagaki, K. & Hatano, G. (1988). Young children's understanding of the mind–body distinction. Paper presented at the Meet. Am. Educ. Res. Assoc., New Orleans.

Inhelder, B. & Piaget, J. (1958). *The Growth of Logical Thinking from Childhood to Adolescence.* London: Routledge & Kegan Paul.

Inhelder, B. & Piaget, J. (1964). *The Early Growth of Logic in the Child: Classification and Seriation.* London: Routledge & Kegan Paul.

Johansson, B. S. & Sjolin, B. (1975). Preschool children's understanding of the coordinates 'and' and 'or'. *Journal of Experimental Child Psychology*, **19**, 233–240.

Karmiloff-Smith, A. & Inhelder, B. (1974). If you want to go ahead, get a theory. *Cognition*, **3**, 195–212.

Keil, F. (1989). *Concepts, Kinds, and Cognitive Development.* Cambridge, MA: MIT Press.

Kotovsky, L. & Baillargeon, R. (1995). Appearance and knowledge-based responses of 10.5-month-old infants to containers. Manuscript submitted for publication.

Kuhn, D., Garcia-Mila, M., Zohar, A. & Andersen, C. (1995). Strategies of knowledge acquisition. *Monographs of the Society for Research in Child Development*, **60**, (4, Serial No. 245).

Labouvie-Vief, G. (1990). Wisdom as integrated thought: Historical and developmental perspective. In R. J. Sternberg (Ed.), *Wisdom: Its Nature, Origins, and Development* (pp. 52–83). New York: Cambridge University Press.

Landau, B,. Smith, L. B. & Jones, S. S. (1988). The importance of shape in early lexical learning. *Cognitive Development*, **3**, 299–321.

Macnamara, J. (1986). *A Border Dispute: The Place of Logic in Psychology.* Cambridge, MA: MIT Press.

Massey, C. M. & Gelman, R. (1988). Preschooler's ability to decide whether a photographed unfamiliar object can move itself. *Developmental Psychology*, **24**, 307–317.

Moshman, D. (1990). The development of metalogical understanding. In W. F. Overton (Ed.), *Reasoning, Necessity, and Logic: Developmental Perspectives* (pp. 205–225). Hillsdale, NJ: Erlbaum.

Moshman, D. (1994). Reasoning, metareasoning and the promotion of rationality. In A. Demetriou & A. Efklides (Eds), *Mind, Intelligence, and Reasoning: Structure and Development* (pp. 135–150). Amsterdam: Elsevier.

Moshman, D. (1995). Reasoning as self-contained thinking. *Human Development*, **38**, 53–64.

Moshman, D. (1998). Cognitive development beyond childhood. In D. Kuhn and R. Siegler (Eds), W. Damon (Series Ed.), *Handbook of Child Psychology (5th edn): Vol. 2: Cognition, Perception and Language.* New York: Wiley.

Newell, A. & Simon, H. A. (1972). *Human Problem Solving.* Englewood Cliffs, NJ: Prentice-Hall.

Nicholls, J. G. (1990). What is ability and why are we mindful of it? A developmental perspective. In R. J. Sternberg & J. Kolligian, Jr (Eds), *Competence Considered* (pp. 11–40). New Haven, CT: Yale University Press.

Osherson, D. N. & Markman, E. (1975). Language and the ability to evaluate contradictions and tautologies. *Cognition*, **3**, 213–226.

Pascual-Leone, J. (1970). A mathematical model for the transition rule in Piaget's developmental stages. *Acta Psychologica*, **32**, 301–345

Pascual-Leone, J. (1983). Growing into human maturity: Towards a meta-subjective theory of adulthood stages. In. P. B. Baltes and O. G. Brim, (Eds), *Life-span Development and Behavior*. Vol. 5 (pp. 117–156). New York: Academic Press.

Pascual-Leone, J. & Goodman, D. (1979). Intelligence and experience: A neo-Piagetian approach. *Instructional Science*, **8**, 301–367.

Phillips, D. A. & Zimmerman, M. (1990). The developmental course of perceived competence and incompetence among competent children. In R. J. Sternberg & J. Kolligian, Jr (Eds), *Competence Considered* (pp. 41–66). New Haven, CT: Yale University Press.

Piaget, J. (1950). *The Psychology of Intelligence*. London: Routledge & Kegan Paul.

Piaget, J. (1952). *The Child's Conception of Number*. London. Routledge & Kegan Paul.

Piaget, J. (1954). *The Construction of Reality in the Child*. New York: Basic Books.

Piaget, J. (1977). *The Development of Thought. Equilibrium of Cognitive Structure*. Oxford: Blackwell.

Piaget, J. & Inhelder, B. (1973). *Memory and Intelligence*. London: Routledge & Kegan Paul.

Piaget, J. & Inhelder, B. (1974). *The Child's Construction of Quantities*. London: Routledge & Kegan Paul.

Platsidou, M. & Demetriou, A. (1995). The processing system: A study of its structure and development. *Psychology: The Journal of Hellenic Psychological Society*, **2**, 41–67.

Quartz, S. R. & Sejnowski, T. J. (in press). The neural basis of cognitive development: A constructivist manifesto. *Behavioral and Brain Sciences*.

Riegel, K. F. (1973). Dialectical operations: The final period of cognitive development. *Human Development*, **16**, 346–370.

Resnick, L. B., Bill, V. & Lesgold, S. (1992). Developing thinking abilities in arithmetic class. In A. Demetriou, M. Shayer & A Efklides (Eds), *Neo-Piagetian Theories of Cognitive Development*. London: Routledge.

Salthouse, T. A. (1991). *Theoretical Perspectives on Cognitive Aging*. Hillsdale, NJ: Erlbaum.

Schaie, K. W., Willis, S. L., Jay, G. &. Chipuer, H. (1989). Structural invariance of cognitive abilities across the adult life-span: A cross-sectional study. *Developmental Psychology*, **25**, 652–662.

Shayer, M., Demetriou, A. & Pervez, M. (1988). The structure and scaling of concrete operational thought; three studies in four countries. *Genetic, Social and General Psychology Monographs*, **114**, 307–376.

Shultz, T. R. (1982). Rules of causal attribution. *Monographs of the Society for Research in Child Development* (Serial No. 194).

Siegler, R. S. (1995). How does change occur: A microgenetic study of number conservation. *Cognitive Psychology*, **28**, 225–273.

Spearman, C. (1927). The Abilities of Man. New York: Macmillan.

Springer, K. &. Keil, F. C. (1989). On the development of biologically specific beliefs: The case of inheritance. *Child Development*, **60**, 637–648.

Sternberg, R. J. & Downing, C. J. (1982). The development of higher-order reasoning in adolescence. *Child Development*, **53**, 209–221.

Sternberg, R. J., Conway, B. E., Ketron, J. L. & Bernstein, M. (1981). People's conceptions of intelligence. *Journal of Personality and Social Psychology*, **41**, 37–55.

Stipek, D. & McIver, D. (1989). Developmental change in children's assessment of intellectual competence. *Child Development*, **60**, 521–538.

Taylor, M. & Flavell, J. H. (1984). Seeing and believing: Children's understanding of the distinction between appearance and reality. *Child Development*, **55**, 1710–1720.

Thatcher, R. W. (1994). Cyclic cortical reorganization: Origins of human cognitive development. In G. Dawson & K. W. Fischer (Eds), *Human Behavior and the Developing Brain* (pp. 232–266). New York: Guilford.

van Geert, P. (1994). *Dynamic Systems of Development: Change between Complexity and Chaos*. New York: Harvester Wheatsheaf.

Vosniadou, S. (1994). Capturing and modeling the process of conceptual change. *Learning and Instruction: The Journal of the European Association for Research on Learning and Instruction*, **4**, 45–69.

Vygotsky, L. S. (1962). *Thought and Language*. Cambridge, MA: MIT Press,

Wagner, S., Winner, E., Cicchetti, D. & Gardner, H. (1981). 'Metaphorical' mapping in human infants. *Child Development*, **52**, 728–731.

Wason, P. C. & Johnson-Laird, P. N. (1972). *Psychology of Reasoning: Structure and Content*. London: Batsford.

Wellman, H. M. (1990). *The Child's Theory of Mind*. Cambridge, MA: MIT Press.

Chapter 6

Social Development

Cornelis F. M. van Lieshout

University of Nijmegen

and

Willem Doise

University of Geneva

INTRODUCTION

Across the life-span, individuals participate in a myriad of interactions. These interactions take place in the here-and-now but also constitute the basic elements of long-lasting relationships. A person is involved in a diversity of relationships that often extend across the life-span. An individual's relationships are mostly embedded in groups: family groups, school groups, sport teams, or professional contexts. In this chapter on social development across the life-span, we will distinguish three hierarchical levels: interactions, relationships, and groups (cf. Hinde, 1997). Interactions, relationships, and groups provide the basic social contexts for individual development, and social context is defined as the opportunities or constraints set by other people on a person's development.

In the course of development, a person is confronted with a sequence of developmental tasks in both the social and nonsocial domains (cf. Baltes, Reese, & Lipsitt, 1980; Havighurst, 1973). We use the developmental task metaphor to describe and understand development. Developmental tasks can stem from three sources: new biological opportunities or limitations

Life-Span Developmental Psychology
Edited by A. Demetriou, W. Doise and C. F. M. van Lieshout. © 1998 John Wiley & Sons Ltd.

(e.g. pubertal maturation or suffering cerebral haemorrhage), new demands or opportunities within the social context (e.g. school entrance or losing your job), and personal engagement in and choice of new opportunities or acceptance of limitations (e.g. engaging in a new professional career or accepting physical handicap). These sources may often overlap and correspond. For example, when a child is mature enough to go to school, compulsory education requires the child to attend school, and most children are eager to do this. However, the sources may also interfere with each other. For example, when parents have children, society expects them to raise and nurture them, but they may reject them.

In new developmental tasks, individuals have to reorganize their behavior in a specific domain. One typically experiences such reorganization as a sequence of problems to solve, often across a number of years. Such reorganization is necessary to adjust to the changes that occur in yourself and your environment. Developmental tasks also leave a person no choice: you cannot evade developmental tasks without serious harm. Engagement in developmental tasks also offers you new opportunities and the competence achieved in earlier developmental tasks is often instrumental for coping with subsequent developmental tasks. For example, proper language skills seem to be a prerequisite for learning to read. The problems confronted in a developmental task often represent a hierarchy of goals or a goal structure that the person is hardly aware of. For example, seeking security with caretakers when threatened relieves children's experience of stress (i.e. a goal at the interaction level) but also reinforces the caretaker–child relationship (i.e. a goal at the relationship level) and contributes to survival (i.e. a goal at the level of the individual and the species).

A person can be engaged in several developmental tasks at the same time although developmental tasks appear to be hierarchically organized. More central developmental tasks have a strong biological background (e.g. language acquisition or attachment to one's caretaker) while more peripheral developmental tasks are determined by historical and cultural demands (e.g. a schooling in modern society). Simultaneous developmental tasks may be in conflict with each other. For a teenage mother, for example, rearing a child may conflict with taking part in an adolescent way of life. More central developmental tasks can less easily be evaded than more peripheral developmental tasks. In sum, the concept of developmental tasks seems to be useful in understanding the interrelatedness of development.

Four modalities can be distinguished in an individual's problem solving in social and nonsocial developmental tasks (see Table 6.1, Col. 5): (i) *cognition*, which is perception, thinking, reasoning, and information processing (see Butterworth, ch. 3 and Demetriou, ch. 5 this volume); (ii) *behavioral execution*, or acting; (iii) *affect*, or emotionality; and (iv) *goal orientation*, which is intentionality, motivation or will. Developmental tasks in the social and nonsocial domains mainly differ in their goal orientation. The goal orientation of development in the nonsocial domain is towards the achievement of standards of excellence in a broad sense. The goal orientation of development in the social domain concerns the interrelatedness or

Table 6.1 Modalities of problem solving in developmental tasks, personality, and interpersonal support in interactions, relationships, and groups

(1) Groups	(2) Dyadic relationships — Dimensions of relationships	(3) Interpersonal support	(4) Interactions	(5) Problem-solving modalities	(6) Developmental tasks — Social domain	(6) Nonsocial domain	(7) Personality dimensions
Shared meaning systems	Expertise	Quality information vs deception	Exchange of knowledge/information	Cognitions (thinking)	Flexibility of information processing		Openness
Dominance hierarchy, coalitions, conformism	Power	Autonomy vs limit setting	Behavior regulation	Behavioral execution (acting)	Active/passive behavioral execution		Extraversion
Cohesion	Trust vs distrust	Warmth vs hostility	Exchange of affect	Affect (Feeling)	Pleasure, interest, vs Aversion, Anxiety		Emotional stability
Group goals, norms, values	Convergence vs opposition of goals	Acceptance vs rejection of goals	Facilitation vs opposition of goal achievement	Goal orientation, intentionality (will)	Inter-related interests	Standards of excellence	Agreeableness / Conscientiousness

Source: Adapted from van Lieshout (1995).

interdependence of an actor's interests with the interests of his or her interaction partners. In the social domain, individuals develop a *prosocial orientation* when they achieve their own goals in interactions and similarly allow their interaction partners to achieve their goals. They develop an *antisocial orientation* when they achieve their own goals without considering the goals of their partners or even at the cost of others. Children achieve *low social competence* when they are shy, withdrawn, or turn away from interactions because they do not want to engage in them or are anxious. Social competence is not limited to an individual's interactions but also concerns the skills needed to develop and maintain a variety of interpersonal relationships and the skills needed to adjust to the demands of such groups as the family, a school class, or professional team. Most developmental tasks concern both the social and nonsocial domains although differences in emphasis may occur.

Personality development framed in terms of the big five personality dimensions (see Kohnstamm & Mervielde, ch. 9 this volume) seems differentially related to the four problem-solving modalities (see Table 6.1, Col. 7). Openness refers to the flexibility of information processing in both the social and nonsocial domains. Extraversion versus introversion concerns the activity versus passivity of one's behavioral execution. Emotional stability refers to the regulation of emotions in both the social and nonsocial domains. And agreeableness is specifically oriented towards the interrelatedness of the partners' interest (i.e. the social domain), while conscientiousness is oriented towards the achievement of certain standards of excellence (i.e. the nonsocial domain). We define personality as the, in part, genetically determined behavioral styles that typify individuals across different situations and different points in time, and manifest themselves in concrete behavioral responses and potential adjustment problems. The adjustment problems confronted by individuals during development and in the sequence of developmental tasks are discussed by Braet and Verhofstadt-Denève (ch. 10 this volume). In the following three sections, we will describe social development in the context of interactions, relationships, and groups.

INTERACTIONS

An interaction can be defined as an action X that person A directs at person B who then responds with action Y (Hinde, 1997). The actions X and Y are described here in a rather neutral way, as if they concerned random actions from an infinite set of possible actions followed by random reaction, from an infinite set of possible reactions. In this definition, interacting partners also seem to meet each other for the first time. Such conditions seldom or never occur. Interactions almost always concern the actions and reactions of people who are involved in interdependent relationships and have an interest in the interactions (Clark & Reis, 1988). Because of their often interdependent nature, interactions are almost always transactions. In sequences of actions and reactions, partners exchange interests, support, hostilities, care, materials, or information. For this reason, interactions (or transactions) almost always make a contribution to the strengthening, maintaining, or weakening of relationships. Interactions have a bi-directional transactional character and transactions take place in interactions. Interactions or transactions are not only the building blocks of relationships but are also determined by relationships.

Descriptions of interactions require specification of the *content*, or what individuals are doing together, which can be talking, caring, feeding, fighting, helping, and so on. In addition, the quality of an interaction, or whether an interaction is pleasant versus threatening and thus has a *positive versus negative valence*, should be specified. In our view, each interaction can be characterized by four behavioral tendencies related to the four problem-solving modalities of cognition, behavior execution, emotionality, and goal orientation. In each interaction, people exchange knowledge or information, regulate each other's behavior, exchange emotions, and provide positive or negative feedback with regard to goal orientation and goal achievement (see Table 6.1, Col 4; also see Kelley, Berscheid, Christensen et al., 1983; Bandura, 1977). Exchange of knowledge corresponds to the cognitive modality; behavioral regulation to behavioral execution; exchange of emotions to affect; and facilitation or interference with goal orientations to motivation or will. Interaction partners can support or oppose each other's goal orientation; they can explain why they do or do not do things; they can encourage each other to take action or abstain from action and they can threaten each other or provide security. Support, provision of information, encouragement, and security provide a positive valence for an interaction, while opposition of goals, withholding information, opposition, and threats provide a negative valence for an interaction.

Information Processing

Although interactions seem simple, several researchers (e.g. Crick & Dodge, 1994) argue that each interaction requires complex information processing. Crick and Dodge assume that people come to a social situation with a set of biologically limited capabilities and a database of memories of past experiences. As input, they receive an array of cues and their behavioral response is the result of a series of steps in the processing of those cues. Initially, people selectively attend to particular situational and internal cues, encode those cues, and interpret them. For example, based on memories of earlier interactions with a person, an individual may attribute intentions and motives to that person and evaluate his or her previous performance in exchange with that person. Next, an individual selects a goal or a desired outcome for the situation (e.g. staying out of trouble, greeting a friend, obtaining a desired toy). Goals function as orientations towards a desired outcome. Persons bring goal orientations to a situation but may also reverse their goals and construct new goals in response to social stimuli. In the next step, people access existing responses to a situation from memory or construct new behaviors in response to social cues. They then evaluate the potential response alternatives and select the most positively evaluated response for enactment. In evaluating the alternative responses, they consider the possible outcome of each response, their own confidence in enacting the response and the appropriateness of each response. In such evaluations, the anticipated pleasure or threat (i.e. emotion) associated with an expected outcome plays a central role. Finally, the selected response is behaviorally enacted. In response, the interaction partners and bystanders evaluate and react to the enacted response leading to subsequent interactive chains. The ensuing events can then be conceptualized as new cycles of information processing. During social-interaction sequences, these information processes are used over and over, very rapidly in real time, often at a nonconscious level, and often more simultaneously than in sequence. Deficiencies in the interactions may result from deficiencies in any of the component steps. For example, children can misinterpret their interaction partner's intentions, motives, and affective states; they may not properly evaluate the potential consequences of their own actions; or they simply may not be able to enact a response because of low interactive competence.

The four modalities commonly involved in interactions are all involved in the foregoing information processing; that is, recognition of emotions, inference of intentions, processing of social cognitions, and enactment of behavioral responses. In a broader sense, a 'theory of mind' (see Demetriou, ch. 5 this volume) or understanding of others as psychological beings having such mental states as beliefs, desires, emotions, and intentions, seems to be a prerequisite for effective interactions. It is beyond the scope of this chapter to discuss the development of all four of the modalities involved in interactions. Because the goal orientations or intentionality of the individual is of critical importance in interactions, we will consider the development of intentionality more closely below.

Goal orientation and intentionality

One's efficiency in modifying one's goals in response to the goal orientations or intentions of others is essential for competent interaction. Therefore in social interactions one must not only infer the goals and intentions of the interactive partners but also coordinate these and to a certain degree deal with incompatibility.

Some authors (Meltzoff, 1995; Searle, 1983) assume several levels in the development of children's understanding of intentions. The first coordinations of intentions occur when newborns match their own body movements with the motor patterns perceived in adults. Studies on the imitation of such simple motor patterns in newborns as tongue protrusion or sequential finger movements (see Butterworth, ch. 3 this volume) have shown newborns able to match their own motor activities to the motor patterns of adults. Observational studies of infants in the first years of life have further shown meaningful social interactions to occur among infant peers as well as between infants and adults. Infants can react positively to peers and interactively match the rhythm of a peer: infant peers engage in mutual imitation, demonstrate turn-taking interactions, and play coordinated games. Such matching provides them with opportunities for learning about themselves and about other people, and how to use the objects in their physical environment. In developing an attachment relationship with a primary caretaker (see Kohnstamm & Mervielde, ch. 9, Weinert & Weinert, ch. 1 this volume), infants learn to use their caretaker as a secure base, for protection under conditions of stress, and for offering support in exploring their environment. The matching of behavior patterns with those of others does not stop in infancy but continues across the life-span and may then involve more complex intentions or goal orientations.

Meltzoff (1995) suggests that a second level in understanding is reached when children perceive the behavior of others as *intentions in actions* or as the *intentions of actors* at the age of 18 months. Infants become capable of imitating or re-enacting actions that they have previously never seen by understanding the intention behind the action. Meltzoff (1995) demonstrated how 18—month-old infants can infer the intention behind actions that adults have tried but failed to perform (see Figure 6.1). The infants saw how adults tried to pull a toy apart or push a button with a stick but failed to do so. The infants were then offered opportunities to re-enact or imitate these acts (which they had actually not observed because the adults failed to reach the goal of their actions). The infants were clearly found to enact the targeted acts as if they had observed them. The 18 month olds apparently understood the intention behind the behavior of the adults. Proper understanding of intentions was further evident when the children showed a completely different reaction to a mechanical device performing the same (failed) movements. The toddlers did not produce the target actions in this case and thus seemed to understand that intention implies the presence of an intending actor.

Only at the age of about 3 years can children reflect on intentions as mental states or prior intentions (i.e. mental states that occur prior to the action being performed and can be described as 'I am going to do X' or 'A is going to do Y'). From this age onwards, inference of the intentions in others will become increasingly intertwined with other concerns and thus become more and more adult-like. Such additional concerns are relevant for a balanced evaluation of intentions. One important concern involves conditions of personal responsibility. In evaluating a person's responsibility for the occurrence of harm, Ferguson and Rule (1983) assume that the following criteria will be applied: (i) Association, harm should not occur; (ii) Causality, one should not cause harm; (iii) Avoidability, one should not cause harm carelessly; (iv) Intentionality, one should not mean to cause harm; and (v) Justification, one should not mean to cause harm with malevolent motives. Olthof (1990) demonstrated how children between 5 and 15 years of age become more and more capable of *interpreting* and *assigning variable importance* to the foregoing dimensions of responsibility in the evaluation of harmdoers. When harm has been inflicted on a victim,

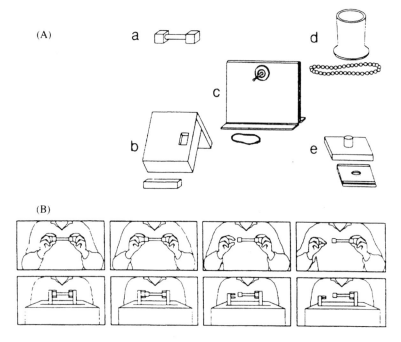

Figure 6.1   A: Meltzoff used five test objects as stimuli to investigate the under-standing of the intentions of others in 18-month-old toddlers: (a) a dumbbell-shaped toy could be pulled apart and put back together again; (b) a buzzer could be activated by pushing a stick on the recessed button on the front of a box; (c) a nylon loop could be hung on a horizontal prong attached to a plastic screen; (d) a loop of beads could be put in a cup; and (e) a transparent plastic square with a round hole could be placed over a wooden dowel. An adult experimenter tried to carry out the actions but failed. After observing the failure of the experimenter, the toddlers were found to enact what the adult had intended to do and not what the adult actually did. B: Next, Meltzoff compared toddlers' imitation of the same actions by either a person or an inanimate mechanical device. Toddlers were found to correctly carry out the actions that a person had tried and failed to execute (pictures in top row), but *not* when a mechanical device tried but failed to execute the same actions (pictures in bottom row)
From Meltzoff, A. N. (1995), Understanding the intentions of others: Re-enactment of intended acts by 18-month-old children. *Developmental Psychology*, **31**, 838–850. Copyright © 1995 by the American Psychological Association. Reprinted with permission.

even kindergarten children evaluate whether the perpetrator intended to inflict harm or not (purposeful versus accidental infliction), whether the perpetrator had acceptable versus unacceptable motives (e.g. wanted to help versus hurt), and whether the harm could have been avoided or not (i.e. an actor could have easily avoided the harm versus took a great risk of inflicting harm). Even when the children distinguish between these different sources of causal information, they do not consider them equally important. Like adults, children at all age levels blame perpetrators with a strong desire to inflict harm (i.e. bad motives) the most. Bad motives resulting in harm (versus good motives resulting in harm) are more morally blameworthy, elicit more anger, and create a stronger tendency to want to retaliate than in the accidental or unavoidable infliction of harm. (For further consideration of the evaluation of harm in the course of development and in different cultures, see Haste, Markoulis & Helkama, ch. 7 this volume).

Developmental Processes in the Coordination of Intentions

From a very early age onwards, infants appear to evaluate and coordinate their own intentions and actions with those of others. Investigators claim that a number of related processes, called *socioconstructivism*, explain how children develop this capacity. In interdependent or matched actions including imitation, cooperation, and conflict and also in such socio-cognitive conflicts as disagreement, contradiction, discussion, or exchange of views, children cannot maintain so-called autistic or egocentric orientations.

In interactions with others, children must coordinate their own approach to reality with that of others (cf. Doise & Mugny, 1984). Such social coordination extends far beyond interdependent or matched actions in particular interactions and produces generalized coordination structures. When children's performance under conditions eliciting independent individual performance versus interdependent cooperative or collective performance was compared, for example, children initially showed the highest performance in the cooperative condition. Only after the children have interiorized these skills as coordinated interdependent actions does the individual performance reach the level of cooperative performance. That is, children who participate in various social coordinations often become capable of executing these coordinations on their own. At the same time, some stability and generality are achieved: social coordinations are transferred to other situations and materials. Certain characteristics of social interactions may nevertheless hinder coordinated performance. For example, when the asymmetry between the contributions of the two partners is too great or when the coordination is achieved through mere compliance, performance may not be optimal. Under such conditions, the structured intervention of adults may help to accomplish proper coordination.

As already mentioned, socio-cognitive conflict also plays an important role in development of coordinated actions and intentions. Socio-cognitive conflict exists when different cognitive approaches to the same problem socially manifest themselves in one and the same situation. Under appropriate conditions, the confrontation and subsequent coordination of the different approaches may result in a new approach that is more complex and adapted to solving the problem than any one of the previous approaches alone. Investigators have elicited socio-cognitive conflicts in children by instigating them to take a perspective and offer a solution for a problem that seemed obvious from their standpoint but was nevertheless incompatible with the perspective and solution offered by another child. After being confronted with such incompatibility, children initially tend to comply with the other child. Requiring the children to give a succession of incorrect or contradictory answers, reminding them of the contradictions, and/or further questioning of the children may lead them to give up their 'egocentric' position and construct a solution with the seemingly contradictory perspectives more or less socially integrated. Such results cannot be explained as an effect of imitation or modeling because the children were never exposed to the correct solution. Doise and Mugny (1984) conclude that keeping one's own point of view in mind while having to take another incompatible view into account can produce progress in the coordination of views.

In the above, performances under conditions with clear standards of excellence and logical consistency were investigated. Most social interaction and social communication involves interpersonal interests, morality and/or ethical considerations, however. Studies have shown children to construct principles of justice in the social domain similarly to principles of truth in the nonsocial domain. Oser (1986, p. 922) describes the characteristics of socio-cognitive conflict situations that may promote development of moral judgment in educational settings as follows:

> 1. presentation of the subjective truth completely and exhaustively . . . as conceived by the participants in the conflict; 2. absence of an authority presenting an outside or observer's point of view as the 'right' answer; 3. creation of a disequilibrium by presenting different arguments and different opinions to stimulate development of moral judgment on increasingly complex grounds; 4. interaction among students (discussants) coordinated in such a way that everyone reacts openly and fairly to one another's point of view (positive climate and transactional discourse); 5. linking of the principles of discourse to the principles of justice.

These characteristics are consistent with the main assumptions of studies on the role of the socio-cognitive conflict: confrontation and coordination of viewpoints, avoidance or compliance, induction of socio-cognitive conflict, articulation of organizing social principles in accordance with external standards and abstract logical principles (for the social construction of problem solutions at the nonsocial domain), or with fundamental principles of justice or reciprocity (for the social construction of morality and ethics at the social domain).

Persistent Interactive Orientations

Thus far we have largely discussed social interactions as if they were independent of the characteristics of the actors themselves. In the course of development, most individuals in fact show a great variety of interactional patterns depending on their interests and situational demands. There is also a significant degree of consistency in an individual's interactions, and many people show fairly stable behavioral orientations in their interactions. Recently, Hartup and van Lieshout (1995) have traced the developmental pathways for three central behavioral orientations; (i) antisocial behavior; (ii) behavioral inhibition and social withdrawal; and (iii) social responsibility.

Antisocial behavior

In aggressive or antisocial interactions, individuals pursue their own goals and interests without considering the interests of others. Such emotions as anger, fear of retaliation, and pleasure from the suffering or misfortune of others are often involved in such aggressive or antisocial interactions.

Terry Moffitt (1993) has distinguished two developmental patterns for aggressive, antisocial behavior: the life-course-persistent and the adolescent-limited patterns. The life-course-persistent pattern concerns a small group of 3–5% of all boys and a much smaller group of girls who show a high level of aggressive and antisocial behavior from a very early age and across the life-span. The adolescent-limited pattern concerns a much larger group of mostly adolescent boys who show a temporary increase in aggressive and antisocial behavior during a short period of a few months to several years but nevertheless limited to the adolescent years.

Life-course-persistent pattern.   The early starters show an early onset of aggressive behavior along multiple pathways (Loeber, Wung, Keenan et al., 1993). The aggression begins along the authority-conflict pathway with coercive, stubborn, oppositional, and disobedient behavior within the family and later authority avoidance in the form of truancy, running away, and staying out late. In the middle-childhood years, both covert and overt aggressive antisocial pathways are added to the authority-conflict pathway. The covert pathway includes early and frequent lying followed by stealing, property damage, and vandalism, and it may culminate in serious delinquency in the form of theft, burglary, and fraud in later years. The overt pathway may start with aggression in the form of bullying, harassing, and annoying others, and it may culminate in such violent acts as assault, battery, and rape. Life-course-persistent aggressive individuals show a consistently high level of generalized aggression and clearly may end up as criminals. In many instances, emotional problems, depressive symptoms, psychopathological disturbances and drug use accompany such adult aggression.

The exact conditions leading to the onset and persistence of such life-course aggression are not clear, but a cumulative chain of determinants may be operating. Early onset of aggression is related to biological factors (e.g. low autonomous activity and reactivity), temperament (e.g. high irritability, low fear, impulsiveness), and later personality characteristics (e.g. high extraversion, low agreeableness, low conscientiousness). The conditions in which these individuals live are often extremely unfavorable (e.g. poverty, high exposure to and tolerance of aggression, hostile parent–child relationships, low monitoring of the child, large or single-parent families, exposure to stress, power conflicts within families and peer groups). Children born with specific genetic or neurological deficiencies and a difficult temperament do not match their parents' expectations and may also be difficult to handle. Such children may also elicit sibling aggression. While parents may share specific genetic deficiencies and temperamental characteristics with their child, such a temperamental 'misfit' between the parents and the child can produce insensitive, rejecting, hostile, and inconsistent parenting behaviours (Moffitt, 1993).

When the parents experience a high level of stress and low support from the birth of their child onwards, the parents and the child may develop an insecure attachment relationship. Such children may distrust close personal relationships as a result and tend to attribute hostile intentions to others in ambiguous situations. They are less able to estimate the effects of their own behavior on the feelings of others and may even experience pleasure in seeing others in distress, in need or injured. Reciprocal escalation of the aggression may occur between the parents and the child or a coercive system may develop between the parents and the child (Patterson, Capaldi & Bank, 1991). Children often appear to win such power conflicts and may thereby learn—even before they enter school—that persistent aggression is ultimately rewarding. Parents may feel less and less effective in controlling their child's aggression and give up: in the end, they no longer care and exert less and less or increasingly inconsistent control. More than one child within a single individual family may become delinquent, which shows the commonality among the determinants. Marital conflict and biased treatment of the siblings within a family can increase aggression among children. Higher levels of aggression among the siblings in a family are related to higher levels of aggression for these children outside the family. Conger and his colleagues (1995) have incorporated family-context variables, parental behavior, and children's antisocial behavior into a single model, which suggests that the effects of family-context variables on children's antisocial behavior may be mediated by parental behavior. For example, stress related to economic hardship forecasts depression and demoralization in parents, marital conflict/hostility, and inconsistency in dealing with the children. Such conditions, in turn, are clearly correlated with antisocial behaviors in adolescence.

When early starters go to school, their aggressive behavior tends to extend to the school and the wider community. They disturb the educational process and are often difficult for the teachers to handle. As a consequence, they get less involved in educational activities and are often rejected by teachers as well as by peers. Lower achievement can produce an aversion to scholastic tasks, flunking, and—as a consequence—disruption of the existing peer network. The parents tend to lose control over their child; school achievement may further deteriorate; additional flunking may mean changes of school, rejection by classmates, dropping out, complete disruption of the peer network (see Patterson, Capaldi & Bank, 1991). These adolescents run an increased risk of involvement in deviant peer groups. Their friendships may foster delinquent behavior, and their life course may be increasingly marked by aggression and delinquency (Dishion, Andrews & Crosby, 1995).

Adolescent-limited pattern. According to Moffitt (1993), the antisocial orientation is much more part of the personality development of early starters than of late starters. The motivation of adolescent-limited aggressive behavior is a consequence of the increasing discrepancy in modern societies between the earlier biological and social maturation of adolescents and their later access to adult obligations, rights, and privileges. Adolescent-limited antisocial behavior is regulated by social-learning principles and may be elicited in the first place by the perceived enviable status and privileges of early starters. As a result of their antisocial behavior, early starters often appear to have access to more money, more gadgets, and greater adult rights and privileges. They are able to resist and avoid adult control and authority and gain more freedom by being truant. Early starters make attractive models and may elicit antisocial behavior in other adolescents and especially boys.

Although the antisocial behavior of early and late starters is difficult to distinguish during adolescence, there are some differences. The clearest difference is of course the time of onset. For the late starters, antisocial behavior is less a part of their personality than for early starters and much more under the control of social-learning principles. The antisocial behavior of late starters when compared to that of early starters is less stable over time, less generalized across situations, more often covert than overt, more often a part of group activities, and less frequently directed at people. Parents also have a very different orientation towards the antisocial behavior of late starters. Such antisocial behavior may in fact occur as a consequence of low parental monitoring; should these adolescents get caught, however, parents become alarmed in many cases and increase their monitoring and control. As they gradually gain access to adult rights, privileges, and responsibilities or discover that their antisocial behavior may endanger their access to adult privileges in the long run, late starters also appear to give up their antisocial behavior more easily than early starters. Their antisocial behavior is thus under the control of such social-learning principles as the expected rewards for no more aggression and the anticipated aversive outcomes of continuing antisocial behavior.

Behavioral inhibition and social withdrawal

Socially withdrawn behavior is rather heterogeneous in form, development and the degree to which it constitutes a problem for the individual. In cases of social withdrawal, individuals are restrained in the pursuit of goals in relation to others. The relevant emotions are shyness, anxiety, and pleasure in self-contained activities. Rubin and Asendorpf (1993) make a distinction between children who are inhibited because they fear novelty or the unknown (*inhibited* children), children with a fear of negative evaluation by others (*socially anxious* children), and children with a low interest in or lack of motivation for social engagement (*solitary or reserved* children). These three groups of children have in common that they may miss the opportunities in interactions to acquire the social skills they may later need in relationships with others (see also Hartup & van Lieshout, 1995).

Inhibited children.   In some individuals more than in others, encounters with strangers or unknown situations may lead to behavioral inhibition. Neurological, endocrine, and genetic factors presumably play a part in such behavioral inhibition. People who display high levels of inhibition as a child in particular show some stability of inhibition in adolescence. The inhibition usually manifests itself for some time after entering such new environments as school, a new school, or a new home. There is a small but significant relation of social inhibition in early childhood to later low self-esteem and social anxiety (cf. Asendorpf & van Aken, 1994). A small but significant relation also exists with such internalized problems as anxiety, somatic complaints, depressive symptoms, and social withdrawal, and—especially in adult males—greater wariness about and delay in marriage and professional career (Caspi, Elder & Bem, 1988). Asendorpf has further shown that such personality characteristics as intelligence may help children to overcome inhibition. Asendorpf's longitudinal studies have also shown that social inhibition at school entrance is not a good predictor of social engagement and peer acceptance after the children have become acquainted with the group. There is no clear relation between social inhibition and the quality of the mother–child attachment although securely attached children may use their mothers to overcome their fear in novel situations and children with an insecure attachment relationship simply do not have this option.

Social anxiety.   Fear of novelty should be sharply distinguished from social anxiety and solitary or reserved behavior. The latter forms of socially withdrawn behavior manifest themselves most in rejected and/or neglected children (Box 6.4). The group of children with a rejected sociometric status contains a subgroup in which rejection is paired with anxious-dependent behavior. These children are socially withdrawn, rejected children (cf. Cillessen, van IJzendoorn, van Lieshout, & Hartup, 1992). They are often perceived by classmates and themselves as the victims of bullying; they also suffer from their isolation in class and often have internalized problems combined with low self-esteem.

Solitary or reserved children.   A second group of socially withdrawn children consists of individualists or self-contained children. Individualists with low impact on groups are usually not rejected by classmates but neglected. They do not show such conspicuous behavioral or emotional problems as fighting, disruptive behavior, bullying, or being the victim of bullying. Their social engagement in class is very low. They are also low in cooperation, offering help, and have very few friends. Social engagement is presumably not very relevant for them and a small subgroup is perceived by classmates as extremely withdrawn (de Poorte, Veling, Haselager, & van Lieshout, 1994).

   Given the heterogeneity of social withdrawal and the fact that socially withdrawn children are often not further differentiated, the developmental pathways for such children are hard to trace. In a number of studies, parents have been found to accept socially withdrawn behavior more easily from girls than from boys. Depressiveness in parents, marital conflicts, and family stress are more often related to extremely high levels of social withdrawal in children than low socio-economic status and poverty. Observational studies and self-reports by mothers have shown kindergarten children with extremely withdrawn class behavior to be very dependent on their mothers, with the mothers exerting more negative and controlling behavior towards their children than other mothers. In the elementary school years, both the parents and the socially withdrawn children themselves perceive their relationships as unsupportive. They show greater disagreement on the support behavior provided by parents (and experienced by the children) than other children and their parents. Conger and his associates (1995) found that the relation between family-context variables and internalizing problems may be mediated in a manner similar to externalizing problems by parent inconsistency and hostility. Poverty and economic hardship forecast more depression and demoralization in parents, and this—in turn—can produce more marital conflict, inconsistency and hostility in dealing with the children. Moreover, parental inconsistency and hostility similarly correlate with internalizing and externalizing problems for children.

Social responsibility

Children are oriented towards socially responsible goals when they take the interests of their interaction partners into consideration and avoid pursuing their own goals at the cost of those of their partners. Social responsibility refers to an 'other orientation' and may involve such prosocial behaviors as cooperation, sharing, comforting, helping/altruism, conscientiousness, and reparation of wrongdoing. The relevant emotions are empathy, discomfort with wrongdoing, fear of deviation and retaliation, guilt, and shame. Socially responsible behaviors can be observed at an early age when children comply with parents; show empathic reactions and prosocial actions when they themselves have caused distress; and provide assistance when they witness distress in others and are not the cause of it. There is some evidence for a genetic contribution to individual differences and variability in the stability of social responsibility. In general, the prosocial behaviors associated with social responsibility stabilize during early and middle childhood.

Development of social responsibility.   At an early age social responsibility appears to be associated with individual differences in two aspects of temperament (cf. Kochanska, 1995). First, some children appear to experience emotional conflict and affective discomfort, guilt, and anxiety in connection with wrongdoing while others do not (i.e. they remain unanxious and unfearful under such conditions). The individual differences that have been observed for such fearful arousal and anxiety appear to have some longitudinal stability and correspond to consistent physiological patterns (e.g.

sympathetic reactivity, increased level of cortisol, and heart rate variability). Second, children appear to differ in the development of behavioral control (i.e. the ability to inhibit a prohibited action, suppress an antisocial or destructive impulse, and perform a more prosocial or desirable behavior). Such individual differences in the regulation of purposeful action may be the temperamental underpinnings to a cluster of behavioral qualities associated with impulse control; such as delay of gratification, control of affect expression or planfulness.

Kochanska and her colleagues (cf. Kochanska, Aksan & Koenig, 1995) have distinguished two forms of compliance in 2- to 6-year-old children. *Situational compliance* is when the child was cooperative with its mother but lacked the sincere commitment and feeling of internal obligation. *Committed compliance* is when the child eagerly embraced and endorsed the mother's agenda. Situational compliance requires sustained and repeated maternal control, seems shaky and is not fully endorsed by the child. Committed compliance, in contrast, reflects an internal eagerness to follow obligations and accept prohibitions. Toddlers and preschoolers with high levels of situational compliance show less committed compliance. Girls show more committed and less situational compliance than boys. Between the toddler and preschool ages, situational compliance decreases while committed compliance increases. Moreover, committed compliance has been found to be related to later *internalization of norms and values* when examined both in the laboratory and at home. Internalization implies that children comply with norms and values without supervision. In the relevant studies by Kochanska and her co-workers, internalization has been measured as task completion without surveillance; meeting obligations and following prohibitions on one's own; and refraining from cheating under seductive circumstances. The links between early committed compliance and internalization appear to be quite context-specific. Differences have been shown, for example, between compliance with standards for restraint (prohibitions or proscriptions) and compliance with standards for production (obligations or prescriptions).

Some correlates of committed compliance and internalization can also be found in the mother–child relationship. Shared positive affect at the toddler stage has been found to predict child internalization at the preschool age. Mother–child positive affect shows some ability across the toddler and preschool ages, but shared positive affect at the preschool age does not predict internalization at the same age. The early mother–child affective bond thus seems particularly important for the development of committed compliance and internalization. In later years, social responsibility appears to be specifically associated with the personality characteristics of agreeableness and conscientiousness (Graziano & Eisenberg, 1994).

Parents and social responsibility in children.   An intriguing question is how individual differences and parental behaviors relate to the internalization of social responsibility. What accounts for the shift from external control of socially responsible behavior in early childhood (other-regulation) to individual compliance with an internalized set of standards for social responsibility (internalization or self-regulation)? Some authors (see Baumrind, 1989) claim that constellations of authoritative child-rearing behaviors (mutually positive affect, gentle control, and respect for the child's autonomy) consistently produce optimal social competence and socially responsible children. Numerous studies have indeed shown authoritarian child-rearing (high-power parenting behavior associated with punitive-coercive control and hostile affect exchanges) to be almost universally detrimental for the socialization of social responsibility. However, the socialization outcome of authoritarian child-rearing is not the same for temperamentally fearful and anxious versus unanxious and unfearful children. In children with low fear and anxiety and proneness to anger, authoritarian parenting may elicit increased anger and resentment in the child, resulting in rejection of the parental message and externalizing problem behaviors. Fearful children, in contrast, may react with such internalized problems as feelings of guilt and anxiety for the punitive hostile parent, instead of empathy with the victim of their wrongdoing and need for reparation (Kochanska, 1995). Also authoritative parenting interacts with affective and behavioral temperamental differences.

Nowadays most theorists assume that parents seldom practice just one single style in responding to childrens misbehavior. Grusec and Goodnow (1994) suggest that information processing determines how parents respond to each of their children's transgressions. This information processing resembles that described earlier for children's interactive initiations (Crick & Dodge, 1994; see above). The parent is one of the partners in the interaction. In evaluating the child's transgression, the parent first decides whether the child's behavior is convergent or opposed to an appropriate goal. Parents in different cultures may respond differently depending on the nature of the transgression, but also quite similarly with regard to specific transgressions. For example, parents in several cultures tend to react with power assertion and reasoning in response to lying and stealing, while damage to physical objects more often elicits physical interference or punishment. Parental responses depend not only on the type of transgression but also on the characteristics of the child, including the child's developmental level, temperament, mood, and past history with respect to discipline. Individual differences between the parents with respect to temperament, personality characteristics, and responsiveness to the children's wishes may also play a role in the parental responses. Parents have quite an arsenal of disciplinary behaviors that vary in content and structure. After assessing the child's goal orientation, effective parents match their choice of disciplinary technique to the type of misdeed. The content of the disciplinary techniques may vary in terms of: affect arousal (empathy arousal, arousal insecurity, threat to the autonomy of the child), quality of information (justification of the discipline in relation to the transgression), and behavioral regulation (requiring reparation of wrongdoing or long-term alterations of behavior). The structure of the parental discipline is determined by such factors as the clarity of the rules and messages; the consistency, relevance, and redundancy of the messages;

and whether the message is signalled as important and the child's attention is captured or not.

Discipline is most effective when it is most likely to lead to long-term alterations of behavior and/or internalization of the relevant norms and values. Grusec and Goodnow assume that internalization is based on a child's accurate perception of the parental message and acceptance (or rejection) of it. Mechanisms promoting acceptance are (i) perception of the parent's discipline as appropriate to the transgression, (ii) motivation to accept the parental position, and (iii) understanding that the target value or standard should be self-generated by the child.

RELATIONSHIPS

Thus far, interactions have been discussed without considering their role in the formation and maintenance of relationships. Interactions and especially long chains of interactive sequences clearly contribute to the formation of relationships. Individuals participate in a network of personal relationships including parent–child, child–sibling, teacher–student, and friendship relationships (see Box 6.1). Each relationship concerns one person and a single other person. Relationships are dyadic in nature. They can also differ in origin. For example, relationships with parents and siblings have a biological background; other relationships arise from societal roles such as teacher–student and boss–worker relationships; still other relationships are based on personal engagement, such as friendships. Many relationships have a multiple background. Think of relationships between parents and their adopted children or stepchildren and relationships among classmates. Relationships not only differ in their origin but also in several other ways (Clark & Reis, 1988). Some relationships are more symmetrical, for example, among colleagues and classmates, while others are more asymmetrical, for example a teacher–student relationship. Some are voluntary, such as friendships and partner relationships in Western societies, and others are more involuntary, such as relationships in your family of origin. Some concern a person's full functioning as in an early mother–child relationships, and others are limited to specific functional domains as among teammates in sports. Some are more permanent, and some are more fleeting.

Despite these differences between relationships, *each* relationship can be characterized by *four common dimensions of relationships* (see Table 6.1, Col. 2). These dimensions corresponded to the four problem-solving modalities of cognition, behavioral execution, emotionality, and goal orientation. The two people in a relationship can be different or similar in their level of *expertise*, knowledge and skill within a specific domain or in a number of domains. They can also differ with regard to *power*; that is, the degree to which one person can prompt or urge the other to execute specific behaviors and the degree to which the other accepts such prompting. The degree to which the people in a relationship *trust or distrust* each other can vary, and the degree to which they share *convergent or opposite goal orientations*

Box 6.1 Relationships

Relationships are not always beneficial for the partners involved. The following vignette shows how an accumulation of problematic relationships together with specific child characteristics can provide for a disastrous outcome. The manner in which the relationships are embedded in the family or the school class, for example, may exacerbate the individual risk. In this instance, the murder of the mother shows the boy's relationship with his mother to have been low quality. The sibling relationships with his stepbrother and his sister may have contributed to the murder as well. The composition of rivalrous and conflictuous relationships within the family group may have enhanced the risks for the child's social development. At school, the boy suffered from severe bullying. He may have been the victim in several bully–victim relationships and was certainly the victim of bullying at the group level. The boy has characteristics of a provocative victim (Olweus, 1993); he was previously involved in open antisocial behavior, caused extreme irritation and tension around him, and was described as hyperactive and having concentration problems. Although the boy's friends were described as 'good friends', these friendships may also have contributed to the murder.

'On February 16, 1995, in the small Minnesota town of Delano, a 14-year-old boy and his best friend ambushed and killed his mother as she returned home. The circumstances surrounding this event were described in the next edition of the *Minneapolis Star Tribune* (February 18, 1995): The boy had "several learning disabilities—including attention deficit disorder". He had been "difficult" for a long time and, within the last year, had gotten in trouble with a stepbrother by wrecking a car and carrying a gun to a movie theater. The mother was described as having a wonderful relationship with her daughter but having "difficulties" with her son. The family dwelling contained guns.'

'Against these child, family, and ecological conditions is a significant social history: The boy was ". . . a lonely and unliked kid who was the frequent victim of schoolmates' taunts, jeers, and assaults. He had trouble with school work and trouble with other kids. . . . He was often teased on the bus and at school because of his appearance and abilities. . . . He got teased bad. Every day, he got teased. He'd get pushed around. But he couldn't really help himself. He was kind of skinny. . . . He didn't really have that many friends."'

'The boy actually had two good friends: One appears to have had things relatively well put together. Together with this friend, the subject ". . . passed [a] gun safety course for hunting; they took the class together." The second friend (with whom the murder was committed) was a troublesome child. These two boys described themselves as "best of friends," and spent much time together. The boys admitted to planning the ambush (one saying they had planned it for weeks, the other for a few hours). They were armed and waiting when the mother

arrived from home from work. One conclusion seems relatively certain: this murder was an unlikely event until these two antisocial friends reached consensus about doing it.'
Reproduced with permission from: Hartup, W. W. (1996). The company they keep: Friendships and their developmental significance. *Child Development*, **67**, 1–13.

can vary. Each relationship is characterized by a mixture of these four relational dimensions. For example, a parent–child relationship is mostly characterized by inequality of expertise (parent has greater expertise, child has less), inequality of power (parent regulates behavior, child is being regulated), complementary emotions (parent provides, child seeks trust), and convergent goal orientations (for example, parent provides education, child seeks to be educated). A friendship relationship is mostly marked by equal or similar levels of expertise, nearly equal power, reciprocity in the provision of and search for emotional support, and convergent or mutually attuned goal orientations. In general, friends have the same level of knowledge or their expertise oscillates around the same level; they are equally able to regulate each other's behavior; they mutually or reciprocally provide security or intimacy; and their goal orientations are convergent in at least a few functional domains.

The four dimensions of relationships are paralleled by four dimensions of interpersonal support (see Table 6.1, Col. 3). These dimensions concern acceptance (convergence) versus rejection (opposition) of each other's goal orientations; provision of quality information versus withholding of information or provision of misleading information; the balance between respecting autonomy and setting limits (i.e. co-regulation of behavior); and warmth versus hostility in emotional exchanges.

The convergence versus opposition of goal orientations within a relationship seems to affect the other dimensions of relational support. Under conditions of convergent goal orientations, interactions will be more frequently characterized by warmth than by hostility; partners will more frequently respect each other's autonomy than consider it necessary to regulate each other's behavior by setting strict limits; and they will tend to communicate and exchange information openly. When goal orientations converge, even conflict may constructively contribute to the realization of common goals. Conflicts may concern the opposition of behavior in interactions, differences in opinion, disagreement on how common goals can be reached, disagreement about the content and exchange of information, disagreement on the regulation of behavior, and conflicting exchanges of emotions (cf. Laursen & Collins, 1994). When goals converge conflicts mostly lead to a more accurate specification of goals in subsequent interactions, further explanation of information and points of views, more efficient co-regulation of behavior, and clarification of the feelings of the interaction partners. In such conflicts, the common goal orientations of the interaction partners are not at stake. Opposition of goal orientations, in contrast, can break up voluntary friendships and turn involuntary relationships into a problem. Under conditions of opposing goal orientations, the interactions will tend to be contradictory. Then, conflicts with regard to the ways to achieve goals, the exchange of information, the regulation of behavior, and the exchange of feelings will be destructive and much more intense.

Relationships in a personal network

Some theorists focus on the network of a person's relationships. Adopting such a network perspective, Furman and Buhrmester (1985, 1992) have systematically compared the perceptions of conflict, relative power, and six types of support for different types of network members (i.e. mother, father, sibling, grandparent, teacher, same-sex friend and romantic friend). The perceptions of conflict, relative power, and degree of support examined in this study correspond to three of the four dimensions of relational support specified earlier. The findings are largely in keeping with the major theories rewarding the development of personal relationships. In particular, mothers and fathers were seen as the most frequent providers of emotional support in middle childhood. Same-sex friends were perceived to be just as supportive as parents in early adolescence and were the most frequent providers of support in middle adolescence. Romantic partners moved up in rank with age until late adolescence when they, along with friends and mothers, received the highest ratings for support. Gender effects show that fathers and mothers are perceived as more supportive to same-sex children. Differences in the young adults showed that males experience romantic relationships as most supportive while females experience the most support from mothers, friends, siblings, and romantic partners. Age differences were also observed in the perceptions of relationships with grandparents, teachers, and siblings. Finally, age differences in perceived conflict, punishment, and relative power suggested that the tension in parent–child relationships and also sibling relationships peaks in early and middle adolescence. In other words, relationships appear to play different roles at different points in development.

According to Furman and Buhrmester (1985, 1992), a number of factors may contribute to the developmental shifts in the perceived support from different people in one's network. Adolescents seem to distance themselves from their families and invest more in peer relationships (initially in primarily same-sex relationships and later romantic relationships as well). Advances in cognitive abilities can facilitate self-exploration and consensual validation of the adolescent's self-concept. Adolescents may join agemates in discussing matters related to sexual maturation and physical appearance. An interest in and concern for matters outside the family may emerge in association with the adolescent's search for autonomy and increasing emotional independence from their parents. And young adults may seek a romantic relationship in order to fulfil their need for a long-lasting relationship and sexual intimacy.

The study of the network of relationships deserves further attention. Most of the research thus far concerns separate specific relationships such as parent–child, friendship, or partner relationships. We will now turn to the most important relationships in childhood and adolescence. As the parent–child relationship is discussed in full in other chapters in this volume (Kohnstamm & Mervielde; Weinert & Weinert), we will not consider it in great detail here.

Parent–Child Relationships

In earlier chapters, security of attachment has been shown to be the most important indicator of the quality of the parent–child relationship. The provision of a secure base from which the child can explore the environment and find security when under stress is the hallmark of secure attachment. In an extension of the attachment relationship, children develop a set of expectations or internal working models with regard to their caretaker and themselves. Children evaluate (a) whether or not the caretaker responds to calls for support and offers protection when the child feels in danger or experiences stress, and (b) whether or not the self is the sort of person to whom the attachment figure is likely to respond in a helpful way (Bowlby, 1973). These expectations with regard to the caretaker and themselves are internalized by the child and constitute the base for his or her attachment to the parent in later years as well. In the case of a secure attachment relationship, the goal orientations of the parents and the children are complementary but nevertheless converge to a high degree. Under conditions of child abuse or maltreatment, the goal orientations of the parent and the child are in conflict and typically accompany insecure attachment.

Security of attachment has a clear developmental function. Securely versus insecurely attached toddlers are better problem solvers, more cooperative and compliant in interactions with their mothers, and share more positive emotions with their mothers in subsequent years as well. In addition, they are more attractive playmates for their peers. Some theorists (cf. Bartholomew & Horowitz, 1991) have argued that the combination of the internalized working models of the parent and the self constitute the base for the development of further intimate relationships (e.g. best friends, romantic love) and that later intimate relationships can be represented by similarly internalized working models. The mental representations of the other (image of other) and one's self (self-image) may be positive or negative ('other people are trustworthy and available vs unreliable and rejecting' and 'I am worthy of love and support or not', p. 227). The combination of the representations of the other and one's self can produce four prototypic attachment patterns (see Figure 6.2). The *secure* attachment pattern indicates a sense of self-worth with an expectation that others will be accepting and responsive. The *preoccupied* attachment pattern indicates a lack of self-worth combined with a positive evaluation of others. The *fearful-avoidant* pattern combines a lack of self-esteem with an expectation that

Model of Self

	Positive	Negative
Positive **Model of Other** **Negative**	<u>Secure</u> Comfortable with intimacy and authority	<u>Preoccupied</u> Preoccupied with relationships
	<u>Dismissing</u> Dismissing of intimacy; Counter-dependent	<u>Fearful</u> Fearful of intimacy; Socially avoidant

Figure 6.2 This model of adult attachment combines the two internal working models positive vs negative self-image and positive vs negative image of others, and leads to four prototypes of attachment
Adapted from: Bartholomew, K. &. Horowitz, L. M. (1991), Attachment styles among young adults: A test of a four-category model. *Journal of Personality and Social Psychology*, **61**, 226–244.

others are untrustworthy and rejecting. The *dismissive-avoidant* pattern combines a sense of self-worth with a negative disposition towards others.

Sibling Relationships

Sibling relationships start with the birth of a second child in the family and continue throughout life. Judy Dunn and her co-workers (cf. Dunn & Kendrick, 1982) are among the pioneers of research on siblings and have shown sibling relationships to resemble parent–child relationships. Sibling relationships are more vertical (except in the case of twins) and less voluntary than friendship relationships. Older siblings may take on some parental roles towards younger siblings. First, older siblings may *teach* their younger brothers and sisters many skills. Like parents, even 2–4 year olds can adapt their speech to the understanding level of their siblings when instructing them to play games. They speak slower, use less complex sentences, articulate clearly, and repeat more often (Shatz & Gelman, 1973). Not only younger siblings learn from those instructions but the older sibling teachers may learn the most from their own explanations. Learning by teaching of younger siblings by older ones is one of the explanations for the small average higher IQ of older children compared to younger ones in families (cf. Zajonc, Marcus & Marcus, 1979). Throughout childhood and adolescence, and maybe even in later years, older siblings also serve as highly valued role models in many situations in the social domain for younger children, although sibling relationships are less intense and more egalitarian with increasing age. Second, older siblings may—like adults—*structure and manage the behavior* of

younger brothers or sisters. Such caretaking may be both close and supportive and oppositional and conflictual. There is more negotiation between
siblings than with parents while siblings are less capable of disengaging
themselves from sibling interactions than from friendship interactions. Third,
older siblings may—like adults—provide *emotional security* to younger
brothers and sisters under stress, comfort them, and support them in coping
with such stressful situations as parental divorce or poor peer relationships.
Fourth, the *goal orientations* of siblings may be both complementary and
oppositional. The different goal orientations within a single sibling relationship may shift more easily than in parent–child relationships, however.
Sibling relationships also reveal marked individual differences. Many sibling
relationships are characterized by rivalry or even anger and aggression when
it comes to, for example, gaining the attention, approval, or affection of
parents. In general, however, children and adolescents experience their
sibling relationships as mutually supportive, enduring and reliable (cf. Boer &
Dunn, 1992; Burhmester & Furman).

Individual differences in the positive and negative behavior of siblings
towards each other show considerable stability from preschool age through
early adolescence and especially after the age of 5 years. These stabilities
apply to first-born as well as later-born children and may be related to the
stability of the personality characteristics of individual children or the
stabilities of parent–child relationships and other family dynamics. Despite
this stability, marked changes in sibling relationships may also occur across
the same time span. Experience of negative and/or aversive life events may
be related to a general increase of behavior and emotional problems within a
family. For sibling relationships, however, these associations seem even
more complex. Sibling relationships may deteriorate and sibling conflict
may increase when families suffer from such internal family stress as marital
disharmony or difficult step parent relationships, even though, siblings may
provide each other with considerable support when the sibling relationships
are basically very close. In the face of more external adversity, in contrast,
such as difficulties at school, maternal illness or illness of a child, sibling
relationships may become closer, more friendly, and more affectionate.
Changes in sibling relationships may also occur with new friendships outside the family in early adolescence and especially when ties are formed by
first-born boys with other boys and/or a male peer group outside the family.
The adoption of values and mores from outside the family lowers the
interest of early adolescents in their younger siblings (Dunn, Slomkowski &
Beardsall, 1994).

For first-born and only children, parents often serve the functions commonly served by older siblings. It is often thought that only children become
spoiled little tyrants. This means that the single-child policy of the People's
Republic of China is producing a nation of little emperors. The weight of the
research evidence (Falbo & Polit, 1986) shows, however, that only children
are typically more obedient and intellectually competent than first-born
children with siblings. Only children have also been found to be socially
competent in interactions with their peers.

Friendships

Most individuals are involved in friendships throughout their lives, and most friendships are long-lasting relationships. Reciprocity, commitment, and equality are essential to friendships, and friendship must be acknowledged by both partners: friends are mutually loyal, affectionately tied, and see themselves as more or less equals. Friendships can most easily be identified by asking individuals who their best friends are and determining whether such choices are reciprocated or not. Social attraction is often difficult for outsiders to evaluate; the individuals themselves are the final authorities on who their best friends are. Mutuality is an essential prerequisite for friendship. Every person can almost always name a few friends when asked to do so. Such unilateral or unreciprocated friendship differs from mutual friendship, however. Mutual friendships take a great variety of forms at different ages, different stages of friendship, and with different types of partners (e.g. male versus female). Hartup and Stevens (1997) refer to such differences in the social exchanges between friends as the surface structure of friendship. The deep structure, in contrast, consists of the reciprocity that is typical of each friendship at whatever age in whatever form.

For further specification of the developmental significance of friendships we distinguish between differences in having versus not having friends and in the identity of one's friends (e.g. the personality characteristics of one's friends) (see Bukowski, Newcomb, & Hartup, 1996; Hartup, 1996; Hartup & Stevens, 1997).

Friends versus no friends

A recent meta-analysis comparing behavioral and affective characteristics of friend versus nonfriend relationships among children revealed differences in four domains (Newcomb & Bagwell, 1995). Friendships were characterized by more *positive engagement*. When compared with nonfriends, friends spent more time together, cooperate more, and exchange more positive affect (i.e. talk, smile, and laugh more). Friends were found to be more efficient in *conflict management* than nonfriends. They do not instigate conflicts more frequently than nonfriends, but when conflicts arise they are more concerned about conflict resolution and refrain more from power assertion than nonfriends. In joint tasks, friends are more oriented towards *on-task activities* as opposed to off-task activities. Joint activities or tasks concern the content of friendships. The content of friendships may be very specific (e.g. being on the same team or in the same class) or cover a diversity of domains when friends share many interests and activities. *Relational properties* constitute the fourth domain. Friendships are marked by reciprocal and intimate affiliation. Similarly, equality, mutual liking, closeness, and loyalty are all higher in friends than in nonfriend dyads while dominance and power assertion are lower.

Hartup (1996, p. 4) relates the observed differences between friends and nonfriends to four 'cognitive and motivational conditions' that are very close to the four behavioral modalities and concomitant characteristics of relationships specified earlier in this chapter.

1. Friends know one another better than nonfriends and share joint domains of interest. They are thus able to communicate with one another more efficiently and more effectively, share common expertise, and exchange information with regard to the content of their friendship.
2. Friends versus nonfriends have more common expectations, particularly with regard to assistance and support. In regulating each other's behavior, equality and similarity prevail over dominance and power assertion.
3. An affective climate more favorable to exploration and problem solving exists between friends as opposed to nonfriends.
4. The content of friendships implies common goals and convergent goal orientations. Friendships are voluntary, and a serious opposition of goals can clearly disrupt a friendship. Friends more readily seek ways of resolving disagreements and thereby support continued interaction more than nonfriends.

Having friends provides a context for social and emotional growth. Between 80% and 90% of all individuals have a mutual friendship that may nevertheless depend on age, gender or such living conditions as being at school or having a job. Children who have friends are more socially competent and less troubled than children who do not have friends. Troubled children or those referred to a clinic more often have no friends than nontroubled or nonreferred children. Friends provide security and emotional support in the face of stress related to maltreatment, parental divorce, rejection by parents or bullying at school. Friends also provide security and support in adjusting to new environments, for example, when young children first go to school or older children change schools.

Several studies have shown friendships to provide contexts for cognitive development and the exploration of moral regulations and norms. The higher motivation for conflict resolution among friends can elicit higher levels of empathy and role taking; that is, the tendency to take the perspective of others in conflicts may be enhanced through friendships. Finally, friendships certainly prepare children and adolescents for later romantic and adult love relationships. Friendships, romantic relationships and adult love relationships have many relationship characteristics in common: equality, similarity, intimacy, mutual liking, disclosure, and closeness. Although most friendships are same-sex relationships and thus differ from most adult love relationships, the empirical findings nevertheless confirm Sullivan's (1953) claim that child and adolescent friendships prepare them for stable adult partnership.

The identity of friends

Who is a friend? In many different languages, similar but contradictory expectations appear to exist. For example, 'les extrêmes se touchent' or 'opposites attract' versus 'gleich und gleich gesellt sich gern' or 'birds of a feather flock together'. In contrast to the variable folk wisdom, the empirical findings univocally support the *similarity–attraction hypothesis* (cf. Hartup, 1996). Individuals generally choose those who resemble themselves the most for friendship. Common ground provides the background for the formation of friendships. Such common socio-demographic characteristics as chronological age, neighborhood, school, school grade, and ethnic background may all contribute to the similarity of friends. Even under such conditions of diversity as mixed gender, mixed-age, and mixed-ethnicity schools, children often choose friends who resemble themselves. The similarity of friends also extends to behavior. After a few sessions of interacting as strangers, children were found to be more similar in sociability and cognitive maturity with preferred than nonpreferred partners (Rubin, Lynch, Coplan, Rose-Krasnor & Booth, 1994). In school classes, moreover, friends are found to be more similar than nonfriends in prosocial and antisocial behavior, shyness/dependency, sociometric status, and depressive symptoms. Friends are also more similar than nonfriends in their social perception of others. That is, evaluations of classmates' behaviors resemble each other more among friends than nonfriends (Haselager, Hartup, van Lieshout & Riksen-Walraven, in press).

The similarity of friends effectively fosters within-friendship support. Friends who have a more similar background, who are more similar in expertise and skill, who have similar affective orientations, and who share common goals are most effective in supporting each other. Friends provide mutual socialization within their domains of interest and independent of whether such goals are prosocial or antisocial from a broader societal perspective. Desirable and normative as well as undesirable and antisocial behavior increases in friendships. That is, the content of friendship may be prosocial or extremely deviant (cf. Hartup, 1996).

Bully–Victim Relationships

The pioneering work by Dan Olweus (1978, 1991, 1993; see also Farrington, 1993) in Scandinavia has produced an increasing interest in bullying/victimization and resulted in the implementation of some large-scale intervention and prevention programs in several countries. In this chapter, we discuss bullying under relationships although this is by no means the complete story. Haselager (1997) has recently provided evidence for a three-level model of bullying and victimization (i.e. at the individual, relational, and group levels). As individuals, the perpetrators and victims have different characteristics; bully–victim relationships typically occur within the context of a larger group, however. The bully–victim relationship is clearly the opposite of supportive friendship. In a bully–victim relationship, the individuals have opposite goal orientations ('I am looking for him/her' vs 'I want to avoid him/her'), similar expectations with regard to the interaction ('When we meet, there will be bullying'), opposite behaviors in an asymmetric power relationship ('I will attack him/her; I will exert my power' vs 'I will be attacked/I will not be able to defend myself'), and opposite emotions ('I will have fun' vs 'I will be afraid and distressed').

Olweus (1993) defines bullying as follows: An individual is being bullied or victimized when he or she is exposed, repeatedly and over time, to negative actions on the part of one or more others. The negative actions are essentially aggressive behaviors and can take many forms, including *direct* bullying (i.e. relatively open verbal or physical attacks on a victim) and *indirect* bullying (i.e. intentional exclusion from a group and social isolation). The different forms of bullying often co-occur and are highly interrelated. Bullying can be distinguished from a single incidental aggressive act as the negative actions involved in bullying are deliberately aimed at the same target person repeatedly and over time. Characteristic of bullying is the imbalance of power and strength between the perpetrator and the victim: victims are unable to effectively defend themselves in actions, words, or to make alliances against the bullying. A bully–victim relationship is thus an asymmetric power relationship, and this power asymmetry very clearly distinguishes the bully–victim relationships from friendship and all other peer relationships.

After discussing the definition of bullying and victimization with the children in a school class, bullying can be assessed through self reports, peer evaluations, and also through teacher evaluations. Self reports are the most direct source of information concerning an individual's involvement in bullying starting around the age of 8 years. Peer-nomination procedures can provide reliable insight into the children's involvement in bully–victim relationships and about the involvement of the class as a group in such bullying. Teacher or parent reports are often incomplete because a large part of the bullying in school classes tends to go unnoticed by most teachers and parents. The results using different methods tend to be moderately to highly correlated (Smith & Sharp, 1994).

The incidence of bullying has been assessed in a great number of countries using the same Bully/Victim Questionnaire (Olweus, 1993). In these countries, 15% or more of the students in elementary school and the first four years of secondary school have been found to be involved in bully/victim problems with some regularity; approximately 9% are involved as victims (*passive or submissive victims*), 7% as *bullies*, and 1. 5% to 2% as both victim and bully (*bully/victims* or *provocative victims*). More than 5% are involved in bullying once or more a week across a period of at least a half year and often many years. The bullying is generally hidden from adults and, when noticed, difficult to stop. In higher grades, the number of victims decreases steadily. The number of perpetrators remains more or less the same. Boys tend to be exposed more than girls to physical forms of direct bullying in particular. Indirect bullying is equally frequent for boys and girls. Boys are also more frequently—up to four times more frequently—the perpetrators of bullying than girls. Boys are chiefly bullied by boys, and boys chiefly carried out the bullying of girls as well.

Research has shown typical *passive/submissive victims* to be characterized by an anxious or submissive reaction pattern combined (in the case of boys) with physical weakness. These victims signal that they are insecure, worthless, and will not retaliate when attacked or insulted (Olweus, 1993). The prevalence of external deviations in victims (e.g. wearing glasses, obesity, red hair, skin color, etc.), is open to dispute (Farrington, 1993). Such deviation is nevertheless known to be a motive for bullying. Cautiousness and sensitivity appear to characterize submissive victims from an early age. They may have difficulty in asserting themselves within the peer group and may often be disliked by age mates. These characteristics may contribute to making them the victims of bullying, and repeated bullying may increase their anxiety, insecurity, and low self-esteem. This vicious circle can then affect their learning at school. Victims may be truant in order to avoid being bullied, have concentration problems, suffer physical illness, and have sleeping problems (cf. Smith & Sharp, 1994).

The smaller group of *provocative victims* is characterized by a combination of both anxious and aggressive reaction patterns. Some of these victims may also have concentration or hyperactivity problems and disturb other children as a result. Long-term follow-up shows the lives of former victims to largely normalize in early adulthood although many of them may still tend to show depressive tendencies, have lower self-esteem, and find it difficult to develop close relationships, trust others, and become intimate.

Typical bullies tend to be aggressive in a variety of settings and over a number of years: they often show aggression towards peers but also towards both parents and teachers (Olweus, 1993). Bullying can be viewed as part of a conduct-disordered behavior pattern, but not all highly aggressive youngsters become bullies. According to Olweus (1993), three interrelated motives appear to underlie bullying. First, typical bullies have a strong tendency to exert power and dominance; they enjoy control and like to subdue others. Second, their aggression is malicious and hostile; they clearly derive satisfaction from the infliction of injury and suffering upon others. Finally, their aggression has an instrumental component; they coerce their victims into providing them with money, food, or other things of value and clearly feel rewarded by the power and prestige that their aggression brings them. The early antecedents to bullying resemble the factors that lead to life-course persistent aggression (Moffitt, 1993). Typical bullies learn to get their own way by abusing the power in their relationships and thereby run a clear risk of adult criminality. In a Swedish study the incidence of relatively serious, recidivist criminality recorded in official crime records was four times higher among former bullies when compared to other young adults (Olweus, 1993). In addition to typical bullies, so-called *passive bullies* or *followers* can also be distinguished. Passive bullies do not usually take the initiative but support typical bullies, either because of peer pressure or the appeal of the bully.

School intervention and prevention programs are in the interest of the

Box 6.2   The school-wide approach to bullying (Olweus, 1993)

The goal of the program is to reduce—ideally to eliminate—existing bully/victim problems in and out of the school setting and to prevent the development of new problems. Expressed more positively: To achieve better peer relations at school and to create conditions that make it possible for both victims and bullies to get along and function better in and out of the school setting. The program is based on a small set of key principles aimed at the modification of aggressive behavior in school. The school environment should be characterized by (i) warmth, positive interest, and involvement from adults; (ii) class rules or firm limits to unacceptable behavior; (iii) in cases of violations of these limits and rules, consistent application of nonhostile, nonphysical sanctions; (iv) monitoring and surveillance of the activities of the students both in and out of school; and (v) authoritative adult-child interaction.

   These principles were translated into a number of specific measures to be used at the school, class, and individual levels. It is considered important to work at all of these levels. A general prerequisite is (i) awareness of all adults in the school (teachers and parents) of the extent of bully/victim problems in their school, and (ii) support of the school director and staff in changing the situation. Awareness can be created by undertaking a bully/victim survey. The following activities should then be undertaken at the school level:

1.   Formation of a coordinating group responsible for the implementation of the intervention program.
2.   A school conference day to create collective commitment and responsibility for the selected program.
3.   Better supervision during recess and lunch time, when most of the bullying takes place. Supervisors must also be prepared to intervene quickly and decidedly when bullying occurs.
4.   A general meeting of the staff and parents (or a representative of the parents) to discuses the planning of the intervention program and evaluate its progress.

The following measures should be undertaken at the level of the class:
1.   Discussion with students of bully/victim problems and involvement of students in discussions on class rules regarding bullying (e.g. We will not bully other students; We will try to help students who are bullied; We will make a point of including students who are easily left out.) The rules should be posted in a visible place and the students must agree to follow the rules.
2.   Regular class meetings are held for follow-up evaluations of the situation in the class. Concrete behavioral instances and sanctions should be discussed with the students. Also passive participation and the role of neutral students may be discussed.

3. Other activities at the class level are cooperative learning, shared positive activities, and meetings with the parents of these students in their class.

The following measures should be undertaken at the level of the individual: (i) serious talks with the individual victims and bullies after bullying has occurred; (ii) serious talks with the parents of the students involved; (iii) consideration together with the parents of the victims and bullies of what can be done.

individual victims and bullies but also in the interest of the educational goals of the schools. Aggression in schools and, more specifically, bully/victim problems are among the foremost threats to effective education. Several large-scale programs and numerous small-scale interventions have been implemented, but only a very few have been properly evaluated: one in Bergen, Norway (Olweus, 1991) and one in Sheffield, England (Smith & Sharp, 1994). In Box 6.2, the program proposed by Olweus is summarized.

Olweus evaluated the program in a three-year longitudinal study. Three repeated measurements were made with four grade/age cohorts consisting of 600–700 students each. The average ages of the students were 11, 12, 13, and 14 years, respectively. First measurement occurred 4 months prior to the intervention. The second and third measurement occurred after the program had been implemented 8 and 20 months. The main results were as follows:

1. Bully/victim problems were reduced by about 50% in terms of numbers of students involved in bullying as either victims or bullies. Reductions were obtained after 8 and 20 months, for boys and girls, across all cohorts, and for different measures.
2. There was no displacement of bullying from the school setting to outside the school setting.
3. There was a clear reduction in such general antisocial behavior as vandalism, fighting, pilfering, and truancy.
4. Marked improvements occurred in various aspects of the social climate in the class (order and discipline, positive social relationships, more positive attitude) and in student satisfaction with the school
5. A clear dosage effect or input–output relation was found, which stresses the need for continuous support; larger reductions of bully–victim problems were found in those classes where the main components of the program were implemented (class rules on bullying, regular class meetings) (see also Smith & Sharp, 1994).
6. Alternative explanations such as underreporting by the students, a repeated measurement effect, or concomitant changes in other factors were very unlikely to have caused the results.

In sum, the effects of a school-wide approach to bullying were found to be remarkable; other intervention programs aimed at the reduction of aggressive and antisocial problem behavior at the individual and school levels have not been particularly successful. The success of Olweus' program also shows that schools can indeed take effective action against bullying (see also Smith & Sharp, 1994, p. 55).

Groups

Interpersonal relationships take place in groups. Groups, such as class groups and family groups, consist of collections of individuals forming interpersonal relationships in a systemic context. The group structure can be described in terms of the nature, quality, and patterning of the relationships (cf. Hinde, 1976). The patterning of the relationships may determine the structure of the group but is itself influenced by the dynamics of the group resulting from explicit or implicit group goals and group norms/values, and possible subgroup coalitions (see Hartup, 1983). The interactions in groups show similar modalities of interaction and dimensions of relational support as interactions in interpersonal relationships (see Table 6.1, Col. 1). In groups, the exchange of information can be colored by *shared meaning systems*. Such shared meaning systems can be determined by a particular philosophy of life or shared cultural background. They may also be more determined by *group goals* than by rules governing interpersonal relationships or by logical rules governing the exchange of matter-of-fact information. The *behavioral regulation* in groups is not only determined by interpersonal relationships but also by such group characteristics as dominance hierarchies, coalition formation, or group conformism. The *emotional exchanges* in groups can exceed feelings in interpersonal relationships and reflect feelings of group cohesion (i.e. feelings of attraction or rejection in multiple dyadic relationships and in subgroups). In groups, not only the content of the relational support in the interpersonal relationships is important, but also the degree of cross-relational consistency and continuity over time. Below we will consider family groups and school classes in greater detail. It should be kept in mind that such groups are embedded in societies and may therefore vary across cultures (see Box. 6.3).

Family groups

A family is a complex interconnected system of individuals and relationships (Belsky & Isabella, 1987). Each family member has a unique position or role in the group (e.g. mother, father, daughter, youngest child, stepfather). Each family member has a person-specific and role-specific behavior pattern and a specific developmental orientation and developmental trajectory. Relationships in family groups have the characteristics specified earlier for relationships in general but also complementary developmental trajectories as well. For example, a parent–child relationship typically involves the developmental trajectories of two people with complementary

Box 6.3   Societies and cultures

Interactions, relationships, and the groups all evolve within a societal and cultural frame. The importance of studying individual development with the more general framework has already been stressed by Baldwin (1913, pp. 107–108):

The society into which the child is born, is, therefore, not to be conceived merely as a loose aggregate, made up of a number of biological individuals. It is rather a body of mental products, an established network of psychical relationships. By this the new person is moulded and shaped to his maturity. ... Society is a mass of mental and moral states and values, which perpetuates itself in individual persons. In the personal self, the social is individualized.

Most developmental tasks can be analyzed as adaptations to the societal and cultural environment. Such an assumption does not necessarily involve a completely relativistic conception of development and the implication that each society or culture produces psychologically completely different individuals. On the contrary, each individual begins development in a relationship of more or less complete dependence and only later attains relative independence in several areas. Every individual, for example, participates in such elementary social interaction schemas as giving and receiving, dominating and submitting, questioning and answering, which are viewed by Feffer (1970) as the basis for more complex interactions. The actions of individuals in interaction necessitate spatio-temporal systems of coordinations such as in front/behind, before/after, above/below, which cannot be executed or followed in an arbitrary manner. It is the universal participation in such social and symbolic systems that enables individuals to understand each other, to communicate across different cultures, and translate the essentials of one language into another language.

Important socio-cultural differences nevertheless exist and may indeed affect the psychological development of individuals. Such differences can again be analyzed in terms of the four modalities outlined in Table 6.1. At the level of group goals, one can distinguish different ecological environments or different economic systems. The influence of ecological factors on spatio-perceptual development has frequently been studied and Berry's (1971) research suggests that hunting people possess better visual discrimination and spatial skills and are socialized with an emphasis on independence and self-reliance. Contemporary studies on collectivism and individualism relate to the more socio-emotional facets of societal and cultural group patterns. These studies consider relationships important for the shaping of personal identity as part of a group or as different or separated from the rest of a group (Oyserman & Markus, 1993). Societal differences in power and status have also been studied in relation to the social construction of gender differences (Lorenzi-Cioldi, 1994). The importance of more general systems of values and particular religious, political, and ideological orientations beliefs is widely recognized. One example is a study of a representative sample of Parisian youth (16–21 years) by Percheron, Chiche and Muxel-Douaire (1988). The opinions of the youth with regard to the judiciary could be organized along a twofold principle and clearly reflected the socio-economic and religious background of the youth. One could trust versus distrust the judicial system (i.e. have confidence in the system as a belief that the rights of the accused will be respected versus no confidence in the system and a belief that the rights of the accused will not be respected). Similarly, one could have a contractual versus a naturalistic conception of justice (i.e. laws did not always exist or are no longer adequate and should therefore be changed versus laws have always existed and remain largely adequate and should therefore not be changed). Younger respondents with a working-class origin and non-catholic background were more frequently found among those near to the poles of distrust and naturalism, while respondents with a higher social origin and students were more frequently found among those near the poles of distrust and contractualism. Catholics and rural youth adhere more frequently to trustful and naturalistic conceptions of the judiciary while the opposite conceptions are more characteristic of those who are already earning their living and are not religious.

and different speeds (parent slower, child faster). The developmental trajectories of siblings may be complementary for reasons related to the gender or the birth order of siblings or different expectations from the parents. The group context or system implies that each family member's behavior depends in part on the behavior of the other family members and thus a more or less unique set of relationships. The family system may also be characterized by a number of organizational features, openness, and dynamics that lie far beyond the behavior of the individuals and their relationships. For example, a certain degree of family continuity may exist despite the addition, mobility or loss of family members.

Families take a wide variety of forms across cultures and time. Since the Second World War in many European countries, the two-generation nuclear family consisting of two biological parents and their children living more or less independent of other family members has largely replaced the multigenerational extended family, consisting of parents and their children living with such other family members as grandparents, aunts, uncles, nephews, and nieces. In recent years in many countries, the 'standard' nuclear family has further changed and now includes a number of different forms: single-parent families, divorced parents, and adopted children from other countries and other ethnic backgrounds. Many children may now grow up in more than one type of family. The family types also differ across countries. For example, the number of unmarried teenage mothers has rapidly increased in the USA and far exceeds the number in Europe. The age at which women first give birth has gradually increased in several countries, and family roles have also changed. The classical pattern of a 'breadwinning' father putting in long hours at the job and a homemaking mother taking care of the children is gradually changing in some families to two parents with (part-time) employment outside the home sharing the homemaking duties and hired child care at an early age. This pattern also varies both within and across the different countries, however.

One characteristic of a family as a system is that the quality of the relationships between two members may affect the interactions and relationship with a third member. In a recent meta-analysis of 68 studies, Erel and Burman (1995) tested two hypotheses concerning the interrelatedness of parental marital relationships and parent–child relationships. The parental relationship was measured in terms of global quality, marital satisfaction and coalition, and absence of overt conflicts. The parent–child relationship was measured in terms of global quality, between- and within-parent consistency, satisfaction, and absence of negative control and harsh punishment. General and strong support was found for the so-called *spillover hypothesis*, which suggests a positive correlation between marital quality and the quality of the parent–child relationships. Parents who have a satisfying and supportive relationship are more available to respond in a sensitive manner to the needs of their child. The spillover hypothesis further suggests that a negative or conflict-filled marital relationships may cause parents to be irritable, emotionally drained, and therefore less attentive and sensitive to their children. No support in the meta-analysis was found for the *compensatory hypothesis*, which suggests that a positive relationship between a child and at least one of the parents may provide a buffer against or compensate for the negative impact of marital discord on children. Despite the absence of such *buffer effects* in the meta-analysis, they may nevertheless occur in specific family contexts and particularly in combination with other so-called *protective factors* (see Braet & Verhofstadt-Denève, ch. 10 this volume).

Many studies (see Grych & Finchman, 1990) have demonstrated a causal relation between increased marital conflicts and increased behavioral and emotional problems in children (e.g. externalizing and internalizing problems, lower school achievement). Similarly, decreased marital conflict has been found mostly to result in a lowering of behavioral and emotional problems in children. The effects of marital conflict are more negative when the conflicts are more frequent, more systematic versus incidental (i.e. concern the quality of the parental relationship and not, for example, the buying of a new house), more open and visible for the children versus more covert, more physical and emotionally distressing for the parents, concern the behavior or the education of the children, and remain unresolved. Divorce is often correlated with a long episode of heated marital conflict, and such conflict often exerts a more negative effect on the children than the divorce itself. Divorce is often suggested, therefore, as better for the children's well-being than continuation of a conflict-ridden marriage. Children are also more negatively affected by divorce when the parental conflict continues with regard to such things as visitation schedules, parent–child interactions/relationships, or the children's education.

The influence of parental conflict in children's behavior may suggest one-way influence, but this is not the complete story. Each family member is active in defining, changing, and shaping the family context, and these influences are always bi-directional. The characteristics and behavior of the parents influence the behavior of their children, and the characteristics of the children elicit certain behaviors from their parents and siblings. These bi-directional effects are part of a transactional process of development (Sameroff & Fiese, 1989) and may lead to very different outcomes for people who originally seemed to have similar developmental outlooks.

Peers in School Classes

Most individuals spend most of their time outside the family in peer groups. Children meet their peers most frequently in their school class where individuals are engaged in networks of friendships, bully–victim relationships and/or romantic relationships. They may segregate into subgroups or cliques according to interests and such demographic characteristics as gender and ethnic status. School classes are not voluntary groups; children have to go to school, and the peer relations within such a setting therefore require attention for several reasons. First, a substantial number of children experience peer problems in school classes. Many children are victimized by aggressive peers and systematic tolerance of such aggression across a number of years at school may 'teach' children that it is acceptable to achieve one's goals using aggressive means and thereby to victimize classmates. Such aggression, as already mentioned, can lead to truancy, school dropout, delinquent behavior in adolescence, and psychopathology in adulthood (cf. Parker & Asher, 1987). Schools should therefore not restrict their mission to the teaching and learning of cognitive skills. Because school is obligatory, some theorists argue that it should guarantee—as a basic right—no exposure to systematic peer aggression and clearly teach both prosocial interaction skills *and* problem-solving skills (see Olweus, 1993). Second, positive peer relations facilitate instruction and learning in class whereas peer problems clearly disturb these activities. In many countries, schools are legally obligated to eliminate factors that may hinder children's effective learning and teachers' effective instruction. Finally, the class group and the school are excellent settings for the support of children and adolescents who experience peer problems. Acceptance and rejection by peers are among the forces motivating children to adapt their behaviors to the groups goals and norms. A favorable class atmosphere can therefore facilitate the utilization of such peer pressure in intervention programs.

Social competence in peer groups

Group relations can be assessed in terms of acceptance and rejection using sociometric procedures (see Box 6.4). This also holds for the social competence of classmates, which can be measured using peer evaluations. For example you can ask children to nominate one or more of the children in their class as best at playing specific roles in an imaginary play. For their Revised Class Play (RCP), Masten, Morison and Pellegrini (1985) selected 30 roles: 15 positive and 15 negative roles within the interpersonal domain. Several studies using RCP have shown children and adolescents to evaluate group members along three basic dimensions of social competence: one with positive valence labelled Sociability-Leadership and two with negative valence labelled Aggressive-Disruptive and Sensitive-Isolated. It should be emphasized that these dimensions of social competence pertain not only to the specific interpersonal skills of individual children but also to their general functioning in relationships and the class group. It seems that, in evaluating the behavior of classmates, children consider not only the characteristics of individual children but also their contribution to group goals and norms, group cohesion, and group hierarchy. It should further be noted that the dimensions produced by an investigation of imaginary class roles may depend on the specific content of the roles. If children are asked to evaluate their classmates in terms of a set of roles derived from the Big Five personality factors (see Kohnstamm and Mervielde, this volume), for example, other dimensions of group functioning may be found.

Sociometric status and social competence

An intriguing question is whether or not and how children's peer acceptance and rejection (see Box 6.4) relates to their social competence and adjustment in groups. In a meta-analysis of 41 studies, Newcomb, Bukowski, and Pattee (1993) compared the four 'extreme' types of sociometric status (i.e. popular, rejected, neglected, controversial) with the average type on several aspects of aggression, sociability, withdrawal, and academic/intellectual ability. The findings were found to be moderately consistent across four different sources of information: direct observation, peer evaluation, adult evaluation, and self-reports. *Popular* children are most liked by peers and best friends, and they also show higher levels of sociability and cognitive abilities with lower levels of aggression and withdrawal. Popular children also have the social abilities to achieve interpersonal goals and maintain positive relationships; while they have the ability to be assertive/aggressive, their behavioral repertoire primarily leads to positive social outcomes for themselves (and for others) and they score low on measures of general aggression, negative affect, and disruption. *Rejected* children show virtually the opposite pattern of behavior. They are more aggressive, more withdrawn, less sociable, and less cognitively skilled than average children. The finding that rejected children are both more withdrawn *and* more aggressive is surprising. Several studies (cf. Cillessen et al., 1992) have recently suggested that the rejected status group is not a single homogeneous group. Nearly half of the rejected children and especially the boys within this group are also aggressive,

Box 6.4   Sociometric status classification of children

Relationships and group structure in peer groups can be assessed using sociometry. The term sociometry was originally proposed by the psychiatrist Jacob L. Moreno (1934). Sociometric methods have regained great interest since the early eighties (for an overview see Williams & Gilmour, 1994). In sociometric procedures, group members evaluate each other—that is, name other children or rate all the children in a group—on one or more criteria. The result is given and received scores for each group member on each criterion. Sociometric procedures can be used in a wide variety of groups and even in groups of very young children. A diversity of criteria can also be used. The general like or dislike of classmates can be measured with such questions as 'Who do you like most?' and 'Who do you least like?' This provides an assessment of peer acceptance and peer rejection although more concrete questions are also often used for measuring likability (e.g. 'Who is your favorite teammate for playing soccer?'). It should be noted, that likability and specific behavioral skills may be confounded in such specific questions. It is impossible to distinguish whether a teammate has been selected because of his or her high skill in playing soccer or because he or she is particularly liked as a playmate.

Peer acceptance ('most liked') and *peer rejection* ('least liked') are typically used to measure interpersonal relationships in class groups. Although peer acceptance and peer rejection were once considered opposite poles of a single dimension, they are not exact antipodes. A low accepted child may not be highly rejected although these facets of popularity tend to be negatively correlated.

Since the early 1980s interpersonal relationships in groups have been measured along two independent dimensions: *social impact* or the sum of acceptance plus rejection and *social preference* or acceptance minus rejection. Social impact or social visibility is a measure of social salience or the relative degree to which children are noticed by their peers, as either liked or disliked. Social preference or likability reflects the extent to which children are liked versus disliked by their peers; children who are highly liked by a relatively large number of classmates obtain a relatively high social-preference score while children who are highly disliked obtain a relatively low social-preference score.

These two sociometric dimensions can be used to classify children into five categories: popular, rejected, neglected, controversial, and average sociometric status. Sociometric classification involves several steps. First, the number of 'most liked' and number of 'least liked' nominations for each child in a group are used to derive acceptance and rejection scores and thereby determine social impact and social preference. Second, the raw scores are standardized in order to control for the variable number of children in a group. Third, children are assigned to sociometric groups on the basis of the standardized scores.

Popular children have high acceptance and low rejection scores; rejected children have high rejection and low acceptance scores; neglected children have low impact scores; controversial children have high impact scores; and average children have intermediate scores on social preference and social impact. Different statistical models were used for the classification of the children in these five sociometric status types: the standard score model is based on the standardized scores (Coie, Dodge & Coppotelli, 1982) and the probability model is based on binomial probability theory (Newcomb & Bukowski, 1983). Other methods use the extreme scores on a single rating scale ('Who do you like most?') for sociometric classification instead of 'like-least' and 'like-most' nominations (Asher & Dodge, 1986). Use of the 'like-most' ratings also avoids the ethical problem of asking children to explicitly name those classmates whom they dislike. These methods have similar psychometric characteristics and result in fairly convergent classifications.

These methods tend to identify across many classes an average of about 15% popular, 15% rejected, 7–8% neglected, 7–8 controversial, and 55% average children. These percentages may vary from group to group depending on the composition of the group and the group atmosphere. For example, very aggressive individual children may elicit numerous rejection scores and new group members may affect the sociometric status of others. Furthermore, cliques, gender and the ethnic composition of the school classes may affect the children's sociometric choices. Children tend to nominate—both positively and negatively—those from the same gender and ethnic subgroup.

impulsive, and disruptive children (i.e. the *aggressive-rejected* subtype). A small but substantial number of the rejected children and more often the girls within this group show high levels of social withdrawal, anxiety, depressive symptoms, and low self-esteem (i.e. the *withdrawn/shy-rejected* subtype). A third group did not appear to vary that much from the average sociometric status type. The withdrawn-rejected subtype can attract a lot of attention through ineffective attention-seeking and extreme dependency on others. Both victimized and bullying children frequently have a rejected sociometric status in class; victimized children are more often of the withdrawn-rejected subtype while bullies are more often the aggressive-rejected subtype. The social development of rejected children in general is at risk. *Controversial* children represent a combination of the characteristics found among rejected and popular children. They can have the highest level of aggressive behavior but compensate for this with significantly better cognitive and social abilities. Bullies, for example, can have a controversial sociometric status. *Neglected* children do not experience particular adjustment difficulties. They seem to opt for a low level of involvement in the group, and their visibility or impact within the group is thus low. They are simply indifferent to the group. They have been found to be less aggressive and to exhibit less sociability than other children but are not socially anxious or withdrawn and do not experience depression. The lack of stability in the neglected status classification and the limited extent/magnitude of the behavioral problems associated with this sociometric status type means it is not an at-risk group. Extensive involvement in the peer group does *not* seem to be a developmental necessity. Neglected children often have a reciprocal best friend, and they generally demonstrate average friendship skills (Newcomb et al., 1993).

Peer relations in developmental perspective

A growing number of longitudinal studies show peer relations and social competence to be related to later social and personality development. The specific role of peer relations in this developmental pathway was considered in earlier sections and found to provide an important link between early parent–child or sibling relationships and later social and personality development and behavior in groups. A controversial issue is whether sociometric status makes a major contribution to such social development or simply represents an epiphenomenon. Several longitudinal studies have recently shown that, as an important group phenomenon and crucial life experience, sociometric status can make both a negative (i.e. for rejected children) and a positive (i.e. for popular children) contribution to developmental outcome in adolescence and early adulthood in association, for example, with children's early personality and behavioral characteristics (see Williams & Gilmour, 1994).

CONCLUSIONS

In closing, we want to stress the relation of social development to two basic developmental concepts: continuity and discontinuity. Both continuity and discontinuity have been found to play major roles in an individual's social development. Let us first consider some partly overlapping sources of discontinuity. The first and largest source of discontinuity consisted of changing intentions, changing situational circumstances, changing relationships, and changing group contexts. The social interactions following such changes may vary so drastically from those prior to the changes that an impression of complete discontinuity can arise. A second source of discontinuity consists of changes in the primacy of different relationships across an individual's life-span. The priority or prominence of child–parent, sibling friendship, partner, and parent–child relationships can clearly change. A third source of discontinuity is the changing of individuals involved in some of these relationships. A person's best friend or partner may change and thereby create discontinuity in the relationship. A fourth source of discontinuity can be a change in the primacy of the groups you are a part of. Your original family, your school, your class, your team, your working environment, and your established family can all change. Finally, at different points in the life-span, individuals are engaged in different developmental tasks that determine to a large extent the content of an individual's interactions, relationships, and group orientations.

The sources of continuity are largely complementary to the sources of discontinuity. The first source of continuity is continuity in the quality of relationships. The security of parent–child relationships predicts the quality of sibling and friendship relationships, which then predict the quality of later romantic and partner relationships. A second source of continuity is the basic deep structure of friendship (Hartup & Stevens, 1997). This pertains to the continuity of friendships throughout an individual's life despite differences in the friendship partners, the actual interactions between the friends, and the content of the friendships. A third source of continuity may be an individual's antisocial, prosocial, or socially withdrawn orientation. These behavioral orientations can be assessed across the life-span using similar measures and thereby provide an indication of the individual stability of these behavioral orientations with age. A fourth and final source of continuity lies in the relational support you experience and provide to others. This may be in different relationships at the same time or in the same relationship across time and involves quality of information, respect for autonomy versus limit setting, feelings of security, and the convergence or opposition of goals. Although there is evidence for continuity in this relational dimensions across several years, the evidence for longer life episodes is still lacking.

In the last 25 years, the study of social development has vastly expanded in terms of social-psychological domains and inclusion of the entire life-span. The mechanisms creating continuity and discontinuity across the life-span and the effects of such continuity/discontinuity have yet to be thoroughly investigated, however, and should therefore be among the most important elements for the study of social development in the future.

REFERENCES

Asendorpf, J. B. & van Aken, M. A. G. (1994). Traits and relationship status: Stranger versus peer group inhibition and test intelligence versus peer group competence as early predictors of later self-esteem. *Child Development*, **30**, 912–919.

Asher, S. R. & Dodge, K. A. (1986). Identifying children who are rejected by their peers. *Developmental Psychology*, **22**, 444–449.

Baldwin, J. M. (1913). *History of Psychology, From John Locke to the Present Time*, Vol. 2. London, Watts.

Baltes, P. B., Reese, H. W. & Lipsitt, L. P. (1980). Life-span developmental psychology. *Annual Review of Psychology*, **31**, 65–110.

Bandura, A. (1977). *Social Learning Theory*. Englewood Cliffs, NJ: Prentice-Hall.

Bartholomew, K. & Horowitz, L. M. (1991). Attachment styles among young adults: A test of a four-category model. *Journal of Personality and Social Psychology*, **61**, 226–244.

Baumrind, D. (1989). Rearing competent children. In: W. Damon (Ed.), *Child Development Today and Tomorrow* (pp. 349–378). San Francisco: Jossey-Bass.

Belsky, J. & Isabella, R. A. (1987). Maternal, infant, and social-contextual determinants of attachment security. In J. Belsky & T. Nezworski (Eds), *Clinical Implications of Attachment*. Hillsdale, NJ: Erlbaum.

Berry, J. W. (1971). Ecological and cultural factors in spatial perceptual development. *Canadian Journal of Behavioral Science*, **3**, 324–336.

Boer, F. & Dunn, J. (Eds) (1992). *Children's Sibling Relationships: Developmental and Clinical Issues*. Hillsdale, NJ: Erlbaum.

Bowlby, J. (1973). *Attachment and Loss*: Vol. 2. *Separation*. New York: Basic Books.

Bukowski, W. M., Newcomb, A. F. & Hartup, W. W. (1996). *The Company They Keep: Friendships in Childhood and Adolescence*. Cambridge: Cambridge University Press.

Burhmester, D. & Furman, W. (1990). Perceptions of sibling relationships during middle childhood and adolescence. *Child Development*, **61**, 1387–1398.

Caspi, A., Elder, G. H. & Bem, D. J. (1988). Moving away from the world: life-course patterns of shy children. *Developmental Psychology*, **24**, 824–831.

Cillessen, A. H. N., van IJzendoorn, H. W., van Lieshout, C. F. M. & Hartup, W. W. (1992). Heterogeneity among peer rejected boys: Subtypes and stabilities. *Child Development*, **63**, 893–905.

Clark, M. S. & Reis, H. T. (1988). Interpersonal processes in close relationships. *Annual Review of Psychology*, **39**, 609–672.

Coie, J. D., Dodge, K. A. & Coppotelli, H. (1982). Dimensions and type of social status: A cross-age perspective. *Developmental Psychology*, **18**, 557–570.

Conger, R. D., Patterson, G. R. & Ge, X. (1995). It takes two to replicate. A mediational model for the impact of parents' stress of adolescent adjustment. *Child Development*, **60**, 80–97.

Crick, N. R. & Dodge, K. A. (1994). A review and reformulation of social information-processing mechanisms in children's social adjustment. *Psychological Bulletin*, **115**, 74–101.

de Poorte, I. M., Veling, G. M., Haselager, G. J. T. & van Lieshout, C. F. M. (1994). Gedragstypering van kinderen met een problematische sociometrische status [Behavior of children with an at-risk sociometric status type]. *Tijdschrift voor Orthopedagogiek*, **33**, 268–283.

Dishion, T. J., Andrews, D. W. & Crosby, L. (1995). Antisocial boys and their friends in early adolescence: Relationship characteristics, quality, and interactional process. *Child Development*, **66**, 139–151.

Doise, W. & Mugny, G. (1984). *The Social Development of the Intellect*. Oxford: Pergamon.

Dunn, J. & Kendrick, C. (1982). *Siblings, Love, Envy, and Understanding*.

London: Grant McIntyre.

Dunn, J., Slomkowski, C. & Beardsall, L. (1994). Sibling relationships from the preschool period through middle childhood and early adolescence. *Developmental Psychology*, **30**, 315–324.

Erel, O. & Burman, B. (1995). Interrelatedness of marital relations and parent–child relations: A meta-analytic review. *Psychological Bulletin*, **118**, 108–132.

Falbo, T. & Polit, D. F. (1986). Quantitative review of the only child literature: Research evidence and theory development. *Psychological Bulletin*, **100**, 176–189.

Farrington, D. (1993). Understanding and preventing bullying. In M. Tonry & N. Morris (Eds). *Crime and Justice*, Vol. 17 (pp. 381–458). Chicago: University of Chicago Press.

Feffer, M. (1970). Developmental analysis of interpersonal behavior. *Psychological Review*, **77**, 197–214.

Ferguson, T. J. & Rule, B. G. (1983). An attributional perspective on anger and aggression. In R. G. Geen & E. I. Donnerstein (Eds), *Aggression: Theoretical and Empirical Reviews*, Vol. 1 (pp. 41–74). New York: Academic Press.

Furman, W. & Buhrmester, D. (1985). Children's perceptions of the personal relationships in their social networks. *Developmental Psychology*, **21**, 1016–1024.

Furman, W. & Buhrmester, D. (1992). Age and sex differences in perceptions of networks and personal relationships. *Child Development*, **63**, 103–115.

Graziano, W. G. & Eisenberg, N. H. (1994). Agreeableness: A dimension of personality. In R. Hogan, J. Johnson, & S. Briggs (Eds), *Handbook of Personality Psychology*, San Diego: Academic Press.

Grusec, J. J. & Goodnow, J. J. (1994). The impact of parental discipline methods on the child's internalization of values: A reconceptualization of current points of view. *Developmental Psychology*, **30**, 4–19.

Grych, J. H. & Finchman, F. D. (1990). Marital conflict and children's adjustment: A cognitive-contextual framework. *Psychological Bulletin*, **108**, 267–290.

Hartup, W. W. (1983). Peer relations. In E. M. Hetherington, (Ed.), *Handbook of Child Psychology*: Vol. 4 *Socialization, Personality, and Social Development* (pp. 103–198). New York: Wiley.

Hartup, W. W. (1996). The company they keep: Friendships and their developmental significance. *Child Development*, **67**, 1–13.

Hartup, W. W. & Stevens, N. (1997). Friendship and adaption in the life course. *Psychological Bulletin*. **121**, 355–370.

Hartup, W. W. & van Lieshout, C. F. M. (1995). Personality development in context. *Annual Review of Psychology*, **46**, 655–687.

Haselager, G. J. T. (1997). *Classmates. Studies on the Development of their Relationships and Personality in Middle Childhood*. University of Nijmegen: unpublished doctoral dissertation.

Haselager, G. J. T., Hartup, W. W., van Lieshout, C. F. M. & Riksen-

Walraven, J. M. (in press). Behavioral similarities between friends and nonfriends in middle childhood. *Child Development*.

Havighurst, R. J. (1973). History of developmental psychology: Socialization and personality development through the life-span. In P. B. Baltes & K. W. Schaie (Eds), *Life-span Developmental Psychology: Personality and Socialization* (pp. 3–24). New York: Academic Press.

Hinde, R. A. (1997). *Relationships. A Dialectical Perspective*. London: Psychology Press.

Kelley, H. H., Berscheid, E., Christensen, A., Harvey, J. H., Huston, T. L., Levinger, G., McClintock, C. G., Peplau, L. A. & Peterson, D. (1983). *Close Relationships*. New York: Freeman.

Kochanska, G. (1995). Children's temperament, mother's discipline, and security of attachment: Multiple pathways to emerging internalization. *Child Development*, **66**, 597–615.

Kochanska, G., Aksan, N. & Koenig, A. L. (1995). A longitudinal study of the roots of preschooler's conscience: Committed compliance and emerging internalization. *Child Development*, **66**, 1752–1769.

Laursen, B. & Collins, W. A. (1994). Interpersonal conflict during adolescence. *Psychological Bulletin*, **115**, 197–209.

Loeber, R., Wung, P., Keenan, K., Giroux, B., Stouthamer-Loeber, M., van Kammen, W. B. & Maughan, B. (1993). Developmental pathways in disruptive child behavior. *Developmental Psychopathology*, **5**, 103–133.

Lorenzi-Cioldi, F. (1994). *Les Androgynes*. Paris: Presses Universitaires de France.

Masten, A. S., Morison, P. & Pellegrini, D. S. (1985). A Revised Class Play method of peer assessment. *Developmental Psychology*, **3**, 523–533.

Meltzoff, A. N. (1995). Understanding the intentions of others: Re-enactment of intended acts by 18-month-old children. *Developmental Psychology*, **31**, 838–850.

Moffitt, T. E. (1993). Adolescence-limited and life-course-persistent antisocial behavior: A developmental taxonomy. *Psychological Review*, **100**, 674–701.

Moreno, J. L. (1934). *Who shall survive? A New Approach to the Problem of Human Interrelations*. Washington, DC: Nervous and Mental Disease Publishing.

Newcomb, A. F. & Bagwell, C. L. (1995). Children's friendship relations: A meta-analytic review. *Psychological Bulletin*, **117**, 306–347.

Newcomb, A. F., Bukowski, W. M. & Pattee, L. (1993). Children's peer relations: A meta-analytic review of popular, rejected, neglected, controversial, and average sociometric status. *Psychological Bulletin*, **113**, 99–128.

Newcomb, A. F. & Bukowski, W. M. (1983). Social impact and social preference as determinants of children's peer group status. *Developmental Psychology*, **19**, 856–867.

Olthof, T. (1990). Blame, anger, and aggression in children. A social-cognitive approach. University of Nijmegen: unpublished doctoral dissertation.

Olweus, D. (1978). *Aggression in the Schools: Bullies and Whipping Boys.* Washington, DC: Hemisphere.

Olweus, D. (1991). Bully/victim problems among school children: Basic facts and effects of a school-based intervention program. In D. J. Pepler & K. H. Rubin (Eds), *The Development and Treatment of Childhood Aggression.* (pp. 411–448). Hillsdale, NJ: Erlbaum.

Olweus, D. (1993). *Bullying at School. What We Know and What We Can Do.* Oxford, Blackwell.

Oser, F. K. (1986). Moral education and values education: The discourse perspective. In M. C. Wittrock (Ed.), *Handbook of Research on Teaching.* 3rd edn. (pp 917–41). New York: Macmillan.

Oyserman, D. & Markus, H. R. (1993). The sociocultural self. In J. Suls (Ed.), *Psychological Perspectives on the Self,* Vol. 4. Hillsdale, NJ: Erlbaum.

Parker, J. G. & Asher, S. R. (1987). Peer relations and later personal adjustment,: Are low-accepted children at risk? *Psychological Bulletin,* **102**, 357–389.

Patterson, G. R., Capaldi, D. M. & Bank. L. (1991). An early starter model for predicting delinquency. In D. J. Pepler & K. H. Rubin (Eds), *The Development and Treatment of Childhood Aggression* (pp. 139–168). Hillsdale, NJ: Erlbaum.

Percheron, A., Chiche, J. & Muxel-Douaire, A. (1988). *Le droit à 20 ans.* Paris: Institut de formation continue du Barreau de Paris/Gazette du Palais.

Renshaw, P. D. & Asher, S. R. (1982). Social competence and peer status: The distinction between goals and strategies. In K. H. Rubin, & H. S. Ross (Eds), *Peer Relationships and Social Skills in Childhood* (pp. 375–395). New York: Springer.

Rubin, K. H. & Asendorpf, J. B. (1993). Social withdrawal, inhibition, and shyness in childhood: Conceptual and definitional issues. In K. H. Rubin & J. B. Asendorpf (Eds), *Social Withdrawal, Inhibition, and Shyness in Childhood.* Hillsdale, NJ: Erlbaum.

Rubin, K. H., Lynch, D., Coplan, R., Rose-Krasnor, L. & Booth, C. L. (1994). 'Birds of a feather . . . ': Behavioral concordances and preferential personal attraction in children. *Child Development,* **65**, 1778–1785.

Sameroff, A. & Fiese, B. (1989). Transactional regulation and early intervention. In S. J. Meisels & J. Shonkoff (Eds), *Early Intervention: A Handbook of Theory, Practice and Analyses.* New York: Cambridge University Press.

Searle, J. R. (1983). *Intentionality: An Essay on the Philosophy of Mind.* New York: Cambridge University Press.

Shatz, M. & Gelman, R. (1973). The development of communication skills: Modifications in the speech of young children as a function of listening. *Monographs of the Society for Research in Child Development,* **38**, (5, Serial No. 152).

Smith, P. K. & Sharp, S. (Eds) (1994). *School Bullying, Insights and Perspectives.* London: Routledge.

Sullivan, H. S. (1953). *The Interpersonal Theory of Psychiatry*. New York: Norton.

Van Lieshout, C. F. M. (1995). Development of social giftedness and gifted personality context. In M. W. Katzko & F. J. Mönks (Eds.), *Nurturing Talent. Individual Needs and Social Ability* (pp. 31–42). Assen, The Netherlands: van Gorcum.

Williams, B. T. R. & Gilmour, J. D. (1994). Annotation: Sociometry and peer relationships. *Journal of Child Psychology and Psychiatry*, **35**, 997–1013.

Zajonc, R. B., Marcus, H. & Marcus, G. B. (1979). The birth order puzzle. *Journal of Personality and Social Psychology*, **37**, 1325–1341.

Chapter 7

Morality, Wisdom and the Life-span

Helen Haste

University of Bath

Diomedes Markoulis

University of Thessaloniki

and

Klaus Helkama

University of Helsinki

BASIC CONCEPTS AND ISSUES

Ask the person in the street about 'morality', and they will describe the qualities which they consider make up a 'good person'. This is typically a mixture of virtues, emotions, good habits, and behaviours. Such 'common-sense' conceptions of 'character', however, have not proved very useful in the systematic study of morality. Early research, by Hartshorne and May in 1932, found low correlations between different elements of 'character' which were remarkably like the commonsense mixture. Since then, researchers have tended to focus on specific aspects of morality, and to ignore others.

This is partly for the sake of precision, but it is also because different theories of moral development are based on rather different definitions of

Life-Span Developmental Psychology
Edited by A. Demetriou, W. Doise and C. F. M. van Lieshout. © 1998 John Wiley & Sons Ltd.

the central issues of 'morality'. This chapter explores the present picture of research on moral development within a life-span perspective, including the difficult question of 'wisdom'.

Moral Development and Life-span Research

Elsewhere in this volume (ch. 1) Weinert and Weinert have discussed the problems of life-span research. These have particular applications to the study of moral development, which we will consider briefly.

It might seem that the best procedure is longitudinal research, but this is expensive, labour-intensive, and takes a long time. Furthermore, not only the respondents and researchers, but the theories underpinning the research get wrinkled and wither. Nevertheless, there are some valuable longitudinal studies in the moral domain. However, most research that feeds into thinking about moral development across the life-span depends on cross-sectional data. It is also the case that much more research has been done on children and adolescents than on adults. This reflects a tradition in developmental research which has treated adulthood as a plateau of undifferentiated 'maturity' and the endstate of childhood and adolescence. Life-span approaches challenge this, and look at development as a continuous process.

This raises some important questions about how we should define moral maturity. Different definitions of 'moral maturity' depend on how we think about development:

1. What is established in the early years remains more or less fixed throughout life; later experiences may expand this, but it is essentially a *cumulative* process; maturity is reflected in the range and depth of knowledge and skill the individual has acquired, and how effectively they are used.
2. Development across the life-span is through continual *change and transformation*; what we know or understand is integrated into successively more complex systems or stages. There is individual variation in the speed and extent of this progression. We expect adults to show more integrated and elaborated morality, but not all adults show equal levels of 'moral maturity'.
3. The life-span has specific *'phases'* or *'developmental tasks'*; these are common to everyone, but they may be negotiated differently by different individuals; 'maturity' is defined by how successfully the individual negotiates the sequence of life phases.

Studies of children and adolescents tell us about the *processes of moral development*; studies of adults can tell us about three things: (i) later stages in progress towards moral complexity; (ii) 'normal'; adult moral functioning; (iii) 'exceptional' and unusual 'moral maturity' or 'wisdom'.

Ways of Thinking about Moral Development

Philosophers distinguish different ways of thinking about morality. Frankena (1973) makes a useful distinction between *deontic* theories, and *aretaic* theories. Deontic theories focus on *judgements of moral obligation*—what we ought to do? how shall we judge what is right? what rules do we need? on what principles should we govern our lives, or evaluate a particular course of action? Aretaic theories focus on *moral value*—the moral worth of persons, traits, motives and deeds, virtues and human qualities.

The two types of moral theory have very different implications for psychologists. Exploring deontic aspects of morality focuses on moral reasoning, judgement and principles. The aretaic approach looks at moral traits and dispositions. Psychologists are directed less often by explicit philosophical positions and more by their preferred psychological tradition, but it is obvious that social learning theory is essentially an aretaic model, whereas cognitive-developmental theory is essentially deontic.

- Different theoretical positions in psychology deem different *aspects* of morality to be important, and researchable.
- They differ in *methods* for studying moral development.
- They differ in the questions they ask about the *processes of development*.
- They differ about the *antecedents* of development—what variables should be investigated, and what assumptions can be made about the effects of these variables.
- They differ in how they conceptualise *life-span development*.

This chapter concentrates mainly on theoretical positions of current significance in research on moral development. All the major theories of psychology have had something to say about moral development, but some are of more historical interest, so they will be dealt with more briefly.

Historical Perspectives

Psychoanalytic theory

Classic Freudian theory located moral development within the framework of tensions between the Ego and the Id. The Superego, comprising the Ego-Ideal and guilt, emerges as a consequence of resolving the Oedipal conflict; the child internalises the parent (to become the Ego-Ideal) and redirected Id energy forms the source of guilt (Freud, 1923/1961).

- This theory focuses on the *aspects* of the Ego's management of conflict with the Superego, external pressures and internal defences.
- The *methods* of study are largely clinical observation of individual conflict and its resolution.
- The *process of development* are primarily the establishment of the Ego and the Superego.

- The significant *antecedents* are parental management of the child's conflicts, and the early parent–child relationship.
- *The life-span model* conceived of development in terms of a series of phases, each of which has key tasks; if the individual fails to negotiate these tasks successfully, it leaves a residue of trauma which interferes with later phases.

Social learning theory

According to social learning theory the individual is socialised largely through reward and punishment, but this includes self-socialisation through modelling, imitation of, and identification with, others.

- The main *aspects* are conditioned behaviour and the motivations which sustain habits. Later theorists included conditioning of cognitive processes and self-monitoring (Mischel & Mischel, 1976; Bandura, 1991). Some theorists (e.g. Eysenck, 1976) argue that guilt is established through classical conditioning.
- The *methods* of investigation are primarily experimental manipulations of reinforcement or the contingencies under which modelling took place.
- The *processes of development* are contingencies of learning and the shaping of behaviour.
- The *antecedents* are the context in which these take place.
- The *life-span* model is cumulative; later experience elaborates or builds upon earlier experience. In principle, inappropriate early learning can be replaced through effective reconditioning.

Cognitive developmental theory—Piaget

- The *aspect* on which this approach focuses is transformation in the complexity of moral reasoning.
- The *method* is the verbal resolution of moral dilemmas, or children's accounts of rules. In his classic study of 1932, Piaget investigated three areas, the rules of the game of marbles, how an actor's intentions were seen to affect their blameworthiness, and the concept of justice, both distributive (fair shares) and retributive (justifications for punishment).
- The *processes of development* are the transformation of understanding into increasingly complex structures, from heteronomy to autonomy. *Heteronomous morality* or moral realism is characterised by the child's unilateral respect for adults and the inability to consider intentions in evaluating a moral transgression. As children develop new logical capacities as a consequence of new forms of cooperation in peer integration, they move into the *autonomous or reciprocal* stage. Now the intentions of the actor enter into the child's evaluations. Moral rules are not simply

accepted unquestionably and morality is based on principles of mutual respect amongst equals.

- The transition between moral stages is a slow process determined mainly by two *antecedents*. The first is the opportunity for interaction among peers, through which the child comes to understand reciprocity in moral behaviour. Increased social interaction also stimulates cognitive disequilibrium which facilitates progress to the next, more adequate, level of moral reasoning. Because of his subsequent influence on a strongly rationalist position, we tend to ignore the social dimensions of Piaget's work on moral judgement (Modgil & Modgil, 1982). Piaget saw morality as rooted in social processes; mutual respect, which he considered to be the basis of reciprocity and moral obligation, is the consequence of social relations rather than the consequence of rational law.

- There were no *life-span implications* of Piaget's original study as his oldest respondents were only 12, but subsequent work in the same tradition by Lawrence Kohlberg extends the theory across the life-span.

Current Perspectives

Post-Freudian approaches

Classic Freudian theory, though rich in its discussion of morality, is rather peripheral to our present concerns. However, one development of traditional psychoanalysis is still salient; the extended life-span model of Erik Erikson, which focuses on ego development rather than the conflicts of the Id and the Superego.

- The *aspects* of development under consideration are ego-strength and the ability to deal with affect, and to integrate cognitive and affective needs.

- The *methods* of investigation tend to be explorations of the individual's self-concept through interviews or open-ended questions, which reveal dominant concerns and strategies for conflict resolution, both within the self and with others.

- The developmental *processes* in question are the mechanisms by which the individual negotiates the life-phase or task successfully, which depend both on the *antecedents* of parent–child interactions and on cultural context.

- The *life-span model* is of phases with specific 'tasks'. Erikson (1963) differentiated eight phases. The Self is constructed through different kinds of tension at each phase—trust v. mistrust, autonomy v. shame and doubt, initiative v. guilt, industry v. inferiority, identity v. identity diffusion, intimacy v. isolation, generativity v. stagnation, and ego integrity v. despair. Morality is closely integrated with selfhood and the capacity to relate to others while sustaining fulfilment of the self, and culminates in 'wisdom' as the successful resolution of the final phase.

Cognitive developmental theory

This is most closely associated with Kohlberg's elaboration of some of Piaget's concerns with the development of concepts of justice.

- Cognitive developmental moral theory focuses on the *aspect* of moral reasoning.
- The *methods* assess complexity of moral reasoning and understanding, through the respondent's resolution and justification of either hypothetical or real-life moral dilemmas.
- The development *processes* under consideration are how concepts are structured in stages, and how disequilibrium is created in those structures, which promotes elaboration into more complex structures—the next stage of development.
- The *antecedents* of development are the conditions which facilitate such disequilibrium, including the general social and educational context, and specific situations or events.
- The *life-span* implication is that development continues throughout life, but at a different pace for different people.

Development of prosocial behaviour

This domain of research is characterised by a set of issues rather than a 'core theory'. The key research question is how people come to be helpful and altruistic. The theoretical assumptions are that empathy develops during the early years out of family interaction. Its form changes with age. Altruism is not dependent solely on affect.

- The *aspects* under consideration are affect (empathy), role and perspective-taking, cognitive understanding of consequences, and moral reasoning.
- The *methods* of investigation are observation of behaviour and affective responses, and eliciting the individual's understanding and reasoning skills.
- The *processes of development* are diverse, involving both the growth of empathic affect, the development of cognitive skills, and the interactions between these.
- The *antecedents* of development include interactions that foster affective development, and conditions that facilitate the acquisition of the cognitive skills.
- The *life-span* implications are that what is established in childhood and adolescence may be enriched in later life by experiences that elicit empathic distress.

Cultural and social approaches

These have emerged in recent years with the increasing appreciation of the significance of language and cultural context in human development. Developmental processes are located in the growing individual's interactions with the social and cultural world; children's understanding comes through negotiating meaning with adults and peers, using language, or initially, through actions which communicate meaning (Rogoff, 1990; Rogoff, Mistry, Göncü & Mosier, 1993). 'Moral development' is the increasing ability to use and understand cultural rules, cultural expectations and particularly cultural meanings (Tappan & Packer, 1991).

- The *aspects* that are in focus are therefore not only what the child understands and enacts, but how that reflects the cultural norms and expectations—expressed through language, in the forms of direct descriptions, narratives and accounts.
- The implication for *methods* therefore is that the investigator must observe naturalistic interactions and interpret their meaning, as well as eliciting accounts of behaviours and values from individuals.
- The developmental *processes* are rooted in social interactions and in the child's skills in negotiating meaning with others.
- The *antecedents* of development are the social context and how it facilitates these processes, and also in cultural values—what is deemed important, and how it is symbolised in everyday life.
- The *life-span* implications are that the individual becomes skilful in living within the cultural context, and interpreting the requirements of the culture.

To Summarise the Picture So Far

Historically, the key questions of moral development research have included:

1. How do conscience and guilt develop, acting as sanctions on our misdemeanours?
2. How do we come to understand the basis of rules and moral principles, so that we can make judgements about our own and others' behaviour?
3. How do we learn the appropriate patterns of behaviour required by our culture?
4. How do we develop the moral emotions that motivate our concern for others?

In the present research climate

1. The first of these questions has largely been sidelined, though there are some signs that it is re-emerging in studies of compliance and internalisation in very young children (e.g. Kochanska, 1994; Kochanska, Aksan & Koenig, 1995).
2. The second question has dominated research on moral development for

three decades, through work within the cognitive developmental theoretical framework. This originally focused on progression through stages of development, but has shifted to looking more at how people reason in different domains.

3. The third question used to be in the domain of social learning theory but is now addressed in cultural psychological approaches which look at language and social interaction, and at how the growing individual makes sense of cultural expectations and becomes a competent member of the culture.

4. The fourth question is incorporated in work on the development of prosocial morality, and on the development of social responsibility.

METHODS

The research questions laid out above require different methodological approaches.

Moral Reasoning

Eliciting reasoning

Formal 'production' methods. Hypothetical dilemmas are presented to respondents, usually in interviews but occasionally in written form, using probes and questions to push the respondent to the limits of his or her reasoning abilities (see Box 7.2). The task of the respondent is to resolve the dilemma, in doing so making explicit the reasoning behind the solution. The advantage of this technique is that it is both a depth measure and it is standardised; the disadvantage may be that the moral dilemma is too removed from the individual's own experience.

Informal methods. Observation of naturalistic moral reasoning, either in natural social situations such as the playground or family, or through interviews which discuss real-life moral experiences of the respondent. Such informal methods may be used either to identify the *level* of moral reasoning, for example, the moral stage according to Kohlberg's formulation, or to classify the content or *type* of reasoning.

Response methods

Several questionnaire measures of moral reasoning developmental level have been devised, especially based on Kohlberg's stage theory. Respondents match their own position to statements which reflect different moral stages. The advantage of these measures is their standardisation, and their reliability. Also, there is now a considerable body of research using these measures from many different samples. The disadvantage is that they do not measure the *production* of reasoning, but *response* to statements at different levels of complexity. While these correlate satisfactorily with production of moral reasoning, they are not as accurate a measure of individual moral stage (Rest, 1979; Gibbs, Basinger & Fuller, 1992; Lind, 1995; Lind, Hartman & Wakenhut, 1985).

Scoring and interpretation

Response methods yield a standardised score on the basis of the scales, which can be treated as quantitative data. Production measures of moral reasoning are scored by reference to the standard interpretive manual (Colby & Kohlberg, 1987). The Moral Judgement Interview is scored by assigning stage ratings either by directly matching interview responses, or through interpreting material in the light of specific criteria.

Cultural Approaches

Cross-cultural studies

Studies of cross-cultural variation in moral development using Kohlberg's measures revealed different levels of moral reasoning in different cultures. This led to researchers looking carefully not only at the moral stage but at the *kind of reasoning, the dominant themes*, that people in different cultures bring to moral discourse even within a formal measure of moral reasoning.

The generation of moral discourse

How moral discourse is negotiated and managed between adults and children, and amongst children, is studied by looking at naturalistic conversations, to see how moral concepts and moral understanding are developed through interaction and through language and symbolic behaviour (Rogoff et al., 1993).

Prosocial Development

This is studied by observation of interaction, ratings of traits, measures of social cognitive skills, and interviews about cognitions and motivations.

Observation of interaction

This is particularly applicable to very small children's sharing or empathic behaviour, whether naturalistically occurring or in an intervention condition.

Ratings of traits

This may be done either by observers or through self-ratings. Some studies, for example, use peer ratings on a range of traits, behaviours or dispositions to select particularly empathic or socially responsible people for study.

Measures of social cognitive skills

These include observers' ratings of individuals, interview measures which assess role-taking and perspective-taking skills, propensity for empathy, and standardised rating scales.

Interviews

These are particularly useful in finding out how people construct a personal identity which is invested in social responsibility or prosocial behaviour. They are also useful in eliciting the nature and extent to which individuals feel personal responsibility to act.

Life-span Methods

Life-span research does not look only at what is present, but also at what is past. In *longitudinal* studies, the same measure is used repeatedly over time, and changes can be observed. In *retrospective* studies, people give accounts of past events or circumstances which they see as significant. Such retrospective accounts are not regarded by researchers as necessarily accurate or wholly objective descriptions of past events; they reflect the individual's *present* perspective on the relationship between their current constellation of moral beliefs, values and motives, and *salient* past experiences.

THEORY AND RESEARCH OVERVIEWS

Cognitive Developmental Theory

Kohlberg

Kohlberg's theory has dominated research in the field of moral reasoning development for 30 years. It focuses on the development of cognitive processes, especially reasoning about obligation, rights and justice. Each successive stage of development reflects more conceptually complex and adequate understanding of social arrangements and increasingly balanced resolutions of conflicts of interest. Kohlberg's scheme is a highly elaborated theory of cognitive developmental transformations, and at the same time is a particular theory of morality, based on justice reasoning. Kohlberg explicitly created a bridge between philosophical and psychological issues (Kohlberg, 1971).

Kohlberg's *method* was to present hypothetical moral dilemmas to his respondents. Their resolutions of the dilemmas, and their justifications, were seen as reflecting their moral cognitive structures. His original study, which formed the basis for his doctorate, involved 72 Chicago boys aged 10–16, and 58 of these boys were followed up at 3-year intervals for 20 years (Kohlberg, 1958, 1984; Colby & Kohlberg, 1987).

Stages of moral reasoning

These studies revealed a developmental sequence of moral reasoning (see Box 7.1). This stage model is held to have the same structural characteristics as Piaget's scheme of *cognitive* development. This scheme is discussed by Demetriou (ch. 5 this volume). Briefly, the main postulates of Piaget's stage theory are:

1. The stages are *invariant*, occurring in all individuals in the same order and with no stage omitted. The rate of progression from one stage to another depends on environmental conditions; not all persons will reach the final stage of development.
2. Stages are '*structural wholes*' with underlying organisation of thought; they are qualitatively, not merely quantitatively, different, involving changes of kind in understanding and in the ability to resolve moral problems.
3. Stages form a *developmental hierarchy of increasing differentiation* in which each stage integrates and transforms the preceding stages.
4. Stages are held to be *culturally universal*, they are not substantially affected by cultural variations or gender differences, though societies may vary in the extent to which they facilitate the speed of development or the attainment of higher stages.

The six stages of moral judgement are distributed across three levels. However, stage 6 disappeared as an empirical position, as none of the longitudinal subjects attained it, though it has been found in a small number of individuals in other studies (see Boxes 7.1–7.3).

The longitudinal study

Longitudinal studies are expensive, both in human resources and in money. Respondents drop out, theories change, and methods suffer mortal critiques. Amendments in midstream create problems of comparability and reliability with earlier data. The Kohlberg longitudinal study survived well; the data were collected regularly, and earlier material was recoded in order to incorporate further developments of the theory. The dataset, now housed in the Henry Murray Centre, at Radcliffe College, is extraordinarily rich, with far more in it than the nine moral dilemmas. The later interviews

Box 7.1   The moral stages: and associated levels of perspective taking

Level I. *Pre-conventional*
Stage 1. Heteronomous Morality, Obedience and Punishment
Orientation to punishment and obedience for its own sake. The *social perspective* of this stage is naïve moral realism and absolute egocentricism. 'The right' is avoidance of rule breaking, and fear of punishment as the main motive of doing right. Intrinsic motivation, such as intention, is absent, and what makes it something right or wrong is dictated by authority figures.

Stage 2. Individualism, Instrumental Purpose and Exchange
Focus is on immediate personal interests; the *social perspective* is concrete and individualistic—the self and the immediate other. What is right is closely connected to rules, in so far as they serve the personal needs of the actor or the acknowledged interest of others. This leads to maximising the realisation of personal needs and desires and minimising the negative consequences for the self. Others are recognised as having the same rights to serve personal needs, so conflicts are resolved by instrumental exchange and coordination of actions for mutual benefit.

Level II. *Conventional*
Stage 3. Meeting Interpersonal Expectations, Interpersonal Conformity
Stage 3 includes a third person, community perspective, and emphasises mutually trusting relationships between people. There is awareness of shared feelings, recognition of other's point of view and particular concern with maintaining interpersonal trust and social approval. Right and good behaviour are conceptualised in relation to the expectations of people with whom one lives and with the more general stereotyped expectations connected to one's role as a husband, wife, citizen, etc.

Stage 4. Social System and Conscience
The fulfilment of duties, the need to maintain social order and the welfare of society, group or institution, constitute the main motives of reasoning and behaviour. Individuals take the perspective of a generalised member of society, the social system is a set of codes and procedures that apply impartially to all members. Therefore laws must be upheld except in extreme circumstances where they conflict with other fixed social duties. Moral judgements are made with reference either to legal systems, or to social institutions.

Level III. *Post-Conventional*
Stage 5. Social Contracts and Individuals Rights
Stage 5 'prior-to-society' perspective is that of a rational moral agent, aware of fundamental values and rights, who enters freely into the social contract. The social system and laws are evaluated in terms of how far they protect non-relative values and rights such as life and liberty. If laws or rules do not serve democratic or social utility

ends—the greatest welfare for the greatest number—they should be changed by democratic process. This 'society creating' rather than 'society maintaining' perspective transcends the social system perspective of stage 4, extending the protection of rights to minority members.

Stage 6. Universal Ethical Principles

The basis of moral decision-making is self-chosen, but universal, ethical principles such as justice, the equality of human rights and respect for the dignity of human beings as persons. Laws or social agreements are valid to the extent that they rest on such principles; if there is a conflict one acts in accordance with the principle. The perspective is that of any rational individual recognising the fact that persons are ends in themselves and must be treated as such; this precedes consideration of particular social arrangements.

Box 7.2   The Heinz dilemma and its resolutions at different stages

In a country in Europe a woman was near death from a kind of cancer. But there was one medicine that the doctor thought might save her. It was a radium medicine that had been developed by a chemist in a nearby town. The medicine was expensive to make, but the chemist was charging ten times what it had cost him. He paid $200 for the ingredients but he was charging $2000 for a small dose of the medicine. The sick woman's husband, Heinz, went to everyone he knew to try to borrow the money, but he could only raise $1000, half of the cost. So he went to the chemist and asked him if he could have the medicine cheaper, or pay later. But the chemist said 'No, I discovered the medicine, and I'm going to make money from it'. So Heinz got desperate and thought of breaking into the chemist's laboratory to steal the medicine for his wife.

Probe questions ask whether he should steal or not, what his obligations are, whether he should steal for a friend or stranger, whether the chemist has the right to charge so much, and whether one should obey the law. All answers are probed for justifications, which reveal the level of moral understanding.

On the surface this is a story about theft to save a life—the conflict of life versus law—but there are also other elements; the rights of inventors of life-supporting commodities, the obligations of the marital role, the prospect of punishment, the provision of law.

Stage 1: reflects an unquestioned belief that the law determines the rightness or wrongness of action, and no recognition of conflict. If Heinz stole the drug he would be a thief, because 'you are not supposed to steal'. Justification for stealing might be based on irrelevant extrinsic reasons such as 'you should steal to save a woman's life, if she is a rich person with lots of possessions'.

Stage 2: recognises the possibility that individual needs and interests might clash with established rules and codes of behaviour. The resolution of the conflict is instrumental—if Heinz steals the drug, he will probably be caught and imprisoned; if he does not steal, his wife will die and he will be deprived of her daily support, so he should steal and hope to get away with it.

Stage 3: wavers between normative role expectations—a good husband provides every possible help to his wife—and the provisions of the law—a good citizen should obey the law. This uncertainty recognises various perspectives in the situation: the husband's, the wife's, the law enforcer's and the wider community. Stealing may set a bad example to the community.

Stage 4: abstract understanding of 'society'. Stealing is against the law and its consequences may set a precedent which could undermine the legal system, affecting not only the individual directly involved, but the wider society as well. However, stage 4 pro-stealing arguments may be justified by marriage placing obligations on the partners for mutual support, or alternatively, because the preservation of life is of greater importance to society than the legal constraints against stealing.

Stage 5: awareness that rules vary from one society to another. The criteria are broad moral principles rather than culturally specific rules: in conflicts between the legal and the moral, the moral should always be chosen, because the law is supposed to serve moral principles. The legal system is supported on the condition that it is a product of a democratic social contract and on the principle that it represents the greatest good for the greatest number. Laws not meeting this criteria should be changed, not defied, though it is recognised that public objections to a bad law may call attention to its inadequacies. So Heinz is justified to steal the drug because the right to life transcends the right to property. The justification for not stealing is that maintaining the social contract is of greater benefit to society, and so more important than individual cases.

covered many areas of personal life and social values (see Hart, 1992). It is also of historical interest; the boys studied in 1956 are the cohort of young men who were later drafted to Vietnam, and who lived through the political upheavals of the seventies.

The primary purpose of the longitudinal study was to establish the developmental sequences of stages that Kohlberg had postulated from his cross-sectional study (Colby & Kohlberg, 1987; Colby, Kohlberg, Gibbs & Lieberman, 1983). It showed that stage 3 is a normal mode of reasoning amongst young US male adults, and that stage 4 surpassed Stage 3 reasoning only at age 24. The future trajectories implied by the pattern of reasoning at age 30–36 suggest increasing stage 4 and (minimally) stage 5, and diminishing stage 3 (see Box 7.3). 'Development' does not stop at adulthood.

The study unequivocally showed that stage 6 must be regarded more as an

Box 7.3   Distribution of stages of moral reasoning, Kohlberg's longitudinal study

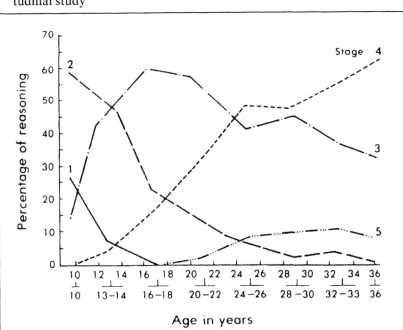

Figure B7.3   Mean percentage of moral reasoning at each stage for each age group
Reproduced with permission from Colby, A. & Kohlberg, L. (1987). *The Measurement of Moral Judgement*, Vol. 1. New York: Cambridge University Press.

abstraction than an empirical phenomenon—but with enormous theoretical significance for the assumptions underpinning the theory of moral reasoning (Kohlberg, Boyd & Levine, 1990). There have been a number of other longitudinal studies which confirm the overall developmental pattern, in Turkey (Nisan & Kohlberg, 1982), in Israel (Snarey, Reimer & Kohlberg, 1985) and in Iceland (Keller & Edelstein, 1993).

Processes of development

Intervention studies of the conditions that facilitate the transition between stages have been done primarily with adolescents, firstly by systematically confronting people with arguments from a higher stage of reasoning than their own (the Socratic method) and, secondly, through participation in a

Box 7.4   What promotes moral development? Case studies of moral transition

Case studies provide insights into stage transition. When the longitudinal cohort entered late adolescence, they appeared to regress from stage 4 reasoning to stage 2 moral relativism, in which no value system was seen to be more valid than any other. This was a consequence of their appreciating possibilities of a wider range of values, as they first became able to step outside the perspective of their own society, which challenged the certainties inherent in stage 4. The 'resolution' of this relativism comes with fully rounded appreciation of the stage 5 prior-to-society perspective (Kohlberg & Higgins, 1984). Case 2, for example, found that his college experience confirmed his view that it was a 'dog-eat-dog world', so he had to put himself first, in order to become successful and survive in that world. He later moved to stage 5 reasoning following a period in which he married, had children, and worked in a 'successful' job that bored him—a period that gave him a sense of responsibility and an appreciation that it was not just getting ahead that mattered, but enjoying what one was doing.

   The Vietnam War provoked moral challenges for many of these young men. Case 23's transitions were closely linked to his political engagements. He came from a deeply conservative, militaristic background. School and college courses prompted a shift to more liberal views, and he was further radicalised by a year at the London School of Economics at the peak of student unrest. On his return, he refused to serve in the army and instead taught in the inner city. These personal changes were reflected in changes in moral stage score (Kohlberg & Higgins, 1984, Weinreich-Haste, 1984; Haste, 1990).

   Lempert (1994) studied German skilled manual workers longitudinally between 23 and 30 years of age. These young men's moral reasoning progressed as a consequence both of occupational and of personal experiences, such as manifest conflicts and involvement in decision-making. Transition from pre-conventional to conventional reasoning depended on the experience of empathy, love and recognition, along with information about the social consequences of behaviour. Movement into post-conventional reasoning required coping with contradictory explanations, rules and values, and taking responsibility for oneself and others.

group which makes moral rules and decisions that have practical consciences for the group (the Just Community approach). Both these methods stimulate questioning of one's own reasoning, and have been shown to promote moral development.

   How much do such experimental studies tell us about 'natural' progression? The longitudinal studies suggest progression of half a stage (for example from 2 to 2/3) over three years during adolescence. But adolescents are intensively exposed to education, and the longitudinal study suggests that once education is complete, stage consolidation takes place.

Further developments in moral reasoning research

There are two strands of theory development; *elaborations* and *diversifications* which initially extend, but eventually go beyond, the theory, and *critiques* which challenge some basic assumptions of the theory, and lead to modifications. In both these strands moral reasoning remains the central concept of moral development. However, the emphasis on moral stage has been replaced by an emphasis on diversity within moral reasoning. Further, there has been a shift away from a narrow focus on internal individual processes that treats social factors and experience as mere catalysts, towards a much more socially embedded model, which also looks at interaction and how moral understanding is socially negotiated between persons. The gap between cognitive developmental models and cultural-social models is narrowing.

Elaborations.   Turiel (1983) argued that 'moral' reasoning could be differentiated in two domains, moral and social-conventional. Nucci (1981) identified a third domain, the personal, concerning the effects upon the actor. Moral obligations were those seen to be binding, irrespective of local conditions—so it was always wrong to hurt someone, even if the teacher seemed to permit it, or children in that town thought it was all right. Social conventions were subject to local *mores*. The important finding was that very young children understood the distinction between the moral and social domains.

Critiques.   We will consider two main critiques of Kohlberg's position. Each has contributed both to increased diversification in how we think of moral reasoning, and to the shift towards a more cultural-social perspective.

Gender issues: Gilligan (1982/1993) argued that women focused on different aspects of moral dilemmas from men, and that, in consequence, women's scores on moral reasoning measures were debased. Men focus on justice, which is the dominant theme of Kohlberg's method of measurement, whereas women focus on caring and responsibility. She argued that these different ethics, or 'moral orientations', rest on a deeper issue, how we think about selfhood. An ethic of justice is the natural outcome of thinking of people as *separate* beings, in continual conflict with one another, who make rules and contracts as a way of handling this. An ethic of caring and responsibility follows from conceptualising selves as being *in connection* with one another.

Her assertion that the Kohlberg scoring system was biased against women was refuted by Walker, who demonstrated that, once education was controlled for, studies did not show a systematic sex difference in moral stage scores (Walker, 1984, 1995). The argument that women 'think differ-ently' about moral issues has also been challenged. Several studies find that sex differences in the use of moral orientations are less important than the kind of dilemmas under consideration. Johnston (1988) suggests that each sex is competent in each mode, but that there are gender-linked preferences. She found that boys tended to use the justice orientation, but if pressed, would also use the care orientation. Girls preferred the care orientation but also switched easily.

Pratt, Golding and Hunter, (1984) asked respondents about real-life dilemmas, and found that sex differences lay in the *type* of dilemma; males reported more non-relational dilemmas, and females more relational di-lemmas, and non-relational dilemmas were almost always scored as reflect-ing a rights orientation. Walker, de Vries & Trevethan (1987) found a similar pattern; women were more likely than men to report relationships or personal real-life moral dilemmas, and men more likely to report impersonal dilemmas. Personal dilemmas were more likely to be scored as using the care orientation, and impersonal dilemmas, the rights orientation, but *within* the type of dilemma, there were no sex differences. Others have argued that involvement counts; people who are involved in a situation, whatever their sex, are more likely to use 'connected' reasoning (Nunner-Winkler, 1984; Markoulis, in press).

These findings support Gilligan's argument that there is more than one moral 'voice', but not her claim that the 'caring' voice was more apparent amongst women. It therefore supports the argument that we should diver-sify our conception of morality, challenging the narrow definition that ties it solely to justice reasoning. This also suggests a cultural rather than an individual explanation; both modes of thinking exist within the culture, but the situation determines which one is accessed (Haste & Baddeley, 1991).

Cross-cultural variation: A second critique comes from interpreting cross-cultural variations in moral stage pattern. Amongst Turkish youngsters both from a rural village and from a city, studied over 12 years, scores were lower than amongst Americans, and rural youngsters scored lower than urban (Kohlberg & Nisan, 1987). In contrast, Israeli youngsters educated in kibbutzim scored higher at each age (from 12 to 24) than American young-sters (Snarey, Reimer & Kohlberg, 1985). These findings suggest that cul-tural factors play a significant role in moral reasoning.

Cultural psychologists argue that we should not be looking for universal moral stages, but trying to understand moral diversity. A focus on justice may be very far from some cultures' primary ethical concerns. If the re-searchers try to measure justice reasoning, rather than eliciting people's usual moral framework, stage scores may be misleading, but more impor-tant, the results would fail to give a true picture of people's moral lives. Edwards argues, for example, that South East Asian culture places family loyalty at the centre of their ethical system, and reasoning has to be under-stood in terms of this (Edwards, 1986). Shweder, Mahapatra and Miller (1987) administered the Heinz dilemma to Indian Hindu villagers. They cite a very morally sophisticated reasoner who came to very different conclusions supported by very different arguments, from that expected within Western culture. This respondent was obviously using a high stage of moral reasoning, but it was impossible to score him on the Kohlberg measure because his arguments were too far away from the Western position (Shweder, 1990).

Cultural-Social Approaches to Moral Development

Seeing moral development as a cultural or social process shifts thinking about morality away from a concentration on individual processes that are 'inside the head'. Cognitive developmental models start with the individual and—if they consider social processes at all—perceive the social world, and interaction with others, as moderating or stimulating individual cognitive processes and development. For the cultural-social position, social processes are central. What 'develops' is the individual's skill in managing the moral expectations of one's culture, which are expressed through linguistic and symbolic practices. Drawing on anthropological methods and perspectives, cultural psychologists such as Shweder and Rogoff locate the individual within a social and cultural context.

Cultural psychology is very close to the tradition of Vygotsky, who argued that one cannot isolate the individual from historical and social context (Vygotsky, 1978, Wertsch, 1985). This also contrasts with the assumption behind cognitive developmental models, that psychological processes are universal. The research agenda of cultural psychology is to explore cultural practices in action, and to see how the individual, as an intentional being, becomes expert in cultural skills. This means focusing less on the final product inside people's heads, and more on what goes on in social and linguistic processes, such as *narrative and discourse*, and how these organise the individual's experiences (Tappan & Packer, 1991).

Work on social interaction in children demonstrates the fine processes of cultural development. Children are very skilled in negotiating moral and social conflict at an early age, invoking appropriate justifications. A study of Japanese nursery school children found that most disputes were resolved by compromise and bargaining, in which children were very skilful, and which used moral justifications (such as 'it's his turn') (Killen & Nucci, 1995). Such activities demonstrate the daily involvement of young children in effectively negotiating moral and social justifications that are acceptable in their peer group. Other studies show how parents and teachers convey values not by direct command, but by *implying* that certain outcomes (harm) will come from the child's actions, or that the child has certain rights to autonomy ('you can choose').

The Development of Prosocial Morality

Approaches to prosocial morality—empathy and concern for others—tend to be more electic than studies of moral reasoning, and take more account of

---

Box 7.5   Cultural variations in the rationale underlying moral judgements

---

Example 1:

Shweder and his colleagues compared Indian Hindu respondents (children and adults) with Chicago-based respondents in a number of 'moral' and 'conventional' examples of behaviour—eating, behaviour after the death of a relative, forms of punishment, dealing with menstruation, and sex roles. There were striking cultural differences but also some similarities. Hindus saw certain behaviours as moral and as binding because it is important to avoid pollution, and to seek salvation for oneself and one's relatives. Avoidance of pollution constrains the behaviour of a menstruating woman. The search for salvation governs rituals which seem wholly trivial to American eyes, such as cutting one's hair, eating chicken or fish, after a relative dies. The underlying rationale makes it entirely understandable why Hindus deem these practices a 'great sin'. In contrast, some American children considered sexual inequality to be a moral issue because it contravenes their ideas of justice.

Example 2:

In a study that compared United States and South Indian adults, Miller and Bersoff (1995) explored different moral perspectives on family relationships. They found that Americans saw family life as existing primarily to meet the needs of every individual member, and they resolved dilemmas about conflicting needs on these terms. Indian respondents saw the family unit as having intrinsic value over and above the needs of the individual members, so dilemmas were resolved in terms of the family's overall needs, rather that the individual's needs. Americans valued psychological support and enhancing relationships, whereas Indian respondents valued selflessness and serving the well-being of others.

Example 3:

Comparing reasoning about the Heinz dilemma in United States and Japan, Iwasa (1992) found no difference in level of moral stage, but qualitative differences in why human life was valued, which reflected cultural norms. Americans were concerned to prolong the length of life, Japanese to make it purer and cleaner. Hence, the majority of Americans thought Heinz should steal, whereas the majority of Japanese thought he should not.

---

aretaic aspects such as traits, skills and dispositions, and a reluctance to separate affect and cognition. Bar-Tal and Nissim (1984) argue that 'mature' helping behaviour demands seven skills; being able to consider a variety of alternative acts, being able to predict the outcome of behaviour, understanding the importance of intention, recognising the needs of others, empathy, understanding moral principles, and having self-regulatory skills.

Empathy

Hoffman (1984, 1991) defines empathy as an affective response to others'
distress, which operates in conjunction with cognitive moral principles (such
as caring or justice) to motivate a response. He distinguishes between 'cool
cognitions', arrived at through cognitive processes, and 'hot cognitions'
where empathic affect is involved.

The development of empathic distress goes though four levels:

1. Global empathy, that characterises infancy, where the child responds to
    another's distress as though it were itself suffering.
2. 'Egocentric' empathy in the second year, where the child is aware that it
    is someone else who is suffering, but the child's reaction is to respond to
    that distress in ways that would be helpful for itself—such as giving a
    distressed adult its comfort blanket or teddy.
3. Empathy for another's feelings affects the child's awareness that others'
    feelings may differ from one's own, and therefore that one has to be
    responsive to cues about the other's state—including cues that the other
    may not wish to be helped.
4. Empathy for another's life condition emerges in late childhood; this
    extends distress at the other's immediate situation, to realisation that
    there is a larger problem, such as deprivation or poverty.

A considerable amount of work has been done on the early development
of empathy (Zahn-Waxler, Radke-Yarrow, Wagner & Chapman, 1992).
Eisenberg and her colleagues' studies include naturalistic observations of
children, quasi-experimental studies—for example of opportunities for do-
nating money or candy—and interview studies of reasoning about prosocial
behaviours (Eisenberg, Miller, et al., 1991; Eisenberg, 1995). In a longitudinal study, Eisenberg identified four stages in the development of prosocial
reasoning, but she does not claim that they are an invariant sequence in the
way that Kohlberg's stages are conceptualised as being. These stages are:
*hedonistic, pragmatic, or 'needs of others' orientation; approval, interpersonal
and stereotype orientation; empathic orientation; and strongly internalised
orientation.*

Antecedents of prosocial development

Studies of interactions in childhood demonstrate the mechanisms of prosocial learning, and the cultural context, especially of sharing, and the
negotiation of helping behaviours. Zahn-Waxler et al. (1992) found for
example that parent–child context was important—and not always healthy;
children with depressed mothers were *more* likely than children with well
mothers to show empathic concern and sympathetic intervention to distressed others. Parents use different kinds of discipline practice for different
transgressions, so children learn to decode not only the context, but the
form of the message, and to recognise its significance; Grusec and Goodnow

(1994) note that parents use power assertion *plus* reasoning in response to moral transgressions, but reasoning alone in response to failure to show concern for others.

Children show early skill in decoding situational demands surrounding helping behaviour. Krappmann and Oswald (1991) found that children's helping behaviour in the classroom was governed by how they interpreted the rights of the requester to expect help, and the goals of the requester—whether they were attempting to take advantage of others.

Social responsibility

A number of studies of adolescents who show unusual social responsibility or helping behaviour focus on the qualities of the individual (trait models), the familial and sociocultural antecedents, and moral reasoning and self-image (see also van Lieshout and Doise, ch. 6 this volume). The overall picture is that the socially responsible adolescent is self-sufficient, able to focus attention and plan, has a future orientation, is adaptable, has a cognitive appreciation of personal responsibility and a belief in his or her own efficacy, and is capable of making a moral commitment to an issue. These qualities are fostered by families in which competence is taken for granted, goals are set, and responsibilities assigned, but they are also fostered by communities which give the individual effective responsibility and the chance to acquire community-related skills (Hart & Fegley, 1995; Hamilton & Fenzel, 1988; Csikszentmihalyi, Rathunde & Whalen, 1993).

Studies of adult prosocial behaviour confirm the importance of social context and cultural expectation. Paolicchi (1995) studied a long-established Italian volunteer group that provides help services such as ambulances, organisation of blood donor activities, and support groups for disadvantaged citizens. Paolicchi's interviews revealed that these people saw themselves as not at all 'special', but situated within a social context. Social relationship was a strong motivation, and the usual route into volunteering was through family or friends. Once engaged, they become part of a microculture with shared life experiences which transcend family and other narrow group boundaries.

MATURITY, WISDOM AND EXTRAORDINARY MORAL RESPONSIBILITY

So far we have presented models of development and considered how the child becomes a morally competent adult, using data from children, adolescents and 'normal' adults. The concept of 'moral maturity' has been defined within each theoretical position, However, the concept of 'wisdom' is not entirely synonymous with 'moral maturity'. We will consider how these concepts are used in commonsense terminology, and how 'wisdom' has been considered both theoretically and empirically by recent psychologists.

Box 7.6   Commonsense ideas about wisdom

The prototype of wisdom is King Solomon, with his famous judgement. But people's ordinary ideas of wisdom involve many other aspects besides moral judgement. Sternberg (1986) first asked people what they thought were characteristics of an ideally wise person, and then asked another to rate how characteristic each behaviour would be of an ideally wise person in their field.

Problem-solving skills occupy a prominent place: a wise person 'has the unique ability to look at a problem or situation and solve it' and has 'a logical mind'. But a wise person also has a number of socio-moral qualities such as 'displays concern for others', 'is fair', 'understands people through dealing with a variety of people'. A wise person 'knows self best' as well. Sternberg also gathered ratings for intelligence and creativity and compared the overlap in the meanings of wisdom, intelligence and creativity in general and also in groups of professors in four fields: art, business, philosophy, and physics. In general, wisdom and intelligence were more closely related to one another (median correlation of 0.68) than the other pairs. The lowest correlation was between wisdom and creativity (a median of 0.27). Indeed, amongst business professors, wisdom and creativity showed a *negative* correlation of −0.24. Thus while in most areas of life we tend to believe that wisdom and creativity go together—to some extent at least—in business organization creativity may be experienced as antithetical to wisdom.

Walker, Pitts, Hennig and Matsuba (1995) interviewed Canadians aged 16–84 years, to investigate lay conceptions of morality. They were asked about what constituted the moral domain, to discuss two personally experienced moral dilemmas and to present an example of something that would for them represent a 'prototypical' dilemma. Finally they were asked to think of two people whom they regarded as 'highly moral' and justify their choice. They found that commonsense thinking departs from the constraints imposed by models of justice-related morality; respondents took account of practical outcomes, and real-life dilemmas were primarily associated with personal relationships and issues such as fidelity and loyalty, abortion and substance abuse. Prototypical dilemmas were more likely to include life and death issues and war.

Walker et al. found that people judge 'moral exemplars' in terms of virtues (including emotions) and interpersonal relations, at least in addition to if not instead of rational decision-making skills. The most frequently cited characteristic of moral exemplars was compassionate/caring; this was followed at some distance by consistency, honesty, self-sacrifice, open-mindedness, thoughtful/rational, socially active, just, courageous and virtuous. In considering the conception of the moral domain and moral values, honesty/truth came out strongest, along with compassion/love and respect for others. Also mentioned frequently were integrity, open-mindedness, religion and the Golden Rule (Do unto others as you would have others do unto you).

Research on Wisdom and Moral Maturity

Our emphasis on a definition of 'moral maturity' in terms of Kohlberg's moral stages is in part due to the availability of data within that paradigm. However there is a wealth of other material in which concepts of 'maturity'—not only moral—abound. There are several intriguing theories of 'wisdom' (see, e.g. Sternberg, 1990a,b; Orwoll & Achenbaum, 1993). We will refer to empirical research on four different aspects of wisdom; wisdom as *socio-moral understanding*; wisdom as *integration of affect and cognition*; wisdom as *reasoning ability and special kind of expertise*; and wisdom as *understanding of knowledge, its nature and limits*.

Do Kohlberg's stages represent increase in wisdom? 'Maturity' in Kohlberg's terminology refers to a combination of cognitive complexity—especially social perspective-taking—and the greater moral 'adaptation' of later stages of morality. This claim for moral adaptation rests on the idea that a more 'just' solution takes into account a larger range of persons who will be affected by actions or policy decisions, who are more 'just'.

Are people whose reasoning on the hypothetical dilemmas is scored stage 5 asked more often for advice than people with a stage 3 reasoning score? Do the former find wiser solutions to real-life moral problems than the latter? Ikonen-Varila (1994) gave Kohlberg's dilemmas to Finnish shop stewards and also asked them to report a moral problem that they had encountered in their work; typical conflicts involved the use of alcohol at work or quarrels among workmates. Ikonen-Varila found good consistency between the stage structures used in solving the real workplace conflicts and those used in solving Kohlberg's dilemmas. Male shop stewards with higher moral judgement scores were more often turned to for advice.

Erikson

Erikson's theory of development differs in important ways from Kohlberg's. Because people move through Kohlberg's stages at different rates, there is a spread of moral stages amongst the adult population. In contrast, Erikson's 'stages' are life phases. Reaching 'maturity' means, firstly, recognising the social roles and relationships that are appropriate at different ages, and secondly, successfully negotiating these life phases. 'Maturity' therefore is not *reaching* these life phases, but *living them well*.

Erikson's final stage, ego integrity (v. despair), is closely related to 'wisdom', but it is also about selfhood as being 'whole'. It is explicitly an 'ethical' stage. Erikson saw moral development as interwoven with ego development; childhood is 'moralistic', adolescence is idealistic and ideological, but this leads into more universal 'adult' ethics (Erikson, 1968). For Erikson, *caring* is a crucial element of ethics. But caring means different things at different stages; identity (adolescence) is about 'what you care to do and whom you care to be'; intimacy (youth) is about 'whom you care to be with' and generativity (adulthood) is about 'what and whom you take care of' (Erikson, 1975).

Wisdom as the Integration of Affect and Cognition

Erikson's conception of wisdom is close to our second definition. Unlike Kohlberg's stage model, this does not depend on education or abstraction. Orwoll and Perlmuter (1990) asked respondents aged 20–90 to nominate a 'wise person'. A substantial proportion of the persons nominated by the respondents as wise did not have university education. There are literary precedents—which of course feed into our cultural norms. In *War and Peace*, Tolstoy provides us with his epitome of wisdom in the figure of Plato Karataev, a simple peasant about 60 years old, who personifies a deep understanding of life, purity of heart and inner harmony. Erikson saw wisdom as a virtue that arises from the conflict which all people are confronted with in the final stage of their life—recognising the physical deterioration and impending death, which inspire despair and disgust, but still seeing one's life as having been meaningful and accepting it as it has been.

What about real life? Ryff and Heincke (1983) developed a scale for integrity, measuring acceptance of one's life as something that has been meaningful, feeling that one has solved past conflicts and is emotionally integrated. Orwoll (Orwoll & Perlmutter, 1990) used this scale to compare people who had been nominated as wise by their acquaintances with people who had been nominated as being creative. She found that 'wise' persons scored significantly higher on this measure of integrity than 'creative' persons (but even the latter had higher scores than a sample of 'ordinary' adults).

Wisdom as Expert Knowledge in Life Pragmatics

This emphasises practical dimensions rather than structures of either moral or ego functioning. Suppose a 14 year old who is pregnant turns to you for advice. Or think of Roberta, a 60-year-old widow who has recently opened her own business and started a new life. She then learns that her son has been left with two small children for whom to care.

These are examples of what Baltes and his associates (e.g. Baltes & Smith, 1990) call *pragmatics of life* tasks, decisions involving important but uncertain issues. The problems are partly moral, but also a lot of practical knowledge is called for. Baltes and his co-workers present their respondents with such problems and ask them to think aloud. The protocols are then analysed in terms of five criteria of wisdom:

1. Rich factual knowledge.
2. Rich procedural knowledge.
3. Life-span contextualism; understanding that people in different life

phases may have different priorities.
4. Relativism: being aware that people coming from different social or
    cultural backgrounds will have a variety of interpretations.
5. Recognising uncertainty and having strategies for dealing with it.

In one study, using life planning problems of the type described above, responses were valued in terms of the five criteria of wisdom. Only some 5% of them came near to satisfying all criteria. Young adults got their poorest performance rating for Roberta's type of problem. By contrast, the oldest subjects performed best precisely on this type of problem.

Kitchener (1986) studied the *uncertainty aspects of wisdom*: what can be known, how can we know something, how certain can we be in our knowing? Kitchener and her associates assume that this develops through seven stages, from naïve conceptions of absolute and certain knowledge (stage 1) through recognition of the contextual and subjective nature of knowing (stage 5) to the mature constructionalist view of knowledge in stage 7. Kitchener and Brenner (1990) report that stage 7 is rare before the age of 30 even in highly educated samples. The roles of education and life experience in the attainment of a wise stage 6 or 7 conception of knowledge is illustrated by the study of Pirttila-Backman (1993) who compared students with samples of employed people from the same field and educational level who had been working for ten years and were in their mid-30s. The groups with more education scored higher on the measure of conception of knowledge, but the role of experience was clearly demonstrated; the 35 year old scored higher than the students in their 20s.

These findings are in line with models of cognitive development which postulate that there are important changes in cognition throughout life (see Demetriou, ch. 1 this volume).

Extraordinary Moral Responsibility

Sustained extraordinary moral responsibility—moral vision and commitment—over the life-span begs several kinds of questions (Haste, 1990). First, there is the question about consistency: what is the *whole* picture of these people? Is their activity isolated from the rest of their selfhood, or is it an integral part? The second question concerns their actual characteristics; what are the qualities, or values, that seem to be essential for facilitating their commitment? Third, what creates this? Where have they come from, and what were the significant shaping forces in their upbringing, the facilitating environmental contexts, or the triggering events in their lives, that have pushed them to where they are? The answers to these questions are interesting not only because they tell us about the exceptional, but because a lifetime of commitment may hold clues for lifetimes less outstanding.

Research on people who behave in morally exemplary ways over a long period of time indicates certain key characteristics. In a seminal study of 'moral exemplars', Colby and Damon (1992) interviewed Americans who had been 'nominated' by a panel of people drawn from a number of professional fields associated with morality. The 'nominators' generated five criteria for moral exemplars, and they suggested named persons whom they felt met those criteria:

1. A sustained commitment to moral ideals including generalised respect for humanity, or sustained moral virtue.
2. Disposition to consistency between actions, intentions, means and ends.
3. Willingness to risk self-interest for the sake of values.
4. Tendency to inspire others to moral action.
5. Realistic humility.

From the 84 people 'nominated' 23 were eventually chosen for interview by Colby and Damon. The moral exemplars were diverse in political and religious beliefs, and in their activities. They were mostly middle-aged or older.

Both the authors (and a number of the nominators) came originally from a cognitive-developmental approach to moral judgement. Moral judgement stage as a predictor of moral commitment was tested by this study; the MJI was administered to the exemplars. However, although they did manifest a spread across the higher stages of reasoning, only half scored at the 'post-conventional' level.

Colby and Damon's exemplars had courage and a willingness to suffer personal risk and deprivation, including deprivation for their families. Furthermore, these people did not engage in careful deliberation about either the rightness of their actions or the possible personal consequences; they were sure and certain; they did not usually experience their moral actions as a matter of choice, they had instead *feelings of moral necessity*, a sense that one could do nothing else. Along with this certainty goes a commitment to honesty, justice, charity, harmony and—for many but not all—religious faith.

The development of the exemplars was marked by stability, but also by flexibility and adaptability, throughout life. Even in their 80s, they were still open to new ideas and challenges. While remaining true to their underlying values, they made quite dramatic changes in how these values were expressed, in different concerns. Colby and Damon stress the importance of social interaction and social influences. This worked in several ways; the exemplars were receptive to the ideas of others, and drew on them for social support. But sometimes resistance to pressures from others could be a catalyst in transforming and developing their convictions.

We will consider two other studies of 'extraordinary moral responsibility' both dealing with 'Rescuers'—Gentiles who rescued Jews from the Nazis. Here there was no ambiguity about danger; to be caught would have meant certain imprisonment and possible death.

A study by Oliner and Oliner (1988) used psychometric measures of the personal characteristics (traits and beliefs) of Rescuers, and their childhood antecedents. These people shared a sense of having control over their lives, strong attachment to others and a feeling of responsibility for them, empathy for others' pain, a willingness to see people as more similar than different, and to befriend people on the basis of personal qualities rather than social group membership. They reported a childhood of family closeness.

In a recent study of Rescuers, Fogelman (1994) analysed interviews with over 300 Rescuers. The 'Rescuer Self' is seen to be part of the individual's larger personal identity, a part evoked by the extreme conditions of war, but not defined only by those conditions. She discovered a range of different motives that seemed to fuel Rescuers. She divided these into four 'profiles'. Those *driven by conscience* most particularly manifested the feeling that they 'had no choice'; when faced with a request for help, they felt that it was the only thing to do. They tended to continue with humanitarian activities after the war. A second category she called '*Judeophiles*', people who had a special sympathy for Jews. Most began by sheltering Jews whom they knew, but extended this to others. In the longer term, they tended to become more identified with Judaism, converting, marrying Jews or emigrating to Israel.

For a third group, rescuing Jews was part of a larger concern to fight oppression; the *network rescuers* were part of cohesive resistance groups. After the War they tended to continue to be active in protest movements; their 'rescuer self' was part of a political self. Fourthly, Fogelman identified '*professionals*'—doctors, social workers, diplomats. For most, this was a seamless part of their professional selves, even though that role sometimes led to conflicts.

The childhood antecedents of the Rescuer Self were varied, but there were commonalities; a nurturing, loving home and the role model of an altruistic parent or caretaker; methods of upbringing which emphasised independence, tolerance of people who are different, and explanation rather than reprisal. A surprisingly frequent element was childhood illness or personal loss which tested resilience and also gave the child the experience of special care.

Studies of extraordinary people tell us about the importance of certain developments in life-span development which apply to all moral development; the role of social interaction and social support, the effects of childhood experience in laying the foundation of values and virtues, the importance of significant life events in facilitating change and re-evaluation. These patterns tell us much of the complexity of lifelong moral development, and point to possible research.

CONCLUDING COMMENTS AND REFLECTIONS ON FUTURE DIRECTIONS

This chapter has concentrated on areas of research on moral development that currently flourish. As in other domains of psychology over the last few decades, cognitive approaches which emphasise active reasoning and reflection superseded models that focused on behaviour. These cognitive models are themselves now being challenged today from a number of sources: efforts to bring emotion more centre-stage; the increasing interest in language and cultural and social processes in the construction of meaning; and thirdly, the emergence of evolutionary psychology which seeks explanations of our present functioning in terms of evolutionary processes of adaptation.

Each of these major developments in psychology is beginning to tackle aspects of moral development, and it will be interesting to review their progress over the next decade, and their effect on how psychologists conceptualise 'morality'. Greater attention to affect may lead us to explore more intensively the 'moral emotions' that are inherent in the existing work on prosocial behaviour, or it may take us again into the presently neglected realm of conscience and guilt (e.g. Kochanska, 1994). The burgeoning work on discourse and social construction takes us away from a concentration on internal reflection and reasoning, towards seeing concepts as the outcome of social processes and the social negotiation of meaning (Tappan & Packer, 1991; Harré & Gillett, 1994; Davidson & Youniss, 1995). Much has already been written within an evolutionary psychology framework about altruism and its adaptive functions (Alexander, 1987; Barkow, Cosmides & Tooby, 1992; Ridley, 1996). This also shifts the focus of attention away from individual cognition and towards adaptive, social mechanisms.

More immediately for the concern of this present volume, taking a life-span perspective on moral development requires us, as we have seen, to pay greater attention to the role of both 'normal' and 'anomalous' life events and crises in the formation and reformation of moral schemas and emotions and their integration into selfhood over eight decades of life, not just the first two. This perspective has also required us to question and elucidate some key concepts: what are the endstates of 'moral development', and to what extent and under what conditions, is 'moral maturity' the same as 'wisdom'?

REFERENCES

Alexander, R. D. (1987). *The Biology of Moral Systems*. Hawthorne, NY: Aldine.

Baltes, P. B. & Smith, J. (1990). Towards a psychology of wisdom and its ontogenesis. In R. J. Sternberg (Ed.), *Wisdom: Its Nature, Origins and Development* (pp. 87–120). Cambridge: Cambridge University Press.

Bandura, A. (1991). Social cognitive theory of moral thought and action. In W. M. Kurtines & J. Gewirtz (Eds), *Handbook of Moral Behaviour and Development*, Vol. 1: *Theory* (p. 45–104). Hillsdale, NJ: Erlbaum.

Barkow, J. H., Cosmides, L. & Tooby, J. (1992). *The Adapted Mind: Evolutionary Psychology and the Generation of Culture*. Oxford: Oxford University Press.

Bar-Tal, D. & Nissim, R. (1984). Helping behaviour and moral judgement among adolescents. *British Journal of Developmental Psychology*, **2**(4), 329–336.

Colby, A. & Damon, W. (1992). *Some Do Care: Contemporary Lives of Moral Commitment.* New York: Free Press.

Colby, A. & Kohlberg, L. (1987). *The Measurement of Moral Judgement.* New York: Cambridge University Press.

Colby, A., Kohlberg, L., Gibbs, J. & Lieberman, M. (1983). A longitudinal study of moral judgement. *Monographs of the Society for Research in Child Development*, **48**, 1–124.

Csikszentmihalyi, M., Rathunde, K. & Whalen, S. (1993). *Talented Teenagers.* Cambridge: Cambridge University Press.

Davidson, P. & Youniss, J. (1995). Moral development and social construction. In W. M. Kurtines & J. Gewirtz (Eds), *Moral Development: An Introduction* (pp 289–310). Needham Heights, MA: Allyn & Bacon.

Edwards, C. P. (1986). Cross-cultural research on Kohlberg's stages: The basis for consensus. In S. Modgil & C. Modgil (Eds), *Kohlberg: Consensus and Controversy* (pp. 419–430). Lewes: Falmer Press.

Eisenberg, N. (1995). Prosocial development: A multifaceted model. In W. M. Kurtines & J. Gewirtz (Eds), *Moral Development: An introduction* (pp. 401–430). Needham Heights, MA: Allyn & Bacon.

Eisenberg, N., Miller, P. A., Shell, R., McNalley, S. & Shea, C. (1991). Prosocial development in adolescence: a longtudinal study. *Developmental Psychology*, **27** (5), 849–857.

Erikson, E. H. (1963). *Childhood and Society*, 2nd edn. New York: Norton.

Erikson, E. H. (1968). *Identity, Youth and Crisis.* New York: Norton.

Erikson, E. H. (1975). *Life History and the Historical Moment.* New York: Norton.

Eysenck, H. J. (1976). The biology of moral development. In T. Lickona (Ed.), *Moral Development and Behaviour: Theory, Research and Social Issues* (pp. 108–123). New York: Holt, Rinehart & Winston.

Fogelman, E. (1994). *Conscience and Courage.* New York: Doubleday.

Frankena, W. K. (1973). *Ethics.* Englewood Cliffs, NJ: Prentice-Hall.

Freud, S. (1923/1961). The Ego and the Id. In J. Strachey (Ed.), *The Standard Edition of the Complete Psychological Works of S. Freud*, Vol. 19 (pp. 3–66). London: Hogarth Press.

Gibbs, J. C., Basinger, K. S. & Fuller, D. (1992). *Moral Maturity: Measuring the Development of Sociomoral Reflection.* Hillsdale, NJ: Erlbaum.

Gilligan, C. (1982/1993). *In A Different Voice.* Cambridge, MA: Harvard University Press.

Grusec, J. & Goodnow, J. (1994). Impact of parental discipline methods on the child's internalisation of values: A reconceptualisation of current points. *Developmental Psychology*, **30**, 4–19.

Hamilton, S. F. & Fenzel, L. M. (1988). The impact of volunteer experience on adolescent social development. *Journal of Adolescence Research*, **3**(1), 65–80.

Harré, R. & Gillett, G. (1994). *The Discursive Mind.* London: Sage.

Hart, D. A. (1992). *Becoming Men: The Development of Aspirations, Values and Adaptational Styles.* New York: Plenum Press.

Hart, D. & Fegley, S. (1995). Prosocial behavior and caring in adolescence:

Relations to self-understanding and social judgement. *Child Development*, **66**, 1346–1359.

Hartshorne, H. & May, M. A. (1928–32). *Studies in the Nature of Character*. New York: Macmillan.

Haste, H. (1990). Moral responsibility and moral commitment: The integration of affect and cognition. In T. Wren (Ed.), *The Moral Domain*, (pp. 315–359). Cambridge, MA: MIT Press.

Haste, H. (1994). *The Sexual Metaphor*. Cambridge, MA: Harvard University Press.

Haste, H. & Baddeley, J. (1991). Moral theory and culture: The case of gender. In W. M. Kurtines & J. Gewirtz, (Eds), *Handbook of Moral Behaviour and Development*, Vol. 1: *Theory* (pp. 223–249). Hillsdale, NJ: Erlbaum.

Hoffman, M. (1984). Interaction of affect and cognition in empathy. In C. E. Izard, J. Kagan & R. B. Zajonc, *Emotions, Cognitions and Behaviour*, (pp. 103–131). Cambridge: Cambridge University Press.

Hoffman, M. (1991). Empathy, social cognition and moral action. In W. M. Kurtines & J. Gewirtz, (Eds), *Handbook of Moral Behaviour and Development*, Vol. 1: *Theory* (pp. 275–301). Hillsdale, NJ: Erlbaum.

Ikonen-Varila, M. (1994). Workplace moral conflicts from the viewpoint of cognitive-developmental moral research [in Finnish]. *University of Helsinki, Dept of Education Research Reports No. 140*.

Iwasa, N. (1992). Postconventional reasoning and moral education in Japan. *Journal of Moral Education*, **21**(1), 3–16.

Johnston, D. K. (1988). Adolescents' solutions to dilemmas in fables: Two moral orientations—two problem-solving strategies. In C. Gilligan, J. V. Ward & J. M. Taylor (1988). *Mapping the Moral Domain* (pp. 49–72). Cambridge MA: Harvard University Press.

Keller, M. & Edelstein, W. (1993). The development of the moral self from childhood to adolescence. In G. Noam & T. Wren (Eds), *The Moral Self* (pp. 255–282). Cambridge: MIT Press.

Killen, M. & Nucci, L. (1995). Morality, autonomy and social conflict. In M. Killen & D. Hart (Eds), *Morality in Everyday Life: Developmental Perspectives* (pp. 52–86). New York: Cambridge University Press.

Kitchener, K. S. (1986). The Reflective Judgement Model: Characteristics, evidence and measurement. In R. A. Mines & K. S. Kitchener (Eds), *Adult Cognitive Development* (pp. 76–91). New York: Praeger.

Kitchener, K. S. & Brenner, H. G. (1990). Wisdom and reflective judgement: Knowing in the face of uncertainty. In R. J. Sternberg (Ed.), *Wisdom: Its Nature, Origins and Development* (pp. 212–229). Cambridge: Cambridge University Press.

Kochanska, G. (1994). Beyond cognition: Expanding the search for the early roots of internalisation and conscience. *Developmental Psychology*, **30**, 20–22.

Kochanska, G., Aksan, N., & Koenig, A. L. (1995). A longitudinal study of the roots of preschoolers' conscience: Committed compliance and emerging internalisation. *Child Development*, **66**, 1752–1769.

Kohlberg, L. (1958). The development of modes of moral thinking and choice in the years ten to sixteen. Unpublished PhD thesis, University of Chicago.

Kohlberg, L. (1971). From is to ought: How to commit the naturalistic fallacy and get away with it in the study of moral development. In T. Mischel (Ed.), *Cognitive Development and Epistemology* (pp. 151–231). New York: Academic Press.

Kohlberg, L. (1984). *Essays in Moral Development*, Vol. 2: *The Psychology of Moral Development*, New York: Harper & Row.

Kohlberg, L., Boyd, D. R. & Levine, C. (1990). The return of Stage 6: Its principle and moral point of view. In T. Wren (Ed.), *The Moral Domain* (pp. 151–181). Cambridge, MA: MIT Press.

Kohlberg, L. & Higgins, A. (1984). Continuities and discontinuities in childhood and adult development revisited—again. In L. Kohlberg, *The Psychology of Moral Development* (pp. 426–497). New York: Harper & Row.

Kohlberg, L. & Nisan, M. (1987). A longitudinal study of moral judgement in Turkish males. In A. Colby & L. Kohlberg, *The Measurement of Moral Judgement*, Vol. 1 (pp. 77–118). New York: Cambridge University Press.

Krappmann, L. & Oswald, H. (1991). Problems of helping among ten-year-old children: Results of a qualitative study in naturalistic settings. In L. Montada & H. W. Bierhoff (Eds), *Altruism in Social Settings* (pp. 142–158). Toronto: Hogrefe & Huber.

Lempert, W. (1994). Moral development in the biographies of skilled industrial workers. *Journal of Moral Education*, **23**(4), 451–468.

Lind, G. (1995). The Meaning and Measurement of Moral Competence Revisited—a Dual Aspect Model. http://www.uni-konstanz.de/ag-moral.

Lind, G., Hartman, H. & Wakenhut, R. (1985). *Moral Development and the Social Environment*. Chicago: Precedent Publishing.

Markoulis, D. (in press). Adopting with blood. The impact gender and sociomoral orientation. *Merrill-Palmer Quarterly Journal of Developmental Psychology*.

Miller, J. G. & Bersoff, D. M. (1995). Development in the context of everyday family relationships: Culture, interpersonal morality and adaptation. In M. Killen & D. Hart (Eds), *Morality in Everyday Life: Developmental Perspectives*. New York: Cambridge University Press.

Mischel, W. & Mischel, H. (1976). A cognitive social-learning approach to morality and self-regulation. In T. Lickona (Ed.), *Moral Development and Behaviour: Theory, Research and Social Issues* (pp. 84–107). New York: Holt, Rinehart & Winston.

Modgil, S. & Modgil. C. (Eds) (1982). *Piaget: Consensus and Controversy*. New York: Holt, Rinehart & Winston.

Nisan, M. & Kohlberg, L. (1982). Universality and cross-cultural variation in moral development: A longitudinal and cross-sectional study in Turkey. *Child Development*, **53**, 865–876.

Nucci, L. (1981). The development of personal concepts: A domain distinct from moral or societal concepts. *Child Development*, **52**, 114–121.

Nunner-Winkler, G. (1984). Two moralities? A critical discussion of an ethic of care and responsibility versus an ethic of rights and justice. In W. M. Kurtines & J. Gewirtz (Eds), *Morality, Moral Behaviour and Moral Development*. New York: Wiley.

Oliner, S. P. & Oliner, P. M. (1988). *The Altruistic Personality: Rescuers of Jews in Nazi Europe*. New York: Free Press.

Orwoll, L. & Achenbaum, W. A. (1993). Gender and the development of wisdom. *Human Development*, **36**, 274–296.

Orwoll, L. & Perlmutter, M. (1990). The study of wise persons: Integrating a personality perspective. In R. J. Sternberg (Ed.), *Wisdom: Its Nature, Origins and Development* (pp. 160–177). Cambridge: Cambridge University Press.

Paolicchi, P. (1995). Narratives of volunteering. *Journal of Moral Education*, **24**(2), 159–174.

Piaget, J. (1932/1968). *The Moral Judgement of the Child* (trans. M. Gabain). London: Routledge & Kegan Paul.

Pirttila-Backman, A. M. (1993). *The Social Psychology of Knowledge Reassessed*. Helsinki: Suomalainen Tiedeakatemia.

Pratt, M. W., Golding, G. & Hunter, W. J. (1984). Does morality have a gender? Sex, sex-role and moral judgement relationships across the adult lifespan. *Merrill-Palmer Quarterly*, **30**(4), 321–340.

Rest, J. R. (1979). *Development in Judging Moral Issues*. Minneapolis: University of Minnesota Press.

Ridley, M. (1996). *The Origins of Virtue*. London: Viking.

Rogoff, B. (1990). *Apprenticeship in Thinking*. Oxford: Oxford University Press.

Rogoff, B., Mistry, J., Göncü, A. & Mosier, C. (1993). Guided participation on cultural activity by toddlers and caregivers. *Monographs of the Society of Research in Child Development, No. 236*. **58**(8).

Ryff, C. & Heincke, S. (1983). Subjective organisation of personality in adulthood and aging. *Journal of Personality and Social Psychology*, **44**, 807–816.

Shweder, R. A. (1990). Cultural psychology: What is it? In J. W. Stigler, R. A. Shweder & G. Herdt, *Cultural Psychology* (pp. 1–45). Cambridge: Cambridge University Press.

Shweder, R. A., Mahapatra, M. & Miller, J. G. (1987). Culture and moral development. In J. J. Kagan & Lamb (Eds), *The Emergence of Morality in Young Children* (pp. 1–82). Chicago: Chicago University Press.

Snarey, J. R., Reimer, R. & Kohlberg, L. (1985). Development of sociomoral reasoning among kibbutz adolescents: A longitudinal cross-cultural study. *Developmental Psychology*, **21**(1), 3–17.

Sternberg, R. J. (1986). Implicit theories of intelligence, creativity and wisdom. *Journal of Personality and Social Psychology*, **49**, 607–627.

Sternberg, R. J. (1990a). *Wisdom: Its Nature, Origins and Development*. Cambridge: Cambridge University Press.

Sternberg, R. J. (Ed.) (1990b). *Wisdom: Its Nature, Origins and Development* (pp. 142–159). Cambridge: Cambridge University Press.

Tappan, M. B. & Packer, M. J. (1991). *Narrative and Storytelling: Implications for Understanding Moral Development*. New Directions for Child Development, Editor-in-Chief, W. Damon, Number 54.

Turiel, E. (1983). *The Development of Social Knowledge: Morality and Convention*. Cambridge: Cambridge University Press.

Vygotsky, L. (1978). *Mind in Society*. Cambridge, MA: Harvard University Press.

Walker, L. J. (1984). Sex differences in the development of moral reasoning: A critical review. *Child Development*, **55**, 677–691.

Walker, L. J. (1995). Sexism in Kohlberg's moral psychology? In W. M. Kurtines & J. Gewirtz (Eds), *Moral Development: An Introduction* (pp. 83–108). Needham Heights, MA: Allyn & Bacon.

Walker, L. J., de Vries, B. & Trevethan, S. D. (1987). Moral stages and moral orientations in real-life and hypothetical dilemmas. *Child Development*, **58**, 842–858.

Walker, L. J., Pitts, R. C., Henning, K. H. & Matsuba, M. K. (1995). Reasoning about morality and real-life moral problems. In M. Killen & D. Hart (Eds), *Morality in Everyday Life: Developmental Perspectives* (pp. 371–408). New York: Cambridge University Press.

Weinreich-Haste, H. (1984). Morality, social meaning and rhetoric: The social context of moral reasoning. In W. M. Kurtines & J. Gewirtz (Eds), *Morality, Moral Behavior and Moral Development* (pp. 325–347). New York: Wiley.

Wertsch, J. (Ed.) (1985). *Culture, Communication and Cognition*. Cambridge: Cambridge University Press.

Zahn-Waxler, C., Radke-Yarrow, M., Wagner, E. & Chapman, M. (1992). Development of concern for others. *Developmental Psychology*, **26**(1), 126–136.

Chapter 8

The Development of Motivation

A. M. Fontaine

University of Oporto

INTRODUCTION

The systematic study of motivation by psychologists has been a fairly recent development in the history of psychology. While motivation is generally considered to be the dynamic aspect of action, attempts to understand the processes underlying this dynamic effect have given rise to numerous theories, each of them shedding light on an important facet of motivational functioning. A brief presentation of these theories seems indispensable, as they progressively lead the reader from a more general comprehension of the reasons for action in simple situations to decision making in more complex ones. These theories form a general background to the introduction of the development of motivation. Until recently, motivation was supposed to develop very early and to remain stable over time, similarly to other personality traits. The interest in the study of the later development of particular motivational characteristics, based on cognitive or social learning theories, is very recent. These theories used to be limited to childhood and adolescence or to describing general principles of social learning that can be applied to all circumstances, including normative transitions. The study of motivation from a life-span perspective is still in its early stages and it needs further research. Thus the outline of research to be presented in this chapter is by no means definitive, but it is intended as a frame for understanding the development of motivation.

Life-Span Developmental Psychology
Edited by A. Demetriou, W. Doise and C. F. M. van Lieshout. © 1998 John Wiley & Sons Ltd.

The chapter is divided into four parts. The first elaborates on *basic concepts and definitions*. This section will first summarize the development of the concept of motivation. All students of motivation agree that motivation is the dynamic aspect of behaviour. However, there is no general agreement as to the inclusion of cognitions and emotions in the concept of motivation. Also, research has suggested that motivation is a very complex construct that involves different components and dimensions. However, if we admit that motivation is associated with the behaviour of individuals when they pursue particular goals, some motivational variables could be associated with the choice of goals and the interpretation of results, others with the strategies of actions, and still others with the perception of the self. These specific concepts will be defined and differentiated in the second part where the theories focusing on these specific aspects will be presented.

The second part of the chapter will be devoted to the principal *theories of motivation*. Although all theories of motivation have been elaborated to answer the same basic question 'Why do people act in different ways?' the explanation varies widely according to the basic assumption about human behaviour common to each period of time. Three trends evolved over time. The first has been narrowed down to a more specific object: the older theories were concerned with the universal explanation of behaviour, while the recent ones select some aspects of motivated behaviour and try to understand the specific underlying processes. The second trend is characterized by the evolution of explanation, from biological to unconscious forces to the influence of cognitive processes and, more recently, the integration of emotional dimensions. The third trend has progressed from an understanding of the origin of motivation in constitutional terms or archaic structures to an emphasis on the importance of interaction between subject and environment, associated with lower stability of motivational variables throughout one's life-span.

The evolution of motivational perspectives will be illustrated with a presentation and discussion of the theories of motivation, from the older to the more recent ones. Indeed, the understanding of motivational processes underlying human behaviour is fundamental to leading the reader to a more comprehensive understanding of this specific class of determinants of human behaviour. Each theory is specifically concerned with a particular problem and has been built to answer some questions. However, their capacity to explain the multiple aspects of human behaviour is limited. These limitations have stimulated the construction of new theories in an attempt to understand the processes underlying other aspects of human functioning; the perspectives presented by the various motivational theories are complementary. The attempt to join several theories in a comprehensive model to explain concrete behaviours in specific settings corresponds to more recent tendencies.

The third part of this chapter will be devoted to the presentation of some of the *methods* used to assess motivational characteristics. Since methods and procedures are strongly dependent on theoretical perspectives, projective tests and clinical interviews associated with dynamic theories have been progressively substituted by questionnaires, rating scales, self-reports, and observations in natural settings. The advantages and disadvantages of each method will be analysed and compared.

The fourth part focuses on the *development of motivation*. Development in a life-span perspective is only indirectly analysed through age and group differences, because longitudinal studies focusing on life-span development are rare. Age differences are viewed as indicators of developmental differences over the years. Also variations of motivational characteristics according to the gender or socio-economic status are viewed as the result of the differential development of motivation in each social group throughout the life-span. This development depends on the experiences lived by individuals and the way they interpret them. Family and school influences on the development of motivation during childhood and adolescence, as well as the influence of professional pressures during adulthood, will illustrate this perspective. The chapter will end with a brief conclusion.

BASIC CONCEPTS AND DEFINITIONS

Motivation is a consensual term frequently used as much in common language as in scientific jargon. Motivation is considered to be necessary for development itself, for learning, and for everyday problem solving. In general terms, motivation is the dynamic aspect of action. The conceptual differentiation between motivation and personality is not easy. In Murray's view, the basis of personality is the motivational system formed by human needs. Although some authors (e.g. Jackson, 1967; Murray, 1953) have considered the same motivation and personality, we assume that motivation and personality are not synonymous but that motivation is a dimension of personality such as agreeableness or conscientiousness, and two of the big-five personality factors are motivational factors (for more details, see Kohnstamm & Mervielde, ch. 9 this volume).

The Main Question: How or Why?

Motivation, in the opinion of Jones (1955), has to do with 'how behaviour gets started, is energized, is sustained, is directed, is stopped and what kind of subjective reaction is present in the organism while all this is going on' (p. vii). Over time, the emphasis on various aspects of motivated behaviour has changed. For instance, researchers in the past were interested in understanding the starting of action, while now they focus on the reasons for choosing among different goals, for shifting from one activity to another, for eliciting specific strategies of action, and for examining the consequences of these options. The main question of motivation is not yet 'how' but 'why': Why do people think and behave as they do? The evolution of theoretical paradigms in this field is closely related with changes in assumptions about the kind of factors underlying motivational development: the motivational

Table 8.1   Evolution of motivational theories: origin and characteristics

Motivational characteristics	Origin of motivation	
	Biological	Social
Static	*Homeostatic theories (1)*[a] Drive Field *Expectancy-value theories (2)* Need for achievement Time perspective	*Expectancy-value theories (2)* Anxiety *Attributional theory (3)*
Dynamic	*Goal theories (5)* Relational	*Action control theory (4)* *Cognitive evaluation theory (3)* *Goal theories (5)* Personal conception of intelligence *Self theories (5)* Self-concept Self-appraisal

[a](1 to 5)=order ranking from older theories to more recent ones.

characteristics may be viewed as more static, that is, biologically or early determined, or as more dynamic, that is, changing with social experiences. In older theories, motivation was viewed as a static attribute. In more recent theories, it is considered to vary with previous experiences and according to the subjective interpretation of personal and situational characteristics. Thus it is considered to be more dynamic (Table 8.1). Behaviour is no longer regarded as an isolated unit. Instead it is integrated as a continuous stream of events with different features which must be explained. Although individual differences are carefully analysed by these theories, only a few of them are concerned with motivational development.

Conscious or Unconscious Aspect of Motivation

Moreover, motivational processes may be assumed to be unconscious processes which can be indirectly assessed, or, depending on cognitive and emotional functioning, which are conscious and can be analysed. Authors also disagree about whether determinants of behaviours should be considered as motivational. According to some authors, such as McClelland (1985), only the intentions must be included in motivation: these intentions, essentially unconscious, must be inferred from observing behaviours. Emotions, as manifestations of unconscious needs, are important but are not studied on their own. In the Weiner perspective (Weiner, 1986), cognitions are essential components of motivation which provoke emotional reactions: emotions are dependent on cognitions. Progressively, the primacy of cognitions gives place to the focus on emotions as a central element in the

Table 8.2 Evolution of motivational theories: nature and degree of rationality

Rationality	Nature of motivation	
	Unconscious	Conscious
Emotions only	Homeostatic theories (1) [a] Drive Field	
Mainly cognitions	Expectancy-value theories (2) Time perspective	Action control theory (4) Cognitive evaluation theory (3)

Emotions and cognitions [b]	Expectancy-value theories (2)
	Anxiety (E=C)
	Need for achievement
	(E>C)
		Attributional theory (3)
		(C>E)
		Goal theories (5)
		  Relational (C>E)
		  Personal conception of
		  intelligence (C>E)
		Self theories (5)
		  Self-concept (E>C)
		  Self-appraisal (E>C)

[a] (1 to 5)=order ranking from older theories to more recent ones.
[b] E=emotions; C=cognitions; C>E=when cognitions determine emotions; E>C=when emotions determine cognitions; (E=C)=when relationship between emotions and cognitions is not oriented.

orientation of behaviour (Table 8.2). Probably the best answer to the 'why' question is one that accounts for the complexity of human behaviour, including conscious or unconscious, as well as rational or emotional determinants of this behaviour. In the next section, this evolution will be illustrated with a brief presentation and discussion of some theories of motivation, from the older to the more recent ones.

Many studies have been conducted in the field of motivation which stimulated the creation of new theories about motivation. A great variety of concepts about motivation have been developed within the specific framework of each theory: achievement motivation, expectations, self-concept, anxiety, self-control, goal-orientation, self-appraisal, attribution, personal causation, and so on. Some of these motivational variables would be associated with the perception of the self (e.g. abilities, skills, attributes), others with the goal of the behaviour (e.g. value, expectations) other with the strategies adopted to attain these goals (e.g. self-control, self-monitoring, avoidance) or the reactions to the results (e.g. causal attributions, anxiety, emotions). Although the theories have little in common and the synthesis of empirical evidence is very difficult, recent theories try to integrate elements of previous theories, thereby enhancing the understanding of the relationship among goals, strategies, representations of self and social context, and task demands. As it would be rather difficult to review all these concepts, only those which are important to the most influential theories will be discussed here.

THEORETICAL PARADIGMS IN THE STUDY OF THE DEVELOPMENT OF MOTIVATION

Homeostatic Theories

Drive theory

Homeostatic theories are among the oldest theories about motivation. Their basic assumption is that the search for satisfaction and well-being is associated with internal equilibrium, which is considered to be a basic condition for the survival of individuals and species. Drive theory (Hull, 1952) assumes that physiological disequilibrium (i.e. change of a factor connected to equilibrium, such as the level of glycosis in the bloodstream) arouses *primary needs* (for food, water, rest, safety, etc.) that are associated with tensions which generate energy (drive) to motivate the organism to act for the restoration of the initial equilibrium. Drive justifies the strength of action but its direction must be explained through habits and other behaviours resulting from learning. First reactions to the aroused need are accidental and non-specific. Some of these actions happen to be more effective in satisfying each need than others. Following the 'law of effect' (Thorndike), the more efficient bonds are reinforced and create habits. Behaviour is the result of interaction between drive and habits: drive is responsible for the intensity of behaviours while habits define the direction of behaviour. The needs for love, self-esteem and knowledge, also important, are *secondary needs* which get their value from their initial association with the primary ones (food and love, for instance). However, this may not be the case. For instance, if there is a theory of mind from the beginning, as many have maintained (e.g. Demetriou, ch. 5 this volume), these are primary needs as well.

Field theory

The field theory proposed by Kurt Lewin (1942) must be synthesized by his famous equation $B = f(P, E)$, which assumes that motivated behaviour, at a given moment, is the function of the interaction between the person (P) and his environment (E), more precisely, between the actual characteristics of the person and his subjective perception of the actual environment. The concept of *life-space* is the representation of this psychological reality. It is divided into two qualitatively distinct kinds of space: the space of the person and the space of the environment, which are themselves divided into regions as shown in Figure 8.1. In the *space of the person*, each region represents a need which must be very specific, such as the need to see a movie or to buy a motorcycle. These needs are directly linked to regions in the space of the environment which represent specific objects or instrumental activities able to satisfy them. The intensity of the need defines the amount of tension in

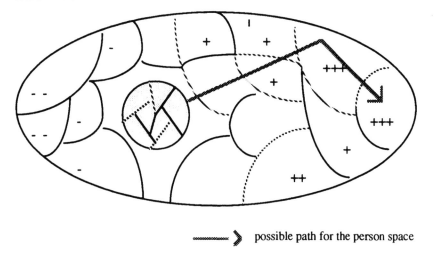

─────── > possible path for the person space

Figure 8.1   Life-space in field theory

each region which must be transferred to adjacent regions if the boundaries between them are permeable.

The degree of permeability of boundaries in the environmental space determines the possibility of crossing them more or less easily. The space of the person moves into the environmental space, following paths through permeable or semi-permeable boundaries, to reach the region able to satisfy a need. This region acquires a positive valence and attracts the person while others which increase the tension in the space of the person acquire a negative valence and repulse him. The strengths of the attractive or repulsive forces determine the strength and direction of current behaviour and, when balanced, explain ambivalent attitudes and conflicts. Tension in the personal region and the corresponding environmental regions disappears after the need has been satisfied, and the behaviour stops as the person has regained his equilibrium and well-being.

Expectancy-Value Theories

The absence of reference to cognitive processes in homeostatic theories introduced strong limitations in the knowledge of psychological processes underlying human behaviour. Expectancy-value theories were grounded on the assumption of the rationality of human behaviour and its liberation from psychological needs. The concept of 'motive' is differentiated from that of 'motivation'. Motives are considered as stable, internal and unconscious dispositions, while motivation is influenced by situational characteristics that stimulate approach or avoidance behaviours (McClelland, 1985). Some of the expectancy-value theories concerned with human behaviour in the field of achievement will be analysed more carefully in the next section.

Need for achievement theory

The achievement motive is considered to be the need 'To accomplish something difficult. To master, manipulate and organize physical objects, human
beings, or ideas . . . To attain a high standard to excel oneself . . . and surpass
others' (Murray, 1953, p. 164). Such a need influences behaviours such as
effort, persistence, competition and goal-orientated activities. Behaviour in
achievement situations is viewed as the result of two antagonic tendencies:
the tendency to approach success and the tendency to avoid failure (T_A =
T_S-T_{AF}) (Atkinson & Birch, 1978). If the tendency to approach success is
stronger than the tendency to avoid failure, the person initiates the activity;
if the opposite occurs, the person does not engage in the activity and he or
she may follow avoidance strategies. Both tendencies are the result of
internal motives and perceptions of the situation. The *motive* to approach
success and the motive to avoid failure are internal and unconscious. The
probability of success vs failure and the anticipation of pride vs shame which
underlies the *incentive value* of success vs failure depends on the difficulty of
the task. Evaluations both of probabilities and of incentives depend on
conscious processes and are assumed to be objective: the probability of
success is higher in an easy task than in a difficult one, but the value of this
success is lower in the easier tasks; the opposite is true for the probability
and value of failure.

Time perspective

In the field of achievement motivation in the academic context, the motivational function of long-term goals has been studied by Raynor (1982), and
more recently by Lens (1987), Tomé and Bariaud (1984), under the label of
Future Time Perspective (FTP). Lens argues that human motivation, in
itself, is future-oriented and he assumes that the FTP is a characteristic of
personality. In FTP, the following motivational dimensions were progressively identified. *Task hierarchy* is formed by the number and sequence of
tasks which people believe they need to carry out to attain future goals: the
greater the number of instrumental tasks, the greater the motivation for the
actual task; *time hierarchy* is evaluated through the period of time people
allow themselves to achieve the goal: when the period of time increases,
achievement motivation decreases (Raynor, 1982). The *extension* of FTP
(Lens, 1987) is short when most of the individual's goals are established for
the near future; it is long when most of them are located in the distant future.
Long FTP individuals have better ability than those with short FTP to
anticipate high values for distant goals, assess a task's utility for future
goals, show capacity to take decisions, delay instant gratification, manifest a
sense of control, anticipate effects of future actions and elaborate complex
planning to attain distant goals. People also show a more or less positive
attitude toward the future and will preferentially *orientate* their thoughts
either to the past, or to the present or to the future (Raynor, 1982). Finally,

people include more or fewer events, projected goals, and aspirations in their personal time perspective (density), and foresee more or fewer realistic and rational paths for attaining their future goals (coherence) (Tomé & Bariaud, 1984). All these dimensions of FTP are viewed as personal dispositions or capabilities (Lens, 1987).

Anxiety

In Atkinsonian theory, the *motive to avoid failure*, or anxiety, has a strong debilitating effect on the individual's performances, particularly in situations of evaluation (Mandler & Sarason, 1952). The pioneers of test anxiety research in educational settings believe that anxiety is a learned psychological drive, characterized by self-directed cognitions which are irrelevant for task resolution (anticipation of failure, punishment or loss of status), and they are associated with worthlessness, feelings of inadequacy, somatic reactions (e.g. perspiration, accelerated heartbeat), passivity, and attempts to avoid the situation. All these symptoms are correlated.

Various dimensions have been progressively enhanced. *Debilitating* anxiety has been differentiated from *facilitating* anxiety. The former has a deleterious effect on performance while the latter has a positive one because it stimulates the adoption of active strategies to avoid failure. Spielberger (1980) has differentiated between anxiety *state* and anxiety *trait*, according to its cross-situational stability: anxiety state is a transitory state whereas an anxiety trait is the chronic tendency to manifest anxiety in a wide range of situations. Other authors have distinguished between *worry* and *emotionality* as the cognitive and the affective dimension of anxiety (Sarason, 1987; Schwarzer, 1986). Worry is the cognitive expression of personal concerns about an inability to respond to situational demands. This is frequently manifested by task-irrelevant cognitions about possible difficulties or implications of failure for the self. As human information processing capability is limited, anxious subjects perform worse because they have to process more information (task-relevant and task-irrelevant information) which overloads their cognitive system. Emotionality is associated with physiological reactions of the autonomic nervous system caused by testing situations but its effect on performances is minimal (Hamilton, 1983, 1988; Hembree, 1988). However, the relationship between anxiety and performances also varies with characteristics of the person, such as intellectual level (Hagtvet, 1983, 1991), sex or socio-economic status (SES) (Fontaine, 1991a).

Attributional Theory

Recent theories have emphasized the importance of the analysis of self-related cognitions. The attributional theory assumes that humans need to understand and control reality, and is interested in explaining how beliefs about causes of events influence cognitions, emotions and behaviours

Table 8.3 Attributional dimensions

	Stability	
Locus	Stable	Unstable
Internal	Capacity	Effort
External	Task difficulty	Chance

(Weiner, 1986). Causes must be organized in causal dimensions (locus, stability and controllability) which have different consequences. The *locus of causality* determines whether the outcome of a particular task depends on factors within the person (internal) or outside the person (external). The *stability–instability* of causes indicates whether causes of events fluctuate with time or are relatively constant. The dimension of *controllability* allows the individual to distinguish between causes that are under his volitional control, such as effort, from others that are beyond his control, such as chance. Table 8.3 shows how these dimensions relate to each other. Causes and their classification into dimensions depend on personal interpretation of reality, that must be taken into account (Weiner, 1982).

Different attributions are associated with different consequences at cognitive, affective and behavioural levels as shown in Table 8.4. The attribution of an event to *stable* causes leads to a high expectation of the occurrence of the same events in the future, while *unstable* attributions permit the anticipation of some change: high expectation of success is associated with persistence and low expectation with desistence. The attribution of success to *internal* factors enhances the concept of competence and self-esteem with manifestations of positive affects, such as satisfaction or pride, while the attribution of failure to internal factors impairs self-esteem with manifestations of negative affects, such as shame or guilt. The attribution to *external* factors has a buffering effect, reducing the cognitive and emotional impacts of these outcomes. The ascription of some outcomes to *controllable* causes underlies subject confidence in his or her ability to change or maintain outcomes through adequate behaviour, and is linked to personal responsibility. People usually attribute good outcomes to themselves and bad outcomes to external factors (or unstable ones). This tendency, which has been called hedonic bias because it improves (or protects) self-esteem, is observed in both achievement and non-achievement situations. Increase in self-esteem commonly activates behaviour, while its decrease has an inhibitory effect. However, regrets or remorse often promote behaviour in order to repair the physical or moral damage (Hoffman, 1975).

Theory of Action Control

Kuhl's (1986) theory of action control is focused on the determinants of volitional control, more precisely on the intentions as they imply personal commitment to an action. The translation of intention into action is possible

Table 8.4 Cognitive and affective effects of attributional dimensions

	Success	Failure
Stability	Expectations of success	Expectations of failure
Unstability	Expectations of outcome change	Expectations of outcome change
Internal locus	Pride	Shame, guilt
	Higher self-esteem	Lower self-esteem
External locus	Buffering effect on self-concept and self-esteem	
Controllability	Responsibility	Remorse; sadness
	Pride	Guilt
Uncontrollabilty	Graceful; luck	Shame; sadness

through access to an individual repertoire of self-regulatory strategies. Self-regulatory efficiency involves two aspects: difficulty of enactment (or difficulty in acting, in performing concrete actions) and self-regulatory abilities. *Difficulty of enactment* depends on three factors: (i) the force of tendencies towards other action competing with the current intention; (ii) the compatibility of expected acting with current intention; (iii) the mode of control currently activated which can be of two types, *action-oriented* or *state-oriented* control. In the first type of control, which is the most efficient, attention is centred on task-relevant characteristics and problem-solving strategies, and interruptions for behavioural evaluations are frequently made. In the latter type, attention is focused on internal or external states, on emotions, on searching for causes of difficulties, or on cognitions related with past, future or present events. This type of control is less efficient. Indeed, excessive centring on planning, on goals or on possible outcomes in state-oriented control occupies memory space, reducing working memory and weakens resistance to failure experience (Kuhl, 1985).

Self-regulatory abilities are formed by action-related strategies. They are stored in long-term memory and they can be activated by an intentional structure, when the difficulty of enactment and the perceived ability to control action exceed critical values. Strategies such as selectivity of stimuli related to current intention, parsimony of information processing, motivational, or emotional or environmental control, facilitate the enactment of current intentions against external pressures. Action-oriented subjects are more effective in using these strategies than are state-oriented ones.

Cognitive Evaluation Theory

The cognitive evaluation theory of Deci and Ryan (1985), better known as the *intrinsic* vs *extrinsic* motivation theory, is based on the postulate that children and adults have a natural inclination to learn and, therefore it is not necessary to exert pressures on them to do so. Intrinsically motivated pupils are mastery-oriented, prefer challenging tasks, take more pleasure in doing the tasks, are actively engaged in them, show more sustained attention and a higher level of conceptual learning, have higher academic competence and sense of self-worth, are less anxious and get better results at school (Ryan, Connel & Deci, 1985).

Two kinds of experience are fundamental to manifest intrinsic motivation in achievement situations: experiences of autonomy which refer to a conviction that personal actions are self-determined and volitional, and mastery or competence (Deci & Ryan, 1985). Perception of *self-competence* depends both on the level of challenge offered by the task and on the kind of feedback provided by other significant people: contingent and positive feedbacks tend to enhance intrinsic motivation, while negative or non-contingent feedbacks have a deleterious effect as they fail to provide feelings of competence. Moreover, the above-mentioned perceptions are dependent on the interpretation of the event as informational or controlling: informational rewards provide competence feedback while controlling rewards are felt as pressures to think, feel, or perform in a particular way, undermining experience of *autonomy*. When the activity becomes instrumental to obtain an extrinsic reward, motivation disappears when the reward is suppressed (Lepper, Greene & Nisbett, 1973).

Educational literature points to a decrease in children's intrinsic motivation during the elementary years and to its differentiation according to school subjects (Gottfried, 1990; Ryan et al., 1985). Although external control is very common in a school context as a means for stimulating students to accomplish goals that are not very exciting, it is important to transform external goals or values into internal and personal ones which can be assumed and pursued in their own right, without external pressures. This purpose can best be achieved by using the principle of 'minimal sufficiency', which includes an amount of pressure strong enough to orientate the behaviour in the expected direction, but sufficiently weak to avoid the attribution of the causes of this behaviour to these pressures. Indeed, the presence of some degree of self-determination in the choice of the task or the strategies to achieve can lower the perception of external pressures and arouse the development of the intrinsic motivational tendencies.

Goal Theories

Personal conception of intelligence model

In Dweck's personal conception of intelligence model, success or failure are only instrumental activities for achieving more internal and personal goals: to increase abilities or to demonstrate abilities. Two distinct *theories of intelligence* could explain subjects' orientation toward these goals: the 'entity' theory and the 'incremental' theory (Dweck, 1986; Dweck & Legget, 1989). The entity theory involves the belief that intelligence is an internal, stable and global 'trait', which may be assessed through performances but cannot be changed. The incremental theory involves the belief that intelligence is composed of a number of different competencies that can be developed through adequate training or experience: effort increases skills and, therefore, intelligence. As shown in Figure 8.2, subjects who adopt the incremental theory of intelligence select *learning goals*, while subjects who adopt the entity theory of intelligence select *performance goals*. The former value the opportunities for learning, the task-solving processes, and the intrinsic interest of activity, while the latter are concerned with the external judgement about outcomes and its consequences on self-image (Dweck & Elliott, 1983). Choice of different goals is linked to the adoption of two distinct *patterns of behaviours, cognitions and affects*, when children cope with failure or obstacles in achievement activities. Performance goals are associated with the adoption of a 'helpless' pattern and learning goals with the use of a 'mastery-oriented' pattern. The 'helpless' subjects give up in the face of difficultly or failure attributed to lack of intelligence, have lower expectation of future successes and feel negative affects such as sadness, shame, guilt, helplessness and worthlessness because they believe that negative outcomes are manifestations of a low intelligence which cannot be improved in any way. Subjects who adopt the 'mastery-oriented' pattern increase their persistence after failure and maintain positive expectations for future successes, analyse the errors in order to obtain more information about the way to solve the task, do not show tendencies for self-depreciation but increase their effort and attention, stimulating positive affects, such as curiosity, self-confidence, sense of personal control, and using intrinsic reinforcement. Indeed, obstacles or difficulties are viewed as an opportunity to improve their intelligence.

Although the two types of oriented behaviours associated with the theories of intelligence have been presented in a dichotomic form, they are poles of a continuous dimension, and each subject must locate her or himself at a particular point of this continuum. From a humanistic perspective, goal setting and goal management have received particular attention in the relational theory of motivation, described below.

Relational theory of motivation

Nuttin's relational theory of motivation considers the choice of goals to be the primary condition for human development in a broader temporal perspective. The nature of human behaviour is based on the need to build significant relationships between the self and the world through action (Nuttin, 1980). Needs are modalities of relationship oriented to self-development, self-enhancement and self-esteem as an attempt to maintain, protect and develop the organism. The steps of action are: (i) the capacity to anticipate goals that should be cognitively manipulated without reality constraints (in the conceptual world); (ii) the capacity to explore the probabilities of reaching these goals; (iii) the anticipation of behavioural strategies to reach these goals and to plan the action according to mental scenarios; (iv) the achievement of the planning actions and appreciation of the goal attainment. All specific goals are oriented to a final goal, uncon-

THEORY OF INTELLIGENCE   **ACHIEVEMENT GOAL**   **COPING PATTERN**

entity theory   ------>   performances goal   ------>   helpless
incremental theory   ------>   learning goal   ------>   mastery – oriented

Figure 8.2 Personal conception of intelligence model

scious and included in a means-end structure. Motivated behaviour follows an ascendant and a descendant phase. The first phase is characterized by the search for disequilibrium and an increase in the complexity of the relationship which the self and the world creates tension. It corresponds to the elaboration of goals as well as of the strategic paths to attain them. The latter phase, the phase of resolution is subordinate to a homeostatic process, as the need satisfaction or goal attainment leads to equilibrium and rest. This phase is always temporary because humans show a strong tendency to create more demanding goals when the less demanding ones have been reached.

Motivation is a very 'personal affair'. Human beings are able to stimulate their own development and personal changes are integrated in the personal project of self-enhancement (Nuttin, 1984). External pressures are inadequate to orientate behaviour as they suppress the dynamic properties of the decision process, personal involvement and personal responsibility (Nuttin, 1984). In a recent study in a classroom setting, Lemos (1993) concluded that sixth graders did not elaborate personal strategies to reach more or less distant goals and presented automated, short-lived, and non-instrumental activities, suggesting a debilitating motivational functioning.

Although other goals theories could present very interesting contributions, it is not possible to review all of them. For instance, Schwartz's taxonomy of values, assumed as motivational goals, is not presented in this chapter. The reader can find a good synthesis of this theory in the chapter by Kohnstamm and Mervielde (ch. 9 this volume) on personality development.

Self-concept and Self-appraisal Theories

Self-concept theories

All motivational theories have emphasized the importance of self-esteem in behavioural orientation. Self-concept must be distinguished from self-esteem. The former refers to the perception of ones own characteristics, and the latter to the affective reaction to this evaluation. Rosenberg (1979, 1985) assumes the unidimensionality of self-concept: self-concept and self-esteem are mixed in a global dimension which manifests a relatively stable way of thinking about oneself, which is to a certain extent independent of objective evaluation. Other authors assume the necessity of separating the assessment of self-concept and self-esteem, and of distinguishing the dimensions of self-concept in different areas of competence (i.e. personal, social, physical, and academic) which may be viewed as totally independent or organized hierarchically (Demetriou, ch. 5 this volume; Harter, 1983, 1985;

Markus, 1977; Marsh, 1987b). Finally, the compensatory model assumes that the various dimensions of self-concept are inversely related: the worse the self-concept is in one field, the better it is in another (for example, bad student but good athlete). All self-concept theories accept the existence of multiple dimensions of self-concept as well as the global one, but do not give them equal importance and identical status. Divergencies among theories also exist about the identification of each self-concept dimensions. According to Markus, each person has many self-representations or 'possible selves'. At each moment, only a few of them are aroused to form the 'working self'. This structure explains both the fluency and the stability of one's self-concept (Cantor, Markus, Niedenthal & Nurius, 1986). The development of self-concept depends on experiences and is achieved in interactional contexts during the socialization process.

For many motivational theories, maintenance of a positive self-image is one of the central pillars of human behaviour: one function of causal attributions is to protect self-esteem through manipulation of pleasure–pain consequences of success and failure; in expectancy-value theories, self-esteem is a central concern that determines the approach or avoidance strategy to cope with challenging tasks; in Dweck's theory, the helpless behavioural pattern is adopted when self-esteem is impaired in specific conditions; in Nuttin's theory, needs are oriented to the development of self-esteem through the choice of adequate goals and strategies.

In his theory of mind, Demetriou distinguishes three main systems: the specialized capacity system, the hypercognitive system, and the processing system (for more information, see Demetriou, ch. 5 this volume). The hypercognitive system involves self-awareness and self-regulation knowledge and strategies, organizes information, guides and controls the behaviours. It is divided into working and long-term hypercognitive systems. Self-concepts and self-esteem belong to the hypercognitive system. The cognitive self-concept, as well as personal theories of intelligence, for instance, are structures of the long-term hypercognitive system. A factorial analysis of self-evaluation scores processed by the hypercognitive system (Demetriou et al., in press), has enhanced the presence of a general factor (G_{hyper}) as well as two more delimited ones (one associated with cognitive functioning, the other with personality and social characteristics). The G_{hyper} factor 'can be taken to represent the effect of general functions underlying self-awareness and self-evaluation, such as . . . one's tendency to have a consistently positive self-image . . . or a negative self-image' (Demetriou et al., in press, p. 46). This factor gives the general orientation for self-evaluation in each specific domain. It is closely related with self-esteem which is viewed as a stable sense of self-worth.

Self-categorization

Wicklund's theory of self-categorization develops this perspective assuming that self-concept is the result of a defence mechanism in social situations.

Empirical results have reported that efficient people are neither more confident nor do they have higher self-esteem, nor is self-appraisal of adolescents
or adults the reflection of their competence to respond to environmental
demands (Wicklund, 1986a, b). Whereas a higher self-concept is not necessarily associated with higher competence, people strongly believe that their
confidence could positively influence their performances and society infers
the individuals' competence from self-descriptions. As society looks at
category membership (e.g. scientific ability, creativity, management competence) to give the member a status (e.g. scientist, artist, manager), the
person who has difficulty in responding adequately to an environmental
demand (for instance, to make a movie) tries, at least, to show external
attributes of associated category (artistic appearance). Thus, he or she
'builds himself into categories in proportion to the lack of actual potential'
(Wicklund, 1986a, p. 166). This person, described as *static-oriented*, is less
concerned with the possibility of learning from situations than with the
manifestation of his or her own competence (creativity) and experiences
negative feelings, such as frustration, irritation, anxiety. Static orientation is
used when a person cannot meet the complexity of environmental demands.
People who respond well to environmental demands are considered to be
dynamic-oriented. These people are not conscious that they perform tasks in
order to define themselves and they are little concerned with their self-image.
They are more willing to learn from the task and improve their behavioural
repertoire from the experience, they are more persistent and they experience
more positive feelings while working. As in ordinary situations everyone
makes evaluative judgements about the self, the important questions are
how frequently it happens and with what intensity.

Learning vs well-being systems

This model, inspired by Dweck's research, describes the interaction between
intelligence, personality and behavioural strategies in a school context
(Boekaerts, 1991, 1993). The students' appraisal is the steering variable
based on an internal working model. The internal working model results
from a continuous comparison process among information about (i) the
task and its context, (ii) personal knowledge and skills, and (iii) personality
traits and self-concept representations. Boekaerts argues that the three
sources of information exert an indirect influence on students' intentions via
self-appraisal. Self-appraisal is positive when personal competence is seen to
be higher than the task demands, and is negative when task demands are
higher than abilities. Figure 8.3 shows that positive appraisal leads to
learning intention, or willingness to make an effort to accomplish learning
goals, but negative appraisal stimulates *coping* intention, or willingness to
use strategies to assure well-being. The former is associated with *learning
processes* and a 'mastery mode' of acting, including self-regulatory skills and
the selection, maintenance or modification of multiple learning strategies,
while the latter is associated with *well-being processes* and a 'coping mode',

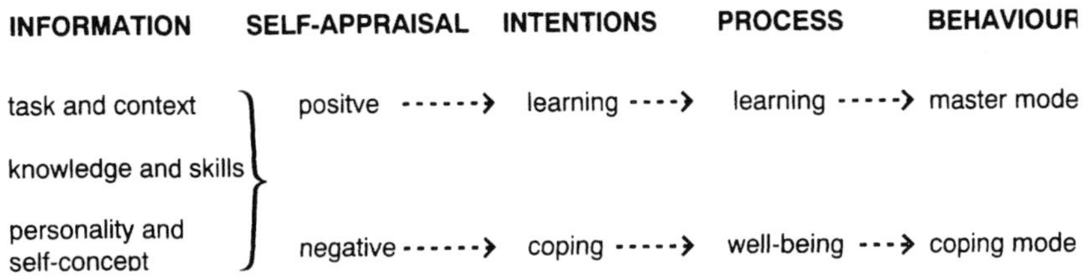

INFORMATION	SELF-APPRAISAL	INTENTIONS	PROCESS	BEHAVIOUR

task and context ⎤

knowledge and skills ⎬   positve ------> learning ----> learning -----> master mode

personality and ⎦
self-concept   negative ------> coping -----> well-being ---> coping mode

Figure 8.3 Learning and well-being systems

the subject regrouping his coping resources to protect his well-being
(Seegers & Boekaerts, 1993). In this model, mastery and coping modes
coexist but in each situation only one is aroused. However, the effect of
self-referenced cognitions on achievement is also associated with cognitive
development and becomes significant only during the secondary school
years (Demetriou, ch. 5 this volume; Helmke, Schneider & Weinert, 1986;
Skaalvik & Hagtvet, 1990). But, it needs to be noted that more study is
needed to specify which is the cause and which is the effect.

Balance of Motivational Theories

Hedonism and unconscious forces

Hedonism is the cornerstone of the first theories of motivation: for the
homeostatic theories, drive reduction is viewed as the sole determinant of
behaviour, while expectancy-value theory assumes that pleasure involves
the break of equilibrium, although some aspects of homeostatic processes
are still present in the fear of failure. These emotions, which are elementary
and affective processes, are not analysed with precision. Recent reflections
have emphasized the importance of the analysis of self-related cognitions in
the motivational field (Sarason, 1987; Heckhausen, Schmalt & Schneider,
1985). For instance, attributional theory, or the personal conception of
intelligence model, subordinates emotions to cognitions. Several studies in
natural settings have also pointed out that the enhancement and protection
of self-esteem are among the most important human goals. However, self-
concept theories seem to be concerned more with the study of the structure
of the self-concept rather than with its motivational relevance. The study of
emotions, as determinants of behaviour, early conceptualized in test anxiety
research, has recently been developed in theories which pursue the integration of results from different theoretical perspectives: the self-appraisal
theories.

   The first motivational theories also considered that human behaviour was
determined by *unconscious* forces, biological in drive theory, external and
integrated in subjective perception of the world in field theory, attributes
early developed—the motives—in expectancy-value theory: people are
pawns, submitted to internal or external forces which determine their behaviour. Conception of human nature, in Nuttin's theory, is also the uncontrol-

lable basis of motivated behaviour: humans need to build significant relationships with the world. However, the choice of specific goals by the person
is able to transform these global needs into personal projects. These choices
must be the best as humans are also fundamentally good. Unfortunately,
Nuttin has not presented the processes used to go from needs to goals and
from projects to actions.

Cognitive processes and objectivity

Nevertheless, references to *cognitive processes* have increased progressively.
In expectancy-value theory, as each person is regarded as a perfect scientist
able to make an absolute rational choice based on total knowledge, always
available, cognitive analysis of reality must be equal for all individuals in the
same situation: behavioural differences exclusively depend on motives. The
incontestable value of *objectivity* was discussed in the light of recent theories, which also call for a more differentiated and deeper analysis of the
cognitions and emotions involved in achievement-oriented behaviour. Attributional theory has analysed an increasing number of cognitive determinants of action to clarify some processes that explain the relationship
between the experience of success or failure (stimuli) and the subsequent
behaviour (response) in the subjective perspective of each individual: the
paradigm of objective rationality and universal goals has been progressively
substituted by another which enhances subjectivity and personal goals, built
from interpersonal experiences in social context. The choice of tasks depends on the possibility they offer to achieve some personal goals, such as
the sense of personal competence or personal autonomy, systematized in the
cognitive evaluation theory. The human being, as a poor information
processor, probably acts less as a scientist than as a judge in making his
decisions. Recent theories have laid more emphasis on the determinants of
the enactment of intentions or volitional control than on those of decision
making.

Temporal perspective

The scope of the analyses of motivated behaviour cannot be limited to the
individual, isolated from the context, from his past and future: the study of
motivation calls for an integration of a broader temporal perspective and
for inclusion of the influence of social context in the analysis of achievement
striving. The *temporal perspective*, initiated in the field of Atkinson's theory,
was developed later from a humanistic perspective. In the relational theory
of motivation, goals transform the undefined need to meet the world into
specific projects which improve individual development: it is a continuous
process, as the attainment of each goal leads to other more demanding ones.

Social context

Within the expectancy-value framework, Horner (1974) questioned the universal value of success, assuming that its attractive power is determined by social context: fear of success, frequently observed in women in the 1970s, depends on the personal analysis of the incompatibility of social constraints and personal values in the decision to strive for success.

A convergence among the cognitive-emotional-behavioural patterns pointed out by recent motivational theories has been observed. Several theories—cognitive evaluation theory, action control theory, Dweck's goal theory and Wicklund's and Boekaerts' self-appraisal theories—describe bipolar patterns of cognitions, emotions and behaviours associated with intrinsic vs extrinsic motivation, state vs action orientation, static vs dynamic conception of intelligence, for static vs dynamic orientation, or coping vs mastery mode of behaviour, respectively. These theories assumed that the adoption of different achievement patterns in challenging situations relates to the representation of social demands. When social demands have a great value but are viewed as too difficult to be adequately responded to, they create a threatening situation. The subject becomes concerned about his or her own capacity to respond to social demands, about the social costs and benefits included in achieving the task, and about the protection of his or her self-esteem: he or she is ego-involved and his or her well-being decreases. When social demands are not very salient, he or she becomes more task-centred, appreciates the characteristics of the task, enjoys the problems to be solved, hopes to learn something and to develop him or herself in achieving the task: he or she is task-involved and experiences positive feelings. These patterns of cognitions, emotions and behaviours may be considered the reaction to the salience of social pressure. Both patterns are coping strategies within situations interpreted as more or less threatening to individual well-being. They represent the poles of a continuum where each concrete behaviour can be located.

METHODS FOR STUDYING THE DEVELOPMENT OF MOTIVATION

The methods used to study motivation will be briefly presented. They vary widely according to the theoretical preferences of the authors and the particular goals of the research.

Direct Observation

A common method used in studies with animals in laboratory settings is the direct observation of some kinds of behaviour associated with motivation, such as activity level, persistence with a task, amount of effort, response latency, frequency of errors, and so on. This method is also used with humans in the framework of drive and field theories. It permits an indirect evaluation of motivational level because it can be inferred from the presence or absence of this or that behaviour. Such observations of motivated behaviour, limited to the presently observable motivational state, progressively give way to the assessment of motivation, assumed to be an internal and stable trait, through verbal productions on projective material. However, more recently, direct observation of children's or preadolescent's behaviours, although rarely used alone, has gained a new popularity, as we shall see later.

Projective Measures

The first attempt to assess human motives directly was achieved by the elaboration of the *Thematic Apperception Test* (TAT) by Murray (1953) which was later adopted by McClelland and Atkinson. This instrument presents some pictures (cues), such as a boy in front of a book, or two men speaking in front of a machine. The subjects must describe the scene, what happened before and what will occur in the future. The motives were evaluated from the content analysis of the fantasy-based productions stimulated by the TAT cues. The frequency of imagery of successful achievement associated with positive feelings in these fantasies is assumed to be a manifestation of the need for achievement, while the reference to frequent failures, shame and misfortune is an expression of fear of failure. This evaluation procedure is strongly influenced by Freudian theory. It is based on the assumption that human motives, being unconscious, are more clearly expressed through free associations than through self-descriptions. However, to be expressed in fantasies, motives need to be aroused, as has been observed in specific circumstances, such as food deprivation experiences: hungry subjects fantasize about food more than non-hungry ones. Before the administration of the TAT, presented as a test of creative imagination, subjects were asked to work on some tasks. It was expected that the manipulation of the task condition would arouse motivation. To test this assumption, two conditions were compared: the relaxed condition and the achievement-oriented condition. In the former condition, the task was described as an exploratory one, its importance was minimized and the identification of the subject was not important; in the latter, the task was presented as a test of important abilities (intelligence) and the task was achieved in an ambience of college examination. As expected, the expression of achievement motives is stronger in the achievement-oriented conditions than in the relaxed ones.

This projective instrument has been widely used to study achievement motives as well as power or social acceptance motives. Nevertheless, the TAT has been much criticized in terms of its psychometric properties. Entwisle (1972) has pointed out its lack of stability test-retest, of interraters' reliability, and of internal consistency (scores among the TAT cues), aspects that seriously question the validity of this instrument. Several authors have pointed out that some of these weaknesses could easily be overcome through careful standardization of the conditions and procedures of the administration of the tests, as well as by adequate training for the scorers, and others are concerned with the specificity of the motives which vary more across situations than other psychological characteristics such as mental abilities, for instance (Atkinson & Birch, 1978; Heckhausen, Schmalt & Schneider, 1985; McClelland, 1985). Atkinson and McClelland, on the basis of research results that are consistent with theoretical expectancies, affirm that it is possible to expect validity despite low internal consistency: inconsistencies in behavioural level are not incompatible with the consistency of this latent dimension.

An additional problem linked to the use of projective instruments is the cost of their scoring. This is based on content analysis and, therefore, it is difficult to use with large samples. To avoid this problem, Schmalt developed a semi-projective instrument for children and young adolescents. This is composed of 18 pictures grouped into six domains (manual activity, musical activity, sports, school, giving help, asserting independence), and subjects must choose, from among the 18 statements available for each picture, one or several of them which would best apply to themselves in each situation, such as 'he feels good doing this'; 'he believes he did everything right'; 'he is afraid he could do something wrong'; 'he thinks he can't do that'; 'he wants to be able to accomplish more than all the others'. The psychometric qualities of this instrument that assesses hope of success, facilitating and debilitating anxieties, are adequate (Heckhausen et al., 1985).

Questionnaires

The problems associated with the use of the projective measures and the need to simplify administration and scoring procedures directed researchers to the use of questionnaires as a means for the assessment of achievement motivation itself and of other motivational characteristics. There are many questionnaires but their quality varies, depending on their origin (intuition or theory-based), their psychometric characteristics, and their adequacy to measure the particular motivational dimension concerned.

Curiously enough, in Atkinsonian achievement motivation theory, fear of failure has always been assessed through a questionnaire (Test Anxiety Questionnaire from Mandler & Sarason, 1952) and not through projective measures. Although this option has never been clearly justified, anxiety has been assimilated to fear of failure, which, in turn, is a manifestation of need for approval because anxious persons anticipate disapproval from significant others (McClelland, 1985). Items of the questionnaire refer to consciousness of psychophysiological symptoms of anxiety, impairment of performances, feeling of uneasiness and worries about performances. Both factorial and conceptual analyses, reported by Heckhausen et al. (1985), suggested that anxiety is a bidimensionality construct.

Instruments based on the hierarchical self-concept theories, for instance, assess the differences in each specific area—physical, social, cognitive, and so on. Moreover, many of them have also included global self-concept (or self-esteem) as one specific dimension of the structure. Indeed, self-esteem is a global feeling about one's worth, and it is not directly dependent on other evaluative dimensions. Some factorial analyses have confirmed this theoretical structure (Marsh, 1987b) while other analyses have pointed to self-esteem as a more general factor (Demetriou et al., in press). The authors have always given importance to the psychometric qualities of these questionnaires, which have been systematically assessed.

The development of a cognitive perspective in the study of motivation emphasizes the relevance of a subjective point of view in achievement-related situations rather than an objective assessment of psychological characteristics. Self-reports have progressively gained importance. In the study of attributions, self-efficacy (perception of one's own competence to achieve some goal) self-concept, or action control, the analysis of individual opinions or representations is not a technical constraint, as was the case for the evaluation of personality traits, but covers a central aspect of the phenomenon: the subjective perception about the self. Various kinds of instruments have been elaborated: questionnaires, inventories, semantically differentiated scales, sentences to be completed, open questions, and so on. In this perspective, the main preoccupation of the authors is to avoid the overdetermination of the subject's point-of-view. This problem has been carefully analysed in the evaluation of action control, self-concept and causal attributions. For other instruments, the overdetermination of subjects' self-ratings by social desirability bias is a main concern common to all testing procedures.

Care should also be taken according to the specific purposes of the study. Oosterwegel (1994), for instance, in the framework of Markus' theory, attempted to differentiate the relationship between actual and ideal self-concept and also between the fantasies about the view of significant others about the self, in real or ideal terms, and enhanced the self-other differentiation. If the objective is to observe the development of the self-referenced thoughts with age as well as their progressive differentiation or organization, the use of unstructured material, open questions or incomplete sentences is better than the administration of a highly structured questionnaire.

Direct Observation with Interview

Direct observation of behaviour has also been used in more recent studies. For instance, in some laboratory experiments which aimed to analyse the cognitive structure of motivation and emotion (e.g. Hamilton, 1983, 1988; Kuhl, 1986), the researchers focused on the information processing structure of motivation. That is, they took information processing parameters, such as reaction speed and short-term memory, as indicators of the activation of cognitive structures or of some interferences in its functioning.

Children's motivated behaviours were also assessed through direct observation. This assessment is not limited only to very young children but it is also used with older ones and preadolescents in laboratory or classroom settings. The observations are frequently videotaped and completed with verbal explanations of self-referenced thought (Dweck & Elliott, 1983; Dweck & Legget, 1989; Lemos, 1993): in general the researchers ask for the pupils' perception of the task, the goals they pursue, their feelings, their internal talk, their personal conceptions of their own characteristics and the strategies adopted, both when confronted with the situation and *a posteriori*. The analysis of pupils' reactions when directly confronted with specific situations in a laboratory setting, as well as with the context-bound approach in a school setting, should lead more directly to educational applications than the studies of general motives and goals, which are not always easily translated into specific contexts.

MOTIVATIONAL CAPABILITIES AND CHARACTERISTICS THROUGHOUT THE LIFE-SPAN

Theories of motivation assume the relative stability of motives from adolescence to adulthood, basing the assumption on the relative stability of environmental pressures throughout the life-span. Early socialization experiences are fundamental for the development of motivation. Achievement experiences in different domains, indirectly dependent on socialization, are progressively integrated into motivational structures to reinforce the previous development: if superficial changes are due to situational variations, deeper changes may be better explained by socialization experiences. However, attempts to introduce changes in non-achievement-motivated subjects through adequate intervention, by McClelland (1985), a researcher who views achievement motivation as a stable trait, are associated with the implicit recognition that relevant modification of daily experiences might lead to changes in motivation, even when they are externally induced. Nevertheless, the stability and generalization of induced changes are current problems in all intervention programmes. The life-span perspective assumes that normative life transitions spontaneously offer everyone relevant experiences which introduce deep changes in motivational attitudes and behaviours. Certain universal demands are associated with life options and life transitions and provoke psychological reorganization. However, these effects have been studied rather more in the field of personality than in the field of motivation.

Most of the studies on motivational development throughout the life-span are limited to the description of motivational development during childhood or early adolescence. In addition, they are based on a cross-sectional rather than on a longitudinal methodology and, as well as the

Table 8.5 Main development tendencies in motivational changes

	Characteristics of developmental steps	Main causes	Mechanism of change
Childhood	Intrinsic motivation Dynamic orientation Dynamic conception of intelligence Little differentiation of causal attributions Task involvement Short time-perspective	Cognitive development	Increase of: self-concept dimensions complexity of cognitive structures Differentiation of dimensions and causal attributions
		Educational practices	Early achievement training and independence training Reward for good behaviour Incipient: personal criterion of excellence
	Positive self-esteem and self-concept Low anxiety	Social comparison	
Early and middle adolescence	Extrinsic motivation State orientation Static conception of intelligence Differentiation of causal attributions	Cognitive development	Formal thinking Inference of internal characteristics from behaviours Negative relationship between capacity and effort
	Ego involvement Long time-perspective Decrease of self-esteem and self-concept	Social norms and values	Identification of social norms and values Differentiation of social norms, values and representations according to social groups Identification of socially valued chatacteristics Normative criterion of excellence
		Social comparison	Use of self-justifications Variables among social groups (conformism, attributions, . . .)
	High anxiety	Educational practices	Reward only when individual performance is better than performances of others
Late adolescence and adulthood	Recuperation of levels of self-esteem and self-concept Reduction of the realism of self-representations	Cognitive development	Formal thinking Best anticipation of consequences of behaviour Social perspective taking
	Variation of the main motivational tendencies during life-span	Social norms and values	Critical evaluation of social norms and values Adhesion to a personal system of norms and values Normative and personal criterion of excellence Efficacy of self-justifications Self-image management
		Social comparison	Comparison between personal and social goals
		Normative transitions	Balance of goal attainment during life-span

specification of the stages of development during childhood and adolescence, they attempt to pinpoint processes which are responsible for specific aspects of motivational development. The difficulties posed by longitudinal studies explain why they are usually limited on their time span: they cover a few months to six years. For this reason, age differences are frequently viewed as indicators of developmental changes over years. Group differences, regularly observed in a motivational domain, might also be considered as the actual result of the motivational development from a life-span perspective, different for each social group. Some results of these studies will be described below. The main developmental tendencies in motivational changes are available in Table 8.5.

Homeostatic Theories

Drive and field theories are not concerned with developmental tendencies in motivation because they focus on the present. However, some studies, which focused on motivation as global characteristic orientating behaviour (Guttman, 1975), have suggested important changes at midlife in both men and women: men switch from an egocentric and assertive orientation to an interpersonal and prosocial one, while women reduce their focus on interpersonal relationships to become more egocentric and assertive, and to accept their aggressive tendencies. Masculine and feminine needs, that are present in everyone, emerge in different periods of life: the less dominant needs call for satisfaction when the more dominant ones (more frequently satisfied during the first part of life) exercise fewer pressures.

Achievement Motivation

Motivational differences and rearing practices

In the expectancy-value framework, the first studies were particularly interested in the effect of early socialization experiences on the development of achievement motivation (Winterbotton, 1958; Crandall, Katovsky & Crandall, 1965). Particular early experiences were associated with stable individual differences in achievement motivation in adulthood: early achievement training and early independence training have been pointed out as the aspects of child-rearing practices which are most relevant to the development of achievement motives. Sex and class differences were also observed. That is, women showed lower levels of achievement motives and higher levels of affiliation motives than men in adulthood, but not in childhood and adolescence (Atkinson & Birch, 1978; Hermans, 1980; Fontaine, 1990a,b, 1994). Achievement motivation in women was higher than in men in relaxed conditions but did not increase between relaxed and achievement-oriented conditions (enhancing capacity and social comparison), while that in men did (Atkinson & Litwin, 1960; Veroff, Atkinson, Feld & Gurin, 1960).

Females showed more fear of success than males (Hoffman, 1975; Horner, 1974); the same kind of differences and variations have been found among SES, ethnic groups, and others. That is, low-status groups are less motivated than high-status groups. These differences vary widely according to culture and have become weaker in recent studies.

The above-mentioned differences among individuals and groups have been attributed to differences in early socialization. In our research (Fontaine, 1990a, 1994), variables were analysed in their components in order to understand better the relationship between motivation differences among social groups and gender and differences in child-rearing practices. It was assumed that these motivational differences result, at least in part, from differences in rearing practices or changes in the impact of these practices. The results of this study do not match the research paradigm, which assumes that the process responsible for the association between motivation and rearing practices is the same whatever the characteristics of the context. On the contrary, they suggest that the association between these variables varies with the context. It demonstrated that training for independence does not stimulate achievement motivation in all cultural contexts: in school settings, obedience was more associated with higher levels of achievement motivation than independence during early adolescence (sixth graders). In the Portuguese culture where this study was made, teachers placed a higher value on conformist behaviour than on independent behaviour. Children who lived in authoritarian families, with more rigid rules and less autonomy, seemed to be more motivated for school achievement than those who did not. These results cannot be overgeneralized. They show, however, that the determinants of achievement motivation are dependent on the kind of behaviour valued as success in a particular context.

This study also showed that intracultural differences do exist. The same rearing practice (internal attribution of responsibility to the child) does not have the same effect on motivation in different social groups: internal attribution was associated with a higher motivation in pupils from average SES, in boys from a high SES and in girls from a low SES, but with a lower motivation in boys from a low SES and in girls from a high SES. The positive effect of internal attribution on motivation seems easy to understand. The mother considers that children are responsible for what has happened to them and are able to change the course of events through adequate behaviours. This maternal conviction, transmitted to the children, will help them to react positively to challenging situations.

However, this effect is not observed for low SES boys and high SES girls. Possibly the effect of internal interpretation of school results depends on the frequency of successes or failures: the belief in children's responsibility for their numerous failures in low SES would have a debilitating effect on achievement motivation, while denial of responsibility would reduce anxiety associated with the threat of failure, protect self-esteem and maintain higher levels of motivation. Results of boys sustain this interpretation which is also compatible with the necessity to reduce the higher levels of anxiety observed in high SES girls, by denying their responsibility for the outcomes.

This interpretation cannot explain the results of low SES girls. Possibly variations of representations about academic intelligence according to this social group may help with understanding these results. In low SES, social stereotypes transmit an image of female incompetence in intellectual tasks. Through their belief in the daughter's responsibility, mothers transmit their conviction about the importance of school achievement and their trust in their daughters's ability in this field, and also encourage their daughters to keep away from those stereotypes and to pursue success in the school area. These results enhance the complexity of interaction effects. Without deeper analysis, they show that the impact of educational practices varies with the context and the characteristics of the target child because school achievement has separate meanings and requires different strategies from males and females of varying SES.

Cumulative effect of ability and motivation

Another stream of research provided evidence about the cumulative effects of initial motivation, ability and performance on the development of achievement motivation during school years. The motivated and capable pupils in the first years of schooling are those who spend more time at work, are more efficient and attain better results. Their successes reinforce their achievement tendencies and the time spent on achievement also increases both their abilities and their knowledge. These cumulative effects explain the rise of the strength of correlations between achievement motivation and school performance with age, associated with changes in beliefs and cognitions. However, the relationships between motivation and performance vary widely with gender and SES (Fontaine, 1990a, 1991a; Weiner, 1992). Recent studies on causal ordering between achievement motivation and performance have shown that performance has more influence on achievement motivation than the other way round (Fontaine, 1995). This finding, limited to junior high school pupils, cannot be overgeneralized as a reciprocal effect may be observed later. The same increase in association between motivation and performance has been observed for anxiety (in the negative direction) and for academic self-concept (in the positive direction). The reasons presented to justify these phenomena are different, although all of them enhance the importance of past experiences, their interpretations and their affective consequences.

Anxiety

Schwarzer (1986), for instance, maintained that anxiety depends on the perception of contingencies between behaviour and performance in past experiences. The subjects' reaction to the first failure experience in a challenging task is not necessarily translated into withdrawal or helplessness. More frequently, in this first stage, increases in effort and persistence are observed because the challenge of the task is stronger than the threat of failure and the feeling of loss of control. These striving tendencies are observed only in people with a positive perception of self-efficacy (perception of capacity to adopt efficient goal-directed behaviours) which is not impaired by the failure experience (Bandura, 1986; Schunk, 1991). In this case, failure raises curiosity, exploration of task characteristics, and investment. However, repetition of failure increases the threat to self-esteem: the subjects maintain strong effort and persistence, essentially to avoid failure, and the emotionality dimension of anxiety is aroused. Mention must be made about facilitating anxiety at this second stage. Anxiety evolves to the third stage when these active behaviours are not able to change the repetition of failure: the threatening aspect of the task arouses the feeling of loss of control with the decrease in challenge; worry about the results and their causes is aroused and debilitating anxiety lowers effort and persistence at the task. Finally, with repetition of the same experiences, the feeling of loss of control becomes more salient, and the helplessness syndrome develops, with the depression and passivity which are the characteristics of the fourth stage. The development of anxiety, exclusively interpreted in terms of the relationship between the subject and his experience of failure, explains the increases in his negative relationships with performance during his life-span, in conditions of repeated and stable failure. As Raynor (1982) has pointed out, repeated failure also reduces the capacity to anticipate goal attainment (expectations) while repeated success increases this capacity. This explains the negative relationship between anxiety and achievement motivation. Although females are more anxious than males, their anxiety impairs their performance to a lesser extent (Fontaine, 1990a, Hermans, 1980; Sarason, 1987).

Self-concept

Although it is assumed that, in each situation, the subject builds an image of the person he believes he is, and acts in accordance with this representation (Reuchlin, 1990), the same working-self must be associated with different behavioural strategies. Most of the theorists assume that self-concept influences behaviour, at least in the specific domain where it has been assessed, but nothing has been said about the processes linking self-concept and behaviour. More recently, researchers have been concerned about the direction of causality in the relationship between self-concept and achievement. Recent empirical studies have shown that achievement determines self-concept rather than the opposite, although a more reciprocal effect appeared with age (Fontaine, 1995; Helmke, 1988; Marsh, 1990; Skaalvik & Hagtvet, 1990). Other studies reported that self-concept of competence predicts affective reactions to success and future intrinsic motivation. Unfortunately, these last studies are based on cross-sectional data (Harter, 1983).

Differentiation and structuration

'A central developmental task during adolescence is the formation of a coherent and articulate self-concept . . . a theory that individuals have constructed about themselves' (van Aken, van Lieshout & Haselager, 1995, p. 169). The association between self-concept and performance is currently assumed to be a consequence of the development of self-concept during childhood and adolescence, sustained by the development of cognitive structures. Cognitive development allows subjects to integrate more and more differentiated information about the self into progressively more complex mental structures. Direct or indirect reference to Piaget's theory is the rule, both for the researchers focused on the differentiation of self-concept and for those interested in the differentiation of other achievement-related constructs.

Harter (1983) has proposed a hypothetical model for self-concept development based on two axes: the content axis and the structure axis (Table 8.6). The *content axis* accounts for the development of the content topics and categories in self-description: from childhood to adulthood, self-descriptions evolved from observable categories (physical attributes, behaviours) to inferred ones, covering psychological aspects (such as emotions and affects, motivations, and cognitions). Simultaneously, progressive differentiation and enrichment of the contents of each category are also observed. However, the evolution of self-descriptive categories does not mean the disappearance of the previous ones. The *structural axis* accounts for the development of the organization of the self-descriptive topics into each category. Harter has differentiated four stages. The first, corresponding to preoperational thoughts, is characterized by self-description in terms of single present-centred attributes, including all-or-none self-concept (always good), and its further temporal differentiation (good in some activities, bad in others). The second stage (concrete operational thoughts), integrates these topics in traits, at first overgeneralized (uncomfortable in all activities), then more differentiated (uncomfortable in some activities, comfortable in others). The third (early formal operational thoughts) integrates these traits in single abstractions, at first overgeneralized (intelligent) and then differentiated (uncomfortable in creative activities, but comfortable in logical activities). The fourth stage pursues this abstraction at a higher level with the same sequence of overgeneralization and differentiation. At each stage, the new information which cannot be explained through the previous structure leads to the differentiation of this structure that exerts cognitive pressures for integration of these contradictory aspects into a more complex structure. Table 8.6 illustrates this evolution through some examples of physical, behavioural and psychological attributes.

The progressive differentiation of the self-descriptive categories has been empirically observed (Fontaine, 1991b,c; Harter, 1985; Huteau & Vouillot, 1987; Marsh, 1989; Reuchlin, 1990; Tomé, 1983). Studies using less structured methods for self-concept evaluation have directly shown the increase in the number of categories with age while those using highly structured

Table 8.6 Harter's model for self-concept development

Content axis Structural axis (operational levels)		Physical attributes	Behavioural attributes	Psychological attributes
Pre-operational	Globalization	Nice boy Nice face *but*	Good at all activities Good at drawing *but*	Good boy Sometimes good behaviour *but*
	Differentiation	Ugly feet Not nice at all	Not so good at reading Uncomfortable in a lot of activities	Sometimes bad behaviour Not very popular
Concrete operations	Globalization	Funny nose *but* Legs and arms too long	Comfortable in solving problems *but* Uncomfortable in group work	Good at understanding feelings *but* Bad at making jokes
	Differentiation	Handsome Athletic body *but*	Low sociability Good friend, Strong relationships *but*	Low assertiveness Good at defending ideas and opinions *but*
Early formal	Globalization	Skin problems	Low attraction for social meetings	Bad at leadership
	Differentiation	Good looking Nice appearance *but*	Independent Independent in professional setting *but*	Tolerant Openness to novelty *but*
Formal	Globalization	Low attractiveness	Dependent in family setting	Traditional values in private life
	Differentiation			

Source: Adapted from Harter (1983).

instruments with pre-defined categories have indirectly shown the same phenomenon through the reduction of correlations between categories with age, an indicator of their progressive independence. Demetriou et al. (in press) have observed that the relationship between cognitive and hypercognitive systems is non-existent among the fifth graders, appears during the sixth grade, but remains weak and dominated by the hypercognitive system, becoming stronger and dominated by the cognitive system one year later. 'Changes traditionally associated with the transition from childhood to adolescence may be related more to the communication between the two knowing levels of mental architecture rather than to the models and the dimensions per se which reside at the levels' (Demetriou et al., in press, p. 50).

Sex differences have also been observed in the various dimensions of self-concept: females have lower self-concept than males in some fields (physical competence, and emotional stability) but higher in other (verbal and school competence, creativity and honesty); in global terms, females are more strict than males in their self-evaluation (Demetriou et al., in press; Harter, 1983; March, 1989). However, sex differences in mathematical self-concept vary widely with cultural context (Fontaine, 1991b,c). Differences among SES are exclusively observed in academic dimensions and vary with school level, as will be shown later.

Differentiations among self- and task-related cognitions

Demetriou (ch. 5 this volume) relates that, at the age of 3, children do have a first representation of causal relations, and from the age of 4, children can make the distinction between psychological and biological or physical causality. Nicholls and Stipek have also focused on the effect of cognitive development on the achievement-related cognitions about the causes of achievement outcomes (Nicholls, Jagacinski & Miller, 1986; Stipek, 1984). They have distinguished between three stages of differentiation for children from 5 to 12 years old. The *first stage* corresponds to a total absence of conceptual distinction among task difficulty, capacity, luck and effort as determinants of outcomes. Children's interpretations of the reasons for outcomes are based more on their own desires than on external information: they cannot perceive that more difficult tasks require greater capacity, cannot differentiate outcomes depending on luck or skills, or relate outcomes, effort and ability. At the *second stage*, some elements of reality are integrated in cognitive structures: complex tasks are viewed as more difficult (puzzles with more pieces are more difficult than those with fewer pieces); effort influences performance not only in tasks depending on ability but also in those depending on luck, but the former is more influenced than the latter; ability also influences outcomes. At this stage, no relationship is established among the different causes. At the *third and fourth stages*, elements from social comparison are introduced in the causal schemata. The difficulty of the task is inferred from the difficulty of execution by the majority of

children: children who can do a task when most of the others have failed are
viewed as more intelligent; children who can perform as well as others with
less effort are also viewed as more intelligent. The level of capacity limits the
effect of effort on performances and effort cannot influence outcomes depending on luck. These results have shown that the influence of social
comparison processes in the construction of personal theories is active only
from the end of childhood: effort can only be viewed as a two-edged sword
by adolescents and adults (Covington, 1984). From adolescence, attribution
of outcomes seems to be relatively stable: no intraindividual change in
causal attributions has been observed from fifth to eleventh grades (Faria,
1995). However, in the same study, differences among school years have
been observed: fifth graders attribute their school results to more internal,
instable and controllable factors than eleventh graders. These differences
have been explained by cohort effects. Some group differences have also
been observed: the self-serving bias has rather more frequently been identified in the attributional pattern of the male than in that of the female
(Weiner, 1986); females are more strict in their self-evaluation than males
(Demetriou et al., in press); and more girls than boys adopt a static conception of intelligence associated with helpless pattern to cope with failure
(Dweck & Elliott, 1983)—such differences have not been observed in all
cultural contexts (Faria & Fontaine, 1994). Children from different SES
attribute their results to different causes (internal, if high SES and unstable if
low SES) and classify the same cause in different categories (effort is stable
for low SES and unstable for high SES pupils) (Bar-Tal, Goldberg &
Knaani, 1984).

Self-concept as a defence mechanism

In the perspective of Wicklund, self-evaluations of adolescents or adults are
not necessarily the reflection of their competence to respond to environmental demands. Wicklund's theory about the development of self-conceptions is quite different from the previous ones. According to self-perception
theories, the self-concept is based on the individual perception of relevant
past experiences in the social or physical domain. According to symbolic
interactionism theory, the self-concept has its origin in the image that others
have of the subject: that is, it is believed that each subject sees himself as
others see him. The perception of others is dependent on what is recognized
as successful behaviours by each society. A subject's perceptions of these
valued aspects in himself can only be formed through social perspective-
taking. Obviously, various errors may be introduced in the building of one's
self-concept: these may come from errors in how others observe the subject's
behaviours or from errors in the subject's ability to see him/herself through
the eyes of others. Therefore, the aspects included in individual self-concept
are limited to the individual's successful behaviours, as perceived directly by
the subject, or indirectly, through the perception of others.

However, according to Wicklund, self-conceptions about social-valued characteristics are not dependent on a successful contact with the demands of reality but on the capacity to establish this contact. When individuals feel that they are not able to respond adequately to the environmental demand, their preoccupations about personal abilities increase. On the other hand, success 'is accompanied by a lack of interest in one's own dispositions' (Wicklund, 1986a, p. 145). To understand Wicklund's point of view, it is necessary to analyse the origin of human description in terms of 'dispositions' that are categories of valued characteristics (intellectual, artistic, . . .). The environment contains different demands that may be more or less complex. If the persons can respond adequately to the environmental demand, their behaviours are assessed as successful ones. It is also the only way for them to know environmental complexity. If a successful behaviour is regularly manifested by everyone (such as walking), no dispositional categories are created to characterize it. If this is not the case, and if behaviours are viewed as important for society (such as artistic or business behaviours), they are labelled in terms of dispositions. These dispositions are socially valued categories which characterize behaviour of subjects who respond perfectly to the environmental demands in a particular aspect.

However, people who are highly competent and exercise that competence are not at all concerned about belonging to any particular category. For them, designation into a particular category is a regression as it cannot cover the specificity, the accuracy, or the functioning of their dynamic interaction with the environment. Although these categories have been created to identify highly competent subjects, they are particularly used by those who cannot do so well. Belonging to categories is an indirect way of coping with environmental demands when the persons cannot directly respond to these demands. In this case, they attempt to use the symbols, self-descriptions, relevant material, or whatever for building up their sense of having the relevant 'competence' to be a member of a specific category. This process has been described by Wicklund and Gollwitzer (1981) in the theory of symbolic self-completion. 'Self-symbolizing' is the main goal of the 'static orientation'; direct response to the environmental demand through adequate behaviour defines the 'dynamic orientation' (Wicklund, 1986a,b).

The use of categorization is aroused when the persons appreciate their difficulty in responding to the environmental demands. This use is only possible when they understand that a 'category system' is valuable for society, and that people are valued for their membership in these categories. Young children whose cognitive competence does not allow them to use the categories would be more affected by their failure to meet environmental demands in terms of self-worth. At the same time, because of difficulty in anticipating whether they will meet the environmental demands or not, they have to be more persistent and able to learn from the tasks. The use of the categories by older children protects the self from consequences of failure. However, this advantage has a side-effect as it is also associated with a lower capability to persist and to learn from experience. Wicklund has not explained why, in failure situations, some children use the categories while others do not.

Social Comparison

Realism of self-concept

The progressive integration of information provided by the task and by the social world necessarily leads to a more realistic self-concept. The increase in realism explains the increase in the relationship between self-concept and performance with age, if both are assessed in the same achievement domain. The force of the association increases when the indicators of performance are more consensual and objective. Realism also justifies the reduction of self-concept levels from childhood to middle adolescence: children progressively substitute an idealistic image of themselves for a realistic one. Relationships between self-concept and performance vary with age, gender, SES and also with the dimension of self-concept considered (Fontaine, 1991a,b,c; Marsh, 1989; Muller, Gullung & Bocci, 1988). Self-evaluation accuracy is associated with age in a sigmoid fashion because the adolescent uses more strict evaluation during the phase of major changes in performance at the beginning of new developmental cycles (Demetriou et al., in press).

The relationship between self-concept and performance is usually positive. This positive relationship is compatible with several models of causality. The self-enhancement model assumes that self-concept has dynamic properties and it influences performance because psychological well-being is essential if one is to take on challenging tasks: this model has inspired many training programmes. The opposite model, the skill development model, claims that self-concept is principally determined by performance. It develops through the integration of past experiences of successes and failures in multiple situations: self-concept is influenced more by performance than vice versa. The third model is the synthesis of the previous ones: it assumes the reciprocal influence of self-concept and performance. These are empirical results in line with each of these models. However, modern methods of analysis, such as structural equation modelling, provide the means for testing these models in a more systematic and straightforward way. Evidence generated by these methods suggests that, in the academic field, the skill development model fits the data for younger students better while the reciprocal model better explains the results for older students. Self-concept becomes less dependent on achievement with age. This phenomenon takes place earlier in boys (Fontaine, 1995; Marsh, 1990; Skaalvik & Hagtvet, 1990).

Influence of reference groups

The development of a more realistic self-concept is dependent on the feedback provided by significant others in different settings, that is the family, the school and the peer groups. A way to appreciate the realism of self-concept is through the comparison between self-descriptions and descriptions of the subject by others. Mutuality has been conceptualized by van Aken and van Lieshout (1991) as the agreement between self-descriptions and descriptions by significant others (parents, teachers, and peers). High mutuality indicates concordance among descriptions of the subject, low mutuality indicates discrepancies. Mutuality is associated with well-being and efficacy in school and social context. In a study with pre- and early adolescents, van Aken et al. (1995) have observed a positive correlation between mutuality and school achievement when the 'other' is the teacher, and between mutuality and self-esteem, social acceptance, whatever the 'significant other'. Peer acceptance, for instance, is a powerful motivational force which leads the child to share the group norms and goals. It can explain children's either social or anti-social behaviour (for more information, see van Lieshout and Doise, ch. 6 this volume).

The influence of reference groups is also important for the understanding of the evolution of self-concept with age. The later recuperation of the levels of self-concepts, observed at the end of adolescence and early adulthood, could be ascribed to different processes: it may be due to the change of the relative position of the subject in the normative comparison group by the modification of the reference groups, or by the substitution of group-reference standards by self-reference standards. Differences in the evolution of adolescents' academic self-concepts in different SES is an example of the influence of the reference group on the self-concept development. Theoretically, subjects from higher SES, as they have higher performance levels at school, must show a higher self-concept related to academic competence. However, a number of studies have reported a higher academic self-concept in subjects from lower SES, compared with those of higher SES, and have explained these results as the consequence of the big-fish-little-pond effect (Marsh, 1987a). The choice of a better school by higher SES families places children in a more demanding comparison group in terms of standards of performance: an average pupil must feel weak in comparison with the others in this reference group. On the other hand, average pupils from low SES, enrolled in a low-status school with weaker pupils, must feel better in comparison: social comparison processes improve their academic self-concept. However, in countries with mixed school populations, the increase of low SES pupils' self-concept occurs only at the end of secondary school (Fontaine, 1991c). The inner school reference group is not favourable to the low SES pupils but the distance between their own level of school attainment and that of their reference groups outside the school (family, neighbours), is highly favourable and it enhances their self-concepts of academic competence. The level of school attainment of low SES pupils is higher than that of other members of this social group, while this is not the case in that of average or high SES pupils.

The impact of normative standards, reinforced by social comparison with others, particularly important during adolescence, should be progressively balanced by more personal standards (Fontaine & Faria, 1989). Indeed, the cognitive development of adolescents allows the use of more complex self-justifications for their behaviours or attitudes, which protect or enhance their self-concept: the self-serving redefinition of reality should not be confused with greater proximity to reality. Indeed, the hypercognitive system simultaneously reflects the reality and, as a part of the human mind, directs the perception and analysis of reality in a personal way (Demetriou et al., in press). Adolescence, as a period of the definition of personal norms and values, also stimulates the differentiation between individual and group reference norms and values. Differences between auto- and hetero-evaluations are not lower in adulthood than in childhood and are greater in areas with less consensual criteria of evaluation (Cairns & Cairns, 1988).

Competitive structures and distribution of rewards in school context

The decrease of motivation with age is dependent partially on cognitive development but also in educational practices. The way to react to environmental challenge depends on socialization experiences. The same evolution has been observed in several motivational characteristics for most of the students throughout school years: from intrinsic to extrinsic motivation, from mastery to performance goals, from better to lower self-concept, from dynamic to static orientation, and from low to high test anxiety (Deci & Ryan, 1985; Ames, 1984; Harter, 1983; Marsh, 1989; Nichols, 1984; Wicklund, 1986b). Some authors have argued that the school context has a negative impact on the development of motivational characteristics of the majority of students. The progressive organization of teaching structures in a way that stimulates social comparison, and the conception of intellectual ability as a static characteristic used to locate the students in a gradient of competence which is relatively stable, are presented as the principal aspects responsible for the negative effects of school context (Ames, 1984; Covington, 1984; Stipek & Daniels, 1988).

Competitive structures value success as a sign of intellectual capacity than enhances students' feelings of competence. In common school settings, children who obtain better marks are rewarded more than children who obtain lower marks. Success creates negative interdependence among subjects because it is evaluated through social comparison: the opportunity to be the best diminishes if others are successful. Information about comparative performances is plentiful and allows the placement of students in gradients of excellence that are relatively stable and are strongly associated with gradients of competence (Marshall & Weinstein, 1986). Failure experiences in these structures are very threatening since they are viewed as signs of incapacity and stimulate feelings of 'nondeservingness' and lower self-esteem. To protect his self-concept of competence, the poor student uses defence mechanisms such as excuses, 'manipulation' of effort, absences, and the like, in an attempt to avoid the attribution of this failure to lack of capacity. While static orientation does not seem the best option in coping with environmental demands, it is useful in a competitive context as it helps the subject to maintain a sense of self-worth in failure situations, building the self into socially valued categories (intelligence). However, it does not stimulate learning as the subject is more concerned with category member-ship than with task-solving strategies: in the long run, most of these mecha-nisms are responsible for the decline in achievement levels, effort, persist-ence, and self-concept, and for the impairment of learning processes and increase in test anxiety.

In competitive structures, differences among the achievement levels of pupils maximize differences in student motivation, and therefore arouse avoidance behaviour and reduce investment in learning activities for the majority of students. To strive against this tendency, teachers use praise, criticism and external rewards. Sometimes, results are different from those expected, with the reduction of effort after praise and increase in effort after criticism (Meyer, 1992). Indeed, the students' perception of praise and criticism is mediated by his inference of teachers' perceptions about his capacity. Praise for the results in an easy task is associated with inference of low capacity while criticism of the results in a difficult task is associated with high capacity. Throughout school, attitudes toward school become more negative. Teachers' pressures are contradictory: on the one hand, they train children to develop dynamic relations with environmental demands, while on the other hand, as members of society, they value them through descrip-tions in terms of categories as a sign of their potential (Wicklund, 1986a). Although intrinsic motivation does not need to be stimulated but only nurtured, it decreases over school years. External rewards reduce intrinsic motivation and genuine interest in learning: students in more controlled and competitive classrooms attribute their outcomes to external or unknown sources and project less self-determined behaviours. They cannot experience autonomy and mastery as their behaviours seem to be entirely determined by external pressures and teacher's orientations. In this context, students do not consider themselves individuals responsible for their behaviour ('ori-gin'), but as 'pawns' pushed round (De Charms, 1984). Ryan, Connell and Deci (1985) studied how to transform this tendency, from extrinsic into intrinsic motivation. For this purpose, they described four levels of regula-tion: (i) *extrinsic regulation* when behaviours are exclusively dependent on the expected external contingencies; (ii) *introjected regulation* when behav-iour is rewarded or punished by the subject himself through intrapsychic, self-esteem-based, contingencies: internal evaluation and its affective conse-quences motivate behaviours; (iii) *identification* when the external regula-tion is experienced as the subject's values or goals, and action is viewed as self-determined: goal pursuing in its own right allows a feeling of autonomy and mastery; (iv) *integration* of the different goals or values into a coherent, non-conflictual hierarchy represents the fourth level of self-regulated behav-iour that is only reached in adulthood?

The educational context of early years seems to sustain and improve motivation better (Stipek & Daniels, 1988). It is more focused on skill mastery and provides more individualized learning without social compari-son. Stipek (1984) suggested maintaining this kind of environment during secondary school to improve the motivation of older children. But, would this environment also be successful with older children?

Age and Cohort Effects during Life-span

The longitudinal study of the US population by Veroff, Reuman and Feld (1984) is one of the few studies that observed the effects of age and cohort on motivational variables during adulthood. They compared random samples of the US population in 1957 and 1976. Age effect has been interpreted as evidence of developmental changes in a life-span perspective; cohort differences as the effect of changes in cultural norms and values across time, transmitted through socialization with visible impact on motivational patterns as well as those of historically relevant experiences shared by the same cohort, such as World War Two. The above authors have compared four major motives: (i) achievement motive as the search for excellence and superiority in comparative terms; (ii) affiliation motive as the tendency to create and maintain emotional relationships; (iii) fear of weakness as a fear of losing influence or being controlled by others; and (iv) power motive as the desire to have influence on both the world of object and the world of persons. Differences across the life-span varied according to motivational characteristics and gender. Women's achievement, affiliation, and power motives decrease with age and this tendency is stronger at midlife; whereas in men, achievement and affiliation motives are almost stable over life cycles while power motive and fear of weakness show a curvilinear evolution over time, with a peak at midlife. These general tendencies varied widely across groups as a function of educational level, professional and parental status (having children or not). Some cohort effects were also observed. Comparing the levels of motives in 1957 and 1976, achievement motivation remained stable in men but increased in women; affiliation motive decreased in men but not in women; fear of weakness increased in both men and women, and power motive increased exclusively in men. Whatever the justifications presented to explain these results, the data sustain the influence of societal norms and values and historical change on motivation, and their differential impact on men and women.

Affiliation motive is more important in the first part of women's life because social networks help to cope with normative transitions (getting a job, getting married, and having children). Indeed, life options are more difficult for women than for men because women's social roles are more conflictual and options need to be taken: social networks reduce the uncertainty of life options, and decrease when this uncertainty decreases. Three exceptions were noticed: young women who were married but childless in 1976, employed women with children, and childless housewives in 1957, showed a low affiliation motive and had a small social network. In reference to the social values of each period of time, these groups of women were counter-normative: obviously, the data cannot define the direction of causality between the dimension of the social network and counter-normative options. The stability of affiliation motive in men was explained by the hypothesis that men are more job centred than women and that uncertainties in job context do not decrease with age. Some empirical results sustain this hypothesis: no decline of affiliation motive in women with high job status and a reduction in men with low job status (less committed with work) were observed.

Decrease in *achievement motive* was noticed in 50-year-old employed women, particularly in those with high school education. Employed women with high school education have higher career aspirations than employed women with elementary school education. These aspirations are cut off early, when they reach the ceiling of their careers. The same is not the case with the better educated women as their jobs offer greater potentialities for advancement, or for lower educated women who do not have career aspirations. Levy-Leboyer (1984) has also questioned the causes of the decrease in achievement motivation at work observed in French society over the last decade. Economic crisis associated with the fear of unemployment reduces mobility as a means of finding more challenging, but less secure, jobs and suppresses the regulatory mechanisms that ensured job satisfaction. Modern workers are over qualified for the available jobs: this situation may lead to disenchantment in terms of investment in future careers and lowers their motivation at work. Therefore they will seek their thrills in leisure activities rather than in work. If was also observed that women who were adolescent or young adults during World War Two had a higher level of achievement motive: responsibilities and achievement experiences in adolescence and early adulthood seem to exert a permanent influence on the development of achievement motivation (Veroff et al., 1984).

Midlife is also the time of reflection and evaluation for men who desire to have influence over others as they have accumulated experience and knowledge to realize their desires. The peak of *power motive* was observed in 50–55-year-old men in 1957, and in younger men in 1976. In 1957, management jobs demanded seniority and experience, while in 1976, they demanded time, energy and risk taking. Men with high school education were concerned with power earlier than others because they had to gain their major advancement when they were young, as their expectations for power late in life were low. This is not true for men with college education who expect continuous advancement throughout their careers, or for lower educated men who do not have high aspirations. On the contrary, fear of weakness is stronger in midlife for lower educated men: according to dominant sex-role expectations, they may be good providers, a goal difficult to reach in midlife when the financial costs and the desire for a comfortable life for their families are higher. Men from this social group are particularly vulnerable to self-accusations. As van Lieshout and Doise (ch. 6 this volume) emphasize, one of the more enduring developmental challenges during the life-span is dealing with incompatibility of personal goals in social and non-social domains, as well as coordinating one's own goal orientations and intentions with those of others. Opposition of goal orientation in relationships and conflictual goals at the individual level may lead to lower behavioural efficiency and negative affects.

Results observed in the life-span perspective explain individual development of motivational tendencies as well as group differences in this develop-

ment. Normative life transitions offer everyone the same kind of developmental tasks, and results show that common tendencies are observed.
However, group differences prove that gender or socio-cultural status are
powerful organizers of life experiences. More important than objective
experience or environmental demand, is the subjective interpretation of the
events, according to norms and social values specific to each group. As we
have seen in a study (Fontaine, 1990a, 1994), for instance, stereotypes of
intellectual competence of the members of each gender or social class may
lead to different interpretations of the same demand in a school context and
different reactions to the same result, and may call for the use of differing
coping strategies to attain the same goal. If it is important, for some groups,
to question and criticize social stereotypes that are threatening to self-
esteem in an academic domain, for others it is better to reinforce the
stereotypes that strengthen motivational tendencies. Studies in the ecological perspective of Bronfenbrenner (Bronfenbrenner, 1986), point out the
importance of the alteration in the relationship among motivation, emotion
and behaviours, and in the underlying processes according to the characteristics of the environmental systems and the interpretation by the subject of
the elements of these systems and their relationships.

CONCLUSIONS

Motivation, being considered as the dynamic characteristic of action, has
been studied in different ways over time. The focus on the identification of
the determinants of the initiation of behaviour has been superseded by the
search for the reasons underlying the selection among different goals or
changes in activity. Various theories have been proposed. The first ones,
such as drive and field theories, were more global and they attempted to
explain all kinds of human behaviours through single laws. Present-centred,
they were based on a mechanical conception of the human being who was
considered to act in order to recover homeostasis through the reduction of
tension. Expectancy-value theories were advanced to explain active behaviors which break equilibrium. Essentially hedonistic, this theory assumes the
rise in tension to be a basic condition for pleasure. Humans were also viewed
as perfect scientists as they were considered able to choose the best option to
maximize pleasure, based on rational analyses of their perfect knowledge of
reality. This value of 'objectivity' was definitively questioned by more recent
theories which provided a deeper analysis of cognitions and emotions and
enhanced the logic of 'subjectivity'. Attributional theory is the first one to
maintain that the subject does not act as a scientist but as a judge. Personal
interpretations of events determine their behavioural, emotional, and cognitive consequences for the subject. The determinants of these interpretations,
not explored by this theory, have stimulated the interests of other researchers. Some of them explored the structure of information processing
functions associated with motivation and emotion, and they considered
them to be similar to those involved in intellectual abilities. These structures

support the theory of action control, which explored the determinants of volitional control. This and the attributional theories centred their concern on the 'expectancy' side of expectancy-value theory, while the cognitive evaluation theory, the goals theory, the self-appraisal model and the relational theory focused more on the 'value' side. The value of the outcome depends on the subjective experiences of autonomy and mastery in the cognitive evaluation theory, on the match of goals and personal theories of intelligence in Dweck's theory, or on the elaboration of personal projects in Nuttin's theory. A task may be viewed as more or less threatening according to the effect of its results on the self. Indeed, the value of the outcomes is linked to their capacity to enhance self-concept and self-esteem. One of the more powerful consequences of cognitive interpretations of events is its effect on the self-concept. The final goals of behaviour seem to be to protect or to develop the self and explain the use of different strategies of action: coping vs mastery strategies, state vs action orientations, static vs dynamic orientations, helpless vs mastery patterns.

Different methods and procedures were adopted to assess motivation. They are adapted to the theoretical perspective of the investigator and to specific goals of the study. The current tendency is to use more questionnaires, self-reports, and rating scales to assess motivational tendencies in large samples at low cost, or to explore a particular aspect of motivation using multiple procedures simultaneously in smaller samples. It is important to adapt the procedure to the specific purpose of the research.

The development of motivation has been the object of recent concern. Few theories are available and their scope is limited in terms of life cycle (childhood or adolescence) or the motivational characteristics included. Differences and changes in motivational characteristics according to gender, SES and age give a base for the interpretation of the effect of social context on motivational development. Whereas the impact of normative transition has been observed, group comparisons permit the identification of individual or social factors which would have a significant impact on motivational development. To highlight the causes and mechanism of the development of motivation, it has been necessary to consider cognitive development, environmental experiences, and societal norms and values together. The results of family and school influences on the development of motivation during childhood and adolescence, as well as the influence of professional pressures during adulthood, have illustrated this perspective. The evolution of motivation has never been the same in all cultures and in different periods in their history. It depends on the experiences they have undergone and the way they have interpreted them. Few life-span studies are available to explore the processes of motivational development and to distinguish the effects of age from those of cohorts. Thus more life-span studies are needed to point out the specificity of developmental paths according to cultural context and to explore the processes of motivational development in adulthood.

NOTE

1. To assess action control, for instance, the subject must choose the answer which better assesses his common behaviour: 'When I stand in front of a movie theatre in which a film that I would like to see is shown, and I have enough time and money to go in (a) I buy a ticket right away; (b) I consider whether I shouldn't be doing something else instead' (Kuhl, 1986).

    In the self-concept domain, the subject must indicate his degree of agreement with sentences that are supposed to describe him: I enjoy doing work in mathematics; Nobody thinks that I am good looking; I make friends easily; etc, (Marsh, 1989).

    As causal attributions as well as their categorizations into attributional dimensions widely vary among subjects, the use of a standardized instrument for all subjects in all contexts is questioned. Some procedures are considered to be better adapted to this evaluation: they start from the exploration of potential causes in a sample of subjects from the same population and allow the subjects of each study, and not the researcher, to organize the particular causes in dimension themselves (Bar Tal et al., 1984; Weiner, 1992, Faria & Fontaine, 1993).

REFERENCES

Ames, C. (1984). Competitive, cooperative, and individualistic structures: A cognitive motivational analysis. In R. Ames & C. Ames (Eds), *Research on Motivation in Education: Student Motivation*, Vol. I (pp. 177–207). New York: Academic Press.

Atkinson, J. W. & Birch, D. (1978). *Introduction to Motivation*, 2nd edn. New York: Van Nostrand.

Atkinson, J. W. & Litwin, G. H. (1960). Achievement motive and test anxiety conceived as motive to approach success and motive to avoid failure. *Journal of Abnormal and Social Psychology*, **60**, 52–63.

Bandura, A. (1986). *Social Foundation of Thought and Action: A Social Cognitive Theory*. Englewood Cliffs, NJ: Prentice-Hall.

Bar-Tal, D., Goldberg, M., & Knaani, A. (1984). Causes of success and failure and their dimensions as a function of SES and gender: A phenomenological analysis. *British Journal of Educational Psychology*, **54**, 51–61.

Boekaerts, M. (1991). Subjective competence, appraisals and self-assessment. *Learning and Instruction*, **1**, 1–17.

Boekaerts, M. (1993). Being concerned with well-being and with learning. *Educational Psychologist*, **28**, 149–167.

Bronfenbrenner, U. (1986). Ecology of the family as a context of human development: Research perspective. *Developmental Psychology*, **22**, 723–742.

Cairns, R. B. & Cairns, B. D. (1988). The socio-genesis of self-concepts. In N. Bolger, A. Cospi, G. Downey & M. Moorehouse (Eds), *Person in Context: Developmental Processes* (pp. 181–202). Cambridge: Cambridge University Press.

Cantor, N., Markus, H., Niedenthal, P. & Nurius, P. (1986). On motivation and self-concept. In R. M. Sorrentino and E. T. Higgins (Eds), *Handbook of Motivation and Cognition* (pp. 96–121). Chichester: Wiley.

Covington, M. (1984). The motive of self-worth. In R. Ames & C. Ames (Eds), *Research on Motivation in Education: Student Motivation*, Vol. I (pp. 78–113). New York: Academic Press.

Crandall, V. C., Katkovsky, W. & Crandall, V. J. (1965). Children's beliefs in their own control of reinforcements in intellectual-academic achievement situations. *Child Development*, 36, 91–109.

De Charms, R. (1984). Motivation enhancement in educational setting. In R. Ames & C. Ames (Eds), *Research on Motivation in Education: Student Motivation*, Vol. I (pp. 275–311). New York: Academic Press.

Deci, E. L. & Ryan, R. M. (1985). *Intrinsic Motivation and Self-determination in Human Behavior*. New York: Plenum Press.

Deci, E. L. & Ryan, R. M. (1986). The dynamics of self-determination in personality and development. In R. Schwarzer (Ed.), *Self-related Cognitions in Anxiety and Motivation* (pp. 171–194). Hillsdale, NJ: Erlbaum.

Demetriou, A., Kazi, S., Platsidou, M., Sirmali, K. & Kiosseoglou, G. (in press). Self-image and cognitive development: Structure, development, and functions of self-evaluation and self-representation in adolescence. *Monographs of Society of Research on Child Development*.

Dweck, C. S. (1986). Motivational processes affecting learning. *American Psychologist*, 41, 1040–1048.

Dweck, C. S. & Elliott, E. S. (1983). Achievement motivation. In P. H. Mussen & E. M. Hetherington (Eds), *Handbook of Child Psychology*, Vol. IV: *Social and Personality Development* (pp. 643–691). New York: Wiley.

Dweck,, C. S. & Legget, E. L. (1989). A social cognitive approach to motivation and personality. *Psychological Review*, 95, 256–273.

Entwisle, D. R. (1972). To dispel fantasies about fantasy-based measures of achievement motivation. *Psychological Bulletin*, 77, 377–391.

Faria, L. (1995). *Desenvolvimento diferencial das concepções pessoais de inteligência durante a adolescência [Differential development of personal conception of intelligence during adolescence]* (PhD dissertation). University of Porto, Portugal: Faculty of Psychology and Education.

Faria, L. & Fontaine, A. M. (1993). Atribuições para o sucesso escolar de adolescentes: Avaliação em contexto natural [Adolescents' attributions for school success: Assessment in natural setting]. *Cadernos de Consulta Psicològica*, 9, 37–47.

Faria, L. & Fontaine, A. M. (1994). Diferenças nas concepções pessoais de inteligência em função do contexto social de existência [Personal conception of intelligence according to social context]. *Psiquiatria Clínica*, 15, 153–158.

Fontaine, A. M. (1990a). *Motivation pour la Réussite Scolaire [Achievement Motivation in School Context]*. Lisboa: INIC (780 pp).

Fontaine, A. M. (1990b). Pratiques éducatives familiales et motivation pour la réussite d'adolescents en fonction du contexte social [Child rearing and adolescent's achievement motivation according to social context]. In S. Dansereau, B. Terrisse & J. M. Bouchard (Eds), *Education Familiale et*

Intervention Prècoce (pp. 209–224). Montréal: Agence d'Arc.

Fontaine, A. M. (1991a). Impact of social context on the relationship between achievement motivation and anxiety, expectations or social conformity. *Personality and Individual Differences*, **12**(5), 457–66.

Fontaine, A. M. (1991b). Desenvolvimento do conceito de si próprio e realização escolar na adolescência [Self-concept development and adolescents' school performances]. *Psychologica*, **2**, 1–19.

Fontaine, A. M. (1991c). O conceito de si próprio no ensino secundário: processo de construção e de diferenciação [Self-concept in secondary school: process of development and differentiation]. *Cadernos de Consulta Psicológica*, **7**, 33–54.

Fontaine, A. M. (1994). Child rearing and achievement motivation in different social contexts. *European Journal of Psychology of Education*, **9**(3), 225–240.

Fontaine, A. M. (1995). Self-concept and motivation during adolescence: Their influence on school achievement. In A. Oosterwegel & R. A. Wicklund (Eds), *The Self in European and North-American Culture: Development and Processes*. Amsterdam: Kluwer Academic.

Fontaine, A. M. & Faria, L. (1989). Teorias pessoais do sucesso [Personal theories of success]. *Cadernos de Consulta Psicológica*, **5**, 5–18.

Gottfried, A. E. (1990). Academic intrinsic motivation in young elementary school children. *Journal of Educational Psychology*, **82**, 525–538.

Guttman, D. (1975). Parenthood: A key to the comparative study of the life-cycle. In N. Datan & L. Girsberg (Eds), *Life-span Development Psychology: Normative Life Crisis* (pp. 167–184). New York: Academic Press.

Hagtvet, K. A. (1983). A construct validation study of test anxiety: A discriminant validation of fear of failure, worry and emotionality. In H. M. Van der Ploeg, R. Schwarzer & C. D. Spielberger (Eds), *Advances in Test Anxiety Research* (pp. 15–34). Hillsdale, NJ : Erlbaum.

Hagtvet, K. A. (1991). Interaction of anxiety and ability on task performance: A simultaneous consideration. In J. J. Sánchez-Sosa (Ed.), *Health and Clinical Psychology* (pp. 109–133). New York: Elsevier.

Hamilton, V. (1983). A cognitive semantic model of anxiety. In V. Hamilton (Ed.), *The Cognitive Structures and Process of Human Motivation and Personality* (pp. 208–233). New York: Wiley.

Hamilton, V. (1988). A unifying information processing system: Affect and motivation as problem solving processes. In V. Hamilton, G. H. Bower & N. H. Frijda (Eds), *Cognitive Perspective on Emotion and Motivation* (pp. 423–411). Dordecht: Kluwer Academic; Nato—Advanced Science Institutes Series.

Harter, S. (1983). Developmental perspectives on the self-system. In E. M. Hetherington (Ed.), *Handbook of Child Psychology* (pp. 275–385). New York: Wiley.

Harter, S. (1985). Competence as a dimension of self-evaluation: Toward a comprehensive model of self-worth. In R. L. Leahy (Ed.), *The Development of the Self* (pp. 55–121). New York: Academic Press.

Heckhausen, H., Schmalt, H. D. & Schneider, K. (1985). *Achievement*

Motivation in Perspective. New York: Academic Press.

Helmke, A. (1988). A longitudinal analysis of the dynamic of interaction of self-concept of math aptitude and math achievement in elementary school children. *European Journal of Psychology of Education, Special Issue 'The child's functioning at school'*, 43–49.

Helmke, A., Schneider, W. & Weinert, F. E. (1986). Quality of instruction and classroom learning outcomes: Result of the German contribution to the classroom environmental study of the IEA. *Teaching and Teacher Education*, **2**, 1–18.

Hembree, R. (1988). Correlates, causes, effects and treatment of test anxiety. *Review of Educational Research*, **58**, 47–77.

Hermans, H. J. M. (1980). *Prestatiemotief en Faalangst in Gezin en Onderwijs tevens Handleiding by de Prestatie Motivatie Test voor Kinderen (PMT-K)* [Achievement Motivation and Fear of Failure: Prestatic Motivation Questionnaire for Children]. Amsterdam: Swets & Zeitlinger.

Hoffman, L. W. (1975). Fear of success in males and females: 1965 and 1971. in M. T. Mendick, S. S. Tangri & L. W. Hoffman (Eds), *Women and Achievement* (pp. 221–230). New York: Wiley.

Horner, M. S. (1974). Performance of men and women in non-competitive and interpersonal competitive achievement oriented situations. In J. W. Atkinson & J. O. Raynor (Eds), *Motivation and Achievement* (pp. 237–254). Washington DC: Winston.

Hull, C. L. (1952). *A Behavior System.* New Haven, CT: Yale University Press.

Huteau, M. & Vouillot, F. (1987). Variations structurales de l'image de soi en fonction du sexe et du niveau scolaire chez les élèves de l'enseignement secondaire [Structural variation of self-image according to sex and grade in a sample of high school pupils]. *Psychologie et Education*, **11**, 15–26.

Jackson, D. N. (1967). *Personality Research Form: Manual.* New York: Research Psychologist Press.

Jones, M. (1955). Introduction. In M. Jones (Ed.), *Nebraska Symposium on Motivation* (pp. vii–x). Lincoln: University of Nebraska Press.

Kuhl, J. (1986). Motivation and information processing: A new look at decision making, dynamic change, and action control. In R. M. Sorrentino and E. T. Higgins (Eds), *Handbook of Motivation and Cognition* (pp. 404–434). New York: Guilford Press.

Lemos, M. S. (1993). *A motivação no processo de ensino/aprendizagem em sala de aula* [Motivation and Learning Process in the Classroom] (PhD dissertation). University of Porto, Portugal: Faculty of Psychology and Education.

Lens, W. (1987). Future time perspective, motivation, and school performance. In E. De Corte, J. Lodewijks, R. Parmentier & P. Span (Eds), *Learning and Instruction. European Research in an International Context*, Vol. 1 (pp. 181–189). Oxford: Pergamon Press.

Lepper, M. R, Greene, D. & Nisbett, R. E. (1973). Undermining children's intrinsic interest with extrinsic rewards. A test of the 'overjustification hypothesis'. *Journal of Personality and Social Psychology*, **28**, 129–137.

Levy-Leboyer, C. (1984). *La Crise des Motivations*. Paris: PUF.

Lewin, K. (1942). Field theory of learning. *Yearbook of the National Society for the Study of Education*, **4**, part 2, 215–242.

Maehr, M. (1984). Meaning of motivation: Toward a theory of personal investment. In R. Ames & C. Ames (Eds), *Research on Motivation in Education: Student Motivation*, Vol. I (pp. 117–143). New York: Academic Press.

Mandler, G. & Sarason, S. B. (1952). A study of anxiety and learning. *Journal of Abnormal and Social Psychology*, **79**, 280–295.

Markus, H. (1977). Self-schemata and processing information about the self. *Journal of Personality and Social Psychology*, **35**, 63–78.

Marsh, H. W. (1987a). The big-fish-little-pond effect on academic self-concept. *Journal of Educational Psychology*, **79**, 280–295.

Marsh, H. W. (1987b). The hierarchical structure of self-concept and the application of hierarchical confirmatory factor analysis. *Journal of Educational Measurement*, **24**, 17–29.

Marsh, H. W. (1989). Age and sex effects in multiple dimensions of self-concept: Preadolescence to early adulthood. *Journal of Educational Psychology*, **81**, 417–430.

Marsh, H. W. (1990). Causal ordering of academic self-concept and academic achievement: A multiwave longitudinal panel analysis. *Journal of Educational Psychology*, **82**, 646–656.

Marshall, H. H. & Weinstein, R. S. (1986). Classroom context of student perceived differential teacher treatment. *Journal of Educational Psychology*, **78**, 441–453.

McClelland, D. C. (1985). *Human Motivation*. Dallas: Scott, Foresman.

Meyer, W. V. (1992). Paradoxical effects of praise and criticism on perceived ability. *European Journal of Social Psychology*, **3**, 259–289.

Muller, J. L., Gullung, P. & Bocci, V. (1988). Concept de soi et performance scolaire: une méta-analyse [Self-concept and school performance: A meta-analysis]. *Orientation Scolaire et Professionnelle*, **17**, 53–69.

Murray, H. A. (1953). *Explorations in Personality*. New York: Oxford University Press.

Nichols, J. G. (1984). Conceptions of ability and achievement motivation. In R. Ames and C. Ames (Eds), *Research on Motivation in Education: Student Motivation*, Vol 1 (pp. 39–73). New York: Academic Press.

Nicholls, J. G., Jagacinski, C. M. & Miller, A. T. (1986). Conceptions of ability in children and adults. In R. Schwarzer (Ed.), *Self-related Cognitions in Anxiety and Motivation* (pp. 265–284). Hillsdale, NJ: Erlbaum.

Nuttin, J. (1980). *Théorie de la Motivation Humaine: Du Besoin au Projet d'Action*. [Theory of Human Motivation: From Need to Project] Paris: PUF.

Nuttin, J. (1984). *Motivation, Planning, and Action: A Relational Theory of Behavior Dynamics*. Hillsdale, NJ: Erlbaum.

Oosterwegel, A. (1994). A multidimensional perspective on the self-system in childhood and adolescence: Do children react upon their own opinion or upon their parents'? Paper presented at the NATO Advanced Research

Workshop no. 930614: The Self in European and North American Cultures—Development and Processes. Chersonissos, Creta, Greece.

Raynor, J. O. (1982). A theory of personality functioning and change. In J. O. Raynor & E. E. Entin (Eds), *Motivation, Career Striving, and Aging* (pp. 249–302). Washington, DC: Hemisphere.

Reuchlin, M. (1990). *Les Différences Individuelles dans le Développement Conatif de l'Enfant* [Individual Differences in the Conatif Child Development]. Paris: PUF.

Ryan, R. M., Connel, J. P. & Deci, E. L. (1985). A motivational analysis of self-determination and self-regulation in education. In C. Ames & R. Ames (Eds), *Research on Motivation in Education: The Classroom Milieu*, Vol. 2 (pp. 13–51). Orlando: Academic Press.

Rosenberg, M. (1979). *Conceiving the Self.* New York: Basic Books.

Rosenberg, M. (1985). Self-concept and psychological well-being in adolescence. In R. L. Leahy (Ed.), *The Development of the Self* (pp. 205–246). New York: Academic Press.

Sarason, I. G. (1987). Tests anxiety, cognitive interference and performance. In R. E. Snow & M. J. Farr (Eds), *Aptitude, Learning, and Instruction: Conative and Affective Process Analyses*, Vol. 3, (pp. 131–142). Hillsdale, NJ: Erlbaum.

Schunk, D. H. (1991). Self-efficacy and academic motivation. *Educational Psychologist*, **26**, 207–231.

Schwarzer, R. (1986). Self-related cognitions in anxiety and motivation: An introduction. In R. Schwarzer (Ed.), *Self-related Cognitions in Anxiety and Motivation* (pp. 1–17). Hillsdale, NJ: Erlbaum.

Seegers, G. & Boekaerts, M. (1993). Task motivation and mathematics achievement in actual task situations. *Learning and Instruction*, **3**, 133–150.

Skaalvik, E. M. &. Hagtvet, K. A. (1990). Academic self-concept: An analysis of causal predominance in a developmental perspective. *Journal of Personality and Social Psychology*, **58**, 292–307.

Spielberger, C. D. (1980). *Test Anxiety Inventory.* Palo Alto, CA: Counseling Psychologists Press.

Stipek, D. J. (1984). The development of achievement motivation. In R. Ames & C. Ames (Eds), *Research on Motivation in Education: Student Motivation*, Vol. I (pp. 145–173). New York: Academic Press.

Stipek, D. J. & Daniels, H. D. (1988). Declining perception of competence: A consequence of changes in the child or in the educational environment? *Journal of Educational Psychology*, **80**, 352–356.

Tomé, H. R. (1983). La connaissance de soi á l'adolescence. *Orientation Scolaire et Professionnelle*, **12**, 203–213.

Tomé, H. R. & Bariaud, F. (1984). *La Perspective Temporelle à l'Adolescence.* Paris: PUF.

van Aken, M. A. G. & van Lieshout, C. F. M. (1991). Children's competence and the agreement and stability of self- and child-descriptions. *International Journal of Behavioural Development*, **14**, 83–99.

van Aken, M. A. G., van Lieshout, C. F. M. & Haselager, G. J. T. (1995).

Low mutuality of self- and other-descriptions as a risk factor for adolescents' competence and self-esteem. In A. Oosterwegel & R. A. Wicklund (Eds), *The Self in European and North-American Culture: Development and Processes* (pp. 162–182). Amsterdam: Kluwer Academic.

Veroff, J., Atkinson, J. W., Feld, S. C. & Gurin, G. (1960). The use of thematic apperception to assess motivation in nation with interview study. *Psychological Monographs*, **74**, 12, 499.

Veroff, J., Reuman, D. & Feld, S. (1984). Motives in American men and women across the adult life-span. *Developmental Psychology*, **20**, 1142–1158.

Weiner, B. (1986). *An Attributional Theory of Motivation and Emotion*, New York: Springer-Verlag.

Weiner, B. (1992). *Human Motivation: Metaphors, Theories and Research*. London: Sage.

Wicklund, R. A. (1986a). Fitting to the environment and the use of dispositions. In R. Schwarzer (Ed.), *Self-related Cognitions in Anxiety and Motivation* (pp. 143–169). Hillsdale, NJ: Erlbaum.

Wicklund, R. A. (1986b). Orientation to the environment versus preoccupation with human potential. In R. M. Sorrentino & E. T. Higgins (Eds), *Motivation and Cognition: Foundations of Social Behaviour* (pp. 64–95). New York; Guilford Press.

Wicklund, R. A. & Gollwitzer, P. M. (1981). Symbolic self-completion, attempted influence, and self-depreciation. *Basic and Applied Social Psychology*, **2**, 89–114.

Winterbotton, M. (1958). The relation of need for achievement to learning experiences in independence and mastery. In J. W. Atkinson (Ed.), *Motives in Fantasy, Action and Society*. New York: van Nostrand.

Chapter 9

Personality development

Dolph Kohnstamm

Leiden University

and

Ivan Mervielde

University of Ghent

BASIC CONCEPTS AND DEFINITIONS

People are born different. With the exception of identical twins, babies are born with unique constitutions. And even identical twins may experience unique prenatal environmental circumstances. Although to some of us all babies look the same, and although they indeed share many of their genes, they are still the unique product of the mixture of genes in the cells of their mother and father. They are also the product of the nine months in their mother's womb. Women differ in what they eat and drink during pregnancy, they differ in habits such as smoking and alcohol use, in the stress they experience and in their health. As a result both of their unique genetic constitutions and of their unique environment during the nine months before birth, infants are different individuals from the very first day in the cradle.

Life-Span Developmental Psychology
Edited by A. Demetriou, W. Doise and C. F. M. van Lieshout. © 1998 John Wiley & Sons Ltd.

Temperament, Character and Personality

With babies it sounds a bit strange to talk about their individual 'personalities'. In most languages this concept (from the Latin 'persona' = role, character) is reserved for older children and adults. This is because the concept *personality* presupposes an individual development during childhood, until a self-directed, more or less independent person emerges acting on his/her environment in his/her typical way. It has become common practice to use the word 'temperament' for individual differences in the typical ways a baby or child, in this early stage of development, acts or reacts. Thus, one well-known book in this field (Buss & Plomin, 1984) was entitled: *Temperament: Early Developing Personality Traits.*

For centuries, even as far back as in ancient Greece, the word temperament has been used for individual differences among adults in basic reaction patterns and emotional states. A typology of temperament in four types, *sanguine, melancholic, choleric* and *phlegmatic*, was originally based on the ancient writings of the Greek physician Hippocrates (460 BC) and the Greek-Roman physician Galen (Galenus; AD 129–201). Hippocrates believed that various ills resulted from the excess or deficiency of the different bodily fluids, whose proper balance was essential to health. These fluids, or humours, were identified as the blood, the yellow bile, secreted by the liver, the black bile supposedly secreted by the spleen, and the phlegm or mucous secretion. Galen applied this theory to individual differences in personality by stating that individuals differ in their temperaments according to which of these humours is relatively more abundant. For example, an abundance of blood would cause a sanguine personality. This typology survived into the early decades of this century and was used to classify adults, usually only males, on the basis of their typical reaction patterns and accompanying emotional states.

Today, the words *temperament* and *temperamental differences* are used to indicate that subclass of personality traits that is inherited and that appears early in childhood. The concept *character* can be used for aspects of *both personality and temperament* . This concept has a *moral* connotation. One can speak about a *good* or *bad* character but not about a good or bad temperament or personality type. With animals, the word *temperament* is generally used, not *personality*. This is another indication of the more basic, constitutional aspects of personality that are covered by the word *temperament*. The boundaries between the three concepts are too fuzzy and open to make more distinguishing definitions possible. In daily language the words *personality* and *character* have a higher frequency than *temperament*. The latter word is often reserved for a particular type of temperament such as the fiery characteristics of Italian cars, as portrayed in image-building, advertisements and commercials. In psychology, however, one can also talk about an easy temperament, or about a temperament characterised by strong negative reactions to novelty—this would be less suitable for use in a commercial for cars or motorbikes.

Individual Differences: Gradual or Also in Distinctive Types?

Human individuals are all similar in that they share the genes typical for man, many of which are also found in the higher animals, such as the genes for the development of five fingers on each hand, two legs, and a nose in the middle of the face. Human fetuses are programmed to develop what is common to man. When defective genes are present anomalic deviations develop and the baby is born with a handicap. Even though all humans share, for example, the genes for a nose in the middle of the face, people differ in shapes of their noses. If we were to measure the length, width, angle, curve and attractiveness of the noses of individuals of a certain age, we could plot the resulting data in a graph. If we collected these data from many individuals of a certain age, say 1000, we would probably obtain a bell-shaped curve, indicating a normal distribution of nose characteristics. The total variance in these characteristics could be represented by the surface under the curve. Most people would have noses with characteristics close to the group mean and a few would score at the extremes of the distribution. In more technical language: The monomorphic 75% of the human genome of in total *c.* 100 000 genes can be distinguished from the 25% polymorphic genes that lead to individual differences. These differences can be the result of monogenetic backgrounds, resulting in specific anomalies, and of poly-genetic-additive or -epistatic backgrounds, as is the case in most individual differences in personality characteristics.

Because of this background in an interaction between several genes (polygenetic) individual differences on most personality traits are spread normally, a bell-shaped curve, when such characteristics are assessed quan-titatively over large groups. In modern personality psychology the categorisation of individuals into distinctive *types* is far less popular than identifying their gradual position on *non-categorical* or *continuous variables*. However, type classification, such as in the classical four-type typology of temperament mentioned above, is also still practised, for example, in clas-sifying the type of attachment-relationship between infants and mothers, and in the diagnosis of psychopathology. The typological approach is more person-centred whereas the continuous approach is more variable-centred. Specific types may sometimes be conceived as consisting of combinations of traits. For example, the opposition of the so-called *easy* and *difficult* child, in the model of temperament developed by the American psychiatrists Thomas and Chess (see below), is based on different scores on the Thomas–Chess temperament dimensions *intensity, negative mood, approach tendencies, adaptability* and *rhythmicity* (e.g. Thomas & Chess, 1977).

Stability

Some sort of continuity is always implied when thinking about personality, temperament and character. A description of an individual as typically reacting in a particular way implies that the individual reacted in such a way today, but also last week and will react similarly next month. How long a time-span is necessary, to permit us to speak about a stable trait or characteristics? There are no rules by which to decide, but it is certainly more a matter of years than days. This depends mostly on the *developmental stage* the individual is in. In his influential book *Stability and Change in Human Characteristics* Bloom (1964) proposed to speak about stability when individuals more or less keep their rank order in a group of individuals over two successive measurements. Thus, a high coefficient of correlation for a group of individuals tested in successive occasions means high stability of the positions of the individuals in that group. In general, the longer the time period between two measures the lower the stability. And also, stability is lowest when development proceeds fastest. The younger the individual, the faster development proceeds. Thus stability is lowest in young children and more obvious in older ages. This phenomenon is commonly referred to as 'Bloom's law'.

Contrary to many physical measures most psychological traits have to be assessed with different instruments at different stages of life. In rare cases a trait can be measured with the same instrument, yielding similar quantitative scores over a range of age periods. For example: a digit-span memory test may remain the same instrument from age 7 upwards. But memory-span at even younger ages should be measured with other means. Also, when we want to measure social inhibition both in infancy and in late childhood we need different instruments. If, however, we were interested in individual differences in motor activity level, and if we chose to measure this trait by fixing actometers to the legs of individuals, we could use the same instruments obtaining similar data, from infancy through old age. For the more complex personality traits the instruments to measure them have to be different for the various stages of life.

The concept stability can also be used for a quite different purpose, namely to see whether the *average* score of a representative group of individuals, on the same instrument, changes over time. For example, when measuring emotional stability with the same personality scale the average self-rating score of girls tends to decrease in the years of early adolescence (Harter, 1990). This type of stability cannot be assessed when using *different* instruments to measure traits that change with age in their behavioural expression. Both types of stability, individual position stability and average score stability assume the continuous presence and influence of the personality characteristics that is being measured, over the period of the life-span under study.

States and Traits: Positive and Negative Emotionality as an Example

Feeling happy or sad and depressed are *states* of emotion which have some persistence over time, lasting for at least a few hours. It is normal that such emotional states alternate, depending on factors such as the circumstances we are in, our health, fatigue. But people differ in their likelihood of their experiencing such states. For some individuals a small cause is sufficient to feel sad, whereas others need a real disaster. Some people seldom feel glad, pleased and cheerful, whereas for others a positive emotional state is usual. They take different positions on a trait that we can label either as *positive* or *negative emotionality*. Thus presented, mood can be seen as a continuous variable, with persistent sadness or depression at one pole and persistent joy and happiness at the other. A bell-shaped curve could be imagined, hovering above a horizontal axis, with the average of all individuals slightly to the (happy) side of a neutral midpoint, because in ordinary circumstances most people are satisfied with their life.

However, empirical results yield a more complex picture of reality. Instead of a single dimension with the opposite poles of happiness and sadness, two independent personality dimensions are usually found. Tellegen for instance found for adults *two* higher-order orthogonal, that means independent, dimensions which he labelled Positive and Negative Affect (Tellegen, 1985; Watson & Tellegen, 1985). These two dimensions can be found when data obtained using questionnaires are analysed by means of factor analysis. A factor identifies which items are heavily loaded by the essential meaning of that factor. Thus, in his *Multidimensional Personality Questionnaire*, Tellegen found two independent factors, which he labelled as *Positive* and *Negative Emotionality*. The first includes feelings of well-being, social potency and pleasurable engagement. The second includes feelings of stress, worry, resentment, and negative engagement (Tellegen, 1985; see also Rothbart, 1989).

The fact that two orthogonal factors can be extracted from such data means that in the views of most people the score on one dimension need not go together with a similar (high or low) score on the other dimension. For temporary *states* of mind, as discussed above, this should be impossible. Because even if we can sometimes shed tears and laugh at the same moment, we cannot feel simultaneously distressed and happy. But with the attribution to persons of more or less stable personality *traits* one can evidently rate oneself and others as usually tending to positive as well as negative affect, or as being usually low on negative mood but also low on positive mood.

THEORETICAL PARADIGMS

Temperamental Distinctions in Infancy and Childhood

The New York psychiatrists Thomas and Chess, and their colleagues from the New York Longitudinal Study (NYLS), are generally given credit for the wave of interest in temperament in infancy and childhood which arose in the 1970s and 1980s (e.g. Thomas & Chess, 1977). This new interest in basic individual differences has probably much to do with the equally new general interest in the biological roots of behaviour and in the fascination of progress in biogenetics and psychopharmacology. The results from some large twin studies caused many to reposition themselves in the nature–nurture controversy. Accepting constitutional propensities for a particular behavioural style was no longer synonymous with a racist or sexist attitude.

There are three major approaches to temperament in childhood and adolescence. The first is the clinically oriented approach of Thomas and Chess and the paediatrician Carey (see e.g. Carey & McDevitt, 1989; Carey, 1997). Whereas the originators of the approach distinguished nine separate temperament dimensions, many of the people choosing to work within this framework have reduced the number of dimensions following the results of factor analyses. The second approach is that propounded by the psychologists Buss and Plomin (1984), who originally discerned four separate dimensions but subsequently reduced their set to three: *Emotionality, Activity* and *Sociability/Shyness* (EAS). The third approach is a theoretically oriented scheme, focusing mainly on infancy, originated by Escalona (1968), and developed by Rothbart and Derryberry (1981), and Goldsmith and Campos (1982). This group has defined temperament as 'constitutionally based individual differences in reactivity and self-regulation, with "constitutional" referring to the person's relatively enduring biological make-up, influenced over time by heredity, maturation, and experience' (Rothbart & Derryberry, 1981). *Reactivity* refers to the arousability of motor activity, affect, autonomic and endocrine response. *Self-regulation* refers to processes that can modulate (facilitate or inhibit) reactivity and these processes include attention, approach, withdrawal, attack, behavioural inhibition, and self-soothing' (Rothbart, 1989). This approach is not very different from one originated in Warsaw and led by Strelau (1985, 1989). Strelau's main temperament concept, derived from Pavlov, is *strength of the nervous system*. According to Strelau's 'regulative theory', individuals differ in their capacity to regulate excitatory and inhibitory processes. Like Rothbart and her colleagues, Strelau uses Gray's neuropsychological concept of *arousability* as a key notion of temperament (Gray, 1982).

Historical Thinking about Individual Differences in Adult Temperament and Personality

The Greek-Roman ideas about individual differences mentioned above were spread throughout Europe during the Middle Ages through the writings of monks and medical schools such as the School of Salerno. Juan Huarte, a Spanish doctor, wrote a book (1575/1578) linking the four classical temperaments to different mixtures of the humours in the brain ventricles, which had been described earlier in the anatomical studies (De humani coporis fabrica, 1534) of the Flemish doctor Andreas Vesalius (1514–1564).

The roots of thinking about individual differences are not only to be found in ancient and medieval medical treatises but also in literary descriptions. Theophrastus (300 BC) described about 30 types of people in a book entitled *Characters*. Here is an example:

> A chatterbox is someone who sits next to an unknown person and starts a eulogy about his own wife. Then he discloses last night's dreams and goes on telling you in great detail what he had for breakfast, lunch and dinner. Once he is warmed up he starts complaining about the fact that people are not the same as they used to be in the 'good old days', that the price of wheat has come down, that there are many foreigners in town . . . (translated from Kouwer, 1963).

Theophrastus' character portraits were translated in the seventeenth century by the French moralist Jean de la Bruyère and published in 1688 as *The Characters or Morals of this Century*. The fact that these portraits are still quite recognisable for contemporary readers shows that stable and coherent patterns of behaviours were being identified in these early works and that such patterns of human behaviour fascinated mankind long before they became the object of scientific study.

Modern Approaches to Individual Differences in Adult Personality

Personality psychology has many roots but most handbooks and textbooks on personality psychology acknowledge the publication of Allport's 1937 book *Personality: A Psychological Interpretation* as the first attempt to define the psychology of personality as a new scientific discipline. This book traces the history of interest in personality as well as the many meanings of the term 'personality'. Allport also provided one of the most cited definitions of personality: 'Personality is the dynamic organisation within the individual of those psychophysical systems that determine his unique adjustments to his environment' (p. 48).

Murray's *Explorations in Personality* (1938) criticised academic psychology for its emphasis on cognitive processes and observable behaviours and provided an account of personality as a motivational system consisting of hierarchically organised needs.

A learning-theory-inspired perspective on personality, based on Hull and Hilgard's S-R theories was first described in *Frustration and Aggression* by Dollard, Doob et al. (1939). This view on individual differences in personality later evolved into the social learning approach exemplified by the work of Bandura and Walters (1963).

Personality psychology also has important roots in clinical psychology. The psychoanalytic theories of Freud and Jung are among the best known examples of process-oriented theories, emphasising the importance of intrapsychics, unconscious processes as determinants of the surface structure of personality.

The dramatic disclosures about the Holocaust during World War Two led to a series of studies about the authoritarian personality (Adorno, Frenko-Brunswick, Levinson & Sanford, 1950), linking psychoanalytic insights and social issues. The publication in 1945 of the *Minnesota Multiphasic Personality Inventory* (MMPI, see below for a short description) is another landmark in the history of personality psychology. Although this instrument was not developed as a personality test but rather as a clinical instrument to diagnose various forms of psychopathology, it is one of the most frequently used personality tests and a source of inspiration for many personality questionnaires.

The descriptive, taxonomic or psychometric analysis of personality was first outlined by the 'London School' of Burt and Cattell and by Eysenck. These authors advocate the use of psychometric methods such as factor analysis to reduce the numerous human traits to a set of dimensions. Cattell reduced the almost 18 000 personality descriptive adjectives, culled from Webster's Dictionary by Allport and Odbert (1936), first to 171 clusters (Cattell, 1943) and later to a set of 35 personality variables (Cattell, 1945). Eysenck, on the other hand derived his dimensions from a thorough study of the scientific literature and initially proposed a two-dimensional system with 'Extraversion' and 'Neuroticism' as two orthogonal dimensions. In Figure 9.1 Eysenck illustrated how his two major dimensions of personality are represented in many specific traits. He also related the classical four temperaments to combinations of his two major dimensions. In contrast to Cattell, Eysenck goes beyond mere description by linking his dimensions of personality to psychophysiological processes (Eysenck & Eysenck, 1985; Eysenck, 1990). From the other side of the Atlantic, Mischel (1968) questioned the basic assumptions underlying personality psychology. He summarised numerous studies pointing to the low degree of consistency of behaviour across situations. His critique fuelled a period of prolonged and heated controversy about personality dispositions and indeed about the construct of personality itself. However, in the past two decades the more severe critiques, such as the claim that personality is a fictional construction in the mind of the perceiver (Schweder, 1975), have been rejected on empirical grounds (Funder, 1989; Kenrick & Funder, 1988; Mervielde & Pot, 1989). One important outcome of this debate was a strong emphasis on person–situation interactions (Endler & Magnusson, 1976; Magnusson & Endler, 1977).

In the last decade, interest in personality psychology has grown significantly. Part of this growth is due to a renewed interest in the lexical approach to personality. Goldberg (1990, 1993) is currently one of the more outspoken advocates of this type of research. He spelled out the basic rationale for this approach as follows:

> Those individual differences that are most significant in the daily transactions of persons with each other will eventually become encoded into their language. The more important such a difference is, the more people will notice it and wish to talk of it, with the result that eventually they will invent a word for it. (Goldberg, 1982, p. 204).

The tradition of lexical research has spread from the US to Europe. Brokken (1978) and Hofstee and De Raad (Hofstee, de Raad & Goldberg, 1992)

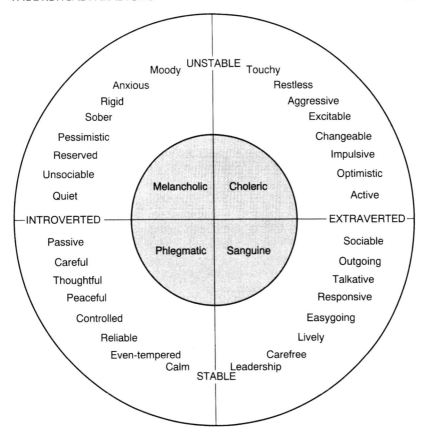

Figure 9.1   Eysenck's illustration of how his two major dimensions of personality are represented in many specific traits

studied the major dimensions underlying the Dutch language. Angleitner, Ostendorf and John (1990) and Ostendorf (1990) did the same for the German language. From these studies there emerged a consensus about the importance of the five-factor model, commonly referred to as the 'Big Five': *Extraversion, Agreeableness, Conscientiousness, Neuroticism* vs *Emotional Stability* and *Openness/Culture/Intellect*. The acronym OCEAN makes these five easy to remember, although in a different order. Particularly in Europe there is now a wave of research investigating the cross-cultural replicability of the Big Five for different languages and cultures (Mervielde & Vandierendonck, 1994; several articles in recent issues of the *European Journal of Personality*). The lexical approach in itself did not succeed in convincing many personality psychologists to adopt this five-dimensional model. It was argued that trait adjectives, the basic units of the lexical analysis, are too abstract or general compared to the typical behavioural items that are the basic units of most personality questionnaires. The development of the NEO-PI, a questionnaire type instrument, by the American researchers Costa and McCrae (1985, 1992) was one of the essential

Table 9.1 NEOPI-R domain and facet scales

FACTOR/DOMAIN	Positive correlates	Negative correlates	NEOPI-R facet scales
EXTRAVERSION	Sociable, active, talkative, optimistic, pleasure-seeking, self-confident, warm	Aloof, withdrawn, shy	Warmth, gregariousness, assertiveness, activity, excitement-seeking, positive emotions
AGREEABLENESS	Soft-hearted, generous, kind, forgiving, sympathetic, warm	Suspicious, headstrong, shrewd, impatient, argumentive, aggressive	Trust, straightforwardness, altruism, compliance, modesty, tendermindedness
CONSCIENTIOUS	Organised, ambitious, energetic, efficient, determined, precise, industrious, persisting	Distractible, lazy, careless, impulsive, hasty, immature, defensive	Competence, order, dutifulness, achievement striving, self-discipline, deliberation:
NEUROTICISM	Worrying, nervous, anxious, moody, inhibited, tense, self-centred	Confident, self-confident, clear-thinking, alert, contented	Anxiety, hostility, depression, self-consciousness, impulsivity, vulnerability
OPENNESS	Wide interests, inventive, original, imaginative, non-traditional, artistic	Conservative, cautious, mild	Fantasy, aesthetics, feelings, actions, ideas, values

Source: Based on Costa and McCrae (1992), p. 49; with permission.

prerequisites to broaden the scope of the Big Five research. These authors not only constructed a reliable questionnaire measuring the five factors but demonstrated, in an impressive series of studies, that most of the variance captured by traditional personality questionnaires could be accounted for by the five factors emerging from the taxonomic and lexical research tradition. Moreover, personality scales that do not correlate significantly with any of the five factors tend to be unique to one or a few personality tests. On the basis of these findings Costa and McCrae argue that the five factors are both *necessary* and *sufficient* for describing the basic dimensions of personality. This statement should be qualified by noting that these authors also distinguish *facet* traits within each of these five dimensions (see Table 9.1). Note that two of these five dimensions are identical to Eysenck's two major dimensions in Figure 9.1.

Once trait theory regained its respectability as a valid perspective on personality, researchers looked for more convincing evidence documenting the stability of traits. Over the last decade, an impressive amount of evidence has been gathered supporting the view that many important personality traits have a sizeable genetic component. This fact supports those who believe in the reliability of stable traits, although genes may also contribute to sudden changes in personality, for example when in the course of life a genetic predisposition for some kind of illness suddenly reveals its influence.

The Genetic Component in the Development of Individual Differences

The question is often asked how much of a particular temperament or personality trait is inherited, or passed on by our genes, the information-bearing structures in the DNA (deoxyribonucleic acid) in every cell of our body. Genes guide the construction of enzymes and proteins thus acting as the blueprints and schedules for development (Loehlin, 1992). The continuous interactions between genes and the succession of environments through which we pass in our development are so complex that it will never be possible to disentangle the relative contributions of genetic and environmental influences on behavioural outcomes. What can be studied is the *hereditability* of traits in a particular *population*, for example by studying large samples of identical and fraternal twins. What cannot be studied is the hereditability of a particular trait in an *individual*. For instance, even if we know that in large samples hereditability accounts for 40–50% of the total variance in intelligence, we cannot apply this probability to every single individual in the sample. Therefore, it makes no sense to think of our own score on an intelligence test as being 40–50% caused by the genes we inherited from our parents. In recent years the field of behavioural genetics has been growing fast, and its methods are becoming more and more sophisticated. Excellent introductions are now available (Loehlin, 1992; Plomin, 1994).

The best instrument that nature has given us for carrying out hereditary research in psychology and medicine is the phenomenon of identical and fraternal twins. Because identical, that is monozygotic (MZ), twins have the same genes, and fraternal, that is dizygotic (DZ), twins just like ordinary siblings share *on the average* only half of their genes, we can take the difference between identical twins resemblances and fraternal twin resemblances on a given trait as indicating half the effect of the genes on the variation in that trait. The correlation between twins is a measure of how much they resemble one another. Thus, twice the difference between MZ correlations and DZ correlations on a trait is an estimate of the genetic influence on it (Loehlin, 1992). For example, if in a large sample of MZ twins a correlation of 0.60 is found for a measure of extraversion, against a correlation of 0.40 in a sample of DZ twins, doubling this difference gives [2 (0.60 − 0.40) = 0.40; which in this case may be interpreted as 40%] a rough estimate of the genetic influence on the *population* variance in extraversion. However, many methodological questions have been raised regarding the interpretation of the data found in such studies. One of the simpler questions is whether for identical (MZ) twins the environmental influences are more similar than for fraternal (DZ) twins. For instance, because parents would raise MZ twins in a more similar way than DZ twins. The sophisticated research designs described in the recent literature (see the sources indicated above) are necessary to cope with such questions. In Europe, the Scandinavian countries have contributed most to this field, because it has been a long tradition in these countries to collect extensive data on twins, beginning in infancy, and often continuing with longitudinal follow-up studies. Twin registers are generally set up to provide a database for both the health and behavioural sciences. Because all twins are registered in such registers it is possible for researchers to draw large representative samples from them. In most other countries researchers are dependent on the voluntary participation of parents or of adult twins in twin clubs. For this reason American researchers have often cooperated with Scandinavian colleagues in analysing the data collected in the Nordic countries. It is only recently that large twin samples have begun to be registered—on a voluntary basis—in countries such as Holland, Belgium and Germany.

Besides showing the importance of genetic factors, behavioural genetic research also has important implications for our conceptualisation of environmental effects. One of the important contributions of behaviour genetic research has been to alert environmental researchers to the importance of measuring differential treatment of children within the same family (unshared environmental influences) rather than focusing solely on the measurement of environment *across* families (Wachs, 1992). The repeated finding that the environment that children share accounts for little variance and hence cannot be considered as an important cause of differences between children from different households is something that contradicts intuitive commonsense. However, more recent studies seem to suggest that when *teachers* are asked to do the personality assessment of siblings (i.e. fraternal twins), instead of *parents*, children of the same family are rated as more similar (Rose, 1995).

Another useful instrument for research into the hereditary basis of behavioural differences is provided by adoption. When children are adopted at a very young age into families with natural children of about the same age, comparative study of both *groups* of children (adopted and natural) can be particularly valuable.

On the Hereditability of Individual Differences in Intelligence

Intelligence is an important aspect of personality. Children, just like adults, differ in intelligence. This is because they live in environments differing in intellectual stimulation and because they have different innate abilities. The central question is, to what extent is intelligence determined by each of the two factors, hereditary and environment.

As we saw above this question can only be answered for *large groups*, not for individuals. Stated simply, on a scale of 0 to 1 the contribution of innate ability varies between 0.4 and 0.8, depending on the environment in which the group lives, and on the scientist interpreting the data. As regards the effect of the environment, if everybody lived under precisely the same conditions then innate ability would have a weight of 1. To the extent that environmental factors such as education, health care, living conditions, social services, and so forth provided by a society are the same for all individuals, the differences in intelligence can be attributed to differences in innate ability. On the other hand, if a society is so structured that children grow up in extremely disparate conditions, which affect the development of their intellectual abilities, then the weight of the environmental factors increases and the weight of the inherited factors decreases.

Brothers and sisters differ from each other in intellectual ability, *on the average*, by about 12 IQ-points. Again this can only be said for large groups and not for individual families. This difference is due to hereditary *and* environment. Differences in *hereditary* occur because children's genes come from both parents, about half from each parent, *and* because siblings only share about half their genes with each other. Differences in *environment* occur because even though the children come from the same family they are not influenced by it in the same way. It is only in the last 20 years that it has become clear how differently a family's surroundings, its circumstances and its child-rearing practices can affect (on the average!) the individual children in it. This is true for the children's intellectual development as well as for other personality characteristics.

While it is certain that heredity plays an important role in intelligence, nobody knows as yet which genes on which chromosomes can account for all the differences between people. There are probably many genes in a variety of locations that work together to produce specific effects that are as yet unknown. It is only in cases of severe deficiency that a single damaged or missing gene can be pinpointed. The normal differences between intelligent and unintelligent children will perhaps never be proved to be attributable to specific genes and gene locations on the chromosomes. Fraternal twins are genetically as similar as normal brothers and sisters. But they are of the same age and they have more in common than normal brothers and sisters as far as position in the family is concerned. Because of this, intelligence scores of fraternal twins are on the average closer than those of normal brothers and sisters (correlations of 0.60 compared to 0.45). It follows that if identical twins, on the average, are more similar to each other in intelligence than are fraternal twins, then the difference between identical and fraternal twins, measured over large groups, could be seen as a measure of the hereditary component of intelligence.

However, the validity of this line of reasoning has been questioned. As we saw above, the first argument against it is always that parents of identical twins treat these children more alike than do parents of fraternal twins; and further, that other adults, children and teachers also have an 'equalising' effect in the way they treat identical twins. In other words identical twins may experience a more similar environment than non-identical twins. There has been a lot of research investigating whether this is the case (for large groups of parents). The net result of all these studies is that it is to some extent true, on the average, but the equalising effects of the environment are not nearly enough to explain the degree of similarity in behaviour of identical twins. It also known that as identical twins approach adult-hood—and the influence of the parents decreases—they actually begin to resemble each other *more* in intelligence (the opposite is the case for fraternal twins).

Adoption studies also play an important role in estimates of the contribution of heredity to intelligence. From these studies there appears to be a clear relationship between the IQs of adopted and natural children in the same family (correlation of 0.30) when the children are young, although as the children grow older the relationship disappears completely. Again, this holds only for large groups, of adoption families. In individual cases an opposite trend is also possible: the adopted and natural children become more and more alike with time. But these cases occur much less frequently.

There has always been discussion about the question of whether people of different race differ in intelligence. In late 1994 the debate surfaced again with the publication of the book *The Bell Curve* by the American authors Herrnstein and Murray. *One* chapter of this book looks at the question of whether the differences found in average intelligence scores between (so-called) 'white' and (so-called) 'black' Americans and the 'black' Americans can be attributed to the innate differences, between the 'white' and the 'black' races. The average difference is approximately 15 IQ-points, which is slightly more than the average differences between brothers and sisters from the same family. But the problem here is that the average difference between 'white' and 'black' goes against 'black'. In contrast to this difference, Americans of East Asian origin score slightly higher than 'white' Americans (average 3 IQ-points). Groups of 'Latin' Americans obtain scores lying on the average approximately halfway between the 'white' and the 'black' averages. For a splendid review of all that is presently known about intelligence see Neisser, Boudoo et al. (1996).

Because there has been a lot of racial intermingling in the US, race differences cannot be investigated there in pure form. Practically all 'black' Americans have at least one 'white' forebear, and it is estimated that 20% of the genes of 'black' people are from 'white' forbears. It goes without saying that the conditions under which the average 'black' in this world lives are much less favourable for the development of the aspects of intelligence measured by intelligence tests, than are the conditions under which the average 'white' lives. Therefore research studies in this area are extremely difficult to interpret. On the one hand there are studies indicating that the children of 'black' American intellectuals and other well-off professionals continue to score on the average lower than children of comparable groups of 'whites' (though the differences is less than 15). This holds for their early childhood years as well as for their later development. On the other hand, there is the study of children of German mothers who shortly after the war became pregnant by American soldiers, without marriage or cohabitation ever taking place. The study found that children fathered by 'black' American soldiers *did* not score lower in their intellectual development than children fathered by 'white' American soldiers.

There are countless studies of this nature, and the net result of all this endeavour is that nothing can be said with certainty about race differences in intelligence. But today the question can be discussed more moderately than it could be 20 years ago. Psychologists and behavioural geneticists who say that it is possible or even probable that races differ in their inborn capacity for certain sorts of achievement, whether physical or mental, are no longer rejected out of hand, as they understandably were a couple of decades after the Second World War.

Values and Personality

Individuals forming a society, a nation or a culture share many values. Values are more than just attitudes. As one value theorist defines the concept: 'Values (1) are concepts or beliefs, that (2) pertain to desirable end states or behaviours, (3) transcend specific situations, (4) guide selection or evaluation of behaviour and events, and (5) are ordered by relative importance. Values, understood in this way , differ from attitudes primarily in their generality or abstractness (see 3) and in their hierarchical ordering by importance' (Schwartz, 1992). Schwartz, an Israeli author, conducts his value research in the social-psychological tradition, following American predecessors such as Rokeach and Bem. His empirical research is directed at finding *universals* in the content and structure of values. *Universals* are values that are valid across language and culture, and are thus world-wide. These goals sound similar to those of personality psychologists, in particular to the goals of the psychologists working with the five-factor model described above.

In addition to the five formal features of values cited above, Schwartz and Bilsky (1987), proposed that the primary content aspect of a value is the type of goal or motivational concern that it expresses. They derived a universal typology of the different contents of values by reasoning that values repre-sent, in the form of conscious goals, three universal requirements of human existence to which all individuals and societies must be responsive: needs of individuals as biological organisms, requirements of coordinated social interaction, and survival and welfare needs of groups. From an evolutionary viewpoint these goals would have crucial survival significance (Schwartz, 1992). Hence, Schwartz and his co-workers concentrate on the motivational types of values. Box 9.1 shows the ten motivational types of values that Schwartz and his co-workers found to be distinguished by people living in 57 different countries. In their surveys they asked respondents to rate the importance of each value 'as a guiding principle in my life'.

In the wordings of the values between parentheses in Box 9.1 you will recognise many adjectives that could also be part of a personality question-naire, such as that used in the research that led to the five-factor model of personality. Using Simple Structure Analsyis to analyse the data obtained from many different samples Schwartz and his associates repeatedly found two independent major dimensions underlying the ten value types. The first was labelled as Self-Transcendence vs Self-Enhancement and the second

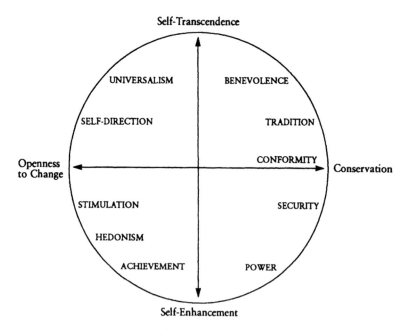

Figure 9.2 Circumplex of two independent value dimensions with the positions of ten different values
Adapted with permission from Schwartz, S. H. (1992). Universals in the content and structure of values: Theoretical advances and empirical tests in 20 countries. In M. P. Zanna (Ed.), *Advances in Experimental Social Psychology*, **25**, 1–65. New York: Academic Press.

Box 9.1 Ten motivational types of values in terms of their goals and (between parentheses) the single values that represent them

Power:	Social status and prestige control or dominance over people and resources. (Social Power, Authority, Wealth, Preserving my Public Image)
Achievement:	Personal success through demonstrating competence according to social standards. (Successful, Capable, Ambitious, Influential)
Hedonism:	Pleasure and sensuous gratification for oneself. (Pleasure, Enjoying Life)
Stimulation:	Excitement, novelty, and challenge in life. (Daring, a Varied Life, an Exciting Life)
Self-Direction:	Independent thought and action-choosing, creating, exploring. (Creativity, Curious, Freedom, Choosing own Goals, Independent)
Universalism:	Understanding, appreciation, tolerance and protection for the welfare of all people and for nature. (Broadminded, Wisdom, Social Justice, Equality, a World at Peace, a World of Beauty, Unity with Nature, Protecting the Environment)
Benevolence:	Preservation and enhancement of the welfare of people with whom one is in frequent personal contact. (Helpful, Honest, Forgiving, Loyal, Responsible)
Tradition:	Respect, commitment and acceptance of the customs and ideas that traditional culture or religion provide. (Devout, Accepting my Portion in Life, Humble, Respect of Tradition, Moderate)
Conformity:	Restraint of actions, inclinations, and impulses likely to upset or harm Parents and Elders. (Obedient, Self-Discipline)
Security:	Safety, harmony and stability of society, of relationships, and of self. (Clean, National Security, Social Order, Family Security, Reciprocation of Favours).

Source: Derived with permission from Schwartz (1992).

was labelled Openness to Change vs Conservation (see Figure 9.2). Looking for a correspondence with the five personality dimensions of the five-factor model it is striking to see that the latter dimension resembles factor V, Openness to Experiences, and that the former dimension appears to be a mixture of the two largest of the Big Five factors, Extraversion and Agreeableness. This dimensions is both a *love* dimension, varying from egoism to altruism, and a *power* dimension varying from social authority to detachment and spiritual life. And did not Peabody and Goldberg (1989) suggest the labels *Power, Love, Work, Affect* and *Intellect* for the Big Five? No wonder that many have commented on the fact that the Big Five also resemble major value dimensions.

This comparison of two quite different types of research, one from social psychology, the other from personality psychology, may help you to recognise the similarities and the differences between culturally valued personality traits and societal values. It may also help you to see how an empirically derived dimensional structure underlying the variability in different traits is dependent on the *selection* of traits to be included in the rating instruments. What is not presented to the raters cannot lead to an underlying factor or dimension, and what is presented in abundance has a higher chance of forming a factor. Thus what is crucial in this striving toward a complete converge of the essential and the universal, is a truly representative selection of items. With the instruments discussed below this item selection has often been guided by biases in one direction or another, sometimes deliberate, mostly unconsciously.

Different Types of Attachment Relationships

Whereas temperament theory postulates inborn tendencies to individual differences in traits such as negative emotionality and sociability, attachment theory postulates that such typical behavioural patterns are the result of the particular type of attachment relation that has evolved between the infant and its primary caretaker, mainly the mother.

Pioneers in the study of attachment relationships are the American psychologist Harlow, studying monkeys, and the British psychiatrist Bowlby, studying humans. In Harlow's early research (Harlow, 1958; Harlow & Zimmerman, 1959) infant monkeys were reared either alone in cages or with 'surrogate' inanimate mothers, for periods varying from three months to a year. One type of surrogate mother consisted of a wire construction covered with soft cloth, with a nipple that gave milk. Infants raised with such a 'mother' became depressed when 'she' was removed from the cage. Secondly, her presence gave them the courage to explore strange environments. Also, when frightened by a mechanical puppet, they fled to this cloth-covered construction for comfort. These three characteristics—an intense emotional tie with caretakers, the use of caretakers as a secure base for exploration, and the comfort received from them when frightened—are also the defining characteristics of human attachment in infancy and early childhood.

Stimulated by Harlow's research and by the maternal-deprivation literature, Bowlby (1958) postulated that humans have an innate need for social interaction that can best be satisfied by the attachment of physical contact with an adult or, as in the case of Harlow's monkey, a surrogate adult. He developed an ethological-evolutionary attachment theory (Bowlby, 1969) that has as its central thesis that infants and others are programmed to develop an attachment relationship. This need of infants is so strong that even if surrogate mothers have little more to offer than their presence, the infant will display its inborn attachment system in variations of the behavioural patterns described above. Because the essential function of the attachment system is the promotion of protective proximity to an adult in the face of threat and of exploration in the absence of threat, the 'Strange Situation' was designed by Mary Ainsworth and her colleagues (Ainsworth, Blehar, Waters & Walls, 1978) to create gradually escalating stress for the baby so that subsequent changes in infant behaviour towards the parent could be observed. This standardised laboratory situation was expressly devised to assess *individual differences* in the way attachment behaviour becomes organised into distinctive patterns. Initially three main patterns were discerned, and eight subpatterns.

> The assessment procedure consists of classification according to the pattern of behaviour shown in the strange situation, particularly in the episodes of reunion after separation. *Eight patterns* were identified, but I shall deal here with only the three main groups into which they fell—Groups A, B, and C. To summarize, Group B babies use their mothers as a secure base from which to explore in the preseparation episodes; their attachment behaviour is greatly intensified by the separation episodes so that exploration diminishes and distress is likely; and in the reunion episodes they seek contact with, proximity to, or at least interaction with their mothers. Group C babies tend to show some signs of anxiety even in the preseparation episodes; they are intensely distressed by separation; and in the reunion episodes they are ambivalent with the mother, seeking close contact with her and yet resisting contact or interaction. Group A babies, in sharp contrast, rarely cry in the separation episodes and, in the reunion episodes, avoid the mother, either mingling proximity-seeking and avoidant behaviours or ignoring her altogether. (Ainsworth, 1979, p. 932).

In 1986 a fourth main category was identified, labelled D, for a *disorganised* and *disoriented* behaviour pattern (Main & Solomon, 1986, 1990). This category was found during the search for common features in cases that were unclassifiable using the original ABC taxonomy. Compared to securely attached (B) and even in insecurely attached (A/C) attachment patterns, the disorganised (D) pattern is conceived as reflecting greater vulnerability to stressful stimulation. In one recent study (Hertsgaard, Gunnar, Erikson & Nachmias, 1995) toddlers who were classified as Ds exhibited higher cortisone concentrations in their saliva, a biological marker of reactivity. Whether this means that the high cortisone level is a cause or a result of the stress shown by these babies is still unclear. Only if it can be demonstrated that it is a *cause* then a constitutional determinant for attachment classifications has been identified. This would be the same as saying that *temperament* influences the quality of the attachment relationship.

With trained coders it has been demonstrated that interjudge agreement on the three major classifications is high. The majority of infants are usually classified as *secure* (B), one-fifth to one-third as *insecure-avoidant* (A), and a small minority as *insecure-ambivalent/resistant.* (C). This is a general trend which has been found in a number of different countries of the Western world in which infants and their parents have been observed in the Strange Situation (Van IJzendoorn & Kroonenberg, 1988). In Asian countries the proportions of A and C tend to be reversed. Although most of the attachment theorising and research comes from the US, some European groups have also made substantial contributions to developing this field (e.g. Grossmann, Grossmann & Schwan, 1986; Van IJzendoorn, 1990; Van IJzendoorn, Goldberg, Kronenberg & Frenckel, 1992; Van den Boom, 1994).

The different types of attachment behaviour patterns that infants display in the Strange Situation are thus thought to be part of the type of attachment relationships that the infant has with the primary caregiver. Infants may show different patterns with different caregivers, for example mother and father. Thus the type of classification is bound to the specific dyad that is classified. Furthermore, the specific type of behaviour pattern the infant displays is thought to be mostly the result of the anteceding behaviour pattern of the caretaker. Researchers have identified several caregiver variables that seem to affect the security of attachment. These include responsiveness to crying, timing of feeding, sensitivity, psychological accessibility, cooperation and acceptance. In sum, responsiveness and sensitivity in maternal caregiving are thought to be major determinants in the development of attachment security in the infant.

In view of the neo-analytical background of Bowlby's theory it is no wonder that attachment researchers traditionally showed little interest in temperamental predispositions of infants as factors which influence the evolving attachment relationships in a secure or insecure direction. Nevertheless, some studies show that temperamental characteristics of infants may condition the type of attachment relationships at least as much as the caregiver characteristics of sensitivity and responsiveness (Goldsmith & Alansky, 1987; Crockenberg, 1981, 1986; Van den Boom, 1994). In fact, the direct influence of both maternal interactive variables and infant distress proneness on the development of the evolving attachment system is still unknown. Debate will continue not only on the *causes* of particular patterns of attachment, but also on their *consequences* after infancy, in childhood, adolescence and adulthood. We will return to this developmental and life-span issue in a later paragraph.

Learning Theories

Could it be that the development of individual differences in personality traits is simply the product of learning? Certainly, the reinforcement of specific types of reaction can be so forceful as to lead to habitual patterns of behaviour. According to classical conditioning theory, children develop through exposure to new reinforcement contingencies. Children discover that the occurrence of a particular unconditioned stimulus is contingent, that is dependent, on the occurrence of a particular conditioned stimulus. By determining the contingency the child can forecast what is going to happen next. Contingency need not be perfect. In real life it rarely is, but people can also operate on imperfect contingencies, expecting the consequences to occur for most of the time. In the theory of instrument conditioning the relevant contingency is between an act and its outcome. When a mobile is attached to a crib in such a way that it starts to move when the infant moves his legs, most infants will begin to include a leg-moving response upon seeing the mobile in their repertoire (Gleitman, 1986).

According to learning theory, personality, or the self, is a repertoire of behaviour created by an organised set of contingencies. As the late king of behaviourism, B. F. Skinner, wrote: 'The behaviour a young person acquires in the bosom of his family composes one self; the behaviour he acquires in, say, the armed services composes another. The two selves may exist in the same skin without conflict until the contingencies conflict—as they may, for example, if his friends from the services visit him in his home' (Skinner, 1974, pp. 164–165). With this example Skinner points to something that many students will recognise from their own self-reflections: the notion that one reacts and behaves differently when in different company or in different surroundings or circumstances. This seems especially true for childhood and adolescence, though less so for later stages in life. How often does one hear of children who are tyrants at home but darlings when visiting the homes of friends and relatives? How can we not be annoyed with ourselves when we notice considerable changes in our stylistic way of behaviour, dependent on the people we are with? What remains of the notion of a stable and unique personality when we change our characteristic ways of behaviour like a chameleon its colours? For Skinner his behaviourist position did not imply the negation of uniqueness for each of us. Nor did it imply constant changeability according to changing environmental circumstances. It only implied that we are not free to change our personalities at will.

> A person is not an originating agent; he is a locus, a point at which many genetic and environmental conditions come together in a joint effect. As such, he remains unquestionably unique. No one else (unless he has an identical twin) has his genetic endowment, and without exception no one else has his personal history. Hence, no one else will behave in precisely the same way. We refer to the fact that there is no one like him as a person when we speak of his identity. (Skinner, 1974, p. 185).

Social-learning Theories

Several theories of personality can be classified as *social-learning theories*. Most influential have been the theories of Miller and Dollard (1941) and Bandura and Walters (1963). Only the latter theory will be described here, because it is the only one that is still very influential. Bandura (1977) disagrees with Skinner, in that he sees the child as an active, thinking being who contributes in many ways to his own development.

The child *is* an originating agent. For example, he/she is free to choose the models he/she will attend to and hence will have some say about what he/she will learn from others. In Bandura's *cognitive* social learning theory *observational learning* requires the observer to actively attend to, encode, and retain

CHILD'S BEHAVIOR   SOCIAL ENVIRONMENT

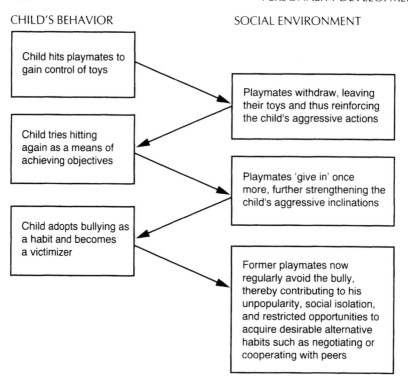

Figure 9.3   Reciprocal determinism: how a child both influences and is influenced by the social environment
From *Social and Personality Development* by D. R. Shaffer. Copyright © 1994, 1988, 1979 Brooks/Cole Publishing Company, Pacific Grove, CA 93950, a division of International Thomson Publishing, Inc. By permission of the publisher.

the behaviours displayed by social models. Children are active information processors, who organise experience by making mental notes about their strengths and weaknesses, and about the likely consequences of their behaviour. In this, Bandura's position is similar to that held by proponents of *attribution* (or social-information-processing) *theory*. Figure 9.3 gives an example from Shaffer (1988) of how social-learning theorists such as Bandura see habitual behavioural styles (or traits) developing from social interaction.

The social-learning approach differs from theories of temperament and present-day mainstream theories of personality in that it puts little or no value on inherited tendencies to act or react in particular ways. Whereas we saw above that Skinner at least recognised the influence of a unique genetic endowment, social-learning theorists seldom pay tribute to what others see as the constitutional basis of personality.

INSTRUMENTS FOR STUDYING INDIVIDUAL DIFFERENCES IN TEMPERAMENT AND PERSONALITY

We have organised this methods section according to four stages in human development: early childhood, school-age, adolescence and adulthood. The methods used at any level, though, may in some cases also be used at another. Thus, questionnaires in which parents or partners express their opinion on the personality characteristics of their children or spouses are instruments that can be used for different age levels. However, questionnaires requiring self-ratings cannot be used for infants and young children, and peer nominations are seldom used with adults. Most of the methods in current use are treated only very briefly and some are not mentioned at all. For instance, arousal and speed of contingency learning are not discussed, not because they are not important, but simply because of the limited number of pages at our disposal. Also, the wealth of standardised personality tests for adults is only briefly treated, just enough to give a rough idea of the different categories of personality tests in current use. Some methods are somewhat arbitrarily placed in a paragraph devoted to one particular age level, for example the Q-sort technique in adolescence. This rating technique may be used at all age levels, though it is seldom used to measure personality traits in adults.

Early Childhood

Two main categories of data-generating instruments can be distinguished: (i) observations of individual differences in concrete behaviour made by trained observers in standardised situations; and (ii) opinions of adults who know the child well, for example, parents and caretakers, as expressed in interviews or in response to items in questionnaires. The main advantages of the first method lie in the objectivity of the measures, the standardisation, and thus comparability, of the situation in which the behaviour of the child is elicited, and in the possibility of audio-visual registration. The main disadvantages lie in the restrictions that are inherent in the selected situation, leading to a limited range of elicited behaviours, and in restrictions resulting from the relatively short duration of such a situation. The observations that are made of this restricted range of behaviour are usually completed within an hour; observations are seldom repeated over several days. The method is expensive in comparison to the questionnaire approach.

This leads us to the main advantage of the second group of measures. Firstly it is a relatively cheap method of data collection allowing the collection of hundreds of opinions of children's characteristics in a relatively short time. Another advantage is that the raters use their memory of how the child typically reacts in a large variety of situations. From living with the child the caretakers have formed a general opinion of the child's temperament and personality, this opinion being more or less differentiated according to their perceptiveness and education, and being based on a period spanning at least several months. The main disadvantage lies, of course, in the subjectivity of ratings obtained from questionnaire items, and in the selection and bias in what is reported about the child in interviews. This unavoidable subjectivity of the opinions expressed by parents and caretakers has led psychologists to refer to parental ratings of children's typical behaviour as a mixture of objective reality and subjective *parental perceptions* (Bates, 1989). Also, parents differ in their skills to observe children's behaviour, which is another source of low comparability of parental data.

More than a century ago a German researcher was probably the first to develop a parent questionnaire, with sections concerning the 'affective and volitional life' of the child. Items in these sections of his questionnaire asked for judgements on characteristics such as mood (is your child predominantly happy or sad?), excitability (is your child easily upset?), obedience, sociability, persistence and patience (Hartmann, 1896).

School-age

Questionnaires

In 1915 Burt published a factor analysis based on data collected in 1911 in Liverpool, from 172 children aged 9–12 and 57 adults (Burt, 1948). The subjects were rated for their positions on 12 'primary emotions' (joy, sex, sociability, assertiveness, anger, curiosity, disgust, sorrow, fear, submissiveness, tenderness and comfort) that Burt had adapted from McDougall. Burt assumed these primary emotions to be the major traits that constituted the emotional domain as opposed to the domain of intelligence. For several decades Burt continued to apply factorial methods to emotional characteristics on lines similar to those already developed for cognitive characteristics. His general aim was to determine what he called the 'highest common factor' for all these traits taken jointly. In 1948 he reported the results of factorial analysis of data collected in the course of over 20 years from 483 boys and girls attending elementary schools in London. The majority of the children were between 9 and 13 years of age and the assessments for the same primary emotions were based on gradings made by teachers. Burt found that three orthogonal factors could explain most of the variance in these 12 traits: a general factor Emotionality (37% of the variance); a bipolar factor distinguishing sthenic (or extravertive) from asthenic (or introvertive) emotions (13%) and a further bipolar factor distinguishing euphoric (or pleasurable) from dysphoric (or unpleasureable) emotions (5%). Analyses like these took enormous effort, since all correlations and all factor loadings had to be computed without calculating machines, and results that are obtained in minutes today took months of computation.

At school, a teacher observing his or her class for several months or longer can make judgements on the typical behavioural style of his or her pupils, *by comparison*. When teachers rate children on questionnaire items they make comparative judgements based on the variance in temperamental differences they observe, not only in this particular class, but also in the classes they have taught before. This is a major advantage over parent reports, especially when parents have only one child at home to observe, or when the age differences between their children are large. Unless parents have had the opportunity to observe other children of about the same age as the child they are asked to report on, they cannot make comparative judgements. If teachers are sufficiently experienced, and motivated, and if they have enough time at their disposal, their reports on a pupil's temperament can be very valid. Of course, a teacher only knows the child from its behaviour at school, and thus he/she reports on typical behaviour in a restricted range of situations. But this is not so different from the situation of parents who also see their child behaving in a restricted range of situations. To help a teacher make comparative, and not absolute, judgements, it is always best to ask him/her to rate several or even *all the* pupils in his or her class, not only the child who is the subject of the study.

Because of the particular characteristics of children's behavioural repertoire of pupils at school and in the classroom, teachers can report on some domains of personality better than on others. In our experience teachers can reliably report on differences in the following areas: socially oriented withdrawn behaviour (extraversion vs introversion), concentration and task orientation, and consideration for other children. The latter includes the frequency of aggressiveness towards other children, and the probability of angry reactions when hindered or attacked by others. The items in questionnaires which measure these three major classroom traits all refer to concretely visible (and audible) behaviour patterns that teachers can observe regularly. On the other hand, a child's typical emotional reactions are more difficult for a teacher to observe, resulting in lower reliability of teacher reports on individual differences in positive and negative emotionality.

Referring back to Skinner's view that our personality differs, depending on the situation we are in, and on our learning history of behaviour appropriate to specific situations, Skinner would not have been surprised to learn that agreement between parent and teacher reports on temperament and personality characteristics of children is in most studies not very high. Therefore, it is preferable to use *both* observers, and to base predictions for future behaviour at school on teacher ratings and predictions for behaviour at home on parent ratings. It is an illusion to think that we can isolate, in school-age children, underlying, general and context-independent traits of temperament and personality, valid for predictions of behavioural patterns in *any* situation.

Peer nominations

A method that has a respectable history in child and school psychology for the assessment of individual differences in popularity and isolation, is the sociometric method of peer nominations. The resulting sociometric status types (*popular*, *rejected*, *neglected*, *controversial* and *average*) may be seen as related with personality types. For example, the child with sociometric status *popular* will end to be high in extraversion and agreeableness. For an extensive description of sociometric instruments see the chapter by van Lieshout and Doise (ch. 6 this volume) on social development.

Adolescence

Self-ratings

In addition to ratings by *others* such as parents, teachers and peers, *self-ratings* can also be obtained from adolescents. It is difficult to say from what age children are capable of making reliable and valid statements about their own temperament and personality characteristics. As we saw above, in relation to judgements by mothers with little or no experiences with other children, some experience in comparative judgements is necessary, because most questionnaires ask the respondent to make statements about how frequent or how typical a certain type of behaviour is. To use such relational terms in a reliable and valid way presupposes a notion about the 'normal range' of behaviour for a particular age and sex. As in all other things, individuals differ in their capacity to reflect on their own behavioural characteristics; and so do children. Some children may be capable of good relational self-observations by age 9 but others may not develop this ability before age 14. Since we are looking for methods that are good for the majority of individuals of a certain age level, we do not recommend the use of self-rating methods before age 12, and we recommend that care be exercised in the selection of behavioural characteristics to be rated during the whole of adolescence.

We prefer teacher ratings or ratings by a group of peers, and parent ratings, to young adolescent self-ratings. However, as an extra, self-ratings may be useful and revealing, especially in individual diagnostics. One technique, popularised by Block, is particularly well suited to use by multiple informants, including adolescents: the Q-sort technique, described below. For the accuracy of self-descriptions see the chapter by Demetriou (ch. 5 this volume) on cognitive development.

Q-sort technique

This is a technique used for scaling a set of personality-descriptive items (Q-items) according to whether they are more or less characteristic of a particular individual. The judges are asked to order the items so that the final order of all the items in the set provides a good representation of the judge's view of the personality of the individual being evaluated. With self-ratings the individual is his own judge. The judge must order the

Q-items into a designated number of categories and, most important, with an assigned number of items placed in each category. At one end of the judgemental continuum are placed those items most characteristic of the person being described or most 'salient' in describing him. At the other end of the continuum are placed the items most uncharacteristic. Conventionally, the Q-items are printed separately on cards, a convenience which permits easy arrangement and rearrangement until the desired ordering is obtained. After the sorting, the placement of each of the items is recorded.

There is a Q-set for adults, the California Q-set, CAQ (Block, 1961/1978) and one for children and adolescents, the California Child Q-set, CCQ (Block & Block, 1980). The CCQ has 100 items and has been translated into many languages. In two recent studies, one Dutch and one American, CCQ-data were used to see whether the factor structure contained in the Q-sort data resembled the five-factor structure of the Big Five. We will return to this question below.

Being obliged to distribute the items in fixed numbers over the piles often causes raters to struggle with choices. The necessity of finding solutions to dilemmas such as: 'Is *this* type of behaviour somewhat more typical for him than *that* kind of behaviour?'; 'Should his talkativeness have been put in pile 4 and his restlessness in pile 5 or vice versa?' forces raters to do a thorough job. Consequently a Q-sort technique takes more time than an ordinary questionnaire. It is also a more costly method when the placing of the cards is done in a face-to-face testing situation, in which a testing-assistant is present in order to ensure that the correct procedure is followed, and to record the composition of the piles assembled by the rater.

Adulthood

Adult personality is usually assessed by self-ratings and in some cases by ratings of the target person by well-known others such as peers, partners or spouses. Clinical psychologists often rely on projective tests such as the Rorschach inkblot test or the Thematic Apperception Test (Murray, 1938). The basic assumption of this approach, that people identify or project their own personality onto ambiguous figures, has been repeatedly challenged. Moreover, the psychometric qualities of these techniques have been extensively investigated, the conclusions generally suggesting low reliability and validity. Still, many clinicians consider projective techniques as a valuable instrument for gaining insight into individual fantasies and for gathering information on the complex organisation of individual perception. However, the richness of the data provided by these techniques is not a sufficient condition for scientific validity.

Personality questionnaires also have their problems, although with careful test construction they can be minimised. Response tendencies, that is systematic tendencies to respond to test items irrespective of their content, are a serious problem. *Acquiescence*, the tendency to answer 'yes' to all questions regardless of content, can be dealt with by keying half of the

answers to 'no', thus ensuring that high scores on the test are not confounded with higher acquiesence tendencies. *Social Desirability* is the tendency to endorse items that refer to behaviour that is considered desirable in
a given society and thus to present a positive image of the self. This response
tendency can be dealt with by forcing subjects to choose between two
equally desirable items with a different descriptive meaning or by administering a scale to measure the tendency itself, such as the Marlowe–Crowne
Social Desirability Scale (Crowne & Marlowe, 1960) or Eysenck's Lie Scale
(see below).

There are many, perhaps too many, personality questionnaires. The lack
of a taxonomic classification of traits has been responsible for a rather
chaotic proliferation of instruments alleging to measure new dimensions of
personality. However, when these new scales are correlated with existing
ones and in particular when they are related to the five-factor model of
personality, new scales often turn out to be newly labelled scales that
correlate significantly with existing ones. With the growing consensus about
the comprehensiveness of the five-factor model, there is hope that the
emphasis will shift towards improving reliability and validity instead of
creating more of the same. Given the plethora of instruments any discussion
has to be limited to a small sample of instruments and is therefore likely to
be selective.

The Minnesota Multiphasic Personality Inventory (MMPI)

The MMPI is undoubtedly the most widely used and researched personality
questionnaire. It is a criterion-reference test which means the items selected
for the individual scales have been found to discriminate between clinical
groups. Hundreds of scales have been constructed to differentiate not only
clinical groups but also all kinds of social deviance. The complete test
contains 566 items. The ten basic clinical scales are Hypochondria (Hs),
Depression (D), Hysteria (Hy), Psychopathic deviate (Pd), Masculinity/
Femininity (Mf), Paranoia (Pa), Psychastenia (Pt), Schizophrenia (Sc),
Hypomania (Ma) and Social introversion (Si). Because the scale construction is based on item–criterion correlations, the internal consistency of the
scales is low and factor analysis at item or scale level does not confirm the
structure. A new version of this instrument, the MMPI-2, was recently
published. The new version was developed to improve the samples from
which the clinical scales were derived and to modify some of the items whose
content became obsolete as well as to widen the behaviour to which the
items refer. It is still too early to judge this new version but given that it was
constructed to resemble the original MMPI as much as possible, the same
objections probably still hold.

The Eysenck Personality Tests

Hans Eysenck has contributed considerably to the construction of psychometrically validated personality tests. Over the years, he has continued to develop and improve his personality test, broadening its scope from a measure of Neuroticism (Maudsley Medical Questionnaire) to the most recent Eysenck Personality Questionnaire–Revised (EPQR), measuring three factors, labelled as Extraversion, Neuroticism or Emotionality and Psychoticism-Ego Control (Eysenck, Eysenck & Barrett, 1992), and including a fourth 'Lie-scale' measuring the social desirability bias. Apart from its good psychometric qualities, the EPQ (Eysenck & Eysenck, 1975) has been used in hundreds of studies to test Eysenck's personality theory, which links Neuroticism to lability of the nervous system, Extraversion to degree of autonomic arousal and Psychoticism to levels of male sex hormones. Eysenck's factors Extraversion and Neuroticism correlate highly with Extraversion and Emotional stability (inverse) as defined in the five-factor model. Psychoticism-Ego Control correlates negatively with both Conscientiousness and Agreeableness as, for example, in comparative studies with the NEO-PI (McCrae & Costa, 1985). The fifth factor, Openness/Culture/ Intellect, is not part of the Eysenckian personality model.

The Jackson Personality Research Form (PRF)

Jackson (1984) constructed a personality test that similarly to the TAT was based on Murray's (1938) theory of needs and 'presses'. He constructed various forms of the test, among them Form E which measures the following 20 Murray needs: *abasement, achievement, affiliation, aggression, autonomy, change, cognitive structure, dependence, dominance, endurance, exhibition, harm-avoidance, impulsivity, nurturance, order, play, sentience (need for physical sensation), social recognition, succourance* (need for social support) and *understanding*. In addition there are two technical scales, one to assess careless responding and the other to measure social desirability bias. The PRF is one of the best tests from a psychometric point of view, because it is based on technically sophisticated forms of item analysis. However, the scales cannot be considered as independent because factor analysis reveals only 6 to 8 orthogonal factors instead of 20. Finally, once again, the scales of this test turn out to be clearly related to the five-factor model (McCrae, 1989).

Five-Factor Model Tests

We have described these tests and their background above (see Table 9.1). Some European adaptations of the NEO-PI have recently been developed (Borkenau & Ostendorf, 1993; Hoekstra, Orwel, & deFruyt, 1996). For a contrary view of the five-factor approach to personality description see Block, 1995).

PERSONALITY CHARACTERISTICS THROUGH THE LIFE-SPAN

Is the Five-Factor Model also Valid for Infancy and Childhood?

As we saw above, influential models for temperament in infancy and childhood were developed by Thomas and Chess (1977), by Rothbart and Derryberry (1981) and by Buss and Plomin (1984). None of these alternative models, however, has as yet acquired sufficient authority to stop the quest for the *best* structure of temperament (and personality) in childhood. Inspired by the success of the five-factor model in adult personality psychology, developmental psychologists have recently begun a search for the antecedents of these five adult factors in childhood. What relevance may this five-factor model have for the search for the essential dimensions of temperament in childhood?

One approach to answer this question is found in studies in which the data produced by old instruments are reanalysed to see how much of the five-factor model can be discerned in the pattern of outcomes. This has been done with Q-sort data obtained with the CCQ, described above. The CCQ was originally intended to measure two traits, *ego-control* and *ego-resiliency* (Block & Block, 1980). A reanalysis of the CCQ-data of a sample of young, adolescent, Pittsburg (US) boys showed that a five-factor solution replicated only three of the Big Five factors (Extraversion, Agreeableness and Conscientiousness), but in a seven-factor principle components analysis (a type of factor analysis) the Big Five were more or less clearly reproduced, supplemented by two extra factors labelled Activity and Irritability (Robins, John & Caspi, 1994; John, Caspi, Robins, Moffit & Stouthamer-Loeber, 1994). In a comparable study, but with larger and more representative samples, van Lieshout and Haselager (1994; see also Hartup & van Lieshout, 1995) also found seven factors: the Big Five, plus Motor Activity and Dependency. Thus a separate Motor Activity factor was found in both CCQ studies. This is a clear indication that motor activity is a specific childhood factor that only in adolescence and adulthood becomes incorporated in the broad factor Extraversion.

When Dutch teachers were asked to rate their pupils in two independent studies, using two very different instruments, three factors very similar to Big Five Extraversion, Agreeableness and Conscientiousness, emerged as the largest factors (Kohnstamm, 1992). In Belgium, studies with teachers revealed that when teachers were asked to give in their own words as many traits as they found relevant for individual differences among pupils, most of the elicited constructs could be located in a FFM factor space (Mervielde, 1994). However, when teachers were asked to rate the pupils in their class on the items of a standard Big Five rating scale, Conscientiousness and Openness to Experience did not emerge as separate factors in their ratings of pupils of the early grades (Mervielde, Buyst & de Fruyt, 1995).

An alternative method is used in research in which parents are asked to freely describe the personalities of their children in their own words. The collection of personality-relevant statements that results from such interviews can then be categorised according to the broad meaning of the five factors. This has now been done for children aged 3, 6, 9 and 12 in countries as diverse as Poland, Greece, Germany, Belgium, The Netherlands, the US and China (Kohnstamm et al., 1995; 1996; 1998). It turns out that in all these countries between 70% and 80% of all descriptors generated by parents can be ascribed to categories covered by the five factors. Whether this *rational* categorisation will pass an *empirical* test is the next question. For this purpose, questionnaires have been constructed with items that are representative of the total domain of what parents report as indicative of child personality. Only the empirical factors resulting from analyses of interitem correlations in these new questionnaires will be able to tell us how much of the variance in the answers to the items is bound by the Big Five, how much is bound by different factors or by combinations of factors, and how much is unexplainable and should be ascribed to chance coincidences and errors of measurement. (For Dutch results see Slotboom & Elphick, 1997.)

It is thus still too early to draw final conclusions about the applicability of a five-factor structure to ratings of individual differences in children made by parents and teachers. Since most adults seem to organise their perceptions of their own personality traits as well as those of other adults according to the five-factor scheme, it is not to be expected that they structure perceived differences among children in a totally different way. On the contrary, a tendency to structure individual differences in children in a way that is *most* consonant with the structure used for adults is to be expected. Only where infants and children differ in behaviour patterns that are very specific to infancy and childhood, and that are important for the care-giver or teacher to cope with—for example, irritability, motor activity level, dependency and manageability—will different factors be found in the structure of adults' perceptions of young and very young persons. Following the same line of thought, one might expect that if personality questionnaires for the elderly were to be constructed, based on free descriptions of the elderly, specific factors such as self-reliance vs dependency, and able-bodiedness would be found, that would not coincide with any of the Big Five. This is because our perceptions of the multitude of individual differences among human beings tend to get organised and structured according to the *interests* of the perceivers. If our major problem with 2 and 3 year olds is that they want to go their own way and are not aware of the dangers in what they are doing, then it is in both our and their interest if we can make reliable predictions about their behaviour; for example to the question; will she jump or not? These interests are so vital that when we describe or rate children of that age who are in our care, or class, our thoughts and utterances will get organised according to these major interests.

There is no structure for individual differences in personality that is given by nature and that exists outside and independent of the brains of the perceivers. There are probably many individual differences *whose origin* is caused by nature, by our genes. But the totality of these differences get *structured* only in our brains, according to our interests. These structures can be revealed by factor analysing large samples of perceiver ratings of individuals they know, on unbiased selections of traits.

More about Stability

Returning now to the issue of stability and change, so central to a developmental approach to personality, we make another methodological distinction. This concerns the differences between studying the stability in a representation sample of the total distribution of a trait, and studying the stability in samples taken only from the two tails of the distribution, not from the middle part. Even when the tails are cut large, so that a quarter of the distribution on each side falls in the sample, the stability coefficients obtained may differ greatly from those obtained in total distribution studies.

The method one chooses is dependent on the assertions one wants to make on the basis of their results. Stability correlation coefficients obtained in extremes-only studies may never be generalised, explicitly or implicitly, to total distributions. However, if one is careful not to make generalised assertions, and explicitly mentions the limitations of the results, there may be good reason to do a tails-only study. For instance, it has been found that the 20% or so of boys scoring highest on aggressive behaviour at age 8 years have a high risk of becoming juvenile delinquents. If one were interested in preventative programmes for juvenile delinquency, one could decide to focus on a small group of extreme-scoring children, if such a predictive relationship had been demonstrated for the extreme-scoring group. Because preventive programmes are usually short of money, one might as well make a decision to focus on high-risk groups only.

Another important issue to keep in mind is the length of the period between measurements. Stability over a period of several months or a year means something different from stability over periods of spanning 5 or 10 years. Most childhood temperament studies involve a relatively short period of time, often less than 12 months. In infancy and childhood the majority of short-term stability coefficients are modest at best (r *between 0.20 and 0.30*), and begin to decline when stability intervals are greater than 6 months, or when different instruments or different tests are used at different ages (Wachs, 1994). When continuity of temperament or personality is assessed across age periods (e.g. from infancy to preschool, from childhood to adulthood), for the most part modest correlations are again the rule. Correlation coefficients in the 0.50 range occur only when aggregated measures are utilised with a temperamentally extreme group of children. Aggregated measures are composed of scores on several specific measures. In Box 9.2 an overview is given of recent stability results in the fields of study: antisocial behaviour and behavioural inhibition/social withdrawal.

One important contribution to this field comes from a Swedish longitudinal study, in which children born between 1955 and 1958 in Stockholm were

---

Box 9.2 Stability of antisocial behaviour and inhibition

- The stability of antisocial behaviour from childhood through ado-lescence is substantial, approximating the consistencies across time, reported for measured intelligence. (This means in the 0.5 to 0.6 range of correlation coefficients for unselected samples.)
- Antisocial behaviour is stable for very aggressive persons but decidedly unstable for many others.
- Some children are aggressive at an early age and remain so, whereas others only become aggressive during the transition to adolescence.
- Inhibition is weakly stable between 16 and 40 months, when negative affect is included in aggregated scores.
- With negative affect not included, inhibition is moderately stable through the first three years, although more so in extreme cases than in representation samples.
- Among older children (4 years through 10 years) stability in be-havioural inhibition is evident when assessed during confronta-tions with strangers.
- Stability from early through late childhood in social withdrawal, peer acceptance, self-attitudes, and internalising symptoms is not clearly evident.

Source: After Hartup & van Lieshout (1995).

---

studied for over 25 years (Kerr, Lambert, Stattin & Klackenborg-Larsson, 1994). The authors searched for stability of position on an inhibition dimen-sion, both for extreme groups (10–15% from each end of the distribution) and for children not rated as extreme. First, stability was measured from an average age of 21 months through age 6 years. Ratings were found to be more stable for children in the extreme groups than for those in the non-extreme groups, for both sexes. Next, stability was measured into adoles-cence. Here, stability was found only for extreme-scoring girls, not for extreme-scoring boys.

In adolescence, the mothers gave the inhibition ratings. Ratings given by these mothers when the children were still 21 months old did not correlate with their own later ratings, not even for the extreme groups. Only the ratings of a psychologist, obtained when the children were aged 21 months, correlated positively with the later maternal ratings, but only for the ex-treme-scoring girls, not for the boys. The initially extreme-scoring boys at age 16 received the same average ratings from their mothers as the initially non-extreme groups from both sexes did.

Most results of longitudinal studies of temperament and personality confirm Bloom's law as cited in the earlier section on stability: Very little stability in infancy, a little more in early childhood, in particular for exter-nalising types of behaviour such as aggressiveness, and still more so at school-age, reaching maximum correlation coefficients of 0.60 after age 7 (time of first measurement) for periods of 4 to 6 years thereafter. For most of the variables of temperament and personality studied so far, scores obtained for individuals with extreme positions on traits such as inhibition, reactivity and aggressiveness.

Before we look at stability from adolescence into adulthood and through adulthood, there is need for a word on the stability of attachment classifications as assessed in infancy and childhood.

Stability of Attachment Classifications

In infancy the stability of attachment classifications between 12 and 18 months varies from study to study (Belsky, Campbell, Cohn & Moore, 1996). It is often shown that many of the relations classified at 12 months as *insecure* are classified as *secure* 6 months later. However, most secure relations at age 12 months tend to be also secure at age 18 months. Particularly in the case of mother–infant relations that are under some kind of stress in the early months of life, an insecure classification at 12 months does not predict insecurity at 18 months. Combining the classifications at 12 and 18 months from three independent Dutch studies, two investigating infants born in Asia and South-America and adopted by Dutch parents (Juffer, 1993; Rosenboom, 1994), and one investigating preterm babies and their biological (Dutch) mothers, reveals that of 110 relations originally classified as *secure* at 12 months 86% were also classified as secure half a year later, whereas of 30 relations originally classified as *insecure* only 33% remained so. On both occasions the same Strange Situation was used to classify the quality of attachment.

For older children the original Strange Situation can no longer be used, so that the quality of the attachment relation must be assessed with other instruments, such as observations in standard situations, interviews and questionnaires. In general, less stability for insecure relations is to be expected over longer time-spans and different assessment methods, compared with early measures of temperament, early attachment classifications do not seem to be more stable.

Transmission of Attachment Classifications over Generations?

Bowlby believed that attachment theory is not only a theory of child development. On a number of occasions he insisted that attachment phenomena are lifelong (e.g. Bowlby, 1988). A major impetus for research in the area of adult attachment was the development of methods for studying attachment styles in adults. One of these methods is the now popular *adult attachment interview*, in which the adult is asked that his or her memory is of attachment-related behaviours in childhood. Since it is evident that such recollections of the first years of life are constructs, perceptions of the past, and not necessarily reports of how things actually were, the research has focused on the content of this mental representation, as an indicator of adults' current feelings about their attachment relations. Present thoughts about the past are assumed to influence the quality of adults' attachment relations with their children. Thus, the search has begun for the intergenerational transfer of individual differences in attachment patterns.

Research in the US, Canada and Australia (see Sperling & Berman, 1994, for a recent overview) and in Europe (Parkes, Stevenson-Hinde & Morris, 1991; Van IJzendoorn, 1995) leads to the conclusion that there is substantial intergenerational transmission of individual differences in attachment patterns. In about 75% of families, the classification of the parents' mental representation of how they were attached themselves (to their parents) is in agreement with measures of the attachment relations they currently have with their infants. In about a quarter of the families, parents classified as *secure* in their mental representations of the past nevertheless are diagnosed as having an *insecure* relationship with their infant, and vice versa. Of course, we should remember in interpreting such data that the distribution of secure and insecure types of attachment is skewed in that most relationships are, luckily, of a secure kind (about 65% in samples from normal populations) and that about 40% of 'hits' may already be reached simply by guessing alone. Another marginal note also seems to be in place: What is cause and what is effect? Is the attachment relation with the child really influenced by the parent's thoughts about their own past, as most researchers in this area seem to think, or is the present quality of the relation with the child actually influencing the parent's memories? Or are both true? As long as this is unclear it would perhaps be better to use the phrase *intergenerational concordance* or *congruence* instead of *intergenerational transmission* of the quality of attachment relations. The latter phrase suggests a one-way causal pathway only.

Stability of Traits from Adolescence to Old Age

Adolescence is commonly thought of as a developmental stage in which important changes take place. The focus here is on changes occurring in the group as a whole rather than on changes in individual differences. According to Harter (1990), self-esteem typically drops slightly at the beginning of adolescence and then steadily rises. By the time they are 19 or 20 years old, boys and girls have a much higher self-esteem than in early adolescence. Research on stability and change in individual differences from adolescence to adulthood requires a common frame of reference. The five-factor model is a likely candidate for such research. As soon as the validity of the model can be established for adolescents and children continuity across developmental stages can be addressed. Most of the available evidence is difficult to judge because personality traits are measured with different instruments and are viewed from different theoretical frameworks, complicating any comparison across stages. These methodological difficulties tend to bias research towards the general conclusion that cross-stage stability is low because differences in measures, raters, reliability and procedures all tend to lower cross-stage correlations.

A notable exception to this general trend is the McCrae and Costa (1990) study about the stability of the 'Big Five' over time. They report substantial correlations over an interval of 6 years for a group of 983 men and women aged 21 to 76 at the first time of testing. The stability correlations for the five factors were: Neuroticism (0.83), Extraversion (0.82), Openness to Experience (0.83), Agreeableness (0.63) and Conscientiousness (0.79). The correlations were essentially similar for men and women and for younger adults (25 to 56 years) and older adults (57 to 84 years); in contrast, first-year students at a military academy showed retest correlations of 0.66, 0.76, and 0.76 respectively for Neuroticism, Extraversion and Openness to Experience over the much shorter interval of 9 months (McCrae, 1993). In general, personality seems to be less stable in adolescents than in adults. Other evidence suggests that over longer periods, such as several decades, the stability is lower but still remarkably good. The fact that personality measures are in general less reliable than cognitive tests suggests that when personality could be measured more reliably individual differences would probably be as stable as individual differences in intelligence.

Sex Differences in Personality Development: Motor Activity Level as an Example

We saw above in the Stockholm study on shyness that it is worthwhile to analyse results of long-term stability or continuity studies separately for the two sexes. In this chapter the expression 'sex differences' is used instead of 'gender differences'. The latter expression is nowadays often preferred because it sounds more civilised, has no association with sexuality and does not imply a biological origin. However, dictionaries still reserve 'gender' for a distinction in grammar and not in human beings. The use of 'gender differences' seems to imply that the differences in question are manmade, cultural phenomena, as linguistic rules of gender are. To choose either word seems to indicate a preference for one explanation: observed differences in behaviour are either inborn or learned. In this way many feminists prefer 'gender' to 'sex' when discussing behavioural differences between males and females. We prefer 'sex' to 'gender' because we want to keep the possibility open that the behavioural differences are, at least partly, caused or facilitated by constitutional factors.

The sex distinction creates two naturally occurring groups in all cultures. In spite of its utmost importance in psychology and sociology, it has not been a well studied subject in the temperament literature. For many centuries adult temperament typology was only applied to males: practically no examples of temperament differences in females were given by writers on this subject. When modern, twentieth-century researchers in the fields of anthropology, psychiatry and psychology began to collect data on temperament in childhood and adolescence, it was a matter of course to include both sexes in the samples studied, without, however, paying much attention to the variable. This situation has now changed considerably. The number of studies reporting sex differences is now so large that meta-analytic studies are published regularly, analysing the results of many different studies in one overall analysis. From such a recent study, over all age levels, Feingold (1994) concluded that males, on average, are more assertive and have slightly higher self-esteem than females. Females are higher than males in extraversion, anxiety, trust, and in particular, tender-mindedness (e.g. nurturance). The totality of studies reported in the literature did not show sex differences in social anxiety, impulsiveness, ideas (e.g. reflectiveness), locus of control, and orderliness. Sex differences were generally constant across ages, years of data collection (cohorts), educational levels, and nations.

The first book to treat the subject at length, though not under the label 'temperament', was Maccoby's (1966) edited volume, later followed more explicitly by Maccoby and Jacklin (1974). The annotated bibliographies in both volumes are goldmines for those interested in the early studies. The earliest study relevant to the subject was on resistive reactions during intelligence testing of 110 children between 6 and 53 months of age (Levy & Tulchin, 1925). This study concluded that boys clung to their mothers more than girls, whereas girls attempted to hide more. The most intense resistive reactions, such as struggling and screaming, reached their peak at 18 months for girls and at 30 months for boys. A similar study, on a considerably larger scale, was published four years later by Goodenough (1929).

There are different ways of looking at sex differences—as *main* effects, and as effects which only show in *interaction* with other variables, such as age. For developmentalists it all starts with this second category of questions. We simply cannot look at sex–temperament interactions without considering the age or the stage of development of the subjects. A more complicated possibility is that at specific developmental stages the *stability* of positions on specific variables is sex-dependent.

Sex differences nowadays are reported in so many studies that we cannot go into detail for all the variables of temperament and personality involved. In this chapter we opted for *motor activity level* as an example, because it is a typical childhood variable, and because a meta-analytic study yields clear results. Eaton and Enns (1986) found boys to be more motorically active in the large majority of studies. Reviewing 127 different studies, they found an average of sex difference of one-half a standard deviation ($d = 0.49$; d has become a popular indicator of effect sizes, see Cohen, 1988), with males being more active in a large majority of the 127 studies reviewed. The effect was age-dependent. Before birth the average difference was 0.33, during infancy 0.29, during preschool 0.44 and at older ages 0.64. Quite unexpectedly, the authors found no differences between three types of study: objective measurement studies using instruments such as actometers; observation studies using professional observers; and rating studies, using ratings by parents and teachers, and self-ratings. The average sex differences found for the three methods are 0.53, 0.47 and 0.50 respectively. This latter finding seems to be very important for the whole field of temperament and personality. Activity level is certainly subject to social sex stereotyping. The Eaton and Enns study indicates that this social stereotyping does not cause the subjective methods, on the average, to *overrate* the difference as measured by objective methods. Concerning the size of the average difference found in their study, these authors write: 'Translated into correlational terms, the obtained effect size presents a point-biserial correlation between sex and activity level of 0.24, and the proportion of total activity level variance associated with sex is about 5%. Expressed in yet another way, the average male subject (at the 50th percentile) is more active than 69% of female subjects.'

Relatively small differences in group means may have strong effects on the proportions of males and females at the *extremes* of the distributions. Eaton and Enns mention the differential proportions in the case of hyperactivity as an illustration. The preponderance of boys with hyperactivity is a well-documented finding. Ratios vary from 2:1 to 8:1. For example, Luk, Leung and Lee (1988) collected teacher ratings on the Conners scale for a sample of 914 Chinese children, aged 6–12 years and living in Hong Kong. Comparing the means and standard deviations on the Conners hyperactivity scale the difference was close to one standard deviation (0.99). Earlier studies with the same scale in the USA and in New Zealand yielded sex differences of 1.00 and 0.71 respectively.

In a huge longitudinal British study (Osborn & Milbank, 1987) 7000 10 year olds throughout Britain were rated by their teachers on several behavioural scales that combined items from the Rutter B-scale and the Conners scale. On the six-item scale called hyperactivity (highest loading item at age 10: 'shows restless or overactive behaviour;) the difference measure was 0.47, and sex 'explained 5.6% of the variance compared with 1.6% for the Social Index score'. In a Dutch study (Kohnstamm, 1992) teachers rated 265 children aged 6–8 years on two different scales for inattentiveness, distractibility and hyperactivity. The sex difference for the two scales (intercorrelation 0.88) were 0.66 and 0.73. On two other scales for introversion and extraversion the teachers rated girls on the average as slightly more extravert than boys. The same was true for the large British study mentioned above: no sex differences in teacher-rated extraversion.

The conclusion with regard to motor activity level must be that boys on the average show somewhat higher levels than girls. This difference increases with age until the early school years. At the high extreme of the scale the proportion of boys is at least twice the proportion of girls. A high level of motor activity is an important component of the behavioural disorder called hyperactivity—which also includes inattentiveness and distractibility. With respect to a causal explanation for this sex difference, some believe in world-wide role-stereotyping, others in world-wide constitutional factors. Most certainly both are true, in combination. This conclusion applies as well to the general field of temperament and personality.

The basic sex differences at any particular age may be small, but culture reacts differently to males and females occupying the same position on specific dimensions. School-age boys and girls in the seventh decile of the common distribution of inhibition or of externalising reactivity following frustration elicit quite different reactions, dependent upon the culture in general and on social class. The more rigidly the sex roles are fixed in a culture or social class, the more different the reactions will be. Further, reactions differ according to the situation in which the behaviour is exhibited and observed. The fact that in some studies teacher ratings produce larger sex differences than parent ratings probably has several reasons. One reason is that the school environment, with its limited space, its many behavioural restrictions and its intensive social interactions of the two sexes, elicits behaviour patterns which parents may not always see at home. Consequently, rather than thinking that teachers in general are more sex-stereotyped in their perceptions than parents are, we think school life elicits more sex-stereotyped behaviours than life at home.

CONCLUSION

The psychology of individual differences in temperament and personality has a rich history, dating back to ancient Greek and Roman observers of mankind. The study of the *development* of personality traits, however, is a relatively new theme for psychologists. True, in Freudian theory the child-hood roots of the *oral, anal* and *genital* character types are of prime concern for both theorist and practitioner, as are the childhood roots of adult traits such as *narcissism* and *neuroticism.* But present-day developmental psychology has rejected these Freudian concepts on the grounds that they have been insufficiently validated and tested within an empirical framework. In Roman countries, however, and in psychoanalytic practice, Freud's developmental theory of personality is still very important. What has replaced Freudian thinking on the development of personality types and personality traits? Very little. Psychologists and psychiatrists of the second half of the twentieth century have modestly concentrated on the best possible classifications, taxonomies, of personality traits—normal and pathological—and on the best ways to measure these traits in individuals. The search for personality *types*, characterised by specific combinations of traits, has come to a halt, as has the search for their life-span antecedents and consequences. Perhaps we shall see a revival of this approach in the twenty-first century. For the time being, taxonomic endeavours, directed at finding the basic dimensions of personality, and their *facets*, will certainly be continued. While giving recognition to the cultural basis of the distinctions we make in perceiving our own personalities and the personalities of others, the search for *universal* dimensions in these perceptions will increase. This is because the trend is more toward cultural integration and conformity than toward segregation and diversity. The striving for more European cooperation and integration—for example the inclusion of Eastern European countries in the EC—is an example of a process that is to be expected on a world-wide scale. With growing economic trade and cooperation, increasing access to information technology and growing prosperity, diversity in cultural values will diminish. Countries, and political and ideological systems, will gradually become more and more alike. And with increasing similarity in cultural values and values systems, the ways in which we perceive, verbalise, evaluate and react to individual differences in personality will also become more alike. This prospect for adult personality psychology does not necessarily mean that our understanding of how children's personalities develop into adult personalities will increase. The longitudinal studies necessary to follow groups of individuals over many years, from infancy into adulthood, and perhaps even into old age, will always require decades of study, large investments of staff and the continuing dedication of the principal researchers. There is no way of *simulating* a life-span development in a time-simulator, of condensing decades of 'natural' development into a few years or, even better, months or weeks. Dependent on such long periods of research on the same subjects, progress in this field will be slow. An extra problem is that as the research continues over a time-span of decades, the world changes. Advances in technology, education, prosperity and mobility change cultures and the people that are part of them. Research findings based on longitudinal studies of subjects who were children in the 1940s will have little relevance for predicting life trajectories of children born in the first decade of the twenty-first century. Such differences in *cohorts* of subjects will remain our most serious handicap.

Progress is to be expected in our knowledge of the genetic base of differences in personality—whether manifested in childhood or at later stages of development. But as we have stressed in this chapter, such knowledge will be valid only for groups of individuals, not for individuals themselves. With the relatively low levels of stability that have been found for personality characteristics assessed in early childhood—and this is also true for intelligence—the predictability of later outcomes, in adolescence or adulthood, will remain low. Thus it is not to be expected that developmental research will produce findings that will make it possible to detect at an early age individuals who will later develop into criminals. The research will certainly lead to more precise likelihood statements. For example, individual children with such and such a combination of characteristics, both genetic and environmental, have a one-in-four chance of later developing such and such patterns of deviant behaviour. But we will not be able to identify the individuals in whom this potential will be realised into actual behaviour. This problem seriously limits the legitimacy of preventive actions. It is legitimate to place groups of children and their families in preventive therapy, because these children have a one-in-four chance of developing into criminals, or psychiatric patients, or of developing other types of seriously deviant behaviour? We are not talking about some kind of neurotransmitting drug, which is in itself harmless but effective as a preventive medicine. It is unlikely that such pharmacological advances will be made. The causation of human individual cases will probably never be identified in sufficient detail for preventive manipulation in childhood to become feasible.

Such a warning of not to expect wonders from this field of research should not depress the reader. The fact that individuals differ so much in personality characteristics, in infancy as well as in old age, will never cease to fascinate those of us who are deeply interested in human behaviour and development.

REFERENCES

Adorno, T. W., Frenckel-Brunswick, E., Levinson, E. & Sanford, R. N. (1950). *The Authoritarian Personality*. New York: Harper.

Ainsworth, M. D. S. (1979). Infant–mother attachment. *American Psychologist*, **34**(10), 932–937.

Ainsworth, M. D. S., Blehar, M. C., Waters, E. & Wall, S. (1978). *Patterns of Attachment: A Psychological Study of the Strange Situation*. Hillsdale, NJ: Erlbaum.

Allport, G. W. (1937). *Personality: A Psychological Interpretation*. New York: Holt, Rinehart & Winston.

Allport, G. W. & Odbert, H. S. (1936). Trait-names: A psycho-lexical study. *Psychological Monographs*, **47** (1, Whole No. 211).

Angleitner, A., Ostendorf, F. & John, O. (1990). Towards a taxonomy of personality descriptors in German: A psycho-lexical study. *European Journal of Personality*, **4**, 89–118.

Bandura, A. (1977). *Social Learning Theory*. Englewood Cliffs, NJ: Prentice-Hall.

Bandura, A. & Walters, R. H. (1963). *Social Learning and Personality Development*. New York: Holt, Rinehart & Winston.

Bates, J. E. (1989). Concepts and measures of temperament. In G. A. Kohnstamm, J. E. Bates & M. K. Rothbart (Eds), *Temperament in Childhood*, Chichester: Wiley.

Belsky, J., Campbell, S. B., Cohn, J. F. & Moore, G. (1996). Instability of infant–parent attachment security. *Developmental Psychology*, **32**, 921–924.

Block, J. (1961/1978). *The Q-sort Method in Personality Assessment and Psychiatric Research*, Palo Alto, CA: Consulting Psychologists Press.

Block, J. (1995). A contrarian view of the five-factor approach to personality description. *Psychological Bulletin*, **117**, 187–215.

Block, J. H. & Block, J. (1980). The role of ego-control and ego-resiliency in the organization of behavior. In W. A. Collins (Ed.), *Development and Cognition, Affect, and Social Relations*. Minnesota Symposia on Child Psychology, Vol. 13 (pp. 39–101). Hillsdale, NJ: Erlbaum.

Bloom, B. S. (1964). *Stability and Change in Human Characteristics*, New York: Wiley,

Borkenau, P. & Ostendorf, F. (1993). NEO-FŸnf-Faktoren-Inventar (NEO-FFI). Gšttingen: Hogrefe.

Bowlby, J. (1958). The nature of the child's tie to his mother. *International Journal of Psychoanalysis*, **39**, 350–373.

Bowlby, J. (1969). *Attachment and Loss*: Vol. 1. *Attachment*. New York: Basic Books.

Bowlby, J. (1988). *A Secure Base. Clinical Applications of Attachment Theory*. London: Routledge.

Brokken, F. B. (1978). The language of personality. Unpublished Dissertation, University of Groningen, Groningen, The Netherlands.

Burt, C. (1948). The factorial study of temperament traits. *British Journal of Psychology* (statistical section), **28**, 178–203.

Buss, A. H. & Plomin, R. (1984). *Temperament: Early Developing Personality Traits*. Hillsdale, NJ: Erlbaum.

Carey, W. B. (1997) *Understanding Your Child's Temperament*. New York: MacMillan.

Carey, W. B. & McDevitt, S. C. (Eds) (1989). *Clinical and Educational Applications of Temperament Research*. Amsterdam/Lisse: Swets & Zeitlinger.

Cattell, R. B. (1943). The description of personality: Basic traits resolved into clusters. *Journal of Abnormal and Social Psychology*, **38**, 476–506.

Cattell, R. B. (1945). The description of personality: Principles and findings in a factor analysis. *American Journal of Psychology*, **58**, 69–90.

Cohen, J. (1988). *Statistical Power Analysis for Behavioral Sciences* (revised edn). New York: Academic Press.

Costa, P. T. Jr & McCrae, R. R. (1985). *The NEO Personality Inventory Manual*. Odessa, FL: Psychological Assessment Resources.

Costa, P. T. Jr & McCrae, R. R. (1992). *Revised NEO Personality Inventory (NEO PI-R) and NEO Five-Factor Inventory (NEO-FFI)*. Odessa, FL: Psychological Assessment Resources.

Crockenberg, S. B. (1981). Infant irritability, mother responsiveness, and social support influences on the security of infant–mother attachment. *Child Development*, **52**, 857–865.

Crockenberg, S. B. (1986). Are temperamental differences in babies associated with predictable differences in care-giving? In J. V. Lerner & R. M. Lerner (Eds), *Temperament and Social Interaction in Infants and Children* (pp. 53–57). San Francisco: Jossey-Bass.

Crowne, D. P. & Marlowe, D. (1960). A new scale of social desirability, independent of psychopathology. *Journal of Consulting Psychology*, **24**, 349–354.

Dollard, J., Doob, L. W., Miller, N. E., Mowrer, O. H. & Sears, R. R. (1939). *Frustration and Aggression*. New Haven, CT: Yale University Press.

Eaton, W. O. & Enns, R. (1986). Sex differences in human motor activity level. *Psychological Bulletin*, **100**, 19–28.

Endler, N. S. & Magnusson, D. (1976). *Interactional Psychology and Personality*. Washington, DC: Hemisphere.

Escalona, S. (1968). *The Roots of Individuality*, Chicago: Aldine.

Eysenck, H. J. (1947). *Dimensions of Personality*. London: Routledge &

Kegan Paul.

Eysenck, H. J. (1990). Biological dimensions of personality. In L. A. Pervin (Ed.), *Handbook of Personality Theory and Research* (pp. 244–276). New York: Guilford Press.

Eysenck, H. J. & Eysenck, S. B. G. (1975). *The Eysenck Personality Questionnaire*. Sevenoaks, Kent: Hodder & Stoughton.

Eysenck, H. J. & Eysenck, M. W. (1985). *Personality and Individual Differences. A Natural Science Approach*. London: Plenum Press.

Eysenck, H. J., Eysenck, S. B. G. & Barrett, P. (1992). *The EPQR*. Sevenoaks, Kent: Hodder & Stoughton.

Feingold, A. (1994). Gender differences in personality: A meta-analysis. *Psychological Bulletin*, **3**, 429–456.

Funder, D. C. (1989). Accuracy in personality judgment and the dancing bear. In D. M. Buss & N. Cantor (Eds), *Personality Psychology. Recent Trends and Emerging Directions* (pp. 210–223). New York: Springer.

Gleitman, H. (1986). *Psychology*. New York: Norton.

Goldberg, L. R. (1982). From Ace to Zombie: Some explorations in the language of personality. In C. D. Spielberg & J. N. Butcher, *Advances in Personality Assessment*, Vol. 1 (pp. 203–234). Hillsdale, NJ: Erlbaum.

Goldberg, L. R. (1990). An alternative 'description of personality': The Big-Five factor structure. *Journal of Personality and Social Psychology*, **59**, 1216–1229.

Goldberg, L. R. (1993). The structure of phenotypic personality traits. *American Psychologist*, **48**, 26–34.

Goldsmith, H. H. & Alansky, J. A. (1987). Maternal and infant temperamental predictors of attachment: A meta-analytic review. *Journal of Consulting and Clinical Psychology*, **55**, 805–816.

Goldsmith, H. H. & Compos, J. J. (1982). Toward a theory of infant temperament. In R. N. Ende & R. J. Harmon (Eds), *The Development of Attachment and Affiliative Systems* (pp. 161–193). New York: Plenum.

Goodenough, F. L. (1929). The emotional behavior of young children during mental tests. *Journal of Investigative Research*, **13**, 204–219.

Gray, J. A. (1982). *The Neuropsychology of Anxiety*. Oxford: Oxford University Press.

Grossmann, K. E., Grossmann, K. & Schwan, A. (1986). Capturing the wider view of attachment: A re-analysis of Ainsworth's Strange Situation. In C. E. Izard & P. B. Read (Eds), *Measuring Emotions in Infants and Children*, Vol. 2 (pp. 124–171), New York: Cambridge University Press.

Harlow, H. F. (1958). The nature of love. *American Psychologist*, **13**, 673–685.

Harlow, H. F. & Zimmerman, R. R. (1959). Affectional responses in the infant monkey. *Science*, **130**, 421–432.

Harter, S. (1990). Processes underlying adolescent self-concept formation. In R. Montemayor, G. R. Adams, & T. P. Gullotta (Eds), *From Childhood to Adolescence: A Transitional Period?* (pp. 205–239). Newbury Park, CA: Sage.

Hartmann, B. (1896). Die Analyse des kindlichen Gedankenkreises als die

naturgemsse Grundlage des ersten Schulunterrichts. Leipzig: Kessel-
ringsche Hofbuchhandlung Verlag.

Hartup, W. W. & Van Lieshout, C. F. M. (1995). Personality development
in social context. *Annual Review of Psychology*, **46**, 655–687.

Hernstein, R. J. & Murray, C. (1994). *The Bell-curve: Intelligence and Class
Structure in American Life*. New York: Free Press.

Hertsgaard, L., Gunnar, M., Erikson, M. F. & Nachmias, M. (1995).
Adrenocortical responses to the strange situation infants with disor-
ganized/disoriented attachment relationships. *Child Development*, **66**,
1100–1106.

Hoekstra, H. A., Orwel, J. & de Fruyt, F. (1996). *NEO-PI-R and NEO-FFI
Big Five Persoonlijkheidsvragenlijsten*. Lisse: Swets & Zeitlinger.

Hofstee, W. K. B., De Raad, B. & Goldberg, L. R. (1992). Interaction of the
Big Five and circumplex approaches to trait structure. *Journal of Personality and Social Psychology*, **63**, 146–163.

Jackson, D. N. (1984). *Personality Research Form. Manual* (3rd edn). Port
Huron, MI: Research Psychologists Press.

John, O. P., Caspi, A., Robins, R. W., Moffit, T. E. & Stouthamer-Loeber,
M. (1994). The 'Little Five': Exploring the nomological network of the
Five-Factor Model of personality in adolescent boys. *Child Development*,
65, 160–178.

Juffer, F. (1993). Verbonden door adoptie (Attached through adoption; an
experimental study on attachment and competence in families with an
adopted baby). Doctoral Dissertation. Utrecht University.

Kenrick, D. T. & Funder, D. C. (1988). Profiting from controversy: Lessons
from the person–situation debate. *American Psychologist*, **43**, 23–34.

Kerr, M., Lambert, W. W., Stattin, H. & Klackenberg-Larsson, I. (1994).
Stability of inhibition in a Swedish longitudinal sample. *Child Development*, **65**, 138–146.

Kohnstamm, G. A. (1992). Factoren in gedragsbeoordelingen van leerlin-
gen. (Factors in ratings of pupil-behaviour). Pedagogische Studi'n, **69**,
12–22.

Kohnstamm, G. A., Halverson, C. F., Jr, Havill, V. L. & Mervielde. I.
(1996). Parents' free descriptions of child characteristics: A cross-cultural
search for the development antecedents of the Big Five. In S. Harkness &
C. M. Super (Eds), *Parents's Cultural Belief Systems: Their Origins,
Expressions and Consequences* (pp. 27–55). New York: Guilford Press.

Kohnstamm, G. A., Halverson, C. F. Jr., Mervielde. I. & Havill, V. (Eds)
(1998). *Descriptions of Child Personality: Development Antecedents of the
Big Five?* Hillsdale, NJ: Erlbaum.

Kohnstamm, G. A., Mervielde, I., Besevegis, E. & Halverson, C. F. Jr
(1995). Tracing the Big Five in parents' free descriptions of their children.
European Journal of Personality, **9**, 283–304.

Kouwer, B. J. (1963). *Het spel van de persoonlijkheid*. Utrecht, Nederland:
Erven J. Bijleveld.

Levy, D. M. & Tulchin, S. H. (1925). The resistant behavior of infants and
children. *Journal of Experimental Psychology*, **8**, 209–224.

Loehlin, J. C. (1992). *Genes and Environment in Personality Development*. London: Sage.

Luk, S. L., Leung, P. W. L., & Lee, P. L. M. (1988). Conner's teacher rating scale in Chinese children in Hong Kong. *Journal of Child Psychology and Psychiatry*, **29**, 165–174.

Maccoby, E. E. (Ed.) (1966). *The Development of Sex-differences*. Stanford, CA: Stanford University Press.

Maccoby. E. E. &. Jacklin, C. N. (1974). *The Psychology of Sex-differences*. Stanford, CA: Stanford University Press.

Magnusson, D. & Endler, N. S. (1977). *Personality at the Crossroads: Current Issues in Interactional Psychology*. Hillsdale, NJ: Erlbaum.

Main, M. & Solomon, J. (1986). Discovery of an insecure-disorganized disoriented attachment pattern. In T. B. Brazelton & M. Yogman (Eds), *Affective Development in Infancy* (pp. 95–124). Norwood, NJ: Ablex.

Main, M. & Solomon, J. (1990). Procedures for identifying infants as disorganized, disoriented during the Ainsworth Strange Situation. In M. T. Greenberg, D. Cicchetti & E. M. Cummings (Eds), *Attachment in the Preschool Years* (pp. 121–160). Chicago: University of Chicago Press.

McCrae, R. R. (1989). Why I advocate the Five-Factor Model: Joint factor analyses of the NEO-PI with other instruments. In D. M. Buss and N. Cantor (Eds), *Personality Psychology: Recent Trends and Emerging Directions* (pp. 237–245). New York: Springer-Verlag.

McCrae, R. R. (1993). Moderated analyses of longitudinal personality stability. *Journal of Personality and Social Psychology*, **65**, 577–585.

McCrae, R. R. & Costa, P. T. Jr (1985). Comparison of EPI and Psychoticism scales with measures of the five-factor model of personality. *Personality and Individual Differences*, **6**, 587–597.

McCrae, R. R. & Costa, P. T. Jr (1990). *Personality in Adulthood*. New York: Guilford Press.

Mervielde, I. (1994). A five-factor model classification of teachers' constructs on individual differences among children aged 4 to 6. In C. F. Halverson, G. A. Kohnstamm & R. P. Martin (Eds), *The Developing Structure of Temperament and Personality from Infancy to Adulthood* (pp. 387–397). Hillsdale, NJ: Erlbaum.

Mervielde, I., Buyst, V. & De Fruyt, F. (1995). The validity of the Big-Five as a model for teachers' ratings of individual differences among children aged 4–12 years. *Personality and Individual Difference*, **18**, 1827–1836.

Mervielde, I. & Pot, E. (1989). Perceiver and target effects in person perception. *European Journal of Personality*, **3**, 1–13.

Mervielde, I. &. Vandierendonck, A. (Eds) (1994). The Five-Factor Personality Model: European contributions. *Psychologica Belgica*, **34**, Whole no. 4. Special Issue.

Miller, N. E. & Dollard, J. (1941). *Social Learning and Imitation*. New Haven, CT: Yale University Press.

Mischel, W. (1968). *Personality Assessment*. New York: Wiley.

Murray, H. A. (1938). *Explorations in Personality*. New York: Oxford University Press.

Neisser, U., Boudoo, G., Bouchard, Th.J., Boykin, A. W., Brody, N., Ceci, S. J., Halpern, D. F., Loehlin, J. C., Perloff, R., Sternberg, R. J. & Urbina, S. (1996). Intelligence: Knows and unknows. *American Psychologist*, **51**, 77–101.

Osborn, A. F. & Milbank, J. E. (1987). *The Effects of Early Education: A Report from the Child Health Education Study*. Oxford: Clarendon Press.

Ostendorf, F. (1990). Sprache und Persönlichkeitstruktur: Zur Validität des Fünf-Faktoren-Modells der Persönlichkeit. Regensburg, Germany: Roderer.

Parkes, C. M., Stevenson-Hinde, J. & Morris, P. (1991). *Attachment across the Life Cycle*. London: Routledge.

Peabody, D. & Goldberg, L. R. (1989). Some determinants of factor structures from personality-trait descriptors. *Journal of Personality and Social Psychology*, **57**, 552–567.

Plomin, R. (1994). *Genetics and Experience*. London: Sage.

Robins, R. W., John, O. P. & Caspi, A. (1994). Major dimensions of personality in early adolescence: The Big Five and beyond. In C. F. Halverson, G. A. Kohnstamm & R. P. Martin (Eds), *The Developing Structure of Temperament and Personality from Infancy to Adulthood* (pp. 267–291). Hillsdale, NJ: Erlbaum.

Rose, R. J. (1995). Genes and human behavior. *Annual Review of Psychology*, **46**, 625–654.

Rosenboom, L. (1994). Gemengde gezinnen, gemengde gevoelens? (Mixed families, mixed feelings? Attachment and competence of adopted babies in families with biological children). Doctoral Dissertation, Utrecht University.

Rothbart, M. K. (1989). Temperament and development. In G. A. Kohnstamm, J. E. Bates & M. K. Rothbart (Eds), *Temperament in Childhood* (pp. 187–247). Chichester: Wiley.

Rothbart, M. K. & Derryberry, D. (1981). Development of individual differences in temperament. In M. E. Lamb & A. L. Brown (Eds), *Advances in Developmental Psychology*, Vol. 1. Hillsdale, NJ: Erlbaum.

Schwartz, S. H. (1992). Universals in the content and structure of values: Theoretical advances and empirical tests in 20 countries. In M. P. Zanna (Ed.), *Advances in Experimental Social Psychology*, **25**, 1–65. New York: Academic Press.

Schwartz, S. H. & Bilsky, W. (1987). Toward a psychological structure of human values. *Journal of Personality and Social Psychology*, **53**, 550–562.

Schwartz, S. H. & Bilsky, W. (1990). Toward a theory of the universal content and structure of value: Extensions and cross-cultural replications. *Journal of Personality and Social Psychology*, **58**, 878–891.

Shaffer, D. R. (1988). *Social and Personality Development*. Pacific Grove, CA: Brooks/Cole Publishing.

Shweder, R. A. (1975). How relevant is an individual difference theory of personality? *Journal of Personality*, **43**, 455–484.

Skinner. B. F. (1974). *About Behaviorism*. New York: Random House. (The quotations are from the Vintage Book edition, 1976).

Slotboom, A. & Elphick, E. (1997) *Parents' Perception of Child Personality.* Doctoral Dissertation. Leiden University.

Sperling, M. B. & Berman, W. H. (Eds) (1994). *Attachment in Adults, Clinical and Developmental Perspectives.* New York: Guilford Press.

Strelau, J. (Ed.) (1985). *Temperamental Bases of Behavior: Warsaw Studies on Individual Difference.* Lisse (Neth.): Swets & Zeitlinger.

Strelau, J. (1989). The regulative theory of temperament as a result of East–West influences. In G. A. Kohnstamm, J. E. Bates & M. K. Rothbart (Eds), *Temperament in Childhood,* Chichester: Wiley.

Tellegen, A. (1985). Structures of mood and personality and their relevance to assessing anxiety, with an emphasis on self-report. In A. H. Tuma & J. D. Maser (Eds), *Anxiety and Anxiety Disorders.* Hillsdale, NJ: Erlbaum.

Thomas, A. & Chess, S. (1977). *Temperament and Development.* New York: Brunner/Mazel.

Van den Boom, D. C. (1994). The influence of temperament and mothering on attachment and exploration: An experimental manipulation of sensitive responsiveness among lower-class mothers with irritable infants. *Child Development,* **65**, 1457–1477.

Van Lieshout, C. F. M. & Haselager, G. J. T. (1994). The Big Five personality factors on Q-sort descriptions of children and adolescents. In C. F. Halverson, G. A. Kohnstamm & R. P. Martin (Eds), *The Developing Structure of Temperament and Personality from Infancy to Adulthood* (pp. 293–318). Hillsdale, NJ: Erlbaum.

Van IJzendoorn, M. H. (1990). Developments in cross-cultural research on attachment: Some methodological notes. *Human Development,* **33**, 23–30.

Van IJzendoorn, M. H. (1995). Adult attachment representations, parental responsiveness, and infant attachment: A meta-analysis on the predictive validity of the adult attachment interview. *Psychological Bulletin,* **117**, 387–403.

Van IJzendoorn, M. H. & Kroonenberg, P. M. (1988). Cross-cultural patterns of attachment: A meta-analysis of the strange situation. *Child Development,* **59**(1), 147–156.

Van IJjzendoorn, M. H., Goldberg, S., Kronenberg, P. M. & Frenkel, O. J. (1992). The relative effects of maternal and child problems on the quality of attachment: A meta-analysis of attachment in classical samples. *Child Development,* **63**, 840–858.

Wachs, T. D. (1992). *The Nature of Nurture.* Newbury Park, CA: Sage.

Wachs, T. D. (1994). Fit, context, and the transition between temperament and personality. In C. F. Halverson, G. A. Kohnstamm & R. P. Martin (Eds), *The Developing Structure of Temperament and Personality from Infancy to Adulthood* (pp. 209–220). Hillsdale, NJ: Erlbaum.

Watson, D. & Tellegen, A. (1985). Toward a consensual structure of mood. *Psychological Bulletin,* **98**, 219–235.

Chapter 10

Developmental Psychopathology

Caroline Braet and Leni Verhofstadt-Denève

University of Ghent

DEFINITION AND CONCEPTUALIZATION

A Developmental Approach to Psychopathology

As the title of this chapter suggests, we will be considering some child disorders from a developmental perspective rather than in terms of psychological or psychiatric syndromes (Rutter & Garmezy, 1983, p. 776). An approach of this type is often represented in so-called longitudinal studies. The examples below are instances of longitudinal studies, and show that adopting a developmental perspective leads to new questions, a new methodology and new insights. This can enhance our understanding of psychopathology in children and in adolescents.

Examples
- When we adopt a developmental approach to studying children who suffer from an anxiety disorder, we find that the anxiety persists in a number of children, whereas in others the disorder disappears after six years (Verhulst, Eussen, Berden, Sanders-Woudstra and Van der Ende, 1993). The point, therefore, is that developmental psychopathology should analyse this phenomenon and try to find the mechanism which explains such differential developmental patterns.

Life-Span Developmental Psychology
Edited by A. Demetriou, W. Doise and C. F. M. van Lieshout. © 1998 John Wiley & Sons Ltd.

- We also know from several longitudinal studies in various countries that
  when we consider the time-span of problematic behaviour, we find
  totally different ages of onset in some psychopathologies, whereas this is
  not (yet) the case in others. Autism is noticeable prior to 3 years of age;
  suicide, however, does not usually occur before the age of 12, and
  depression can occur at any age (Wenar, 1994). Some problems arise
  most typically in adolescence (e.g. headaches) (Hellinckx, De Munter
  and Grietens, 1993). This is yet another example of an issue that developmental psychopathology can tackle: what are the reasons underlying
  the differences in the onset of a number of complaints?
- Recently, Bernstein, Borchardt and Perwien (1996), found that vulnerability to panic disorder is a function of pubertal changes. Theories
  examining complaints such as 'panic disorders' have so far not paid
  adequate attention to the time dimensions, to the developmental aspect.
  Again, this belongs in the domain of developmental psychopathology.

As Cicchetti says, we have to be 'concerned with the origins and *time
course* of a given disorder, its varying manifestations with development, its
precursors and sequelae, its evolutions in the future' (Cicchetti, 1989).
Although it is generally accepted that stability and consistency in children's
behaviour improves with development, very few of the articles published in
journals adopt a developmental psychopathology methodology (Wierson &
Forehand, 1994).

Life-span psychologists have also emphasized that developmental crises
occur in adult life as well and that the way in which problems in childhood
were treated or solved can influence later life (Rutter & Garmezy, 1983). A
developmental approach to psychopathology therefore needs to be *extended*
even into adulthood.

Rather than starting from assumptions about the origins of disorders in
general, a developmental approach starts by using procedures appropriate
to the *development level* and the developmental course of a disorder. This
approach yields a *new theoretical framework* for disorders in children.
Achenbach puts forward the following definition: 'Developmental psychopathology: a general approach to understanding relations between development and its maladaptive deviations' (Achenbach, 1990, p. 3). The
characteristics of the domain 'Developmental Psychopathology' will be
described in the following paragraphs.

The Gap Between Research and Clinical Practice

Although one of the key features of clinical psychopathology in childhood is
its focus on the functioning of the child in different contexts and against the
background of its development, it is regrettable that the study of disorders in
childhood has failed to make the link between psychopathology and development. Researchers may, for example, study 'depression in adulthood',
and evaluate aspects of the treatment programme, differences in prevalence,

diagnostic considerations, and so on. However, they often do not examine whether the development of depression in adulthood is related to other problems at an earlier age (e.g. a trauma in childhood, an identity crisis in adolescence). The problem may also be related to particular 'life-events', for example, the birth of a child. This implies that the specific 'life-context' and the 'developmental tasks' which are related to it must be taken into account. Clinical practice usually does make those links, but research into aspects of psychopathology all too often neglects them.

In considering the longitudinal course of disorders in childhood, researchers have to take into account changes, mechanisms and processes that underlie developmental transitions, and therefore have to use other instruments to assess continuities and discontinuities between infancy, childhood and adult life. This is now one of the challenges for the developmental psychopathologist.

In this context Cicchetti, Toth and Bush (1988) emphasize that a linear, unicausal theory of psychopathology is being abandoned in favour of a transactional model, in which genetic, constitutional, neurobiological, biochemical, psychological and social determinants play a role. There is, moreover, a dynamic relation between these factors.

Example.

In a study on 'Developmental psychopathology and neurobiology of Tourette's syndrome' by Cohen and Leckman (1994) a new model of pathogenesis of the tic syndrome is presented, based on four interrelated areas including history, genetic and environmental factors, and neurobiological substrate. The power of the model derives from the developmental approach and the study of interactional effects. For this study 34 children were selected from 22 families. The criterion for the selection was that either the parents or a direct relative of the children suffered from the syndrome. None of the children suffered from it at the outset of the study, but four years later 68% suffered from some disorder (e.g. depression, anxiety, and particularly the obsessive-compulsive disorder). The authors conclude that Tourette's syndrome is related to a genetic predisposition and to neurocognitive defects. However, the gravity of the syndrome is also influenced by biological as well as environmental factors (e.g. life-events). By contrast, adjustment to the disorder appeared mainly to be dependent on the child's self-image, in its way of coping with specific disorder-bound stress factors (such as its coping with social stigma), and on the family's functioning (e.g. the role of adequate parenthood). The study therefore shows that the following factors have a very 'protective' nature: a positive self-image and adequate functioning of the family. The study also illustrates the implications if an individual suffers from a given disease: this disease is a clear risk factor weighing on healthy development. If a person suffers from Tourette's syndrome, the gravity of the disorder will be determined by the extent to which he or she is faced with additional stressful factors (e.g. life-events).

As a conclusion, we can say that developmental psychopathology attaches great importance to contextual factors. However, the domain reveals several other characteristics as well. These will be highlighted in the following paragraphs.

The Difference Between Developmental Psychopathology and Normative Theories of Child Development

Much of developmental psychology is based on deciphering the mechanisms that describe development in all children. Rutter and Garmezy (1983) suggest that knowledge of these universals is fundamental to any understanding of the developmental process. The developmental psychopathologist wants to know more about the variations in development and about *individual differences* in the developmental process. To that end the developmental psychopathologist needs to use additional research strategies. For example, Masten, Best and Garmezy (1991) want to find out exactly why the development of certain children is so successful in spite of the many difficulties they face. In so doing they describe the mechanisms, predictors, or protective factors which explain why certain risk children manage to cope with their adversities, whereas others do not. This approach requires the strict individualization of the subject, and lays far more stress on specific contextual factors.

In turn, this approach to developmental psychopathology leads to a better understanding of (normal) development. Wenar (1994) stresses the importance of new insights into developmental psychology. One example: in the study of autism, the so-called 'theory of mind' was developed (Premack & Woodruff, 1978) according to which autistic children can be said not yet to have adequately developed the skill of taking perspective. This insight has been taken over by developmental psychology, so that developmental psychology has benefited from this approach and now uses the model of 'development of social role-taking' in describing the normal social and cognitive development of children, such as the development of symbolic games (Leslie, 1986).

Expanding the Scope of Psychopathology

The sections above show that developmental psychopathology sheds new light on the aetiology of psychopathology: in studying developmental aspects of psychopathology, a growing number of clinicians and researchers are concerned with historical and contextual aspects of a disorder and with the long-term outcome. Developmental psychopathologists are interested in infancy, childhood and adult life. Developmental studies of childhood disorders or syndromes lasting into adulthood (e.g. schizophrenia or hyperactivity which persist into adulthood) may shed new light on mechanisms of child psychopathology. And conversely, one will understand a disorder in childhood better when one knows more about the outcome in adulthood.

In addition, greater individualization is sought after. Specific variables in the individual history of a complaint are traced, as well as any interactions which may arise (e.g. between biological and psychological variables).

In this approach, developmental psychopathologists are equally interested in children who are at risk of developing a disorder yet fail to develop it, and in those who in due course manifest the complete pattern of psychopathology (Sroufe & Rutter, 1984). Some subjects remain maladaptive or dysfunctional, some do not. Our understanding of why some do go from maladaptation to health is limited. Those who escape disorder present an interesting case for the study of the so-called 'protective' factors, which provide a framework for prevention programmes. This takes us to the study of 'resilience', which will be dealt with later.

Life-span psychologists have emphasized that developmental tasks and crises occur in adult life as well as in childhood. What is important is the way in which the developmental tasks are tackled. In studying developmental 'crises' in their constructive as well as destructive aspects, we learn more about psychopathology and about development in general. Each task has its own behavioural solutions and its maladaptive counterparts. Children, like adults, may counter the challenge of new tasks by falling back on former strategies for coping, even strategies with little long-term utility. A few examples of developmental tasks during childhood (Loeber, 1990) are the arrival of siblings, school transition and bodily maturation. Studies of individuals in transitional stages of life can yield significant insights. An example is furnished by the studies of Verhofstadt-Denève, Schittekatte and Braet (1993, 1994), in which the authors focus on the transition from adolescence to adulthood (cited below).

Example.

A doctorial study in Belgium (Van den Bergh, 1992) followed, for more than a year, 70 women who were expecting their first baby. The assumption was that the birth of a first baby is a 'developmental task' which can cause a crisis. Consequently, both the mothers and the babies were subjected to anxiety measurements (testing, video-recording) before and after the birth. The results show, among other things, that mothers who had experienced anxiety before the birth had a baby who was more prone to problems. Though no causal deductions can be made on the basis of these results, and though other explanations for this phenomenon remain possible, the study does show that psychopathological cases must always be placed in a wider context, in which our understanding of transitional stages and of the developmental tasks related to these stages can contribute to greater insight into the nature of a problem.

Short History of Developmental Psychopathology and its Cultural Aspects

Short historical survey

The term 'developmental psychopathology' was introduced by Achenbach in 1974. As early as 1983, Rutter and Garmezy wrote an important chapter on developmental psychopathology in the prestigious *Handbook of Child Psychology* edited by Mussen. Subsequently, the first journal on 'development and Psychopathology' (1989) was published, and in 1990 the first

handbook by Michael Lewis and Suzanne Miller came out. In the same year
Charles Wenar published a book with the same title. Today, we can find
more than 100 articles on development and psychopathology, published
between 1986 and 1997.

So the discipline is no more than 20 years old, which makes it a fairly
young one. Studies on a larger scale are now under way and their results are
due to be published over the next few years (see 'Development Psychopathology: A new child in developmental psychology; now an active toddler', Lewis & Miller, 1990).

There are two reasons for the delay in the development of developmental
psychopathology. On the one hand, the description and the scientific study
of child psychopathology form a young research object. On the other,
developmental psychopathology is often based on the follow-up data
gathered in epidemiological studies, and these have only recently become
available.

Epidemiological studies about the prevalence of 'pathology' in children
started in the US with Lapouse and Monk in 1958 (Hellinckx et al., 1993).
Later, a French researcher published a number of articles about child
psychopathology in a representative community sample (Chiland, 1971). At
about the same time, the British psychiatrist Michael Rutter carried out
research on the Isle of Wight (Rutter, Tizard & Whitmore, 1970; see the
section on the longitudinal-epidemiological approach, below), and his study
was a true landmark in child psychiatry. Other countries subsequently
followed, and most of the European countries now have their own epidemiological studies on child psychopathology. It is to be expected that the
growth of developmental psychopathology will accelerate considerably
when all these data are fully available.

Cultural aspects

Since developmental psychopathology needs to take contextual factors into
account, cultural aspects are bound to have an important effect. Therefore
economic crises are an important cultural factor (see below for the discussion of risk groups). Youngsters who spend their childhood or adolescence in poor urban environments will also be considered a risk group and
will be given special attention in developmental psychopathology. In a wider
sense, differences found to exist between native groups and non-native
groups can be classified as cultural factors from the point of view of
developmental psychopathology.

Example.

We find that different cultures react in a different way to a child which still
suffers from enuresis at the age of 10. Assuming a tough attitude to this
situation (as opposed to an understanding one) may in due course result in
new problems. We were recently confronted with the case of a 10-year-old girl
suffering from enuresis. In her culture, enuresis is looked upon as a sign of
disobedience, to which the father thought he was to react with even more
severity. The result was a fully psychopathological evolution: the girl began to

suffer from non-organic abdominal spasms and from psychic paralysis. Without a developmental and cultural approach the disorder could never have been fully understood.

There are important differences between cultures in their emphasis on conformity, obedience and masculine dominance, and this may in turn affect what is considered as normal or deviant. In conduct disorders, for example, there is the objective finding that more boys become involved than girls. Rutter and Garmezy (1983) found that this association was weaker among blacks than among whites in the United States, but stronger among people with Asian backgrounds.

We tend to look at normal development from an Anglo-American point of view. How universal this will turn out to be has not yet been fully established. One of the pioneers in this area was Margaret Mead (Harkness & Super, 1990). Mead described adolescent girls on Samoa and found no evidence of social or psychological 'conflicts'. Mead argued that the troubles of American adolescence could be seen as cultural artifacts. Another example is the attachment theory, which is very important for West European infants because parents may tend to encourage independence in their children, whereas Japanese infants show more lasting attachment, perhaps because they are rarely separated from their mothers (Van IJzendoorn & Kroonenberg, 1988). These are but a few examples showing that anthropological research and cross-cultural studies can play an important role in the field of developmental psychopathology.

A Developmental Overview of Clinical Disorders at Different Ages in Childhood

Before describing some specific disorders occurring in childhood, we will first consider an overview which is unique in that it is presented within a developmental model. Achenbach (1990) presents a table (Table 10.1) with an interesting set of normal achievements as well as behavioural problems and clinical disorders in childhood, from birth to 20 years of age. This information is presented in accordance with the various developmental periods as suggested by eminent developmental psychologists such as Freud, Erikson, Piaget . . .

Classification and Diagnostic Considerations

The value of a diagnosis or classification has always been questioned. By DMS-IV criteria (APA, 1995), a disorder has its time of onset at a certain modal age level. However, many antecedents of the disorder may be observable much earlier and the time of its appearance changes over the life-span. It is for example generally accepted that conduct disorders typically emerge at the age of 8, but actually the first symptoms of antisocial behaviour are

Table 10.1 A Developmental overview

Approximate age	Cognitive period	Psychosexual phase	Psychosocial conflict	Normal achievements	Common behavior problems[a]	Clinical disorders
0–2	Sensory-motor	Oral	Basic trust vs mistrust	Eating, digestion, sleeping, social responsiveness, attachment, motility, sensory-motor organization	Stubbornness, temper, toileting	Organically based dysfunctions, anaclitic depression, autism, failure to thrive
2–5	Preoperational	Anal	Autonomy vs shame and doubt	Language, toileting, self-care skills, safety rules, self-control, peer relationships	Argues, brags, demands attention, disobedient, jealous, fears,[b] prefers older children, overactive, resists bedtime, shows off, shy,[b] stubborn, talks too much, temper, whines	Speech and hearing problems, phobias in socialized behavior
6–11	Concrete operational	Latency	Industry vs inferiority	Academic skills, school rules, rule-governed games, hobbies, monetary exchange, simple responsibilities	Argues, brags,[c] can't concentrate self-conscious, shows off, talks too much[b]	Hyperactivity, learning problems, school phobia aggression withdrawal
12–20	Formal operational	Genital	Identity vs confusion	Relations with opposite sex, vocational preparation, personal identity, separation from family, adult responsibilities	Argues, brags[c]	Anorexia, delinquency, suicide attempts, drug and alcohol abuse, schizophrenia, depression

[a]Problems reported for at least 45% of children in nonclinical samples.
[b]Indicates problem reported for ≥45% of girls only.
[c]Indicates ≥45% of boys only.
Note. The table gives developmental overview of normal achievements in childhood, presented according to the major developmental periods in the domains of cognition (Piaget), psychosexual phases (Freud) and psychosocial tasks (Erikson), and completed with specific problem behaviour and clinical disorders reported at that age (Achenbach, 1990, p. 9).
From *Developmental Psychopathology* (p. 67) by T. M. Achenbach. Copyright © 1982 by John Wiley & Sons Inc. Reprinted by permission of John Wiley & Sons Inc.

already perceptible at a much earlier age. Besides, does everyone think of the same thing when we talk of 'conduct disorder' in a child? For these reasons the developmental psychopathologist does not wholeheartedly support these 'static' classifications.

Nevertheless, we do need a classification. It should be a useful guide to clinical practice, by providing brief, clear and explicit criteria for defining all kinds of childhood disorders. It should also facilitate research and improve communication between clinicians, researchers and teachers.

Clinical classifications are usually categorial: either you have a disorder or you do not. This is the viewpoint taken by, among others, Rutter in his Children's Behaviour Questionnaire (Rutter et al., 1970). There is, however, no generally agreed classification of child psychopathology and it has been a very controversial issue for the past 10 years.

Sometimes clinicians and researchers in child psychopathology classify childhood disorders according to a number of criteria: (i) externalizing problems (e.g. aggression), which project a person's problems on outsiders, internalizing problems (e.g. anxiety), which turn a person's problems on himself; (ii) undercontrolled disorders (e.g. attention deficit disorder), which shows a lack of control in the individual concerned, vs overcontrolled disorders (e.g. obsessions), which shows an excessive degree of control over certain aspects of life. These oppositions have been repeatedly identified in analyses and they reflect a distinction between two broad-band groupings of behavioural problems. Although this can be useful, it is not always very clear where a specific problem is to be located along a dimension. Also, the dimensions are not totally independent of each other. More recently researchers and clinicians have been debating fundamental questions such as: What are the basic criteria of a diagnostic system? These criteria can be put forward from at least two points of view: the traditional approach and the quantitative approach.

The traditional approach

The most traditional approach to a taxonomy of psychopathology in children, adolescents and adults, is the DSM (= the *Diagnostic and Statistical Manual of Mental Disorders*: American Psychiatric Association, 1980, 1987, 1995). This classification is based on the observation of disorders and of problem behaviour, but its implementation in fact depends on the observational skills of the clinician.

Example.
DSM-IV Criteria for Conduct Disorder (APA, 1995) In the DSM-IV we find about 15 criteria which can point to a Conduct Disorder. This includes problematic behaviour such as:

- often initiates physical fights
- has broken into someone else's house or car or into a building
- has shown physical cruelty to animals, etc.
- has engaged in fire setting
- is often truant from school, etc.

If three of them are present for a least six months, the child is classified as having a Conduct Disorder.

Today, the fourth edition of the DSM has been published in various languages and most psychopathologists now use this edition, eight years after the DMS III-R which was published in 1987 by the American Psychiatric Association. In this classification, certain problems are specifically identified as being relevant to childhood and early development. Some examples: attention deficit disorder, separation anxiety, elimination disorders, autism.

The DSM III-R (APA, 1987) is generally accepted as being valid and this is expected of the new DSM-IV as well. Wenar (1994) analysed the preliminary version of the DSM-IV (APA, 1995) and assessed the classification as follows: its rationale is clear, and with regard to objectivity the DSM-IV is behaviour-specific in description. A diagnostic system should at least be comprehensive in its coverage of psychopathologies. In this respect too, the DSM-IV is evaluated as satisfactory.

A comparable system of classification is the ICD-9, compiled by the World Health Organization.

Other approaches to the taxonomy of child psychopathology are based on factor analysis of behavioural checklists. In this context, there is one more taxonomy that is very well known and based on a multivariate statistical approach, and this was developed by Achenbach (1990).

The quantitative assessment of child psychopathology (source: Achenbach, 1990)

Clinicians use a variety of tools in the assessment of child psychopathology: observation, interviews and psychological tests. With the evolution of the discipline, there has been a remarkable change from description (and interpretation) of psychopathology to measurement and quantification of specific problem behaviour. Subsequently, new statistical methods were advanced for questionnaire evaluation and for finding out which higher-order categories (or factors) can be differentiated in assessing the different kinds of problematic behaviour. This led to another taxonomy, based on questionnaire items and their statistical processing at different levels.

Achenbach was one of the first to introduce the concept of 'Behavioural Assessment'. Achenbach's approach is a very objective tool for screening psychopathology in children, because no interpretations or personality traits are accepted. To this end, he developed questionnaires which he analysed extensively.

There are certain areas in which children are not good respondents, such as in their own attention problems, hyperactivity and oppositional behaviours. Several researchers have found that more sources of information and more screenings are necessary for these cases. Although the reliability of many of the instruments is high, there are only modest correlations between respondents. Parents, teachers, psychologists, all seem to obtain important

---

Box 10.1 Psychometric measurement: Child Behaviour Checklist (CBCL)

A widely used questionnaire in the CBCL developed by Achenbach (Achenbach & Edelbrock, 1983). This instrument assesses all kinds of psychopathology in children and adolescents between the ages of 4 and 16. The CBCL consists of 118 items and is filled out by the parents or teachers. The higher the score, the more problematic the behaviour. There are different norm groups for different age groups, separately for boys and girls. These data are collected in epidemiological studies. Today they are available for different European, Australian and American samples. The items are based on the concrete description of problematic behaviour. Some examples:

- destroying objects belonging to others
- suicidal talk
- vomiting, etc.

After factor analysis, based on the 118 items and carried out on large samples of children, the authors found nine syndromes, also called narrow-band syndromes. Some examples of the syndromes:

- depression
- hyperactive behaviour
- delinquency, etc.

These nine syndromes can in turn be subdivided into two wide-band syndromes: internalizing and externalizing syndromes.

According to the scores obtained on the 118 items, a child is given a score on the 'narrow-band' and a score on the 'wide-band' syndromes. A table converts the scores to normalized T-scores, where an average score of 50 is normal. For a score of 63 or higher, a child is said to have a high score, and a score of 70 is considered 'clinically problematic'.

---

information about the child, but the information is based on different points of view and their views are rather complementary. Achenbach concludes that no single informant can substitute for all the others (Achenbach, 1990). He therefore proposed a multi-axial assessment model with different complementary strategies relevant to the assessment of most children. It includes teacher reports (for children of school age), parents' reports, direct assessment of the child (not for very young infants) and psychological and medical reports on the child's cognitive and physical development. Finally, Loeber and Farrington (1994) argue that psychophysiological and neuropsychological measures may complement any of the preceding sources of information.

Lewis and Miller (1990) present a study of 125 children from birth to the age of 9. Their mothers filled out the Child Behaviour Checklist (Achenbach & Edelbrock, 1983) and answered a set of questions about the children. The children filled out a Children's Depression Inventory and answered a set of questions. Teachers filled out a Classroom Behaviour Inventory. From these various sources it was possible to derive a 'depression' score for each child. However, the authors found that, according to one source of information, some children were categorized as depressed, while they were not seen as depressed by other sources. The study shows that there are children who have a high depression score while their mothers do not report such a psychopathology, and that, conversely, there are mothers who report a depression in their child although the child did not report it. This is a difficulty for follow-up studies. The following questions have not yet been answered: Which source of information gives the most objective view? Do we have to rely on one source of information or on all of them? This example illustrates the difficulty of screening problems in childhood. Another problem arises with the study of the prevalence of a disorder. When counting the depression scores from all the sources together, one finds a very large 'problem' group. Lewis and Miller (1990) emphasize that there is no one correct judgement and that multiple measurements are likely and needed.

Edelbrock and Costello (1988) found considerable overlap between the DSM-III categories and the CBCL-syndromes. The DSM-III was evaluated as being more differentiated because there were more specific diagnoses (e.g. Separation Anxiety, etc.). But as far as the issue of classification is concerned, the controversy about using a quantitative or a qualitative approach crops up again. It depends very much on the theoretical framework one uses, on how one interprets the differences between clinical, subclinical and normal development: is the deviation only quantitative or is it also qualitative?

Achenbach in fact belongs to the quantitative school. The fact is that a child's psychopathology depends on its scores in the items of a test, and the more problematic items a child has, the closer its score will come to the level of clinical psychopathology. So children can show low or high degrees of one particular syndrome.

Rutter was one of the first to develop questionnaires for the assessment of psychopathology in children (Rutter et al., 1970), although he insisted on using a categorical system which relies on a qualitative approach: one either has the disorder or one does not. The debate on this issue is still very much alive for the developmental psychopathologist. The assessment of children's problems and skills is central to all the other activities in developmental psychopathology, including research, training, services, evaluation of outcomes, epidemiology and planning (Achenbach, 1990).

METHODS FOR STUDYING DEVELOPMENTAL DEVIATIONS

Areas of Interest

Developmental psychopathology relies on longitudinal studies. The main

advantages of longitudinal studies are summarized by Loeber and Farrington (1994) and by Verhulst and Koot (1991).

In general terms, the following are the major areas of interest of developmental psychopathology (Rutter & Garmezy, 1983; Verhulst & Koot, 1991;
Loeber & Farrington, 1994):

1. To study a disorder that is considered abnormal at any developmental
   stage (e.g. autism).
2. To study problematic behaviour that is also common in normal development (e.g. attachment problems).
3. To study responses to stress and traumas and their interaction with
   the normal developmental process until adulthood (e.g. children in
   institutions).
4. To define those disorders which may have no connection with development (e.g. phobia).
5. To learn more about normal development (e.g. aggressive behaviour in
   adolescence, or the problems that autistic children have in social interaction and which are related to cognitive skills in the development of
   empathy).
6. To learn more about developmental mechanisms (e.g. what is the impact of conflicts during childhood and adolescence on adult life).
7. To learn more about the prevalence of a disorder at given stages, in the
   context of the development of the child and against the background of
   his or her evolving environment.

In the longitudinal approach, there are several traditions of research in
developmental psychopathology which can be used separately or in combination. We will discuss them briefly in the following section.

The most common longitudinal studies are those of specific risk groups
(see below) or of population groups as a whole (epidemiological studies, see
below). In epidemiological studies, it is also possible, of course, to compare
the risk groups with the non-risk groups.

The longitudinal approach to risk groups includes follow-up studies and
follow-back studies. Follow-back studies are studies in which risk variables
and disorder mechanisms are reconstructed respectively instead of prospectively (see below).

The study of risk groups has led to a new object of study, viz. development
trajectories. This is dealt with in greater detail in the section below on
developmental pathways.

With all the emphasis on risk factors, the 'protective factors' have so far
been neglected. This is discussed more extensively below.

An overview of the studies carried out so far shows that only a few of
them are based on a theoretical model. So we find studies which focus
sharply on the relations between variables, but which do not proceed on the
basis of a clear-cut model of individual functioning. Studies based on an
underlying model adopt a conceptual approach and these will therefore be
discussed separately.

The Longitudinal-epidemiological Approach

Single-case studies are sometimes important in showing how a problem expresses itself. However, they are not sufficient for making generalized predictions. If we want a wide survey of all the different kinds of children's psychopathologies, we need to study quite large examples of children. For this reason researchers choose an epidemiological approach.

Rutter conducted highly important work in the study of child psychopathology. He and his colleagues carried out a landmark study on the Isle of Wight (Rutter et al., 1970) where they tested all the children between 9 and 11 years of age (in all, 3500 children) and followed them up after five years. In the first stage, Rutter used the 'Questionnaire for Teachers' and the 'Children's Behavioural Questionnaire for Parents' (Rutter et al., 1970). Both questionnaires focus on 'problematic behaviour'. If the children had a score higher than a 'critical score', they were put in a 'clinical' group for further study in a second stage. This applied to 13% of the 9 to 11 year olds. Next, Rutter and colleagues conducted further analysis which enabled them to focus on a clearly problematic group. This involved 6.8% of the children who suffered from depression, anxiety disorders, obsession, tics, conduct and emotional disorders, and some smaller groups of children with other problems, such as personality disorders. In so doing, Rutter obtained valuable information about the prevalence and evolution of child psychopathology. This kind of work was entirely new since the method of epidemiological examination had not yet been developed.

Later, Rutter's research group did the same in London's inner city (Rutter, Cox, Tupling, Berger & Yule, 1974). Again, all the children ($N = 1689$) were tested and followed for several years (from 10 until 18 years). Here, the prevalence of psychopathology in the first stage was about 25.4%, which is enormous. Apparently, children in an overwhelmingly urban environment run a greater risk of developing some disorder or other. This could be explained by differences in their living conditions. In urban centres, people live much closer together, and children have fewer opportunities for enjoying themselves in their own ways, and moreover they are more likely to come into contact with criminality. It is also possible that the parents of urban children constitute a special group, or that they lead more stressful lives and have less time available for their children.

The positive side of the longitudinal-epidemiological approach is that it looks at a non-clinical group too, so that it can uncover more overall risk factors as well as protective factors (Rutter, 1989). However, it also has a few disadvantages. If we want to study complete populations over a longer time, we need a very efficient screening instrument. However, concern with individuality also affects the choice of measurements that can subtly differentiate the various aspects of child functioning, so that we can look for abnormalities in emotional, social, physical, cognitive, and moral development. Overall, we have to find variations and individual differences. Here one faces the issue of the use of diagnostic instruments. For example, it is a

---

Box 10.2   Prevalence of psychopathology in children

Thanks to epidemiological studies carried out in different countries and using large samples, we actually know more about the prevalence of child psychopathology in different populations. If we consider different studies and meta-analyses on the prevalence of psycho-pathology in children, we generally find that about 10–15% of the children have a disorder. However, there may be some variation depending on the questionnaire used, the age of the children, the region concerned, and so on.

Psychopathology is also very persistent over the years and more frequent in boys than girls. A striking finding from the same studies is that not all problematic children were effectively seeking advice. So far only 1 in 10 who have a disorder are actually looking for help.

---

well known fact that there are major sex differences in emotional development, but so far they have not been described and explained. This is understandable since epidemiological approaches focus on a general population in order to establish prevalence and incidence of disorders or problem behaviour. Second, only a few longitudinal studies are available. The reason is that following a complete population of children over several years, until they are adults, is a very expensive undertaking. As Lewis and Miller (1990) have put it, the cost of this kind of study, both in terms of financial expenditure and in terms of time that the investigator must devote to the project, is forbidding.

Most of the time, researchers work with a general sample of a whole population and then follow the same subjects more easily over a longer period of time. Our own work at our research centre in Ghent is an illustration of this procedure.

Illustration of a longitudinal-epidemiological approach

The transition from adolescence to young adulthood is often characterized by sudden qualitative changes in the physical, social, cognitive, and emotional fields. It is not uncommon during these changes for the individual to experience conflicts. Our team at the Ghent University (Verhofstadt-Denève, Schittekatte & Braet, 1993, 1994; Verhofstadt-Denève, 1996) studied in depth the implications of these conflicts. We selected at random 1000 adolescents between the ages of 15 and 19 years from a list of the whole population of East Flanders. Of these, 820 agreed to participate. In several follow-up stages we followed them for 15 years. The method used was that of the individual survey conducted at the subject's home. Half of the youngsters had a job and the others were still studying. Both 8 and 15 years later, we succeeded in contacting 604 and 537 subjects respectively from the original sample (74% and 65% respectively). This study attempted to answer the following question: Is the experience of conflict linked to psychological growth?

The selection of the independent variables (e.g. level of studies, philosophical and religious conviction, kind of relationship with parents, sexual identity, early sexual experiences, partner relationships, etc.) and the dependent variables (e.g. psychosocial developments, financial status, etc.) aimed to shed light on the effect of conflict experiences and also to specify the long-term effects of phenomena associated with the beginning of the transition from adolescence to young adulthood. The results showed that the experience of conflicts and opposition between opinions and values during adolescence proves to be a signal of positive self-evaluation and well-being in psychosocial matter during adulthood. Moreover, many links were identified between attitudes, behaviour and situations during adolescence, on the one hand, and self-evaluations with regard to psychosocial variables in adulthood, on the other.

Epidemiological follow-up studies were conducted in several other countries as well. Verhulst et al. (1993) presented a recent follow-up study of a group of Dutch children. In a sample of 936 children between the ages of 4 and 11, three subgroups were made on the basis of CBCL scores obtained at four two-yearly intervals. One subgroup consisted of children classified as 'permanents', that is, children who had shown deviant behaviour over the whole of the six-year period of the study. A second subgroup involved the 'climbers', who had shown rising scores of problematic behaviour. The third group comprised children with falling scores. The study found that the 'permanents' had mainly externalizing problems, whereas the 'fallers' had mainly internalizing problems (e.g. anxiety disorders).

Study of a Population at Risk

Many researcher are concerned with children who already have a problem or who are 'at risk', such as the children of alcoholics. This approach also produces very important information about the development of child psychopathology. The following is an illustration of this approach.

The *Journal of Pediatric Psychology* includes a study of a research group from Israel (Levy-Shiff, Einat, Mogilner & Lerman, 1994), who studied the development of prematurely born infants in early adolescence and compared them with control-matched adolescents born at full term. The subjects of the 'at risk' group scored lower on nearly all the measurements: IQ, visual-motor coordination, psychosocial variables and hyperactive behaviour.

The following examples go into two kinds of studies. The first group of studies concerns children born to parents with psychiatric disorders, and the second group concerns youngsters at risk because of delinquency.

> **Box 10.3**   Methodological considerations in studying at risk groups
>
> 1.   Concepts and problems cannot always be defined accurately. For example: 'effects on children who grow up in an institution'. The problem is that so many variables are unknown: which children in the institution are to be studied (All of them? How long did they stay there? Are there differences according to the age of entrance?). And perhaps even more variables depend on the children's social contacts in the institutions, but how can these be operationalized, and how can they be reconstructed?
> 2.   One has to follow a control group as well.
> 3.   If we are concerned with the historical aspects of a given disorder, with its evolution, and with its different manifestations, then we have to find and to follow a great number of children who have the same problem. This approach is expensive and difficult because the children in this population often tend to move to other institutions and are often hard to find after several years.
>
> *Source*: Based on Asarnow (1994); Lester and Tronick (1994).

Follow-up studies of children born to parents with psychiatric disorders

Children born of a schizophrenic mother were compared with a low-risk control group (Rutter & Garmezy, 1983; Asarnow, 1994). Indeed, it was found that they really are at risk. The children of schizophrenic mothers show poorer motor and perceptual functioning, hypersensitivity in responses, and attentional deficits. However, one has to follow such subjects long enough, and so far little is known with any certainty. Other problems are that if the children are separated from their families because of the disorder in the mother, other complications can occur simultaneously. And, again, there is the problem of concept definition: schizophrenia is not always defined using the same criteria.

A second example can be found in a study by Loeber (1988). Loeber carefully examined the early years of children born of depressed parents. In so doing, he used the NIMH/Colorado studies on the regulation of emotion in young offspring of depressed parents. The findings suggested that as early as the first year, children of depressed parents can be distinguished from control children on a number of variables. The central concept of the study is 'regulation of emotion'. The author concludes that the symptomatology of the parents has a profound influence on the children's 'acquisition of developmental competencies'.

Follow-up studies of high-risk groups of delinquent adolescents

Loeber (Loeber, 1982; 1990; Loeber & Dishion, 1983) conducted an extensive study of the risk factors that may precede later antisocial and delinquent behaviour. Youngsters with antisocial behaviour were followed in longitudinal studies and screened for various parameters of psychopathology. This resulted in the specification of various trajectories which are most likely to be followed by risk groups of youngsters with antisocial behaviour. Loeber's overall conclusion (1982, 1990) is that antisocial behaviour tends to persist over time. The 'chronic delinquents' were youngsters who, at a very early age and in various settings (at school, at home, etc.), had shown a wide range of problematic patterns of behaviour. In his review Loeber gives an extensive description of longitudinal follow-up studies which suggest that these youngsters continued their antisocial behaviour later in life.

A study by Moore, Chamberlain and Mukai (1979, in Loeber, 1982), which followed youngsters (average age 9.8 years) for eight years yielded findings in line with this conclusion. That is, at the beginning, a minimum of four complaints, (e.g. thefts) had been lodged against them in a period of four months. Eight years later 84% of them had been arrested (see also Pulkkinen & Tremblay, 1992).

Our study (Verhofstadt-Denève, 1985), however, presents a different picture. In essence this 1985 study was the precursor of the longitudinal epidemiological population study undertaken by Verhofstadt-Denève et al. (1993, 1994, 1996) referred to earlier. The first of these studies, which is described below, yielded evidence contrary to the expectations. The study was set up with juvenile delinquents, a typical group at risk. In the first stage of the study the subjects concerned were in a state reformatory institution and were between the ages of 15 and 21. The sample involved 62 boys and 42 girls. Seven years later they were contacted again.

One of the main findings of this study was that those adolescents who experienced many emotional conflicts (such as refusal of their sex role, body image or identity) during the time they were in the institution, showed a more positive psychosocial evolution during their young adulthood. For example, those adolescents who had attempted suicide were found during the follow-up stage to have succeeded in building up a stable relationship. Similarly, they had been confined to a penal institution less frequently and they had fewer employment problems than the subgroup who had not made any attempt at suicide.

This finding was in sharp contrast with the expectations of the institution's educational staff, who tended to expect more problems in the troublesome conflict group. One explanation for these results is a dialectical view of man in which each transition is seen as a dynamic process propelled by oppositions. Looked at this way, the experience of opposition is an active process linked with change. Anxiety and uncertainty about oneself and about one's own situation in life are no longer considered weaknesses but rather signs of development, signals of a new potential. The dialectic point of view needs to be refined with one fundamental modification: the principle of opposition is a necessary though not in itself sufficient condition for the process of development. And not each and every opposition which the individual experiences will be related to his or her development and growth.

Follow-back studies

Another approach that high-risk studies have taken is to examine the childhood characteristics of people identified as problematic in adult life. Initially, developmental psychopathology made frequent use of these studies, since they were the first to take into account elements of time and context. It was particularly adults with problems who were asked about their antecedents. These retrospective longitudinal studies cover the past only and reconstruct the circumstances of past psychopathology (Loeber & Farrington, 1994). If this enables us to detect 'predictors' of the later disorders, then perhaps we can treat children preventively, teach them how to cope with specific problems and prevent the development of a serious disorder.

Loeber (1990), for example, made an extensive examination of violent offenders when they were young. On the basis of several studies he concluded that 70–90% of violent offenders had been highly aggressive when young.

Follow-back studies have a wider scope than retrospective studies: they may also involve the interviewing of others from the individual's environment, the tracing of specific data (e.g. the person's school results, weight at birth, etc.) or the interviewing of other groups (e.g. children). Nowadays, however, prospective studies are given absolute preference. The fact is that the attraction of follow-back studies is seriously diminished mainly by methodological problems (e.g. some important events were not remembered exactly, because of poor memory, and this can lead to retrospective bias, or else old records of patients from 30 years ago have already been destroyed, etc.). In the examples given below, other problems with follow-back studies will be illustrated.

In a study of the characteristics of schizophrenics, Watt (1974) went back to their childhood. He found that schizophrenics had much lower levels of interpersonal social competence in their childhood, but only about half the sample showed these characteristics. This is an example of another methodological problem of follow-back studies: the data were not convincing enough, so far. And, it may still be too early to embark on prevention programmes.

Miller and Lewis (1990) criticized a study with children identified as abused and non-abused. The mothers of abused children were asked if they had been abused in their childhood. Since 70% replied they had been, it was concluded that being abused as a child is related to abusing one's own children. Lewis and Miller now formulate the following comments. First, there are no data available about mothers who had been abused in their childhood but who now have a family and children who are not abused. So we cannot compare the prevalence rates of sexual abuse in both groups and we can only make assumptions about the incidence of sexual abuse in families of mothers who had been sexually abused in their childhood.

Wenar (1994) reported a follow-back study on alcoholics, of whom 75% had been truants, compared with 26% among healthy individuals. But a follow-up study about truants revealed that only 11% became alcoholics compared with 8% of a non-truant population who became alcoholics. Wenar concludes that the association between truancy and alcoholism is too weak for predictive purposes. These differences are common when one compares follow-up studies with follow-back studies. This example can be completed with another study which examined the development of the children of alcoholics (Johnson, Sher & Rolf, 1991). The authors conclude that only a minority of the children develop a disorder. In this study they could identify two 'risk-variables' for developing a disorder: disturbed family relations on the one hand, and a 'genetically' co-occurring psychiatric disorder in the parents and their children, on the other. As a conclusion, differences between prospective follow-up studies and retrospective follow-back analysis are obvious and both seem to have advantages and disadvantages.

Risk factors

Apart from risk groups, research can also focus on risk factors or risk periods, the so-called 'critical periods'. Several studies begin to trace factors which increase the risk of developing a disorder. A risk factor has a different meaning than a correlate of a later outcome. Correlates usually refer to factors that occur at the same time as the outcome and that statistically covary with it. Risk factors on the other hand refer to events occurring earlier and which predict a later outcome.

The following are examples of studies into risk variables. Loeber (Loeber, 1990; Loeber & Dishion, 1983) and Patterson (Patterson, Debaryshe & Ramsey, 1989) work at the Oregon Social Learning Center; they conclude that, with regard to antisocial behaviour, the greatest risk factor is the family environment, viz. 'poor parental supervision, discipline and monitoring; parental uninvolvement or rejection, marital problems'.

The authors base these conclusions on an extensive survey of retrospective as well as prospective studies. Other 'early predictors of delinquency' (Loeber & Dishion, 1983) are: the child's conduct problems, deviant peers, parental criminality and the child's poor academic performance. In 1990 Loeber qualified his claims. The overt expression of conduct disorders is said to have a strong predictive value, for example, teasing, temper, stubbornness; Loeber added that a strong new predictor had emerged from several prospective studies, notably 'Negative Cognitions': nobody loves him, others try out to get him, he doesn't feel guilty, he is always jealous. Moreover, multiple handicaps increase the risk considerably. This is an example of how other procedures can also enable us to trace 'at risk' groups.

Several studies focused on risk factors with regard to the problem of hyperactivity in children. In hyperactive children, the following antecedent risks have been revealed so far: neurotoxins such as lead, early malnutrition, low birth weight and substance use by the mother during pregnancy (Loeber, 1990). The 'community' studies by Moffitt in New Zealand (Moffit &

Silva, 1988), moreover, show that hyperactivity itself is a risk factor for later delinquency. Their study pointed up later delinquency in 60% of the children with an ADD-diagnosis.

Other studies reveal that biological factors are not unimportant. Loeber (1990) cites a study by Magnusson in which the early onset of menarche in girls was associated with a higher rate of norm violations. This was observed especially in those girls who were associated with older girls. This finding was confirmed in the New Zealand study (Caspi, Lynam, Moffitt & Silva, 1993).

The study by Kolvin (referred to by Loeber, 1990) draws attention to the significance of family conditions. Divorced parents or social deprivation such as marital disruption, parental illness, poor domestic care, overcrowding, poor quality mothering, are said to be an important risk indicator for children younger than 5. Again it is those children with multiple deprivations who prove to end up with most convictions.

Summing up, we can quote Wenar (1994) on a survey of the most frequent risk indicators: (a) risks of physical illness (e.g. tic disorder), brain damage or other biological factors (e.g. menarche); (b) risks in the interpersonal context (e.g. child maltreatment, child rearing, divorce, social class, family history, etc.); (c) risks for ethnic minority children; (d) risks in transitions (e.g. transitions to adolescence, life-events); (e) the child's mental health.

Stress elements are sometimes split up into acute (change of school, birth of a sibling, divorce of the parents, unwanted pregnancy, death of a parent) and chronic (family rows, a chronic disease, recurrent sexual abuse).

Rutter has recently argued that there is a difference between 'knowing which are the risk factors and knowing how to change them'. 'The lesson is that it is essential that our research takes the crucial step of moving from statistical risk indicators to an understanding of how risk processes operate' (Rutter, 1996).

Finally, Loeber (1990) points out that there are also 'risk periods'. With regard to the development of morality, the period between the ages of 9 and 12 is crucial. The prediction of alcoholism in adulthood is better when predictors were measured at ages 11–14 than when measured earlier or later; aggression early in life (< 10 years) is used as a predictor of later deviant outcomes rather than aggression at later points in time. In the same context we have studies on the critical periods for bonding and attachment. They point out that, for children between 6 months and 3 years, adoption at a later age or long-term residence in hospital can have considerable adverse effects on behaviour (Loeber, 1990).

Developmental Pathways

Antisocial youngsters have repeatedly been studied. Hartup and Van Lieshout (1995), Patterson et al. (1989) and Loeber (1988, 1990) describe different categories of antisocial youngsters, such as the late and the early starters, aggressive and non-aggressive types, each with a distinctive development. The prognosis for one type is much more negative than for the other. It was the study of the origin and evolution of individual disorders that gave rise to the concept of 'developmental pathways'.

> *Example*: the developmental trajectory of early starters with aggressive behaviour
> Those who start early with aggressive behaviour often prove to have a difficult temper, causing the parents problems with their upbringing from an early age on. This is thought to raise the chances of aggression on the one hand, and of insecure attachment on the other. It causes the child to distrust new situations, new people, new relations. But they also learn that aggressive behaviour can be successful, so that it is resorted to not only within the family but also outside it. These children tend to be rejected more easily by their teachers as well as by their classmates. Among the consequences we find bad results at school, having to repeat a year, and changing from one school to another, increasingly aggressive behaviour and loss of control by the parents. The child may find a degree of recognition and appreciation in a group of peers. But in this new environment delinquent and aggressive behaviour is often the only outlet and status symbol, and the youngster's further development will be increasingly determined by criminal influences.
> *Source*: Loeber (1990).

Rutter (1989) argues that developmental psychopathology is more than the mere description of different disorders at different ages. It will be clear from our discussion of the development of 'early starters' that we can sometimes trace effective 'trajectories' of particular disorders.

Rutter (1989) also outlines a number of diverse developmental trajectories. For instance, bad school results can predict a given trajectory in which one pathway leads to, among other things, a bad employment situation; and the early experience of divorce can lead to depression in adulthood.

A more detailed example is that of boarding-school girls who in their childhood have an unsatisfactory relation with their parents and who turn out to have a greater chance of sending their own children to a boarding-school. The pathway that most of these girls choose is to leave their home at a fairly early age and live on their own. The risk of pregnancy when still fairly young is greater, and so is that of entering into an early marriage with a partner who has himself been raised in difficult circumstances. The chance of the marriage being a failure is greater, and so is the chance of problems arising in connection with these young mothers rearing their own children.

Loeber's research into antisocial behaviour is well known (1982, 1988, 1990). Loeber contends that the sequence of problematic patterns of behaviour is continuous over time, even though the manifestations of such behaviour may be different at different ages. This has already been illustrated here in the example of the development of antisocial behaviour: we can distinguish early and late starters. Loeber (1990) added another distinction, that is, between aggressive and non-aggressive youngsters. Non-aggressive antisocial behaviour is usually: stealing, lying, truancy, substance abuse. Antisocial behaviour as such does not occur until later, at the beginning of adolescence. Problems at school mainly boil down to 'refusal of authority'. The prognosis in such cases is better than for the aggressive type. Loeber

believes that further research may well find that there are even more different pathways in antisocial behaviour. For instance, there is probably also a
trajectory which begins in adolescence with substance abuse, without there
being other conspicuous behavioural problems, either earlier or at the time
of substance abuse itself.

The notion of progression does not imply that youngsters who engage in
the first step will necessarily engage in all subsequent steps. One danger of
outlining such pathways is that they might be understood as normative, that
is, that they might be thought to 'predestinate' the individual. This would
lead to a rather deterministic view of man, which is definitely not intended,
as Rutter (1989) warns us. For this reason research into protective factors
and into the possibilities of leaving the pathways concerned should be given
more attention. The following section will look into this more extensively.

Nowadays most pathway research is prospective, but Rutter's first studies
(1989) were mainly retrospective. We have already discussed the advantages
and the disadvantages of this method of 'follow-back' studies.

The Study of Protective Factors and Resilience in Children

Garmezy brought another important element into the study of populations
at risk. In focusing on high-risk groups, he examined the effects of stressful
life-events, but they also looked into the prevalence of protective factors. He
looked for the processes and mechanisms that contribute to adaptation in
situations that normally led to maladaptation. A lot of children can cope
effectively with stressful events and do not develop a disorder. Even when a
trauma is very severe, it can have constructive elements. Garmezy focuses on
such aspects as well, in order to acquire a better understanding of the
development of psychopathology.

Rice, Herman and Petersen (1993) wrote an article in the *Journal of
Adolescence* about 'coping with challenge in adolescence'. The team found
that developmental stressors can be viewed as challenges to the coping
responses and resources of adolescents. Some challenges can be risks to
adolescents mental health while others can be opportunities for further
growth and development. Moderators of the positive relation between
challenge and mental health outcome include personal and interpersonal
resources. At a later stage, this model led to an educational programme for
enhancing this positive relation and protecting adolescents from psychopathology.

This new evolution in the study of developmental psychopathology concerns what is today called 'resilience' in children and adolescents and deals
with all components of conflict in its positive, constructive aspects. Other
questions that arise are: 'Who is most vulnerable?', 'Which factors predis-
pose children to psychopathology?', and 'What conditions activate or reverse developmental disorders?'

Garmezy and his colleagues (Masten et al., 1991) distinguish three specific
target groups. The first group is of people who have developed in a positive

470 DEVELOPMENTAL PSYCHOPATHOLOGY

sense against all expectations. The second contains those individuals who have adapted well in spite of a number of stressful experiences and life-events. The third group are people who are recovering from a trauma. Since traumatic experiences are thought to affect the quality of functioning, it is important to stress that the third group is in a process of recovery.

As longitudinal research in this field is of great importance, we will go into the results of each of these three groups somewhat more extensively. Note that retrospective as well as prospective studies have been made.

Type 1: positive development against all odds

Werner conducted one of the most influential studies in this field (Werner, 1993; Werner & Smith, 1992). In this study, Werner followed all children born in the year 1955 on one particular Hawaiian island for 30 years. About one-third of the group was considered to be a risk group because of the presence of four or more risk indicators which became apparent in the first year of life, and which were clearly predictive of maladaptation found at a later age (10–18 years). Among the risk indicators were, for example, poverty, discordant relations in the family, perinatal stress in the mother, and a low educational standard in the family. About one-third of the risk group turned out to have a positive development in spite of expectations (the so-called resilient individuals). What protective factors were responsible for the development of these youngsters in a positive direction? Among the important predictors of a positive outcome had been: temperament, openness to new experiences, fewer stressful life-events, family harmony, better physical health and a good relationship with a carer (implying adequate attention and less separation). Intelligence, positive experiences at school, membership of a group or religion outside the family, also turned out to be positive predictors. The research team draws the conclusion that 'the promotion of competence and self-esteem in a young person is probably one of the key ingredients in any effective intervention process' (Werner, 1993).

Type 2: youngsters who adapt adequately in spite of stressful experiences

Another group of studies focused on children who grow up in economic hardship. For instance, these studies examined the development of children whose parents are long-term unemployed. A second group of 'resilience' studies concentrated on children of parents with a psychic disorder, or on children who have been separated from their biological parents for a long time. The same predictors of adequate adaptation emerged again (Masten et al., 1991): that is the presence of a good relation with one carer or adult, the child's intelligence, self-efficacy and the quality of the environment in which the children are brought up, which means both a stable family environment and good socio-economic circumstances, in the absence of poverty.

Box 10.4   Top ten factors which enhance an individual's resilience

---

- adequate parenthood
- contacts with other socially competent adults
- attractive looks
- keen intelligence
- talents and achievements appreciated by others or by the individual concerned
- feelings of self-efficacy, self-esteem and optimism
- religious conviction or adherence to a religious movement
- a comfortable social-economic position

Source: Masten et al. (1991)

Type 3: recovery after traumatic experiences

Some individuals recover from a trauma in an almost miraculous fashion. The following traumatic experiences have been studied: bus hijacks, children face-to-face with murder or fires, natural diasters and child abuse (Masten et al., 1991). Again, the quality of the care provided by the (substitute) parent proved to be essential to recovery. Intelligence too was shown to be an important indicator. Typically, proximal factors (e.g. the environment in which upbringing takes place) turn out to be more decisive than distal factors (e.g. social class). The above studies enable us to make a selection of the most frequent protective factors. On the basis of the data gathered from studies into protective factors, a list of elements can be compiled which boost the resilience of children and adolescents.

Rutter, in one of his latest studies (Rutter, 1996), suggests that resilience is not only the avoidance of risks or the search for positive experiences. 'For example, immunity to infection, whether natural or therapeutically induced through immunization, derives from controlled exposure to the relevant pathogen and not through its avoidance. In short, resistance to infection comes from the experiences of coping successfully with lesser doses or modified versions of the pathogen. Perhaps the same may apply in the field of psychosocial stress and adversity.' Rutter also draws a clear distinction between protective factors and protective mechanisms. He believes that factors per se can work in a positive sense in one situation, but also in a negative sense in another (e.g. adoption). It is therefore preferable not to trace protective factors but rather to find protective mechanisms. Protective mechanisms can manifest themselves in five different ways:

1. Those that involve reduction in the personal impact of risk experience (e.g. importance of parental supervision and monitoring of their children's activities).
2. Those that reduce negative chain reactions (e.g. good humour).
3. Those that promote self-esteem and self-efficacy (e.g. successful task accomplishment).

Table 10.2 Vulnerabilities, and protective factors

Organic	Intrapersonal	Interpersonal	Superordinate
		Risks	
Genetic Pre- and perinatal influences; neurological damage; inadequate nutrition; difficult temperament	Low intelligence; low self-esteem, low self-efficacy; low self-control; insecure attachment	Marital or familial disharmony; abuse or neglect; poor peer relations; large number of siblings	Poverty
		Vulnerabilities	
Difficult temperament	Sex; poor planning ability	Poor relations with both parents; lack of affectionate care; lack of positive school experiences	
		Protective factors	
Easy temperament	Average or above intelligence; competent; socially engaging	Positive, stable care; competent adult role models	
		Protective mechanisms[a]	
	Reducing risks impact Reducing negative chain reaction Promoting self-esteem and self-efficacy Opening up opportunities		

[a]Both intra- and interpersonal

Source: Reproduced by permission of The McGraw-Hill Companies © 1994 from C. H. Werner, *Developmental Psychopathology*, McGraw-Hill, New York, p. 28, Table 1.1.

4. Those that open up positive opportunities (e.g. geographical move).
5. Positive cognitive processing of negative experiences (e.g. accept the ability of the negative experiences).

Wenar (1994) gives an interesting overview of risks, vulnerabilities, protective factors and protective mechanisms, divided into different categories: organic, intrapersonal, interpersonal and superordinary. In Table 10.2, he describes some examples of each of the categories and factors. Important risk factors on the intrapersonal level are, for example, low intelligence or low self-esteem, while poverty is seen as a risk factor on the superordinary level. Protective factors on the organic level are, for example, an easy temperament, while a competent adult role model is seen as a protective factor on the interpersonal level.

These studies suggest that social support and self-efficacy do function as protective factors for at-risk children. Bandura (1990, p. 327) puts it as follows: 'People's beliefs in their efficacy can be enhanced in four principal ways. The most effective way of developing a strong sense of efficacy is through mastery experiences. Performances and successes build a sense of personal efficacy, failures create self-doubts.' It is important then, that an individual should have the experience of success, which will make him confident of his own abilities. 'After people have become convinced they have what it takes to succeed, they persevere in the face of adversity and quickly rebound from setbacks.'

Another important mechanism is illustrated by Harter (1982). She argues that self-worth and self-efficacy in children are, to a large extent, 'fed' by feedback from important adults. Since self-esteem is partially dependent on the way the child is evaluated by significant others, we can work in high-risk groups in order to change the feedback from those parents who apply negative labels to the child.

Masten et al. (1991) also reflect on the process in which protective factors work. In their view, it explains the protective influence of effective parenthood. Parents whose actions are effective act as models for adequate coping. Children learn this from their parents and thus have more chances of becoming acquainted with mastery. Moreover, these parents are said to create more chance for their children to gain experience, and they give them more feedback on coping. Masten et al. (1991) also refer to this model to explain the protective factors which we find in the attachment theory. Indeed, if one creates a solid bond with a child, the child will see this as a non-verbal expression of one's appreciation of the child as a person. In addition, one provides a basic feeling of security, which stimulates the child to try and seek out new experiences. Finally, religion too can have such a function, that is, it can 'enhance positive beliefs about the self'.

Conceptual Approaches

A number of longitudinal studies were inspired by attachment theories (Sroufe & Rutter, 1984; Kraemer, 1992; Weinert & Weinert, ch. 1 this volume). Most findings are based on Bowlby's theory (Bowlby, 1969). The question raised here is how primary attachments shape later relationships and adaptation to society and new environments. It has been shown that attachment patterns, once established, continue to persist and that they influence a variety of emotional states and behaviour, such as separation anxiety, school failure, victimization and bullying. In later stages of life, most of the dis-attached children are more isolated and feel more rejected than others and they do not have a good relationship with their teachers, which is related to feelings of lower self-appreciation and depression. This framework can help to explain developmental psychopathology and, in later stages of life, greater vulnerability to adult psychopathology.

A newer conceptual approach is based on the principles of 'ego development'. Noam (1991) has been critical of the use of chronological age as a common denominator in the study of psychopathology in any phase of life. He considers the degree of ego maturity as a better measurement of maturity and development than age itself. Furthermore, the manifestation of a psychopathology will depend on ego maturity. For example, no baby will blush, because the ego development is not evolved enough. Blushing emerges as soon as the ego development reaches the level of self-consciousness. Noam gives other examples as well: Feelings of sexual guilt would only emerge after cultural criteria have been internalized, which is situated at the second level of the moral development.

This approach is based on work by Kohlberg (1978), Loevinger and Wessler (1970) and Erikson (1968) among others. All these authors developed theories about stages in particular aspects of ego development. The stages of ego development as developed by Erikson were shown in Table 10.1 in relation to expected normal achievements as well as to behavioural problems and clinical disorders. According to Kohlberg (1978), morality is seen as primarily external to the young child and moral development progresses through three levels, encompassing sequential stages of logically more adequate concepts of justice. Later, it was hypothesized that people showing higher levels of externalizing psychopathology function at lower levels of moral reasoning. Results of studies utilizing objective measures derived from Kohlberg's theory are overwhelmingly supportive of hypothesized relationships between juvenile delinquency and moral reasoning (Smetana, 1990).

The following is another example of a study in which researchers actually start from a theoretical concept in developing their research. The research project was set up by Noam (1991, 1993). The question he raised was whether externalizing behaviour (e.g. aggression, delinquency) was significantly associated with immature ego development, and internalizing symptoms were more strongly associated with mature development. This difference could be very important for understanding why some children develop externalizing disorders and others internalized problems. Noam used the Child Behaviour Checklist developed by Achenbach and Edelbrock (1983) and the parallel self-report form (Youth Self Report). The researchers found that most externalizing adolescent behaviour scales were significantly associated with lower levels of ego development. So they could ascertain a clear relation between earlier developmental stages of ego functioning and psychopathology.

Another study (Borst & Noam, 1993) examines the relation of ego development and suicide risk variables among 139 female in-patients. Their hypothesis is that the self-protective qualities of early development are 'externalizing' and put a person at greater risk for impulsivity, acting out problems or delinquency, but can shield children from directing the aggression against themselves. This explains the low prevalence rate of suicide in children. The authors find that with increasing ego development, adolescents become more vulnerable to suicidal behaviour, because at later stages in ego development, internalizing becomes a central characteristic. According to this theory, it was hypothesized that as long as young adolescents show aggressivity instead of depression, the vulnerability to suicide should not be high.

The researchers also examined the evolution in ego development in relation to changes in symptomatology and coping. The subjects of the study were adolescents who progressed in ego development in contrast with those who regressed or did not develop at all over nine months. The results show that the first group had significantly fewer symptoms and used more coping strategies and adaptive defences.

Conceptual approaches stress the importance of personal experiences as well. Not all crises are real or foreseen. People can feel a crisis as a personal reaction to a series of interpersonal life-events, the so-called perceived crisis. Reactions will be different according to the way they interpret the events. It is assumed that the same events will be experienced differently depending on the subject's level of development and on the interpretations given by the subject. Secondly, behaviour problems are seen as expressions of an internal problem, but they cannot be interpreted without knowing the personal significance. Running away from home can be a sign of a problematic relationship with the parents, a sign of neglect and abuse or the result of an identity crisis (Noam, 1992). Noam (1992) argues that we have to give greater consideration to the *meaning* of symptom expression in adolescence. Study of the self and of subjective experiences is therefore an important field of study.

Rutter and Garmezy (1983) and Bose (1991) agree that Noam's suggestion that higher states of development are more adaptive is supported by evidence. The discovery that ego development correlates with internalized feelings of guilt seems also to be true. However, Noam's suggestion that higher stages of development may also lead to maladaptation needs further expansion. In any case, clinical implications of cognitive immaturity can be drawn from this context: if the person is unable to evolve to higher levels of ego development the development can be stimulated, with the assistance of a counsellor.

One can raise the question whether conceptual models are really necessary. Finding relations by means of empirical research is only one phase in scientific work; interpreting these relations is an equally delicate matter. In so doing, it is appropriate to indicate one's conceptual model explicitly. This explains the controversy surrounding another study by the Moffitt team, notably on 'the inverse relation between IQ and delinquency'. Different explanatory accounts for the relation were examined empirically, using data on 13-year-old boys who were the subjects of a high-risk longitudinal study. Findings were most consistent with the hypothesis that the direction of effect runs from low IQ to delinquency. The IQ–delinquency relation was still robust after the effects of race, class, and observed test motivation were statistically removed (Lynam, Moffitt & Stouthamer-Loeber, 1993). Specifically, the role of impulsivity in understanding this relation was discounted. For this reason the conceptual, operational and analytical bases of the Lynam et al. report were strongly criticized. Their neurologically based view of 'executive dysfunction' as underlying delinquency was portrayed selectively. IQ scores, used as an index of brain–behaviour relations, are only remotely related to specifiable neurological functioning. The Lynam et al. conclusions that impulsivity cannot appreciably explain the relation between IQ and delinquency is shown to depend on the analytical approach used. Analysed alternatively, impulsivity emerges as the more important predictor that can mediate the observed IQ and delinquency relation. The social policy implications of these differing interpretations are important.

AREAS OF DEVIATION FROM THE NORMAL COURSE OF DEVELOPMENT

The DSM-IV (APA, 1995) provides an overview of the most frequently occurring psychopathological problems which occur in childhood and adolescence. Box 10.5 below presents a survey of widespread DSM disorders. Next, a number of these disorders will be discussed from the viewpoint of developmental psychopathology. In so doing, we will use a particular taxonomy which will highlight the link between developmental psychopathology and normative developmental psychology.

The psychopathologies were organized in a taxonomy according to the domain of development in which their deviant manifestation was most clearly perceptible. For example: if a given disorder makes a child deviate most in its social or cognitive development, the disorder will be presented as a social or cognitive disorder. It needs to be noted that this is only one of several taxonomies, and the others can be made. One example is the classification into internalizing vs externalizing disorders, or a classification based on the age at which the complaints first manifest themselves. In developmental psychology, children are usually described from the point of view of a number of areas, such a cognitive, social, emotional or moral development, behavioural and motoric development. In this chapter we will use the same approach in describing some illustrations of psychopathology in childhood. Box 10.5 gives an overview of some relevant clinical syndromes arranged according to various areas of child development.

This section presents a number of illustrations and research data in which

---

Box 10.5   Examples of child psychopathology

Emotional area:
anxiety disorders (e.g. overanxiety, school phobia, separation anxiety disorder), obsessive-compulsive disorder; depression, adolescent suicide
Cognitive area:
mental retardment, attention deficit/hyperactivity disorder, learning disorders
Behavioural aspects:
conduct disorder, motor skills disorder, tic disorders
Social area:
autism and pervasive developmental disorders, oppositional defiant disorder, childhood schizophrenia
eating and elimination (early socialization): pica, rumination disorder, enuresis, encopresis

---

the context and the temporal evolution of a complaint are taken into account. The studies under discussion will mainly be follow-up or developmental studies about child psychopathology.

Problems in Early Socialization

Here the developmental psychopathology has to consider the course taken by various kinds of disorder which can occur in early infancy. Most common are sleeping problems, problems in eating situations and problems in the socialization of elimination, or toilet training.

It is important to note that the meaning of the same behaviour (e.g. refusing to eat) changes with development. In infancy it is intimately connected with attachment, in the toddler period with negativism or non-compliance, in preadolescence with conflicts and overdependency.

The following is another illustration of a developmental study of early socialization problems.

A developmental study on enuresis

With regard to elimination problems, bedwetting (enuresis) is very common in childhood. Since enuresis can go together with many different problems, and since sometimes the problems can persist for years, it is an important field of study. The following describes one of the few longitudinal studies of enuresis (Kaffman & Elizur, 1977). It is a widely renowned study, and it is also described in Rutter and Garmezy (1983) and in Wenar (1994):

> In the kibbutz, children spend about four hours daily with their parents. For the rest of the time, they are cared for by a trained care in a communal

children's house. It is this care, rather than the parents, who has the responsibility for toilet training. In the study of Kaffman and Elizur (1977) 161 children were followed from infancy to the age of 8. The study found the usual predisposing factors of enuresis such as smaller functional bladder capacity, but it also found that enuretic children had more behavioural problems. Two high-risk personalities could be distinguished. First: 30% were hyperactive, aggressive and negative in response to discipline, with low frustration tolerance and problems in adapting to new situations. Second: a smaller group were dependent and unassertive, with low achievement and mastery motivation. In later stages of life, the two groups became more problematic.

Wenar (1994) concluded that longitudinal studies that include intrapersonal and interpersonal variables help the clinician in detecting groups which are at risk in later development. When parents ask for help of enuresis in 4-year-old children, assessment of these variables can help in differentiating between children who will develop normally and children in which the problems are likely to persist.

Cognitive area

Deviations from the normal course of cognitive development are usually associated with mental retardment and school achievement problems.

The study of mental retardation over the last century has uncovered a variety of causes and developmental paths that all lead to mental retardation. Thus, mental retardation is now seen as multiply determined and multiply evolving.

One of the most common reasons why children are referred for psychological treatment is ADD, Attentional Deficit Disorder, classified as a cognitive disorder. The DSM-IV (APA, 1995) describes the cognitive deficiencies in the first place, but also points out additional behavioural problems (see below). If a child that suffers from ADD also shows symptoms of hyperactive behaviour, this is called ADHD (Attention Deficit Hyperactive Disorder).

The disorder is characterized by undercontrolled attention. In the last ten years, a growing number of studies have argued that the symptom is associated with a developmental delay in the ability to sustain attention or concentration on activities, relative to same-age peers (Barkley, 1981, 1990). Research suggests that between 3 and 5% of the school-age population have ADD. Some of the symptoms of deviation in attention are the following (from the DSM-IV, APA, 1995): easily disturbed by external stimuli; does not seem to listen, . . . This attention deficit is related to poor impulse control and poor regulation of activity, both being noticeable mainly in rule-governed behaviour, for example:

- difficulties in task orientation
- impulsivity
- not being able to follow instructions
- losing things

- not being able to organize tasks and activities
- failure to complete a task

For a better understanding of Attention Deficit Disorders, and for a definition and diagnosis, the work of Barkley (1981, 1990) is essential. The following deals with his contribution to developmental psychopathology.

Developmental aspects of ADD-children

Barkley draws the following conclusions from his follow-up studies of ADD-children (Barkley, 1990):

1. Symptoms of ADD arise early in childhood, and most have been identified prior to the age of 7.
2. Infants (0–3 years) who are temperamentally difficult to care for because of their high activity level, irritability and unpredictability are at risk of developing subsequent problems.
3. By age 3 one notes difficulties with managing these children, and problems within toilet training crop up.
4. Between 3 and 6 the ADD symptoms are likely to be at their peak of severity and correlated to deviant and non-compliant behaviour.
5. By age 6 the development of symptoms is completed and ADD children display all kinds of problem behaviour often associated with a number of other developmental, academic, social and family problems.
6. During adolescence, the severity of the primary symptoms (in attention and impulsivity) is less pronounced, but nevertheless a number of problems continue into adulthood.
7. Many ADD children continue to have problems (sometimes different ones) in adulthood. Perhaps a genetic or biomedical approach is necessary to understand the continuity of problems throughout development (Deutsch & Kinsbourne, 1990).

Some hyperactive children will be more difficult to socialize than others; similarly, some families will cope better with the problem than others,

Here too we need more research on protective factors. It is, for example, still unknown whether positive peer experiences can help a hyperactive child to overcome some of the problems. Also, we need to know more about the role of the carer. In this respect there is an interesting hypothesis: sensitive persons are perhaps more helpful than intrusive ones, and children living in disorganized, punitive or inconsistent environments tend to do poorly.

Social Area

Some children have more problems than others with regard to manifest social behaviour: attachment problems, autism, problems in peer relationships, and so on. Some studies suggest a biological abnormality in the capacities of social understanding, others put more emphasis on environmental factors, suggesting some form of continuity between early parent–child attachments and late aspects of social functioning. Wenar (1994) argues that in the first two years of life, the attachment to the parents is crucial: it is at the heart of human development and communication.

Below we describe research into the course taken by a severe disorder in social development, notably autism. What is typical of an autistic child? In the DSM-IV (APA, 1995) a number of symptoms are listed: among others, lack of social and emotional reciprocity, minimal facial expression, impaired use of eye contact, failure to develop peer relations appropriate to the child's age, stereotype patterns of interests and activities, delayed or total absence of spoken language. Wenar (1994) describes different models which compare the disorder with normal behaviour. The first is a qualitative one in which the behaviour of autistic children has little or no counterpart in normal development. The second model emphasizes the relationship between variables rather than a single variable itself. Some variables progress normally, while others follow an idiosyncratic course. This is called 'asynchrony'. A third model is based on the concept of 'fixation', which means that autism is seen as a developmental delay and the differences between normal and autistic children are only quantitative. Research is needed to verify or reject a given model.

Developmental aspects of autism

It is to be expected that this severe and pervasive disorder, which occurs so early in life, will have enormous implications for future development. Follow-up studies indicate that fewer than 10% will do well in adult life. About 60% will be completely dependent on others in all aspects of life (Wenar, 1994). More research in developmental psychopathology is needed to sketch a more differentiated developmental picture. Longitudinal studies not only focus on the developmental course of the disorder until adulthood, but sometimes they are also more concerned with aetiology and with identifying risk factors. There is, for example, a longitudinal study by Chess (1971), in which 243 children were followed who had been infected with congenital rubella in utero; later, 10 of them showed symptoms of autism. But other studies contradict this finding, and there is as yet no consensus.

A survey of the literature suggests that autism is not necessarily associated with a particular precipitating event (an infection or trauma) or with an inadequate relationship with the mother. According to one hypothesis, a genetic component may be partly responsible, not just for autism, but for sociability in general. Clearly, further study is needed before final conclusions can be drawn.

The role of genetic influences is still subject to misconceptions. We must abandon a number of stereotypes about the role of genetic factors. The fact is that the discovery of a genetic factor does not mean that other influences are insignificant or can fix a limit. Because it may be important for the developmental psychopathologist to clearly understand the specific role of

---

Box 10.6   Misconceptions about the role of genetic influences

As Rutter (1991, p. 128) puts it: 'Genetic findings indicate that for most psychological characteristics within the normal range, as shown by individuals reared in non-extreme environments, non-shared influences are probably much more important.' He discusses 11 misconceptions:

1. Strong genetic effects mean that environmental influences must be unimportant.
2. Genes provide a limit to potential.
3. Genetic strategies are of no value for studying environmental influences.
4. Nature and nurture are separate.
5. Genes for serious diseases are necessarily bad.
6. Diseases have nothing to do with normal variation.
7. Genetic findings will not help to identify diseases.
8. Genetic influences diminish with age.
9. Disorders that run in families must be genetic.
10. Disorders that seem not to run in families cannot be genetic.
11. Single major genes lead only to specific rare diseases that follow a Mendelian pattern.

Source: Rutter (1991).

---

genetic influences, Rutter's contribution in Box 10.6 may have a clarifying value.

Emotional Area

In the DSM-IV (APA, 1995), we find the following clinical syndromes for the emotional area: anxiety disorders, for example, overanxious children, school phobia and other phobic reactions, separation anxiety, avoidance disorder, obsessive-compulsive disorder, depression, hypochondriasis, adolescent suicide.

Based on epidemiological studies one might suspect a prevalence of emotional disorders of about 2–8% in the overall population of children. Cross-sectional population studies conclude that up to 20% of children met the criteria for at least one DSM disorder. Rutter and Garmezy (1983) did not discover such a clear picture of different emotional disorders in children; what they did find could be termed 'mixed forms'. Ollendick and King (1994) have recently found that, although the pattern of findings varies somewhat from study to study, it is clear that there exists a lot of so-called 'comorbidity'. Within the anxiety disorders, it is the rule, not the exception, that different forms of anxiety problems occur together, for example, a child with separation anxiety and school phobia or a child with social phobia and

---

Box 10.7   Research issues in the area of social development

Which aspects of autism are genetically determined? And how is the mechanism translated into autistic behaviour? Another hypothesis has it that autism can also be related to brain damage. A large number of questions remain unanswered. Just as in the discussion of all kinds of aetiology of psychopathology, here again we come up against the nature–nurture controversy.

Today attention is also focusing on problems such as social isolation, elective mutism, the abused child, attachment problems, childhood precursors of adult schizophrenia, and children with oppositional deviant behaviour.

Some abnormalities in the social area differ in kind as well as in degree from normal social development. However, children's reactions to given social situations are not only triggered by something within the child (temperament, etc.), but are also the result of social attachment processes and a wider social context. Research issues in this context:

1.   What is the impact of the different conditions in which the child is reared (e.g. negative relationship with one parent, children in day-care, etc.)?

2.   Children in brief periods of separation from their parents (for example when admitted to hospital for one week): connection with later adaptation and early attachment?

3.   Is there any continuity between early parent–child attachments and later aspects of social functioning? What are the implications for institutional children?

---

agoraphobia. Furthermore, the comorbidity is even more pronounced in these cases, where children suffer both from anxiety and depression or from anxiety and disruptive disorders.

Lewis and Miller's handbook (1990) puts forward some arguments for the role of temperamental characteristics in the aetiology of emotional disorders. One example: children with a low threshold for fear and threat tend to show more inhibitory reactions. The following concerns three examples of psychopathology.

Developmental aspects of anxiety in children

Developmental patterns have been found for childhood anxieties as well as for the frequency of children's fears and anxiety. The number of fears that children report declines with age. The frequency of early childhood fears and anxieties seems to peak between 2 and 4 years of age (Lewis & Miller, 1990). These fears are functionally related to the child's developing autonomy. During infancy, fears of loud noises or of other excessive or unfamiliar stimuli, or of separation from one or both parents predominate (Rutter & Garmezy, 1983). Sexual fears appear more frequently in adolescence, and school phobia is related to school-age children.

However, certain kinds of fears are more stable over the years. Lewis and Miller (1990) mention some 'common' fears occurring in almost all age groups: fires, not being able to breathe, a burglar breaking into the house, getting hit by a car, death or dead people, looking foolish, getting poor grades, being in a war. One possible explanation is that these fears involve fundamental existential anxieties and concern for one's own life.

From a developmental viewpoint, Lewis and Miller (1990) give three categories of fears. One category includes fear of doctors, injections, darkness and strangers. Fears of this kind have their onset in early childhood, but with increasing age there is a drastic reduction. The second group includes fear of animals, heights, storms, enclosed places and social situations. These fears appear to show a more persistent course. The third category of fears includes fear of crowds, death, injury, illness and separation. These fears have a later developmental onset.

Other studies focus on the development of children with an abnormal fear or anxiety disorder. This is a topic which requires much further research. Little is known about the history and outcome of many psychiatric disorders in children and adolescents, including the internalizing disorders. The limited research available suggests that anxiety and affective disorders may be more persistent than we used to think (Ollendick & King, 1994). Whereas Rutter's Isle of Wight studies (Rutter et al., 1974) found that up to 21% of children with internalizing problems proved to remain deviant in later stages of life, as did 31% of children with externalizing problems, the picture now appears to be the reverse. For instance, a Dutch follow-up study by Verhulst, on 104 children with internalizing problems, finds that 36% remain deviant in the fourth follow-up stage, six years later (Verhulst et al., 1993). And Ollendick and King (1994) refer to a study by Offord and colleagues on a random sample of 881 children in the Ontario community. Psychiatric diagnosis was determined in part by prenatal response to the Child Behaviour Checklist. For emotional disorders, 26.2% of the children with such a disorder persisted in that disorder four years later. In addition, at follow-up, 14% of these children were categorized as hyperactive and 18.2% as conduct-disordered. Thus, although the persistence of emotional disorder per se was not particularly high, emotional disorder acted supplementarily (32.2%) as a risk factor for later psychopathology.

Some research issues in the emotional area are: Can fears at age 3 predict the development of a neurotic disorder in later life? What about longitudinal data for children developing school phobia?

Studies on depression

With regard to depression in children, developmental psychopathology can make a fundamental contribution. Sroufe and Rutter (1984) and Marks

(1971) find that children diagnosed as depressive are not likely to be diagnosed as depressive adults and when adult depression has been preceded by a psychiatric disorder, the child generally had not been diagnosed as depressed. Time and context appear to play a role in the aetiology of depression.

Moreover, a multi-factorial model seems obviously necessary for a better understanding of the onset of depression, in which the following factors are seen as important contributors: cognitive appraisals of events, life-stress, interpersonal variables (e.g. attachment, difficulties in peer, family and social interactions) and biological processes. This developmental psychopathology model of depression is proposed by Hammen (1992).

Studies on Growth Failure

It has been hypothesized that emotional deprivation causes growth failure as a psychosomatic effect on endocrine function. It is now clear, however, that the only real cause of limited growth is undernourishment (Rutter & Garmezy, 1983). But undernourishment can be related to psychological factors such as depression in the child, causing loss of appetite or impaired gastrointestinal function. Cicchetti et al. (1988) provide further illustrations of how psychological factors affect biological functioning and how shortcomings in caretaking may contribute to the emergence of neuroendocrine and other biological system complications. They find, for example, that children with non-organic growth failure are more likely to have insecure attachments.

Behavioural Area

The most typical disorders in the behavioural area are conduct disorders in children (CDC). Psychologists, psychiatrists and parents are very much concerned about these problems. In the DSM-IV (APA, 1995) a CDC is defined as a disorder which lasts at least six months, during which at least three signals of described problems are presented. Many heterogeneous problems are included: aggression, delinquency, stealing, running away from home, lying, fire-setting, cruelty, and so on. Prevalence rates differ from one study to another.

One frequently advanced hypothesis for the cause of this disorder is that CDC youngsters are often deficient in the development of their impulse control. Moreover, their antisocial behaviour proves to be very persistent. Patterson et al. (1989) even talk in term of a 'developmental trait'. In their view one of the most important tasks of the developmental psychopathologist is to determine the mechanisms explaining the stability of antisocial behaviour. They look upon ineffective parenting practices as the determinant of CDC. This resulted in the so-called 'control' theory. That is, CDC is seen as a consequence of poor monitoring and supervision of the child's activities. Patterson et al. (1989) also point out that there is an alternative explanation of CDC, notably one which builds on elements of social interaction. In this model, children are thought to learn antisocial behaviour through the observation of family interactions; in addition, they find that aggressive/coercive behaviour can be very successful, and in this way a vicious circle is created which maintains and even escalates this unwanted type of behaviour.

Aggressive behaviour seems to be very pervasive across time and generations. Some researchers have suggested genetic influences on the development of aggression (see the comment on genetic influences in Box 10.6). Moffitt (1993) suggests a neurobiological explanation. It is argued that neurophysiological variables warrant further study as possible causal factors for CDC. A developmental perspective on how neuropsychological problems might contribute to the risk of CDC is put forward. There is some evidence from neuropsychological tests suggesting that brain dysfunction is a correlate of conduct disorder (Moffitt, 1993). Neuropsychological measurements are related to some of the best indicators of poor outcomes for children with CDC symptoms, such as early onset, stability across time, hyperactive symptoms, and aggressiveness. It remains to be seen if the future, and future findings in developmental psychopathology, will be able to decide on the validity of these hypotheses and to say whether they contradict or complement each other.

Clearly, more research is needed before any final conclusions can be made that would lead to the prognosis of later antisocial behaviour in aggressive children. We believe, with Loeber and Farrington (1994) that developmental psychopathology can play an important role here. A number of indicators should be screened routinely from an early age: such as impulsiveness, intelligence, achievements at school, parental skills in upbringing, social isolation, and more biological variables such as weight at birth, testosterone levels.

The following paragraphs focus on research into follow-up data for the evolution of conduct disorders.

Follow-up studies on the evolution of conduct disorders

Many retrospective and prospective studies of children with aggressive behaviour have been undertaken. Well-known research is that of Robins (as early as the 60s) and of Farrington (cited by Rutter and Garmezy, 1983; Loeber, 1990; Patterson et al., 1989; Martin & Hoffman, 1990). Robins was concerned with the extent to which manifestations of antisocial behaviour in children continue in adulthood. His findings and those of others (Offord & Bennett, 1994) can be summarized as follows:

- only 50% of antisocial children become antisocial adults;
- 50–75% of adolescent delinquents become adult offenders;
- a particular type of childhood deviance is not a good predictor of adult deviance, e.g. emotional disorders in childhood rarely lead to antisocial

behaviour in adult life;

- the overall level of deviant behaviour in childhood (with all its variations and manifestations), is a better predictor of adult deviance. These relationships do not depend on the continuation of the same behaviour, e.g. antisocial symptoms and hyperactivity predict criminality, alcoholism and personality disorder in adult life;
- 70% of adult antisocial behaviour is related to antisocial behaviour in childhood, e.g. an adult antisocial personality is predicted by conduct disturbances in childhood;
- the prognosis for conduct disorders is generally worse than for emotional disorders.

Some considerations on sex differences

The study of psychopathology might reveal something about normal development and about sex differences which are noticeable even in normal development. A typical example is the prevalence of conduct disorders, which are far more common in boys than in girls. Another remarkable finding is that disorders with an onset early in life (e.g. autism, conduct disorders) have a higher prevalence in boys, whereas disorders which typically arise in adolescence (e.g. eating disorders, depression) occur rather more often in girls (Masten et al., 1991).

Several explanations of these sex differences have been put forward. One acceptable explanation suggests a biological basis for aggression. Another is that boys are more susceptible to stress than girls; aggression is seen as an externalizing of stress problems. This hypothesis has been subjected to a great deal of replication research in the UK and the US, using different measurements for family conflicts and conduct disorders. Yet another hypothesis suggests that boys and girls elicit different responses from their parents: from girls we expect controlled behaviour, and aggression is not permitted at all. The social learning approach comes up with another explanation: fathers are the model of aggression for the boys. A very recent hypothesis suggests that girls too develop antisocial patterns, but that their aggression is more internalized, resulting in somatic complaints, unfriendliness or underachievement (Zahn-Waxler, 1993).

Research into developmental psychopathology has also produced other interesting observations on aggression in boys. It looks now as if it is apparent from early childhood on and these sex differences are noticeable across different cultures and even in subhuman primates. This could shed new light on the explanations put forward for sex differences in antisocial behaviour.

Psychological correlates of conduct disorders

Conduct-disordered young people are frequently found to have lower intelligence and to show poorer academic performances than non-delinquent young people (Martin & Hoffman, 1990; Patterson et al., 1989). A great deal of empirical research on the relation between conduct disorders and school results is available. The association is particularly strong between reading and deviant behaviour in boys. This can be explained indifferent ways. A developmental approach will be necessary to gain a better understanding.

1. Antisocial behaviour in the classroom leads to educational failure and school dropout.

   However, developmental studies now argue that delinquency sometimes starts only after leaving school.

2. Educational failure generates lower self-esteem, more emotional disorders and problems at school, which may contribute to the development of conduct disorders.

   More evidence for this comes from Rutter's above-mentioned study on the Isle of Wight and from his Inner London study (Rutter & Garmezy, 1983). Three groups were compared with each other in different characteristics: children with reading difficulties, children with pure conduct disorders and children with both problems. The third group, the one with the two problems combined, was more similar to the group with pure reading difficulties, and not similar to the pure conduct disorder group. These are arguments for the theory that social problems are more likely to be the result of educational failure. However, other studies do not produce a clear-cut answer to this question. It has repeatedly been demonstrated that programmes improving the skills of antisocial youths do not reduce other antisocial symptoms (Patterson et al., 1989). A third explanation can therefore be put forward.

3. To some extent, cognitive deficits and conduct disorders share a common aetiology.

   Here, researchers have turned to the role of temperamental characteristics and family variables. Since other explanations are no longer acceptable, this is the only one left. Loeber (1990) suggests a hypothesis: impulsiveness could underlie behavioural problems on the one hand, and academic failure on the other (lack of concentration could cause problems with arithmetic calculations). And there is also the hypothesis of Moffitt (1993) as described above.

TREATMENT AND PREVENTION

Despite the logical links that exist between the provision of psychotherapeutic interventions to children and adolescents, and developmental theory and research, too few bridges have been laid between these two areas (Cicchetti & Toth, 1992). When we consider the treatment of psychopathologies, we find studies on the short-term and long-term evaluation of various kinds of treatment given within a number of theoretical frameworks, such as the Psychoanalytic Approach, the Client-Centred Approach, Behaviour Therapy, Family Approach of Group Psychotherapy. These

---

Box 10. 8   Definitions of treatment models

Psychodynamic theories: Freudian and neo-Freudian theories, which aim to understand the basic motivations of human behaviour. Emotions as well as unconscious motivations play a major role.

Client-centred therapy: therapy based on Roger's therapeutic model, which utilizes warmth, acceptance and reflection of the client's ideas and feelings to remove the obstacles to self-actualization.

Behaviour therapies: a group of therapies characterized by attention to specific current behaviour, objective measurement and reliance on learning paradigms and principles of the social learning approach.

Family therapy: based on the assumption that it is necessary to treat the entire family to correct the mechanism responsible for producing a disorder in one particular member.

Group psychotherapies: in order to solve their problems, individuals work together guided by a trained leader. Social interaction and social support play an important role.

Source: Wenar (1994).

---

approaches to treatment depend on a specific model: the medical model, the social-learning approach, dynamic or interactional models and learning paradigms. These models differ in the way they look at the origin and evolution of a disorder. They also differ in the extent to which they take account of developmental psychopathology and/or study its potential.

With regard to the treatment of conduct disorders, Kazdin (1987) describes the potential of the different therapies, their focus and their key processes (Table 10.3). However, Kazdin is not very optimistic about the chances of success for the treatment of conduct disorder. It is only parent-training for preadolescents which shows any favourable outcome. As a complement to this, academic remediation and child social skill training are also thought to be useful.

Other studies evaluate the effects of a specific kind of treatment, for example institutionalization. Many negative effects of institutionalization are known, with one hopeful statement: if we can provide at least one close human contact, a more positive evolution is possible for the institutionalized child. Others argue that institutional environments appear to have marked influence on current behaviour, but that the benefits do not persist when the young people return home to a totally different environment.

Wierson and Forehand (1994) observe quite rightly that long-term follow-up studies are the only means for determining the real effectiveness of therapy as compared with temporary treatment gains. Forehand refers to his own studies, which follow children up to 14 years after treatment. Loeber and Farrington (1994) also recently advocated an approach to research in child psychopathology which would no longer be cross-sectional or correlational:

The use of longitudinal and experimental treatment methods represented a great step forward in methodology . The time is now ripe to combine these strong designs to capitalize on the advantages of both. Multiple-cohort longitudinal-experimental studies should now be mounted, ones which include several years of personal contacts with the subjects before and after an intervention and that also have repeated frequent data collection from a variety of sources (p. 897).

Consequently the studies mentioned above prove again that the longitudinal approach can be exceptionally useful.

In going through the research into 'treatment; and 'developmental psychopathology', one finds only a small number of studies in this new field. It is worth looking at the situation in some greater detail. Kazdin (1993) offers an agenda for future research. Several priorities are suggested, including:

- expanding the criteria for evaluating therapy outcome
- expanding the range of research issues
- testing a broader range of treatments and treatment combinations
- evaluating long-term treatment effects
- expanding models of developing and assessing treatment

Cicchetti et al. (1988) were among the first to point out the potential of developmental psychopathology for the therapeutic domain. For a number of frequently occurring psychopathologies in children they describe a series of implications for the treatment of the disorders concerned. It appears to be possible to intervene and/or take corrective measures quite early on in development. In so doing, one proceeds on the basis of developmental differences which have already been traced and described at an early age, such as adaptation after birth, homeostatic regulation of sleeping, eating and elimination processes, reactions to tensions, attachment, development of the self, symbolic play, peer relations and school functioning. So children who are depressive, or who are reared by depressive mothers, can be described according to the above dimensions at an early age; and this also goes for the problems of child maltreatment and for children with Down's Syndrome or with growth failure. Potential interventions could be management of tension, secure attachment, development of an autonomous self and establishing stable peer relations.

An analysis of the factors that pull subjects toward or away from increased risk at various stages will provide us not only with a deeper understanding of development but also with valuable information for prevention. Consequently, interventions can be made by way of preventative actions. These will be aimed at particular groups of the population, and attempts will be made to prevent the emergence of psychopathologies by way of, for example, education, the stimulation of self-responsibility, and so on. A classic example is the television programme 'Sesame Street', which was aimed at children from the lower economic classes. When prevention is geared to specific risk groups (e.g. pregnant minors or hyperactive children in one-parent families), it is referred to as secondary prevention, as opposed to primary prevention, which is geared to the community at large.

Offord and Bennett (1994), in 'Conduct Disorder: long-term outcomes

Table 10.3 Therapeutic focus and processes of major classes of treatment for antisocial behaviour

Treatment type	Focus	Key processes
Child focused		
Individual psychotherapy	Focus on intrapsychic bases of antisocial behaviour, especially conflicts and psychological processes that were adversely affected over the course of development.	Relationship with the therapist is the primary medium through which change is achieved. Treatment provides a corrective emotional experience to providing insight and exploring new ways of behaving.
Group psychotherapy	Processes on individual therapy, as noted above. Additional processes are reassurance, feedback, and vicarious gains by peers. Group processes, such as cohesion and leadership, also serve as the focus.	Relationship with therapist and peers as part of the group. Group processes emerge to provide children with experiences of others and opportunities to test their own views and behaviours.
Behaviour therapy	Problematic behaviours presented as target symptoms. Prosocial behaviours are trained directly.	Learning new behaviours through direct training, modelling, reinforcement, practice, and role playing. Training in the situations (e.g., at home and in the community) in which the problematic behaviours occur.
Problem-solving skills training	Cognitive processes and interpersonal cognitive problems-solving skills that underlie social behaviour.	Teach problem-solving skills to children by engaging in step-by-step approach to interpersonal situations. Use of modelling, practice, rehearsal, and role playing to develop problem-solving skills. Development of an internal dialogue or private speech that uses the processes of identifying prosocial solutions to problems.

Treatment	Description	Notes
Pharmacotherapy	Designed to affect the biological substrates of behaviour, especially in the light of laboratory-based findings on neurohumours, biological cycles, and other physiological correlates of aggressive and emotional behaviour.	Administration of psychotropic agents to control antisocial behaviour. Lithium carbonate and haloperidol have been used because of the antiaggressive effects.
Residential treatments	Means of administering other techniques in day treatment or residential setting. Foci of other techniques apply.	Processes of other techniques apply. Also separation of the child from parents or removal from the home situation may help to reduce untoward processes or crises that contribute to the clinical problem.
Family focused Family therapy	Family as a functioning system rather than the identified patient serves as focus. Interpersonal relationships, organization, and roles and dynamics of the family.	Communication, relationships, and structure within the family and processes as autonomy, problem solving, and negotiation.
Parent management training	Interactions in the home, especially those involving coercive exchanges.	Direct training of parents to develop prosocial behaviour in their children. Explicit use of social-learning techniques to influence the child.
Community based Community-wide interventions	Focus on activities and community programmes to foster competence and prosocial peer relations.	Develop prosocial behaviour and connections with peers. Activities are seen to promote prosocial behaviour and to being compatible with antisocial behaviour.

Source: A. E. Kazdin, Treatment of antisocial behavior in children: Current status and future directions, *Psychological Bulletin,* **102**, 2, 187–203; © 1987 by the American Psychological Association. Reprinted with permission.

and intervention effectiveness', present a critical analysis of four intervention strategies for preventing or treating conduct disorder: parent and family targeted programmes, social-cognitive programmes, peer and school-based programmes and community programmes. However, their conclusion provides only limited evidence of the effectiveness of either primary or secondary prevention. This is also the conclusion drawn in the latest study by Dishion and Andrews (1995). The latter had attempted to prevent the further escalation of problematic behaviour in a high-risk group of adolescents (drug use prior to age 15, substance use, etc.). Only if the parents are involved in the prevention programmes is the outcome slightly more positive.

Another application of a possible link between treatment aspects and prevention is found in an interesting study by Marvin (1992). Marvin provides a brief treatment protocol for paediatric psychogenic pain condition. The principles of protocol are based on the attachment theories and in fact use an approach along the lines of developmental psychopathology. In the study 19 families participated in a 4-day programme; subsequently, in a 6-month follow-up, 17 children proved to have remained symptom-free.

Wenar (1994) presents two prevention programmes based on development-oriented research.

The STEEP-Programme

This programme was developed by Erikson, Korfmacher and England in 1992 and it was designed to offset the risk of an insecure attachment. They selected a target population of mothers at risk as a result of poverty and other life circumstances. Home visits started when they knew the mother was pregnant and were based on insight therapy. Follow-up research is still in progress to evaluate the effects of this prevention programme on the attachment relationship.

The Fast Track Programme

This programme was developed by the Conduct Problems Prevention Research Group in 1992. The target population consists of first-graders with signs of disruptive behaviour such as aggression, impulsiveness, and so on. The programme uses various techniques. Some members of the team work with the parents on disciplinary practices, others try to increase the child's social skills. There is also a school programme designed to avoid school failure, in which the emphasis lies on a positive relationship with the child's teacher. Studies on the effectiveness of the programme are not available yet.

CONCLUSION AND FUTURE PERSPECTIVES

The aim of this chapter is to review the fairly new field of developmental psychopathology. To this end, we focused on a longitudinal and context-related view of children and their psychopathologies. It goes without saying that this approach has implications for the method of research. The studies we have cited clearly show that the longitudinal and context-related view can make major contributions to clinical and developmental psychology. Among the most important discoveries one should note, for instance, the discovery of alternative developmental pathways (e.g. for conduct disorders) and the discovery of the effects of various risk variables, life-events and protective factors (e.g. in so-called resilience studies). Causal inferences can now be drawn more safely than before. It would therefore be advisable to redirect treatment and prevention and incorporate these new findings.

However, on a number of issues the domain of developmental psychopathology is still in its infancy. For one thing, longitudinal studies require work and financial resources over a long period of time. For another, research into risk groups or risk variables does not always enable one to draw general conclusions. Moreover, definitions of children's psychopathologies derive from classifications made for adult psychiatry, and they are not always fully geared to the complete range of childhood psychopathology. It is still too early to define an overall theory of psychopathological development of children. Many areas remain as yet unexplored, such as the impact of early life experiences on later behaviour and development. Researchers in the field also need to acquire clinical experience in order to better conduct their research. Most researchers focused on the changes that take place in early childhood, so little is known about the transition to adolescence. A number of important questions therefore still remain unanswered: What is the relation between adolescence and the increased frequency and intensity of feelings of depression, delinquent activities, the onset of anorexia nervosa, and so on? These are topics which remain a challenge for the clinicians and researchers in the promising field of developmental psychopathology.

Nevertheless, there have over the past few years been a number of new developments which have greatly benefited developmental psychopathology and which constitute a sound basis for further intervention and prevention. We refer to 'our knowledge of the incidence of various child and adolescent risk conditions' (Cicchetti & Toth, 1992) and to protective factors (Masten et al., 1991). As a consequence, aetiological models of disorders increasingly reflect the true complexity inherent in the emergence and development of psychopathology. Rutter and Garmezy (1983) and Loeber (1990) outline the following perspectives for future work: improvements in diagnosis and classification of childhood disorders; availability of adequate assessment methods; better studies into causal factors; integration of biological, psychological, sociological and family factors in the child during its development along normal as well as abnormal lines; the formulation of new questions and hypothesis (e.g. the impact of developmental processes on the outcome of interventions).

Together with Cicchetti and Toth (1992, p. 491), we can conclude that 'ontogenesis is an integrated and complicated process, characterized by multiply-determined pathways and outcomes that interact in a complex system of biological, psychological and environmental factors . . . '. This also means that developmental psychology and psychopathology will tend to become increasingly interrelated. This may have far-reaching consequences for understanding both the normal course of development and the deviations from this course. This understanding will further enhance our ability and skills in formulation of models, diagnosis, treatment and prevention regarding the threat posed by the problems of the developing person.

REFERENCES

Achenbach, T. M. (1990). Conceptualization of developmental psychopathology. In M. Lewis and S. M. Miller (Eds), *Handbook of Developmental Psychopathology*. New York: Plenum Press.

Achenbach, T. M. & Edelbrock, C. S. (1983). *Manual for the Child Behavioral Checklist and Revised Child Behaviour Profile*. Burlington, VT: Dept. of Psychiatry, University of Vermont.

American Psychiatric Association (1980). *Diagnostic and Statistical Manual of Mental Disorders*, 3d edn. Washington, DC.

American Psychiatric Association (1987). *Diagnostic and Statistical Manual of Mental Disorders*, 3d edn, revised. Washington, DC.

American Psychiatric Association (1995). *Diagnostic and Statistical Manual of Mental Disorders*, 4th edn. Washington, DC.

Asarnow, J. R. (1994). Annotation: Childhood-onset schizophrenia. *Journal of Child Psychology and Psychiatry*, **35**, 8, 1345–1371.

Bandura, A. (1990). Conclusion: Reflections on nonability determinants of competence. In R. H. Sternberg & J. Kolligan, Jr (Eds), *Competence Considered* (pp. 315–362). New Haven, CT: Yale University Press.

Barkley, R. A. (1981). *Hyperactive Children: A Handbook for Diagnosis and Treatment*. New York: Guilford Press.

Barkley, R. A. (1990). Attention Deficit Disorders. History, definition and diagnosis. In M. Lewis & S. M. Miller (Eds), *Handbook of Developmental Psychopathology*. New York: Plenum Press.

Bernstein, G. A., Borchardt, C. M. & Perwien, A. R. (1996). Anxiety disorders in children and adolescents: A review of the past 10 years. *Journal of the American Academy of Child and Adolescent Psychiatry*, **35**, 9, 1110–1120.

Borst, S. R. & Noam, G. G. (1993). Developmental psychopathology in suicidal and nonsuicidal adolescent girls. *Journal of the American Academy of Child and Adolescent Psychiatry*, **32**, 3, 501–508.

Bose, S. (1991). Observation on Noam's article. *Newsletter of the International Society for the Study of Behavioural Development*. Berlin: Max Planck Institute, **1**, 5.

Bowlby, J. (1969). *Attachment and Loss*, Vol. 1. New York: Basic Books.

Caspi, A., Lynam, D., Moffitt, T. E. & Silva, P. A. (1993). Unraveling girls' delinquency: Biological, dispositional, and contextual contributions to adolescent misbehavior. *Developmental-Psychology*, **29**, 1, 19–30.

Chess, S. (1971). Autism in children with congenital rubella. *Journal of Autism and Childhood Schizophrenia*, **1**, 33–47.

Chiland, C. (1991). L'enfant de six ans et son avenir. *Collection de la Psychiatrie de l'enfant*. Paris: PUF.

Cicchetti, D. (1989). Developmental psychopathology: some thoughts on its evolution. *Developmental Psychopathology*, **1**, 1–4.

Cicchetti, D. & Toth, S. L. (1992). The role self developmental theory in prevention and intervention. *Development and Psychopathology*, **4**, 489–493.

Cicchetti, D., Toth, S. & Bush, M. (1988). Developmental psychopathology and incompetence in childhood. In B. B. Leahey & A. E. Kazdin (Eds), *Advances in Clinical Child Psychology*, Vol. 11 (pp. 73–124). New York: Plenum Press.

Cohen, D. J. & Leckman, J. F. (1994). Developmental psychopathology and neurobiology of Tourette's syndrome. *Journal of the American Academy of Child and Adolescent Psychiatry*, **33**, 1, 2–15.

Deutsch, C. K. & Kinsbourne, M. (1990). Genetics and biochemistry in Attention Deficit Disorder. In M. Lewis & S. M. Miller (Eds), *Handbook of Developmental Psychopathology*. New York: Plenum Press.

Dishion, T. J. & Andrews, D. W. (1995). Preventing escalation in problem behaviors with high-risk young adolescents: Immediate and 1-year outcomes. *Journal of Consulting and Clinical Psychology*, **63**, 4, 538–548.

Edelbrock, C, & Costello, A. J. (1988). A typology of child behaviour profile patterns: Distribution and correlates for disturbed children age 6–16. *Journal of Abnormal Child Psychology* , **16**, 219–231.

Erikson, E. (1968). *Identity: Youth and Crisis*. New York: Norton.

Hammen, C. (1992). Cognitive, life stress, and interpersonal approaches to a developmental psychopathology model of depression. *Development and Psychopathology*, **4**, 1, 189–206.

Harkness, S. & Super, C. H. (1990). Culture and psychopathology. In M. Lewis & S. M. Miller (Eds), *Handbook of Developmental Psychopathology*. New York: Plenum Press.

Harter, S. (1982). A developmental perspective on some parameters of self-regulation in children. In K. Karoly & F. H. Kanfer (Eds), *Self-management and Behaviour Change* (pp. 165–204). New York: Pergamon Press.

Hartup, W. W. & Van Lieshout, C. F. M. (1995). Personality development in context. *Annual Review of Psychology*, **46**, 655–687.

Hellinckx, W., De Munter, A. & Grietens, H. (1991, 1993). *Gedrags- en emotionele problemen bij kinderen*, Vols 1 and 2. Leuven-Apeldoorn: Garant.

Johnson, J. L., Sher, K. J. & Rolf, J. E. (1991). Models of vulnerability to psychopathology in children of alcoholics. An overview, special focus: Alcohol and youth. *Alcohol Health and Research World*, **15**, 1, 33–42.

Kaffman, M. & Elizur, E. (1977). Infants who become enuretics: A longitudinal study of 161 kibbutz children. *Monographs of the Society for Research in Child Development*, **42**, 2.

Kazdin, A. E. (1987). Treatment of antisocial behavior in children: Current status and future directions. *Psychological Bulletin*, **102**, 2, 187–203.

Kazdin, A. E. (1993). Treatment of conduct disorder: Progress and directions in psychotherapy research. Special issue: Toward a developmental perspective on conduct disorder. *Development and Psychopathology*, **5**, 1–2, 227–310.

Kohlberg, L. (1978). Revisions in the theory and practice of moral development. In W. Damon (Ed.), *New Directions in Child Development* (pp. 83–89). San Francisco: Jossey-Bass.

Kraemer, G. W. (1992). A psychobiological theory of attachment. *Behavioural and Brain Sciences*, **15**, 3, 493–541.

Leslie, A. M. (1986). Getting development off the ground: Modularity and the infant's perception of causality. In P. Van Geert (Ed.), *Theory Building in Developmental Psychology*. Amsterdam: North Holland.

Lester, B. M. & Tronick, E. Z. (1994). The effects of prenatal cocaine exposure and child outcome. *Infant Mental Health Journal*, **15**, 2, 107–120.

Levy-Shiff, R., Einat, G., Mogilner, M. B. & Lerman, M. (1994). Biological and environmental correlates of developmental outcome of prematurely born infants in early adolescence. *Journal of Paediatric Psychology*, **19**, 1, 63–78.

Lewis, M. & Miller, S. M. (1990). *Handbook of Developmental Psychopathology*. New York: Plenum Press.

Loeber, R. (1982). The stability of antisocial and delinquent child behaviour: A review. *Child Development*, **53**, 1431–1446.

Loeber, R. (1988). The natural history of juvenile conduct problems, delinquency, and associated substance use: Evidence for developmental progressions. In B. B. Leahey & A. E. Kazdin (Eds), *Advances in Clinical Child Psychology*, Vol. 11 (pp. 73–124). New York: Plenum Press.

Loeber, R. (1990). Development and risk factors of juvenile antisocial behavior and delinquency. *Clinical Psychological Review*, **10**, 1–41.

Loeber, R. & Dishion, T. (1983). Early predictors of male delinquency: A review. *Psychological Bulletin* , **94**, 68–99.

Loeber, R. & Farrington, D. P. (1994). Problems and solutions in longitudinal and experimental treatment. Studies of Child psychopathology and delinquency. *Journal of Consulting and Clinical Psychology*, **62**, 5, 887–900.

Loevinger, J. & Wessler, R. (1970). *Measuring Ego Development*, Vols 1 & 2. San Francisco: Jossey-Bass.

Lynam, D., Moffitt, T. E. & Stouthamer-Loeber, M. (1993). Explaining the relation between IQ and delinquency: Class, race, test motivation, school failure, or self-control? *Journal of Abnormal Psychology*, **102**, 2, 187.

Marks, I. (1971). Phobic disorders four years after treatment: A prospective follow-up. *British Journal of Psychiatry*, **118**, 683–688.

Martin, B. & Hoffman, J. A. (1990). Conduct disorders. In M. Lewis & S. M. Miller (Eds), *Handbook of Developmental Psychopathology*. New York: Plenum Press.

Marvin, R. S. (1992). Attachment- and family-system-based intervention in developmental psychopathology. Special issue: Developmental approaches to prevention and intervention. *Development and Psychopathology*, **4**, 4, 697–711.

Masten, A. S., Best, K. M. & Garmezy, N. (1991). Resilience and development: Contributions from the study of children who overcome adversity. *Development and Psychopathology*, **2**, 425–444.

Moffitt, T. E. (1993). The neuropsychology of conduct disorder. Special issue: Toward a developmental perspective on conduct disorder. *Development and Psychopathology*, **5**, 1–2, 135–151.

Moffitt, T. E. & Silva, P. A. (1988). Self-reported delinquency, neuropsychological deficit, and history of attention deficit disorder. *Journal of Abnormal Child Psychology*, **16**, 553–569.

Noam, G. G. (1991). Clinical developmental psychology. *Newsletter of the International Society for the Study of Behavioural Development*. Berlin: Max Planck Institute, **1**, 1–4.

Noam, G. G. (1992). Development as the aim of clinical intervention. Special issue: Developmental approaches to prevention and intervention. *Development and Psychopathology*, **4**, 4, 679–696.

Noam, G. G. (1993). Ego development: True or false? *Psychological Inquiry*, **4**, 1, 43–48.

Offord, D. R. & Bennett, K. J. (1994). Conduct disorder: Long-term outcomes and intervention effectiveness. *Journal of American Academy of Child and Adolescence Psychiatry*, **33**, 8, 1069–1078.

Ollendick, T. H. & King, N. J. (1994). Diagnosis, assessment and treatment of internalizing problems in children. *Journal of Consulting and Clinical Psychology*, **62**, 5, 918–927.

Patterson, G. R., Debaryshe, D. & Ramsey, E. (1989). A developmental perspective on antisocial behavior. *American Psychologist*, **44**, 2, 329–335.

Premack, D. & Woodruff, G. (1978). Does the chimpanzee have a theory of mind? *The Behavioural and Brain Sciences*, **4** 515–526.

Pulkkinen, L. & Rönkä, A. (1994). Personal control over development, identity formation. Future orientation as components of life orientation: A developmental approach. *Developmental Psychology*, **30**, 2, 260–271.

Pulkkinen, L. & Tremblay, R. E. (1992). Patterns of boys' social adjustment in two cultures and at different ages: A longitudinal perspective. *International Journal of Behavioral Development*, **15**, 4, 527–553.

Rice, K. G., Herman, M. A. & Petersen, A. C. (1993). Coping with challenge in adolescence: A conceptual model and psycho-educational intervention. Special Issue: Stress and coping in adolescence. *Journal of Adolescence*, **16**, 3, 235–251.

Rutter, M. (1989). Pathways from childhood to adult life. *Journal of Child Psychology and Psychiatry*, **30**, 23–51.

Rutter, M. (1991). Nature, nurture, and psychopathology: A new look at an old topic. *Development and Psychopathology*, **3**, 125–136.

Rutter, M. (1996). Psychosocial adversity: Risk, resilience and recovery. In L. Verhoftstadt-Denève, I. Kienhorst & C. Braet (Eds), *Conflict and*

Development in Adolescence. Leiden, DSWO Press.

Rutter, M., Cox, A., Tupling, C., Berger, M. & Yule, W. (1974). Attainment and adjustment in two geographical areas: I. The prevalence of psychiatric disorder. *British Journal of Psychiatry*, **126**, 493–509.

Rutter, M. & Garmezy, N. (1983). Developmental psychopathology. In P. H. Mussen (Ed.), *Handbook of Child Psychology*, Vol. IV, *Socialization, Personality and Social Development* (pp. 775–911). New York: Wiley.

Rutter, M., Tizard, J. & Whitmore, K. (1970). *Education, Health and Behaviour.* London: Longmans.

Smetana, J. G. (1990). Morality and conduct disorders. In M. Lewis & S. M. Miller (Eds), *Handbook of Developmental Psychopathology*. New York: Plenum Press.

Sroufe, L. A. & Rutter, M. (1984). The domain of developmental psychopathology. *Child Development*, **55**, 17–29.

Van IJzendoorn, M. H. &. Kroonenberg, P. M. (1988). Cross-cultural patterns of attachment: A meta-analysis of the strange situation. *Child Development*, **59**, 147–156.

Van den Bergh, B. (1992). Maternal emotions during pregnancy and fetal and neonatal behaviour. In J. G. Nijhuis (Ed.), *Fetal Behaviour. Development and Perinatal Aspects* (pp. 157–178). Oxford: Oxford University Press.

Verhofstadt-Denève, L. (1985). Crises in adolescence and psycho-social development in young adulthood: A seven-year follow-up study forma dialectical viewpoint. In C. J. Brainerd & V. F. Reyna (Eds), *Developmental Psychology*. Amsterdam/New York/Oxford: North-Holland.

Verhofstadt-Denève, L. (1996). Adolescents have become adults. A 15–year follow-up. In L. Verhofstadt-Denève, I. Kienhorst & C. Braet (Eds), *Conflict and Development in Adolescence*. Leiden: DSWO Press.

Verhofstadt-Denève, L., Schittekatte, M. & Braet, CC. (1993). From adolescence to young adulthood: a follow-up survey over eight years of psycho-social development. *International Journal of Adolescent Medicine and Health*, **6**, 37–57.

Verhofstadt-Denève, L., Schittekatte, M. & Braet, C. (1994). Conflict experience and opposition in the transition from adolescence into young adulthood. *Swiss Journal of Psychology*, **4**, 220–229.

Verhulst, F. C., Eussen, M., Berden, G., Sanders-Woudstra, J. & van de Ende, J. (1993). Pathways of problem behaviors from childhood to adolescence. *Journal of the American Academy of Child and Adolescent Psychiatry*, **32**, 2, 388–396.

Verhulst, F. C. & Koot, H. M. (1991). Longitudinal research in child and adolescent psychiatry. *Journal of the American Academy of Child and Adolescent Psychiatry*, **30**, 361–368.

Watt, N. F. (1974). Childhood roots of schizophrenia. In D. Ricks, A. Thomas and M. Roff (Eds), *Life History Research in Psychopathology*, Vol. 3. Minneapolis: University of Minnesota Press.

Wenar, C. H. (1994). *Developmental Psychopathology*, 3rd edn. New York: McGraw-Hill.

Werner, E. E. (1993). Risk, resilience and recovery. Perspectives from the Kauai Longitudinal Study. *Development and Psychopathology*, **5**, 503–515.

Werner, E. E. & Smith, R. S. (1992). *Overcoming the Odds: High Risk Children from Birth to Adulthood*. Ithaca, NY: Cornell University Press.

Wierson, M. & Forehand, R. (1994). Introduction to special section: The role of longitudinal data with child psychopathology and treatment. Preliminary comments and issues. *Journal of Consulting and Clinical Psychology*, **62**, 5, 883–886.

Zahn-Waxler, C. (1993). Warriors and worriers: Gender and psychopathology. Special issue: Toward a developmental perspective on conduct disorder. *Development and Psychopathology*, **5**, 1–2, 79–89.

KEY CONCEPTS

A QUICK REFERENCE

1 History and Systems of Developmental Psychology

- Preyer's central contribution to developmental psychology was to ensure that behavioral observation became the primary method of the discipline. (p. 6)
- In developmental psychology, the name Alfred Binet (1857–1911) is primarily associated with the construction of the first intelligence test, and the concept of 'intellectual age.' (p. 7)
- The main contribution of J. B. Watson to the history of developmental psychology was his introduction of the experimental method to infant research. (p. 9)
- For Freud the motor of psychic development was a set of psychosexual drives. These drives dominate behavior and appear in a regular sequence over childhood and adolescence. (p. 9)
- In contrast to both maturation and learning perspectives, Piaget stressed the child's activity and self regulation. (p.16)
- According to Vygotsky, higher mental functions do not develop in the individual, but in the social interaction. (p.18)
- From a psychological point of view, attachment describes the emotional bond that develops between a child and his or her caretaker. (p. 22)
- The focus of life-span research was not just to expand the range of developmental research to include adulthood and old age. Rather, it presented a fundamentally new theoretical orientation. (p. 23)
- Age got its status as an indicator variable simply because the timing and length of many maturational processes, many learning processes, and many culturally normed educational opportunities are highly correlated with chronological age. (p. 30)
- All reliable, valid empirical findings and all empirically supported theoretical models help to increase our understanding of practical problems. (p. 31)

2 The Growing and Aging Brain: Life-span Changes in Brain and Cognitive Functioning

- Neural functions are not strictly localized. (p. 36)
- Mental activity involves three principal functional brain systems: the reticular activation system, the information system, and the action system. (p. 39)
- Neural development during the embryonic period takes place at an extremely rapid rate. (p.44)
- Postnatal neural development includes formative and regressive changes. (p. 46)
- Aging is difficult to define. (p.53)
- Neural aging includes gross and regional changes. (p. 54)
- Environmental influences may promote brain growth during development and reduce brain decline associated with aging. (p. 57)
- The brain is malleable but not a chalkboard. (p. 61)
- Stage-wise cognitive development may be driven by brain-growth cycles. (p. 69)
- Frontal lobes are the last to mature and the first to decline. (p. 73)
- All elements of the information processing system mature at a similar rate. (p. 79)
- But motor processes may be more sensitive to aging than perceptual processes. (p. 83)

3 Perceptual and Motor Development

- The paradox to be resolved by any theory of perceptual development is that the two dimensional surface of the eye, the retina, on which visual images of the world are projected lacks the third dimension and yet we perceive the world as three dimensional and extended in space. (p.102)
- Piaget suggested that the visual world of the newborn is two-dimensional and lacking in depth. Perception of shape and size develop only slowly, during the first 6 months of life. (p. 103)
- A radical alternative to the traditional view of visual perception was developed by James Gibson (1966). He argued that perception should be considered as an active process of seeking after information, with no one sense being more important than any other. (p. 104)
- The fact that babies show spontaneous perceptual preferences means that it is possible to study what the infant chooses to look at. (p.105)
- Relative to adult standards, the acuity of vision in the newborn is poor. (p. 106)
- It is becoming increasingly clear that infants are attentive to sounds from before birth. (p. 107)
- Evidence against the theory that 'touch tutors vision' came from ingeni-

ous experiments which demonstrated that infants are capable of picking up visual information that an object is about to collide with them. (p. 110)

- As adults we know that when one object is occluded by another, the hidden object continues to exist and retains its physical and spatial properties. (p. 111)
- De Vries, Visser and Prechtl (1984) have described 15 distinctively different movement patterns in the 15-week fetus, these include foetal breathing movements, where the amniotic fluid is regularly inhaled and exhaled, stretching movements, turning movements, and slightly later, thumb sucking. (p. 117)
- Gibson and Gibson (1955) argued that repeated perception of the figures enabled the subjects progressively to isolate the relevant dimensions along which the stimuli varied from the standard. They call this process 'perceptual differentiation'. (p. 125)
- Luquet (1927), one of the early students of child art, argued that children's drawing passes through several stages. (p. 128)
- Contemporary evidence suggests that infants are much better able to perceive reality than had been traditionally assumed. (p. 131)
- Motor development is similarly richly endowed from the outset. Development consists in selective retention of some aspects of an innate repertoire of motor abilities, the coordination and hierarchical integration of actions with perception. (p. 131)

4 Communication and Language Development

- For thirty years, the study of the development of communication and language has become increasingly specialized, and the studies more and more specific. (p. 137)
- Language has two major functions: representation and communication. (p. 138)
- Four levels of language analysis are defined: phonological, syntactic, semantic, and pragmatic. (p. 140)
- Formal studies on the development of communication and language only date back to the beginning of the twentieth century. (p. 143)
- Research in the field of language acquisition relies on both the experimental method and observation. (p. 148)
- There are four main periods in the development of communication and language: the prelinguistic period, the one-word utterance period, the two-word utterance period, and the sentence period, with its long and complex evolution which continues until adulthood and sometimes even beyond. (p. 150)
- There are more people in the world who use two or more languages than there are who use only one. (p. 159)
- Acquisition of the written language is a major step in the life of a child: it determines proper adjustment and success in school. (p. 161)

- Research conducted in areas such as memory has provided some interesting information on communication and language during adulthood and old age. (p. 162)
- Four main theoretical bases can be proposed to account for language acquisition: empiricism, innatism, constructivism, and functionalism. (p. 164)
- A recent view stresses the link between the child's socialization and the development of language and communication. (p. 174)

5 Cognitive Development

- The psychology of cognitive development studies how people understand the world and solve the problems they face and how these processes improve and expand with growth. (p. 179)
- For Piaget, intelligance is at one and the same time the means and the ultimate end of adaptation in the environment as it makes the person increasingly able to avoid errors. (p. 184)
- Cognitive development takes place along a sequence of stages (sensorimotor, pre-operational, intuitive, concrete and formal operational), each of which is based on a different kind of mental structure. (p. 144)
- Cognitive development is the result of conflicts between what is known and the present situation, active interaction with the aspect of the environment concerned, and abstraction from and elaboration on error-free actions. (p. 198)
- Although Piaget's theory faces many problems because Piaget was not aware of many phenomena that we study today, whenever investigators remained close to the original Piagetian conditions, the phenomena that he discovered were observed in more or less the same way at more or less the same age. (p. 200)
- The information processing metaphor of the mind assumes that development comes from improvements in registering, storing, and processing information about the environment. (p. 202)
- Neo-Piagetians believe that the mind involves two hierarchical levels, one defined by content-free information processing capacity and functions and one defined by Piagetian-like cognitive operations and knowledge. (p. 204)
- Case's stages (sensorimotor, interrelational, dimensional, and vectorial) coincide by and large with Piaget's main stages. (p. 206)
- Although total processing capacity remains constant throughout life, the space available for the storage of information increases because processing becomes more efficient and automated so that it takes less processing capacity. (p. 210)
- Dynamic systems theory aims to highlight how the interaction between different processes generates different forms of development. (p. 217)
- Reasoning involves inference, which involves processes that enable

thinkers to transfer meaning from one representation to another systematically and coherently. (p. 219)

- Deductive reasoning is inference which builds concepts by generalizing
  from particular instance or experiences. (p. 221)
- Deductive reasoning proceeds from the general to the specific and it
  serves verbal interaction and integration of information received from
  different sources or at different times. (p. 224)
- Although the basic forms of inductive and deductive inference may be
  part of the human makeup, all forms of reasoning develop as a result of
  social interaction, increasing mastery of language, and increasing awareness of one's own mind. (p. 229)
- Some scholars believe that children and laymen think like scientists, that
  is they organize their knowledge about the world into theories concerned
  with different domains of the world, such as the physical, the biological,
  and the psychological world. (p. 232)
- Minds are representational systems which are aware of their own and of
  each other's representational nature. (p. 235)
- Research on the appearance/reality distinction strongly indicates that
  changes in the appearance of objects or living beings make young
  children believe that they also change in their very identity. (p. 240)
- The mind is a three-level hierarchical universe which involves (i) domain-specific systems of thought which are oriented to knowing different aspects of the environment (categorical, quantitative, causal, spatial,
  and propositional thought), (ii) self-oriented systems which enable self-
  awareness and self-regulation (a theory of mind, a theory of intelligence,
  and a cognitive self-image), and processing functions which constrain
  what can be known at each of these two knowing levels (speed of
  processing, control of processing, and storage. (p. 246)
- Cognitive development takes place along multiple roads because the
  various systems at each of the levels of the mind may change in relative
  autonomy of each other. (p. 251)
- Cognitive change is made necessary by variations in the environment
  which first affect a related system of mind and may then propagate to
  other systems via mechanisms which vary according to the system
  affected. (p. 254)
- In the years of maturity a gradual slowing in mental efficiency goes hand
  in hand with an increase in relativism and wisdom, but late in life limited
  efficiency, flawed reasoning, and even cognitive disengagement may
  prevail. (p.259)

6 Social Development

- Interactions, relationships, and groups provide the basic social contexts
  for individual development. (p. 271)
- Four modalities are distinguished in an individual's problem solving in
  developmental tasks: cognition or thinking, behavioral execution or

KEY CONCEPTS: A QUICK REFERENCE

acting, affect or emotionality, and goal orientation or will. (p. 272)
- In each interaction people exchange knowledge, regulate each other's behaviour, exchange emotions, and provide positive or negative feedback with regard to goal orientation and goal achievement. (p. 275)
- One's efficiency in modifying one's goals in correspondence to the goal orientations or intentions of others is essential for competent interaction. (p. 276)
- In aggressive or antisocial interactions, individuals pursue their own goals and interests without considering the interests of others. (p. 281)
- A distinction has been made between inhibited children, socially anxious children, and solitary or reserved children. (p. 283)
- Children act in a socially responsible way when they take the interests of others into consideration and avoid pursuing their own goals at the cost of others. (p. 285)
- Two people in a relationship can be different or similar in expertise, in power, in offering each other security or threat, and in the degree to which they share convergent or opposite goal orientations. (p. 288)
- Dimensions of interpersonal support concern convergence of goals; provision of quality information; respecting autonomy and setting limits; and warmth versus hostility. (p. 290)
- Anti-bullying programs in schools are in the interest of the individual victims and bullies but also in the interest of the educational goals of the schools. (p. 299)
- Interpersonal relationships take place in groups, like school classes and families; groups consist of individuals forming interpersonal relationships in a systemic context. (p. 302)
- Children meet their peers most frequently in their school class where individuals are engaged in networks of friendships, bully–victim relationships and/or romantic relationships. (p. 306)

7 Morality, Wisdom and the Life-span

- Commonsense conceptions of 'character' are typically a mixture of virtues, emotions and good habits; they have not proved very useful in the systematic study of morality. (p. 317)
- Different definitions of 'moral maturity' depend on how we think about development. (p. 318)
- The four key questions about moral development have been about *conscience and guilt, understanding rules and principles, learning appropriate behaviour* and *developing moral emotions.* (p. 323)
- Studies of cross-cultural variation in moral development using Kohlberg's measures revealed different levels of moral reasoning in different cultures. This led researchers to look not only at moral stage but at the *kind of reasoning* that different cultures use. (p. 325)
- Kohlberg's scheme is a highly elaborated theory of cognitive developmental transformations, and at the same time is a particular theory of

morality, based on justice reasoning. (p. 326)

- The longitudinal study showed that stage 3 is a normal mode of reasoning among young US male adults, and that stage 4 surpassed stage 3 only at age 24. (p. 330)
- The findings support Gilligan's argument that there is more than one moral 'voice' but not that the 'caring' voice was more apparent among women. (p. 334)
- Cultural psychologists argue that we cannot isolate the individual from historical and social context; this also contrasts with the assumption behind cognitive developmental models, that psychological processes are universal. (p. 335)
- The socially responsible adolescent is self-sufficient and adaptable, able to focus attention and plan, has a sense of personal efficacy and is capable of moral commitment. (p. 338)
- Four different aspects of wisdom: as *socio-moral understanding*, as *integration of affect and cognition*, as *reasoning ability and special kind of expertise*, as *understanding of knowledge, its nature and limits*. (p. 340)
- 'Moral exemplars' had courage and willingness to suffer personal risk and deprivation, and they had feelings of moral necessity – that one could do nothing else. (p. 343)
- Taking a life-span perspective requires us to pay attention to both 'normal' and 'anomalous' life events and crises, and their integration into selfhood over eight decades of life, not just the first two. (p. 345)

8 The Development of Motivation

- The evolution of theoretical paradigms in this field is closely related with changes in assumptions about the kind of factors underlying motivational development. (p. 353)
- Their basic assumption is that the search for satisfaction and well-being is associated with internal equilibrium, which is considered to be a basic condition for the survival of individuals and species. (p. 356)
- Expectancy-value theories were grounded on the assumption of the rationality of human behaviour and its liberation from physiological needs. (p. 357)
- The attributional theory is interested in explaining how beliefs about causes of events influence cognitions, emotions and behaviours. (p. 359)
- The translation of intention into action is possible through access to an individual repertoire of self-regulatory strategies. (p. 360)
- Two kinds of experience are fundamental to manifest intrinsic motivation in achievement situations: experiences of autonomy and mastery. (p. 362)
- Choice of different goals is linked to the adoption of two distinct patterns of behaviours, cognition and affects. (p. 363)
- For many motivational theories, maintenance of a positive self-image is one of the central pillars of human behaviour. (p. 365)

- The first studies were particularly interested in the effect of early socialization experiences on the development of achievement motivation. (p. 375)
- The association between self-concept and performance is currently assumed to be a consequence of the development of cognitive structures. (p. 379)
- Self-evaluations of adolescents or adults are not necessarily the reflection of their competence to respond to environmental demands. (p. 382)
- The progressive integration of information provided by the task and by the social world necessarily leads to a more realistic self-concept. (p. 384)
- The influence of reference groups is also important for the understanding of the evolution of self-concept with age. (p. 385)
- The same evolution has been observed in several motivational characteristics for most of the students throughout school years. (p. 386)
- Normative life transitions offer everyone the same kind of developmental tasks but group differences prove that gender or socio-cultural status are powerful organizers of these life experiences. (p. 390)

9 Personality Development

- In modern personality psychology the categorisation of individuals into distinctive *types* is far less popular than identifying their gradual position on *non-categorical* or *continuous variables*. (p. 401)
- In general, the longer the time period between two measures the lower the stability. And also, stability is lowest when development proceeds fastest. The younger the individual, the faster development proceeds. Thus stability is lowest in young children and more obvious in older ages. This phenomenon is commonly referred to as 'Bloom's law'. (p. 402)
- The psychoanalytic theories of Freud and Jung are among the best known examples of process oriented theories, emphasising the importance of intra-psychic, unconscious processes as determinants of the surface structure of personality. (p. 405)
- 'Those individual differences that are most significant in the daily transactions of persons with each other will eventually become encoded into their language. The more important such a difference is, the more people will notice it and wish to talk of it, with the result that eventually they will invent a word for it'. (p. 406)
- What can be studied is the *hereditability* of traits in a particular *population*. (p. 409)
- Psychologists and behavioural geneticists who say that it is possible or even probable that races differ in their inborn capacity for certain sorts of achievement, whether physical or mental, in various types of sporting and intellectual activities, are not longer rejected out of hand, as they understandably were a couple of decades after the Second World War. (p. 413)

- Whereas temperament theory postulates inborn tendencies to individual differences in traits such as negative emotionality and sociability, attachment theory postulates that such typical behavioural patterns are the result of the particular type of attachment relation that has evolved between the infant and its primary caretaker, mainly the mother. (p. 415)
- What remains of the notion of a stable and unique personality when we change our characteristic ways of behaviour like a chameleon its colours? (p. 419)
- This unavoidable subjectivity of the opinions expressed by parents and caretakers has led psychologists to refer to parental ratings of children's typical behaviour as a mixture of objective reality and subjective *parental perceptions*. (p. 422)
- It is an illusion to think that we can isolate, in school-age children, underlying, general and context-independent traits of temperament and personality, valid for predictions of behavioural patterns in *any* situation. (p. 423)
- We do not recommend the use of self-rating methods before age 12, and we recommend that care be exercised in the selection of behavioural characteristics to be rated during the whole of adolescence. (p. 424)
- Many clinicians consider projective techniques as a valuable instrument for gaining insight into individual fantasies and for gathering information on the complex organisation of individual perception. However, the richness of the data provided by these techniques is not a sufficient condition for scientific validity. (p. 425)
- Our perceptions of the multitude of individual differences among human beings tend to get organised and structured according to the *interests* of the perceivers. (p. 429)
- With increasing similarity in cultural values and value systems, the ways in which we perceive, verbalize, evaluate and react to individual differences in personality, will become more alike. (p. 438)
- Is it legitimate to place groups of children and their families in preventive therapy, because these children have a one-in-four chance of developing into criminals, or psychiatric patients, or of developing other types of seriously deviant behaviour? (p. 438)

10 Developmental Psychopathology

- Developmental psychopathology: a general approach to understanding relations between development and its maladaptive deviations. (p. 448)
- Focus on the functioning of the child in different contexts and against the background of its development. (p. 448)
- Developmental psychopathologists are equally interested in children who are at risk of developing a disorder yet fail to develop it, and in those who in due course manifest the complete pattern of psychopathology. (p. 450)

- The term 'developmental psychopathology' was introduced by Achenbach in 1974. (p. 451)
- We tend to look at normal development from an Anglo-American point of view. (p. 453)
- With the evolution of the discipline, there has been a remarkable change from description (and interpretation) of psychopathology to measurement and quantification of specific problem behaviour. (p. 456)
- We generally find that about 10–15% of children have a disorder. (p. 461)
- Following a complete population of children over several years, until they are adults, is a very expensive undertaking. (p. 461)
- If we are concerned with the historical aspects of a given disorder, with its evolution, and with its different manifestations, then we have to find and to follow a great number of children who have the same problem. (p. 463)
- Differences between prospective follow-up studies and retrospective follow-back analysis are obvious and both seem to have advantages and disadvantages. (p. 466)
- The sequence of problematic patterns of behaviour is continuous over time, even though the manifestations of such behaviour may be different at different ages. (p. 468)
- A lot of children can cope effectively with stressful events and do not develop a disorder. This new evolution in the study of developmental psychopathology concerns what is today called 'resilience'. (p. 469)
- Finding relations by means of empirical research is only one phase in scientific work; interpreting these relations is an equally delicate matter. (p. 475)
- When parents ask for help for enuresis in 4-year-old children, assessment can help in differentiating between children who will develop normally and children in which the problems are likely to persist. (p. 478)
- Many ADD children continue to have problems (sometimes different ones) in adulthood. (p. 479)
- The discovery of a genetic factor does not mean that other influences are insignificant or can fix a limit. (p. 480)
- Although the persistence of emotional disorder per se is not particularly high, emotional disorder acted supplementarily as a risk factor for later psychopathology. (p. 483)
- Aggressive behaviour seems to be very pervasive across time and generations. (p. 485)
- A particular type of childhood deviance is not a good predictor of adult deviance. (p. 485)
- It appears to be possible to intervene quite early on in development. (p. 489)

INDEX

Related titles of interest...

Handbook of Child Psychology, 5th Edition

Editor-in-Chief: William Damon

Volume 1: Theoretical Models of Human Development; Volume 2: Cognition, Perception and Language; Volume 3: Social, Emotional and Personality Development; Volume 4: Child Psychology in Practice

0-471-05527-1	Volume 1	1392pp	November 1997
0-471-05730-4	Volume 2	1120pp	November 1997
0-471-07668-6	Volume 3	1232pp	November 1997
0-471-07663-5	Volume 4	1120pp	November 1997
0-471-17893-4	4 Volume Set	4864pp	November 1997

Handbook of Child and Adolescent Psychiatry

Editor-in-Chief: Joseph D. Noshpitz,

Volume 1: Infancy and Pre-school: Development and Syndromes; Volume 2: The Grade-School Years: Development and Syndromes; Volume 3: Adolescence: Development and Syndromes; Volume 4: Varieties of Development.

0-471-55079-5	Volume 1	622pp	April 1997
0-471-55075-2	Volume 2	720pp	April 1997
0-471-55076-0	Volume 3	478pp	April 1997
0-471-55078-7	Volume 4	704pp	April 1997
0-471-17640-0	4 Volume Set	2524pp	April 1997

Volume 5: Clinical Assessment and Intervention Planning; Volume 6: Basic Psychiatric Science and Treatment; Volume 7: Advances and New Directions.

0-471-19330-5	Volume 5	800pp	March 1998
0-471-19331-3	Volume 6	608pp	March 1998
0-471-19332-1	Volume 7	624pp	March 1998
0-471-19328-3	7 Volume Set	4300pp	March 1998
0-471-19329-1	3 Volume Set (5,6,7)		March 1998

Understanding and Teaching Children with Autism

Rita Jordan and Stuart D. Powell

This book explores the roles played by emotion and cognition in the autistic condition and the way in which these affect teaching and learning.

0-471-95888-3 188pp 1995 Hardback
0-471-95714-3 188pp 1995 Paperback

Culture and the Child

A Guide for Professionals in Child Care and Development

Daphne M. Keats

This is a handy practical guide for professionals dealing with children whose cultural backgrounds differ from those of the mainstream of the society in which they live.

0-471-96625-8 200pp 1996 Paperback

Visit the Wiley Home Page at http://www.wiley.co.uk